A HOUSE FOR THE MOST HIGH:
The Story of the Original Nauvoo Temple

A HOUSE FOR THE MOST HIGH:
The Story of the Original Nauvoo Temple

Matthew S. McBride

GREG KOFFORD BOOKS
SALT LAKE CITY 2007

Paperback printing, 2013. ISBN: 978-1-589586-574

Also available in ebook.

www.gregkofford.com

Library of Congress Cataloging-in-Publication Data

McBride, Matthew S.

A house for the Most High : the story of the original
Nauvoo Temple/ Matthew S. McBride.
      p.cm.
Includes bibliographical references and index.
  ISBN: 1-58958-016-8 (alk. paper)
  ISBN: 1-58958-021-4 (Limited Leather: alk. paper)

1. All things in readiness : August 1840 to January 1841.
2. Laying the foundation : February 1841 to October 1841.
3. The font of the temple : November 1841 to April 1842.
4. The walls rise : May 1842 to December1842.
5. The work continues : January 1843 to December 1843.
6. The death of Joseph : January 1844 to June 1844.
7. The ascendancy of the Twelve : July 1844 to December 1844.
8. Setting the capstone : January 1845 to May 1845.
9. The roof and tower : June 1845 to September 1845.
10. Conference in the temple : October 1845 to November 1845.
11. Endowed with power : December 1845 to February 1846.
12. Monument to a people : March 1846 to August 1848.
13. The temple's fate : September 1848 to 1937.
BX8685.N3 M24 2003
246/.95/0977343 21
                   2002151064

Table of Contents

The Arsonist
Tornado Destroys Temple
Fate of the Stones and the Lot
The LDS Temple-Building Traditions Continues

List of Illustrations

ILLUSTRATION CREDITS

The following illustrations are in the publisher's personal collection: 7, 81, 175, 181, 259, 311, 321, 363

The following illustrations are courtesy of Don O. Thorpe: 185, 379

The following illustrations are used with permission from LDS Church Archives: 11, 255, 305

The following illustrations are used with permission from LDS Historical Department: 363

The following illustrations are used with permission from Cedar City, Utah, Daughters of the Utah Pioneers: xviii

PREFACE

*The architectural magnificence of the Nauvoo Temple is not the most important
thing to remember this day. The significance of this temple rests in the impact it had
in the lives of those Saints who lived and labored in Nauvoo to finish a temple unto
the Lord that he had commanded them to build.*

—Elder M. Russell Ballard[1]

The story of Nauvoo centers on the story of the Nauvoo Temple. Few
aspects of life in Mormon Nauvoo excited more curiosity among visitors, solicited
more contempt from critics and apostates, or inspired more zeal on the part of
Church members than the construction of the temple and the introduction of its
related doctrines and practices.

Thomas L. Kane, the Church's staunchest non-Mormon defender during the
nineteenth century, quipped, "Since the dispersion of Jewry, probably, history
affords us no parallel to the attachment of the Mormons for this edifice."[2]

The temple was the fruit of fervent religious devotion on the part of thousands
of Nauvooers and members of the Church throughout the world. The writings of
those who funded, built, and worshiped in the Nauvoo Temple relate a remarkable
story of dedication, a story worth retelling.

—What was it like to participate in building the temple?
—How did individual members of the Church contribute to the project?
—What were the feelings and attitudes of those who administered ordinances and
     received them in the temple?

These questions are best answered by participants and witnesses. This work is
an attempt to provide a glimpse—to paint a picture in broad strokes—of the Nauvoo
Temple experience using primarily the words of the Nauvoo Saints.

In referring to the Nauvoo Temple, I speak not only of the physical edifice,
but also of what President Boyd K. Packer has called the "invisible temple." This
"invisible temple within," he explains, "is the same in all temples."[3]

---

1. M. Russell Ballard, "The Legacy of Hyrum," *Ensign* (September 1994): 55.

2. Thomas L. Kane, "The Mormons: A Discourse Delivered Before the Historical Society of
Pennsylvania, March 26, 1850," quoted in Daniel Tyler, *A Concise History of the Mormon Battalion
in the Mexican War, 1846-1847* (Chicago: Rio Grande Press, 1964), 80.

3. Boyd K. Packer, *Things of the Soul* (Salt Lake City: Bookcraft, 1996), 200. See also Lucile C.
Tate, *Boyd K. Packer: A Watchman on the Tower* (Salt Lake City: Bookcraft, 1995), 206.

It consists of the doctrines, covenants, and ordinances associated with Latter-day Saint temple worship. The years in Nauvoo saw the culmination of the process by which the invisible temple was restored. With the introduction of the doctrine of vicarious ordinance work, the endowment, and celestial marriage, including polygamy, the invisible temple reached an unprecedented state of completion. Indeed, temple worship as known by Latter-day Saints today largely came into being in Nauvoo.

While citizens and visitors alike admired the Nauvoo Temple, it was the invisible temple that commanded the reverence and respect of the faithful. The promised blessings of the invisible temple served as the catalyst—the great motivating force behind the colossal building effort. There is no way to adequately tell the story of the Nauvoo Temple without relating the primary events connected with the maturity of the invisible temple.

The ceremonies of the temple are held sacred by Latter-day Saints around the world. As a believing member of The Church of Jesus Christ of Latter-day Saints, I am mindful of the sacred nature of temple ordinances and have sought to be respectful, guarded, and appropriate in my references to those ordinances. I have used as my guides the writings of Church leaders and other faithful members on this subject.

I first became fascinated in the Nauvoo Temple story while doing family history research. My ancestor Abigail Mead McBride, the first in her family to join the Church, moved to Nauvoo with her children in 1839 along with many other Saints who had fled from Missouri. Her husband Daniel, a Baptist preacher in New York, had died in 1823. She and several of her children participated in the temple's construction and received ordinances within its walls. Her son Reuben was the first person baptized for the dead in the temple. Their love for the temple captivated my interest. This was clearly more than the story of a building of stones, wood, mortar and brick. It was a human story with many facets—a drama of community and conflict, toil and tears, finances and faith. I have since felt that the most worthwhile approach to studying the Nauvoo Temple lies not in examining its architecture, as valuable as that may be, but in understanding the people who built it. Hence, I have tried to emphasize the participants' perspective as much as possible. I hope to have accomplished this in part by letting the participants speak for themselves. Of the records of the Church and its members in Nauvoo, Heber C. Kimball stated: "What a pleasure it will be for our children to look upon these books, while we are in our grave, sleeping. They can see what an interest, and labor, and toiling, their fathers accomplished, when we were building the Temple in order to get our endowments."[4]

4. "Speech Delivered by Heber C. Kimball," *Times and Seasons* 6 (15 July 1845): 972.

The diaries, journals, and correspondence of Heber C. Kimball, William Clayton, William Huntington, Charlotte Haven, Brigham Young, Abraham O. Smoot, Zina Diantha Huntington Jacobs, Willard Richards, Thomas Bullock, and many others are among the most important contemporary sources available on the subject. Of course, the periodical literature of any period is also a key to understanding the unfolding of events in their context. Hence, the *Nauvoo Neighbor*, *Times and Seasons*, *Millennial Star*, and *New York Messenger*, all owned by the Church, and the *Warsaw Signal*, and *Hancock Eagle*, two Hancock County papers, are particularly important sources. In addition to these primary sources, many key figures in the Nauvoo Temple story later wrote reminiscences or autobiographies that contain their perspectives and feelings on their experience. Among the most relevant accounts are those by Norton Jacob, Helen Mar Whitney Kimball, Louisa Barnes Pratt, and Truman O. Angell. Other essential sources include a short history of the temple authored by William Clayton in 1845, the day books and ledgers of the various organizations charged with gathering funds for the temple and carrying out its construction, the work of historians such as B. H. Roberts, Andrew Jenson, Stanley B. Kimball, and T. Edgar Lyon, archeological evidence gathered when the temple site was excavated in 1962, and last but not least, the six-volume *History of the Church*. Nearly all of these sources can be found in the Church Historical Department Library and Archives, the Harold B. Lee Library at Brigham Young University, and/or the Marriott Library at the University of Utah.

The introduction of this book discusses briefly the temple-building efforts of the fledgling Church of Jesus Christ of Latter-day Saints prior to its arrival in Nauvoo in 1839, and the early development of temple-related doctrines. The body of the history in thirteen chapters moves chronologically through the major stages of the temple's construction and use from 1840, when the temple was first contemplated, to 1850, when its walls were toppled by a tornado.

An epilogue completes the story by recounting the story of the repurchase of the temple lot by the Church in 1937, the lot's excavation in 1962, and the announcement by President Gordon B. Hinckley on 4 April 1999, that the temple would be rebuilt. The appendix contains important eyewitness descriptions of the temple from contemporary sources.

I have arranged the narrative chronologically, placing events in a definite context. However, as the story develops the reader will notice several recurring themes that encapsulate the Nauvoo Temple's importance, both in its effects during the Nauvoo period and in its lasting impact on the Church:

1. Together with its sister project, the Nauvoo House, the temple had a tremendous impact on the economy of the young city. The Church undertook to

build the temple in adverse circumstances. This giant edifice represented such a tremendous strain on their meager resources that many criticized Joseph Smith and Brigham Young for insisting on its completion. The fact remains, however, that the great building project and the attraction of the temple itself did much to stimulate the economy and provide employment.

2. The temple was largely responsible for Nauvoo's rise to national prominence, attracting the attention of dozens of newspapers across the country. The distinctiveness of the temple's design and its unusual approach to funding and labor drew both praise and scorn from the press. Scores of articles kept America apprised of the status of the building throughout its construction.

3. In Nauvoo, the temple emerged as one of the dominant themes of Joseph Smith's teaching. Many of the most prominent doctrinal developments in Nauvoo came as a result of or laid the groundwork for temple worship. During the last five years of his life, Joseph's activities centered on planning and building a temple-centered kingdom.

4. Custodianship of the authority necessary to administer temple ordinances played a critical role in the succession crisis following Joseph Smith's death in 1844. The ascendancy of Brigham Young and the Twelve was due in part to their claim that Joseph had initiated them into all of the temple ordinances and bestowed upon them the sealing power and authority necessary to perform these ordinances for others.

5. The temple and its associated theology acted as a sieve. For the faithful, the building effort and newly revealed ordinances affirmed the prophetic calling of Joseph Smith and Brigham Young. They viewed calls to contribute to the temple's construction and to receive ordinances within its walls as a great privilege. For others, temple theology symbolized Joseph Smith's fall from his standing as God's mouthpiece.

6. Several procedures and organizations put in place for the purpose of completing the temple left an indelible impression on church organization and policy. The creation of the ward unit, the formation of the Female Relief Society, and the establishment of tithing as the means to fund Church needs are examples of the influence of the Nauvoo Temple upon the course of the Church.

7. Above all, the temple represented a tremendous sacrifice. It is a monument to the faith of the Nauvoo Mormons. According to Elizabeth Ann Smith Whitney, who participated in those sacrifices, "The people were most of them poor, and they denied themselves every comfort they possibly could to assist in finishing the Lord's house."[5] Their efforts afford an example worthy of emulation for

5. Elizabeth Ann Smith Whitney, "A Leaf from an Autobiography," *Woman's Exponent* 7 (August 1878): 191.

modern Saints who have been challenged by one of Joseph Smith's successors, to "establish the temple of the Lord as the great symbol of their membership."[6]

These seven themes permeate the writings of the participants. They seem to have had a prescient awareness of the theological, architectural, and historical significance of what they did.

I express thanks to Tom Kimball, Greg Kofford, and James Summerhays for their encouragement on this project, Milton V. Backman, Scott Christensen, the volunteers at the Hancock County Historical Society, and many others for sharing resources and time, Julie Maddox for her helpful suggestions, Lavina Fielding Anderson for her insightful editing, and my dear wife Mary for her unfailing support.

---

6. Howard W. Hunter, "The Great Symbol of Our Membership," *Ensign* (October 1994): 2.

Nauvoo Temple Daguerreotype circa 1846-1848

Introduction

THE TEMPLE IN PRE-NAUVOO CHURCH HISTORY

Early Temple Building Efforts

Temple building has been as a part of Mormon theology from the very beginning. The first references to a temple in Mormon history were paraphrases of Old Testament prophecy. When Moroni appeared to Joseph Smith on 21 September 1823, he quoted Malachi 3, among other biblical prophecies, which declares that the Lord "shall come suddenly to his temple." Moroni further stated that these prophecies were about to be fulfilled (JS-H 1:36, 40). On 9 February 1831, less than a year after the Church was organized in April 1830, Joseph Smith received a revelation with instructions on building a modern city of Zion. In addition to describing social and economic aspects of the city, the revelation specifies that the city was to be built that "my covenant people may be gathered in one in that day when I shall come to my temple" (D&C 42:36).

These revelations made it clear that the Church was to play a role in fulfilling the ancient prophecy of the Lord's coming to his temple and that the temple would be the vital center of the gathering of God's people in the last days.[1] On 20 July 1831, the desire of the Church and its prophet to bring about this prophetic

---

1. Joseph Smith Jr. et al., *History of the Church of Jesus Christ of Latter-day Saints*, edited by B. H. Roberts (Salt Lake City: Deseret News Press, 6 vols. published 1902-12, Vol. 7 published 1932), 1:189.

event compelled Joseph Smith to pray, "When will Zion be built up in her glory, and where will thy Temple stand, unto which all nations shall come in the last days?" The Lord revealed in response, "The land of Missouri ... is the land which I have appointed and consecrated for the gathering of the saints. Behold, the place which is now called Independence is the center place; and a spot for the temple is lying westward, upon a lot which is not far from the courthouse" (D&C 57:1-4).

It is clear, even at this early date, that temple building was to be a distinctive part of the Mormon way of life. As time passed, the temple would assume even greater importance in this gathering of Israel to Zion. On 11 June 1843 in Nauvoo, Joseph Smith taught, "What was the object of gathering the Jews, or the people of God in any age of the world?... The main object was to build unto the Lord a house whereby He could reveal unto His people the ordinances of His house and the glories of His kingdom, and teach the people the way of salvation."[2]

Shortly after receiving the revelation on the location of the temple in Independence, Joseph Smith selected a site "about three-quarters of a mile from Independence"[3] and, on 3 August 1831, dedicated it. The temple itself "was laid out in the year 1831, and the cornerstone laid."[4] However, because the Saints were forcibly removed from Jackson County by Missourians hostile to their goal of gathering, the construction of the temple never progressed beyond the laying of the cornerstones.[5]

By December 1832 with plans for the Jackson County Temple indefinitely suspended, the attention of Church members shifted to the construction of a temple in Kirtland, Ohio, then headquarters of the Church. On 27 December the Prophet Joseph received a revelation, formally commanding the Saints to build a temple in Kirtland (D&C 88:119). On 4 May 1833, Hyrum Smith, Jared Carter, and Reynolds Cahoon were appointed a committee to obtain funding for the temple.[6]

---

2. Ibid., 5:423.

3. Ibid., 1:199.

4. Orson Pratt, 1 August 1880, *Journal of Discourses*, 26 vols. (London and Liverpool: LDS Booksellers Depot, 1855-86), 21:330-31.

5. Although plans for this temple were temporarily set aside, Latter-day Saints anticipate returning to Independence to build the temple eventually. It continues to hold a place of particular importance among temples as the temple to which the prophecies of Christ return applied specifically. See, e.g., Joseph F. Smith, "Redemption of Zion," *Improvement Era* 7 (May 1904): 512.

6. *History of the Church*, 1:342-43. Hyrum Smith (1800-44), elder brother of Joseph Smith, was one of the eight witnesses of the Book of Mormon. He later served as a counselor to Joseph in the First Presidency and as Patriarch to the Church. He took the place of Elias Higbee on the Nauvoo Temple Building Committee in 1843 and was martyred with Joseph on 27 June 1844 in Carthage Jail. Jared Carter (1801-49) was baptized in 1831. He served as a member of both the Kirtland and Far West high councils. Reynolds Cahoon (1790-1861) joined the Church in 1830, was a counselor to Bishop Newel K. Whitney in Kirtland, and was a member of the stake presidency in Adam-Ondi-Ahman. He also served as a member of the Nauvoo Temple Building Committee (1840-44). See chap. 1.

On 5 June, Smith and Cahoon began to dig a trench for the walls of the new temple. "On ... July 23rd [1833] ... the corner stones of the Lord's House were laid in Kirtland, after the order of the Holy Priesthood."[7] In early 1836, the final touches were completed; and the temple was dedicated on Sunday, 27 March 1836.

The Saints were not long allowed to enjoy the Kirtland Temple. Late in 1837, persecution drove them from their Kirtland homes. Although Joseph Smith, as trustee for the Church, still legally owned the temple, the Church abandoned the structure.[8] The body of the Saints journeyed to Missouri and joined their struggling brothers and sisters there. In addition to the Saints that had been driven from Jackson County, other converts had joined them to form branches in Caldwell, Clay, and Daviess counties, far enough from their hostile former neighbors in Jackson County, they hoped, to be safe.

On 4 July 1838, the Saints celebrated the nation's birthday with a uniquely Mormon ceremony. They gathered at Far West in Caldwell County to lay temple cornerstones for the third time. During the following months, they began to excavate this site. Later that summer, Joseph Smith selected a fourth temple site, which Brigham Young dedicated in Adam-ondi-Ahman, Daviess County, at some date after 6 August 1838. Apostle Heber C. Kimball, later Brigham Young's counselor, recalled:

> While there we laid out a city on a high elevated piece of land, and set the stakes for the four corners of a temple block, which was dedicated, Brother Brigham Young being mouth.... This elevated spot was probably from two hundred and fifty to five hundred feet above the level of Grand River, so that one could look east, west, north or south, as far as the eye could reach; it was one of the most beautiful places I ever beheld.[9]

---

7. *History of the Church*, 1:400.

8. The disposition of these various temple properties has been a matter of dispute since the death of Joseph Smith. In 1867, the Church of Christ, a group of former Latter-day Saints led by Granville Hedrick, took possession of portions of the temple lot in Independence. Other portions were purchased by the Reorganized Church of Jesus Christ of Latter Day Saints (now Community of Christ). In 1895, the Reorganized Church attempted unsuccessfully to regain possession of the Church of Christ's part of the lot in a legal suit known as the "Temple Lot case." Today, portions of the lot are owned by the Hedrickites, the Community of Christ (which has built a new temple on the grounds), and The Church of Jesus Christ of Latter-day Saints, which has established a visitors center on its part of the lot.

Ownership of the Kirtland Temple was also in dispute during the latter half of the nineteenth century. Eventually, Joseph Smith III, the heir to Joseph Smith Jr.'s trusteeship, deeded it to the Reorganized Church (Community of Christ) in 1880. The Community of Christ continues to own and maintain the building as a historic property open to visitors.

9. Quoted in Orson F. Whitney, *Life of Heber C. Kimball* (Salt Lake City: Kimball Family, 1888), 209.

Unfortunately, the Church's hasty departure from Missouri during the winter of 1838-39 meant that these two temple sites were also abandoned. The Far West Temple was little more than a hole in the ground and work on the Adam-ondi-Ahman Temple was never started.

Preparatory Doctrinal Developments

During the 1830s, the doctrinal foundation for the Mormon temple experience in Nauvoo was laid in place, line upon line and precept upon precept through the Prophet Joseph Smith.

ORDINANCE WORK ON BEHALF OF THE DEAD

The doctrine that living members of the Church could stand as proxies for the dead in performing gospel ordinances was introduced at Nauvoo in 1840. However, preparation for this concept had begun much earlier. One influential event was the 1823 death of Joseph Smith's eldest brother, Alvin, at age twenty-four.[10] The Smith family grieved the loss of Alvin and were disturbed when a Reverend Stockton of the Presbyterian Church, in his funeral sermon, "intimated very strongly that [Alvin] had gone to hell, for [he] was not a church member." William Smith, Joseph's brother, remembered that their father, Joseph Sr., "did not like it" because he knew that "Alvin was a good boy."[11] Because the whole family was familiar with New Testament teachings about the necessity of baptism, Alvin's status in the next life thus became a cause of concern for the young prophet and his family.

Joseph's concern for his brother's salvation doubtless intensified when, while translating the Book of Mormon in 1829, his translation reiterated the requirement of baptism by proper authority. This led to a prayer of inquiry, in company with his scribe Oliver Cowdery, which resulted in the visitation of John the Baptist to restore the Aaronic Priesthood—the authority to baptize.[12] The necessity of baptism was again reinforced in February 1832 when Joseph and Sidney Rigdon, Joseph Smith's scribe and confidant, received a remarkable vision in Kirtland, which introduced the doctrine of the three degrees of glory. This vision reaffirmed that

---

10. Although History of the Church, 1:6 dates Alvin's death as 1825, subsequent research supports the 1823 date. Russell R. Rich, "Where Were the Moroni Visits?", BYU Studies 10, no. 3 (Spring 1970): 255.

11. "The Testimony of William Smith," Millennial Star 61 (26 February 1894): 132-34.

12. Joseph Smith—History 1:68-71, in Pearl of Great Price; hereafter cited as JS-H.

those who entered into the highest or celestial degree of glory were those "who received the testimony of Jesus, and believed on his name and were baptized after the manner of his burial, being buried in the water in his name" (D&C 76:51).

Then in January 1836, shortly before the dedication of the Kirtland Temple, Joseph had a vision of the celestial kingdom:

> I saw ... my brother Alvin that has long since slept;
>
> And marveled how it was that he had obtained an inheritance in that Kingdom, seeing that he had departed this life before the Lord had set his hand to gather Israel the second time and had not been baptized for the remission of sins.
>
> Thus came the voice of the Lord unto me saying: All who have died without a knowledge of this gospel, who would have received it had they been permitted to tarry, shall be heirs to the celestial kingdom of God. (D&C 137:5-7)

This vision not only settled the issue of Alvin's salvation and gave great comfort to the Smith family, but it also set the stage for subsequent revelations. While it confirmed the possibility of saving those who had died without hearing the gospel, it did not explain that saving ordinances would still need to be performed for them.

In 1837 and 1838, the idea of salvation for the dead became more widespread among church members. On 3 January 1837, Wilford Woodruff received a blessing from seventies president Zebedee Coltrin when he (Woodruff) was ordained to the office of seventy in Kirtland. Coltrin promised Woodruff "that I should visit Kolob and preach to the spirits in prison and that I should bring all of my friends or relatives forth from the terrestrial kingdom by the power of the gospel."[13] Warren Cowdery, Oliver Cowdery's brother and editor of the Church's newspaper in 1837, editorialized: "If it be a point sustained by the word of God, that all who do not have, or have not had, the privilege of embracing or rejecting the gospel here in the flesh, have that privilege in God's own time before the judgment day; then will the character of God be vindicated."[14] In support of his view that the dead could also receive salvation, Cowdery cited 1 Peter 3:19 and 4:6 stating that, after Christ's death, he "went and preached unto the spirits in prison.... For this cause was the gospel preached to them that are dead, that they might be judged according to men in the flesh." These verses have remained among the clearest biblical proof texts for those explaining and defending work for the dead.

---

13. Wilford Woodruff, *Wilford Woodruff's Journal*, 1833-1898, typescript, edited by Scott G. Kenny, 9 vols. (Midvale, UT: Signature Books, 1983-85): 1:119.

14. Warren Cowdery, "Love of God," *Messenger and Advocate* 3 (March 1837): 471. The article is signed "Ed." (for editor).

In July 1838, Joseph Smith, responding to the question, "What has become of all those who have died since the days of the apostles?" answered: "All those who have not had an opportunity of hearing the gospel, and being administered to by an inspired man in the flesh, must have it hereafter before they can be finally judged."[15]

Although these developments added to the Saints' understanding of the status of those who died without the gospel, the matter of how the dead could fulfill the requirement of baptism continued to be one of speculation. Joseph Fielding, a British convert whose sister Mary married Hyrum Smith, later described his thoughts:

> For some time I had thought much on the subject of the redemption of those who died under the broken covenant, it is plain they could not come forth in the kingdom of God, as they had not been adopted, legally into it ... yet how would those who died martyrs and all those who have lived up to the best light they have had, and would no doubt have rejoiced in the fulness of the gospel had they had it, be denied this privilege? I thought, perhaps those who receive the priesthood in these last days would baptize them at the coming of the Savior ... but a touch of the light of revelation has at once dispelled the darkness and scattered the doubts which once perplexed my mind and I behold the means which God hath devised that his banished ones may be brought back again.... When I have listened to the teachings of the servants of God under the new covenant and the principle of Baptism for the Dead the feelings of my soul were such as I cannot describe.[16]

The perplexity that Joseph Fielding and others felt was laid to rest in August 1840 with the introduction of baptism for the dead in Nauvoo. (See chap. 1.)

The Kirtland Endowment

Although the Kirtland Temple, first of the temples of this dispensation, did not function in the way Latter-day Saints think of temples today, it served a unique purpose in preparing for future temples. In addition to serving as a site for congregational meetings, prayer meetings, and the administration of the sacrament, the

---

15. Joseph Smith, (untitled article), *Elders Journal* 1, no. 3 (July 1838): 43. The article's first sentence is: "In obedience to our promise, we give the following answers to questions, which were asked in the last number of the Journal."

16. Joseph Fielding, Letter to the editor, 28 December 1841, *Times and Seasons* 3 (1 January 1842): 648-50.

Kirtland Temple was a place of revelation, particularly the revelation of temple-related doctrines and the authority to perform temple ordinances.

On Sunday, 3 April, one week following the temple's dedication, the Lord appeared to Joseph Smith and Oliver Cowdery in the temple. He promised to "manifest myself to my people in mercy in this house. Yea, I will appear unto my servants, and speak unto them with mine own voice, if my people will keep my commandments, and do not pollute this holy house" (D&C 110:7-8). Immediately following this visitation, Moses appeared and "committed unto [them] the keys of the gathering of Israel." Another divine messenger named Elias "committed the dispensation of the gospel of Abraham, saying that in us and our seed all generations after us should be blessed." Finally, Elijah appeared and declared to Joseph and Oliver:

> Behold, the time has fully come, which was spoken of by the mouth of Malachi—testifying that he [Elijah] should be sent, before the great and dreadful day of the Lord come—To turn the hearts of the fathers to the children, and the children to the fathers, lest the whole earth be smitten with a curse.
>
> Therefore, the keys of this dispensation are committed into your hands. (D&C 110:14-16)

Latter-day Saints understand Elijah's commission as transmitting to Joseph the sealing power which would be used later to perform such temple ordinances as the sealing of husband to wife and parents to children. The bestowal of these keys and powers was a critical precedent to their use in the Nauvoo Temple. Twentieth-century Apostle Joseph Fielding Smith taught: "The Kirtland Temple was but a preparatory temple which was built before the nature of temple ordinances was revealed. The primary purpose of its erection was to provide a sanctuary where the Lord could send messengers from his presence to restore priesthood and keys held in former dispensations, so that the work of gathering together all things in one in the dispensation of the fulness of times might go on."[17]

While most temple ordinances were not introduced until Nauvoo, the Kirtland Temple did serve as a dedicated structure in which some ordinances were performed. One of the stated purposes of the Kirtland Temple was that the elders of the Church might receive what Joseph Smith called an "endowment." In November 1835, the Prophet taught:

> You need an endowment, brethren, in order that you may be prepared and able to overcome all things, and then those who reject your testimony will be

---

17. Joseph Fielding Smith, *Doctrines of Salvation: Sermons and Writings of Joseph Fielding Smith*, compiled by Bruce R. McConkie, 3 vols. (Salt Lake City: Bookcraft, 1954-56), 2:236.

damned. The sick will be healed, the lame made to walk, the deaf to hear and the blind to see through your instrumentality.... [W]hen you are endowed and prepared to preach the Gospel to all nations, kindreds and tongues in their own languages, you must faithfully warn all, bind up the law and seal up the testimony, and the destroying angel will follow close at your heels and execute his tremendous mission upon the children of disobedience, and destroy the workers of iniquity: while the Saints will be gathered out from among them, and stand in holy places ready to meet the Bridegroom when he comes.[18]

When Latter-day Saints use the term "Kirtland Endowment," they mean one of two things. The first is the general outpouring of spiritual manifestations that accompanied the temple's completion and dedication, described by Joseph Smith as "a Pentecost and an endowment indeed."[19] George A. Smith, Joseph's cousin and a future apostle, who was present for many of these manifestations, recalled: "On the evening after the dedication of the temple, hundreds of the brethren received the ministering of angels, saw the light and personages of angels, and bore testimony of it. They spake in new tongues, and had a greater manifestation of the power of God than that described by Luke on the day of Pentecost."[20] Among these manifestations were the visitations by prophets of earlier dispensation who came, as already described, to restore particular priesthood keys.

The second meaning of the term refers to a series of ordinances introduced in Kirtland which were a precursor to the temple ordinances introduced in Nauvoo. Again, George A. Smith, who received these ordinances, explained:

Four hundred and sixteen Elders, Priests, Teachers, and Deacons met in the Kirtland Temple on the evening of its dedication.... The Lord poured His Spirit upon us, and gave us some little idea of the law of anointing, and conferred upon us some blessings. He taught us how to shout hosannah, gave Joseph the keys of the gathering together of Israel....

We were instructed to wash each other's feet, as an evidence that we had borne testimony of the truth of the Gospel to the world. We were taught to anoint each other's head with oil in the name of the Lord, as an ordinance of anointing.[21]

These washings and anointings were to prepare the elders for their ministry and to make their testimony to the world binding. Apostle Orson Pratt later explained:

18. *History of the Church*, 2:309.

19. Ibid., 2:432.

20. George A. Smith, 8 April 1855, *Journal of Discourses*, 26 vols. (London and Liverpool: LDS Booksellers Depot, 1855-86), 2:214-15.

21. Ibid.

When the [Kirtland] Temple was built, the Lord did not see proper to reveal all the ordinances of the Endowments, such as we now understand. He revealed little by little. No rooms were prepared for washings; no special place prepared for the anointings, such as you understand, and such as you comprehend at this period of the history of the Church! Neither did we know the necessity of the washings, such as we now receive. It is true, our hands were washed, our faces and our feet. The Prophet Joseph was commanded to gird himself with a towel, doing this in the temple. What for? That the first elder might witness to our Father and God, that we were clean from the blood of that wicked generation, that then lived. We had gone forth according to our best ability, to publish glad tidings of great joy, for thousands of miles, upon this continent. After this we were called in, and the washing of hands and feet was to testify to God that we were clean from the blood of this generation. The holy anointing was placed upon the heads of his servants, but not the full development of the Endowments in the anointing.... Great were the blessings received. We were commanded to seek to behold the face of the Lord; to seek after revelation; to seek after the spirit of prophecy, and the gifts of the Spirit; and many testify to what they saw.[22]

This endowment would be superseded in May 1842 when Joseph Smith introduced an altered and more complete ceremony in its place. (See chap. 4.)

CELESTIAL MARRIAGE

As early as 1835, Joseph Smith began to teach an expansive view of marriage as an eternal relationship. W. W. Phelps intimated in a May 1835 letter to his wife that he had learned at least the concept of marriage lasting beyond this life: "A new idea, Sally, if you and I continue faithful to the end, we are certain to be one in the Lord throughout eternity; this is one of the most glorious consolations we can have in the flesh."[23]

In November 1839, Joseph Smith traveled to Washington, D.C., to petition the federal government for redress of the property lost when the Saints were expelled from Missouri in 1838-39. En route, Joseph taught Parley P. Pratt some of the basic principles of eternal marriage, which Pratt later reported in these terms:

It was at this time that I received from him the first idea of eternal family organization, and the eternal union of the sexes in those expressibly endearing relationships which none but the highly intellectual, the refined and pure in heart, know how

22. Orson Pratt, 20 May 1877, *Journal of Discourses*, 19:17.

23. W. W. Phelps, Letter to Sally Waterman Phelps, 26 May 1835, *Journal History of the Church of Jesus Christ of Latter-day Saints* (chronology of typed entries and newspaper clippings, 1830-present), Historical Department Archives of the Church of Jesus Christ of Latter-day Saints, Salt Lake City (hereafter LDS Church Archives).

to prize, and which are at the very foundation of everything worthy to be called happiness.

Till then I had learned to esteem kindred affections and sympathies as pertaining solely to this transitory state, as something from which the heart must be entirely weaned, in order to be fitted for its heavenly state.

It was Joseph Smith who taught me how to prize the endearing relationships of father and mother, husband and wife; of brother and sister, son and daughter.

It was from him that I learned that the wife of my bosom might be secured to me for time and all eternity; and that the refined sympathies and affections which endeared us to each other emanated from the fountain of divine eternal love. It was from him that I learned that we might cultivate these affections, and grow and increase in the same to all eternity; while the result of our endless union would be an offspring as numerous as the stars of heaven, or the sands of the sea shore.

It was from him that I learned the true dignity and destiny of a son of God, clothed with an eternal priesthood, as the patriarch and sovereign of his countless offspring. It was from him that I learned that the highest dignity of womanhood was to stand as a queen and priestess to her husband, and to reign for ever and ever as the queen mother of her numerous and still increasing offspring.

I had loved before, but I knew not why. But now I loved—with a purness—an intensity of elevated, exalted feeling, which would lift my soul from the transitory things of this grovelling sphere and expand it as the ocean. I felt that God was my Heavenly Father indeed; that Jesus was my brother, and that the wife of my bosom was an immortal, eternal companion; a kind ministering angel, given to me as a comfort, and a crown of glory for ever and ever. In short, I could now love with the spirit and with the understanding also.

Yet, at that time, my dearly beloved brother, Joseph Smith, had barely touched a single key; had merely lifted a corner of the veil and given me a single glance into eternity.[24]

In Nauvoo the principle of eternal marriage was taught to and practiced by a select group of the Prophet's confidants. Polygamy, an extension of this same principle, was also introduced; and many such marriages were solemnized in the temple and in other locations while the temple was under construction.

Founding the City of Nauvoo

In late 1838, Governor Lilburn Boggs of Missouri issued an order to drive the Mormons from the state or exterminate them. Joseph Smith and several other Church leaders were incarcerated at Liberty, in Clay County, pending trial. During the winter of 1838-39, between ten and twelve thousand Saints were forced to

24. Parley P. Pratt, *Autobiography of Parley P. Pratt,* edited by his son Parley P. Pratt (1874; Salt Lake City: Deseret Book Company, 1985 printing), 259-60.

leave Missouri. Most of them traveled east across Missouri, crossed the Mississippi River, and found shelter in Illinois. Many of them spent the winter in Quincy, a riverside town. During the move to Illinois, several men were dispatched to explore the surrounding area. One of them, David W. Rogers, recalled:

> When the saints were crossing the Mississippi River in their exodus from the state of Missouri I was appointed (by the then authorities of the Church who had crossed over) one of a committee of three to reconnoiter the upriver country in the state of Illinois and in the then territory of Iowa, in order to ascertain if there were any chance for the saints to find shelter from the inclemency of the season. Bro[ther] S. Bent and Bro[ther] Israel Barlow were to be my colleagues. Bro[ther] Bent was taken sick in a few hours after we started and returned home. Barlow and myself went on and were nine days in our exploration and found in the towns of upper and lower Commerce about 40 empty dwellings for which we made conditional arrangements.... We then found Dr. Isaac Galland who professed to have possession of the buildings and the right to sell 20,000 acres of land known as the half-breed reservation formerly belonging to the Sax and Fox Nations of Indians and also proposed his terms of sale.[25]

In February 1839, Dr. Galland's offer was forwarded to the Prophet, still in Liberty Jail, who responded, "We will purchase it of you at the proposals that you made to Mr. Barlow."[26] This land formed the nucleus of the future city of Nauvoo. Joseph and Hyrum Smith, who were allowed to escape in April 1839, joined their families in Quincy, Illinois, and Joseph took immediate steps to gather his scattered flock. That same month, he purchased the 135-acre farm of Hugh White. Joseph and his family moved into a log home standing on that property on 10 May; and the Saints began to flock to Commerce. The land was "regularly laid off into blocks, containing four lots of eleven by twelve rods each making all corner lots."[27] The name of the city (Commerce) was changed to Nauvoo, which Joseph Smith explained was a word of Hebrew origin meaning "beautiful."[28]

As Mormon immigrants gathered to the new town, several additions were made to the original plat. On 4 April 1840, a local landowner, Daniel H. Wells, allowed his eighty-four-acre property to be annexed to the growing city. The Wells

---

25. David W. Rogers, quoted in David and Della Miller, *Nauvoo: The City of Joseph* (Salt Lake City: Peregrine Press, 1974), 21. David White Rogers (1787-1881) was baptized in 1837 by Parley P. Pratt.

26. Dean C. Jessee, ed., *The Personal Writings of Joseph Smith* (Salt Lake City: Deseret Book, 1984), 424.

27. "Nauvoo," *Times and Seasons* 3 (1 October 1842): 936.

28. Louis C. Zucker, "Joseph Smith As a Student of Hebrew," *Dialogue: A Journal of Mormon Thought* 3 (Summer 1968): 41.

property was located on a bluff east of the original settlement and was divided into twenty-four blocks by 1839.[29] On one of these blocks, the temple would be built.

The Saints had left one temple in Ohio and had, for the time being, abandoned plans to build three others in Missouri. Yet only a year after their arrival at Nauvoo—destitute, afflicted with malaria from mosquitoes in the swampy river bottom, and challenged by all of the tasks of reclaiming the land and building a city—they began to speak of building a temple. Thus, the stage was set for the next great effort in temple building.

---

29. Miller and Miller, *Nauvoo: City of Joseph*, 36, 38.

Chapter 1

ALL THINGS IN READINESS: AUGUST 1840 TO JANUARY 1841

Announcement of the Nauvoo Temple

Although no 1839 records from Nauvoo hint of building a temple, the press of building a new city had only postponed, not displaced this important goal. William Clayton indicates that, early in 1840, "the authorities began to talk upon the subject of building a temple, wherein to administer the ordinances of God's house. Several Councils were held and a place selected whereon the Temple was contemplated to be built."[1] Clayton's statement affirms that these discussions were initially limited to private meetings, though we do not know exactly which "authorities" were involved. However, talk of temple building became public during the summer. A contributor to the *Times and Seasons*, the new Church paper in Nauvoo, indicated in the 8 June issue that there were "several large stone buildings

---

1. George D. Smith, *An Intimate Chronicle: The Journals of William Clayton* (Salt Lake City: Signature Books, 1995), 526. William Clayton's history of the construction of the Nauvoo Temple, a holograph document composed in 1845, is in the LDS Church Archives, titled, "William Clayton's Journal, etc." Andrew Jenson made a typescript copy which appears in the Journal History of the Church of Jesus Christ of Latter-day Saints (chronology of typed entries and newspaper clippings, 1830-present), LDS Church Archives, under the date 31 December 1844.

now in contemplation to be erected this season, one of which is designed as a place of worship."[2] It seems likely that this passage has reference to the temple.

On 19 July 1840, the Prophet made the first recorded public announcement that clearly identifies his intention to build a temple in Nauvoo:

> Now from this hour bring every thing you can bring and build a Temple unto the Lord, a house unto the mighty God of Jacob. We will build upon the top of this Temple a great observatory, a great and high watch tower and in the top thereof we will suspend a tremendous bell that when it is rung shall rouse the inhabitants of Madison, wake up the people of Warsaw, and sound in the ears of men in Carthage. Then come the ancient records, yea all of them. Dig them; yes bring them forth speedily.
>
> Then shall the poor be fed by the curious who shall come from all parts of the world to see this wonderful temple. Yea, I prophecy that pleasure parties [sh]all come from England to see the Mammoth and like the Queen of Sheba shall say the half never was told them....
>
> Now brethren I obligate myself to build as great a temple as ever Solomon did, if the church will back me up. Moreover, it shall not impoverish any man but enrich thousands.... And if it should be (stretching his hand towards the place and in a melancholy tone that made all hearts tremble) [the] will of God that I might live to behold that temple completed and finished from the foundation to the top stone I will say, "O Lord it is enough Lord let thy servant depart in peace," which is my earnest prayer in the name of the Lord Jesus, Amen.[3]

This remarkable discourse gives a sweeping overview of Joseph's vision for the temple. It is clear at this early date that some of the design imperatives, including the tower, observatory, and bell, had already been considered. He also mentions, with characteristic foresight, the impact the building project would have on Nauvoo's culture and economy, and the curiosity it would generate even outside of the surrounding country. Finally, he poignantly foreshadows his death which tragically prevented him from seeing the temple completed.

Furthermore, as the mention of "ancient records" suggests, Joseph may have intended to use a portion of the temple as a museum to house and display antiquities, including these papyri. After Joseph showed one visitor the mummies and the Egyptian papyri from which he was translating the Book of Abraham, the visitor exclaimed: "What an ornament it would be to have these ancient manuscripts handsomely set in frames, and hung up about the wall of the temple which

---

2. "Immigration," *Times and Seasons* 1 (8 June 1840): 124.

3. Dean Jessee, "Joseph Smith's 19 July 1840 Discourse," *BYU Studies* 19 (Spring 1979): 390-94. From a discourse of Joseph Smith reported by Martha Jane Knowlton, 19 July 1840.

you are about to erect at this place." Joseph replied, "Yes ... and the translations hung up with them."[4] Furthermore, the revelation commanding the Saints to build a temple, which was received in January 1841, included the provision, "Come ye ... with all your antiquities" (D&C 124:26). The temple was never used as a museum, although plans for another museum in Nauvoo were made in 1843. Alluding of this museum, John Taylor commented: "We expect that ere long Nauvoo will be the great emporium of the west, and take the lead in the arts, sciences, and literature, as well as in religion."[5]

As the summer wore on, Church authorities continued to discuss the temple, and word of the anticipated construction circulated. On 31 August, the First Presidency issued a letter to the Church reiterating their commitment to build a temple:

> Believing the time has now come, when it is necessary to erect a house of prayer, a house of order, a house for the worship of our God, where the ordinances can be attended to agreeably to His divine will, in this region of country—to accomplish which, considerable exertion must be made, and means will be required—and as the work must be hastened in righteousness, it behooves the Saints to weigh the importance of these things, in their minds, in all their bearings, and then take such steps as are necessary to carry them into operation; and arming themselves with courage, resolve to do all they can, and feel themselves as much interested as though the whole labor depended on themselves alone. By so doing they will emulate the glorious deeds of the fathers, and secure the blessings of heaven upon themselves and their posterity to the latest generation.
>
> To those who feel thus interested, and can assist in this great work, we say, let them come to this place.[6]

This passage makes it clear that one purpose of the proposed structure would be to house ordinances that could not be appropriately performed elsewhere.

Among the most interesting aspects of the statement is the appeal to gather to Nauvoo for the purpose of erecting the temple. Saints who felt "interested" and who had the means were to come assist in the project. This almost hesitant request contrasts sharply with later instructions from Joseph and his successors about the temple's construction which treated it as a matter of salvation.[7] No doubt

4. Unknown author, "A Glance at the Mormons," *Alton (Illinois) Telegraph* 5 (14 November 1840): 2.

5. "To the Saints Among All Nations," *Times and Seasons* 4 (15 May 1843): 210.

6. Joseph Smith, Jr., et al., *History of the Church of Jesus Christ of Latter-day Saints*, edited by B. H. Roberts (Salt Lake City: Deseret News Press, 6 vols. published 1902-12, Vol. 7 published 1932, 1st printing), 4:186.

the importance of the temple was impressed more deeply in the minds of Joseph Smith and his followers with the passage of time.

Appointment of the Temple Committee

At a general conference of the Church held the first week of October 1840, the Saints took the first substantive steps toward organizing the temple-building effort. During the conference session on 3 October Joseph "spoke of the necessity of building a 'House of the Lord' in this place." The conference voted affirmatively "that the saints build a house for the worship of God" and decided to start construction in ten days.[8]

The conference also appointed a temple committee, three "men of tried integrity" who would manage the day-to-day tasks associated with the construction of and funding for the temple. In appointing the committee, the Saints were following the precedent set in Kirtland where Hyrum Smith, Jared Carter, and Reynolds Cahoon had served as the building committee to oversee the construction of the Kirtland Temple. The new committee consisted of Cahoon, Elias Higbee, and Alpheus Cutler. Higbee, a convert to the Church in 1832, brought his experience in working on the Kirtland Temple to the project. Fifty-six-year-old Cutler, who had joined the Church in 1833, was the oldest member of the committee. The conference resolution concluded with a plea "to hold up, and strengthen their hands" so that the temple could be erected.[9]

The duties of the temple committee were many and varied. During the initial stages of construction, Higbee "kept the books and work accounts, and generally wrote the receipts for tithing. This branch of the business occupied nearly the whole of his time."[10] The duty of writing tithing receipts was later transferred to the office of Joseph Smith's clerk. (See chap. 9.)

The committee's primary role was that of operations management. They hired workers, authorized the purchase of materials, monitored the workflow and watched for bottlenecks in the process.[11] For example, during the autumn of 1842, the committee could not get "sufficient stone quarried to supply the stone cutters

7. See chap. 2. In January, a revelation would command the Church to gather and build a temple or risk their salvation (D&C 124:32).

8. (untitled article), *Times and Seasons* 1 (October 1840): 184. The first sentence is: "In this number we lay before our readers the minutes of the conference held at this place on the 3rd [of October]."

9. Ibid.

10. George D. Smith, *An Intimate Chronicle*, 529.

11. Ibid..

at the Temple, and ... some of them have been obliged to quit work in consequence."[12] Later, the quarry was "blockaded," being "filled with rock," but the
stonecutters were still idle because no teams were available to haul the rock to the
temple grounds.[13] On other occasions, the stone setters were obliged to wait
because the cutters had not yet dressed the stones.[14] In such cases, the committee
assessed the needs and joined with other authorities in petitioning the Saints in the
community for additional help. Occasionally they made announcements in print
and from the pulpit, addressing the specific needs of the day. For example, at a special conference held in Nauvoo in October 1843, Cutler and Cahoon addressed
specific concerns of committee with respect to the construction:

> Elder Alpheus Cutler, on the part of the Temple Committee, represented the work
> of the Temple to be retarded for want of team work and provisions; also of iron,
> steel, powder and clothing—giving as his opinion that the walls could easily be com-
> pleted next season, if these embarrassments were removed, and the brethren would
> come forward to sustain them in the work with the means that were in their hands.
>   Elder Reynolds Cahoon followed, seconding the remarks of [E]lder Cutler, and
> setting forth the importance of the saints using their utmost exertions to fulfill the
> revelation concerning the Temple earnestly exhorting the saints, here and abroad,
> to roll in the necessary means into the hands of the Committee, that the work may
> advance with rapidity.[15]

In the spring of 1841, a small shed known as the "committee house" was
erected at the temple site from which the committee operated.[16] The committee
members were paid $2 per day for their services in coordinating the construction.[17]

Purchasing the Land

During the months after October conference, the newly appointed committee "contracted with Daniel H. Wells, Esq., for the land whereon to build the
temple."[18] In the beginning, the contract was informal, possibly verbal. Wells, a

12. "The Temple," *Times and Seasons* 3 (1 October 1842): 938.

13. "Conference Minutes," *Times and Seasons* 5 (1 August 1844): 596-97.

14. George D. Smith, *An Intimate Chronicle*, 533; see also History of the Church, 7:323.

15. Minutes of Special Conference, 9 October 1843, *Journal History of the Church of Jesus Christ
of Latter-day Saints* (chronology of typed entries and newspaper clippings, 1830-present), LDS Church
Archives.

16. William Clayton, Journal, *Journal History*, 23 October 1842, 4.

17. Brigham Young, quoted in Wilford Woodruff, *Wilford Woodruff's Journal*, 1833-1898, typescript, edited by Scott G. Kenny, 9 vols. (Midvale, Utah: Signature Books, 1983-85): 5:360.

non-Mormon resident who would later become mayor of Salt Lake City and a counselor to Brigham Young, was well disposed toward the Saints. He subdivided his farm on the bluff or bench overlooking the river into building lots and sold them at low prices and easy terms to the new settlers.[19] This land was known as the Wells addition. The temple lot was block 20, bordered by Knight Street on the north, Woodruff Street on the east, Wells Street on the west, and Mulholland Street on the south.[20]

The agreement to purchase the four-acre plot for $1,100 was concluded during late 1840; and on 15 December 1840, Joseph wrote to the Twelve that the Church had "secured one of the most lovely sites for [the temple] that there is in this region of country."[21] Wells did not actually transfer the deed to Joseph Smith until 4 February 1843.[22]

Frederick Piercy, a British convert who passed by Nauvoo in August 1854, noted that the site was "situated on the highest eminence of the city" where it became to Nauvoo "what the capstone is to a building."[23] From its perch on "the Mississippi bluff," wrote Illinois representative John Reynolds, the view it commanded "reached as far the eye extends over the country up and down the river."[24] Josiah Quincy, the somewhat skeptical mayor of Boston who visited Nauvoo in 1844, expressed the belief that "it would have required a genius to have designed anything worthy of that noble site."[25]

18. George D. Smith, *An Intimate Chronicle,* 527.

19. Junius F. Wells, "Wells Family," *Utah Genealogical and Historical Society Magazine* 6 (January 1915): 4. Wells joined the Church in August of 1846 and joined the Saints in Winter Quarters that fall. He later served as a counselor to Brigham Young in the First Presidency.

20. B. H. Roberts, *Comprehensive History of the Church of Jesus Christ of Latter-day Saints,* 6 vols. (Salt Lake City: Deseret News Press, 1930), 2:200.

21. Dean C. Jessee, ed., *The Personal Writings of Joseph Smith* (Salt Lake City: Deseret Book, 1984), 484. *The History of the Church,* 4:229, contains a slightly variant version of this statement but misdates it at 19 October 1840, which is almost certainly too early.

22. Hancock County, Deeds, Book M, 397, microfilm, LDS Church Archives. The deed was recorded on 8 July 1844, less than two weeks after the murder of the Smith brothers. The wording of the deed identifies the sellers as "Daniel H. Wells and Eliza R., his wife," while the recipient was "Joseph Smith, sole Trustee in Trust for the Church of Jesus Christ of Latter-day Saints." "Nauvoo 'Operahouse' Acquired by Wilford C. Wood," *Improvement Era* 40 (June 1937): 638.

23. Frederick H. Piercy, "Route from Liverpool to Great Salt Lake Valley," *Improvement Era* 57 (August 1954): 557. Excerpts from Piercy's 1855 publication, *The Route from Liverpool to the Great Salt Lake Valley Illustrated.*

24. John Reynolds, *My Own Times: Embracing the History of My Life* (Belleville, IL: Perryman and Davison, 1855), 587, microfilm, L. Tom Perry Special Collections, Harold B. Lee Library, Brigham Young University, Provo, Utah. Reynolds (1788-1865), not a member of the Church, was an Illinois politician who visited Nauvoo several times.

25. Josiah Quincy, *Figures of the Past from the Leaves of Old Journals* (Boston: Roberts Brothers, 1883), 390.

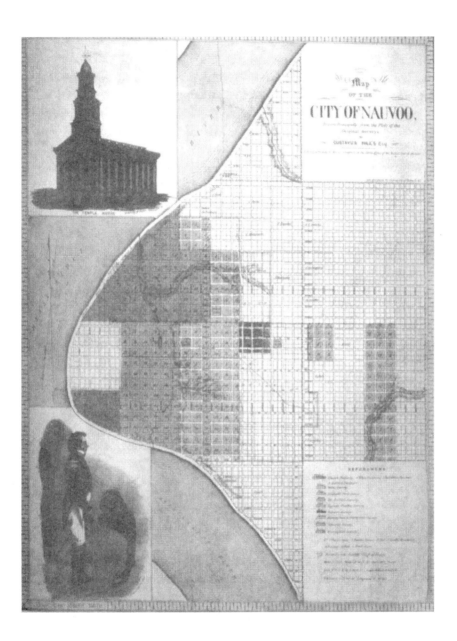

1841 Map of Nauvoo with an early sketch of the temple in the top left corner

Architect William Weeks

The two great contributors to the temple design were Joseph Smith and William Weeks. Soon after the October 1840 conference, Joseph "advertised for plans for a temple." According to William Clayton, his personal secretary during this period, "Several plans were made and submitted by various individuals."[26] According to tradition none of the plans was satisfactory to the Prophet until Weeks showed Smith his plans. Then "Joseph grabbed him, hugged him and said, 'You are the man I want.'"[27]

Twenty-seven-year-old Weeks had joined the Church in the South and had arrived at Nauvoo in 1839 with his wife. Although details of his architectural training are scarce, one historian believes he was tutored under William Strickland, a leading proponent of the neo-classical Greek Revival style.[28] What is clear, however, is that he was familiar with and influenced by that style.[29]

The exact nature of the relationship between Weeks and Smith and the extent to which each participated in the design is a matter of speculation, since only a few anecdotes have survived. On 5 February 1844, when the temple was well under way, Weeks attempted to overrule a particular design element that Joseph Smith had suggested. Smith firmly corrected him: "I wish you to carry out my designs. I have seen in vision the splendid appearance of that building illuminated, and will have it built according to the pattern shown me."[30]

It is clear that Joseph was responsible for the general concept as well as many of the details. Josiah Quincy, after visiting the temple site in 1844, remarked, possibly with some sarcasm: "It was a wonderful structure, altogether indescribable by me. Being, presumably, like something Smith had seen in a vision."[31] John Pulsipher, a teenager in the 1840s, recalled in his autobiography that the temple

---

26. Joseph Earl Arrington, "William Weeks, Architect of the Nauvoo Temple," *BYU Studies* 19 (Spring 1979): 340. While the exact date of the sweepstakes for the temple design is unknown, it almost certainly occurred in October. The December issue of the *Millennial Star* published in England, contains this brief report of the October conference: "They have began to build a house of worship in Nauvoo, which will be built of stone, 110 feet by 120 in breadth and length." "News from America," *Millennial Star* 1 (December 1840): 216. The *Star* regularly included a report of happenings in America that was two months behind in its news. In order for word of the temple's proposed dimensions (although they later changed) to be published in England in December, they would have most certainly been established in October.

27. George D. Smith, *An Intimate Chronicle*, 526.

28. T. Edgar Lyon, quoted in Charles Mark Hamilton, "Authorship and Architectural Influences on the Salt Lake Temple" (M.A. thesis, University of Utah, 1972), 9.

29. Ibid., 9.

30. *History of the Church*, 6:196.

had been "built according to the pattern that the Lord gave Joseph."[32] Parley P. Pratt later testified to a congregation of Saints in Utah that "angels and spirits from the eternal worlds" had instructed Smith "in all things pertaining to ... sacred architecture."[33] Joseph Smith himself declared that it was "built by direct revelation."[34] Benjamin Winchester wrote, "Its plan for convenience, surpasses any thing that I ever saw, and well it may; for the Lord has had something to do with it."[35]

Wandle Mace, likely repeating what he had learned from Joseph Smith, indicates that the Book of Revelation served as inspiration for the design: "The order of architecture was ... a representation of the Church, the Bride, the Lamb's wife. John the Revelator, in the 12 chapter [and] first verse of [the book of Revelation,] says, 'And there appeared a great wonder in heaven; a woman clothed with the sun, and the moon under her feet, and upon her head a crown of twelve stars.' This is portrayed in the beautifully cut stone of this grand temple."[35a]

Despite Joseph Smith's direct involvement, however, he admitted to a reporter in 1843: "I am not capacitated to build according to the world. I know nothing about architecture and all that."[36] Weeks thus played a critical role in realizing Joseph's ideas. His contributions included formalizing the design, drafting the plans, planning the building's structural engineering, and supervising the design's implementation on-site.

There may never have been a complete set of finished drawings for the temple. The design was fluid and evolved as Joseph (and later Brigham Young) saw the need for change. Revisions to the design are known to have taken place as late as 1845. (See chap. 9.) In the spring of 1844, a reporter for the *St. Louis Gazette* commented that the temple was to be built

in a style of architecture which no Greek, nor Goth, nor Frank ever dreamed.... Indeed, as I heard it from the lips of the Prophet himself, the style of architecture is exclusively his own, and must be known henceforth and forever I suppose as the "Mormon order!"... Its interior structure and arrangement, we were informed by the prophet, had not yet been decided on—(he did not tell me "had not yet

31. Quincy, *Figures of the Past*, 390.

32. John Pulsipher, Autobiography, typescript, 8-9, Perry Special Collections, Lee Library.

33. Parley P. Pratt, 6 April 1853, *Journal of Discourses*, 26 vols. (London and Liverpool: LDS Booksellers Depot, 1855-86), 2:44.

34. Joseph Smith, quoted in I. Daniel Rupp, *An Original History of the Religious Denominations at Present Existing in the United States* (Philadelphia: J. Y. Humphreys, 1844), 409.

35. Benjamin Winchester, Letter to Erastus Snow, 12 November 1841, *Times and Seasons* 3 (15 November 1841): 605.

35a. Wandle Mace, Autobiography, 207, typescript, 8-9, Perry Special Collections, Lee Library.

36. David Ney White, "The Prairies, Nauvoo, Joe Smith, the Temple, the Mormons, etc.," *Pittsburgh (Pennsylvania) Weekly Gazette* 14 September 1843, 3; reprinted in Dean C. Jessee, ed., *The Papers of Joseph Smith* (Salt Lake City: Deseret Book, 1989), 1:438-44.

been revealed to him," as he did to many others) and indeed he was by no means certain he should erect the edifice externally in accordance with the plan proposed and published."[37]

Several of the temple drawings have been preserved in the LDS Church Archives. These include a rendering of the temple's exterior and two front eleva-

TABLE 1

CHANGES IN THE EXTERIOR DESIGN FOR THE TEMPLE

Drawing 1.[38] Rendering in Corner of Hill's Map	Drawing 2.[39] First Front Elevation	Drawing 3.[40] Second Front Elevation	DUP Daguerreotype[41]
Square tower made of stone and wood	Square tower made of stone and wood	Octagonal tower made of wood	Octagonal tower made of wood
Triangular pediment[42]	Triangular pediment	Square pediment	Square pediment
One semicircular window in pediment	One semicircular window in pediment	Five semi-circular windows in pediment	Four square windows in pediment
Trumpet stone capitals	Sunstone capitals	Sunstone capitals	Sunstone capitals
No weather vane	No weather vane	Angel weather vane	Angel weather vane
Peristyle[43] temple	Engaged pilasters[44]	Engaged pilasters	Engaged pilasters

37. Date of original publication not given; reprinted as "The Temple of Nauvoo," *Journal History*, 12 June 1844, 6.

38. Drawing by William Weeks in top right corner of Gustavus Hill's Nauvoo plat (ca. 1841). Poster reproduction of map obtained from Nauvoo Restoration, Inc., in my possession.

39. Front elevation of Nauvoo Temple by William Weeks (ca. 1841), original in LDS Church Archives.

40. Ibid.

41. Southwesterly view of temple (ca. 1847), daguerreotype in possession of Daughters of the Utah Pioneers, Cedar City, Utah.

42. A pediment is the decorative ornament that crowns the front of a classical building. It rests on the architrave, or beam that spans the columns or pilasters that support the structure.

43. Peristyle means "encompassed by a row of columns."

44. Pilasters are square columns. An engaged pilaster is set within a wall and projects only about one quarter of its diameter from the wall.

Two drawings of the temple by William Weeks. On the left is an early rendering that appeared on Gustavus Hill's 1842 map of Nauvoo; to the right is a front elevation showing how his design evolved.

tions, each revealing key changes made over time. When compared to daguerreotypes of the finished structure's exterior, it becomes apparent that many other radical changes occurred before the design was final. Table 1 compares the three progressive design drawings with each other and with the photographs.

Interestingly, the third drawing has the marks of extensive use. Pinholes have been pricked through the corners of the sheet, suggesting that it may have been posted near the building site for reference.

It is also evident that a scale model of the working temple design was made and shown to visitors. It was from this model that many visitors to the incomplete temple obtained an idea of what the finished temple would eventually look like.[45]

Impressions of the Design and Architectural Style

During the five-year building project, newspapers and travelers published a wide array of opinions about the temple's appearance and assessments of its architectural style. The design defied categorization according to conventional architec-

---

45. Unidentified visitor, *St. Louis Gazette*, ca. June 1844.

tural styles or traditions. One editor declared, "Nothing can be more original in architecture."[46] Charles Lanman, a traveling essayist who visited the temple in 1846, believed that the temple was patterned "principally after the Roman style of architecture, somewhat intermixed with Grecian and Egyptian."[47] Henry Lewis, an artist who painted the temple in 1848 offered his opinion: "It bears a nearer resemblance to the Bysantium or Roman Grecian style than any other although the capitals and bases are entirely unique. Still the cornices are Grecian in part.... [C]onsidering ... that is of no particular style it [does] not in the least offend the eye by its uniqueness like almost all innovations from established standards do."[48] John Greenleaf Whittier, the famous Quaker poet from New England, thought the design embodied "the Titan idea of the Pyramids, and the solemn and awe-inspiring thought which speaks from the Gothic piles of the middle ages."[49]

Thomas Ford, governor of Illinois from 1842 to 1846 and a frequent visitor to Nauvoo, wrote disparagingly in his 1854 history of the state:

> It has been said that the church architecture of a sect indicates the genius and spirit of its religion. The grand and solemn structures of the Catholics point to the towering hierarchy and imposing ceremonies of the church; the low and broad meeting houses of the Methodists formerly shadowed forth abhorrence of gaudy decoration; and their unpretending humility, and the light and airy, and elegant edifices of the Presbyterians, truly indicate the passion for education, refinement and polish, amongst that thrifty and enterprising people. If the genius of Mormonism were tried by this test, as exhibited in the temple, we could only pronounce that it was a piece of patch-work, variable, strange, and incongruous.[50]

Josiah Quincy also disliked the design and called the temple a "grotesque structure" covered with "queer carvings of moons and suns." According to him it "produced no effect that was commensurate with its cost."[51] But the temple's appearance and sheer size, as a rule, impressed those who saw it. The statements below are typical of the reactions of most:

---

46. *New York Spectator,* 9 November 1844, reprinted in Cecil B. McGavin, *Nauvoo Temple* (Salt Lake City: Deseret Book, 1962), 50.

47. Charles Lanman, *A Summer in the Wilderness* (Philadelphia: n.pub., 1847), 31; see also Reynolds, My Own Times, 586-87.

48. Henry Lewis, *Valley of the Mississippi Illustrated* (St. Paul: Minnesota Historical Society, 1967), 292.

49. John Greenleaf Whittier, "A Mormon Conventicle," *Littell's Living Age* (October-November 1847), reprinted in William Mulder and A. Russell Mortensen, eds., *Among the Mormons: Historic Accounts by Contemporary Observers* (New York: Alfred Knopf, 1958), 159.

St. Louis Gazette (spring 1844): The appearance presented by this edifice in the diagram model, which was shown me by the Prophet, is grand and imposing.... [It] will certainly represent one of the most extraordinary architectural structures since the era of the erection of the massive sanctuaries of the Nile—of descriptions of the ruins of which the spectator is by this reminded.... The external layer of stone is dressed with considerable neatness, and each of the range of pilasters by which it is ornamented, bears upon it a sculptural representation of the crescent, with the profile of a man's face in strong relief, much in the style of that edifying picture of the moon you may have been wont to admire, as well as myself, in the primer when a boy! The effect of this image is semi-solemn, semi-laughable, and certainly more than semi-singular.[52]

John Reynolds (ca. 1846): I was in the Mormon Temple at Nauvoo and examined it. It was a large and splendid edifice ... and its grandeur and magnificence truly astonished me.[53]

Joseph Fielding (December 1845): The temple is indeed a noble structure, and I suppose the architects of our day know not of what order to call it, Gothic, Doric, Corinthian or what. I call it heavenly. The upper room is finished.... I entered it for the first time and I truly felt as though I had gotten out of the world.[54]

Henry Lewis (1848): Taking into consideration the circumstances under which it was built it is a wonderful building and considering too that it is of no particular style it does not in the least offend the eye like almost all innovations from old established standards do.[55]

J. B. Newhall (24 April 1846): The Nauvoo Temple is a very singular and unique structure.... It is different from anything in ancient or modern history. Everything about it is on a magnificent scale, and when finished and seen from the opposite side of the river, will present one, if not the most beautiful, chaste and noble specimens of architecture to be found in the world.[56]

John Greenleaf Whittier (1844): The Nauvoo Temple ... when completed, will be the most splendid and imposing architectural monument in the new world ... it stands upon the highest elevation of the most beautiful city in the west, overlooking the "Father of Waters"—a temple unique as the faith of its builder.[57]

50. Thomas Ford, *History of Illinois, from Its Commencement as a State in 1818 to 1847* (Chicago: S. Griggs & Co., 1854), 491.

51. Quincy, *Figures of the Past*, 390.

52. "The Nauvoo Temple," *Journal History*, 12 June 1844, 3.

53. Reynolds, *My Own Times*, 587.

54. Andrew F. Ehat, ed., "'They Might Have Known He Was Not a Fallen Prophet:' The Nauvoo Journal of Joseph Fielding," *BYU Studies* 19 (Winter 1979): 158-59.

Tithing on Labor and Possessions

At the October 1840 conference, Joseph Smith "explained to the Saints the law of tithing and the plan upon which the building of the temple was to be conducted."[58] The temple was to be constructed by the tithes of the people. Saints were to donate "one tenth of all they possess when they enter into the new and everlasting covenant; and then one tenth of their interest, or income yearly afterwards."[59] William Huntington, a fifty-seven-year-old convert from New Hampshire who had joined the Church in 1835, wrote in his journal that one "tenth of all we possess ... has been handed over to the trustee-in-trust for the purpose of building the house of the Lord."[60]

In the 15 December 1841 issue of the *Times and Seasons*, the Quorum of the Twelve, most of whom who had recently returned from missions in Great Britain, issued an epistle to the Church emphasizing tithing as the primary means of funding the temple project:

> The Temple is to be built by tithing and consecration, and every one is at liberty to consecrate all they find in their hearts so to do; but the tithings required, is [sic] one tenth of all any one possessed at the commencement of the building, and one tenth part of all his increase from that time till the completion of the same, whether it be money or whatever he may be blessed with. Many, in this place, are laboring every tenth day for the house, and this is the tithing of their income, for they have nothing else; others would labor the same but they are sick, therefore, excusable, when they get well let them begin: while there are others who appear to think their own business of more importance than the Lord's: to such we would ask, who gave you your time, health, strength, and put you into business? and will you not begin quickly to return with usury that which you have received? Our God will not wait always.[61]

Joseph Fielding, noting the peculiarity of this "bootstrapping" method of financing the temple, especially given the crushing poverty of the Saints, speculat-

---

55. Lewis, *Valley of the Mississippi Illustrated*, 292.

56. J. B. Newhall, extract from discourse published in *Salem Advertiser and Argus*, quoted in *History of the Church*, 5:432.

57. Whittier, "A Mormon Conventicle," 159.

58. William Clayton, "An Interesting Journal," in George D. Smith, *An Intimate Chronicle*, 526.

59. "An Epistle of the Twelve to the Church of Jesus Christ of Latter-day Saints," *Times and Seasons* 6 (15 January 1845): 779-80.

60. William Huntington, Sr., "Journal of William Huntington" (1784-1846), typescript, 13, Perry Special Collections, Lee Library.

61. "Baptisms for the Dead: An Epistle of the Twelve to the Saints of the Last Days," *Times and Seasons* 3 (15 December 1841): 626.

ed, "I suppose the men of England would not attempt to build such a house unless they had some thousands of pounds to start with, but it seems as though the Lord saw that money is the god of this generation, and to shew the folly of it, is manifesting to the world that he can do his own work."[62]

Although workers began to be hired as early as 1842 to perform such specialized tasks as carpentry and intricate stone carving, much of the work on the temple was accomplished by labor tithing. The success of the labor tithe was so marked that it became the means of tithing requested from all able-bodied men who lived in or near Nauvoo. An epistle of the Twelve in April 1842 explained: "The building of the Temple of the Lord in this city ... is and must be accomplished by the united exertions of the labors of the brethren who reside here, and the tithings and contributions of those who are scattered abroad in the different states."[63]

In February 1841, after several months of work in the quarry, Elias Higbee, one of the building committee, commended the men of Nauvoo for their tithing labor:

> Most of the brethren here, have manifested a disposition worthy of imitation by the remainder in the good cause, by working every tenth day, since last Conference, by which some materials are made ready for the building: those who live in this place, who have not been able to put in their tenth day, will, I hope, not fail to put in an equivalent against Spring. Those who live at a distance, who cannot put in work, will, I trust, send in their tithing speedily, so that the work may be accomplished speedily.[64]

Speaking a year later, Joseph Smith lauded the dedication of the tithing laborers and appealed to the Mormon citizens not to let other interests take precedence over the building effort: "The heart of the Trustee is daily made to rejoice in the good feelings of the brethren, made manifest in their exertion to carry forward the work of the Lord, and rear His Temple; and it is hoped that neither planting, sowing, or reaping will hereafter be made to interfere with the regulations hinted at above."[65]

Aroet Hale, who turned fourteen in 1842, recalled that his father, Jonathan Harriman Hale, was one of those who understood the principle of tithing labor and kept careful account of his obligations to labor on the temple: "Father moved to

62. Joseph Fielding, Letter to the Editor, datelined January 1842, Nauvoo, *Millennial Star* 3 (August 1842): 78.

63. "An Epistle of the Twelve," *Times and Seasons* 3, no. 13 (2 May 1842): 767.

64. Elias Higbee, "Ecclesiastical," *Times and Seasons* 2 (1 February 1841): 296.

65. Joseph Smith, "To the Brethren in Nauvoo City," *Times and Seasons* 3 (28 February 1842): 517. Joseph here refers to the regulations of labor tithing.

Nauvoo in the spring of 1841.... On arriving at Nauvoo, he unloaded his wagon ... and commencing hauling rock on the temple and never ceased until he had paid up two and a half year's back tithing here at Nauvoo."[66]

In Nauvoo's cash-strapped economy, labor tithing was a versatile medium of exchange. Workers aboard the *Maid of Iowa*, a ferryboat purchased by the Church, had tithing for the temple deducted automatically from their pay.[67] Some worked to pay tithing owed by a third party or in exchange for other services. Mercy Fielding Thompson, the sister of Joseph Fielding, received a receipt from the building committee in September 1842 certifying that she had "two dollars in work for the building of the Temple; work paid by Zihen Ballonis."[68] John McDonald, who turned ten in 1843 "worked his father's tithing on the Nauvoo Temple," but because he was "so young" his hours were figured at "only half of the going rate."[69]

Unfortunately, some abused the practice of collecting money in exchange for a promise to work on the temple. The trustees issued this warning late in 1844:

> There have been instances wherein men have gone amongst the branches of the church, collecting money and agreeing to pay the same amount in labor on the Temple, which they represent will answer as good a purpose as the money. We have to say on this subject that all such transactions are regarded as fraud, and is only a more crafty way of cheating the brethren. It would be folly for us to tell a man that ten days labor on the Temple would answer the law of tithing as well as ten dollars in money, when he was possessed of one hundred dollars in money.... Whoever will read the history of the ancients with care will find that the law was, that they must pay one tenth of all in its kind, whether cattle, horses, sheep, or the fruits of the field. 'Tis true there were laws of redemption, whereby a man might redeem "ought of his tithing" but it was so strict, that it is far easier to pay the tithing in kind rather than redeem it.[70]

Many members of the Church paid tithing in the form of cash, particularly those who lived at great distances from Nauvoo. These contributions were espe-

---

66. Aroet Hale, "Diary of Aroet Lucius Hale," typescript, 6, Perry Special Collections, Lee Library. Although this document is titled "Diary," it is in reality an autobiography and appears to have been written after 1850.

67. Donald L. Enders, "The Steamboat *Maid of Iowa*: Mormon Mistress of the Mississippi," *BYU Studies* 19, no. 3 (Spring 1979): 329.

68. Certificate dated 28 September 1842, Mercy Fielding Thompson Papers, microfilm, LDS Church Archives.

69. "John McDonald," in Andrew Jenson, *LDS Biographical Encyclopedia*, 4 vols. (Salt Lake City: Andrew Jenson History Co., 1901-37; reprinted Salt Lake City: Greg Kofford Books, 2007), 2:11.

70. N. K. Whitney and George Miller, "A Voice from the Temple," *Times and Seasons* 5 (1 December 1844): 729.

cially significant because some needed materials for the temple could be purchased only with cash or traded for high-quality goods. Luman Andros Shurtliff
wrote, "The best of the property was of necessity taken to buy nails, glass, paints,
and such things as our labor would not produce."[71]

During the first year of work on the temple, members usually paid their
tithes directly to the temple committee who issued receipts to the donors.
However, Joseph Smith himself received many donations for the temple.
Apparently he would accumulate these donations and then periodically forward
them to the building committee. On 12 April 1841, the building committee issued
a receipt to him for such contributions, signed by all three committee members:
"Received of Joseph Smith Sole Trustee in trust for the Church of Jesus Christ of latter day Saints One hundred and eighty six dollars, and fifty one cents in notes and
orders and also one hundred and eighty six dollars and twelve and half cents in
cash to be expended by the building Committee to the use of the house of the Lord
in this City."[72]

Often, members paid tithes in-kind, meaning that they offered goods or
services instead of cash. Tithe-payers would bring their donations to the temple
committee who would appraise them and record their equivalent as tithing credit. In December 1841, the *Times and Seasons* published a typical plea for tithing
support:

> Large stores of provisions will be required to complete the work [on the temple],
> and now is the time for securing it, while meat is plenty and can be had for one
> half the value that it can at other seasons of the year, and the weather is cool and
> suitable for packing. Let the brethren for two hundred miles around drive their fat
> cattle and hogs to this place, where they may be preserved, and there will be a
> supply till another favorable season rolls round, or till the end of the labor.—Now
> is the time to secure food. Now is the time that the trustee is ready to receive
> your droves.—Not the maimed, the lean, the halt, and the blind, and such that you
> cannot use; it is for the Lord, and he wants no such offering: but if you want his
> blessing give him the best; give him as good as he has given you. Beds and bed-
> ding, socks, mittens, shoes, clothing of every description, and store goods are
> needed for the comfort of the laborers this winter; journeymen stonecutters,
> quarrymen, teams and teamsters for drawing stone, and all kinds of provision for
> men and beast, are needed in abundance.[73]

71. Luman Andros Shurtliff, "Biographical Sketch of the Life of Luman Andros Shurtliff," typescript, 52, Perry Special Collections, Lee Library. Shurtliff (1807-84), was baptized on 21 August 1836
and was a member of Nauvoo Legion.

72. Receipt, Newel K. Whitney Papers, Perry Special Collections, Lee Library.

73. "Baptism for the Dead," *Times and Seasons* 3 (15 December 1841): 626-27.

No doubt some contributors were not satisfied with the valuation placed on their donations; but as this notice makes plain, the committee must have also experienced dissatisfaction with some of those contributions. On 20 January 1861 in Salt Lake City, Brigham Young complained sarcastically about some of the difficulties of appraising non-cash tithing donations in Nauvoo:

> In the days of Joseph, when a horse was brought in for tithing, he was pretty sure to be hipped, or ringboned, or have the pole-evil,[74] or perhaps had passed the routine of horse-diseases until he had become used up. The question would be, "What do you want for him?" "Thirty dollars in tithing and thirty in cash." What was he really worth? Five dollars, perhaps. They would perhaps bring in a cow after the wolves had eaten off three of her teats, and she had not had a calf for six years past; and if she had a calf, and you ventured to milk her, she would kick a quid of tobacco out of your mouth. These are specimens of the kind of tithing we used to get. If you give anything for the building up of the kingdom of God, give the best you have.[75]

The records of the trustees, bishops, and temple committee indicate that among the most common goods donated and dispensed were flour, corn, bacon, sugar, coffee, beef, pork, potatoes, clothing, and blankets. These items were used to pay the hired temple hands and also to assist the poor.[76] The Nauvoo Temple day books also show that tithing played an important and versatile role in Nauvoo's economy. Albert P. Rockwood, the quarry foreman, was credited 50 cents toward his tithing on 25 February 1842, for repairing Gustavus Hills's watch. On 12 April 1841, Reynolds Cahoon was credited $4.50 for "tools furnished the House." Other interesting donations included a map of the United States, silver spoons, watch chains, copies of the Book of Mormon, and a box of pills (ailment not specified).[77] Obviously, some of these items were more useful than others; and at April 1844 general conference, Hyrum Smith pled for relevant donations: "We want provisions, money, boards, planks, and any thing that is good; we don't want any more old guns or watches."[78]

---

74. "Ring-bone" is a callus growing in the hollow circle of a horse's pastern, near the hoof. "Hipped" means to have dislocated hips.

75. Brigham Young, 20 January 1861, *Journal of Discourses*, 8:46.

76. Nauvoo Temple Committee, Day Books and Ledgers (1840-44), LDS Church Archives; Newel K. Whitney Papers, Perry Special Collections, Lee Library.

77. Nauvoo Temple Committee, Day Book A, 1841-42, LDS Church Archives.

78. "Conference Minutes," *Times and Seasons* 5 (1 August 1844): 596.

Zadoc Judd, who was seventeen in 1844, worked in Springfield, Illinois, as a tailor. His autobiography includes the story of one cash donation he made to the Nauvoo Temple:

> In my young apprenticeship I was encouraged to take in such jobs of work from my associates or others as I could and to do it at odd spells ... and by so doing I could get a little money to go to the theater or to get any extras I chose ... but my wants were few and necessities less and I soon found I had quite a lot of little change, so I went to a pawn-brokers shop and told the man I wanted a five dollar gold piece for a whole handful of silver. He gave me a very nice piece, which I carried as a pocket piece for quite a while. Now I thought I was rich, but it soon became an old story and I changed it for a five-dollar bill and sent it in a letter to my good stepmother in Nauvoo, requesting her to give it to the temple building. I soon received a kind letter from her. She was much in need of money at the time and her boy should work on the temple stone quarry and give me the credit. I was satisfied and glad I had sent it to her.[79]

After October 1842, the store near the temple itself was the primary locus for receiving and disbursing contributions. (See chap. 4.) Although it contained a wide variety of items and was a central institution in Nauvoo's economy, some donations were not useful and sometimes contributions were scanty. This meant that hired hands often had to be turned away when they came to the store for pay. William Adams, one of the hired stonecutters, later wrote: "The temple was built by tithing and other donations of the saints and the committee had much difficulty to furnish the workmen means to live upon so that their families had to be many times stinted in their food. I had worked on the temple four weeks [in early 1844] and had received no pay as very little tithing had been received at the temple store.[80]

To remedy these shortages, the General Authorities, the temple committee, and the recorder took various measures. On 21 February 1843, Joseph Smith spoke to the temple workmen, encouraging the contribution of more useable materials:

> The banks are failing and it is a privilege to say what currency we want: gold and silver to build the Temple and Nauvoo House. We want your old nose rings and finger rings and brass kettles no longer. If you have old rags, watches, guns go and peddle them and bring the hard metal. If we will do this by popular opinion

---

79. Zadoc Judd, Autobiography, 1903, typescript, 19, Perry Special Collections, Lee Library.

80. William Adams, "History of William Adams, Written by Himself" (1894), 10-11, typescript, LDS Church Archives. Adams (1822-1901) was baptized in England on March 26, 1842.

you will have a sound currency. Send home bank notes and take no paper money. Let every man write his neighbor before he starts to get gold and silver. I have contemplated these things a long time, but the time has not come till now to speak till now.[81]

At the 15 October 1843 Sunday services, he repeated the same message: "Oh, all ye rich men of the Latter-day Saints from abroad, I would invite you to bring up some of your money—your gold, your silver, and your precious things, and give to the Temple. We want iron, steel, spades, and quarrying and mechanical tools."[82]

Authorities often petitioned for help in assuring that the tithing goods in store were commodities useful to the workers.[83] For example, in July 1844, temple recorder William Clayton issued this notice in the Nauvoo Neighbor, requesting that members come trade life-sustaining goods for the nugatory wares that abounded at the store:

THOSE brethren who want to exchange their grain, pork, beef, potatoes etc., for property, wearing apparel etc., would do well to give the Temple committee a call. They would be glad to exchange any kind of property in their hands for grain, inasmuch as provisions are most wanted to carry on the works.

N. B. A good new turning lathe for sale at the Committee office.[84]

Sarah M. Kimball's Temple Contribution

The following reminiscence of Sarah Melissa Granger Kimball illustrates the good humor of Joseph Smith, the tender regard of a husband for his wife, and the sincere desire of one sister to contribute to the temple:

I went with my husband, Hiram Kimball, to his home in Nauvoo, Illinois, three weeks after my marriage. When my eldest son was three days old,[85] the Church was in need of help to assist in raising the Temple walls. I belonged to The Church of Jesus Christ of Latter-day Saints, but my husband was not yet a member. I wished to help on the Temple, but did not like to ask my husband (who owned considerable property) to help for my sake.

My husband came to my bedside, and as he was admiring our three-day-old darling, I said, "What is the boy worth?"

He replied, "Oh, I don't know; he is worth a great deal."

I said, "Is he worth a thousand dollars?"

81. Faulring, An American Prophet's Record, 310.

82. History of the Church, 6:58-59.

83. Faulring, An American Prophet's Record, 476.

84. William Clayton, "To the Farmers around Nauvoo and Vicinity," Nauvoo Neighbor 2 (7 August 1844): 3.

The reply was, "Yes, more than that if he lives and does well."

I said, "Half of him is mine, is it not?"

"Yes, I suppose so."

"Then I have something to help on the Temple."

Pleasantly, "You have?"

"Yes, and I am thinking of turning my share right in as tithing."

"Well, I'll think about that."

Soon after the above conversation, Mr. Kimball met the Prophet and said, "Sarah has got a little the advantage of me this time. She proposes to turn out the boy as church property."

President Smith seemed pleased with the joke, and said. "I accept all such donations, and from this day the boy shall stand recorded, church property."

Then turning to Willard Richards, his secretary, he said. "Make a record of this; and you are my witness."

Joseph Smith then said, "Major (Mr. Kimball was major in the Nauvoo Legion), you now have the privilege of paying $500 and retaining possession, or receiving $500 and giving possession."

Mr. Kimball asked if city property was good currency.

President Smith replied that it was.

"Then," said Mr. Kimball, "how will that block north of the Temple suit?"

President Smith replied, "It is just what we want."

The deed was soon made out and transferred in due form.

President Smith said to me, "You have consecrated your first born son. For this you are blessed of the Lord. I bless you in the name of the Lord God of Abraham, of Isaac and of Jacob. And I seal upon you all the blessings that pertain to the faithful."[86]

Quarry Opened

The decision to erect an edifice of stone, rather than a frame building, made the construction of the temple an even more demanding project, since quarrying and dressing stone were demanding and time-consuming trades. The Saints were fortunate to find several large limestone beds within miles of the city. The bed which would be the primary source for temple stone was located at the north end of the city but within the city limits. This quarry is now between Hyrum Street and Joseph Street, just west of Main Street, and near the riverbank. The stone had been

---

85. Hiram Kimball, son of Hiram Kimball and Sarah Melissa Granger Kimball, born 22 November 1841.

86. "Autobiography of Sarah Kimball," *Woman's Exponent* 12 (1 September 1883): 51.

87. Lanman, *A Summer in the Wilderness*, 31. A hydroelectric dam from Hamilton, Illinois, to Keokuk, Iowa (downriver from Nauvoo), was completed in 1913. The river level at Nauvoo rose over thirty feet, submerging the original quarry. Ida Blum, Nauvoo: Gateway to the West (n.p.: Ida Blum, 1974), 64.

exposed by a stream, now dry, that had run through the area.[87] The limestone was a beautiful white-gray.

The Saints did not delay in availing themselves of this stone. On 12 October 1840, recorded William Clayton, "the brethren commenced the opening of a quarry from which to obtain stone for the building."[88] Perrigrine Sessions recalled that they "commenced with out hardly the first tool even to a spade to begin to quarry the stone."[89] William Clayton recorded that "Brother Elisha Everett was the man who struck the first blow on the works."[90]

Jesse Crosby, a twenty-year-old at the time, later recalled: "I was present to assist. Joseph the Prophet was also there and assisted, in company with some 200 or 300 brethren in opening a beautiful quarry of lime rock, almost as white as marble."[91] Although Joseph Smith had no particular experience in stonework, he returned often to the quarry. According to John Pulsipher, Joseph "worked with his own hands, quarrying the stone for its walls when his enemies were not pursuing him."[92] Charles Barnum's biographical sketch proudly records that he was also among those that did the first quarrying.[93] Joseph Grafton Hovey recalled having "got out several hundred feet of stone during the [first] season."[94] Isaac Manning, one of the few African American members of the Church in Nauvoo, was reportedly among these stoneworkers.[95] Albert Rockwood was appointed "the overseer or captain of the stone quarry," assisted by Charles Drury.[96]

---

88. George D. Smith, *An Intimate Chronicle*, 526.

89. Perrigrine Sessions, Journal, 1814-86, 6, microfilm of holograph, LDS Church Archives. Perrigrine Sessions (1814-93) was baptized on 17 September 1835 and was a Seventy while living in Nauvoo.

90. George D. Smith, *An Intimate Chronicle*, 526. Elisha Everett (1810-90) was baptized in 1835 and later served in the Mormon Battalion.

91. Jesse Crosby, "History and Journal of Jesse Wentworth Crosby," ca. 1846, 10, Perry Special Collections, Lee Library. Crosby (1820-93) was baptized 13 July 1838 and was ordained a Seventy on 6 October 1840, following the conference which resolved to begin the temple.

92. John Pulsipher, Autobiography, typescript, 6, Perry Special Collections, Lee Library. Pulsipher (1800-94), a stonemason by trade, was baptized 25 July 1836. A captain in the Nauvoo Legion, he joined the Seventh Quorum of Seventy in 1844.

93. "Charles Barnum," in Jenson, *LDS Biographical Encyclopedia*, 3:594.

94. Joseph Hovey, "Autobiography of Joseph Grafton Hovey," typescript, 16, Perry Special Collections, Lee Library. Grandson M. R. Hovey copied and arranged this document from Hovey's journal in 1933.

95. Isaac Lewis Manning, Obituary, *Deseret News*, 17 April 1911, reprinted in Kate B. Carter, ed., *Our Pioneer Heritage*, 20 vols. (Salt Lake City: Daughters of Utah Pioneers, 1958-77): 8:509.

96. William Clayton, Journal, in *Journal History*, 31 December 1844, 14.

97. *History of the Church*, 6:242. On 7 March 1844, at a meeting called to forward the work of the temple, Hyrum Smith declared, "We shall call upon this vast multitude for a donation to buy pow-

Blasting was the usual method of obtaining blocks. The records of the building committee and trustee show frequent purchases of black powder and patent fuses. These materials were often purchased in St. Louis, with donated goods.[97] Powder cost about 20 cents a pound.[98] Rockwood estimated that by the spring of 1845 (near the closing of the quarry), they had "burned ... about one hundred casks of powder" at the quarry.[99] Each keg contained from 50 to 100 pounds of blasting powder—a total of between two and four tons of powder to quarry the temple rock.

Workmen bored holes in the limestone using brace and bit drills, then tamped powder into the holes. Next, rope fuse was inserted and lit. The workers were required to move a safe distance away—about sixteen rods or 250 feet—and take cover. After the blast, the workmen would return and do rough shaping of the larger stones, using hammer and chisel. Some of the largest stones weighed as much as two tons.[100]

The building's design required thousands of cut stones, including dozens of decorative pieces. Each of these stones had to be carefully selected and prepared to meet strict specifications. After the stones were extracted from the quarry and hauled to cutters, they were examined and rough-cut to fill specific niches in the building. This necessitated a high degree of communication and coordination between the architect, the quarry workers, and the stonecutters.

The smaller stones scattered by the blasts were used, among other things, to line the wells in the temple basement from which water came for the baptismal font and to build the chimneys. The smallest chips were spread on Nauvoo's streets on "the flat" to combat the mud that resulted after storms. A charming story shows Joseph Smith solving two problems simultaneously with these chips. When several young men in Nauvoo were convicted of property damage and sentenced to six months in jail, Joseph Smith asked that they be released to his custody for those six months, explaining:

> "Our Nauvoo streets are difficult to travel because of mud holes. We'll employ them to haul stone chips from the temple quarry and gravel from the river banks to improve our streets. We'll pay them fifty cents a day to reimburse the man whose property was destroyed. This will save the county money as they won't

---

der and fuse-ropes to blast the rocks in the quarry." *History of the Church*, 6:236. At the close of the meeting, "a collection was taken up to buy powder and fuse rope. About $60 dollars was received." Woodruff, *Journal*, 3:359; see also *History of the Church*, 6:230.

98. "Cost of a Charge for the 'Big Gun,'" *Nauvoo Neighbor*, 24 April 1844, 3.

99. *History of the Church*, 7:381.

100. George D. Smith, *An Intimate Chronicle*, 545.

101. T. Edgar Lyon, "Oral History: Recollections of Old Nauvooers," *BYU Studies* 18, no. 2 (Winter 1978): 146.

have to be fed for six months at county expense. Let them pay the costs of the court procedures and all will be better off than a jail sentence would achieve."

One of the boys later remarked, "That was the greatest training I ever had not to wantonly or willfully destroy the property of another. It was the best training to work consistently and earn an honest day's pay I ever had."[101]

Work in the quarry was not glamorous. It was dangerous and physically demanding.[102] Orson Hyde, a member of the Quorum of the Twelve, in a sardonic letter to the Church-owned *New York Messenger*, recommended: "When a man comes [to Nauvoo] ... and wants an appointment to some lucrative station, but does not join the church ... my counsel would be to give him an appointment in the stone quarry, and he will soon show how much love and sympathy he has got for the church."[103]

Like other workers on the temple who depended on tithing contributions for their sustenance, the quarry workers were often on skimpy rations. Quarry worker Luman Shurtliff recalled:

The committee did the best they could but they had nothing better in their hands to give us. We labored ten hours a day, and got something to take to our families for supper and breakfast. Many times we got nothing; at other times we got a half pound of butter or three pounds of fish, beef, and nothing to cook it with. Sometimes we got a peck of cornmeal or a few records [sic] of flour and before any more provisions would come into the office, the hands that worked steadily would sometimes be entirely out of provisions and have to live on herbs, boiled, without any seasoning except salt, or on parched corn or anything we could get to sustain us. I had some milk from my cows and by putting it half water and, if we could get corn or meal, we could live well for these times. For breakfast we would eat a little of this mush and then take a pint of milk in a bottle and some mush in a cup for dinner, go to the boat at six and at noon eat dinner and thank God that I and my family were thus blessed. And often I worked until dark before I could get home. Then if our cows did not come home, we had to take our mush alone and thank God that we were thus blessed.

The reader may think the above-mentioned scarcity of provisions was confined to my family. Not so. My family was as well off as the majority of my neighbors. I have seen those that cut stone by the year eat nothing but parched or browned corn for breakfast and take some in their pockets for their dinner and go to work singing the songs of Zion. I mention this not to find fault or to com-

---

102. Apparently only one death occurred in the quarry. See chap. 8.

103. Orson Hyde, Letter to the editor, *New York Messenger* 1 (6 September 1845): 77.

104. Luman Shurtliff, "Biographical Sketch of the Life of Luman Andros Shurtliff," typescript, 52, Perry Special Collections, Lee Library.

plain, but to let my children know how the temple of Nauvoo was built, and how their parents as well as hundreds of others suffered to lay a foundation on which they could build and be accepted of God.[104]

James Leithead, another quarry worker, recounted his experience: "Many times I have worked on the stone quarry on the banks of the Mississippi River, had nothing for dinner but corn bread, when dry dipped in the river, and worked drilling rock day after day as cheerful and contented as I ever was in my life."[105]

Because the native limestone was so abundant, stone from several privately owned quarries was also used in the construction of the temple. Hiram Kimball owned one of these quarries, and Robert D. Foster owned another.[106] William Goforth Nelson, age ten in 1840, worked in his father Edmund's privately owned quarry: "Father paid his temple work and most of his tithing in rock from this quarry, all of which was used in the temple."[107] Joseph Smith III, the oldest surviving son of Joseph Smith Jr., remembered that temple stone also came from a quarry owned by Chauncey Loomis "along the river" below the city.[108] The Loomis quarry was also known as the "lower quarry."[109] It was apparently stone from this quarry that Luman Shurtliff recalled transporting to the city site: "I had helped lay the foundation of our temple in Nauvoo and now wished to do something more towards the building of it," he wrote. "Accordingly I went to the temple committee and hired [with] them to work on a boat to boat rock, timber and wood."[110] James Holt, also "boated a great deal of rock from the quarry."[111]

105. James Leithead, "Life and Labors of James Leithead," LDS Church Archives, typescript in my possession. Leithead (1816-1907) was born in Scotland, immigrated to Ontario, Canada, and was baptized there on 6 March 1837. He moved to Nauvoo in 1841.

106. According to Blum, *Nauvoo: Gateway to the West*, 64, the Foster quarry was located at Robison and Ripley Streets.

107. Mansel H. Nelson, "Life of Edmond Nelson," 4, typescript in possession of Dora Fitch, Provo, Utah; photocopy in my possession. This document is taken from a history written by Edmond Nelson's son, William Goforth Nelson.

108. Mary Audentia Smith Anderson, ed., *Joseph Smith III and the Restoration* (Independence, MO: Herald House, 1952), 100.

109. Nauvoo Temple Committee, Day Book A, 1841-42. References to the "lower quarry" abound in the committee books.

110. Shurtliff, "Biographical Sketch," 52.

111. "James Holt—1852," in *Our Pioneer Heritage*, 13:470. Holt (1804-94) was baptized in 1839 and ordained a Seventy in 1844.

Hauling Stone to the Temple Site

Most of the stones were hauled to the temple site by ox carts, even those that made part of the trip on the water, since they still had to be brought up the hill from the riverbank to the top of the bluff. Joseph III, who turned nine in 1841, remembered that he used to wander around the temple site "to see the stones being brought in on great carts drawn by oxen, with the stones swinging under the axle of the great high, broad-tired wheels, usually two yoke of cattle drawing them."[112] The stones were probably suspended by wide leather straps. They were pried high enough with levers so that the straps could be slipped under them.

William Allred and Lorenzo Brown were the first two drivers to haul loads of stone to the building site. Allred later recalled, "I started with the first load of stone that was hauled for the temple, but as I had an ox team, Lorenzo Brown got to the temple ground first as he had a horse team."[113]

Members also supplied ox teams. Lewis Barney "furnished a team and wagon to haul rock for the Nauvoo Temple."[114] Joseph Fielding reported that, in January 1842 when the frozen roads would make for easier pulling, "from ten to twenty teams [were] at work, bringing the stones to the place."[115] Tithing laborers often acted as teamsters.

Joseph Lee Robinson, an early convert and close friend of Joseph Smith, recollected a personal miracle associated with his drayage for the temple:

> One tithing day for our ward in the Fall a great many were sick and I was quite sick myself but not confined to bed. I took my team and started for the quarry for to haul rock for the Temple. While on my way to the quarry I felt inspired to say "In the name of the Lord, I am going to haul rock for the Temple, but I am sick wilt thou help me on, O Lord." Yes, the Lord will heal me, I know he will, and surely he did heal me at that time. Yes I was healed there and then. I drove to the quarry but found no one there but heavy rocks quarried out. Presently Brother John Taylor came with his team. He was in grunting order [not feeling well] but we went to work with a will and we rolled rocks on to our wagons—we two alone, that should astonish the world; rocks that to my judgment would weigh from ten to twenty hundred pounds or upwards. We hauled all day. The Lord helped us.[116]

---

112. Anderson, *Joseph Smith III and the Restoration*, 100.

113. William Moore Allred, Autobiography, 1885, typescript, 7-8, LDS Church Archives.

114. Lewis Barney, in Jenson, *LDS Biographical Encyclopedia*, 2:594.

115. Joseph Fielding, Letter, datelined January 1842, Nauvoo, 78.

116. Joseph Lee Robinson, "History of Joseph Lee Robinson," typescript, 18, Perry Special Collections, Lee Library.

117. Clayton, Journal, in *Journal History*, 31 December 1844, 5. Ephraim John Pearson (1825-1902) was baptized in 1841 and later served in the Mormon Battalion. William H. Dane (1819-unknown) was baptized in May 1841 and was ordained a Seventy in 1844.

At the temple site, stonecutters did the final cutting and shaping. Then teams hauled the stones into position near the cranes that would hoist them upon the walls. William Clayton later recalled, "For the most part of the time there was only one team to draw the stone to the cranes. Brother Ephraim J. Pearson attended the most of the time. After he left Alma N. Shennan took his place. When the second team was put to work Brother William H. Dame was appointed to attend to it."[117]

Joseph Smith roamed freely about these sites, lending a hand with almost everything, as this delightful story illustrates:

> It was Temple Tithing Day ... This boy's father had hitched his team to his wagon and with his son had gone to the quarry to load a large stone into the wagon; then, they started for the temple. Pulling out of the quarry with its stone floor was no problem, but when they started across the "Flat" their wagon became stuck in a mud hole. The father whipped the horses and they lurched forward against their collars, but this sudden pull merely jiggled the wagon and made it sink a bit deeper in the mire. The father handed the reins to his son telling him to stay with the team while he went up to the temple and secured someone to come down with a team or two of oxen and pull his wagon out of the mud.
>
> His father had just stepped off the wagon when a man walking along the side of the street called to him and said, "I see you are having trouble, Brother Bybee." "Yes," replied the latter, "I'm going to the temple to get someone to pull me out." The man waded into the mud and said to the father, "Brother Bybee, you get by that left rear wheel and put your right shoulder under a spoke. I'll get my left shoulder under a spoke of the right wheel." Then to the nine year old boy he said: "Get your whip ready and when I say 'Lift,' we'll lift with our shoulders, and don't you spare the horseflesh."
>
> So saying, each in position, the man said "Lift." Each did his part. The horses jumped at the sting of the whip, the wagon moved a bit, and the horses were able to keep it going. After going about a hundred feet onto dry ground the boy let the team rest. The two men caught up with the wagon and as Brother Bybee climbed up to the driver's seat and took the reins from his son, the father called out, "Thank you, Brother Joseph."[118]

The Purpose of Temples

If asked the purpose of temples, most members of the Church today would respond, "to do work for the dead" or "to seal families together for eternity." While Joseph Smith may have understood these elements of the temple theology he was instrumental in revealing, he did not make them known to the Church during the

118. "Brother Bybee" quoted by Lyon, "Recollections of 'Old Nauvooers,'" 147-48.

early years in Nauvoo. Rather, it was more typical for him to describe the purpose of the temple as a meetinghouse or a place of revelation. Elias Higbee of the building committee gave a good indication of what members of the Church understood the purpose of the temple to be in a letter published in the 1 February 1841 issue of the *Times and Seasons*:

> When the house is finished, the priesthood will be set in order, an acceptable offering can then be offered unto the Lord of Hosts.... Then can the oracles of God be daily received if necessary for the salvation of the people, by those who are appointed to minister in the holy place. Then can God be worshipped in the beauty of holiness: then will those who are appointed to minister be as a watchman on a tower, who can warn the church of approaching danger, or dispense unto them, through the priesthood, the words of eternal life.[119]

At the April 1841 conference held on the temple site, Joseph Smith spoke of the "necessity which existed of building the Temple, that the Saints might have a suitable place for worshiping the Almighty."[120]

These explanations of the temple's purpose indicate a strong connection for Church members between the uses of the Kirtland Temple and the Nauvoo Temple. They emphasize the temple as a place of revelation and congregational worship. Although we no longer stress the importance of the temple as a place of assembly, this purpose was clearly evidenced by the fact that these edifices (including the early Utah temples as well) were designed to accommodate large congregations. However, over the course of four years, from 1841 through 1844, Joseph Smith began instructing his followers in the pivotal role that the temple played as a place for performing sacred rites and ordinances. In 1840, the Church stood on the threshold of a revolution in its understanding of temples.

Baptism for the Dead Introduced

On 15 August 1840, Joseph Smith preached his first public sermon on baptism for the dead. This sermon, given at the funeral of Seymour Brunson,[121] marked the beginning of a remarkable four-year period during which the Prophet would introduce to the Church most of the core doctrines and ordinances that would comprise Mormon temple worship. While baptism for the dead was not initially a

---

119. Higbee, "Ecclesiastical," 296.

120. *History of the Church,* 4:339.

121. Seymour Brunson (1799-1840) served in the War of 1812 and joined the Church in January 1831. He was serving as a member of the Nauvoo High Council at his death on 10 August 1840.

temple ordinance, it became associated with the temple in January 1841. Brigham Young, speaking in Idaho in 1873, recalled how the doctrine of baptism for the dead had been revealed:

> Do you recollect that in about the year 1840 ... Joseph had a revelation concerning the dead? He had been asked the question a good many times; "What is the condition of the dead, those that lived and died without the Gospel?" It was a matter of inquiry with him. He considered this question not only for himself, but for the brethren and the Church. "What is the condition of the dead? What will be their fate? Is there no way today by which they can receive their blessings as there was in the days of the Apostles, and when the Gospel was preached upon the earth in ancient days?"

Young explained that the Prophet Joseph received "knowledge by the spirit of revelation how the dead could be officiated for"; and when called to speak at Brunson's funeral, he began to elucidate this doctrine.[122] No contemporary account of the sermon has survived, but Simon Baker later recalled the address in a speech:

> I was present at a discourse that the prophet Joseph delivered on baptism for the dead August 15, 1840. He read the greater part of the 15th Chap[ter] of Cor[inthians] And remarked that the Gospel of Jesus Christ brought glad tidings of great joy, and then remarked that he saw a widow in that congregation that had a son who died without being baptized, and this widow in reading the sayings of Jesus; "Except a man be born of water and of the spirit he cannot enter the Kingdom of heaven," and that not one jot or tittle of the Saviour's words should pass away, but all should be fulfilled. He then said that this widow should have glad tiding [sic] in that thing. He also said that the Apostle was talking to a people who understood Baptism for the dead, for it was practiced among them. He went on to say that people could now act for their friends who had departed this life, and that the plan of salvation was calculated to save all who were willing to obey the requirements of the law of God. He went on and made a very beautiful discourse.[123]

---

122. Brigham Young, 31 August 1873, *Journal of Discourses*, 16:165.

123. *Journal History*, 15 August 1840, 2. This excerpt is included with the following description: "Following is a statement made by Simon Baker in a speech which he delivered." No date is given for the speech. Baker (1811-64) was born in New York and joined the Church there on 16 April 1839, was ordained a Seventy in Nauvoo, and was endowed in the Nauvoo Temple on 6 January 1846.

124. Ibid., Statement by Jane Neymon made "in History office G.S.L. City Nov 29th, 1854 half past 10 o'clock a.m." This statement said to have been discovered in 1908 by Andrew Jenson, "while undertaking a careful perusal of original documents."

In an 1854 statement, Jane Neymon, another witness to the discourse, recounted: "Joseph preached Seymour Brunson's funeral sermon and then first introduced the subject of baptism for the dead and said to the people: 'I have laid the subject of baptism for the dead before you, you may receive it or reject it as you choose.'"[124] Vilate Murray Kimball wrote to her husband, Apostle Heber C. Kimball, then in England on a mission, describing the circumstances of Joseph's discourse, "It was attended by thousands of people.... A more solemn sight I never witnessed; and yet the day was joyful, because of the light and glory which Elder Smith set forth. I can truly say my soul was lifted up."[125]

Four months after Brunson's funeral, Joseph Smith wrote to members of the Twelve in Great Britain. This epistle contained the first official news of the new doctrine:

> I presume the doctrine of "Baptism for the dead" has ere this reached your ears, and may have raised some inquiries in your mind respecting the same. I cannot in this letter give you all the information you may desire on the subject, but aside from my knowledge independent of the Bible, I would say, that this was certainly practiced by the ancient Churches and St. Paul endeavours to prove the doctrine of the resurrection from the same, and says "else what shall they do who are baptized for the dead," etc., etc. I first mentioned the doctrine in public while preaching the funeral sermon of Brother Brunson, and have since then given general instructions to the Church on the subject. The saints have the privilege of being baptized for those of their relatives who are dead, who they feel to believe would have embraced the gospel if they had been privileged with hearing it, and who have received the gospel in the spirit through the instrumentality of those who may have been commissioned to preach to them while in prison. Without enlarging on the subject you will undoubtedly see its consistency, and reasonableness, and [it] presents the gospel of Christ in probably a more enlarged scale than some have viewed it.[126]

Wilford Woodruff was among those who received their first knowledge of the ordinance from this epistle. He remembered, "The moment I heard of it, my

125. Vilate Kimball, Letter written 6 September 1840, Nauvoo, extract published in *Millennial Star* 1 (November 1840): 191. Kimball further explained: "A short time before his death, he [Brunson] told Brother J. Smith not to hold him any longer; for said he, I have seen Elder David Patten, and he wants me, and the Lord wants me, and I want to go. They then gave him up. At one time, as Elder Joseph Smith entered the room, he told him there was a light encircling him above the brightness of the sun; he exclaimed, the room is full of angels, they have come to wait my spirit home. He then bade his family and friends farewell, and sweetly fell asleep in Jesus. He requested Elder Smith to preach his funeral sermon, which he did."

126. *History of the Church*, 231, misdated as 19 October 1840. See Jessee, *The Personal Writings of Joseph Smith*, 486.

127. Wilford Woodruff, 9 April 1857, *Journal of Discourses*, 5:85.

soul leaped with joy; for it was a subject in which I felt deeply interested."[127] Brigham Young reacted similarly:

> It was [in England] I got the glad tidings that the living could go forth and be baptized for those who had fallen asleep. This doctrine I believed before anything was said or done about it in this church; it made me glad when I heard it was revealed through his servant Joseph, and that I could go forth, and officiate for my fathers, for my mothers, and for my ancestors, to the latest generation who have not had the privilege of helping themselves; that they can yet arise to the state of glory and exaltation as we that live, have a privilege of rising to ourselves. The next year I came home and requested Brother Joseph to preach upon the subject, which he did. I also heard many of the elders preach upon the same subject.[128]

Three aspects of this new doctrine gave it immense power. First, as Brigham Young mentioned, nearly everyone would think immediately of departed loved ones who had not had the privilege of accepting the gospel in this life, so the doctrine would be a source of great joy and hope. Second, by affirming that baptism was absolutely necessary for salvation and by showing that God had prepared a way for all to receive this ordinance, it strengthened the Saints' faith both in God's justice and in his mercy. Third, because the Apostle Paul referred explicitly to the practice of vicarious baptism in 1 Corinthians 15:29, it strengthened the Saints' understanding that they were participating in a restoration of primitive Christianity.

Naturally, the Saints were eager to learn more. The doctrine of vicarious baptism immediately became a popular topic at meetings. On 11 October 1840, John Smith, Joseph's uncle, was among the first Mormons after Joseph Smith to give a public sermon on the topic when he "gave some instruction on baptizing for the dead as spoken by Paul in the 15 Chap[ter] of Corinthians" at the Sunday services in Montrose, Iowa, across the Mississippi River from Nauvoo.[129] Joseph Smith and his associates took every opportunity to defend the doctrine in print and from the pulpit. An editorial on 15 April 1842 in the *Times and Seasons*, then being edited by Joseph Smith, is typical:

> When speaking about the blessings pertaining to the Gospel, and the consequences connected with disobedience to the requirements, we are frequently asked the question, what has become of our fathers? Will they all be damned for not obeying the Gospel, when they never heard it? Certainly not. But they will

128. Brigham Young, "Speech," *Times and Seasons* 6 (1 July 1845): 954.

129. John Smith, Journal, 11 October 1840, typescript, 5, George Albert Smith Papers, Special Collections, J. Willard Marriott Library, University of Utah, Salt Lake City.

possess the same privilege that we here enjoy, through the medium of the ever-lasting priesthood.... [A]nd in order that they might fulfill all the requisitions of God, living friends were baptized for their dead friends, and thus fulfilled the requirement of God, which says, "Except a man be born of water and of the Spirit, he cannot enter into the kingdom of God," they were baptized of course, not for themselves, but for their dead.

A view of these things reconciles the Scriptures of truth, justifies the ways of God to man, places the human family upon an equal footing, and harmonizes with every principle of righteousness, justice and truth. We will conclude with the words of Peter: "For the time past of our life may suffice us to have wrought the will of the Gentiles." "For, for this cause was the Gospel preached also to them that are dead, that they might be judged according to men in the flesh, but live according to God in the spirit."[130]

The Saints did not wait for a fuller understanding of the doctrine before joyfully commencing the work of vicarious salvation. William Allred recalled being "present when the first person was baptized in the Mississippi River for the dead."[131] One of the first to be baptized was Jane Neymon, who "was baptized for her son Cyrus Livingston Neymon, by Harvey Olmstead." She stated that Vienna Jacques witnessed the ceremony "by riding into the river on horseback to get close so as to hear what the ceremony would be." That evening, Joseph Smith "asked what [Olmstead] said. On his telling what the ceremony was it proved that Father Olmstead had it right."[132]

John Smith, just days after his sermon on the subject, wrote in his journal: "Thursday, October 15. This day for the first time we met on the bank of the Sugar Creek to baptize for our departed friends, which was a day of rejoicing time for many who was present. 22 was baptized as agents for their departed friends and then for themselves. I assisted to confirm them."[133]

Little-known Nehemiah Brush was the most active proxy during the first year after the ordinance was commenced. In 1841 he was baptized for 111 people. Sarah M. Cleveland, who later became a counselor to Emma Smith in the Relief

---

130. "Baptism for the Dead," *Times and Seasons* 3 (15 April 1842): 760-61; see also "On Future Punishments," *Millennial Star* 3 (February 1843): 181.

131. William Allred, Autobiography, typescript, 8, LDS Church Archives. See also "Recollections of the Prophet Joseph Smith," *Juvenile Instructor* 27 (1 August 1892): 471-72. Allred (1819-unknown), a Tennessee native, was baptized 10 September 1832 and was a member of Zion's Camp.

132. Neymon, Statement, 6.

133. John Smith, Journal, typescript, 5, George A. Smith Papers, Special Collections, Marriott Library.

134. M. Guy Bishop. "'What has Become of Our Fathers?': Baptism for the Dead at Mormon Nauvoo," *Dialogue: A Journal of Mormon Thought* 23 (Summer 1990): 90.

Society presidency was the most active woman, being baptized for forty.[134] Judge James Adams of Springfield, while visiting Nauvoo in November of 1840, was baptized a member of the Church. Erastus Snow, later an apostle, later wrote in his autobiography: "As the doctrine of baptism for the dead had just previously been revealed to the Saints, he also wished to be baptized for his deceased friends. I accordingly baptized him four times while I was at Nauvoo."[135] Adams apparently found this doctrine deeply comforting, for during the next year, he was baptized for sixty-seven of his friends and relatives, including President John Adams, whom he listed as a friend.[136]

Joseph Smith Sr. was on his deathbed when word of the new ordinance reached him. Lucy Mack Smith recalled that when Joseph Jr. "informed his father that it was then the privilege of the Saints to be baptized for the dead.... Mr. Smith was delighted to hear [it] and requested that Joseph should be baptized for Alvin immediately."[137] Joseph's brother Hyrum fulfilled his father's wish by being baptized for Alvin.[138]

At that early date, the practice of baptizing for the dead was almost entirely unregulated. Speaking to a congregation in Idaho in August 1873, Brigham Young recalled:

> When this doctrine was first revealed, and in hurrying in the administration of baptism for the dead ... sisters were baptized for their male friends, ... for their fathers, their grandfathers, their mothers and their grandmothers, etc. I just mention this so that you will come to understanding, that as we knew nothing about this matter at first, the old Saints recollect, there was little by little given, and the subject was made plain, but little was given at once. Consequently, in the first place people were baptized for their friends and no record was kept.[139]

---

135. Erastus Snow, "A Journal or Sketch of the Life of Erastus Snow," 62, typescript, Perry Special Collections, Lee Library. This entry is undated, but the event would have occurred in November or December 1840.

136. Bishop, "What Has Become of Our Fathers?" 90.

137. Lucy Mack Smith, *Biographical Sketches of Joseph Smith the Prophet and His Progenitors for Many Generations* (1853), 265-66, photomechanical reprint by (Orem, Utah: Grandin Books, 1995).

138. "Nauvoo Baptisms for the Dead," Book A, 1841, 145, 149, Family History Library, Church of Jesus Christ of Latter-day Saints, Salt Lake City. Because the baptisms in the 1841 book are not dated, the date on which Hyrum performed this proxy ordinance for his brother is not known. Joseph Sr. died on 14 September 1840.

139. Brigham Young, 31 August 1873, *Journal of Discourses*, 16:166-67. Wilford Woodruff gave a similar reminiscence on 9 April 1857: "When that was first revealed, we rejoiced in it; and, as soon as we had an opportunity, we began to be baptized for our dead. A man would be baptized for both male and female ... I went forward and was baptized for all my dead relatives I could think of, both male and female, as did others." Ibid., 5:85.

John D. Lee, an 1837 convert who served as a recorder in the Nauvoo Temple during the winter of 1845-46, recorded that "when the doctrine of baptizing for the dead was first introduced, the families met together, down by the river side, and one of their number, of the order of the Melchizedek Priesthood, officiated."[140] In addition to being baptized for deceased kin, many Saints generously extended the privilege of baptism to noted historical figures. George Washington, John Adams, Thomas Jefferson, James Madison, and other prominent men were baptized, often more than once. Charlotte Haven, a non-Mormon resident of Hancock County, left a somewhat skeptical account of some baptisms for the dead that she observed being performed in the Mississippi River in the spring of 1843:

> We followed the bank toward town, and rounding a little point covered with willows and cottonwoods, we spied quite a crowd of people, and soon perceived there was a baptism. Two elders stood knee-deep in the icy water, and immersed one after another as fast as they could come down the bank. We soon observed that some of them went in and were plunged several times. We were told that they were baptized for the dead who had not had the opportunity of adopting the doctrines of the Latter Day Saints. So these poor mortals in ice-cold water were releasing their ancestors and relatives from purgatory!... [We] heard several names repeated by the elders as the victims were doused, and you can imagine our surprise when the name George Washington was called. So after these fifty years he is out of purgatory and on his way to the "celestial" heaven![141]

Robert Horne recalled witnessing baptisms in the river as well: "I saw the Elders baptizing for the dead in the Mississippi River. This was something new to me, and the beauty of this great principle dawned upon me. I had never heard of such a doctrine then. Orson Pratt was baptizing. Brother Joseph stood on the banks holding a child in his arms."[142]

---

140. John D. Lee, *Mormonism Unveiled; or, The Life and Confessions of the Late Mormon Bishop, John D. Lee* (St Louis, MO: Bryan and Brand, 1877), 168-69.

141. Charlotte Haven, "A Girl's Letter from Nauvoo," *Overland Monthly* (San Francisco) 16 (December 1890): 630.

142. Robert Horne, *Millennial Star* 55 (September 1893): 584, reprinted in N. B. Lundwall, *Temples of the Most High* (Salt Lake City: Bookcraft, 1993), 70. Horne (1814-unknown) joined the Church in 1842 in England.

Revelation on the Temple

On 19 January 1841, five months after Joseph Smith preached Seymour Brunson's funeral sermon, he received an important revelation on the temple. Appropriately recorded on the first page of the Book of the Law of the Lord, it contained several doctrinal statements that impacted work on the temple and greatly expanded Smith's view of temples and temple worship. This revelation makes the first statement linking the ordinance of baptism for the dead—then being performed in the Mississippi River—with the temple. Just one month earlier, in introducing the doctrine of work for the dead to the Twelve and reviewing the efforts to build a temple, Joseph had not mentioned any connection between the two. Furthermore, a letter from Joseph to the Twelve published in the *Times and Seasons* just four days prior to the revelation states that the temple, when constructed, would "enable all the functions of the priesthood" without mentioning baptism for the dead.[143] Thus, this revelation represented a bold new development, forever linking ordinance work for the dead with the temple:

> For a baptismal font there is not upon the earth, that they, my saints, may be baptized for those who are dead—
> For this ordinance belongeth to my house, and cannot be acceptable to me, only in the days of your poverty, wherein ye are not able to build a house unto me. (D&C 124:29-30)

The revelation then gives the Church an ultimatum that proved to be a fantastically effective motivator:

> But I command you, all ye my saints, to build a house unto me; and I grant unto you a sufficient time to build a house unto me; and during this time your baptisms shall be acceptable unto me.
> But behold, at the end of this appointment your baptisms for your dead shall not be acceptable unto me; and if you do not these things at the end of the appointment ye shall be rejected as a church, with your dead, saith the Lord your God.

---

143. Joseph Smith, "A Proclamation to the Saints Scattered Abroad," *Times and Seasons* 2 (15 January 1841): 274. On 18 May 1884, John Taylor, speaking to a congregation assembled for the dedication of the Logan Temple, stated, "Immediately after these baptisms, the prophet had a revelation which more clearly developed the order in relation to such baptisms. According to that revelation it appeared that, notwithstanding all the visions, revelations, keys, etc., that had heretofore been given, there was not a place, not even in the Kirtland Temple, wherein those things could be carried out, and hence a font, such as we have in this temple, was built in the temple at Nauvoo, and it was there, under proper circumstances and proper administration, and according to the principles that he had laid down, that those ordinances were administered then, and are administered now." *Journal of Discourses*, 25:182-83.

> For verily I say unto you, that after you have had sufficient time to build a
> house to me ... your baptisms for your dead cannot be acceptable unto me.
> (D&C 124:31-33, 37)

This passage evoked a strong response from the members of the Church. Most accepted the challenge and considered it a sacred duty to fulfill the commandment. It would be repeated on occasion as a reminder of the importance of the temple and to stimulate activity on the works. Joseph Robinson recalled in his autobiography, "Knowing this to be the words of the Lord it inspired the saints to exert themselves exceedingly to use all diligence on that House."[144] Luman Shurtliff, in his autobiography, cast it in even more energetic terms: "We would rather live poor and keep the commandments of God in building a temple than to live better and be rejected with our dead."[145]

But there were some who felt tried by this demand, as was often the case when the Joseph Smith revealed new requirements. Ebenezer Robinson, then editor of the *Times and Seasons*, was one who reacted negatively. In an 1891 article for a newspaper he founded to criticize the RLDS Church for its denial of some of Joseph Smith's temple-related teachings, Robinson commented:

> Many felt that it was more than a matter of life and death, for if they failed to have
> the work accomplished by the time appointed, they lost not only their own soul's
> salvation, but also that of their dead friends for whom they had been baptized....
>
> I confess that it was too strong meat for me. I could not believe our Heavenly
> Father would make our dead friends responsible for the performance, or non performance of any duty assigned to the living ... neither could I believe he would
> reject the innocent for the acts of the guilty, therefore I came to the conclusion
> that the Lord did not give that revelation.[146]

The pronouncement that baptisms would be performed in the temple also required an adjustment to the design. The decision was made to modify the basement story so that a large font, suitable for baptisms, could be accommodated.

The revelation continues with a comprehensive listing of the intended functions of the new temple: anointings, washings, baptisms for the dead, solemn assemblies, sacrifices, oracles, revelations, and endowments (v. 39). This temple was clearly intended to house a variety of activities never associated with the Kirtland Temple. The Lord also promised to reveal new ordinances, including

---

144. Robinson, "History of Joseph Lee Robinson," 10.

145. Shurtliff, "Biographical Sketch," 52.

146. Ebenezer Robinson, "Items of Personal History of the Editor—Including Some Items of Church History Not Generally Known," *The Return* 3 (January 1891): 12-13.

"things which have been kept hid from before the foundation of the world, things that pertain to the dispensation of the fulness of times" (v. 41). Not only would the new temple exceed that of Kirtland in size and grandeur, but it would facilitate a greater variety of ordinances than its predecessor.

The Lord promised to "show unto my servant Joseph all things pertaining to this house, and the priesthood thereof, and the place whereon it shall be built" (v. 42). He confirms the chosen site saying that it was the "spot which I have chosen for you to build it" (v. 43). Finally, the Lord assures the Church, "If ye labor with all your might, I will consecrate that spot that it shall be made holy" (v. 44).

The Nauvoo House

Also near the close of 1840, Joseph Smith "had suggested the propriety to [George Miller] of building a house suitable for a tavern or hotel, answering to the growing importance of the city."[147] This date of this suggestion coincided closely with the initial phase of planning for the temple. Joseph Smith's desire to see such a hotel was solidified on 19 January 1841, when the above-mentioned revelation on the temple also mandated the construction of the hotel, giving it the status of a commandment. The name of the hotel, as prescribed in the revelation, would be the "Nauvoo House" (D&C 124:60). Thus, understanding the history of the Nauvoo House is critical to understanding many of the developments in the story of the Nauvoo Temple.

The house was to be built on the corner of Main Street and Water Street, just west of Joseph Smith's residence at the time, the "Homestead," which he had purchased from Hugh White in 1839. It would be a three-story, L-shaped structure, built of red brick. Thomas Carlin, then governor of Illinois, signed an act to incorporate the Nauvoo House Association on 23 February 1841, authorizing the trustees of the house to issue $150,000 in $50 shares.

The Nauvoo House and the Nauvoo Temple were twin projects. Their construction achieved the status of commandment in the same revelation. The temple was to be a habitation for God, the Nauvoo House a habitation for humans. They shared building materials and competed for labor resources. The committees of both buildings met in conference frequently to coordinate their efforts in obtaining

147. George Miller, *Correspondence of Bishop George Miller with the Northern Islander from His First Acquaintance with Mormonism Up to Near the Close of His Life*, 1855, compiled by Wingfield Watson (Burlington, WI: Wingfield Watson, 1916), 7; copy in Perry Special Collections, Lee Library. The letters in this pamphlet were originally published in 1855 in the *Northern Islander*, a newspaper published by followers of James Strang, who claimed the right of succession after Joseph Smith's death in 1844.

supplies and dividing labor. Together they formed the heart of the public works in the city.

The differences between the modes of financing the two buildings are likewise instructive. The temple was to be funded entirely by consecration, the Nauvoo House primarily by the sale of stock. The owners of Nauvoo House Association stock had a financial stake in the building. Those who contributed to the temple did so only with the expectation of spiritual recompense. Investment in the Nauvoo House was a business opportunity, albeit with the sanction of revelation. Tithing for the temple was treated as a religious duty.

Despite these differences, both houses were considered solemn obligations. Speaking to the workmen on the temple construction site on 21 February 1843, Joseph Smith declared, "The building of the Nauvoo House is just as sacred in my view as the Temple. I want the Nauvoo House built. It must be built. Our salvation depends upon it."[148] These two buildings were to take precedence over all other real estate development in the growing city. Joseph continued by expressing his dismay at those who neglected the Nauvoo House in favor of private real estate interests:

> I will whip Hiram Kimball and Esquire Wells, and everybody else, over Dr.
> Foster's head, who, instead of building the Nauvoo House, build a great many little skeletons. See Dr. Foster's mammoth skeletons rising all over the town; but
> there is no flesh on them; they are all for personal interest and aggrandizement.
> But I do not care how many bones there are in the city; somebody may come
> along and clothe them. See the bones of the elephant yonder, (as I pointed to the
> big house on Mulholland Street, preparing for a tavern, as yet uncovered,) the
> crocodiles and man-eaters all about the city, such as grog shops, and card shops,
> and counterfeit shops, etc., got up for their own aggrandizement, and all for speculation, while the Nauvoo House is neglected.[149]

---

148. *History of the Church*, 5:285.

149. Ibid. Hiram Kimball (1806-63) would not be baptized until 20 July 1843, although his wife, Sarah Melissa Granger Kimball, was. "Esquire Wells" is Daniel H. Wells, who owned most of the property surrounding the temple and was selling it by lots. Dr. Robert D. Foster (1811-unknown) joined the Church in 1839, was excommunicated in April 1844, and was one of the owners of the *Nauvoo Expositor*, the abatement of which led to the death of Joseph Smith in June 1844.

150. The original manuscript for the Book of Mormon was placed in its cornerstone, and the bodies of Joseph and Hyrum were temporarily buried in the basement. Lewis Bidamon, Emma Smith's second husband, completed a portion of the building in the 1850s, after which it served as a hotel and home to their combined families. Emma died here in 1879. The Community of Christ (formerly RDLS Church) owns the completed portion, which it renovated and maintains as a boarding house.

Like the temple, the Nauvoo House was never completed according to the original plans, and only one wing of the proposed "L" was finished. However, it was a significant structure in the landscape for many years.[150]

Chapter 2

LAYING THE FOUNDATION:
FEBRUARY 1841 TO OCTOBER 1841

Division of Nauvoo into Wards

Responding to the revelation of 19 January 1841, Church leaders took steps to hasten the temple's construction. On 22 February, "the temple committee organized the city into Wards and called upon the men to come forward and labor every tenth day."[1] William Huntington wrote that there were ten wards formed. Except on Sundays, "each ward works once in ten days. Consequently there is laborers every working day of the week."[2] This new arrangement was intended to accelerate work on the temple and provide a more even distribution of tithing labor. This goal was apparently successful early on. Nathan Cheney stated that after

---

1. George D. Smith, ed., *An Intimate Chronicle: The Journals of William Clayton* (Salt Lake City: Signature Books, 1995), 527.

2. William Huntington, Sr., "Journal of William Huntington" (1784-1846), 8 March 1841, typescript, 12, L. Tom Perry Special Collections, Harold B. Lee Library, Provo, Utah. Huntington (1784-1846) was a stonecutter, and "by particular request the stones which he cut were laid in a column from the basement to the top of the chimney of the southwest corner." Andrew Jenson, *Latter-day Saint Biographical Encyclopedia,* 4 vols. (Salt Lake City: Andrew Jenson History Co., 1901-37; reprinted Salt Lake City: Greg Kofford Books, 2005), 1:369.

the ward divisions were made, there were "probably from fifty to seventy people to work every day on the house."[3]

When there were large tasks to accomplish, several wards were called to work together. For example, in November of 1842 the temple committee

> requested all the brethren who had teams to turn out and with their teams, assist in hauling the lumber to the Temple. The first, second, third, fourth and fifth wards of the city were requested to be on the ground on Monday, Tuesday and Wednesday; and the sixth, seventh, eighth, ninth and tenth on Thursday, Friday and Saturday.[4]

After their early compliance, the men of the city gradually allowed their personal business to take precedence over the day assigned to their ward. A year after these ward subdivisions, Joseph Smith published a stern letter to the Nauvoo brethren about complying with this coordinated labor tithing schedule:

> It is highly important for the forwarding of the Temple, that an equal distribution of labor should be made in relation to time; as a superabundance of hands one week, and none the next, tends to retard the progress of the work: therefore every brother is requested to be particular to labor on the day set apart for the same, in his ward; and to remember that he that sows sparingly, shall also reap sparingly, so that if the brethren want a plentiful harvest, they will do well to be at the place of labor in good season in the morning, bringing all necessary tools, according to their occupation, and those who have teams bring them also, unless otherwise advised by the Temple Committee. Should any one be detained from his labor by unavoidable circumstances on the day appointed, let him labor the next day, or the first day possible.

He then adds this important detail concerning early ward organization and its function with respect to the construction of the temple: "The captains of the respective wards are particularly requested to be at the place of labor on their respective days, and keep an accurate account of each man's work, and be ready to exhibit a list of the same when called for."[5]

---

3. Nathan Cheney, Letter to Beloved Friends (Charles Beebe et al.), 17 October 1841, in Eliza Rawson, "Letters and Sketches," 2, LDS Church Archives. Cheney (1811-52), baptized in 1836, was among those who covenanted to help move Church members from Missouri in 1838-39.

4. "The Temple of God in Nauvoo," *Times and Seasons* 4 (15 November 1842): 10.

5. Joseph Smith, "To the Brethren in Nauvoo City," *Times and Seasons* 3 (28 February 1842): 517.

Presumably these captains were appointed at the time the wards were organized. It is significant that they were not bishops and that these wards were not ecclesiastical units.[6] Two years later on 20 August 1842, the Nauvoo High Council took these existing ward divisions into consideration when they created ecclesiastical wards and appointed bishops to look after the temporal needs of Church members in their respective wards.[7]

Commencement of Work at the Temple Site

During the winter of 1840-41, the tithing hands were busy quarrying rock in preparation for early spring when actual construction would begin. Elias Higbee published a notice in the newspaper lauding the willingness of the brethren to labor "every tenth day, since last Conference, by which some materials are made ready for the building."[8]

Work at the temple site itself began in mid-February. According to William Clayton's record, "Elder Alpheus Cutler, assisted by Elder [Reynolds] Cahoon and others, laid out the foundation of the temple."[9] The building's dimensions were roughly 128 feet east to west by 88 feet north to south, making it one of the largest buildings in the western United States with over 11,000 square feet.

Once the position and dimensions of the temple had been determined and marked, excavation for the foundation began. On February 18, "the brethren began to dig the cellar."[10] Clayton indicated that "Old Thomas Travis, a faithful brother from England ... was one of the first who commenced to dig the foundation."[11] William McIntire, recalled, "My hands assisted to remove the earth to lay

6. Nauvoo had been divided into voting wards as early as 1840. Initially, there were three (upper, lower, and middle) with a fourth following in February 1842. The ward divisions made by the temple committee differed from these wards. It was not until a high council meeting on 20 August 1842 that the wards began to be viewed as ecclesiastical units. The divisions made on that occasion corresponded to the ten wards created earlier by the temple committee.

7. Nauvoo High Council, Minutes, 20 August 1842, in *History of the Church*, 5:119.

8. Elias Higbee, "Ecclesiastical," *Times and Seasons* 2 (1 February 1841): 296.

9. George D. Smith, ed., *An Intimate Chronicle: The Journals of William Clayton* (Salt Lake City: Signature Books, 1995), 527.

10. Ibid.

11. William Clayton, Journal, in Journal History of the Church of Jesus Christ of Latter-day Saints (chronology of typed entries and newspaper clippings, 1830-present), 31 December 1844, 13, LDS Church Archives. Andrew Jenson included portions of this Nauvoo journal in the Journal History, but it was not reprinted in the *Juvenile Instructor* and hence does not appear in George Smith's edition of Clayton's diaries, *Intimate Chronicle*.

12. William McIntire Patterson, Journal, holograph, 2, William Patterson McIntire Papers, Perry Special Collections, Lee Library.

13. Jesse Crosby, Autobiography, in "Autobiographies of Early Seventies," typescript, 51, LDS Church Archives. The autobiographies in this collection were extracted from the Seventies Record,

the foundation or basement stone."[12] Twenty-year-old Jesse Crosby also wrote of having "worked on [the temple] the first day."[13]

Assuming that the men used techniques common to the period, they used horse-drawn scrapers to loosen the dirt. Then workmen using shovels and wagons removed it from the foundation area. According to Clayton, excavation began with "the corners."[14] Norton Jacob, who would become one of the prominent workers on the temple, confirms this statement with his description of the project's status on 6 April 1841: "Not much had been excavated then except about the corners where trenches had been sunk to the depth of the intended basement."[15]

These trenches were about five feet deep and sufficiently wide to accommodate the large foundation stones which were being prepared at the quarry. Archeological evidence suggests that these stones were irregular in size, ranging from four to five feet wide.[16]

On 8 March, William Huntington, among others (including Luman Shurtliff), "commenced laying the foundation stone" and helped position "the first stone that was laid in the bottom of the foundation of the temple."[17] The foundation stones had no footings but rather were set directly on the clay floor, then cemented together with lime mortar.[18] Work on this phase of the foundation continued for approximately two weeks.

On 5 April, "the wall was raised five feet [and] was in readiness for to receive the cornerstone for the hewed stone of the basement story," wrote William Huntington.[19] Thus the foundation, at least at the corners, was raised to ground level in preparation for laying the cornerstones. Although this ceremony has become, by tradition, a minor ritual just moments before the formal dedication of a modern temple, in Nauvoo, the cornerstones were literally the stones on which the edifice was erected, and their laying was a lengthy and significance-fraught event.

---

a series of books kept by the seventies quorums in Nauvoo, including minutes of meetings, records of donations, and autobiographies of quorum members.

14. George D. Smith, *An Intimate Chronicle*, 527.

15. Norton Jacob, Journal, 1804-52, typescript, 5-6, L. Tom Perry Special Collections, Harold B. Lee Library, Brigham Young University, Provo, Utah. Jacob (1804-79), joined the Church in 1841. The basement between the foundation walls was not excavated until after April conference.

16. Virginia S. Harrington and J. C. Harrington, *Rediscovery of the Nauvoo Temple* (Salt Lake City: Nauvoo Restoration, Inc., 1971), 16.

17. Huntington, Journal, 12; Luman Andros Shurtliff, Autobiography, typescript, 52, Perry Special Collections, Lee Library.

18. Harrington and Harrington, *Rediscovery of the Nauvoo Temple*, 16. The footing of a building is the base of the foundation walls, usually wider than the foundation walls so as to distribute the weight of the building.

19. Huntington, Journal, 12.

Laying the Cornerstones

On 1 April 1841, the *Times and Seasons* reported that the temple would "be ready to have its corner stone laid with due solemnity, at our approaching conference."[20] Advertisements also appeared in Hancock County's only other newspaper: the *Western World*, later known as the *Warsaw Signal*. Thomas C. Sharp, its editor, was invited to the service.[21] Robert B. Thompson, Joseph Smith's scribe reported:

> For some days prior to the sixth, the accession of strangers to our city was great, and on the wide spread prairie, which bounds our city, might be seen various kinds of vehicles wending their way from different points of the compass to the city of Nauvoo, while the ferry boats on the Mississippi, were constantly employed in wafting travellers across its rolling and extensive bosom.[22]

The events connected with the cornerstone ceremony on 6 April 1841, the day before the conference commenced, are well documented. The *Times and Seasons* of 15 April contains two detailed accounts of the laying of the cornerstones.[23] Shortly after 6:00 a.m., the Nauvoo Legion assembled at its parade ground on the flat below the temple. At 7:00 a.m., a volley of "artillery" (rifle fire) saluted the arrival of Generals William Law and Don Carlos Smith. The citizenry, alerted by the sound, "began to pour in from all quarters [in] a continuous train, for about three hours and continued to swell the vast assembly."[24] By 9:00 a.m., a crowd, officially estimated at between seven and ten thousand were present.[25]

Shortly after 9:00 a.m., Joseph Smith, acting in his capacity as Lieutenant General of the legion, reviewed the troops, which were under the command of Major General/Mayor John C. Bennett. Immediately afterward, Bennett "organized the procession, to march to the foundation of the temple," a task that took "a considerable

20. "The Temple," *Times and Seasons* 2 (1 April 1841): 369.

21. "The More We Reflect," *Warsaw Signal* 2 (9 June 1841): 2. According to Sharp, Nauvoo's Mayor John C. Bennett issued the invitation. The *Western World* had changed its title to the *Warsaw Signal* starting 12 May.

22. Robert B. Thompson, "Communication," *Times and Seasons* 2 (15 April 1841): 380.

23. "Celebration of the Anniversary of the Church—Military Parade—Prest. Rigdon's Address—Laying the Corner Stones of the Temple," *Times and Seasons* 2 (15 April 1841): 375-77, appears to be taken from the official minutes. The second article is Robert B. Thompson, "Communication," ibid., 380-82.

24. Thompson, "Communication," 380.

25. "Celebration of the Anniversary of the Church," 376; Huntington, Journal, 12; Sharp, "The Mormons," *Western World* (Warsaw, IL), 7 April 1841, 3.

length of time."[26] The procession included not only the legion but many civilians who marched, eight abreast between the two cohorts of the Legion.

The parade arrived at the temple site at about noon and formed a hollow square three deep around the area where the walls would rise.[27] In the center of what would soon be the temple's footprint were "Major General Bennett, Brigadier Generals Law and Smith, their respective staffs, guard, field officers, distinguished visitors, choir, [and] band, etc."[28] The women in the company had their place immediately outside the walls, with "the gentlemen and infantry behind." The Nauvoo Legion's mounted units took up positions behind the three-deep militia units.[29] Joseph Smith, Sidney Rigdon, and several others took their seats on a stand or scaffolding that had been erected at the southeast corner.[30] Joseph Smith III, who was nine at the time, later recalled: "I remember being present upon that occasion, going to the grounds with Father who left me during the ceremonies in charge of someone who would not let me go upon the platform for fear I would be in the way."[31]

Norton Jacob, who was much impressed by the occasion, recorded it in minute detail in his autobiography:

> [The] countless multitude thronged around the Marshaled lines [was] filled with much wonder and curiosity to know what all this would amount to. Many strange murmurs ran through the waving throng to see the prophet, the master spirit of the glittering scene, mount a scaffold at the south-east corner in full military costume, accompanied by many of his fellow officers and friends. T[homas] C. Sharp ... with other visitors took his seat beside the prophet.[32]

The program opened with the choir, under the direction of B. S. Wilbur, singing the hymn on page 65 from the "new hymnbook."[33] Sidney Rigdon next

---

26. Thompson "Communication," 381.

27. Norton Jacob, Autobiography, 6. See also "Celebration of the Anniversary of the Church," 375. A hollow square was a common military formation.

28. "Celebration of the Anniversary of the Church," 375.

29. Thompson "Communication," 381.

30. "Celebration of the Anniversary of the Church," 375. See also Jacob, Autobiography, 5-6.

31. Mary Audentia Smith Anderson, ed., *Joseph Smith III and the Restoration* (Independence, MO: Herald House, 1952), 99.

32. Jacob, Autobiography, 5-6. Concerning Sharp's attendance, Jacob added: "I believe he here imbibed that spirit of rancor which since has been so freely manifested against the Saints for he envied that majesty and magnanimity which he had not the honesty and courage to emulate."

33. The book was the 1841 (second) printing of Emma Smith's hymnal: *Collection of Sacred Hymns for the Church* (Nauvoo: Ebenezer Robinson, 1841). The first stanza of the hymn sung at the ceremony reads: "Thou, Lord, through ev'ry changing scene, / Hast to the saints a refuge been; / Through every age, eternal God! / Their pleasing home—their safe abode."

addressed the gathering "for more than an hour." He noted that this was the third time he had spoken at the laying of temple cornerstones and remarked, "that not every people can build a house to [the Lord], but those only whom he himself directs."[34] According to the *Times and Seasons* report, "He rejoiced at the glorious prospect which presented itself of soon completing the edifice, as there were no mobs to hinder them in their labors, consequently their circumstances were very different than before."[35] The choir sang another hymn, and Rigdon closed the meeting with prayer, invoking "the blessings of Almighty God upon the assembly, and upon those who should labor on the building."[36]

At this point in the services, the southeast cornerstone was laid under the First Presidency's direction. At the laying of the Salt Lake Temple cornerstones, Brigham Young later explained that the southeast or chief stone is traditionally laid first, since it represents "the corner from whence light emanates to illuminate the whole fabric that is to be lighted."[37] The *Times and Seasons* noted that "the architects" (presumably William Weeks and some of the principal workmen) "lowered the first stone."[38] William Huntington was also "selected with others in laying the four cornerstones."[39] Joseph Smith pronounced this benediction: "This principal corner stone, in representation of the First Presidency, is now duly laid in honor of the great God; and may it there remain until the whole fabric is completed; and may the same be accomplished speedily; that the Saints may have a place to worship God, and the Son of Man have where to lay his head."[40]

Rigdon added a further benediction: "May the persons employed in the erection of this house be preserved from all harm while engaged in its construction, till the whole is completed; in the name of the Father, and of the Son, and of the Holy Ghost; even so, Amen."[41]

The meeting was then adjourned for one hour—presumably for lunch—after which the remaining three stones were laid.

34. "Celebration of the Anniversary of the Church," 375. See also Sharp, "The Mormons," 3. Rigdon had spoken at the cornerstone laying of both the Kirtland and Independence temples.

35.Thompson, "Communication," 382.

36. Ibid.

37. Brigham Young, 6 April 1853, *Journal of Discourses*, 26 vols. (London and Liverpool: LDS Booksellers Depot, 1855-86), 1:135.

38. "Celebration of the Anniversary of the Church," 376.

39. Huntington, Journal, 12. Huntington, a member of the Nauvoo High Council, would have also assisted in laying the third cornerstone.

40. "Celebration of the Anniversary of the Church," 376.

41. Ibid.

The second (S. W. corner) stone, by the direction of the Pres't. of the High
Priesthood, with his Council, and Pres't [William] Marks, was lowered to its place
when the Pres't. of the High Priesthood pronounced the following: "The second
corner stone of the temple now building by the Church of Jesus Christ of Latter-
day Saints, in honor of the Great God, is duly laid, and may the same unanimity,
that has been manifested on this occasion continue till the whole is completed
that peace may rest upon it to the laying of the top stone thereof, and the turning of the key thereof; that the Saints may participate in the blessings of Israel's
God within its walls, and the glory of God rest upon the same. Amen.

The third (N. W. corner) stone, superintended by the High Council, as repre-
sentatives of the Twelve, (they being in Europe.) was then lowered to its place,
with the benediction of Elias Higbee as follows: "The third corner stone, in representation of the Twelve, is now duly laid; and as they are, in some measure the
support of the church, so may this stone be a firm support to the corner, that the
whole may be completed as before purposed, and according to the order of the
Priesthood.

The fourth (N. E. corner) stone, superintended by the Bishop, was then lowered to its place, and Bishop Whitney pronounced the following, "The fourth and
last corner stone, expressive of the Lesser Priesthood, is now duly laid; and may
the blessings before pronounced, with all others desirable, rest upon the same
forever; Amen.[42]

At the conclusion of the ceremonies, the Nauvoo Legion marched back to
the parade ground and the crowd dispersed.[43]

The laying of the cornerstones with its pomp and ceremony was largely
responsible for giving the temple its first regional, even national publicity. The story
on the ceremony in the *Western World* spread to other regional papers such as the
Sangamo Journal and *Quincy Whig*, and eventually to papers around the country.
For example, the *Maysville Eagle* in Kentucky, the *Telegraph* in Painesville, Ohio,
and the *New York Observer* would carry stories on the laying of the cornerstones.[44]

"Send Ye Swift Messengers"

The following day, during the first formal session of the general conference,
Gen. John C. Bennett, at Sidney Rigdon's request, read the revelation of January 19

---

42. Ibid., 377.

43. Jacob, Autobiography, 6; See also Thompson, "Communication," 382.

44. See *Sangamo Journal* (Springfield, IL), 10 (16 April 1841): 4; *Quincy (IL) Whig* 3 (24 April
1841): 2; *Mayfield Eagle* (Maysville, KY), 6 (24 April 1841): 3; *Painesville (OH) Telegraph* 7 (28 April
1841): 3; *New York Observer* (Utica, NY), 19 (10 May 1841): 75.

concerning the temple. Prompted by this review of its instructions, the conference resolved: "That John Murdoch, Lyman Wight, William Smith, Henry William Miller, Amasa Lyman, Leonard Soby, Gehiel Savage, and Zenos H. Gurley be appointed to travel and collect funds for the [Temple]."[45] Their call answered to the mandate of the revelation, "Send ye swift messengers, yea, chosen messengers" (D&C 124:26). These men and others, appointed during the following months, traveled to branches of the Church in the eastern United States and Canada, gathering funds for building the temple. Each was given a certificate of authority such as this one, carried by Ira T. Miles, who was appointed as an agent in 1842, and signed by the building committee:

> To all whom it may concern
> This may certify that the bearer of this Elder Ira S. Miles has been appointed by the Temple Committee to collect funds for the building of the Temple now erecting in this place.
> Given under our hands at Nauvoo this 11th day of October A. D. 1842.[46]

Benjamin Clapp's letter of authority to collect funds in the Southern States gave explicit instructions about the agents' duties. They were "required ... to keep a correct list of all the donors' names and the description and amount of property donated by each, that they may be duly recorded on his return in the record of tithing and consecration." It further warned, "Should any donor require a receipt for the property donated it must be distinctly understood that it will not be recorded until the receipts are returned to the Recorder's Office in the City of Nauvoo."[47]

Since the Church was not incorporated during the 1840s , it could not own property. To facilitate ownership, the Church used the legal vehicle of "trustee in trust," which gave an appointed person authority to oversee organizational property. The temple agents turned over their gleanings to the temple committee or to Joseph Smith, who had been appointed trustee in trust for the Church on 30 January 1840.[48] The trustee or committee then issued receipts to the agents.

45. Joseph Smith Jr. et al., *History of the Church of Jesus Christ of Latter-day Saints*, edited by B. H. Roberts (Salt Lake City: Deseret News Press, 6 vols. published 1902-12, Vol. 7 published 1932, 2d printing), 4:342.

46. Ira S. Miles, Certificate of Authority, 11 October 1842, microfilm of holograph, Newel K. Whitney Papers, Perry Special Collections, Lee Library. See also certificate issued to Peter Haws in "Thought and Action," *Courage: A History of History* 1 (September 1970): 51.

47. "A Copy of a Letter of Authority Given to Benjamin D. Clapp," 18 October 1844, microfilm of holograph, Whitney Papers, Perry Special Collections, Lee Library.

48. Beginning in December 1841, donations were no longer given to the committee. See section on the Temple Recorder in chap. 3. Joseph Smith had been elected "Trustee-in-Trust" for the Church unanimously "at a special conference of the Church," on 30 January 1840. *History of the Church*, 4:286.

In a letter to Joseph Smith in November 1842, James M. Adams, a temple agent, reported his experience gathering funds for the temple in Andover, Ohio:

> Notwithstanding our poverty we are anxious to send up our mites to assist in accomplishing the great work of God in building the temple according to revelation. I have therefore used my best endeavors to gather what I could for this most glorious object. As an opportunity is offered us of sending by Brother Russell. It is but a little that we shall be able to send at this time as we had only a day or two notice that there would be an opportunity of sending this haul. We shall calculate to send something more in the spring when Br[other] Lyman Wight returns. I will give below a list of the articles sent together with the names of those who sent them and wish the amount placed to their credit to apply on their tithing:

James M. Adams

Donor Names		Articles Sent
James M. Adams		Cash $10.00
		one pair shoes
		one pair socks
David H. Parsons		two yards and three fourths of fulled cloth
		two pair socks
		one pair mittens
Samuel Arnold		one veal skin
		two sheep skins
		one pair socks
Gamaliel R. Grover		one pr. boots
John Riggs		one pr. boots
Benjamin Soles	Erie Pa.	Cash five Dollars
James VanNatta	D[itt]o	Cash five Dollars
Clarinda Gleason		one quilt
Susan Holman		four ½ yards muslin
Susan Tyler		one pr. socks
Sally Geer		one pr. socks
Jonathan Willson		one pr. mittens[49]

Elijah Malin Jr., newly baptized in 1843, wrote to Joseph Smith on 15 May 1843 from "Brandywine Branch," in Chester County, Pennsylvania. His letter gives further insight into the willing hearts that greeted the appeal for funds: "Bro. Joseph,

---

49. James M. Adams, Letter to Joseph Smith, 16 November 1842, Whitney Papers, Perry Special Collections, Lee Library. James Marvin Adams (1806-unknown) joined the Church in Ohio and received his patriarchal blessing in 1837.

by request of a poor brother I enclose two dollars to go to the temple, or to the building of it, his Name is Andrew Main."[50]

Many agents were bonded, meaning that they signed a document that made them personally liable, up to the dollar amount stated in the bond, for any collected temple donations that they did not faithfully transfer to Joseph Smith. William Smith, Joseph's brother, signed this bond on 13 April, just days after the conference:

> Know all men by these presents that I William Smith of the County of Hancock and State of Illinois am held and firmly bound to Joseph Smith of the County and State aforesaid in the sum of one thousand dollars for the payment of which well and truly to be made I bind myself my heirs and assigns firmly by these presents.
>
> Now the condition of the above obligation is such that if the said William Smith shall well and truly perform the office of agent to collect funds for building the temple in this place, and shall make just and true returns of all monies and properties he may receive for building the temple as aforesaid and faithfully pay over said monies or properties to the said Joseph Smith without delay then this bond to become null and void, otherwise to be and remain in full force and virtue
>
> In testimony whereof I have hereunto set my hand and seal at the City of Nauvoo this thirteenth day of April A. D. 1841
>
> Wm. Smith (signed)
Acknowledged in presence of R. B. Thompson[51]

The practice of bonding temple agents would continue over the life of the project, even though not all agents entered into this type of obligation. After Joseph Smith's death, the agents were bonded to the new trustees of the Church.[52]

Thomas C. Sharp's Criticisms

After attending the laying of the temple cornerstones, Thomas C. Sharp published what would be his last impartial article on Joseph Smith and the building up of Nauvoo. Sharp, a New Jersey born lawyer, moved to Illinois in 1840 and

---

50. Elijah Malin Jr., Letter to Joseph Smith, 15 May 1843, Whitney Papers, Perry Special Collections, Lee Library.

51. "Bond of William Smith," 13 April 1841, Whitney Papers, Perry Special Collections, Lee Library. This collection also includes Leonard Soby's bond for $2,000, written to Joseph Smith and issued two days after William's on 15 April 1841. William Clayton, in his 1845 history of the temple, claimed that the practice of bonding agents began in 1843: "Thus the Twelve were the first agents who were ever placed under bonds, when sent to collect funds for the Church." George D. Smith, An *Intimate Chronicle*, 539. These documents prove otherwise.

52. From 1844-46, George Miller and Newel K. Whitney, both Nauvoo bishops, acted as "Trustees-in-Trust." Several bonds dating from this period are in the Whitney Papers, Perry Special Collections, Lee Library.

began editing the *Western World* in November of that year. His first article on the cornerstone ceremony praised the Nauvoo Legion for a "very respectable appearance," commended General Bennett for acquitting himself in a "very officer-like manner," and described the exercises as "pass[ing] off with the utmost order."[53] However, during the months that followed, Sharp would engage in a bitter editorial exchange with Joseph Smith and his brother William, editor of the *Nauvoo Wasp*, over John C. Bennett's mayoralty and what Sharp saw as Joseph's lack of fitness as a leader.[54] From 2 June forward, Sharp relentlessly attacked Smith, Nauvoo, and the efforts of the Church to build the temple.

In a second article about the cornerstone laying, published on 9 June, Sharp sarcastically reported that during a break in the ceremonies he had "tried our hardest to steal off and make for home." He felt he was "caressed and having all manner of affection paid us, in order to bribe us to flattery and make a great noise over their splendid parade in our editorials, and then after disappointing them, how exceedingly ungrateful must we be to make an attack upon them."[55]

Sharp also criticized the method of raising funds. In a fictional epistle, purportedly written by "Moroni" and published only weeks before Joseph Smith's murder, Sharp chided Joseph Smith about the system of tithing labor and the measures being taken to complete the construction:

> Bring your tithings for the temple, for Brother Joseph hath need of all the gold silver and merchandise that belong to the saints—and even this is not enough to answer his extraneous purposes. The poor can build the temple, and when they become weary, Joseph knows how to curse them, and threaten them with hell, if they do not try away. He then calls on the Bishop to warn them out of the different wards—again Hercules like they put their shoulders to the wheel, and the stone again begins to roll. After this he pats them on the back, and calls them fine fellows and promises them great wealth.[56]

A month earlier, Sharp had referred to the revelation of 18 January 1841, and mocked: "It appears that the time allotted [to build the temple] has been nearly exhausted, and the work not half completed. What are the consequences, if no temple is erected in the allotted time? Friend Jo tells his sycophants that they will

---

53. Sharp, "The Mormons," 2.

54. Marshall Hamilton, "Thomas Sharp's Turning Point: The Birth of an Anti-Mormon," *Sunstone* 13 (October 1989): 5, 21.

55. Sharp, "The More We Reflect," *Warsaw Signal*, 9 June 1841, 2.

56. Moroni [pseud.], "Spiritual Wife System," *Warsaw Signal*, 8 May 1844, 5. Although this epistle is not signed by Sharp, it matches Sharp's other denunciations of Joseph Smith and Mormonism in content and style.

be rejected, and their dead with them. This failed in producing the necessary energy."[57]

When endowments began in the temple just before the exodus from Nauvoo, Sharp published a lurid exposé of the ceremony intended to "let the cat out of the bag," as he put it, and reveal what he called "the obscene rites."[58] He wrote:

> This endowment consists in an abrogation of all existing marriages and every good saint is at liberty to cast away his present wife, and take any other who may suit him better. The consequence is, all Nauvoo is in commotion and the Saints are running around perfectly wild with excitement.
>
> The reason why the Lord concluded to endow his saints in this singular manner, was because, some husbands were willing to go to Oregon and the wives objected and vice versa; so they being mismatched, the Lord concluded to prevent the difficulty by giving all willing ones a chance to select new partners for the expedition.[59]

While these venomous attacks lay, for the most part, years in the future, Norton Jacob believed it was at the cornerstone ceremony that Sharp first "imbibed that spirit of rancor which since has been so freely manifested against the Saints for he envied that majesty and magnanimity which he had not the honesty and courage to emulate."[60]

Progress on the Foundation During the Summer

During the summer of 1841, activity at the temple site focused on completing the excavation of the basement and building the remainder of the foundation walls. Some idea of the depth of the excavation was given by David White in 1843. He reported that the completed basement was "about twelve feet in the clear, the half of which is underground."[61] While the basement near the exterior walls was excavated to a depth of five or six feet, the center was excavated to a depth of over eight feet and sloped gradually upward as it approached the outside walls. Hiram Gano Ferris, a student who visited the temple in 1846, wrote that the

---

57. An Exile [pseud.], "The Nauvoo Block and Tackle," *Warsaw Signal*, 25 April 1844, 3.

58. Thomas C. Sharp, "Ceremony of the Endowment," *Warsaw Signal*, 18 February 1846, 4.

59. Thomas C. Sharp, "Great Commotion in Nauvoo," *Warsaw Signal*, 24 December 1845, 2.

60. Jacob, Autobiography, 5-6.

61. David White, "The Prairies, Nauvoo, Joe Smith, the Temple, the Mormons, etc.," *Pittsburgh Weekly Gazette* 58 (15 September 1843): 3, as quoted in Dean C. Jessee, ed., *The Papers of Joseph Smith*, 2 vols. (Salt Lake City: Deseret Book Company, 1989), 1:442.

floor "has a gradual descent from the sides and ends to the font."[62] This unusual basin-shaped floor was undoubtedly intended to help accommodate the baptismal font, the floor of which would be three feet above ground.[63]

Piercing the exterior walls surrounding the basement were semicircular windows. By late summer, "the temple walls were up to the arch of the basement windows."[64] Peter Conover, a recent convert to the Church, related the circumstances under which the stone for the window arches was obtained: "The Prophet called me to get men to go with me to get some rock for the circle windows in the basement story of the temple. I called for volunteers at a meeting held at my house. I soon had all the men I wanted. We worked all the week and got all the rock that was needed."[65]

A traveler writing in the St. Louis Gazette commented, "The solidity of the buttresses and the port hole aspect of the basement apertures for windows, lend the pile more the appearance of a fortress than a sanctuary."[66]

William Clayton wrote that "after the corner stones were laid and the conference was over, the work upon the temple seemed to progress more rapidly."[67] One factor was that the tithing labor force was increasing, as the city's population swelled with newly arriving immigrants from around the United States, Canada, and Great Britain.

Perhaps the most important reason for the acceleration in the work, however, was the decision to hire eighteen full-time stonecutters to dress the roughly hewn stones from the quarry. "Up to this time," explained Clayton, "the work performed was nearly all done by tenth days' labor. But after this the Saints began to bring in some provisions, property and money; and the committee was enabled to employ a number of stonecutters and keep them constantly at work."[68] Hired labor would become even more important the following year. In summarizing the data in temple committee's books, historian Don F. Colvin reports that 885 people were employed by the temple works between 1842 and 1845, for periods of from one to twelve months.[69]

---

62. Hiram Gano Ferris, "A Description of the Mormon Temple," Carthage Republican, 19 March 1890, 2. Ferris's description was penned in 1846.

63. History of the Church, 4:446.

64. Mary Ann Stearns Winters, Autobiography, ca. 1855, typescript, 10, LDS Church Archives. Winters (1833-unknown) was the stepdaughter of Apostle Parley P. Pratt.

65. Peter Conover, "Autobiography of Peter Wilson Conover," 1884, typescript, 2, Nauvoo Restoration Lands and Records Office, Nauvoo Illinois. Conover (1807-92), a former Campbellite, was baptized 17 May 1840.

66. "The Temple of Nauvoo," St. Louis Gazette, ca. 12 June 1844, in Journal History, 12 June 1844, 5.

67. George D. Smith, An Intimate Chronicle, 529.

68. Ibid.

69. Don F. Colvin, "A Historical Study of the Mormon Temple at Nauvoo, Illinois" (M.A. thesis, Brigham Young University, 1962), 62.

On 13 June, William Huntington, who was hired as a stonecutter, wrote in his journal: "Through this summer and fall the work of the House of the Lord is prospered the basement story almost up."[70] On 2 August 1841, a contributor to the *Times and Seasons* encouraged readers to visit the site where "they will see the foundation of a building laid, which is expected to astonish the world, and show how much can be done by a concentration of action."[71]

Carving the Baptismal Font

In response to the 19 January revelation about baptisms for the dead as a temple ordinance, William Weeks prepared architectural drawings detailing the font's appearance. William Clayton wrote, "President Joseph approved and accepted the draft for the font," which was to be placed "in the cellar floor near the east end of the temple."[72] In addition to the obvious convenience of locating at ground level such a heavy object, which must be filled with water and drained, the Prophet Joseph later explained that the font was "instituted as a simile of the grave, and was commanded to be in a place underneath where the living are wont to assemble" (D&C 128:13).

Although no records exist of Joseph Smith providing instructions to William Weeks concerning the font, there is no doubt he suggested its design, which was directly inspired by the "brazen sea" of Solomon's temple (1 Kings 7:23-26).[73] Like Solomon's font, the Nauvoo Temple font would rest on the backs of twelve oxen arranged like the spokes of a wheel, facing outwards.

Weeks's drawings were completed sometime between February and June 1841. The 1 July number of the *Times and Seasons* contained this report concerning progress on the font: "The building committee are making every preparation to erect the baptismal font in the basement story as soon as possible. The font, is intended to be supported by twelve oxen, several of which are in a state of forwardness, and are certainly good representations of that animal, and do great credit to the mechanics who are engaged in carving the same."[74]

---

70. Huntington, Journal, 12.

71. "War! War! And Rumors of War!!!" *Times and Seasons* 2, no. 19 (2 August 1841): 496. The article is unsigned. Joseph Smith edited the 2 August issue of the paper but it is unclear whether he authored the article.

72. George D. Smith, *An Intimate Chronicle*, 532.

73. See also Benjamin Winchester, Letter to Erastus Snow, 12 November 1841, *Times and Seasons* 3 (15 November 1841): 605.

74. "The Temple of the Lord," *Times and Seasons* 2 (1 July 1841): 455. The article is unsigned. The editors for that issue were Robert B. Thompson and Don Carlos Smith.

Although this article does not identify the "mechanics," or woodcarvers, William Clayton wrote that William Weeks "began carving the oxen, twelve in number, upon which the font was to stand. After carving for six days, he consigned this branch to Brother Elijah Fordham, the principal carver, who continued until they were finished."[75] The *History of the Church* reports that this endeavor "occupied eight months of time."[76]

When the font was finished in November, it was described as

> constructed of pine timber, and put together of staves tongued and groved, oval shaped, sixteen feet long east and west, and twelve feet wide, seven feet high from the foundation, the basin four feet deep, the moulding of the cap and base are formed of beautiful carved work in antique style. The sides are finished with panel work. A flight of stairs in the north and south sides lead up and down into the basin, guarded by side railing.
>
> The font stands upon twelve oxen, four on each side, and two at each end, their heads, shoulders, and fore legs projecting out from under the font; they are carved out of pine plank, glued together, and copied after the most beautiful five-year-old steer that could be found in the country and they are an excellent striking likeness of the original; the horns were formed after the most perfect horn that could be procured.[77]

Joseph Fielding, in a letter to the *Millennial Star* the next summer, observed, "What I call the vault, is in part occupied by the baptismal font, supported by twelve oxen, which are of wood, now painted white, but eventually to be overlaid with gold."[78] Albert C. Koch, a German visitor to Nauvoo in 1844 noted that the oxen were "painted with white oil paint."[79] Some understood that only the horns would be gilded.[80] If or when any gold-leaf was ever applied to the font is

---

75. George D. Smith, *An Intimate Chronicle*, 532. Elijah Fordham (1798-1879) joined the Church ca. 1836 and was a carpenter in Nauvoo.

76. *History of the Church*, 4:446. William Clayton states that the work of carving took two months and gives 11 August as the starting date. George D. Smith, *An Intimate Chronicle*, 532. However, the carving of the oxen was underway as early as 1 July. "The Temple of the Lord," *Times and Seasons* 2 (1 July 1841): 455. It is possible that Clayton meant that carving the font basin had taken eight weeks.

77. *History of the Church*, 4:446.

78. "Joseph Fielding's Letter" (dated January 1842), *Millennial Star* 3 (August 1842): 78. See also "The Temple of the Lord," 455.

79. Albert C. Koch, *Journey Through a Part of the United States of North America in the Years 1844 to 1846*, translated and edited by Ernest A. Stadler (Carbondale: University of Illinois Press, 1972), 67. Koch also mentions that the oxen "like the water container they carry, will be gilded."

80. Nathan Cheney, Letter to "Beloved Friends," in Eliza Jane Cheney Rawson, "Letters and Sketches," typescript, 3 LDS Church Archives.

unknown. It seems unlikely given the Saints' desperate poverty and the fact that the wood font was replaced in 1845 due to rotting.

However, because the font was such a distinctive feature and was finished by October 1841, it became the most talked-about aspect of the new building. Articles about Nauvoo and the temple that appeared in newspapers across the country almost invariably featured the writer's reaction to the curious font and oxen. A New York paper printed this commentary in 1844: "The execution of the twelve oxen evidences a degree of ingenuity, skill and perseverance that would redound to the reputation of an artist in any community. When they are finally gilded, as intended, and the laver is made to resemble cast brass, together with the finishing up of the place in which the unique apparatus of the church is lodged—as a whole that part of the temple will be one of the most striking artificial curiosities in this country."[81]

A less complimentary description appeared in the lengthy *St. Louis Gazette* article printed in the spring of 1844:

> In the centre of the basement, resting upon the backs of eight[82] white oxen carved from wood with passable skill, stands the baptismal font, a rectangular box of some twelve feet square, and half as many in depth.
>
> From each side of this box appear the heads and shoulders of two oxen up to their knees in brick work, with most inexpressive eyes, most extensive ears, a remarkable longitude of face, and a protrusion of horns perfectly prodigious with a single exception, one horn of one unhappy ox having been torn off by some more than usually rude grasp at the "altar!" The effect of all this is of a character somewhat mixed.
>
> It is certainly a little startling in the dim religious duskiness of the spot, to stumble upon these eight white oxen, standing so still, and stiff, and stark, and solemn, with their great stony eyes staring sternly at you for the intrusion; and yet, the first inclination, after recovering from your surprise is to laugh, and that most heartily. The idea of this font seems to have been revealed to the prophet directly by the plan of the molten sea of Solomon's Temple, which we are told in the old scriptures, stood upon twelve oxen, three looking to the north, three to the south, three to the east, and three to the west; all their hinder parts inward.[83]

The Saints took great pride in the font. Benjamin Winchester, a Church member in Nauvoo, described the oxen as "ingeniously carved, and strikingly

---

81. *New York Spectator*, 9 November 1844, reprinted in Cecil B. McGavin, *Nauvoo Temple* (Salt Lake City: Deseret Book, 1962). For more descriptions of the basement and font, see Appendix: Eyewitness Descriptions of the Temple.

82. Contrary to this report, there were twelve oxen.

83. "The Temple of Nauvoo," *St. Louis Gazette*, ca. June 1844, in Journal History, 12 June 1844, 3.

resemble the living original."[84] Nathan Cheney believed that "the oxen look as natural as though they were alive."[85] Joseph Fielding recorded his reaction when he first saw the font: "It would be vain to attempt to describe my feelings on beholding this interesting sight; but if you have the same faith as myself in the great work of God ... you may judge of my feelings."[86]

This font was temporary, to be used "until the temple shall be finished, when a more durable one will supply its place."[87]

The Temple Basement

According to Lyman Littlefield, who wrote in 1845, the basement was "divided off into thirteen rooms, the one in the centre is one-hundred feet in length from east to west, and fifty feet wide."[88] This large center room held the baptismal font. The other twelve rooms were smaller, six each lining the north and south walls of the basement. The *St. Louis Gazette* reporter wrote, "The basement story, as you look down into it, reminds you more of a wine cellar, with its dozen apartments or crypts, each divided from the other by ponderous masonry."[89] Another visitor later recorded his impression that the basement was "a damp, gloomy looking place and very chilly."[90] Nathan Cheney wrote this description of the basement to his family:

> You would be surprised to see the city that there has been laid out in the basement story of the temple. There is thirteen different rooms in the basement story, one room is 40 feet square, the room that is 40 square has got a baptismal font in it.... The other rooms are for the different quorums to meet in. The work that has been done is done in the best kind of manner.[91]

84. Benjamin Winchester, Letter to Erastus Snow, dated 12 November 1841, *Times and Seasons* 3 (15 November 1841): 604. Winchester (1817-1901) joined the Church in February 1833 in Erie, Pennsylvania, and was a member of Zion's Camp.

85. Cheney, Letter to "Beloved Friends," 3.

86. Joseph Fielding, Letter, January 1842, 78.

87. Joseph Smith, *History of the Church*, 4:446. For information on the stone font that replaced the wood one, see chap. 8.

88. Lyman Littlefield, "From Nauvoo to the Editor of the Messenger," *New York Messenger*, 30 August 1845, 67, photocopy in LDS Church Historical Department Library.

89. "The Temple of Nauvoo," *St. Louis Gazette*, 3.

90. Author unknown, Illinois Journal, 9 December 1853, reprinted as "Recollections of the Nauvoo Temple," *Journal of the Illinois State Historical Society* 38 (December 1945): 482; photocopy in LDS Church Historical Department Library.

91. Cheney, Letter to "Beloved Friends," 3.

While Cheney and perhaps others believed early on that the rooms in the basement were intended for meetings, the commandment to build a font in the temple changed their use. The rooms were called variously "preparation and reception rooms"[92] or "robing rooms"[93] and were used "for the person who had been baptized to change their clothes."[94] Doors to these side rooms had been installed to provide privacy by May 1844.[95]

To fill the font, the Saints dug a well in the basement floor. The first plans called for a well at the west end of the basement, but a well ten feet deep, dug in 1841, did not produce enough water to fill the font. This well was later enclosed in a chamber "under the portico of the temple ... and situated in a room to which there was no entrance except by an opening made in the floor" of the vestibule above.[96] Walling off the room in this way may have been a safety precaution to prevent accidents. A visitor to the temple in the summer of 1844 commented on this room, "A chamber is in this huge [west] wall without door or window—the wall is about three feet thick."[97]

After this well proved disappointing, workmen excavated a new well approximately twenty-seven feet from the eastern wall of the basement. Hyrum Oaks and his brother-in-law, Jesse McCarrol, dug the well. According to family tradition, "they had to penetrate ten feet of solid rock before they struck water. When they struck water, they lost the drill and the water spurted up with great force. Grandfather [Hyrum] put his hat over the hole until Jess could get a block of wood to stop the water."[98]

92. Unknown author, untitled article containing quotations from J. M. Davidson, "Nauvoo: The Past and Present of That City: Visits of 1846 and 1864 Contrasted," *Carthage Republican,* 25 February 1864, 1, and quoted in E. Cecil McGavin, *The Nauvoo Temple* (Salt Lake City: Deseret Book, 1962), 93-95. McGavin mistakenly cites Davidson as the author of the article, rather than as "quoted by unknown author."

93. J. H. Buckingham, "Letter from Nauvoo, July 1847," to the *Boston Courier* in "Illinois as Lincoln Knew It," edited by Harry E. Pratt, *Papers in Illinois History and Transactions for the Year 1937* (Springfield, IL.: n.pub., 1938), 171; photocopy at Nauvoo Restoration, Inc., Nauvoo, Illinois.

94. William Gallup, Diary, 29 July 1848, photographic reprint of pages 129-30 accompanied by introduction by William Powell, photocopy, Perry Special Collections, Lee Library. See also John Reynolds, *My Own Times: Embracing the History of My Life* (Belleville, IL.: B. H. Perryman and H. L. Davison, 1855), 586-87.

95. Sissimus (pseud.), "To the Editor of the Neighbor," *Nauvoo Neighbor* 2 (1 May 1844): 1. Internal evidence indicates that the letter was authored by a nonmember who visited Nauvoo in April 1844.

96. *St. Louis (MO) Morning Republican,* 24 September 1846, quoted in Harrington and Harrington, *Rediscovery of the Nauvoo Temple,* 30.

97. "To the Editor of the *Neighbor,*" 1.

98. Larraine Wissler King, "Life of Hiram Oaks," n.d., in her Book of Remembrance, in possession of Bill Burnard, Newton, Utah, photocopy of typescript at Nauvoo Restoration, Inc., Nauvoo, Illinois.

This second well was thirty feet deep.[99] It was lined with small stones taken from the temple quarry. A reporter noted, "A pump stands by it to supply it with water."[100] According to John Reynolds, who visited Nauvoo in 1844, "arrangements were made to heat the rooms and the water in the baptismal font."[101] Church members visiting Nauvoo in 1937, at the time the temple lot was repurchased, claimed that "residents of Nauvoo" knew "that although, in drought seasons, other lower wells have failed in Nauvoo, the high temple site well has never been without water."[102]

The Call to Gather

Soon after Joseph Smith's arrival in Illinois, he "cried 'Lord what will thou have me to do?' And the answer was, 'build up a city and call my saints to this place!'"[103] Thus, almost as soon as the refugees from Missouri had established themselves in their new home, the call to gather went out to members of the Church worldwide. One of the earliest formal calls to gather to Nauvoo was the revelation received on 19 January 1841 in which the Saints were commanded: "Come from afar ... and build a house to my name" (D&C 124:25, 27). Following this pronouncement, the Quorum of the Twelve reiterated the call in an epistle in March 1841:

> Having been instrumental in the hands of our heavenly Father in laying a foundation for the gathering of Zion, we would say, let all those who appreciate the blessings of the gospel, and realize the importance of obeying the commandments of heaven, who have been blessed of heaven with the possession of this world's goods, first prepare for the general gathering—let them dispose of their effects as fast as circumstances will possibly admit, without making too great sacrifices, and remove to our city and county—establish and build up manufactories in the city, purchase and cultivate farms in the country—this will secure our permanent inheritance, and prepare the way for the gathering of the poor.—This is agreeable to the order of heaven, and the only principle on which the gathering

99. *History of the Church*, 4:446.

100. White, "The Prairies, Nauvoo, Joe Smith, the Temple, the Mormons, etc.,"1:442. According to Charlotte Haven, *A Girl's Letters*, 620, who also visited Nauvoo in 1843, "Pumps are attached to the font to supply it with water when necessary."

101. Reynolds, *My Own Times*, 586-87.

102. Marba Cannon Josephson, "Church Acquires Nauvoo Temple Site," *Improvement Era* 40 (March 1937): 284.

103. Scott H. Faulring, ed., *An American Prophet's Record: The Diaries and Journals of Joseph Smith* (Salt Lake City: Signature Books, 1989), 362.

can be effected—let the rich, then, and all who can assist in establishing this place, make every preparation to come on without delay, and strengthen our hands, and assist in promoting the happiness of the Saints.... The elders are hereby instructed to proclaim this word in all the places where the Saints reside in their public administrations, for this is according to the instructions we have received from the Lord.[104]

The revelation of 19 January 1841 had definitely linked the gathering with the building of the temple. (See vv. 26-27.) Two years later, the Prophet Joseph would expand upon this connection:

What was the object of gathering the Jews together or the people of God in any age of the world? The main object was to build unto the Lord an house whereby he could reveal unto his people the ordinances of his house and glories of his kingdom and teach the people the ways of salvation. For there are certain ordinances and principles that when they are taught and practiced, must be done in a place or house built for that purpose. This was purposed in the mind of God before the world was and it was for this purpose that God designed to gather together the Jews oft but they would not. It is for the same purpose that God gathers together the people in the last days to build unto the Lord an house to prepare them for the ordinances and endowments, washings and anointings, etc.[105]

Thousands answered the call. Nauvoo's population, which was approximately 3,000 in early 1841, doubled by the summer of 1842. Before the departure of the Saints in 1846, Nauvoo's population had swelled to over 12,000 inhabitants, most of whom were members of the Church.[106] A reported 4,200 came from England alone.[107] These immigrants greatly enlarged the workforce and increased the economic base from which tithes were paid. The influence of these emigrants in supporting and working on the temple is inestimable.

Ezra T. Benson, a thirty-year-old who joined the Church in nearby Quincy in 1840, was among those who gathered to Nauvoo:

About the first of March, 1841, the spirit of gathering rested upon me and I told the brethren I thought of moving to Nauvoo, Illinois. They thought I had better

---

104. "Extracts from an Epistle to the Elders in England," *Millennial Star* 1 (March 1841): 270-71.

105. *History of the Church*, 5:423.

106. Stanley B. Kimball, "The Mormons in Early Illinois: An Introduction," *Dialogue: A Journal of Mormon Thought* 5 (Spring 1970): 9.

107. Dean May, "A Demographic Portrait of the Mormons, 1830-1980," in *New Mormon History: Revisionist Essays on the Past,* edited by D. Michael Quinn (Salt Lake City: Signature Books, 1992), 122.

remain where I was a little longer, but I was not satisfied and started to Nauvoo to get counsel from Brother Joseph Smith.... I sold out my nursery, settled my affairs, paid tithing and by the first of April, was on my way to Nauvoo, and arrived in time to attend the April conference and to see the cornerstones of the temple laid.[108]

The immigrants flooding into Nauvoo were met with enthusiasm. Eliza R. Snow recalled how one company of newcomers was greeted when they disembarked at Nauvoo on 12 April 1843:

The time of the arrival had been announced, and many hearts (mine not excepted) were anxiously and expectantly beating, and when the steamer came in sight, every eye was turned in the direction, and as it neared the landing, white handkerchiefs were waving along the shore, up and down, for a great distance. President Joseph Smith, with a large number of brothers and sisters, was present to greet our friends, and he gave notice to the newcomers to meet at the temple on the next day at ten o'clock, to receive instructions.[109]

Job Smith, age fifteen, described one of these instructional sessions after his family's arrival from England:

The Sunday [following our arrival] ... found us at the "stand" or place where meetings were held. This stand was in a grove of trees in front of the temple, the walls of which at that time were halfway up the first tier of tall windows. The Prophet was present, also several of the apostles who each discoursed to the new arrivals advice as to how to succeed in becoming permanently settled. We took occasion to visit the basement of the new building and saw there the baptismal font which had already been prepared with the carved oxen underneath it as apparent support. The artistic work of the whole excited much admiration.[110]

The contribution of these immigrants to the construction of the temple was invaluable. Without this infusion, it is unlikely that a sufficiently large, adequately skilled workforce could ever have been mustered to complete the structure.

---

108. Ezra T. Benson, "Ezra Taft Benson I: An Autobiography," *Juvenile Instructor* 80 (July 1945): 103. Benson (1811-69) later served as a member of the Quorum of the Twelve.

109. Eliza R. Snow, *Biography and Family Record of Lorenzo Snow* (Salt Lake City: Deseret News, 1884), 67. See Faulring, *An American Prophet's Record*, 360, for one of Joseph's speeches to the immigrants.

110. Job Smith, Autobiography, 1854, typescript, 5, LDS Church Archives. Smith (1828-1913), a native of England, was baptized 18 May 1940.

The Temple as a Public Works Project

In 1840 and 1841, the populace of Nauvoo was extremely poor. Luman Shurtliff reminisced, "The citizens of Nauvoo, when this temple was begun, was most of them who had been driven from Missouri and stripped of all they then possessed."[111] The missionaries' tremendous success in converting new Saints and bringing them to Nauvoo only compounded the problem of providing food, shelter, and work, for many among these newcomers also had no money or property of any value. Parley P. Pratt apprised church members in Nauvoo of the plight of many of the British emigrants:

> A few of those who come over in the *Tyrean*[112] will have a little money, and perhaps they will do some little for the temple; but it will take what they have to provide them a home; indeed many of them will land without a shilling. The distress is such in this country that the saints will go to Zion whether they can carry any thing with them or not. They had rather be slaves in America than to starve in this country. I cannot keep them back, go they will, and go they must, or perish.[113]

New arrivals were often disappointed to find that the struggling community offered little in the way of work. In addition to employing skilled workers, the temple committee also assumed the burden of providing employment to many of the new arrivals and the poor as a form of work relief. George Miller, then bishop of the Nauvoo First Ward, explained:

> The poor had to be cared for, and labor created that they might at least earn part of their subsistence, there not being one in ten persons that could set themselves to work, to earn those indispensable things for the comfort of their families.
>
> My brethren of the Committee of the Nauvoo House Association, and the Committee of the Temple all bore a part in the employment of laborers, and the providing food for them....
>
> The residue of the summer and fall [1841] were taken up with providing the means for paying the wages of the laborers on the Temple.... The workmen were kept all winter, as we necessarily had to feed them whether we discharged them from the work or not; they having no means of buying their winter's food without our aid.[114]

---

111. Shurtliff, Autobiography, 52.

112. The *Tyrean* departed from Liverpool, bound for New Orleans, on 21 September 1841, carrying 204 Latter-day Saints under the direction of Joseph Fielding. On 24 December, the company arrived at Warsaw, Illinois.

113. "Letter from P. P. Pratt," 12 August 1841, *Times and Seasons* 3 (15 December 1841): 625.

The temple works employed hundreds of poor. These workers were paid with food, clothing, and other necessities, which had been donated as tithing. Every tenth day they worked without pay, donating their labor on that day as tithing.[115]

Employment of the poor on the temple works was an ingenious system of welfare, but it was also an important aspect of Nauvoo's economy that benefited both the poor and the temple. The religious duty to pay tithing and the commandment to build the temple combined to increase the exchange of goods and to stimulate the barter economy. Speaking to church members in Nauvoo on 15 October 1843, Joseph Smith lauded the benefits of donating to the temple to assist the poor: "Some say it is better to give to the poor than build the Temple. The building of the Temple has sustained the poor who were driven from Missouri, and kept them from starving; and it has been the best means for this object which could be devised."[116]

Despite its obvious advantages, however, this work relief system did not always successfully match supply and demand. Brigham Young later lamented that many of the workers "labored on that house with not a shoe to their feet, or pantaloons that would cover their limbs, or a shirt to cover their arms."[117] This occurred for several reasons:

Poverty prevailed and tithing payments were meager. Two or three years was not long enough to overcome the devastating economic blow suffered by Mormon exiles from Missouri who had lost most of their property or immigrants who had sold much of what they owned to obtain passage to Nauvoo.

It was widely believed that those with means frequently withheld tithing. George Miller recalled,

> The rich among us pretended to be too poor to barely feed themselves and nurse their speculations which they were more or less engaged in, and those who were poor could not help themselves.[118] [Joseph Smith reportedly] pronounced a curse on the merchants and the rich who would not assist in building [the temple].[119]

The process of collecting tithing and donations from members was time consuming and expensive. Agents sent to collect funds frequently used a portion of the funds they collected for their own support and passage.

114. George Miller, *Correspondence of Bishop George Miller with the Northern Islander from His First Acquaintance with Mormonism Up to Near the Close of His Life, 1855*, compiled by Wingfield Watson (Burlington, WI: Wingfield Watson, 1916), 7; copy in Perry Special Collections, Lee Library.
115. Joseph Earl Arrington, "Story of the Nauvoo Temple," ca. 1970, unpublished manuscript, microfilm of typescript, Perry Special Collections, Lee library.
116. *History of the Church*, 6:58-59.
117. Brigham Young, 6 October 1863, *Journal of Discourses*, 10:252-53.
118. Miller, *Correspondence of Bishop George Miller*, 8.
119. Faulring, *An American Prophet's Record*, 244.

Members of the Church naturally sold their more negotiable items to purchasers from outside Nauvoo who could pay more. A typical rebuke of this practice appeared in the *Nauvoo Neighbor* in August 1844, asking the Saints to bring their

> wheat, corn, and other provisions to Nauvoo, for the benefit of the temple, and store them. It is folly to let every thing in the provision line, go to other cities, as was the case last year, and leave a large portion of poor people destitute of the means of subsistence.[120]

It required the constant efforts of the trustee, the recorder, his clerks, the temple committee, the bishops, dozens of collecting agents, and other Church authorities to raise and manage the enormous volume of supplies needed to care for the poor and forward the building project.

British convert and immigrant John Wortham was among those who were employed on the temple in 1842. He later reflected on this experience:

> I used to walk through the city every day looking for work (was hired to work on the temple). Began to feel the want of bread. Returning home tired and hungry one day, I told the Lord I would not murmur. I had gathered in accordance with [His] will. The saying of an Apostle came to mind. After much tribulation, cometh the blessings. Went on rejoicing. The Lord opened my way, and although I often went to work on the temple without eating, I never got starved to death.... I agreed to work on the temple until it could be dedicated if I had to live on parched or boiled corn, did so.[121]

The Purchase of Mills in Wisconsin

In addition to the stone required for the exterior walls, much lumber would be needed to frame the interior of the temple. However, lumber was scarce and expensive in Illinois. During the late summer of 1841, George Miller suggested a meeting of the temple and Nauvoo House committees to "deliberate on the best plan of operations for procuring lumber for the building of the Temple and the Nauvoo House."[122] As a result of this conference, the joint committees agreed to buy a saw mill owned by Horatio Kirtz (Curts) and George Crane, two Wisconsin settlers. Miller describes the circumstances surrounding the purchase:

120. "Wheat and Provisions!," *Nauvoo Neighbor* 2 (28 August 1844): 7.

121. John Wortham, Autobiography, in "Autobiographies of Early Seventies," typescript, 75, LDS Church Archives. Wortham (1817-unknown) joined the Church in England in 1840 or 1841 and immigrated to Nauvoo, probably in 1841-42.

122. Miller, *Correspondence of Bishop George Miller*, 8.

Crane and Kirtz were sent for, (their residence twenty miles off.) They came. The bargain was made upon representation of Crane and Kirtz, and Peter Haws, of the Nauvoo House Committee, and Alpheus Cutler of the Temple Committee, were appointed to take immediate possession of the mills, and take a company of laborers, with nine months provisions and clothing, and enter into the business of lumbering, for the joint benefit of both buildings, each furnishing an equal portion of the accruing expenses. The outfit was provided for a large company, (I do not remember the precise number,) and they all forthwith set out on their undertaking.[123]

The accord with Crane and Kirtz was reached on 9 September 1841. The Mormons agreed to pay $1,400 in three installments by 14 April 1843. All three members of the temple committee and the principals of the Nauvoo House Association signed this document.[124] The cost of the venture would be divided equally by the two committees, as would the lumber thus produced.

The mill was located in Wisconsin on the Black River, a tributary of the Mississippi, roughly 500 to 600 miles north of Nauvoo.[125] During the 1840s, this region became the most important supplier of timber to the Mississippi River Valley. An 1845 article in the *Missouri Republican* observed, "Ten years ago there was not a mill in this country, and now lumber is turned out to the value of over $100,000."[126] The Church's purchase of sawmills in that region was a part of this boom.

On 15 September, a *Times and Seasons* article announced the purchase and reported that "a company of several men, in their employ, will leave here in a few days for that country."[127] The company, headed by Cutler and Haws, departed on 25 September. The members of the party were "Tarlton Lewis, Jabez Durfee, Hardin Wilson, William L. Cutler, Horace Owens, Octavus Pauket, Blakely W. Anderson, James M. Flake, Nathaniel Childs and mother, Child's wife and daughter and Peter M. Conover."[128] George Miller later summarized the early activities of the company: "Haws and Butler returned with a raft of hewed timber at the close of navigation, and twelve of the men. They left a man in charge at the pineries. They

---

123. Ibid., 8. For a more in-depth look at the pinery mission, see Dennis Rowley "The Mormon Experience in the Wisconsin Pineries," *BYU Studies* 32 (Winter and Spring 1992): 127.

124. Rowley, "The Mormon Experience in the Wisconsin Pineries," 127.

125. *History of the Church,* 4:417.

126. "Lumber Business of the Upper Mississippi," *Nauvoo Neighbor* 3 (28 May 1845): 4.

127. "The Church and Its Prospects," *Times and Seasons* 2 (15 September 1841): 543.

128. George D. Smith, *An Intimate Chronicle,* 530.

remodeled, or rather almost made anew the mill, but made but little or no lumber, and left the men to get logs ready for spring sawing."[129]

The Wisconsin sawmills were in operation during most of the temple's construction. Work crews felled the trees, dragged them to the Black River (which emptied into the Mississippi River), and organized the logs into rafts. The crews did this by fastening the logs together with wooden pins and hickory withes. They would ride on the pine rafts with their provisions. When they stopped to sleep or purchase supplies, they would lash the large rafts to trees or rocks at the riverside. While preparing to make one such stop, Lyman Curtis attempted to anchor his raft to a young tree, but the force of the current pulled the tree down into the water. Curtis, still holding tightly to the tree, was also forced under the water, evoking the sarcastic comment from a bystander, "There's one Mormon gone to hell." Fortunately, the tree's roots held and it sprang back, lifting him out of the river.[130]

Allen Stout, who worked at the pineries in the summer and fall of 1843, penned the following description to his older brother Hosea:

> We are now on the bank of Black River under a shady black oak this is the handsomest country I ever saw. The sons of Laman look like Sioux. Rock Island is the handsomest place I ever saw. We are about 80 miles above Prairie du Chein [sic]....
>
> Black River runs a west course and in some places is very rapid, [in] others exceedingly deep. The water [is] black but pure, her tributaries clear as crystal. This is the greatest water privilege I ever saw. The river has the rapidest kind of a fall and the dam is at the head of the falls and there is a natural race [channel or canal] cut around rock that forms the lower bay at the lower end of which the Mill stands. From thence there is a race cut by art on down to the foot of the rapids. There is a small creek [that] empties in right opposite the race of the big mill on which there is a small saw and grist mill turning lathe and grindstone. This creek is as good and as cold water as any spring and soft to wash in. The big mill runs 2 saws and there is water pour enough to run all creation, the river being navigable for keels at low water.... Timber is no object here.... The two saws will cut 10000 feet in 24 hours we are going to put up 2 more mills.[131]

Of members of the pineries mission, George Miller later wrote: "Too much cannot be said in praise of these faithful brethren. They really performed wonders. We were in the midst of a howling wilderness, and the aspect of our affairs to some

129. Miller, *Correspondence of Bishop George Miller*, 8.

130. (No author listed), "Lyman Curtis, Pioneer of 1847," in *An Enduring Legacy*, compiled by the Daughters of Utah Pioneers Lesson Committee, 12 vols. (Salt Lake City: Daughters of the Utah Pioneers, 1978-88), 9:215.

131. Allen Joseph Stout, Letters to Hosea Stout, Wisconsin Territory, 25 July and 10 September 1843, holograph of microfilm, LDS Church Archives.

might seem forbidding; but we were buoyant with hope of better days, and resolved on accomplishing the work we had undertaken."[132]

Deposit in the Cornerstone

Joseph Smith's journal entry for 30 June 1842 records: "On the 25th day of September 1841, a deposit was made in the south east corner of the temple."[133] By this he meant that items were sealed into the hollowed-out cornerstone. The fact that the cornerstone was still exposed at that point is the best evidence available that workmen had used the summer to complete the excavation and foundation walls. Nancy Naomi Alexander Tracy, who was present when the cornerstone deposit was made, wrote:

> I looked over toward the temple and saw a large crowd gathered with some two or three women present; so I thought I would [go] over. I put on my bonnet and shawl and made my way over. Brother Joseph was there and seemed busily engaged over something. Finally, he looked up and saw us women. He said for the brothers to stand back and let the sisters come up. So they gave way, and we went up. In the huge chief corner stone was cut out a square about a foot around and about as deep lined with zinc, and in it Brother Joseph had placed a Bible, a Book of Mormon, hymn book, and other church works along with silver money that had been coined in that year. Then a lid was cemented down, and the temple was reared on the top of this.[134]

Samuel Miles, age fifteen at the time, estimated that the crowd consisted of nearly two hundred onlookers. His account provides this interesting detail:

> When a Bible was presented for deposit it was thought necessary that it should be complete—containing the Apocrypha. As there seemed to be none within reach, except large, highly-prized family Bibles, Brother Reynolds Cahoon volunteered to go to his home, which was nearby and cut out the Apocrypha from his large family Bible, which was accepted and the Bible thus made complete. After several books, coins, periodicals and publications had been accepted and

132. Miller, *Correspondence of George Miller*, 11.

133. Entry for 30 June 1842, Jessee, *Papers of Joseph Smith*, 2:396. See also George D. Smith, *An Intimate Chronicle*, 532. J. C. Dowen, who was a justice of the peace in Kirtland, Ohio, was present in Nauvoo when "they put the trinkets in the south-east corner near the road." Statement, 2 January 1885, Chicago Historical Society, Chicago.

134. Nancy Naomi Alexander Tracy, Autobiography, 1816-85, typescript, 26, LDS Church Archives. Tracy (1816-1902) was baptized in Ellisburg, New York, on 10 May 1834.

deposited a poem was presented the Prophet to be laid away with the other things. Joseph handed it to one of the brethren requesting him to read it. When he was through Joseph said, "What does it amount to?"

"See saw, Margery Daw,

Sold her bed and laid in the straw."

So the poor poem was left out in the cold.[135]

Evidently, the items deposited in the cornerstone were not recovered when the southeast corner of the temple was destroyed by a tornado in 1848.

October 1841 General Conference

At the October general conference that fall, Joseph Smith preached on the subject of baptism for the dead, "by request of some of the Twelve."[136] It had been a year and six weeks since he had first explained this doctrine at Seymour Brunson's funeral and ten months since the important revelation of 19 January 1841, had linked it to temple work. His sermon, given 4 October, reflects several important developments in the development of this doctrine. Among other things, he made the following observations about its scriptural underpinnings:

The speaker [Joseph Smith] presented baptism for the dead as the only way that men can appear as saviors on Mount Zion.... Men, by actively engaging in rites of salvation substitutionally, became instrumental in bringing multitudes of their kin into the kingdom of God. It is no more incredible that God should save the dead, than that he should raise the dead.... There is a way to release the spirit of the dead; that is, by the power and authority of the Priesthood—by binding and loosing on earth. This doctrine appears glorious, inasmuch as it exhibits the greatness of divine compassion and benevolence in the extent of the plan of human salvation. This glorious truth is well calculated to enlarge the understanding, and to sustain the soul under troubles, difficulties, and distresses.

This doctrine, he said, presented in a clear light, the wisdom and mercy of God, in preparing an ordinance for the salvation of the dead, being baptised by proxy, their names recorded in heaven, and they judged according to the deeds done in the body. This doctrine was the burden of the scriptures. Those saints who neglect it, in behalf of their deceased relatives, do it at the peril of their own salvation.[137]

---

135. Samuel Miles, "Recollections of the Prophet Joseph Smith," *Juvenile Instructor* 27 (June 1892): 174. Miles (1826-1910) converted to Mormonism during the winter of 1833-34 and served in the Mormon Battalion.

136. "Minutes of a Conference," *Times and Seasons* 2 (15 October 1841): 578.

137. Ibid.

The Prophet Joseph next confirmed that the doctrine of salvation for the dead had been revealed to him by God; "The only way to obtain truth and wisdom, is not to ask it from books, but to go to God in prayer and obtain divine teaching." According to Warren Foote, a Nauvoo schoolteacher, Joseph also taught that "the Saints could be baptized for any of their dead relatives, or friends, who had not been murderers. Such could not be baptized for. The Lord had other ways of dealing with murderers."[138]

Perhaps the most significant remark of the conference came at the close of Joseph Smith's sermon on 4 October. According to Foote, "all at once his countenance brightened up"[139] and he announced: "There shall be no more baptisms for the dead, until the ordinance can be attended to in the font of the Lord's House; and the church shall not hold another general conference, until they can meet in said house. For thus saith the Lord!"[140]

This deferral of baptisms for the dead seems to be connected with the 19 January revelation, which allotted a "sufficient time" for the construction of a temple. Hyrum Smith intermingled Joseph's words at conference with words from the revelation in a letter to the Church on 31 October: "There shall not be a general assembly for a general conference assembled together until the House of the Lord and baptismal font shall be finished, and if we are not diligent the church shall be rejected and their dead also, 'saith the Lord.'"[141] While some baptisms for the dead continued to be performed in the Mississippi River after this date, the overwhelming majority were deferred until the baptismal font in the temple was completed in November 1841. (See chap. 3.)

Likewise, conferences of the Church continued to be held at regular intervals. However, these conferences were not considered "general conferences." Reuben Hedlock, a British Saint, in a letter published in the *Millennial Star* in 1845, explained that the Prophet "said there would not be another General Conference until the temple was completed, and it has been so; all the Conferences held in

---

138. Warren Foote, Journal, 1817-1903, typescript, 46, Perry Special Collections, Lee Library. This document begins as a reminiscence, and he begins daily/weekly entries 10 May 1837. The entry for 3 October 1841 containing the quoted passage from Joseph Smith's discourse on baptisms for the dead appears to have been written that very day. The published minutes indicate that Joseph said: "All are within the reach of pardoning mercy, who have not committed the unpardonable sin, which hath no forgiveness, neither in this world, nor in the world to come." "Minutes of a Conference," 578. Foote's statement may represent his interpretation of Joseph's comment. Foote (1817-1903) had become a believer in Mormonism in 1835 but was not baptized until 24 March 1842.

139. Ibid.

140. "Minutes of a Conference," 578.

141. Hyrum Smith, "Extract of a Letter to a Member of the Branch in Kirtland," *Times and Seasons* 3 (15 October 1841): 589.

Nauvoo since that time, have been special Conferences."[142] William Clayton also called the very next conference, held 6 April 1843, a "special conference."[143]

Offers to Board Temple Workers

Arrangements needed to be made to accommodate the influx of workers from outlying settlements who had come to Nauvoo in answer to the call to work on the temple. This was accomplished principally by Nauvoo homeowners who volunteered to lodge the laborers. Writing on 12 October to the "brethren scattered abroad on the continent of America," the Twelve reported: "Scores of brethren in this city, have offered to board one and two laborers each till the temple is completed."[144] The temple committee took the names of those who volunteered to provide room and board to temple workmen, and this list was given to new arrivals. One such list of volunteers, signed by the committee, includes twenty-four names:[145]

[John] Pack
[Ezra T.] Clark
Joseph Younger
[illegible] Edwards
Eleazer King, Sr.
Eleazer King, Jr.
Reuben Hedlock
Charles C. Rich
John H. Tippets
James Carrol
O. M. Allen
Ezra Parrish
John Bills
John Taylor
L[ewis]. D. Wilson

142. Reuben Hedlock, "Address to the Saints," *Millennial Star* 5 (January 1845): 128. Special conferences were gatherings of a regional nature. The first special conferences were called in Kirtland in 1831, continued to be held on an ad hoc basis well into the twentieth century. Special conferences were replaced with regional conferences in the 1960s. See *History of the Church*, 1:235; "The Church Moves On," *Improvement Era* 44 (November 1941): 579.

143. George D. Smith, *An Intimate Chronicle*, 98.

144. "An Epistle of the Twelve," *Times and Seasons* 2 (15 October 1841): 567.

145. "List of People Who Would Board Men Working on the Temple at Nauvoo," n.d., microfilm of holograph, Newel K. Whitney Papers, Perry Special Collections, Lee Library. This document, though not dated, must have been created in 1842.

William Aldrich
Stephen Winchester
L[yman]. Wight
Melvin Wilbur
John H. [illegible]
Philander Colton
Windsor Lyon
Daniel Allen
L[evi]. S. Nickerson

Despite the generosity of the volunteers, only a few workmen initially accepted their offer. In December, the Twelve again encouraged workers to come to Nauvoo, reminding them of the proffered lodging:

Probably some may think they ... cannot labor, as they have no means of board-ing themselves, but let such remember that several score of brethren and sisters in this city, offered at the general conference, to board one or more laborers on the temple till the same should be completed, and but few of those as yet have had the opportunity of boarding any one. To all such we would say, you are not forgotten, we have your names also, and we expect soon to send someone to your table, therefore put your houses in order and never be ready to refuse the first offer of a guest.[146]

James and Drusilla Hendricks were among those who opened their home to temple hands in late 1841. She recorded in her autobiography:

I began to take boarders and we still had one yoke of cattle so my son, William, took them and hauled rock for the Temple to pay our tithing. He also paid some for others in the same way and they paid us in something we needed. I boarded the carpenters and masons and paid them to put us up a brick house; we bought the brick and paid the money for them.[147]

---

146. Twelve Apostles, "Baptism for the Dead," 13 December 1841, *Times and Seasons* 3 (15 December 1841): 626.

147. Drusilla Dorris Hendricks, "Historical Sketch of James Hendricks and Drusilla Dorris Hendricks," typescript, 16, LDS Church Archives. Drusilla Hendricks dictated this account after her husband's death in 1877.

Chapter 3

THE FONT OF THE TEMPLE: NOVEMBER 1841 TO APRIL 1842

Dedication of the Temple Font

The suspension of baptisms for the dead until they could be performed in the temple[1] motivated Church members to move forward with greater vigor to prepare the basement of the temple for enclosure. The impending winter made it necessary to construct a temporary roof over the basement so that ordinance work could begin. This task was completed by the first week of November, and Joseph Smith described the results in a letter to the Twelve: "The font was enclosed by a temporary frame building sided up with split oak clapboards, with a roof of the same material, and was so low that the timbers of the first story were laid above it."[2] This roof was still in place at least as late as September 1843, for David White, a reporter from Pittsburgh who visited Nauvoo that month, observed that the font was "protected from the weather by a temporary roof."[3]

1. Joseph Smith Jr. et al., *History of the Church of Jesus Christ of Latter-day Saints*, edited by B. H. Roberts (Salt Lake City: Deseret News Press, 6 vols. published 1902-12, Vol. 7 published 1932, 1st printing), 4:426.

2. Ibid., 4:446

3. David White, Letter, *Pittsburgh Gazette*, 14 September 1843, reprinted in Dean C. Jessee, ed., *The Papers of Joseph Smith* (Salt Lake City: Deseret Book, 1989), 1:443.

On 8 November 1841, Brigham Young, at Joseph Smith's invitation, dedicated the font in a public meeting. Brigham Young wrote in his journal that day: "I attended the dedication of the baptismal font in the Lord's House; President Smith called upon me to offer the dedicatory prayer. This is the first font erected and dedicated for the baptism for the dead in this dispensation."[4]

First Baptisms in the Font

Less than two weeks later, the first baptisms for the dead were performed in the font. The History of the Church records on Sunday, 21 November: "At four o'clock, repaired to the baptismal font in the basement of the Temple. Elders Brigham Young, Heber C. Kimball and John Taylor baptized about forty persons for the dead. Elder Willard Richards, Wilford Woodruff and George A. Smith confirming. These were the first baptisms for the dead in the font."[5]

Wilford Woodruff and Brigham Young also noted this event in their diaries. Woodruff wrote:

> I [was] at B[righam] Young's until 4 o'clock at which time we repaired to the baptismal font in the Temple for the purpose of baptizing for the dead, for the remission of sins and for healing. It was truly an interesting scene. It was the first font erected for this glorious purpose in this last dispensation. It was dedicated by President Joseph Smith and the Twelve for baptizing for the dead etc. and this was the first time the font had been prepared for the reception of candidates. [6]

Brigham Young's entry was succinct: "Brothers Hyrum Smith and John Taylor preached. At 4 p.m., Brothers Kimball, Taylor and I baptized about forty persons in the font, for the dead; Brothers Richards, Woodruff and George A. Smith confirming. These were the first baptisms for the dead in the font."[7]

---

4. Elden J. Watson, ed., *Manuscript History of Brigham Young, 1801-1844* (Salt Lake City: Elden J. Watson, 1968), 111-12. See also *History of the Church*, 4:446: "At five o'clock p.m., [Joseph Smith] attended the dedication of the baptismal font in the Lord's House. President Brigham Young was spokesman."

5. *History of the Church*, 4:454.

6. Wilford Woodruff, *Wilford Woodruff's Journal, 1833-1898*, typescript, edited by Scott G. Kenny, 9 vols. (Midvale, UT: Signature Books, 1983-85), 2:138. Woodruff's statement that the font was dedicated by "President Joseph Smith and the Twelve," may have reference to the fact that they were all present on the occasion. Brigham Young clearly offered the prayer.

7. Watson, *Manuscript History of Brigham Young*, 112.

William Clayton added a further detail: "Brother Reuben McBride was the first person baptized, under the direction of the President."[8] Later in life, McBride wrote a letter to his sister, Martha McBride Knight, containing an account of that evening's events. Joseph Smith had assigned McBride to settle Church affairs in Kirtland and wanted him to be baptized in the Nauvoo Temple font before his departure for Ohio. McBride's letter was to provide an account of "the first work that I done for our dead relatives." He said that Joseph "had the font in the temple filled with water from the wells. He said he wished me to be baptized in the font before I went back to Ohio. We met. Joseph spoke and the font was dedicated and he, Joseph, said, 'Blessed is the first man baptized in this font.' Brigham Young baptized me. I was baptized six times."[9] McBride's reference to the font's dedication occurring on the same evening of his baptism is enigmatic. Perhaps he is referring to another prayer given on the occasion.[10]

Unlike endowments and sealings, which were initially introduced to few during Joseph Smith's lifetime, baptisms for the dead were practiced by many, from members of the leading priesthood quorums to the newest converts. Between five and ten thousand baptisms in the font were performed between 1841 and 1844.[11]

In this early period, the Quorum of Twelve and other authorities were usually responsible for performing the baptisms. On 20 February 1842, Brigham Young noted in his journal that he "officiated with the Twelve at the font, in baptizing and confirming for the dead."[12] On 20 March 1842, Wilford Woodruff recorded in his journal, "There was probably eighty baptized and confirmed for their dead relatives at the font by the Twelve. H[eber] C. Kimball baptized about forty in the font. I assisted in confirming about twenty. It was truly an interesting day."[13] They partici-

---

8. George D. Smith, ed., *An Intimate Chronicle: The Journals of William Clayton* (Salt Lake City: Signature Books, 1995), 532. Reuben McBride (1803-91), a New York native, was baptized in June 1833 and was a member of Zion's Camp.

9. Reuben McBride, Letter to Martha Knight, 1 November 1886, photocopy of holograph at Nauvoo Restoration, Inc., Nauvoo, Illinois.

10. Although William Clayton and Reuben McBride seem to indicate that the first baptisms in the font occurred the night of the dedication, their records were written years after the fact while the Woodruff and Young accounts are contemporary.

11. Records are lacking for 1842. In an untitled article, the *Deseret News*, 26 November 1882, 6, reported that 15,626 baptisms for the dead were performed in Nauvoo from 1841 to 1846, many in the river. Nearly 7,000 were performed during 1841, probably most of them before the font was finished. See M. Guy Bishop, "'What Has Become of Our Fathers?': Baptism for the Dead at Mormon Nauvoo," *Dialogue: A Journal of Mormon Thought* 23, no. 2 (Summer 1990): 85.

12. Watson, *Manuscript History of Brigham Young*, 115.

13. Woodruff, *Journal*, 2:164.

pated as proxies as well. Willard Richards recorded that he and his wife were baptized for several of their relatives on 13 December 1843.[14]

The opportunity to participate in saving ordinances for deceased friends and relations stimulated genealogical work in Nauvoo. On 19 May 1843, Jonah Ball wrote some of his relatives asking for "a list of father's relations his parents and uncles and their names, also mother's. I am determined to do all I can to redeem those I am permitted to."[15] Sally Randall, a thirty-nine-year-old Mormon mother, wrote to her non-Mormon relatives on 24 April 1844 requesting genealogical information:

> What a glorious thing it is that we believe and receive the fulness of the gospel as it is preached now and can be baptized for all of our dead friends and save them as far back as we can get any knowledge of them.
>
> I want you should write me the given names of all of our connections that are dead as far back as grandfather's and grandmother's at any rate. I intend to do what I can to save my friends and I should be very glad if some of you would come and help me for it is a great work for one to do alone. It is father's privilege to save his friends if he will come into the church. If not, some other one must do it. I expect you will think this is strange doctrine but you will find it to be true. I want to know whether Lettice was over eight years old when she died. Oh, mother, if we are so happy as to have a part in the first resurrection, we shall have our children just as we laid them down in their graves.[16]

The public continued to react to the distinctive LDS practice of baptism for the dead with curiosity and perplexity, even after the locale shifted from the Mississippi River to the Nauvoo Temple font. Thomas L. Kane later reflected on what he had heard about the font in Nauvoo and its use:

> They said, the deluded persons, most of whom were immigrants from a great distance, believed their Deity countenanced their reception here of a baptism of regeneration, as proxies for whomsoever they held in warm affection in the countries from which they had come. That here parents "went into the water" for their lost children, children for their parents, widows for their spouses, and young persons for their lovers. That thus the Great Vase [the font] came to be for them associated with all dear and distant memories, and was therefore the object, of

---

14. Willard Richards, Journal, 1838-46, holograph, LDS Church Archives.

15. Quoted in Bishop, "'What Has Become of Our Fathers,'" 85.

16. Sally Randall, Letter to Dear Friends, 21 April 1844, in Kenneth W. Godfrey, Audrey M. Godfrey, and Jill Mulvay Derr, *Women's Voices: An Untold History of the Latter-day Saints, 1830-1900* (Salt Lake City: Deseret Book, 1982), 139.

all others in the building, to which they attached the greatest degree of idolatrous affection.[17]

On at least some occasions when the font was being cleaned or repaired, baptisms for the dead were again performed in the river. For example, in April 1843, the Twelve appointed several elders "to administer baptism for the dead, in the river, while the font could not be used."[18]

Other Uses of the Font

One practice associated with the font in the Nauvoo Temple and also that of early Utah temples, but which is no longer practiced, was baptism for healing from illness or injury.[19] The first recorded instance of using the font for health purposes occurred in February 1842: "Samuel Rolfe washed his hands in the font, being seriously affected with a felon,[20] so that the doctors thought it ought to be cut open; others said it would not be well before spring. After washing in the Font his hand healed in one week."[21] William Clayton also recorded some details about this healing:

> Brother Samuel Rolfe ... being seriously afflicted with a felon on one hand president Joseph instructed him to wash in the font, and told him he would be healed, although the doctors had told him it would not be well before spring, and advised him to have it cut. He washed his hands in the font and in one week afterwards his hand was perfectly healed.

---

17. Thomas L. Kane, "The Mormons: A Discourse Delivered Before the Historical Society of Pennsylvania, March 26, 1850," quoted in Daniel Tyler, *A Concise History of the Mormon Battalion in the Mexican War, 1846-1847* (Chicago: Rio Grande Press, 1964), 67.

18. "Elders' Conference," *Times and Seasons* 4 (1 April 1843): 158.

19. D. Michael Quinn, "The Practice of Rebaptism at Nauvoo," *BYU Studies* 18, no. 2 (Winter 1978): 226, discusses this practice and its discontinuance during President Joseph F. Smith's administration, priesthood blessings being considered sufficient. James Ririe, "James Ririe: 1827-1905," *Our Pioneer Heritage,* compiled by Kate B. Carter, 20 vols. (Salt Lake City: Daughters of Utah Pioneers, 1966), 9:371, recorded being baptized in June 1886 in the Logan Temple font because "I was still so lame I could only walk very slowly and not far at a time. I was so poorly that I crippled into the font at one end with much exertion, but as I went out at the other end, I could walk quite briskly. I had not dressed myself without help for a long time previously to this, but I now dressed myself alone. My lameness was gone and has been ever since except when I over-do."

20. A felon is a painful inflammation of the tissues in the fingers or toes.

21. Jessee, *The Papers of Joseph Smith,* 2:396.

After this time baptism was continued in the font, and many realized great blessings both spiritually and bodily.[22]

Helen Mar Whitney, daughter of Heber C. Kimball and Vilate Murray Kimball, was baptized for health in "the fall of 1842." Her autobiography contains this account of her remarkable healing:

In the early part of March in 1842 ... my eldest brother [William] and myself were invited to attend an evening party in the neighborhood.... I was wrapped in a good shawl but as we drove in an open carriage, the cold bleak wind pierced through to my vitals, and the consequence was that I was thrown into what was considered a quick consumption,[23] from which there was but little hope of my recovery, though I was kept in ignorance of my true condition until after the danger was over. I was not sick in bed, but I looked like a walking ghost, and it took but a few steps to exhaust what little strength I had. No pains were spared and nothing that affection could prompt, or faith and skill accomplish that was left untried, though I sometimes noticed their anxious and careworn looks. Early one morning in the fall of the year my father had William hitch up his horse and buggy and take me up to the temple, where he met us. He took me to the font under the temple into which the water had been pumped the day before and there baptized me for my health, which I regained more rapidly from that time.[24]

It is also apparent that baptisms for the remission of sins were sometimes performed in the font. On 7 May 1842, six months after the font had been dedicated, Wilford Woodruff recorded in his journal that he baptized "about one hun-

22. William Clayton, Journal, 1840-45, 21, LDS Church Archives. Clayton's account gives the impression that Rolfe's healing took place the night of the font's dedication, on 8 November 1841. However, Clayton wrote his account in 1845, while Joseph Smith's journal entry for 30 June 1842 gives the date as February 1842. Jessee, The Papers of Joseph Smith, 2:396. Clayton may have used Smith's journal as one of his sources when writing his 1845 account. Smith's entry begins: "On the 8th of last November at about 5 o'clock in the evening, the baptismal font was dedicated. In February 1842 Samuel Rolfe washed his hands in the font....." Perhaps Clayton copied the information from Smith's journal hastily, missed the second date, and thus mistakenly dated the healing to 8 November 1841.

23. Consumption was a term used generally for any wasting disease, but probably here refers to pneumonia.

24. Helen Mar Kimball Smith Whitney, "Scenes and Incidents in Nauvoo," Woman's Exponent 11 (15 September 1882): 57. For a similar account, see Larkin H. Southworth, in Susan Easton Black, Early Membership of the Church of Jesus Christ of Latter-day Saints, 50 vols. (Provo, UT: BYU Religious Studies Center, 1984-88), 33:217. Southworth, not baptized until December 1845), reported hearing an Elder Adams preach in Boston that, while he was in Nauvoo, "he was sick with fever, and that he was baptized and was instantaneously healed."

dred for the remission of sins, the healing of the body, and the dead."[25] In December 1844, William W. Phelps wrote: "The fount in the basement story is for the baptism of the living, for health, for remission of sin, and for the salvation of the dead, as was the case in Solomon's temple, and all temples that God commands to be built."[26]

Ward Pack recalled that he was "baptized when eight years old in the font in the basement of the Nauvoo Temple by Charles C. Rich" in April 1842. At the general conference, also in April 1842, Hyrum Smith clarified: "Baptisms for the dead, and for the healing of the body must be in the font, those coming into the Church, and those re-baptized may be baptized in the river."[27]

Office of Recorder Opened

During 1840-41, "there had been no general tithing record opened. The money and other property contributed had all been paid over to the committee, and receipts were issued to the several donors."[28] On 13 December 1841, Joseph Smith appointed Willard Richards "Recorder for the Temple, and the scribe for the private office of the President, just opened in the upper story of the new store, and the recorder entered on the duties of his office."[29] Willard Richards was a member of the Quorum of the Twelve and had begun to function as Joseph's scribe in September.[30] He was now given the additional duty of acting as temple recorder. This change centralized the process of gathering funds.

The decision to appoint a temple recorder resulted from a discussion between Joseph Smith and the Twelve two days earlier. In that meeting, Smith "directed Brigham Young, President of the Twelve Apostles, to go immediately and instruct the building committee in their duty, and forbid them receiving any more property for the building of the Temple, until they received it from the Trustee in Trust [Joseph Smith]."[31] On 13 December Brigham Young delivered this message to the three members of the temple committee—Reynolds Cahoon, Alpheus Cutler,

25. Woodruff, Journal, 2:175.

26. W. W. Phelps, Letter to William Smith, *Times and Seasons* 5 (December 1844): 759.

27. *History of the Church*, 4:586. Ward Eaton Pack (1834-1907) was baptized in the temple font on 17 April 1842.

28. George D. Smith, An Intimate Chronicle, 529.

29. Jessee, *The Papers of Joseph Smith*, 2:336-37.

30. Robert B. Thompson, Joseph's previous scribe, died 27 August 1841, and Richards was named scribe on 13 September 1841. George Q. Cannon, *The Life of Joseph Smith the Prophet* (Salt Lake City: Deseret Book, 1986), 381.

31. *History of the Church*, 4:470.

and Elias Higbee—in the presence of Apostles Heber C. Kimball and Wilford Woodruff, and Willard Richards, the new recorder.[32]

On the same day, 13 December, the Twelve wrote an epistle to the Church, instructing that "all money and other property designed for tithing and consecrations to the building of the Temple must hereafter be presented to the Trustee in Trust, President Joseph Smith, and entered at the recorder's office."[33] Two days later on 15 December, the *Times and Seasons* printed a notice of Richards appointment, announcing that he would "receive all property devoted to the building of the Temple and enter the same, at the Recorder's office in the lower room of the store."[34] Joseph Smith's red brick store on Water Street quickly became a hub of activity for the city. Joseph had opened this general merchandise store in January 1841. A small room behind the main display area on the first floor served as the recorder's office. Here Richards appraised and recorded tithes. In the front of the building, many of the tithing goods received in kind were dispersed to men hired by the temple committee.[35]

Those responsible for supervising on-site the temple labor, such as the committee or the foremen they appointed over certain tasks, issued receipts to the laborers which were redeemable at the store. For example, Nathaniel Richmond received a certificate from William F. Cahoon, later a carpenters' foreman, stating, "I hereby certify that Nathaniel Richmond has labored on the Temple at Carpenter work to this date, 34 ½ days at $1.50 per day."[36]

James Rollins, age twenty-five in 1841, worked as a clerk and left this glimpse of typical activities:

---

32. Ibid., 4:472. As late as April conference 1843, Joseph Smith repeated his instructions that contributions should not be made directly to the temple committee: "If [the members of the Committee] appropriate any property where they ought not, they are liable to me for it; and the church are running to them, with funds every day, and thus make a bridge over my nose. I am not responsible for it. If you put it into the hands of the Temple Committee, I, nor my clerk, know nothing of it.... Who are the Temple Committee that they should receive the funds? They are nobody." "Special Conference," *Times and Seasons* 4 (1 May 1843): 181-82. No doubt Joseph used this stern language because he was legally responsible for the temple as trustee and wished to be certain that he could account for all donations.

33. "Baptism for the Dead," *Times and Seasons* 3 (15 December 1841): 627.

34. Joseph Smith, "To Whom It May Concern," *Times and Seasons* 3 (15 December 1841): 638.

35. The store stood on the northwest corner of the block upon which Joseph's Nauvoo residence stood. Although he did not operate the store himself, Joseph assisted the store clerks on occasion. The first temple endowments were performed in the large room above the store. See chap. 4 for a discussion of the uses of this room.

36. Certificate of Nathaniel Richmond for work on the temple, August 1845, holograph, L. Tom Perry Special Collections, Harold B. Lee Library, Brigham Young University, Provo, Utah.

At this time a good deal of work was being done on the Temple which the work-men received orders for their labor on the store. It was very much crowded for two or three days, and as I stood in the counting room door looking at faces in the house, there were a great many very familiar to me, and they came to me as they were waiting for their pay, asked me if I could wait on them.

Joseph, being in the store at the time, said to me, "Why don't you wait on those people?" I told him when I was ordered to I would do so with pleasure. He then said, "Go and wait on them." I then went to work behind the counter on the grocery side, and paid off many orders this day and the next, the store being crowded constantly, and at least fifty to one hundred people to be waited on from morning until night, and being so very close with so many present was very oppressive to all of us. When Joseph came in and saw us looking tired and pale, he told us to shut up the store that night and not open again for two or three days, which we did, until we got rested, then opened again for business.[37]

In addition to the store, the trustee owned a corral where animals donated for tithing were kept. A notice in the *Nauvoo Wasp* for 8 July 1842 identifies this tithing yard:

STRAYED

From the enclosure of the Trustee in Trust, a large red ox, about 8 years old, the tithing of Dr. Lenox M. Knight; any person who will secure and return him to the recorders office shall have our thanks, and will add so much to his own interest in the building of the Temple.

The notice was signed by Joseph Smith as trustee and by William Clayton as clerk.[38]

William Clayton was the temple recorder from 1842 to 1846.

37. James Henry Rollins, "A Sketch of the Life of James Henry Rollins, 1898, typescript, LDS Church Archives.
38. "Strayed," *Nauvoo Wasp*, 1 (8 July 1842): 4. *The Wasp*, edited by Joseph Smith's brother

Willard Richards's responsibilities as temple recorder and as scribe for Joseph Smith multiplied quickly. In a letter to his brother Levi three months after his appointment, he enumerated his duties:

> I am acting as President Joseph's private secretary, and scribe and clerk. General for all the office—the general business office, counting room; store, (in transfer of papers, accounts, notes etc.), printing office, book binding, stereotype foundry, engraving, etc. and as recorder for the temple, city recorder and for register of deeds, etc.—All these things I have to attend to. The general business office includes all land contracts for Brother Joseph and the Church. I could tell of more but I will stop.[39]

Richards's duties as temple recorder occupied much of his time, making it difficult for him to attend to some of his other responsibilities. In January 1842, a year after his appointment, he published this notice in the *Times and Seasons*:

> From this time, the Recorder's office will be opened on Saturday of each week for the reception of the tithings and consecrations for the brethren, and closed on every other day in the week. This regulation is necessary, to give the Trustee and Recorder time to arrange the Book of Mormon, New Translation and [sic] of the Bible, Hymn Book, and Doctrine and Covenants for the press; all of which the brethren are anxious to see, in their most perfect form; consequently, they will be particular to bring their offerings on the day specified until further notice, but not relax their exertion to carry on the work.
>
> The Elders will please give the above notice in all public meetings, until the plan is understood.[40]

Limiting the recording of tithing to Saturdays, though freeing up weekdays for other duties, made it virtually impossible for Richards to keep pace with tithing contributions. It became necessary for Joseph Smith and others to assist him on Saturdays in the time-consuming work of appraising the various in-kind donations.[41] Joseph Fielding, after visiting the recorder's office several times, observed that the donations "often exceeded 1,000 dollars per week."[42] Richards "counseled with his

William and published from April 1842 to April 1843, was the *Nauvoo Neighbor's* predecessor. It was edited by William Smith, Joseph's brother.

39. Willard Richards, Letter to Levi Richards, 9 March 1842, Richards Family Letters, typescript, ca. 1929, not paginated, LDS Church Archives.

40. Willard Richards, "Tithings and Consecrations for the Temple of the Lord," *Times and Seasons* 3 (15 January 1842): 667.

41. Jessee, *Papers of Joseph Smith*, 2:355, 357, 359, 360.

42. Joseph Fielding, Letter to the editor (Parley P. Pratt), *Millennial Star* 2 (August 1842): 78.

brethren of the Twelve; and, having received permission from President Joseph," hired William Clayton as his assistant on 10 February 1842.[43] Heber C. Kimball was requested to go to Clayton's house and inform him that he "must go to Joseph Smith's office and assist Brother Richards." Clayton "accordingly got ready and went to the office and commenced entering tithing for the Temple."[44] Clayton's role as a record keeper for the temple continued until he left Nauvoo in February 1846.

The Book of the Law of the Lord

The recorder and his clerks logged the temple donations in a ledger called the Book of the Law of the Lord. Historian Dean Jessee describes this record as "a large leather-bound book measuring 11 5/8 × 17 inches, containing 477 pages.... The first three leaves of the book are blank; the fourth contains the title 'The Book of the Law of the Lord' in very ornate hand lettering in black ink.... The front and back covers are unmarked, but the spine of the book is labeled 'Law of the Lord.'"[45] In addition to the records of tithing and donations, this book contained the text of several revelations, the first being that of 19 January 1841, regarding the temple (now D&C 124) and Joseph Smith's daily journal for 1842.

In 1845, William Clayton penned the following description of the accounting procedures used in entering donations in the book:

> All tithings, consecrations, donations, and sacrifices presented for the building of the temple are recorded in a book kept for that purpose in the form of a history, wherein is recorded the names of the donors, the kind of property donated, and the price of the same, or if in money, the amount, all under the respective dates when the same is deposited in the hands of the Trustee in Trust, except in cases where authorized agents have collected funds and given receipts to those who donated. Wherever receipts are given for property, we do not enter it in the general record until those receipts are presented at the recorder's office. Consequently we are under the necessity of making a separate list of all properties received where receipts have been given, and keeping that list until the receipts are presented for record.
>
> Now inasmuch as the "books will be opened" as evidence of our faithfulness in the day of the Lord and not "the receipts," we would advise all to bring their receipts as early as possible and have them duly recorded, that their names may

43. George D. Smith, *An Intimate Chronicle*, 531.

44. Ibid., 90.

45. Jessee, *The Papers of Joseph Smith*, 2:335.

be found amongst the number of the faithful in that book which will bear testimony as to our faithfulness in attending to the law of tithing and consecration.[46]

From that point on, this procedure was normally followed in lieu of issuing receipts for donations. On 24 February 1842, Joseph Smith wrote to an unidentified Church member:

BELOVED BROTHER—Yours of the 24th is received, in relation to certain tithings of your neighborhood being transferred to your account, which you hold against the Church to the amount of $305, including $150 of your own.

There are no receipts issued for property received on tithing; but an entry is made in the Book of the Law of the Lord, and parties living at a distance notified of the same.

If the parties named will pay you the sum specified in your letter, and you will endorse the same, i.e. $305, on the obligation you hold against the Church, and give me notice accordingly, with a schedule of individuals' names and payments, the same shall be entered to their credit on tithing.[47]

Willard Richards entered the first donation in this book on 1 December 1841. "It was one gold sovereign, valued at $5.00, to the credit of John Sanders, late from Cumberland, on the borders of Scotland, Europe."[48]

To have one's name entered in this book was an important privilege. Shortly before he died, Joseph Smith, speaking in Nauvoo on 7 March 1844, made it clear that "those whose names are found in the Church books shall have the first claim in that house. I intend to keep the door at [the] dedication myself and not a man shall pass who had not paid his bonus."[49] Heber C. Kimball spoke of the "pleasure it will be for our children to look upon these books, while we are in our graves sleeping. They can see what an interest and labor and toiling their fathers accomplished when we were building the temple."[50] Church members "throughout the world" were encouraged to "send up their tithings, with their names to be recorded in the Book of Law of the Lord, by so doing they will not only keep the commandments of the Lord, but will own their share in the house, and have a right

---

46. William Clayton, "To the Friends of the Temple," *Times and Seasons* 5 (15 October 1844): 675-76.

47. "Letter of the Prophet's to an Unknown Brother on Tithing," *History of the Church*, 4:518.

48. George D. Smith, *An Intimate Chronicle*, 531.

49. Scott H. Faulring, ed., *An American Prophet's Record: The Diaries and Journals of Joseph Smith* (Salt Lake City: Signature Books, 1989), 456. "Bonus" refers to the premium paid for a privilege granted. On 4 March 1844, Joseph Smith told the Twelve and the temple committee: "When the Temple is completed, no man shall pass the threshold till he has paid $5.00." *History of the Church*, 6:230.

50. "Speech Delivered by Heber C. Kimball," *Times and Seasons* 6 (15 July 1845): 972.

to all the promised blessings, ordinances, oracles, and endowments which will not only benefit them, but their posterity to the latest generation."[51] John Fullmer, who would later be appointed one of the trustees of Church property in Nauvoo by Brigham Young, suggested to a relative that he make a donation to the temple "that your name might be entered as a donor upon the 'Book of the Law of the Lord' ...; the day will come when you would give more than that for such a privilege."[52] Agents in remote branches took care to record donations "in a book, and keep a copy with us, and also send a copy of the same with the money to Nauvoo, that it may be recorded in the book of the Law of the Lord."[53]

Payment of Tithes Required for Use of Font

One important Church policy that emerged during the winter of 1841-42—the restriction of temple use to faithful tithe payers—is still in effect today. In the 15 December 1841 *Times and Seasons*, the Twelve issued this statement:

> The command is to "all the saints from afar," as well as those already gathered to this place; to arise with one consent and build the Temple ... But some may say how can this be, I am not there, therefore I cannot meet in the Temple; cannot be baptized in the Font?
>
> The command of heaven is to you, to all, gather: and when you arrive here, if it is found that you have previously sent up of your gold or your silver, or your substance, the tithings and consecrations which are required of you, for this building, you will find your names, tithings, and consecrations written in the Book of the Law of the Lord, to be kept in the Temple, as a witness in your favor, showing that you are a proprietor in that building, and are entitled to your share of the privileges thereunto belonging.
>
> One of those privileges which is particularly attracting the notice of the saints at the present moment, is baptism for the dead, etc. in the font ... but while we have been called to administer this ordinance, we have been led to enquire into the propriety of baptizing those who have not been obedient, and assisted to build the place for baptism, and it seems to us unreasonable to expect that the Great Jehovah will approbate such an administration; for if the church must be

---

51. Wilford Woodruff, "To the Officers and Members of the Church of Jesus Christ of Latter-day Saints in the British Islands," *Millennial Star* 5 (January 1845): 140.

52. John Solomon Fullmer, Letter to Almon Fullmer, ca. June 1843, holograph, LDS Church Archives. Fullmer (1807-93), a Pennsylvania native, was baptized on 29 July 1839. In 1846, he was appointed a trustee of Church property in Nauvoo with Almon Babbitt and Joseph Heywood, charged with selling the temple. See chaps. 11 and 12.

53. Woodruff, "To the Officers and Members," 140.

brought under condemnation and rejected with her dead if she fail to build the house, and its appurtenances, why should not individuals of the church, who thus neglect, come under the same condemnation?[54]

As this statement suggests, those who paid tithing became "proprietors" in the building and were thereby entitled to the blessings of the temple. According to Erastus Snow, later an apostle, the Prophet Joseph "instructed the brethren in charge, to the effect that none should be allowed to participate in the privileges of the House of God excepting those who shall produce a certificate from the General Church Recorder, certifying to the fact that they had paid up their tithing."[55] Snow added that many Saints had "preserved among their old papers certificates of this character, issued by Brother William Clayton." Apostle Franklin D. Richards had such a receipt, signed by Joseph Smith himself.[56] Some of these certificates, cherished by their recipients and descendants, have survived. The practice of issuing these certificates—the predecessors to modern Mormon temple recommends—continued after Joseph's death in 1844. One such certificate reads:

This may certify that George Morris is entitled to the privilege of the baptismal font, having paid his property and labor tithing in full to April 12th 1846,

City of Joseph, April 29th 1846.

William Clayton recorder

by James Whitehead, Clerk[57]

At a special conference in Nauvoo on 6 April 1842, Joseph Smith stated: "A box should be prepared for the use of the font, that the clerk may be paid, and a book procured by the monies to be put therein by those baptized, the remainder to go to the use of the Temple."[58] Perhaps the Prophet intended this regulation for those who had not paid tithing.

---

54. "Baptism for the Dead," *Times and Seasons* 3 (15 December 1841): 626.

55. Erastus Snow, 15 May 1878, *Journal of Discourses*, 26 vols. (London and Liverpool: LDS Booksellers Depot, 1855-86), 19:339. See also John D. Lee, *Mormonism Unveiled: or the Life and Confessions of the Late Mormon Bishop John D. Lee* (St. Louis: Bryan, Brand & Company, 1877), 169: "No person, however, is allowed the privilege of this baptismal fount ... unless they have paid their tithings promptly, and have a certificate to that effect."

56. Franklin D. Richards, 30 August 1885, *Journal of Discourses*, 26:299.

57. George Morris, Autobiography, 1823-91, typescript, 40-41, Perry Special Collections, Lee Library. Other examples include David P. Rainey, "Recommend Privilege to Use Baptismal Font," 25 October 1845, photocopy of holograph, LDS Church Archives; Nathaniel Richmond, "Certificate," August 1845, holograph. Perry Special Collections, Lee Library.

58. "Conference Minutes," *Times and Seasons* 3 (15 April 1845): 763.

Work During the Winter Season

The winter of 1841-42 set in with the last few weeks of November marked by severe storms. The snow spelled an end to favorable building weather that year, and work slowed somewhat during the ensuing months. Benjamin Winchester observed the decrease in construction activities: "There does not appear to be so many to work on [the Temple] at present as heretofore; for many are engaged in fitting up their private dwellings for the coming winter, and preparing that they may attack it with renewed vigour and zeal in the coming spring."[59]

At the close of the 1841 building season, William Clayton noted: "The walls on the south side were built up to the water table,[60] a part of which also was laid. On the north side the walls were only about two feet high. In this state the structure remained until the Spring of 1842."[61] Joseph Fielding, who reached Nauvoo from Great Britain in December 1841, noted in his journal: "We soon passed the sacred place and foundation of the temple. The arches of the vault [basement] windows were not all finished. The sight of this though by the light of the moon only gave me peculiar feelings. The idea that it was done at the special command of the Almighty was a new thing in this age. It seemed to fill the mind with solemnity and to give a sacredness to the whole place."[62]

The next month, he wrote to the Saints in Britain: "The temple is going on well, though the building itself is at a stand, because of the frost, but I suppose scores of men are at work in the stone quarry, and from ten to twenty teams are at work, bringing the stones to the place." He also indicated that the temple was "not yet quite up to the floor of the building,"[63] meaning to the level upon which the first story floor would be laid.

Joseph Smith reported in the spring of 1842 that there had been "during the winter, as many as one hundred hands quarrying rock, while at the same time multitudes of others have been engaged in hauling, and in other kinds of labor."[64]

---

59. Benjamin Winchester, Letter to Erastus Snow, 12 November 1841, *Times and Seasons* 3 (15 November 1841): 605.

60. A water-table, in architectural terms, is a ledge that skirts a building about two feet above the ground.

61. George D. Smith, *An Intimate Chronicle*, 529.

62. Andrew F. Ehat, ed., "'They Might Have Known He Was Not a Fallen Prophet': The Nauvoo Journal of Joseph Fielding," *BYU Studies* 19 (Winter 1979): 141.

63. Joseph Fielding, "Joseph Fielding's Letter," from Nauvoo, January 1842, *Millennial Star* 3 (August 1842): 77-78.

64. History of the Church, 4:608.

Generous Benefactors

The temple continued to be funded by a slow steady flow of tithing and donations. Occasionally, larger donations provided some relief from the tremendous financial burdens imposed by the temple project.[65] On 21 February 1842, a notice of just such a gift appeared in the *Times and Seasons*, complete with Willard Richards's expression of gratitude and joy:

> This day a certificate of deposit of $145, in the Auburn Bank, was received at this office, and passed to the credit of the twelve individuals of West Niles, named in the accompanying letter of W[illia]m. Van Orden, in the Book of the Law of the Lord, page 83, with their respective items attached to the individual names, as specified in the schedule.
>
> Such receipts can never come amiss, but this arrived at a moment when it will prove peculiarly useful, as we knew not what course to pursue to raise that amount of cash, which could not be dispensed with without immense loss, or sacrifice of the property of the church.[66]

In the spring of 1842, another generous donation was received in the form of a "certificate of deposit in the 'Butchers and Drovers Bank,' New York, by Doct[or] John M. Bernhisel, in favor of the Trustee in Trust." The notice of this donation was accompanied with the admonition, "Go and Do Likewise."[67] In early 1841, Edward Hunter, a wealthy convert who had been baptized in October 1840, "gave Brother Hyrum $200 for the Temple and $200 for the Nauvoo House." He later donated several parcels of real estate as well.[68]

A Year of Jubilee

On 12 April 1842, the Twelve met with Joseph Smith and "agreed to unite [their] influence with the brethren to consecrate their old notes, deeds and obligations which they hold against each other, to the building of the temple in Nauvoo."[69] Willard Richards was authorized to write an epistle for the Twelve, which appeared in the Times and Seasons on 2 May. This letter recounted how,

---

65. One of the largest and best-known contributions to the temple was made by Joseph Toronto. See chap. 8.

66. Willard Richards, "Temple Friends," dated 21 February 1842, *Times and Seasons* 3 (1 March 1842): 715.

67. "Temple Funds," *Times and Seasons* 3 (2 May 1842): 782. John Bernhisel (1799-1881), a medical doctor, joined the Church in 1837 in New York. He was a close friend of Joseph Smith.

68. "Edward Hunter," *Our Pioneer Heritage*, 6:322. This biographical sketch (no author identified) contains lengthy excerpts from Hunter's autobiography.

69. Watson, Manuscript History of Brigham Young, 69; see also *History of the Church*, 4:589.

when the Church was driven from Ohio and Missouri and its members found themselves without shelter, clothing, food, or any means to obtain necessities, that

> many of the brethren stepped forward to their rescue, and not only expended all they possessed for the relief of suffering innocence, but gave their notes and bonds to obtain more means, with which to help those who could not escape the overwhelming surge of banishment from all that they possessed on earth[;] ... and all the means which could possibly be obtained from each other, in addition to the noble charities of the citizens of Illinois, were brought into requisition to sustain a remnant of the Saints, who now mostly inhabit this place.
>
> To accomplish this, the President and Bishops loaned money and such things as could be obtained, and gave their obligations in good faith for the payment of the same; and many of the brethren signed with them at different times and in different places, to strengthen their hands and help them carry out their designs; fully expecting, that, at some future day, they would be enabled to liquidate all such claims, to the satisfaction of all parties.

While some of these financial obligations had been fulfilled, many were yet outstanding. The epistle called for a "year of jubilee ... a time of release to Zion's sons":

> Yes, brethren, bring all such old accounts, notes, bonds, etc., and make a consecration of them to the building of the Temple, and if anything can be obtained on them, it will be obtained; and if nothing can be obtained, when the Temple is completed, we will make a burnt-offering of them, even a peace-offering, which shall bind the brethren together in the bonds of eternal peace, and love and union; and joy and salvation shall flow forth into your souls, and you shall rejoice and say it is good that we have harkened unto counsel, and set our brethren free, for God hath blessed us.
>
> How can we prosper while the Church, while the Presidency, while the Bishops, while those who have sacrificed everything but life, in this thing, for our salvation, are thus encumbered? It cannot be. Arise, then, brethren, set them free, and set each other free, and we will all be free together, we will be free indeed.[70]

The extent to which this request was honored is not known, but the trustees' papers do contain a list of several bonds donated to the temple. These may have been among those given up in response to this plea for jubilee.[71] John Fullmer, in writing to a family member to whom he was indebted, pleaded, "Make a donation of said claim toward building our beautiful temple."[72] A receipt issued in September 1843 to Lyman Wight, an agent for the temple committee, recorded

---

70. "Epistle of the Twelve," *Times and Seasons* 3 (2 May 1842): 767-69.
71. "List of Bonds and Deeds Belonging to the Temple," n.d., Newel K. Whitney Papers, Perry Special Collections, Lee Library.
72. John Fullmer, Letter, Letter to Almon Fullmer, ca. June 1843, holograph, LDS Church Archives.

Olive Case's donation of a "note against Lehasa Hollister of seven dollars with the interest on the same from the date all to be paid to the building of the temple in Nauvoo."[73] James M. Monroe, who was teaching grammar school in Nauvoo the April after Joseph Smith's murder, published a notice in the newspaper requesting his students "who have not paid up their subscriptions . . . to go and work it out on the Temple."[74]

A New Form of Volunteer Labor

At the October 1841 conference, "two or three hundred Elders . . . offered to go out on missions, some six months, others one year, and some two years, and had their missions assigned them at the general conference to labor on the Temple."[75] On 2 October Brigham Young addressed the conference on "the propriety of many of the Elders remaining at home, and working on the Lord's House; and that their labors will be as acceptable to the Lord as their going abroad, and more profitable for the church."[76] Most of these volunteers had yet to make good on their offer to labor in December. The Twelve stated in an epistle: "We wish [those Elders] to call and take their names away, and give them up to the building committee."[77] In early 1842, many of those original volunteers and several others answered the call to work on the temple full time with little or no compensation. Elijah Funk Sheets, a twenty-one-year-old blacksmith, was among those who "volunteered to work six months on the Nauvoo Temple without pay."[78] A family tradition suggests that Hyrum Oaks likewise contributed one and a half years of labor to the temple:

> When the time came to build the Nauvoo Temple, Joseph was going to borrow
> some money from a man to pay the men for working in the timber, but when the

73. Nauvoo Temple Committee, Receipt issued to Lyman Wight, 3 September 1843, Newel K. Whitney Papers, Perry Special Collections, Lee Library. Another record in the same collection recorded the donation on 16 February 1844 of a "promissory note of Ute Perkins and Williams Prior, payable to Daniel Woods ... for Forty dollars."

74. James M. Monroe, "Notice," *Nauvoo Neighbor* 2 (21 April 1845): 4.

75. "Baptism for the Dead," *Times and Seasons* 3 (15 December 1841): 626.

76. "Minutes of a Conference," *Times and Seasons* 2 (15 October 1841): 578. See also Elden J. Watson, ed., Manuscript History of Brigham Young, 180144 (Salt Lake City: Elden J. Watson, 1968), 110.

77. "Baptism for the Dead," *Times and Seasons* 3 (15 December 1841): 626.

78. Elijah Funk Sheets, in Andrew Jenson, *LDS Biographical Encyclopedia*, 4 vols. (Salt Lake City: Grek Kofford Books, 2007)), 614. This source also gives the number of "about a hundred men." Sheets (1821-1904) was baptized 5 July 1840 in Pennsylvania and moved to Nauvoo in 1841.

time came the man disappointed him and he had to call for volunteers. Grandfather Oaks was one of the 50 men who volunteered to work, even though his health was very poor. Joseph told him that if he would do the Lord's work, the Lord would bless him with health and strength. He worked for a year and a half without pay, during which time he did enjoy good health and strength, as Joseph had promised. When the job was finished, Joseph told him that he could consider his tithing paid, until his hair turned gray.[79]

Joseph Smith was quick to acknowledge the liberality of this group of laborers who had foregone other employment to focus on the building project. In a letter to Church members abroad, he praised them:

Many brethren here, instead of a "tenth," labor almost continually upon the house of the Lord, and where is the charity of the churches abroad if they neglect to furnish clothing, against the chilly winds of winter? Do ye not know that Paul said to Timothy: "Now the end of the commandment is charity, out of a pure heart, and good conscience, and faith unfeigned." What a joy and gratification it must be to the saints, who possess such principles as Paul, and have this world's goods, to have a chance to manifest their love of the commandments and brethren, by sending cloth, clothes, or means that will bring them. Remember, brethren, that beautiful expression, "the laborer is worthy of his hire."[80]

The Temple Stonecutters

During the first year of the construction, most of the work on the temple was accomplished by tithing labor. As mentioned previously, following the cornerstone ceremony on 6 April 1841, "the Saints began to bring in some property and money and provisions, which enabled the committee to employ a number of the stonecutters and keep them constantly to work."[81] Initially, about eighteen stonecutters were thus employed. William Clayton's list, reconstructed in 1845, identified some of those who "were among the first who commenced cutting stone for the Temple" and who continued until the building was complete: Alvin Winegar, James Standing, Harvey Stanley, Daniel S. Cahoon, Andrew Cahoon, Stephen Hales Jr., William Jones, John Keown, Rufus Allen, Samuel Hodge, Bun Anderson, and George Ritchey. According to Clayton, "Pulaski S. Cahoon, John Dresdale and

79. Larraine Wissler King, "Life of Hiram Oaks" in her Book of Remembrance, in possession of Bill Burnard, Newton, Utah, date of writing unknown; photocopy of typescript at Nauvoo Restoration, Inc., Nauvoo, Illinois.

80. "To the Saints Abroad," *Times and Seasons* 3 (15 September 1842): 923.

81. George D. Smith, *An Intimate Chronicle*, 529.

Aaron Johnson also commenced to cut stone at the beginning, but did not continue long."[82]

Over the next four years other stonecutters were hired to augment the original group. Clayton added these individuals to his list: William Huntington Sr., Samuel Williams, John Anderson, David B. Dille, Augustus Stafford, Jerome Kimpton, Buckley B. Anderson, Edwin Cutler, Franklin B. Cutler, William L. Cutler, Charles Lambert, John Pickles, James Sharp, Joseph G. Hovey, Welcome Chapman, Joshua Armstrong, James Henry Rollins, Lucius Merchants, John Harper, James D. Miller, John Miller, Peter Campbell, Samuel Heath, Morgan Thomas, Ira K. Hillman, Foster Curtis, Joseph Bates, Henry Parker, Andrew Smith, Benjamin T. Mitchell, Isaac Allred, Wiley Allred, Wilson Lund, Parmelia A. Jackman, William Jackman, William Adams, Thomas McLellan, Chancy Gaylord, Thomas Johnson, David Burrows, and William Cottier.[83]

During the first two to three years of work on the temple, the stonecutters worked outdoors, on or near the temple grounds. In April 1842, *The Wasp*, newly founded by William Smith, the Prophet's brother, published a description of work on the temple site: "We passed the temple, and was [sic] delighted at the prospect that here presented itself. A scene of lively industry and animation was there. The sound of the polisher's chisel—converting the rude stone of the quarry into an artful shape—sent forth its busy hum; all were busily employed—the work was fast progressing."[84]

No later than 1844, a workshop was constructed near the temple to accommodate the stonecutters. Gilbert Belnap, who was twenty-three in the summer of 1844, recorded visiting "the stone cutters shop" and described the scene: "The sound of many workmen's mallets and the sharp ring of the smith's anvil all bore the unmistakable evidence of a determined purpose to complete the mighty structure."[85]

An unnamed visitor in June 1844 reported to a St. Louis paper described the inside of the shop: "In the workshop beside the structure, in which a large number of stone cutters are employed, may be seen divers other carvings on stone, designed for the holy edifice, still more novel than that I have named. Among them

---

82. William Clayton, Journal, in Journal History of the Church of Jesus Christ of Latter-day Saints (chronology of typed entries and newspaper clippings, 1830-present), 31 December 1844, 13, LDS Church Archives. "Bun" Anderson may be a nickname for Buckley Burnham Anderson, who lived in Nauvoo during the right time period.

83. Ibid. "Permelia" may be a scribal error for Parmenio Adams Jackman, a son of Levi Jackman born 6 August 1822 in New York and baptized 28 October 1833.

84. William Smith, "Nauvoo," *The Wasp* 1 (23 April 1842): 4.

85. "Autobiography of Gilbert Belnap," typescript, 30, Perry Special Collections, Lee Library.

are suns, full moons, and half the constellations of the firmament, to say nothing of the human faces of expression weird enough for an English obelisk."[86]

Instead of receiving a daily wage, the stonecutters were paid set prices for decorative stones and were compensated by the foot for other stones cut. For example, shortly after the death of Joseph Smith, in a meeting in August 1844, the stonecutters agreed to "the following specified prices, viz., that the cutting of capital be reduced to two hundred dollars each, also that of the bush-hammer and droved work be reduced to fifty cents per foot. That of the axed work to twenty-five cents per foot."[87]

The stonecutters, like other temple hands, were usually paid in tithing goods such as food and clothing. On one occasion, when tithing provisions were scarce and the committee was unable to compensate the workers, the temple committee assigned the stonecutters to visit outlying Mormon settlements near Nauvoo and preach tithing. William Huntington wrote in his journal about this experience:

> The affairs of the Church have [been] very prosperous through the winter with the exception of a scarcity of provision at the temple. The committee recommended to the stone cutters to go out into the branches and preach to the people the necessity of pay[ing] in their tenth. I went over the River into Iowa and preached one week in the different branches and the people brought wagon loads of provision for the temple. All who went out were blessed and much provision was brought into the temple.[88]

Joseph Hovey, one of the hired stonemasons, wrote in his autobiography of his arduous labor: "I worked hard on the temple of the Lord cutting and sawing stone and I do get so fatigued when I leave my labors that I have not much courage to write my life.... I am a poor man in the things of this world and have to work hard. But thanks be unto [the] God of Israel that I am here in Nauvoo."[89]

---

86. "The Temple of Nauvoo," *St. Louis Gazette*, ca. June 1844, Journal History, 12 June 1844, 5.

87. William H. Cahoon, Minutes of a meeting of the stonecutters for the temple, Journal History, 15 August 1844, 8. A bushhammer is a hammer with several rows of pyramidal points on the face of the hammer head, used for dressing stone. "Droved" refers to stonework accomplished with a drove, or broad chisel. These tools were used for medium- and fine-grade stone dressing. "Axed" work was rough-grade finishing.

88. William Huntington, Sr., "Journal of William Huntington" (17841846), 1 January 1844, typescript, 14, Perry Special Collections, Lee Library.

89. Joseph Grafton Hovey, "Autobiography of Joseph Grafton Hovey," typescript, 16, Perry Special Collections, Lee Library. Grandson M. R. Hovey copied and arranged this document from Hovey's journal in 1933. It begins with an autobiography, then moves to daily entries in 1842. Hovey (1812-68) was baptized 4 July 1839 in Illinois.

Although Joseph Smith did not work directly on the stones, he paid frequent visits to the shop and became friends with the workers. Thirty-four-year-old Mary Alice Cannon Lambert recorded a visit in May 1844: "He went to the stone shops where the men were working on the Nauvoo Temple and blessed each man by the power of his priesthood. Brother Lambert (whom I afterward married) he gathered right in his arms and blessed, and it was ever his testimony that he was thrilled from head to foot by that blessing."[90] On another occasion, Joseph gave a banquet for the stone workers in the Mansion House.[91]

Although quarrying and hauling stone could be considered unskilled labor, finishing the temple stone required considerable expertise. Charles Lambert, who was responsible for shaping many of the decorative stones, was a skilled stonemason before he reached Nauvoo. Others learned the art of stonecutting on the job. For instance, William Adams, another of the hired stone workers, took up the trade because of the lack of other work in Nauvoo's saturated labor market. He reached Nauvoo in 1844 at age twenty-two and recorded his struggle:

> [My brother-in-law] John Harper [was] a stone cutter by trade and was working at the temple since he arrived in Nauvoo.... The situation in Nauvoo discouraging to make a living, I was at lost [sic] what course to pursue. To leave the city and hunt for work was against my feelings. I considered with Brother Harper how the situation looked to me. He told me he thought I might get work at the temple, that the committee were anxious to push the work along as fast as possible, and that he had a few tools he could lend me, that I could get along at the present and he being a stone cutter by trade, he would give me all the help he could to assist me to cut stone. I was pleased with the proposition, and with the consent of [Reynolds] Cahoon, one of the committee, I went to work and continued to the fall of 1846.[92]

Similarly, George Patten, who was fifteen in 1843, became a stonecutter when his father, William, arranged to have him "work under Jerome Kempton to learn stone cutting at the temple yards."[93] James Henry Rollins arranged to become Harvey Stanley's apprentice to learn stonecutting, "he agreeing to furnish me with provisions if he had to divide his portion which he drew from the tithing office. I

90. Mary Alice Cannon Lambert, "Recollections of Joseph Smith," *Young Woman's Journal* 16 (December 1905): 554.

91. "Elizabeth Murphy McLelland," *Daughters of the Utah Pioneers and Their Mothers*, edited by James T. Jakeman (Salt Lake City: Western Publishing Company, 1916), 59.

92. William Adams, Autobiography, 1894, typescript, 10-11, Perry Special Collections, Lee Library.

93. "George Patten," *Our Pioneer Heritage*, 7:256. Patten (1828-1914) was baptized in Nauvoo on 15 June 1843, about the time he started learning the trade of stonecutter. Jerome Bonaparte Kempton (1820-1899), a New York native, was a lifelong stonecutter.

commenced work the next day and cut with Mr. Stanley's help, one of the diamond arch stones which counted to him five dollars when finished. This was my first work in the stone shop. I soon became so [sic] I could cut one of these arch stones with out help."[94]

As part of the finishing work, the workmen polished many of the prominent stones. Lyman Curtis and his father, Nahum, were among those who performed this particular task. "Sand was poured on a cut stone then another large flat one was laid on top and ground back and forth until the under stone was polished." According to a Curtis family tradition, it sometimes took days to polish the larger stones.[95] The *New York Messenger* praised their work in November 1844: "Their finish is admirable and as complete as any of the best specimens of chiseling on the Girard College of Philadelphia."[96]

---

94. James Henry Rollins, Autobiography, 1898, typescript, 1819, LDS Church Archives. These diamond arch stones were the keystones of the arches over the semicircular windows.

95. "Lyman Curtis, Pioneer of 1847," in *An Enduring Legacy*, compiled by Daughters of Utah Pioneers Lesson Committee, 12 vols. (Salt Lake City: Daughters of the Utah Pioneers, 1978-88), 9:215.

96. *New York Spectator*, 9 November 1844, quoted in Cecil B. McGavin, The Nauvoo Temple (Salt Lake City: Deseret Book, 1962), 51. The Girard College near Philadelphia boasted a marble build-ing that was considered one of the finest in America. *Charles Dickens, American Notes for General Circulation* (Avon, CT: Limited Editions Club, 1975), 170, described this building under construction in 1842: "Near the city [Philadelphia], is a most splendid unfinished marble structure for the Girard College ... which, if completed according to the original design, will be perhaps the richest edifice of modern times."

Chapter 4

THE WALLS RISE:
MAY 1842 TO DECEMBER 1842

First Endowments Given

The month of May 1842 was among the most important periods in Latter-day Saint temple history. It was during this month that a new temple-related ordinance was first administered by Joseph Smith to a few of his trusted associates. The endowment, as it would later be called, differed significantly from the endowment associated with the Kirtland Temple.[1] The Kirtland experience was an endowment of spiritual power given to the elders of the Church, preparing them for their missionary duties. Consisting mainly of washings and anointings, it encompassed the general spiritual outpouring experienced by the Saints in conjunction with the dedication and use of the temple. (See "Introduction.")

The endowment Joseph introduced in May 1842 expanded upon the original: The recipient wore a white garment under his or her street clothing,[2] entered

1. Brigham Young thought that if that the Saints had been allowed to remain in Kirtland, they would eventually have performed the endowment in its fullness there. See his address, 6 April 1853, *Journal of Discourses*, 26 vols. (London and Liverpool: LDS Booksellers Depot, 1855-86), 2:32.

2. Eliza M. A. Munson reported that Joseph Smith asked her grandmother, seamstress Elizabeth Warren Allred to make these garments:

into certain covenants and obligations, and received from the officiator key words and signs symbolic of those covenants. These significant new changes meant that those who had received the Kirtland endowment would need to receive it again.

Much has been written about the origin of the 1842 endowment. Joseph did not document how the endowment came to be revealed. There is no revelation such as those found in the Doctrine and Covenants outlining the ordinance or explaining its content. Masonry is also often cited as a source of inspiration for certain aspects of the ritual, Joseph having been admitted to the Masonic brotherhood just weeks earlier in March 1842. This theory is supported by several of Joseph's contemporaries. For example, Joseph Fielding's diary entry for 22 December 1843 declares, "Many have joined the Masonic institution. This seems to have been a stepping stone or preparation for something else, the true origin of Masonry."[3] Heber C. Kimball wrote to Parley P. Pratt on 17 June 1842: "There is a similarity of Priesthood in masonry. Brother Joseph says Masonry was taken from priesthood but has become degenerated, but many things are perfect."[4] These statements hint that Masonry, though "degenerated," was instrumental in the revelation of the Nauvoo endowment, perhaps in the same way that biblical Christianity, though

---

It was while they were living in Nauvoo that the Prophet came to my grandmother [Elizabeth Warren Allred], who was a seamstress by trade, and told her that he had seen the Angel Moroni with the garments on, and asked her to assist him in cutting out the garment. They spread unbleached muslin out on the table, and he told her how to cut it out. She had to cut the third pair, however, before he said it was satisfactory. She told the Prophet that there would be sufficient cloth from the knee to the ankle to make a pair of sleeves, but he told her he wanted as few seams as possible and that there would be sufficient whole cloth to cut the sleeves without piecing. The first garments were made of unbleached muslin and bound with turkey red and were without collars. Later on the Prophet decided he would rather have them bound with white. Sister Emma Smith, the Prophet's wife, proposed that they have a collar on as she thought they would look more finished, but at first the Prophet did not have the collars on them. After Emma Smith had made the little collars, which were not visible from the outside... The garment was to reach to the ankle and the sleeves to the wrist. The marks were always the same. Eliza M. A. Munson. "Early Pioneer History," n.d., typescript, 1-2, LDS Church Archives.

3. Andrew F. Ehat, ed., "The Nauvoo Journal of Joseph Fielding," *BYU Studies*, 19 [Winter 1979]: 145, 147). Others of Joseph's contemporaries use Masonic terms such as tyler (guard) in speaking about the ceremony, and Dimick B. Huntington has Joseph exulting, in reference to the first bestowal of the endowment: "I have done what Solomon ... and Hiram Abiff could not do: I have set up the Kingdom, no more to be thrown down forever nor to be given to another people" (Statement, undated, photocopy in Mary Brown Firmage Papers, L. Tom Perry Special Collections, Harold B. Lee Library, Brigham Young University, Provo, Utah).

4. Heber C. Kimball, Letter to Parley Pratt, 17 June 1842, qtd. in Stanley B. Kimball, "Heber C. Kimball and Family: The Nauvoo Years," *BYU Studies* 15 (Summer 1975): 458.

apostate, was clearly a springboard to the restoration of the fullness of the gospel and the establishment of the Church.[5]

Although these ceremonies were not announced publicly in the same way baptisms for the dead had been discussed, Joseph made reference to this new ordinance in a sermon on 1 May. He preached on the subject of the keys of the kingdom:

> The keys are certain signs and words by which false spirits and personages may be detected from true, which cannot be revealed to the Elders till the Temple is completed. The rich can only get them in the Temple, the poor may get them on the mountain top as did Moses.... There are signs in heaven, earth and hell; the Elders must know them all, to be endowed with power, to finish their work and prevent imposition. The devil knows many signs, but does not know the sign of the Son of Man, or Jesus. No one can truly say he knows God until he has handled something and this can only be in the holiest of holies.[6]

This sermon was probably Joseph's most detailed public description of the new endowment. Two days later, he called upon a group of men to prepare the large room in the second story of his store on Water Street for the presentation of the endowment.[7] This room had been the location for the organizational meeting of the Relief Society one month earlier on 17 March 1842 and would yet host some of the most significant gatherings in Church history.[8] Lucius N. Scovil, who was among those selected to prepare the room, later recalled the events of Tuesday, 3 May:

---

5. While the endowment does not represent a wholesale borrowing from Masonry, it shows clears signs of Masonic influence. Many scholars point to ancient sources and note striking similarities between the endowment and hermeticism, mysticism, and ancient Egyptian, Jewish, and Christian initiation rituals. The sources they cite, most of which were unavailable to Joseph Smith in 1842, strongly suggest an ancient foundation to the endowment. For further reading on this subject see Hugh Nibley, *The Message of the Joseph Smith Papyri: An Egyptian Endowment* (Salt Lake City: Deseret Book, 1975). See also David John Buerger, "The Development of the Mormon Temple Endowment Ceremony," *Dialogue: A Journal of Mormon Thought* 20 (Winter 1987): 33.

6. Joseph Smith, Jr., et al., *History of the Church of Jesus Christ of Latter-day Saints*, edited by B. H. Roberts (Salt Lake City: Deseret News Press, 6 vols. published 1902-12, Vol. 7 published 1932), 4:608.

7. Lisle G. Brown, "Sacred Departments for Temple Worship in Nauvoo," *BYU Studies* 19 (Spring 1979): 363. The room was painted white, had three large windows overlooking Water Street, and had initially been used as a storage room.

8. Franklin D. Richards, "A Tour of Historic Scenes," *Contributor* 7 (May 1886): 301, later reminisced that Joseph's store had been "sanctified by [the Lord's] presence, by his ministration, and by the promulgation of some of the grandest principles ever given of God to lead mortality into the higher life." He continued:

I can testify that on the 3rd day of May, 1842, Joseph Smith the Prophet called upon five or six, viz: Shadrach Roundy, Noah Rogers, Dimick B. Huntington, Daniel Kearns, and myself (I am not certain but that Hosea Stout was there also) to meet with him (the Prophet) in his business office (the upper part of his brick store). He told us that the object he had was for us to go to work and fit up that room preparatory to giving endowments to a few Elders that he might give unto them all the keys of power pertaining to the Aaronic and Melchizedek Priesthoods.

We therefore went to work making the necessary preparations, and everything was arranged representing the interior of a temple as much as the circumstances would permit, he being with us dictating everything. He gave us many items that were very interesting to us, which sank with deep weight upon my mind, especially after the temple was finished at Nauvoo, and I had received the ordinances.... I can and do testify that I know of a surety that room was fitted up by his order which we finished in the forenoon of the said 4th of May, 1842.[9]

Dimick B. Huntington, another of those called upon to assist in preparing the room that day, later wrote that he, William Felshaw and Samuel Rolfe assisted in preparing the "lodge room in the brick store chamber for the first endowments; took some bars of lead to hold up the trees of the garden and a piece of carpet for a curtain, Joseph Smith giving directions how to prepare all things."[10] "Archeological evidence suggests that the men further prepared the room by painting a pastoral mural in the northwest corner and then arranged various plants to represent the Garden of Eden."[11]

The necessary preparations having been made, Joseph Smith could now proceed. On that same day—Wednesday, 4 May—in the afternoon, he called upon nine men to join him above the store. George Miller, one of those who received

---

Here were prepared the political doctrines contained in "View of the Powers and Policy of the General Government, by Joseph Smith"; and his letters to Henry Clay and John C. Calhoun. Here he received the revelation on the eternity and plurality of the celestial marriage covenant. Here was organized a Council of the Kingdom, and here, when the spirit prompted him that his life's work was drawing to a close, and when he saw that his earthly days might be ended before the completion of the temple, he called a chosen few and conferred upon them the ordinances of the holy endowments, so that the divine treasures of his mind might not perish from the world with his death. Even bricks and stones are made sacred by such associations; and my mind has often dwelt upon this place with a feeling of sublime reverence.

9. Lucius N. Scovil, Letter to the Editor, 2 January 1884, quoted in "The Higher Ordinances," *Deseret Evening News*, 11 February 1884, 2.

10. The word carpet may have referred to a large table covering. Dimick B. Huntington, Statement, undated, Lee Library.

11. Roger D. Launius and F. Mark McKiernan, *Joseph Smith's Red Brick Store*, Western Illinois Monograph Series, number 5 (Macomb, Illinois: Western Illinois University, 1993), 28.

the endowment that day, later wrote a statement indicating that Joseph had received specific instructions about who should receive the ordinance: "Joseph washed and anointed as King[s] and Priests to God, and over the House of Israel, the following named persons, *as he said he was commanded of God,* viz: James Adams (of Springfield), William Law, William Marks, Willard Richards, Brigham Young, Heber C. Kimball, Newel K. Whitney, Hyrum Smith, and myself; and conferred on us Patriarchal Priesthood."[12]

Because those who participated were instructed not to reveal or write down the specifics of the proceedings, only two extant records—one an entry in the Book of the Law of the Lord, and the other in Brigham Young's history—provide sketchy contemporary glimpses of what transpired. The first reads: "May 4, 1842, Wednesday. In council in the Presidents and General offices with Judge Adams, Hyrum Smith, Newel K. Whitney, William Marks, W[illiam] Law, George Miller, Brigham Young, Heber C. Kimball, and Willard Richards [blank] and giving certain instructions concerning the priesthood. [blank] etc. on the Aaronic Priesthood to the first [blank] continuing through the day."[13]

Brigham Young's entry for that day is also very brief: "I met with Joseph, Hyrum, Heber, Willard, Bishops Whitney and Miller, and General James Adams, in Joseph's private office, where Joseph taught the ancient order of things for the first time in these last days, and received my washings, anointings and endowments."[14]

Willard Richards, who wrote the official account of those events two and a half years later in December 1844, combined these two contemporary journal entries and added insights gleaned from conversations with the Prophet. The resulting entry in the *History of the Church* is what Andrew F. Ehat has called "the most comprehensive statement made by an original participant, providing us [with] Joseph Smith's explanation of the meaning of the endowment."[15] Richards cast the account as if it were in Joseph's own words, a technique frequently used in the *History of the Church*:

---

12. George Miller, Letter to James J. Strang, 26 June 1855, in H. W. Mills, "De Tal Palo Tal Astilla," *Annual Publications—Historical Society of Southern California* 10 (Los Angeles: McBride Printing Company, 1917) 364; emphasis mine.

13. Dean C. Jessee, ed., *The Papers of Joseph Smith,* 2 vols. (Salt Lake City: Deseret Book Company, 1992), 2:380.

14. Elden J. Watson, ed., *Manuscript History of Brigham Young* 1801-44 (Salt Lake City: Elden J. Watson, 1968), 116.

15. Andrew F. Ehat, "'Who Shall Ascend into the Hill of the Lord?' Sesquicentennial Reflections of a Sacred Day: 4 May 1842," in *Temples of the Ancient World: Ritual and Symbolism,* edited by Donald W. Parry (Salt Lake City: Deseret Book, 1994), 51.

I spent the day [of May 4] in the upper part of the store, that is in my private office (so called because in that room I keep my sacred writings, translate ancient records, and receive revelations) and in my general business office, or lodge room (that is where the Masonic fraternity meet occasionally, for want of a better place) in council with General James Adams, of Springfield, Patriarch Hyrum Smith, Bishops Newel K. Whitney and George Miller, and President Brigham Young and Elders Heber C. Kimball and Willard Richards, instructing them in the principles and order of the Priesthood, attending to washings, anointings, endowments and the communication of keys pertaining to the Aaronic Priesthood, and so on to the highest order of the Melchizedek Priesthood,[16] setting forth the order pertaining to the Ancient of Days, and all those plans and principles by which any one is enabled to secure the fullness of those blessings which have been prepared for the Church of the First Born, and come up and abide in the presence of the Elohim in the eternal worlds. In this council was instituted the ancient order of things for the first time in these last days.[17]

Corroborating these accounts are two cautiously worded statements by Heber C. Kimball about this historic occasion. In a letter to Parley P. Pratt the next month, Kimball wrote, "We have received some precious things through the Prophet on the priesthood that would cause your soul to rejoice. I cannot give them to you on paper for they are not to be written. So you must come and get them for yourself."[18] He later wrote that he "was initiated into the ancient order was washed and anointed and sealed and ordained a Priest, and so forth in company with nine others."[19]

The next day, Thursday, 5 May, Joseph received the endowment from those to whom he had previously administered it. This order followed the pattern established when Joseph and Oliver Cowdery were ordained to baptize, and then baptized one another (JS-H 1:69-71). All those who attended the ceremony on 4 May were present the next day except James G. Adams who had returned to Springfield, Illinois that morning. Once again, the entry for 5 May in the *History of the Church* is a synthesis of the Brigham Young account and the entry in Book of the Law of the Lord: "Thursday, 5.—General Adams started for Springfield, and the

---

16. This statement is not entirely accurate in terms of contemporary understanding of temple theology. The highest order of the Melchizedek Priesthood can be obtained only by a couple who have been sealed and who enter into this order by an ordinance known as the "second anointing." D. Michael Quinn, "Latter-day Saint Prayer Circles," *BYU Studies* 19 (Fall 1978): 79.

17. *History of the Church*, 5:1-2.

18. Heber C. Kimball, Letter to Parley Pratt, 17 June 1842, qtd. in Stanley B. Kimball, "Heber C. Kimball and Family: The Nauvoo Years," *BYU Studies* 15 (Summer 1975): 458.

19. Stanley B. Kimball, ed., *On the Potter's Wheel: The Diaries of Heber C. Kimball* (Salt Lake City: Signature Books, 1987), 55.

remainder of the council of yesterday continued their meeting at the same place, and myself and Brother Hyrum received in turn from the others, the same that I had communicated to them the day previous."[20]

It is not clear why this entry says Hyrum Smith received his endowment on 5 May, since he had apparently received the endowment from his brother on 4 May like the others. Brigham Young's diary does not shed additional light but simply records that the group of men "administered to Brother Joseph the same ordinances"[21] which he had previously administered to them. The entry in the Book of the Law of the Lord does contain an incomplete sentence stating that they "continued in Council as the day previous and Joseph and Hyrum were [blank]."[22] Hyrum's role in this second meeting thus remains uncertain. He may have assisted Joseph in the first meeting in some way that necessitated his receiving the ordinance a second time.

Meetings of the "Quorum of the Anointed"

The gatherings on 4-5 May were the first of many such occasions. During the twenty-five months before his death, Joseph held private meetings in which he administered the endowment to more than sixty people, including several women. Brigham Young recorded the essentials of three such meetings in May 1843:

> May 26—Met with the Prophet Joseph S., the Patriarch Hyrum S., Brothers Kimball and Richards, Judge James Adams, and Bishop N. K. Whitney, receiving our endowments and instructions in the priesthood. The Prophet Joseph administered to us the first ordinances of endowment, and gave us instructions on the priesthood and the new and everlasting covenant.
> May 28—I met with Brothers Joseph, Hyrum, Heber, Willard, Bishop Whitney and Judge Adams when we administered to Brother Joseph the same ordinances of endowment, and of the holy priesthood which he administered unto us.
> May 29—Met at 9 a.m., with the same brethren, when Joseph instructed us further in principles pertaining to the holy priesthood.[23]

This group of trusted friends would come to be known as the "Holy Order" or the "Quorum of the Anointed." At the time, Heber C. Kimball noted, "[Joseph] has got a small company that he feels safe in their hands; he can open his bosom

20. *History of the Church*, 5:2.

21. Watson, *Brigham Young Manuscript History*, 116.

22. Jessee, *The Papers of Joseph Smith*, 2:380.

23. Watson, *Brigham Young Manuscript History*, 129.

to and feel himself safe."[24] Nine men were present in the first council in addition to Joseph, although two of the accounts mention only seven. William Law and William Marks were later stricken from these accounts after they apostatized.[25] Significantly, Brigham Young led one of these meetings on an occasion when Joseph could not be present.[26] In 1877, Young described the manner in which such meetings of the "Holy Order" were conducted:

> When we got our washings and anointings under the hands of the Prophet Joseph at Nauvoo we had only one room to work in with the exception of a little side room or office where we were washed and anointed.... Then after we went into the large room over the store in Nauvoo. Joseph divided up the room the best that he could hung up the veil, marked it gave us our instructions as we passed along from one department to another.[27]

Bathsheba Wilson Bigler Smith, who was among the first women to receive the endowment from Joseph, speaking in a "sisters meeting" of Salt Lake Temple workers in 1899, told them:

> The endowments were given under the direction of the Prophet Joseph Smith, who afterwards gave us a lecture or instructions in regard to the endowment ceremonies.... It was in the lodge room over the store.... There were two rooms over the store. In one room they had a sheet hung up as a veil, and the first endowments were given there.... Joseph gave me permission to stand by the veil and listen to the ceremony, which I did.[28]

Often these Quorum meetings would last the entire day, the participants pausing only for meals.[29] Although *Times and Seasons* editor Ebenezer Robinson

---

24. Heber C. Kimball, Letter to Parley Pratt, 17 June 1842, qtd. in Stanley B. Kimball, "Heber C. Kimball and Family: The Nauvoo Years," *BYU Studies* 15 (Summer 1975): 458.25. On 21 December 1845, a meeting of endowed persons was held in the temple. William Clayton recorded that Heber C. Kimball addressed this group: "About 4 years ago next May nine persons were admitted into the Holy order 5 are now living. B. Young W. Richards George Miller N. K. Whitney and H. C. Kimball two are dead, and two are worse than dead." George D. Smith, *An Intimate Chronicle*, 222. By these last two, he meant Law and Marks.

26. Watson, *Brigham Young Manuscript History*, 156.

27. Quoted in L. John Nuttal, Diary, 7 February 1877, typescript, Perry Special Collections, Lee Library.

28. Quoted in Salt Lake Temple, Sisters Meeting, Minutes, 16 June 1899, typescript, 67, LDS Church Archives.

29. Ebenezer Robinson, "Items of Personal History of the Editor—Including Some Items of Church History Not Generally Known," *The Return* 2 (April 1890): 252.

was never endowed, he recorded attempting to visit the Prophet in the upper rooms of the store during one of these sessions:

[We] encountered John Taylor, one of the twelve Apostles, in a long white garment, with a white turban on his head, and a drawn sword in his hand, evidently representing the "cherubims and flaming sword which was placed at the east of the garden of Eden, to guard the tree of life." He informed us Brother Joseph was in the room. Here, we understand, and firmly believe, the ceremony originated, as practiced in the endowment house in Utah.[30]

The Kirtland endowment, which was designed to prepare elders for proselytizing missions, was administered only to men. Similarly, the new endowment in Nauvoo was initially administered only to men. However, Joseph Smith and others who had received it indicated that the time would soon come when all members of the Church, would be eligible to receive the endowment. Joseph taught:

There was nothing made known to these men but what will be made known to all the Saints of the last days, so soon as they are prepared to receive, and a proper place is prepared to communicate them, even to the weakest of the Saints; therefore let the Saints be diligent in building the Temple, and all houses which they have been, or shall hereafter be, commanded of God to build; and wait their time with patience in all meekness, faith, perseverance unto the end, knowing assuredly that all these things referred to in this council are always governed by the principle of revelation.[31]

As months passed, word began to spread that the endowment had been introduced. George Q. Cannon recalled:

When [Joseph] did communicate the endowments to a few persons before the Temple was completed, the whole people were moved with desire to complete the Temple, in order that they might receive these great blessings therein. They were valued beyond price. A man that could go in and get his endowments was looked upon as though he had received some extraordinary blessing—something akin to that which the angels received—and it was estimated and valued in that way.[32]

---

30. Robinson, "Items of Personal History," 252.

31. *History of the Church* 5:1-2. This statement is part of the entry for 4 May, the day the endowment was given for the first time. Though authored by Willard Richards, it likely reflects Joseph's ideas on the matter.

32. George Q. Cannon, 14 January 1894, *Collected Discourses*, 6 vols., edited by Brian H. Stuy (Salt Lake City: B.H.S. Publishing, 1987-92), 4:13.

Arrival of William Player

In June, William Player, a skilled builder from England, arrived "with the full intention of working on the temple."[33] Player would become one of the heroes of the Nauvoo Temple saga. While he was expert in stonecutting and -engraving,[34] his ability to set stone proved to be his most valued contribution to the building project. He supervised the setting of the remainder of the temple stones from the moonstone plinths, which rested at the base of the each pilaster, to the capstone.[35] He was a paid laborer, receiving compensation from tithing funds.[36]

When Player commenced work on the stone walls on 8 June, his first undertaking was to adjust some of the stones "which had not been done very well."[37] Truman O. Angell later recalled that the original work that had been done on the walls had been "much botched."[38] On 11 June, Player set the first plinth "on the southwest corner of the south side." William Jones had carved the stone.[39]

The moonstone plinths had a downward-facing crescent moon carved in each. One journalist, visiting Nauvoo shortly before the death of Joseph Smith, described them:

> The external layer of stone is dressed with considerable neatness, and each of the range of pilasters by which it is ornamented, bears upon it a sculptural representation of the crescent, with the profile of a man's face in strong relief, much in the style of that edifying picture of the moon you may have been wont to admire, as well as myself, in the primer when a boy! The effect of this image is semi-solemn, semi-laughable, and certainly more than semi-singular.[40]

One visitor thought that the face on the moonstone was "Joe Smith's profile."[41]

The *Times and Seasons* published an over-optimistic appraisal of the temple's progress on 2 May 1842: "This noble edifice is progressing with great rapidi-

---

33. George D. Smith, *An Intimate Chronicle,* 532. William Warner Player (1793-unknown) was converted in England by Wilford Woodruff in 1841.

34. Wilford Woodruff, 26 March 1841, *Wilford Woodruff's Journal, 1833-1898,* typescript, edited by Scott G. Kenny, 9 vols. (Midvale, UT: Signature Books, 1983-85), 1:524.

35. A plinth is the bottom stone of a column or pilaster.

36. William Clayton, Letter to Brigham Young, 30 May 1843, holograph, Brigham Young Papers, LDS Church Archives.

37. George D. Smith, *An Intimate Chronicle,* 532.

38. Truman O. Angell, Letter to John Taylor, 11 March 1885, holograph, John Taylor Papers, LDS Church Archives.

39. William Clayton, Journal, in Journal History, 31 December 1844, 13.

40. "The Temple of Nauvoo," *St. Louis Gazette,* ca. June 1844, Journal History, 12 June 1844, 5.

41. John Rowson Smith, *A Descriptive Pamphlet of Smith's Leviathan Panorama of the Mississippi River Now Exhibiting at Mason Hall Philadelphia* (Philadelphia: n.pub., 1848), 3-4.

ty ... and by next fall we expect to see the building enclosed; if not the top stone raised with 'shouting of grace, grace, unto it.'"[42]

As the walls began to rise higher above ground level, setting the massive stones became more difficult. The building committee decided to have cranes erected to hoist the stones and asked Wandle Mace, age thirty-three, to build the cranes. He wrote in his autobiography: "The temple committee found difficulty in getting an experienced hand to frame some masts to hoist the stone onto the walls of the temple so applied to me. I thereupon engaged to do the work of building three masts and cranes to be used for that purpose, which when completed was perfectly satisfactory to the temple committee."[43]

As Mace suggests, the cranes were made of wood. These structures, which supported pulleys, were mobile. They had wheels, and tracks or runways were made around the temple allowing the cranes to be more easily positioned.[44] Draft animals were probably used to assist in hoisting the heavier stones. Teams of workers, known as "windlass men," were assigned to the cranes.[45] William Clayton recorded: "The names of the constant hands who attended Brother Player's crane are Tarlton Lewis, Archibald Hill, John Hill, Hans Christian Hansen and Charles W. Patten."[46]

As each stone was hoisted, using the crane, workmen spread mortar in the space designed to receive it, then pounded the stone with a heavy mallet for the snuggest possible fit.[47] The mortar was made of lime, which could be obtained near the stone quarry at one of several lime kilns.[48]

William Niswanger owned one of the most important lime kilns in Nauvoo and provided much of the lime used in the temple.[49] Niswanger advertised his busi-

42. "The Temple," *Times and Seasons* 3 (2 May 1842): 775.

43. Mace built one crane in 1842. The second and third cranes, also by Mace, were added later. George D. Smith, *An Intimate Chronicle*, 533; Wandle Mace, Autobiography, 1890, typescript, 82, Perry Special Collections, Lee Library. Mace's account is retrospective but contains notes and entries recorded earlier. Mace (1809-90), baptized in 1838 in New York, supervised the framing of the temple's tower.

44. Requests to the Trustees to Credit Various Individuals for Work Contributed as Tithing, 16 April 1845, microfilm of holograph, Newel K. Whitney Papers, Perry Special Collections, Lee Library; George D. Smith, *An Intimate Chronicle*, 538.

45. *History of the Church*, 7:249. A windlass was any wood-framed structure used for hoisting, usually equipped with a block and tackle. Many wells and mines were outfitted with a windlass. In this case, the windlass was used as a crane for the stones.

46. Clayton, Journal, in Journal History, 31 December 1844, 13.

47. *History of the Church*, 7:417.

48. Virginia S. Harrington and J. C. Harrington, *Rediscovery of the Nauvoo Temple* (Salt Lake City: Nauvoo Restoration, Inc., 1971), 16.

49. "Lime," *Nauvoo Neighbor* 3 (24 April 1844): 4. Bathsheba Wilson Bigler Smith, Letters to George A. Smith, 12 September 1843, 127, LDS Church Archives, wrote, "I got 10 bushel of lime of Niswanger." Others who owned lime kilns in Nauvoo were Joseph Owens, Thomas Mendenhall, Josiah Boyce, Edmund Nelson, John Van Naten, and Peter Shirts.

ness in the newspaper: "All kinds of country Produce, or Store Goods will be taken in exchange for lime, at his kilns, at the Temple Stone Quarry, on Main Street."[50]

Limestone is composed of gases, carbonic acid, and lime. When limestone is burned, the gases and acid are released, and the white lime is left behind. This lime was crushed and mixed with other materials to make mortar, plaster, whitewash, and other building and finishing materials. The powdery lime acted as a bonding agent. Mortar was made using a mixture of crushed lime, sifted sand, and water. These were mixed together in buckets until the lime was distributed evenly throughout. The resulting mortar took several days to dry completely. According to William Clayton, "Old Thomas Travis, a faithful brother from England, was the man who mixed the mortar. This was his business from the beginning of the works; he was sometimes assisted by the tithing hands."[51]

The construction of the exterior walls began in the summer of 1841 and continued from the spring of 1842 until May 1845. During the warm seasons of those four years, the stonesetters were almost constantly at work. Nancy Alexander Tracy recalled:

> My husband went up on the hill near the temple and bought a small lot and built another house ... and to the south just one lot and a street separated us from the temple. Here we hoped would be our permanent home. My husband did his own carpenter work and also helped to work on the temple. Out of my bedroom window I could see the masons at work and could hear the click of their hammers and hear their sailor songs as they pulled the rock in place with pulleys. It was grand to see.[52]

Mary Ann Stearns also remembered the workmen singing on the site: "The songs of the earnest workers as they tugged at the ropes, pulling up the heavy stones to the top of the building were cheering and inspiring as they floated out on the morning air."[53]

Joseph Smith made frequent visits to the site during the latter half of 1842 to ascertain the progress on the walls. His journal records several rides to the temple, both alone and with his family. On one occasion he wrote that he "was pleased

---

50. Niswanger, "Lime," *Nauvoo Neighbor* 3 (24 April 1844): 4.

51. Clayton, Journal, in Journal History, 31 December 1844.

52. Nancy Naomi Alexander Tracy, "Life History of Nancy Naomi Alexander Tracy," 1885, typescript, 25, LDS Church Archives. Nancy Naomi Alexander (1816-1902) married Moses Tracy in 1832 and the two were baptized 10 May 1834.

53. Mary Ann Stearns Winters, "An Autobiographical Sketch of the Life of the Late Mary Ann Stearns Winters," 1855, typescript, 12, LDS Church Archives. Winters (1833-1912) was born in Maine. Her father died when she was an infant; and her mother, Mary Ann Frost Stearns, joined the Church in 1836 and married Parley P. Pratt.

with the progress made in that sacred edifice" and that he spent time "conversing with several of the brethren and shaking hands."[54]

During the 1842 season, stone-setting progressed slowly because Player and the windlass men could set stone faster than the stonecutters could prepare it. William Clayton recalled that Reynolds Cahoon's sons, who were cutting moonstones, caused some of the delay by "playing in the stone shop much of their time."[55] Still, by autumn, Player "had got all the rock-work laid around as high as the window sills, together with all the window sills including that of the large east Venetian window. He had also two courses of pilaster stones on the plinths all around."[56] When work on the walls ceased in the late fall because of the onset of winter, "the rock-cutters continued their labor with the intention of having a goodly number of the stones ready for the Spring."[57]

Children and the Temple

Because of its unusual design, enormous size, and the religious fervor their parents expended on its construction, the children of Nauvoo were captivated by the temple. Mary Ann Stearns, who turned ten in 1843, remembered playing on the rising walls as a child: "One of our most enjoyable pastimes was to visit the temple and run around on its walls, until it grew so high that it was considered dangerous, and we were prohibited from that pleasure."[58]

Matilda McClellan, who was thirteen in 1842, ran errands for her mother to the temple:

> How well I can remember being very pleased when my mother would let me take father's dinner to him while he was working on the Nauvoo Temple. I seemed to understand the importance and the holiness of the building. Father was always so pleased to have us children come with his dinner and would tell us all about the temple of God he was assisting to build. Being a blacksmith, he had a shop nearby where he worked. When necessary, he did all kinds of labor.[59]

According to family tradition, Martin Bushman, who frequently hauled stone to the temple for his tithing with the aid of his teenage sons, took "all of [his] children into the Temple and showed them the beautiful building which they have

---

54. 29 October 1842, Jessee, *The Papers of Joseph Smith*, 2:489; see also 381, 490-91.

55. George D. Smith, *An Intimate Chronicle*, 533.

56. Ibid.

57. Ibid., 537.

58. Winters, "An Autobiographical Sketch," 12.

59. Matilda McClellan Loveless, Autobiography, n.d., 1, typescript, Perry Special Collections, Lee Library.

never forgotten especially the font resting on the back of twelve bronze oxen."[60] Joseph Moesser, age ten in 1846, later wrote of a visit to the completed temple: "We went on the top [of the Temple] I looked over the railing that was around there. It seemed so far down that I became very frightened."[61]

Hannah Hill, only four years old in 1846, recalled, "Father worked on the temple. He took me to the temple one day to meeting.... After meeting, father took me up on top of the temple and I saw the Mississippi River. It looked like an ocean to me then as I had never seen such a great body of water."[62]

Changes at the Recorder's Office

On 29 June 1842, an important change was made at the recorder's office. Joseph Smith gave Willard Richards leave from his duties as recorder to travel east to bring his family to Nauvoo. Smith's journal states, "The recorder being about to start east on a journey committed the Law of the Lord to W[illia]m Clayton to continue this journal, etc. in his absence and the keys etc. to the President and Clayton."[63] Clayton's history of the temple also records this transfer of responsibility:

[Richards] transferred the "Law of the Lord" and books belonging to the temple to the care and charge of William Clayton. One or two days later Elder Richards started away.

About nine o'clock on the evening of Saturday, September 3rd, the President was at Bishop N. K. Whitney's but was about to leave that place to go to Edward Hunter's. He called William Clayton to him and said:

"Brother Clayton, I want you to take care of the records and papers; and from this time I appoint you Temple Recorder; and when revelations are to be transcribed, you shall write them."

This was done because Elder Richards had more work than he could attend to, he being engaged upon the Church History, which the President was anxious should progress as fast as possible.[64]

---

60. Jacob Bushman, Autobiography, 1902, typescript, 1, Perry Special Collections, Lee Library.; "Martin B. Bushman," in Jenson, Latter-day Saint Biographical Encyclopedia, 1:507. Martin Bushman (1802-70) joined the Church 1840 and moved to Nauvoo 1842.

61. Joseph Moesser, "Sketch of the Life of Joseph Hyrum Moesser," 1922, typescript, 1, LDS Church Archives.

62. Quoted in "Hannah H[ood] Hill Romney," Our Pioneer Heritage, compiled by Kate B. Carter, 20 vols. (Salt Lake City: Daughters of the Utah Pioneers, 1958-77), 5:262. Hannah (1842-1929), the daughter of Isabella Hood Hill and Archibald Hill, married Miles P. Romney in 1862.

63. Jessee, The Papers of Joseph Smith, 2:395.

64. George D. Smith, An Intimate Chronicle, 535-36.

Naturally, other personnel changes occurred periodically. Two weeks earlier on 11 June, Clayton asked James Whitehead to be his assistant clerk. Upon Richard's departure, Whitehead became Clayton's clerk, much as Clayton had acted as Richard's clerk. John P. McEwan was hired as an assistant clerk early in 1845 to help with the increasing workload at the recorder's office. Joseph C. Kingsbury became the trustee's disbursing agent, meaning that he helped distribute store pay to the workers.[65] Curtis Bolton worked in the recorder's office for a period of time in 1845 while Whitehead was ill. He wrote in his journal:

> One day towards Autumn [1845], Brother [Samuel] Rolfe recommended me as a writer ... to the temple time keeper [William F. Cahoon] to straighten up his accounts and enter them in a book, which I had to do from the very beginning as they had been kept on loose pieces of paper. This I did to his entire satisfaction and to the satisfaction of the trustees. Some little time after one of the clerks named Whitehead being taken very ill I was sent for from the temple [where he was a workman] to take his place in the tithing office where I remained two weeks—where he returned to his place and I returned to mine.[66]

The Temple Store

In addition to the important changes in personnel at the recorder's office, the office itself was relocated to be closer to the temple site. The move was approved on 1 October 1842. William Clayton wrote:

> It was ... agreed that the recorder's office should be removed to the Committee House near the temple for the better accommodation of the business.
> Accordingly the committee built a small brick office for the recorder; and on Wednesday, November 2nd, the recorder moved his records, books, papers, etc., to the new office and began business there forthwith.[67]

A notice in the *Times and Seasons* alerted the Saints that "the Recorder's Office [is] henceforth removed to the Committee house near the Temple; all property and means must therefore be brought to that place, where it will be recorded in due form."[68]

---

65. William Clayton, Journal, in Journal History, 31 December 1844.

66. Cleo H. Evans, comp. and ed., Curtis Edwin Bolton: *Pioneer, Missionary, History, Descendants, and Ancestors* (Fairfax, VA: Author, 1968), 7.

67. George D. Smith, *An Intimate Chronicle*, 537.

68. William Clayton, "To the Saints in Nauvoo, and Scattered Abroad," *Times and Seasons* 3 (11 October 1842): 957.

The new recorder's office also functioned as the "temple store,"[69] replacing Joseph Smith's store as the location where temple hands received their wages. One advantage of the move was that the weary workmen were not required to walk two miles from their worksite to the store. Another advantage was that the upper room of Joseph's store, one of the city's few large meeting rooms, had become the Prophet's preferred location for holding important councils and giving endowments. Obviously more privacy was desirable.

The new temple store was an important commercial center in Nauvoo. The transactions at the store were not limited to the receipt and disbursement of tithing goods. Ordinary citizens frequently bought and bartered at the store. Wilford Woodruff wrote, "I bought two wagons, one of the Temple committee for $70."[70] I. R. Tull, a merchant from Pontoosuc, a town a few miles up the Mississippi, came frequently to Nauvoo to sell produce. When he was unable to sell his wares in regular channels, he took it to the temple store, where he "could always trade it off for something." He noted that the store had "almost every conceivable thing, from all kinds of implements and men's and women's clothing, down to baby clothes and trinkets, which had been deposited by the owners as tithing, or for the benefit of the Temple."[71]

Joseph's Letters on Baptism for the Dead

On 8 August 1842, Joseph Smith was accused as an accessory in the attempted murder of Lilburn W. Boggs, the former governor of Missouri. For three weeks he eluded arrest by remaining hidden in the homes of friends. Edward Hunter recalled that "Brother Joseph hid up at my house.... During that time Joseph revealed that last part of baptisement for our dead."[72] Wilford Woodruff noted in his diary about six weeks later on 19 September 1842: "Joseph has been deprived of the privilege of appearing openly and deprived of the society of his own family because sheriffs are hunting him to destroy him without cause. Yet the Lord is with him as he was upon the Isle of Patmos with John.... He has appeared occasionally in the midst of the Saints which has been a great comfort to the Saints."[73]

68. William Clayton, "To the Saints in Nauvoo, and Scattered Abroad," *Times and Seasons* 3 (11 October 1842): 957.

69. Thomas Bullock, Diary, 1845-46, typescript, LDS Church Archives, repeatedly calls it "the Temple Store."

70. Woodruff, Journal, 3:39.

71. Quoted in Thomas Gregg, *History of Hancock County* (Chicago: Charles C. Chapman, 1880), 374-75.

72. "Edward Hunter," in *Our Pioneer Heritage*, 6:319. This article on Hunter (no author identified) contains a lengthy excerpt from his autobiography from which I took this quotation.

73. Woodruff, 19 September 1842, Journal, 2:187.

One such "appearance" took place on 31 August when the Prophet addressed the Nauvoo Relief Society. On that occasion he "remarked that a few things had been manifested to him in his absence, respecting the baptisms for the dead, which he should communicate next Sabbath if nothing should occur to prevent." He added as an intriguing "preview": "All persons baptized for the dead must have a recorder present, that he may be an eyewitness to testify of it. It will be necessary in the grand Council, that these things be testified—let it be attended to from this time, but if there is any lack it may be at the expense of our friends—they may not come forth."[74]

The next day, Joseph wrote a letter to the Church reiterating the necessity of having a recorder present during all baptisms for the dead. The letter contained the following revelation, now in Doctrine and Covenants 127:

> Verily, thus saith the Lord unto you concerning your dead: When any of you are baptized for your dead, let there be a recorder, and let him be eye-witness of your baptisms; let him hear with his ears, that he may testify of a truth, saith the Lord;
>
> That in all your recordings it may be recorded in heaven; whatsoever you bind on earth, may be bound in heaven; whatsoever you loose on earth, may be loosed in heaven; ...
>
> And again, let all the records be had in order, that they may be put in the archives of my holy temple, to be held in remembrance from generation to generation, saith the Lord of Hosts. (D&C 127:6-7, 9)

On 8 September, Joseph wrote another letter to the Church:

> I have had a few additional views in relation to this matter, which I now certify.... Now, in relation to this matter it would be very difficult for one recorder to be present at all times, and to do all the business. To obviate this difficulty, there can be a recorder appointed in each ward of the city, who is well qualified for taking accurate minutes; and let him be very particular and precise in taking the whole proceedings, certifying in his record that he saw with his eyes, and heard with his ears, giving the date, and names, and so forth, and the history of the whole transaction; naming also some three individuals that are present, if there be any present, who can at any time when called upon certify to the same, that in the mouth of two or three witnesses every word may be established.
>
> Then, let there be a general recorder, to whom these other records can be handed, being attended with certificates over their own signatures, certifying that the record they have made is true. Then the general church recorder can enter the record on the general church book, with the certificates and all the attending

74. *History of the Church*, 7:142.

witnesses, with his own statement that he verily believes the above statement and records to be true, from his knowledge of the general character and appointment of those men by the church. And when this is done on the general church book, the record shall be just as holy, and shall answer the ordinance just the same as if he had seen with his eyes and heard with his ears, and made a record of the same on the general church book. (D&C 128:2-5)

Even before the Prophet gave these instructions, recorders had been appointed in different areas to keep records of baptisms for the dead. For example, John Patten, a member of the High Council in the Iowa Stake, was the recorder for baptisms for the dead in Iowa, beginning in July 1841.[75] The fact that some proxy baptismal records exist for 1840 and 1841 is evidence of a system of recording, though incomplete and certainly not uniform. These 1840-41 baptismal records simply give the name of the deceased individual, the name of the proxy, and their relationship (father, mother, wife, husband, nephew, friend, and so on). The most important changes brought about as a result of these letters were: (1) the requirement that two additional witnesses be present to attest to each baptism, and (2) the requirement that the recording system be more detailed, complete, and uniform.

Immediately following the receipt of these letters, each ward appointed its own recorder of baptisms. For example, Jonathan Hale, bishop of the Nauvoo Ninth Ward, was also "appointed recorder for baptisms for the dead, August 1842" for his ward. In July 1843, Joseph M. Cole, George Walker, and J. A. W. Andrews were appointed to the same duty in their respective wards by Nauvoo Stake President William Marks.[76] James Sloan, the Nauvoo City Recorder, was given charge of the general record of baptisms for the dead. Upon his appointment he drafted what appears to be a model certificate for recording baptisms. Note the precision with which it complies to the requirements set forth in Joseph's letters:

I certify that upon the day of the date hereof, I saw and heard the following Baptisms take place in the Font in the Lord's House in the City of Nauvoo, Illinois; to wit [blank] and that [blank] and [blank] were present as Witnesses to said Baptisms, and also that said Record has been made by me, and is true.

Dated September 1842

Recorder of Baptisms for the Dead appointed for the first tithing Ward of the City of Nauvoo, Illinois.

---

75. Joseph Smith's journal, Journal History, 12 July 1841. There were several Mormon settlements west of the Mississippi River across from Nauvoo in Iowa.

76. *History of the Church*, 5:522.

I certify that from my knowledge of the general Character of [blank], whose name is subscribed to the foregoing certificate, and also of his appointment by the Church of Jesus Christ of Latter-day Saints as a Recorder of Baptisms for the Dead for the tithing Ward number one in the City of Nauvoo, I verily believe the above Statement and Record to be true.

Dated September 1842

James Sloan general Church Recorder, and also of Baptisms for the Dead in the Church of Jesus Christ of Latter-day Saints.[77]

Thomas Bullock later served as the general recorder for baptisms. His 1845 journal indicates that he copied the records of baptisms for the dead into a general record which he "sent off ... to be bound."[78] John D. Lee who served as a temple recorder in 1845-46, described the procedure followed by these Nauvoo recorders of proxy baptisms:

[A] clerk must make a record of it, and two witnesses must be present, and the name of the person baptized and for whom he or she was baptized, and the date of baptism, together with the name of the officiating elder, and the name of the clerk and witnesses entered in the register or record. All persons who are baptized must also be confirmed. Male and female alike pass through the same ceremony, and the fact entered in the record kept for that purpose.[79]

Temporary Floor Laid

In September 1842 while Joseph was still in hiding, he received a visit from Reynolds Cahoon of the temple committee. During the course of the visit, Joseph "requested Brother Cahoon, as soon as he should return home, to call upon the Saints to put a temporary floor in the temple, that we might be enabled to hold our meetings within its sacred walls."[80]

On 23 October during the regular Sabbath services, the committee "laid before the Saints the propriety and advantages of laying a temporary floor on the Temple that the brethren could henceforth meet in the Temple to worship instead of meeting in the grove." They indicated that "a large raft of pine lumber had late-

77. Loose certificate inserted inside front cover of Baptisms for the Dead, Book C, September 1842-June 1843, microfilm of holograph, LDS Church Family History Library, Salt Lake City.

78. Thomas Bullock, "Journal of Thomas Bullock, 31 August 1845 to 5 July 1846," edited by Gregory R. Knight, *BYU Studies* 31 (Winter 1991): 32.

79. John D. Lee, *Mormonism Unveiled: or the Life and Confession of the Late Mormon Bishop John D. Lee* (St. Louis: Bryan, Brand, & Co., 1877), 168-69.

80. George D. Smith, *An Intimate Chronicle*, 536.

ly arrived and was now laying in the river at this place. They requested all the brethren who had teams to turn out and with their teams, assist in hauling the lumber to the Temple."[81] The committee assigned wards to haul wood to the site from Monday to Thursday, then "requested all the carpenters to come together on Thursday to prepare the timbers for the first floor of the Temple, and all the brethren who could, to assemble on Friday and Saturday and lay a temporary floor and prepare seats inside the walls of the Temple."[82] William Clayton recorded:

> Accordingly, when Monday came we had a cheering assemblage of wagons, horses, oxen and men who began with zeal and gladness to pull the raft to pieces and haul it up to the Temple. This scenery has continued to the present date and the expectations of the committee more than realized.
>
> On Thursday we had a large assemblage of carpenters, joiners &c. who succeeded in preparing the lumber and laying the joists preparatory to laying the temporary floor and fixing seats etc.
>
> This day a large number of brethren were on the ground and commenced their operations and whilst we are writing they are busy at work and will soon have all things prepared for the comfort and convenience of the Saints.[83]

On Friday evening, 28 October, Reynolds Cahoon reported that "the work is completed and the seats etc. formed ready for meeting next Sabbath." Joseph Smith declared, "This day the brethren finished laying the temporary floor, and seats in the Temple, and its appearance is truly pleasant and cheering. The exertions of the brethren during the past week to accomplish this thing are truly praiseworthy."[84]

The *Niles Register* of Baltimore, Maryland, noted that the temple was "progressing by the voluntary labor of the Saints, who turn out with their teams, tools, etc, to aid in its construction. The timbers for the first floor of the Temple were thus laid."[85]

---

81. Jessee, *The Papers of Joseph Smith*, 2:488. The grove was a clearing on the hill near the temple where meetings were frequently held. This flooring was evidently planking that had been cut from logs floated down the Black River in Wisconsin to Church-owned sawmills, also on the Black River, then transported on log rafts down the Mississippi River to Nauvoo. Apparently the cut lumber was dry enough for immediate use by this method.

82. William Clayton, "The Temple of God in Nauvoo," *Times and Seasons* 4 (15 November 1841): 10.

83. Ibid.

84. *History of the Church*, 5:180-81.

85. "Mormons," *Niles National Register*, 10 December 1842, 4, microfilm, Lee Library. This paper, published by William Ogden Niles in Baltimore, Maryland, takes unusually frequent notice of happenings in Nauvoo for so distant a paper. Articles on the Mormons, Joseph Smith, and the temple appeared at least once a month from 1842 to 1844.

On Sunday, 30 October, the first meeting was held on the temporary floor and seats. "This day the saints met to worship in the Temple and notwithstanding its largeness it was well filled. It had been expected that president Joseph would address them, but he sent word that he was so sick that he could not meet with them; consequently E[lde]r John Taylor delivered a discourse."[86]

From this date, many gatherings of the Saints were held on this platform in the unfinished temple. Charlotte Haven, a nonmember visiting in Nauvoo, wrote to her mother in New Hampshire on 3 January 1843:

> I know, dear Mother, you would be highly amused were you now to look from our parlor window at the crowd of people that are passing from their devotions in the Temple. As that edifice has neither roof nor floor, preaching is held there only on pleasant Sundays. Then planks are laid loosely over the joists and some boards are placed for seats, but not half enough to accommodate the people; so men, women, and children, take with them chairs, benches, stools, etc. They are now returning with them.[87]

Pleas for Increased Faithfulness

Throughout the five and a half years of the construction, Church authorities and the temple committee unwaveringly and consistently urged the temple as a priority. They used every opportunity, both at the pulpit and in print, to campaign for greater commitment. Dozens of articles published in Church papers during that period alternately lauded the faithful, warned the disobedient, and prodded everyone to sacrifice more, as these quotations show:

> Joseph Smith, 2 May 1842: Never since the foundation of this church was laid, have we seen manifested a greater willingness to comply with the requisitions of Jehovah; a more ardent desire to do the will of God; more strenuous exertions used; or greater sacrifices made, than there has been since the Lord said, "Let the Temple be built by the tithing of my people." It seemed as though the spirit of enterprise, philanthropy, and obedience rested simultaneously upon old and young; and brethren and sisters, boys and girls, and even strangers, who were not in the church, united with an unprecedented liberality in the accomplishment of this great work; nor could the widow, in many instances, be prevented, out of her scanty pittance, from throwing in her two mites.

---

86. Jessee, *The Papers of Joseph Smith*, 2:490.
87. Charlotte Haven, "A Girl's Letters from Nauvoo," *Overland Monthly* 16 (December 1890): 624.

We feel at this time to tender to all, old and young, both in the church and out of it, our unfeigned thanks for their unprecedented liberality, kindness, diligence, and obedience which they have so opportunely manifested on the present occasion.[88]

Temple committee, 1 September 1842: As many false reports are circulated to delay the building of the Temple of God at Nauvoo, we take this public method of stating that the saints are constantly engaged in rearing this great house for their salvation, by tithing and donations according to the commandments; and in order that the work may progress more speedily; we call upon the churches abroad and near by, to bring or send us their tithes or donations, that we may be enabled to go on prosperously and finish it in an acceptable time to the Lord. The work hands upon this house need provisions and clothes, and the brethren have these things and other means, and can, if they will help us. Brethren remember the commands of the Lord and help fulfill them.[89]

Joseph Smith, 1 October 1842: It behooves us as [God's] people to use the most untiring diligence, and to exert all our energies in the accomplishment of an object so desirable for us to attend to; and so pregnant with importance to the inhabitants of this city.... This is a commandment which is binding, which is imperative upon all God's people, and if we consider ourselves his people, we shall feel ourselves bound under the strongest obligations ... and as the building of the Temple is principally depending upon the tenth day's labor of the inhabitants of this place, when many are slack, as has been the case of late, it has a great tendency to retard the work—to dispirit those who are actively engaged, and who feel zealous in the work, and to derange very materially the plans and designs of the committee.

The committee find themselves very much perplexed in consequence of the brethren not coming forward as usual from their different wards, to perform their tenth of labor. They state ... that unless strenuous exertions are immediately made, and the brethren come up promptly to their duty, the work will be greatly retarded, and perhaps have to stop.... Brethren, such things ought not to be.[90]

The Quorum of the Twelve, February 1842: The first great object before us, and the saints generally, is to help forward the completion of the Temple and the Nauvoo House ... and if there are those among you, who have more than they need for the gathering, and for assisting the destitute, who desire to gather with

88. Joseph Smith, "The Temple," *Times and Seasons* 3 (2 May 1842): 775-76.

89. Temple Committee, "To the Churches Abroad and Nearby," *Times and Seasons* 3 (1 September 1842): 909.

90. Joseph Smith, "The Temple," *Times and Seasons* 3 (1 October 1842): 938.

them they cannot make a more acceptable offering unto the Lord, than by appropriating towards the building of his Temple.[91]

Parley P. Pratt, October 1841: There is one thing to which we would call the special attention of the saints at this time, and that is, the BUILDING OF THE TEMPLE at Nauvoo.... A few individuals in England, have already sent some twenty-eight or thirty pounds, for this purpose, by the two last ships, and we hope the exertion will be more general hereafter.[92]

Quorum of the Twelve, 2 May 1842: Although all things are more prosperous concerning the Temple than at any former period, yet the Saints must not suppose that all is done, or that they can relax their exertions and the work go on. It is a great work that God has required of His people, and it will require long and unwearied diligence to accomplish it; and redoubled diligence will be necessary with all, to get the building enclosed before another winter, so that the joiner can be employed during the cold weather; and we would again call upon all the Saints abroad to unite in making their deposits in banks known to be good and safe, and forward their certificate to the Trustee in Trust, as speedily as possible; when trusty men are not coming immediately to this place who can bring your offerings. All will want the privileges and blessings of the sanctuary, when it is completed; and all can have their wishes; but they can obtain them only by faithfulness and diligence in striving to build.

While there are those who of their abundance have built unto themselves fine houses, and who ride in fine carriages and on horseback, and regale themselves with the good things of the land, and at the same time they have left the Lord's house untouched, or, if touched at all, have touched it so lightly as scarce to leave the print of their little finger: their reward will be according to their deeds, and unless they speedily repent, and come up with their abundance to the help of the Lord, they will find in the end that they have no part nor lot in this matter; their gold and silver will become cankered, their garments moth eaten, and they will perish in their own slothfulness and idolatry, leaving none to mourn their absence.

But, brethren, the Temple will be built. There are hundreds and thousands who stand ready to sacrifice the last farthing they possess on the earth rather than have the building of the Lord's house delayed, all while this spirit prevails no power beneath the heavens can hinder its progress: but we desire you all to help with the ability which God has given you; that you may all share the blessings which will distil from heaven to earth through this consecrated channel.

---

91. "An Epistle of the Twelve," *Millennial Star* 2 (February 1842): 146.
92. Parley P. Pratt, untitled announcement, *Millennial Star* 2 (October 1841): 105-6.

This is not all. It will be in vain for us to build a place where the Son of Man may lay his head, and leave the cries of the widow and the fatherless, unheard by us, ascending up to the orphan's God and widow's Friend. It is in vain, we cry Lord, Lord, and do not the things our Lord hath commanded; to visit the widow, the fatherless, the sick, the lame, the blind, the destitute, and minister to their necessities; and it is but reasonable that such cases should be found among a people who have but recently escaped the fury of a relentless mob on the one hand, and gathered from the half-starved population of the scattered nations on the other.[93]

Charges Against the Temple Committee

Early in the fall of 1842, rumors began to circulate "to the effect that the committee was not making a righteous disposition of property consecrated to the building of the temple, and there appeared to be some dissatisfaction among the laborers on account of these reports."[94] Joseph Smith gathered the committee members, Clayton, and Bishop Newel K. Whitney together on 1 October to settle the dispute. Clayton wrote of this meeting:

After carefully examining the books and making inquiry into the entire proceeding of the committee, President Joseph expressed himself as being perfectly satisfied with the committee and its work.

The books were balanced between the Trustee-in-Trust and the committee, and also each individual account was carefully examined.

The wages of the Trustee-in-Trust, the members of the committee and the recorder were also fixed by the President; and it was agreed that each should receive two dollars per day for his services.

The parties separated perfectly satisfied, and the President said that he would have a notice published stating that he had examined the accounts and was satisfied.[95]

The notice, published on 15 October, read:

This may certify that President Joseph Smith, the Trustee in Trust, for the Temple, called upon the Temple Committee on the 1st inst. to present their books and accounts for examination, and to give account of the work at the Temple. After carefully and attentively examining and comparing their books

---

93. "An Epistle of the Twelve," *Times and Seasons* 3 (2 May 1842): 767.

94. George D. Smith, *An Intimate Chronicle*, 536.

95. Ibid., 536-37.

and accounts, the Trustee expressed himself well satisfied with the labors and proceedings of the Committee, and ordered that this be published in the Times and Seasons, that the saints may know the fact and be thereby encouraged to double their exertions and forward means to roll on the building of the Temple in Nauvoo.[96]

Further difficulties arose a month later in November. The stonecutters preferred charges against Reynolds Cahoon and Elias Higbee of the temple committee for "oppressive and unchristian conduct ... an unequal distribution of provisions, iron, steel, tools, etc.; also alleging that favors were shown by the committee to the sons of its members."[97] On 28 November, Joseph Smith called the parties involved to a meeting at his house. The Prophet's journal contains an account of the proceedings:

W[illiam] Law [and] Pres[iden]t Hyrum acted as council for the defendants and E[lde]r H. G. Sherwood[98] on the part of the accusers. The hearing of testimony lasted until about 4 o'clock at which time the meeting adjourned for half an hour. On coming together again Pres[iden]t Hyrum addressed the brethren at some length showing the important responsibility of the Committee also the many difficulties they had to contend with. He advised the brethren to have charity one with another and be united etc. E[lde]r Sherwood replied to Pres[iden]t Hyrum's remarks. Pres[iden]t H[yrum] explained some remarks before made. E[lde]r W[illia]m Law made a few pointed remarks after which President Joseph arose and gave his decision which was that the Committee stand as before. He likewise showed the brethren that he was responsible to the State for a faithful performance of his office as sole Trustee-in-Trust etc. The Temple Committee were responsible to him and had given bonds to him to the amount of $12,000 for a faithful discharge of all duties devolving upon them as a Committee etc. The trial did not conclude until about 9 o clock P. M.[99]

William Clayton, in his record of this event, commented that Joseph "gave much good instruction to all parties correcting the errors of each in kindness." He summarized: "The decision was marked by judgment and wisdom and cannot fail to produce a good effect."[100]

96. William Clayton, "To the Saints in Nauvoo and Scattered Abroad," Times and Seasons 3 (15 October 1842): 957.

97. Ibid., 537-38.

98. Henry Garlic Sherwood, baptized in 1832, was the clerk of the Nauvoo High Council and also a city marshal in Nauvoo.

99. Jessee, The Papers of Joseph Smith, 2:494.

100. George D. Smith, An Intimate Chronicle, 537-38.

The Temple Inspires Poets and Artists

The temple inspired literary descriptions, poetry, and art.[101] In May 1842, Lyman Littlefield, a member of the Church in Nauvoo, wrote a rhapsodic description of Nauvoo contrasting "the gaudy palaces where aristocracy sits gorged in the lap of affluence," with the simple majesty of the temple rising above the Mississippi. He looked forward to the day "when its magnificent walls of grandest architect and most skillful masonry, will post their ponderous and polished fronts upon that beautiful eminence, and become the beacon of Zion to sentinel the enchanted land."[102]

The temple inspired several poems. Some were composed for particular occasions such as laying the capstone in 1845.[103] This poem by W. W. Phelps was motivational, encouraging the Saints to greater efforts:

Ye servants that so many prophets foretold,
Should labor for Zion and not for the gold,
Go into the field ere the sun dries the dew,
And reap for the kingdom of God at Nauvoo.

Go carry glad tidings, that all may attend,
While God is unfolding "the time of the end"
And say to all nations, whatever you do,
Come, build up the Temple of God at Nauvoo.

Go say to the Islands that wait for his law,
Prepare for that glory the prophets once saw,
And bring on your gold and your precious things, too,
As tithes for the Temple of God at Nauvoo.

Go say to the great men, who boast of a name;
To kings and their nobles, all born unto fame,
Come, bring on your treasures, antiquities, too
And honor the Temple of God at Nauvoo.

Proclaim the acceptable year of the Lord,
For now we have prophets to bring forth his word,
And reveal to the church what the world never knew,
By faith in the Temple of God at Nauvoo.

---

101. See Stanley B. Kimball, "Nauvoo as Seen by Artists and Travelers," *Improvement Era* 69 (January 1966): 38-43.

102. Lyman O. Littlefield, "Sights from the Lone Tree," *Times and Seasons* 3 (15 November 1841): 587.

103. William Pitt and W. W. Phelps each composed works for the capstone ceremony. See chap. 8.

To spirits in prison the gospel is sent,
For on such a mission the Savior once went;
And we are baptiz'd for the dead surely, too,
In the font at the Temple of God at Nauvoo.

Up; watch! for the strange work of God has begun,
And now things are opening, now, under the sun:
And knowledge on knowledge will burst to our view,
From Seers in the Temple of God at Nauvoo.[104]

One of the most interesting poems about the temple was composed by beloved Mormon poetess Eliza R. Snow. In her poem "The Temple of God," composed in the summer of 1841, she captured the kinship the Saints felt with the children of Israel who built the tabernacle of Moses and the sense they had of fulfilling biblical prophecy by building the temple:

Lo, the Savior is coming, the prophets declare
The times are fulfilling; O Zion, prepare!
The Savior is coming: but where shall he come?
Will he find in the palace of princes, a home?
No! O no, in his temple he'll surely attend;
But O where, is the "temple," where Christ shall descend?

Since the ancient apostles and christians [sic] are dead
The heavens have been seal'd—they are brass o'er the head
Of a world of professors, presuming to claim
A belief in the gospel of Jesus' blest name;
Who profess to believe it, yet boldly deny
Its most prominent feature, the gifts from on high,
And deny that the word of the Lord should come forth,
As it anciently did, to the saints upon earth!
Then, to whom shall Jehovah his purpose declare?
And by whom shall the people be taught to prepare
For the coming of Jesus—a "temple" to build,
That the ancient predictions may all be fulfil'd?
When a Moses of old, was appointed to rear
A place, where the glory of God should appear;
He receiv'd from the hand of the high King of Kings,
A true model a pattern of heavenly things.
The eternal Jehovah will not condescend,

---

104. W. W. Phelps, "The Temple of God at Nauvoo," *Times and Seasons* 3 (15 June 1842): 830.

His pure wisdom, with human inventions to blend;
And a temple—a house, to the name of the Lord,
Must be built, by commandment, and form'd of his word.
Or he will not accept it, nor angels come down
In the light of His presence, the service to crown,
O! then who, upon earth, uninstructed, will dare
Build a house to the Lord? But the scriptures declare
That Messiah is coming—the time's drawing nigh!
Hark! a scheme is divulg'd—'twas concerted on high;
With divine revelation the saints have been bles't—
Every doubt has subsided—the mind is at rest.

The great God, has establish'd, in mercy and grace
The "strange work," that precedes the concluding of days—
The pure gospel of Jesus again is restor'd;
By its power, thro' the prophet, the word of the Lord
Is again coming forth; and intelligence rolls
From the upper eternity, cheering our souls.
"Build a house to my name," the Eternal has said
To a people by truth's holy principles led:
"Build a house to my name, where my saints may be blest;
Where my glory and pow'r shall in majesty rest,"
When its splendor will gladden the heavenly choir,
And high Gabriel's own hand shall awaken the lyre.

Oh, ye saints, be admonish'd by Time's rolling c[ar;
It is rapidly onward! Hear, ye from afar!
Come, and bring in your treasures your wealth from abroad:
Come, and build up the city and Temple of God:
A stupendous foundation already is laid,
And the work is progressing—withhold not your aid.
When you gather to Zion, come, not "looking back"—
Let your hearts not be faint—let your hands not be slack,
For great honor, and glory, and grace, and renown,
Shall appear on their heads, whom the Savior will crown;
And the Savior is coming, the prophets declare,
The times are fulfilling—to Zion repair:
Let us "watch and be sober"—the period is near
When the Lord in his temple, will surely appear.[105]

---

105. Eliza R. Snow, "The Temple of God," *Times and Seasons,* 2 (2 August 1841): 493-94.

Even nonmembers were moved to write. One visitor exclaimed in verse:

Though wild and visionary schemes, their doctrine seems to me,
Yet on that temple, when I gaz'd involuntarily,
Escaped my heart a prayer to God, sincere and fervent too,
That he will bless the people of the young and fair Nauvoo.[106]

The temple also inspired other artistic endeavors. During the 1840s, at least four painters created enormous panoramas of the Mississippi River and the cities along its shores. These panoramas, some measuring one mile in length, were taken to East Coast cities and to Europe where they were exhibited to the delight of huge audiences. Frequently included among the scenes chosen for their works was Nauvoo, dominated by its rising temple. The four known panoramists were John Rowson Smith, Samuel B. Stockwell, Leon de Pomarede, and Henry Lewis, each of whom depicted the temple in 1848, just prior to its destruction by fire.[107] Although Smith's panorama did not survive, an engraving of his view of the Nauvoo Temple was published in 1849 in *Graham's American Monthly Magazine*.[108] He depicts the temple with the baptismal font standing outside but explains, "in the basement is its real situation."[109]

Henry Lewis recorded his impressions of the edifice in his journal on 16 June 1848:

Taking into consideration the circumstances under which it was built it is a wonderful building and considering too that it is of no particular style it does not in
the least offend the eye by its uniqueness like most all innovations from old estab-

106. Laura, a visitor (pseud.), "Nauvoo," *Nauvoo Neighbor* 2 (16 October 1844): 6.

107. John Rowson Smith (1810-64), was born in Boston and began his career as a painter in the 1830s in Philadelphia. Samuel B. Stockwell (1813-54) was also from Boston. Leon de Pomarede was born in Tarbes, France, in about 1807 and studied painting in France, Italy, and Germany before coming to the United States in 1830. Henry Lewis (1819-unknown) was a self-taught painter from England. The Nauvoo portions of the four panoramas were produced between 1847 and 1848 and showed the completed temple.

108. "Mormon Temple, Nauvoo," *Graham's American Monthly Magazine*, 26 (April 1849): 257; photocopy of engraving and relevant excerpt from Smith's pamphlet in Perry Special Collections, Lee Library. The editors have added this explanatory note: "By permission of Mr. J. R. Smith, we have caused a view of the Mormon Temple at Nauvoo to be engraved from his splendid Panorama of the Mississippi, and we give the engraving in this number. As the building has been recently destroyed by fire, our engraving, the first ever published acquires additional value."

109. John Rowson Smith, *A Descriptive Pamphlet of Smith's Leviathan Panorama of the Mississippi River Now Exhibiting at Mason Hall Philadelphia* (Philadelphia: n.p., 1848), 3-4. This pamphlet is in the Lovejoy Library, Southern Illinois University, Edwardsville.

lished standards do.... It bears a nearer resemblance to the Byzantium or Roman Grecian style than any other although, the capitals and bases are entirely unique still the cornices are Grecian in part.[110]

In addition to the panoramists, others painted the temple. Joseph and Emma's youngest son, David Hyrum Smith, grew up in Nauvoo. He made paintings of several townscapes, including the temple and the Nauvoo House.[111]

One unusual piece of artistry inspired by the temple was a Staffordshireware plate. This piece of china, depicting the temple surrounded by the names of the members of the Quorum of the Twelve, was made in 1846 in England. The plates were marked with the name of "J. Twigg," the proprietor of a pottery in Kilnhurst, Yorkshire, England, during the mid-nineteenth century. Missionary Lucius Scovil, commissioned the work.[112]

---

110. Henry Lewis, Diary, 51-52, quoted in Joseph Earl Arrington, "Panorama Paintings in the 1840s of the Mormon Temple in Nauvoo," BYU Studies 22, no. 2 (Spring 1982): 202.

111. His painting of the Nauvoo House has been reproduced in Robert B. Flanders, Nauvoo: Kingdom on the Mississippi (Urbana: University of Illinois Press, 1965), 118.

112. Arthur H. Merritt, "A Postscript to American Churches Pictured on Old Blue China," New York Historical Society Quarterly 34, no. 1 (January 1950): 19-23.

Chapter 5

THE WORK CONTINUES:
JANUARY 1843 TO DECEMBER 1843

New Arrangements for Collecting Funds

April conference 1843 convened in the open air on the temporary floor of the temple. The *Times and Seasons* reported: "The foundation of the Temple was crowded to excess, with thousands of saints, whose faces beamed with gladness as they listened to the Prophet, and others who officiated at the conference. The walls were also covered and the ground outside, for some distance around the Temple."[1] Speaking to the congregation, Hyrum Smith reported caustically about a band of men who "pretend to be strong in the faith of the doctrine of the Latter-day Saints; but they are hypocrites ... and they hold that it is right to steal from any one who does not belong to the Church, provided they consecrate one-third of it to the building of the Temple. I wish to warn you all not to be duped by such men, for they are the Gadiantons of the last days."[2]

---

1. "Conference," *Times and Seasons* 4 (1 April 1843): 154. The issue, though dated 1 April, was released over a week late due to a paper shortage. It therefore included a brief report of the conference which concluded, "The minutes of the conference will be given in full, and most of the discourses." The minutes were published one month later in *Times and Seasons* 4 (1 May 1843): 180-85.

2. Joseph Smith, Jr., et al., *History of the Church of Jesus Christ of Latter-day Saints*, edited by B. H. Roberts (Salt Lake City: Deseret News Press, 6 vols. published 1902-12, Vol. 7 published 1932,

Among the most important issues addressed at the conference was the very familiar topic of collecting funds for the temple. No strict organization had been observed up to this point about appointing agents, and Joseph Smith explained the problems that had resulted: "It has been customary for any elder to receive moneys for the temple when he is traveling, but this system of things opens a wide field for every kind of imposition, as any man can assume the name of a Mormon elder, and gather his pockets full of money and go to Texas. Many complaints have come to me of money being sent that I have never received." He believed that "agents have had too great latitude to practice fraud, by receiving donations and never making report" and directed that "no money should ever be sent by any man except it be some one whom you have appointed as agent, and stop every other man from receiving moneys." The Prophet then proposed:

> The Twelve are the most suitable persons to perform this business; and I want the conference to devise some means to bind them as firm as the pillars of heaven, if possible. The Twelve were always honest, and it will do them no hurt to bind them.... I go in for binding up the Twelve, solid, putting them under bonds; and let this conference institute an order to this end, and that the traveling expenses of the agents shall not be borne out of the funds collected for building these houses, and let no man pay money or stock into the hands of the Twelve, except he transmit an account of the same immediately to the Trustee in Trust; and let no man but the Twelve have authority to act as agent for the temple and Nauvoo House.
>
> We cannot give an account to satisfy the people, on the church books, unless something is done. I propose that you send your moneys for the Temple by the Twelve, some one, or all; or some agent of your own choosing, and if you send by others, and the money is lost, 'tis lost to yourselves; I cannot be responsible for it.—Every thing that falls into my hands shall be appropriated to the very thing it was designed for.[3]

The conference voted to appoint the Twelve to receive funds for the temple and also voted that they should "give bonds for the safe delivery of all funds." W. W. Phelps then proposed to the conference that the Twelve also sign triplicate receipts for all donations.

1st printing), 5:332-33. Hyrum mentioned the names of David Holman and James Dunn in connection with these crimes. Holman (1808-unknown) joined the Church in 1837. His farm and house just outside of Nauvoo were burned by a mob in 1845. Dunn (1810-unknown) was a Seventy living in Nauvoo.

3. Joseph Smith, "Special Conference," Times and Seasons 4 (1 May 1843): 181-83.

Brigham Young objected, and said he should never give receipts for cash, except such as he put into his own pocket, for his own use; for it was calculated to make trouble hereafter, and there were better methods of transacting the business; and more safe for the parties concerned; that he wished this speculation to stop, and would do all in his power to put it down: To which the Twelve responded, amen. Elder Young asked if any one knew any thing against any one of the Twelve, any dishonesty; if they did, he wanted it exposed.[4]

Despite his objections to the receipts, Brigham and the Twelve agreed to being bonded for $2,000 each "previous to their going East, which bonds were filed in the office of the Trustee in Trust."[5] Brigham Young's bond, which is almost identical to those of the other Twelve reads:

Know all men by these presents, that we, Brigham Young and John M. Bernhisel, are held and firmly bound unto Joseph Smith, as sole trustee-in-trust for the Church of Jesus Christ of Latter-day Saints, in the penal sum of two thousand dollars, lawful money of the United States; for the payment of which sum, well and truly to be made, we bind ourselves, our heirs, assigns and administrators firmly by these presents.

Dated at Nauvoo, this 30th day of May, 1843.

The condition of the above obligation is such that the above bounden Brigham Young who has been appointed an agent to collect funds for the Nauvoo House Association and for the Temple now building in the city of Nauvoo, shall faithfully pay to the said trustee-in trust [Matt, hyphen missing in original before "trust"?] as aforesaid, all moneys that he may collect for either house, then this obligation be null and void, otherwise to remain in full force and virtue.

Signed, sealed and delivered the day and year first above written.[6]

Then Joseph Smith, in his role of trustee, signed a certificate of authority for each of the Twelve. Heber C. Kimball's certificate, dated 1 June 1843, read:

To all Saints and honorable men of the earth, greeting:

Dear brethren and friends: I, Joseph Smith, a servant of the Lord and trustee-in-trust for the Church of Jesus Christ of Latter-day Saints, do hereby certify that the bearer hereof, Heber C. Kimball, an elder and one of the Twelve Apostles of the Church of Jesus Christ of Latter-day Saints, has deposited with me his bond

4. Ibid., 183.

5. William Clayton, Journal, in Journal History of the Church of Jesus Christ of Latter-day Saints (chronology of typed entries and newspaper clippings, 1830-present), 9 October 1843, 2, LDS Church Archives.

6. *History of the Church*, 5:414. Bernhisel signed the bond as a witness.

and security to my full satisfaction, according to the resolution of the conference held in this city on the 6th day of April last. He therefore is recommended to all Saints and honorable people as a legal agent to collect funds for the purpose of building the Nauvoo House and temple of the Lord, confident that he will honor this high trust, as well as ardently fulfill his commission as a messenger of peace and salvation, as one of the Lord's noblemen, I can fervently say may the Lord clear his way before him and bless him and bless those that obey his teachings, whenever there are ears to hear and hearts to feel.

He is in the language of the Hebrews (Haura-ang-yeesh-rau-ale). The friend of Israel, and worthy to be received and entertained as a man of God; yea, he has, as had the ancient apostles (O logos o kalo) the good word, even the good word that leadeth unto eternal life. Laus Deus. Praise God. Wherefore brethren! and friends, while you have the assurance of the integrity, fidelity, and ability of this servant of the living God, trusting that your hearts and energies will be enlivened, and deeply engaged in the building of these houses, directed by revelation for the salvation of all Saints, and that you will not rest where you are, until all things are prepared before you, and you are gathered home with the rest of Israel to meet your God, I feel strong in the belief and have a growing expectation that you will not withhold any means in your power that can be used to accomplish this glorious work.

Finally as one that greatly desires the salvation of man, let me remind you all to strive with a godly zeal, for virtue, holiness and the commandments of the Lord. Be good, be wise, be just, be liberal and above all, be charitable always, abounding in good works. And may health, peace and the love of God our Father, and the grace of Jesus Christ our Lord be and abide with you all, is the sincere prayer of your devoted brother and friend in the everlasting gospel, Joseph Smith.[7]

William Clayton commented on these arrangements: "The wisdom of this order was soon manifest; for, although it was well understood and universally believed that the Twelve would invariably make correct returns, there were others who might not be so careful or scrupulous. And, inasmuch as members of this first quorum were required to give bonds, no other man could justly complain if he were brought under the same rule."[8]

Despite these measures, six months after the Prophet's death, the temple committee published a warning in the *Times and Seasons* that there were agents

7. Joseph Smith, Certificate of Authority for Heber C. Kimball, 1 June 1843, quoted in Helen Mar Kimball Smith Whitney, "Scenes and Incidents in Nauvoo," *Woman's Exponent* 11 (August 1882): 74. Brigham Young's certificate appears in *History of the Church* 5:416-417. For that of Wilford Woodruff, see Wilford Woodruff, *Wilford Woodruff's Journal, 1833-1898*, typescript, edited by Scott G. Kenny, 9 vols. (Midvale, UT: Signature Books, 1983-85), 2:237-238. Each has a similar wording.

8. George D. Smith, ed., *An Intimate Chronicle: The Journals of William Clayton* (Salt Lake City: Signature Books, 1995), 539.

"who are going round amongst the branches of the church to collect funds for the temple without authority" who kept "the property for their own individual benefit." The notice reminded the Saints "not to credit any man's testimony as to his being an agent unless he can shew written authority from us or the quorum of the Twelve." Even worse, "men who are not Latter day Saints, but on the contrary our most bitter enemies" had chosen this means of "gulling the churches and professing to be Mormons and agents to collect funds." He also counseled those in remote branches of the Church who wished to donate but who rarely saw an authorized agent:

> In such cases, when they want to send up their donations, let them do it by some man with whom they are well acquainted, and who they are well satisfied will do right, and carry their donations safe to its destination. And it would be well in all cases, where the brethren abroad send donations by authorized agents, to send a letter by mail (post paid,) to the trustees in trust, informing them of the facts, and by whom their donations were sent, etc., and a good man will not blame you for being thus careful, for the same law that guards your rights will guard his rights, and the rights of every man.

The temple committee, in the same article, also stated its intention "to publish the names of our agents in the '*Nauvoo Neighbor*' and '*Times and Seasons*,' which we consider to be safer and better than written authority, inasmuch as the latter can be 'forged,' but the former cannot, and the agents can carry a copy of the paper, having their authority with them wherever they go." The committee also requested the Saints not to give donations to agents who claimed they would return to Nauvoo and pay an amount in labor.[9]

Further Tensions with the Temple Committee

During 1843 several complaints were made against the temple committee. On 6 April during the opening session of the spring conference, Joseph Smith announced, "There has been [a] complaint against the Temple Committee for appropriating the Church funds to the benefit of their own children, to the neglect of others who need assistance more than they do."[10] William Clayton had

---

9. Ibid. These measures were later amended. Beginning in early 1845, agents were to carry "written authority from us [the Twelve] to which shall be attached the private seal of the Twelve and their names published as above stated. Those men that we shall select for agents will be men of honor, men of integrity and respectability, in whom we can confide, and who are responsible, and able, and willing to enter into bonds for the faithful performance of their duty." "An Epistle of the Twelve," *Times and Seasons* 6 (15 January 1845): 780.

10. Scott H. Faulring, ed., *An American Prophet's Record: The Diaries and Journals of Joseph Smith* (Salt Lake City: Signature Books, 1989), 345.

made this accusation, claiming that he was "able to prove by the books that Cahoon and Higbee have used property for their own families to the exclusion of others." Joseph suggested that a trial be held the following day. On the 7th, the conference reconvened and heard the charges against the committee. According to the minutes:

> William Clayton said: Some may expect I am going to be a means of the downfall of the Temple committee. It is not so; but I design to show that they have been partial. Elder Higbee has overrun the amount allowed by the trustees about one-fourth. Pretty much all Elder Higbee's son has received has been in money and store pay. Higbee's son has had nothing credited on his tithing. William F. Cahoon has paid all his tenth; the other sons of Cahoon have had nothing to their credit on tithing. The committee have had a great amount of store pay. One man, who is laboring continually, wanted twenty-five cents in store pay when his family were sick; but Higbee said he could not have it.... Alpheus Cutler said he did not know of any wrong he had done. If any one would show it, he would make it right. The conference voted him clear.
>
> Reynolds Cahoon said: This is not an unexpected matter for me to be called up. I do not want you to think I am perfect. Somehow or other, since Elder Cutler went up into the pine country, I have, from some cause been placed in very peculiar circumstances. I think I never was placed in so critical a position since I was born. When President Smith had goods last summer, we had better property; goods would not buy corn without some cash: instead of horses, etc., we took store pay. I have dealt out meal and flour to the hands to the last ounce, when I had not a morsel of meal, flour or bread left in my house. If the trustee, Brother Hyrum, or the Twelve, or all of them will examine and see if I have too much, it shall go freely. I call upon the brethren, if they have anything against me, to bring it forward and have it adjusted.... Reynolds Cahoon said, when Brother Cutler was gone, Brother Higbee kept the books, and they have found as many mistakes against Brother Higbee as in his favor.
>
> The conference then voted Cahoon clear.
>
> Elias Higbee said: I am not afraid or ashamed to appear before you. When I kept the books, I had much other business on my hands and made some mistakes. The conference voted in favor of Elder Higbee unanimously.[11]

During the week of the conference, a misunderstanding between the committee and William Weeks also came to the attention of the Prophet. Joseph Smith took quick steps to resolve this disagreement in favor of Weeks. On 6 April, Joseph's diary shows: "I gave a certificate to William Weeks to carry out my designs and the architecture of the Temple in Nauvoo, and that no person or persons shall

---

11. History of the Church, 5:337-38.

interfere with him or his plans in the building of the Temple."[12] A month later on 5 May, William Clayton wrote in his journal: "President Joseph told the Temple committee that he had a right to take away any property he chose from the Temple and they had no right to stand in the way. It was the people who had to dictate to him and not the committee. All the property he had belongs to the Temple and what he did was for the benefit of the Temple and the committee had no authority only as they receive it from him."[13] No details of these particular grievances have been preserved, but apparently the chronic shortness of goods in an environment of continuing poverty exacerbated dissatisfactions. At October conference only a few months later, "charges were again preferred against the temple committee, and a public investigation was entered into; and it was again voted that the members of the committee should be retained in their standing."[14]

Further Logging Operations

Meanwhile, work had continued at the "pineries" in Wisconsin, supplying the lumber for construction in Nauvoo. By the summer of 1843, the small group that had initially been sent to operate the mill had established a semipermanent settlement with several frame houses for members of the company, which had reached about 150 in number.[15]

The year 1842 had been a challenging one for the new enterprise. The workmen managed to send to Nauvoo "a large raft of first-rate pine lumber" by July 1842, which reportedly "brightened the prospects of the work very much."[16] On 6 July 1842, "two keel boats, sloop-rigged, and laden with provisions and apparatus necessary for the occasion, and manned with fifty of the brethren, started [from Nauvoo] this morning on an expedition to the upper Mississippi, among the pineries, where they can join those already there, and erect mills, saw boards and plank, make shingles, hew timber, and return next spring with rafts."[17] As a result of this infusion of manpower and supplies, a "raft of about 90,000 feet of boards and 24,000 cubic feet of lumber" arrived at Nauvoo on 13 October.[18] This lumber was used to construct the temporary floor in the temple just days later. (See chap. 4.)

---

12. Ibid., 5:353.

13. George D. Smith, *An Intimate Chronicle*, 100.

14. Ibid., 539.

15. Allen Joseph Stout, Journal, 1815-89, typescript, 17, L. Tom Perry Special Collections, Harold B. Lee Library, Brigham Young University, Provo, Utah. Stout (1815-89) was baptized on 22 April 1838 in Missouri and was a bodyguard to Joseph Smith. This document begins with an autobiographical reminiscence, then continues with daily entries.

16. Journal History, 14 February 1842.

17. *History of the Church*, 5:57.

18. Journal History, 13 October 1842.

However, when Joseph Smith sent Bishop George Miller to Wisconsin later in October, the operation was "in debt $3,000, and the amount of lumber so little that our work was almost brought to a stand."[19] Miller's task was to extricate the venture from debt. He had a lawsuit pending against Jacob Spaulding, the owner of several mills in Wisconsin, but the two men settled their differences in late 1842 by swapping the old sawmill, which Miller described as "of little or no value" for a new mill that Spaulding had just constructed.[20]

About a hundred workmen stayed at Black River during the winter of 1842-43 and endured snow that reached depths of twenty-one feet. After the spring thaw, Miller, accompanied by a few workmen, shepherded "a raft of 50,000 feet of pine lumber for the Temple and Nauvoo House" downriver to Nauvoo, arriving 12 May 1843.[21] Only thirteen days later, Miller returned to the pineries. Joseph Holbrook, who traveled with Miller, remembered this summer:

> I left Nauvoo for the Black River pinery with Bishop George Miller.... We went as far as Prairie La Cross on the Mississippi by the steamboat, then took it on foot for 100 miles up the Black River. There being no regular trail we could find, we were lost some two days, but at length found ourselves within 40 miles of the mills on the Black River Falls... . The river being high and the current strong, we were forced to bushwhack[22] our way by taking hold [of a] bush at the bow of each boat and running back to the stern and so continuing through the day. We were [sic] 25 miles per day. After arriving at the mills, all hands were employed in rafting logs to the saw mills and rafting lumber, shingle[s], square timber, etc., for about six weeks when we had a raft of 150,000 feet.... Brother Cummingham was drowned this summer above the mills. In rafting logs, he got in a whirl in the river and was seen no more. I returned with Bishop Miller to Nauvoo on the raft and arrived at Nauvoo July 8, 1843.[23]

On 12 July 1843, the *Nauvoo Neighbor* reported this arrival:

> A large raft of pine lumber from the pinery of Wisconsin, arrived in this city on Monday last. It contained about 157,000 feet of boards, etc. for the Nauvoo House,

19. George Miller, *Correspondence of Bishop George Miller with the Northern Islander from His First Acquaintance with Mormonism Up to Near the Close of His Life, 1855*, compiled by Wingfield Watson (Burlington, WI: Wingfield Watson, 1916), 10, 15.

20. Ibid.

21. *History of the Church*, 5:386.

22. Allen Stout, Journal, 17, indicated that at times they poled (used long poles to push off the river bottom) and cordelled (pulled themselves using ropes) their way up the river.

23. Joseph Holbrook, Autobiography, 1871, typescript, 58, Perry Special Collections, Lee Library. Holbrook (1806-85), a New York native, was baptized 6 January 1833.

Temple, and other buildings. This is the second raft, which has come down this season, expressly for the above mentioned houses, and, with those already landed by
traders, makes quite a respectable lot of lumber, for the use of the "beloved city."[24]

The amount of lumber including the sawed shingles totaled 170,000. He
reported that the raft he brought to Nauvoo "was all sawed [in Wisconsin] in two
weeks and brought down in two more; says he has bought all the claims on those mills
for $12,000 payable in lumber at the mills in three years, one third already paid for.
Two saws did this job. Chance for as many mills as they may have a mind to build, and
every saw can run five thousand feet per day, year round. Two saws now running, can
deliver 157,000 every fortnight."[25] By midsummer of 1843, the pinery operation was
clearly recovering from the financial struggles it had faced the previous year.

Pausing for barely two days in Nauvoo, Miller made his third trip of the season to the Black River sawmill, departing on 20 July with $290 that Joseph Smith
gave him "for the expedition" and accompanied by "about one hundred fifty persons
... consisting of men, women, and children," including Apostle Lyman Wight and
his family.[26] The group reached the mill on 4 August 1843.[27] Allen Stout indicated
that those in the camp attempted to live according to the laws of consecration and
stewardship. He wrote to his brother Hosea:

---

24. "Lumber," *Nauvoo Neighbor* 1 (12 July 1843): 4. As this article mentions, the Church also
purchased lumber from other timber merchants who stopped at Nauvoo. For example, on 1 May
1845 Brigham Young among others, purchased $1,600 of lumber from one such trader and "gath-
ered teams to draw it to the Temple." Journal History, 1 May 1845, 1.

25. *History of the Church*, 5:512. Although Miller reports his arrival date at 18 July, this shipment
was the same lumber that he and Stout had brought down together, arriving probably on 8 June. The
date is in questions since the *Nauvoo Neighbor's* statement that it arrived "Monday" would have
dated the arrival to 11 June instead of 8 June. This difference is probably not significant; but given the
anxiety for more building materials, the June date fits the known facts better than the July date.

26. Ibid., 5:515. Lyman Wight, Journal, quoted in Heman C. Smith, *History of the Reorganized
Church of Jesus Christ of Latter Day Saints*, 7 vols. (Independence, MO: Herald House, 1903-14; 2d
printing, 1967), 2:649-50. Wight wrote: "I was busy .... making preparations to move my family to the
lumber country in Wisconsin Territory, on Black River, distance from this place about five hundred
miles.... I accordingly started on the 22d of July, with my family, and about one hundred and fifty persons besides, consisting of men, women, and children, with no other purpose in view only to procure
lumber to build the temple, the Nauvoo House, and to assist in building up the city of Nauvoo."

27. George Miller was not completely pleased with this large group and later (1855) wrote that
Joseph and Hyrum Smith had privately arranged with him to include Lyman Wight in the company to
get him out of Nauvoo—he "had become wholly disqualified for business of any kind, in consequence
of his indulgence in a habit that he was occasionally addicted to." Wight was assigned to "gather up
a company of young men and families to go with me to the pineries. Lyman readily agreed to enter
into the arrangement, and forthwith raised quite a crowd ready for the undertaking, a number of wid-
ows and children among them, that we really supposed would be a great encumbrance to our estab-

> We have gone into the whole law of God on Black River that is every man has given a schedule of his property to the bishop and we have all things common according to the law in the Book of Covenants every man has his own goods to do what he pleases with the thing is we are on an equality [each] man ... labours alike, eats, drinks, wears alike but at the same time he lives to himself and at his own control.[28]

Miller returned to Nauvoo on 25 September with the report that they had had to leave the last raft behind for the winter as "the water in Black River [was] so low that they could not get their raft into the Mississippi River."[29] He was dismayed to discover that

> a great deal of the lumber that we had (the last two seasons of toil and sacrifice) made for the temple and Nauvoo House had, to my great mortification, been used for other purposes than those intended. The Temple Committee said that the workmen must needs have houses, and they had to pay their men. But the truth of the case was, that that committee had become house builders; they were not alone content to have fresh eggs to set themselves, but they wanted eggs to set all their numerous brood of chickens, and that it was really convenient to use the material provided for the Nauvoo House (as its operations were temporarily suspended,) as in like manner the temple materials also, as we had in common such productive mills in the pinery.[30]

Joseph Smith soothed the outraged Miller: "Joseph told me to be content, and that he would see by and by that all would be made right."[31] Obviously it still rankled years later.

The Mormon efforts in the pineries of Wisconsin continued during the next summer, with at least two more rafts reaching Nauvoo before the assassinations of Joseph and Hyrum Smith in late June 1844 threw the Wisconsin missionaries into turmoil. The first raft, which contained 87,000 feet, arrived late on 5 July, and the second, a batch of nearly 68,000 feet, reached the city on 16 July.[32] Then, under the leadership of the Quorum of the Twelve, lumber operations recommenced and

---

lishment, but Lyman persisted in taking them, as they had to be cared for and fed, and I was the proper person to do it; and furthermore that they would earn their living by cooking, washing and mending for the men, and making their clothes." Miller, Correspondence, 15.

28. Allen Joseph Stout, Letter to Hosea Stout, Wisconsin Territory, 13 September 1843, microfilm of holograph, LDS Church Archives. What Stout calls "the whole law of God" refers to consecration and stewardship and was later known as "the United Order" or the "Order of Enoch."

29. *History of the Church*, 6:37.

30. Miller, Correspondence, 15.

31. Ibid.

32. Journal History, 16 July 1844; Andrew Jenson, "Nauvoo Temple," *Historical Record: A Monthly Periodical Devoted Exclusively to Historical, Biographical, Chronological and Statistical Matters* 8 (July 1886): 866.

continued through the early months of 1845. Sometime prior to March 1845, Lyman Wight, disenchanted with Brigham Young's claim to Church leadership, sold the mills and moved to Texas with 150 followers. Because of the continued need for lumber Miller continued well into the summer to travel up and down the river looking for rafts of lumber to direct to Nauvoo. Miller, writing to his fellow bishop Newel K. Whitney on 28 April 1845, summarized his efforts to obtain lumber:

D[ea]r Sir

I hasten to lay before you the present prospects of getting Lumber. I am turning all the lumber I can see to Nauvoo. They all ask from 12 to 15 dollars per thousand. There was a very large raft passed here last night I could not get on it but the bearer of this letter says he will overtake them and turn [them] to Nauvoo. And I shall continue to send all I can see, or otherwise influence [to go to] our place. I shall leave [on] the first boat going up, and not stop until I get logs to make the thick lumber. The course I am taking will land all the lumber at our place.... I do not expect to pay out any money except for the logs and my expenses you may therefore make your calculations accordingly.... You shall hear from me every opportunity.[33]

Miller's strenuous efforts produced several rafts of lumber that spring and summer including one of 140,000 feet which arrived at Nauvoo during the first week of May.[34] When the pinery mission closed in late 1845, it had produced hundreds of thousands of feet of lumber, not only providing raw materials for the temple and the Nauvoo House, but also furnishing the citizens with wood for dozens of frame houses. The location of the camp and mills would be called the "Mormon clearings" and the nearby rapids the "Mormon Riffles" by local citizens for decades to come.[35]

Hyrum Smith Replaces Elias Higbee

On 3 June 1843, Elias Higbee, who had served faithfully on the temple committee since October 1840, became ill and died five days later on 8 June, age forty-seven. William Clayton wrote: "His death was unexpected and deeply lamented by all his brethren. He had proved himself a worthy man, and was much respected by all who knew him." Eliza R. Snow expressed her concern in her diary: "It is to us a mysterious providence at this time, when every talent and exertion are

33. George Miller, Letter to N. K. Whitney, Mississippi River, 28 April 1845, Newel K. Whitney Papers, Perry Special Collections, Lee Library.

34. *History of the Church*, 7:407.

35. F. W. Draper, "Timber for the Nauvoo Temple: From an Unwritten Page of Early Clark and Jackson County History," *Improvement Era* 46 (February 1943): 88.

peculiarly needed for the erection of the Temple; that one of the Committee should be so suddenly called from time to eternity."[36] The *Nauvoo Neighbor* eulogized him:

> Our old esteemed and much respected friend Judge Higbee, one of the Temple Committee is dead.... When the revelation for the building of the Temple was received, the unanimous voice of the church elected him a member of the Committee which was incorporated to supervise its erection. His untiring perseverance in prosecuting this important work, and the strict fidelity that characterizes his stewardship, are too well known, in this community, to require any comment from us.[37]

Obviously, despite the complaints that had periodically been made against Higbee's work on the temple committee, he would not be an easy man to replace. Clayton recorded that "several applications were made by men to be appointed to fill the vacant place of Elder Higbee. Elder Jared Carter was very anxious to have the appointment and, for some cause or other, claimed it as his right. But the Spirit whispered that it would not be wisdom to appoint him."[38] Carter's previous service as a member of the building committee for the Kirtland Temple was probably the reason he felt most qualified to fill the position. However, after two days of consultation, Hyrum Smith "was appointed, by the voice of the Spirit"[39] through Joseph Smith, to take Higbee's place, "with the consent of the other committee [members]," and "on the morning of the 23rd day of October, 1843, he entered upon the duties of his office, amidst the greetings and good feelings of the workers universally."[40]

Women Receive the Endowment

While the endowment was given only to men from its inception on 4 May 1842, until September 1843, its blessings were, from the outset, clearly intended for women as well. On 27 May 1842, three weeks after the endowment was first given, Bishop Newel K. Whitney addressed the two-month-old Nauvoo Relief Society, intimating that the sisters of the society would eventually also receive the new endowment:

> In the beginning God created man male and female and bestow'd upon man certain blessings peculiar to a man of God, of which woman partook, so that with-

---

36. Maureen Ursenbach Beecher, ed., *Personal Writings of Eliza Roxcy Snow* (Salt Lake City: University of Utah Press, 1995), 75-76.

37. "Death of Elias Higbee," *Nauvoo Neighbor* 1 (14 June 1843): 27.

38. George D. Smith, *An Intimate Chronicle*, 538.

39. *History of the Church*, 6:53.

40. George D. Smith, *An Intimate Chronicle*, 538.

out the woman all things cannot be restored to the earth—it takes all to fully restore the Priesthood. This perfect restoration is the intent of the society. That by humility and faithfulness, in connection with their husbands, they may be found worthy. I rejoice while contemplating the blessings which will be poured out on the heads of the Saints. God has many precious things to bestow, even to our astonishment if we are faithful.[41]

Reynolds Cahoon later implied that the purpose of the Relief Society itself was to prepare the sisters for the blessings of the temple. Eliza R. Snow recorded his address to the society on 13 August 1843, "This Society is raised by the Lord to prepare us for the great blessings which are for us in the House of the Lord in the Temple."[42] Joseph Smith likewise told the Relief Society sisters he intended to "organize the Church in its proper order as soon as the Temple is completed.... He spoke of delivering the keys of the Priesthood to the Church, and said that the faithful members of the Relief Society should receive them in connection with their husbands."[43]

The first woman to receive the endowment was Emma Smith. This occurred on or before 23 September 1843.[44] She then officiated in the washings, anointings, and endowments of other women in the months that followed, including the Prophet's mother Lucy Mack Smith.[45] Bathsheba Wilson Bigler Smith, the wife of Apostle George A. Smith, was also endowed during this period. "I received the ordinance of anointing in a room in Sister Emma Smith's house in Nauvoo," she later recalled, "and the same day, in company with my husband, I received my endowment in the upper room over the Prophet Joseph Smith's store. The endowments were given under the direction of the Prophet Joseph Smith, who afterwards gave us lectures or instructions in regard to the endowment ceremonies."[46]

At age eighty-one, Bathsheba Smith, then the general president of the Relief Society, told a congregation of Saints in Ogden about the day she and her husband "received our first ordinances." She repeated: "Joseph Smith ... was present with us and lectured and talked with us ... and I have met him many times at councils which

41. "Relief Society Notes," *Woman's Exponent* 21 (15 March 1893): 149.

42. Ibid.

43. *History of the Church*, 4:602, 604-5.

44. Because 28 September was the day that Emma received her second anointing, she must have received her endowment on or before this day as well. Interestingly, she had been sealed to Joseph earlier, on 28 May 1843.

45. Helen Mar Kimball Whitney, "Scenes in Nauvoo and Incidents from H. C. Kimball's Journal," *Woman's Exponent* 12 (15 June 1883): 18.

46. Bathsheba B. Smith, quoted in Joseph Fielding Smith, *Blood Atonement and the Origin of Plural Marriage: Discussion between R. C. Evans and Elder Joseph Fielding Smith* (Salt Lake City: Deseret News, 1905), 87. Joseph Fielding Smith was the grandson of Hyrum Smith.

were held and he told us many things and explained them to us, showed us how to pray, and how to detect them when true or false angels come to us, and many other true things he taught us, and he instituted the endowments through the Lord."[47]

A total of forty-seven women received the endowment before the Nauvoo Temple was sufficiently finished that endowments could be bestowed upon the general membership beginning in December 1845. Twenty-eight of these women were endowed during Joseph's lifetime.[48]

The Introduction of Further Ordinances

In 1843, Joseph Smith introduced additional ordinances that would become temple ceremonies. The first of these was that of celestial marriage. The term "celestial marriage" referred both to the idea that marriages could be valid after this life and to plural marriage. Joseph had evidently received revelation on this subject years earlier and discussed aspects of it privately with a trusted few.[49] He had even "sealed" several couples for eternity.[50] However, it was not until the summer of 1843 that he dictated the formally worded revelation. William Clayton recorded the circumstances of recording this important revelation:

> On the morning of the 12th of July, 1843; Joseph and Hyrum Smith came into the office in the upper story of the brick store, on the bank of the Mississippi river.

47. Bathsheba W. B. Smith, quoted in *Deseret Evening News*, 23 June 1903, Journal History, 12 June 1903, 4. Bathsheba Wilson Bigler Smith (1822-1910), a West Virginia native, was baptized 21 August 1837 in Harrison, West Virginia, and married George A. Smith, Joseph Smith's first cousin, in Nauvoo in 1841.

48. See Andrew F. Ehat, "Joseph Smith's Introduction of Temple Ordinances and the 1844 Mormon Succession Crisis" (M.A. thesis, Brigham Young University, 1982).

49. See Introduction. See also Benjamin F. Johnson, Letter to George Gibbs, 1903, typescript, 10, Huntington Library, San Marino, California. Johnson stated that "the revelation to the Church at Nauvoo, July 21, 1843, on the Eternity of the Marriage Covenant and the Law of Plural Marriage, was not the first revelation of the law received and practiced by the Prophet. In 1835, at Kirtland, I learned from my sister's husband, Lyman R. Sherman, who was close to the Prophet, and received it from him, 'that the ancient order of Plural Marriage was again to be practiced by the Church.'" Johnson also stated: "The Prophet ... said that years ago in Kirtland the Lord had revealed to him the ancient order of plural marriage, and the necessity for its practice, and did command him then to take another wife."

50. Joseph sealed Heber C. and Vilate Kimball in 1841 and Newell K. and Elizabeth Ann Whitney in 1842. Orson F. Whitney, *Life of Heber C. Kimball* (Salt Lake City: Kimball Family, 1888), 334-39; Carol Cornwall Madsen, "Mormon Women and the Temple: Toward a New Understanding" in *Sisters in Spirit: Mormon Women in Historical and Cultural Perspective*, edited by Maureen Ursenbach Beecher and Lavina Fielding Anderson (Urbana: University of Illinois Press, 1987), 86.

They were talking on the subject of plural marriage. Hyrum said to Joseph, "If you will write the revelation on celestial marriage, I will take it and read it to Emma, and I believe I can convince her of its truth, and you will hereafter have peace." Joseph smiled and remarked, "You do not know Emma as well as I do." Hyrum repeated his opinion, and further remarked, "The doctrine is so plain, I can convince any reasonable man or woman of its truth, purity and heavenly origin," or words to that effect. Joseph then said, "Well, I will write the revelation and we will see." He then requested me to get paper and prepare to write. Hyrum very urgently requested Joseph to write the revelation by means of the Urim and Thummim, but Joseph in reply, said he did not need to, for he knew the revelation perfectly from beginning to end.

Joseph and Hyrum then sat down and Joseph commenced to dictate the revela tion on celestial marriage, and I wrote it, sentence by sentence, as he dictated. After the whole was written, Joseph asked me to read it through, slowly and carefully, which I did, and he pronounced it correct. He then remarked that there was much more that he could write on the same subject, but what was written was sufficient for the present.

Hyrum then took the revelation to read to Emma. Joseph remained with me in the office until Hyrum returned. When he came back, Joseph asked him how he had succeeded. Hyrum replied that he had never received a more severe talking to in his life, that Emma was very bitter and full of resentment and anger.

Joseph quietly remarked, "I told you you did not know Emma as well as I did." Joseph then put the revelation in his pocket, and they both left the office.

The revelation was read to several of the authorities during the day. Towards evening Bishop Newel K. Whitney asked Joseph if he had any objections to his taking a copy of the revelation; Joseph replied that he had not, and handed it to him. It was carefully copied the following day by Joseph C. Kingsbury. Two or three days after the revelation was written Joseph related to me and several others that Emma had so teased, and urgently entreated him for the privilege of destroying it, that he became so weary of her teasing, and to get rid of her annoyance, he told her she might destroy it and she had done so, but he had consented to her wish in this matter to pacify her, realizing that he knew the revelation perfectly, and could rewrite it at any time if necessary.[51]

That revelation, now Doctrine and Covenants 132, laid the foundation for several important marriage-related doctrines:

• Marriage between a man and a woman could be "sealed" by the priesthood thereby permitting the union to persist after this life (v. 19).

---

51. William Clayton, quoted in B. H. Roberts, *A Comprehensive History of the Church of Jesus Christ of Latter-day Saints*, 6 vols. (Salt Lake City: Deseret News Press, 1930), 2:206-7.

• Marriages "for time," performed by civil authority, were not valid after death (vv. 7-15).
• One man could be sealed to more than one woman for time or eternity (vv. 34-44).
• Being married for eternity was necessary in order to inherit a fullness of the glory of God (vv. 18, 20).

On 16 July 1843, four days after dictating the revelation, Joseph Smith preached in the grove near the temple on certain aspects of this revelation. According to Clayton, "President Joseph ... showed that a man must enter into an everlasting covenant with his wife in this world or he will have no claim on her in the next. He said that he could not reveal the fulness of these things until the Temple is completed."[52] As this statement indicates, the authority to seal marriages should be exercised in a temple. The introduction of marriage added a major requirement to Joseph's salvation theology and assumed the role of the "welding link" between generations previously accorded to baptism for the dead.

As Emma Smith's reaction shows, the most controversial element of the law of celestial marriage was that of plural marriage. Even those whom the Prophet trusted with knowledge of the revelation struggled to accept it. Brigham Young, speaking to a congregation of the Saints in Utah in 1855, recalled, "It was the first time in my life that I had desired the grave, and I could hardly get over it for a long time. And when I saw a funeral, I felt to envy the corpse its situation, and to regret that I was not in the coffin."[53] For many, the struggle was resolved by spiritual manifestations that confirmed the divinity of the new doctrine. For example, Joseph Smith introduced Benjamin F. Johnson to the doctrine and, at the same time, asked him to teach it to his sister Almera. He later recalled in a letter to George F. Gibbs:

"But how," I asked, "Can I teach my sister what I myself do not understand, or show her what I do not myself see?" "But you will see and understand it," he [Joseph] said, "And when you open your mouth to talk to your sister, light will come to you and your mouth will be full and your tongue loose....

I now bear an earnest testimony that his ... prediction was more than fulfilled, for when with great hesitation and stammering I called my sister to a private audience, and stood before her shaking with fear, just so soon as I found power to open my mouth, it was filled, for the light of the Lord shone upon my understanding, and the subject that had seemed so dark now appeared of all subjects

52. George D. Smith, *An Intimate Chronicle*, 110.
53. Brigham Young, 14 July 1855, *Journal of Discourses*, 26 vols. (London and Liverpool: LDS Booksellers Depot, 1855-86), 3:266.

pertaining to our gospel the most lucid and plain; and so both my sister and myself were converted together, and never again did I need evidence or argument to sustain that high and holy principle.[54]

Elizabeth Ann Smith Whitney, the wife of Bishop Newel K. Whitney, had a more unusual experience in that she and her husband received a joint confirmation. She recounted this trial of her faith:

> Joseph had the most implicit confidence in my husband's uprightness and integrity of character; he knew him capable of keeping a secret, and was not afraid to confide in him.... He therefore confided to him, and a few others, the principles set forth in that revelation, and also gave him the privilege to read it and to make a copy of it, knowing it would be perfectly safe with him. It was this veritable copy, which was preserved, in the providence of God, that has since been published to the world; for Emma afterwards becoming indignant, burned the original, thinking she had destroyed the only written document upon the subject in existence. My husband revealed these things to me; we had always been united, and had the utmost faith and confidence in each other. We pondered upon them continually, and our prayers were unceasing that the Lord would grant us some special manifestation concerning this new and strange doctrine. The Lord was very merciful to us; He revealed unto us His power and glory. We were seemingly wrapt in a heavenly vision, a halo of light encircled us, and we were convinced in our own minds that God heard and approved our prayers and intercedings before Him.[55]

The Whitneys were so convinced "that we were willing to give our eldest daughter, then only seventeen years of age, to Joseph, in the holy order of plural marriage.... She was the first woman ever given in plural marriage by or with the consent of both parents."[56]

While not elucidated in Section 132, two other doctrines related to celestial marriage were introduced in 1843:

> • Children born to sealed couples were born heirs to the covenant.
> • If one spouse died before the couple could be sealed, the sealing of the marriage could be performed by proxy.

---

54. Benjamin Johnson, Letter to George Gibbs, 1903, 10.

55. Elizabeth Ann Whitney, "A Leaf from the Autobiography of Elizabeth Ann Whitney," *Woman's Exponent* 7 (15 November 1878): 105. Sister Whitney (1800-82), who married Newel K. Whitney in 1822, was baptized with him in November 1830. They were the parents of eleven children.

56. Ibid. This daughter was Sarah Ann Whitney (1825-73).

Joseph first preached that children born to sealed parents were heirs of the covenant, automatically sealed to their parents, on 13 August 1843 at the funeral of Elias Higbee. He taught that "when a father and mother of a family have entered into [this sealing], their children who have not transgressed are secured by the seal wherewith the parents have been sealed."[57] Elizabeth and Newel K. Whitney's youngest daughter, Mary Jane, was born in January 1844. Elizabeth considered this birth to be a great blessing:

> She was the first child born heir to the holy priesthood in the new and everlasting covenant in this dispensation. I felt she was doubly a child of promise, not only through the priesthood, but through Joseph's promise to me when I gave him my eldest daughter to wife. He prophesied to me that I should have another daughter, who would be a strength and support to me to soothe my declining years; and in this daughter have these words been verified.[58]

Mercy Rachel Fielding Thompson was the first person to have a deceased spouse sealed to her by proxy. She described the ceremony in a reminiscence:

> A revelation had been given stating that marriages contracted for time only lasted for time and were no more one until a new contract was made, for all eternity and for those who had been separated by death a proxy would have to be obtained to act for them. Of course no time was lost by those who had an opportunity of securing their companions and the first presidency and as many of the Twelve as were [available] and the Presiding Bishop of the Church were all invited to meet in an upper room in the Prophet's house each man bringing his wife. Of course such a wedding I am quite sure [had] never [been] witnessed before in this generation. Of course my case was a singular one and had to be considered but the Prophet soon concluded that his Brother Hyrum had the best right to act for Robert B. Thompson. My sister Mary Smith of course standing with Hyrum for Jerusha Barden. Perhaps some may think I could envy Queen Victoria in some of

---

57. Howard and Martha Coray Notebook, quoted in *The Words of Joseph Smith*, compiled and edited by Andrew F. Ehat and Lyndon W. Cook (Provo, UT: BYU Religious Studies Center, 1980), 241. William Clayton's account of this statement reads: "When a seal is put upon the father and mother it secures their posterity so that they cannot be lost but will be saved by virtue of the covenant of their father." Ibid., 42.

58. Elizabeth Ann Whitney, "A Leaf from the Autobiography of Elizabeth Ann Whitney," *Woman's Exponent* 7 (15 February 1879): 191. Little is known of the life of Mary Jane Whitney. She received some attention in Nauvoo as the first "child of promise," and was given a special blessing by the Quorum of the Twelve. George D. Smith, *An Intimate Chronicle*, 169; Stanley B. Kimball, *On the Potter's Wheel: The Diaries of Heber C. Kimball* (Salt Lake City: Signature Books, 1987), 125.

her glory. Not while my name stands first on the list in this dispensation of women seal[e]d to a dead husband through divine Revelation.[59]

Another ordinance that Joseph introduced in 1843 was an extension of the endowment: receiving the fulness of the priesthood through a second anointing. Part of the existing endowment was a preparatory anointing of the recipients to become kings and priests or queens and priestesses. However, on 6 August 1843, Brigham Young pointed out: "If any in the Church had the fulness of the Melchizedek Priesthood, he did not know it. For any person to have the fullness of the priesthood, he must be a king and priest. A person may have a portion of that priesthood, the same as governors or judges of England have power from the king to transact business; but that does not make them kings of England. A person may be anointed king and priest long before he receives his kingdom."[60] This statement contains the suggestion that, at some future time, endowed members would, if faithful, receive further ordinances and blessings.

On 28 September 1843, the Prophet introduced the capstone of the temple endowment, the second anointing.[61] Joseph and Emma Smith were the first to receive this ordinance. The Prophet's journal contains a record of that momentous event:

> At 7 [o'clock in the] eve[ning] met at the Mansion's upper room front with W[illiam] L[aw] [and] W[illiam] M[arks]. Baurak Ale [Joseph Smith] was by common consent and unanimous voice chosen President of the quorum and anointed and ord[ained] to the highest and holiest order of the priesthood (and companion [Emma Smith]) Joseph Smith, Hyrum Smith, Geo[rge] Miller, N[ewel] K. Whitney, Willard Richards, [Uncle] John Smith, John Taylor, Amasa Lyman, Lucien Woodworth, J[ohn] M. Bernhisel, W[illia]m Law, W[illia]m Marks. President [Joseph Smith] led in prayer that his days might be prolonged, have dominion over his enemies, all the households be blessed and all the church and world.[62]

---

59. Mercy Rachel Fielding Thompson, "Reminiscence of Mercy Rachel Fielding Thompson," in *In Their Own Words: Women and the Story of Nauvoo*, edited by Carol Cornwall Madsen (Salt Lake City: Deseret Book, 1994), 195. Mercy (1807-93) joined the Church with her brother Joseph and sister Mary in Canada, was baptized 21 May 1836, and married Robert B. Thompson in 1837. He died in August 1841.

60. *History of the Church*, 5:527. Heber C. Kimball stated in a temple meeting on 21 December 1845: "You have been anointed to be kings and priests, but you have not been ordained to it yet, and you have got to get it by being faithful." George D. Smith, *An Intimate Chronicle*, 226.

61. See David John Buerger, "The Fulness of the Priesthood': The Second Anointing in Latter-day Saint Theology and Practice," *Dialogue: A Journal of Mormon Thought* 16 (Spring 1983): 10-44.

62. Faulring, *An American Prophet's Record*, 416.

Thirty-five other individuals received this ordinance from Joseph's hand before his death the following summer.[63]

Prayer Meetings

Another feature new to the 1842 endowment was instructions about a new manner of praying. Bathsheba Smith recollected: "Once when speaking in one of our general fast meetings, he [Joseph Smith] said that we did not know how to pray to have our prayers answered. But when I and my husband had our endowments, in February, 1844, Joseph Smith presiding, he taught us the true order of prayer."[64] To pray in this new order, endowed men and women gathered in a circle, clothed in their endowment robes. After reviewing the signs and symbols associated with endowment covenants, they then united in prayer under the direction of a designated leader. During the remainder of Joseph Smith's lifetime, the group of endowed members met frequently to pray for desired blessings, including deliverance from their enemies. Bathsheba Smith recollected, "I met many times with Brother Joseph, and others who had received their endowments, in company with my husband in an upper room dedicated for that purpose and prayed with them repeatedly in those meetings."[65]

After the Prophet's death, these prayer meetings acquired even more urgency. In December 1845, Heber C. Kimball told a group of endowment recipients in the temple: "From seven to twelve persons ... have met together every day to pray ever since Joseph's death, and this people have been sustained upon this principle."[66]

George A. Smith, in a similar meeting on 21 December 1845, explained:

When we come together ... and act as one mind, the Lord will hear us and will answer our prayers. He [George A. Smith] related an instance of some children being healed and cured of the whooping cough in one night through the prayers of himself and Elder Woodruff in Michigan, while they were there on a mission. Said that whenever they could get an opportunity they retired to the wilderness or to an upper room they did so ... and were always answered. It would be a good thing for us ... every day [to] pray in private circles.[67]

63. Buerger, "The Fulness of the Priesthood," 23, identifies these twenty men and "at least sixteen women" by name.

64. Bathsheba W. B. Smith, "Recollections of the Prophet Joseph Smith," Juvenile Instructor 27 (1 June 1892): 345.

65. Bathsheba W. B. Smith, Autobiography, ca. 1906, entry under date of 1843, holograph, LDS Church Archives.

66. George D. Smith, An Intimate Chronicle, 224.

67. Helen Mar Kimball Whitney, "Scenes in Nauvoo and Incidents from H. C. Kimball's Journal," Woman's Exponent 12 (15 July 1883): 14.

Even after the majority of the Saints had left Nauvoo, several of those who remained held "regular meetings with the brethren in the temple for prayers, to continue, so long, as we stayed in the place, beginning near the hour of sunset."[68]

Contributions of the Relief Society

The Nauvoo Female Relief Society was organized 17 March 1842 in the assembly room above Joseph Smith's store. According to Sarah Melissa Granger Kimball, the society had its origin in an effort to organize the women of Nauvoo to help the temple workers. Kimball and her seamstress, Margaret Cook, discussed the possibility of organizing for that purpose:

> In the summer of 1843, a Miss Cooke was seamstress for me. The subject of combining our efforts for assisting the Temple hands came up in conversation. She desired to help, but had no means to furnish. I told her I would furnish material if she would make some shirts for the workmen. It was then suggested that some of our neighbors might wish to combine means and efforts with ours, and we decided to invite a few to come and consult with us on the subject of forming a Ladies' Society. The neighboring sisters met in my parlor and decided to organize. I was delegated to call on Sister Eliza R. Snow and ask her to write a constitution and by-laws, and submit them to President [Joseph] Smith prior to our next meeting. When she read them to him, he replied that the constitution and by-laws were the best he had ever seen. "But," he said, "this is not what you want. Tell the sisters their offering is accepted of the Lord, and he has something better for them than a written constitution. I invite them all to meet with me and a few of the brethren next Thursday afternoon, and I will organize the women under the priesthood after the pattern of the priesthood."[69]

Supporting the temple-building effort and caring for the poor were the primary interests of the newly organized society. Emma Smith was elected as the first president with Elizabeth Ann Whitney and Sarah M. Cleveland as counselors, and Eliza R. Snow as secretary. During a meeting on 16 June 1843, Sister Whitney declared that she had "received instructions that we might not only relieve the wants of the poor but also cast in our mites to assist the brethren in building the

---

68. Samuel W. Richards, Diary, 12 February 1846, typescript, 3, Perry Special Collections, Lee Library. These meetings continued intermittently in stakes and wards throughout the Church until 3 May 1978 when they were suspended by policy. D. Michael Quinn, "Latter-day Saint Prayer Circles," *BYU Studies* 19 (Fall 1978): 105.

69. Sarah Melissa Granger Kimball, "Autobiography of Sarah M. Kimball" *Woman's Exponent* 12 (1 September 1883): 51.

Lord's House—said she had felt a deep interest on the subject since last Sabbath hearing President Smith's remarks—wished the sisters to express their feelings—our President Mrs. Smith said we might speak to the Temple Committee, and whatever they wished and we could, we might do.... The sisters expressed their feelings one by one—an unanimous sentiment seemed to pervade the hearts of all present, to wit, a desire to assist in forwarding the Temple and in aiding the cause of Zion."[70]

The Relief Society minutes reveal the extraordinary zeal with which its members offered their time and talents. The following excerpt from 16 June 1843 is typical:

> The sisters proceeded to volunteer various means and services to help. Mrs. Durfee said if the heads of the Society wished, she is willing to go abroad with a wagon and collect wool etc. for the purpose of forwarding the work.
>
> Mrs. Smith suggested that merchant's wives donate material that others may be employed.
>
> Miss Wheeler—said she is willing to give any portion or all of her time—Mrs. Granger willing to do anything, knit, sew or wait on the sick, as might be most useful.
>
> Miss Ells said she had felt willing to go out and solicit donations etc.
>
> Mrs. Angell said she was willing to repair old clothes if necessary when new material cannot be obtained.
>
> Mrs. Smith proposed getting wool and furnish old ladies with yarn to knit socks, to supply the workmen on the Temple next winter.
>
> Sis[ter] Stringham offered to make men's clothes and take work on the Temple.
>
> Sis. Felshaw proposes to give some soap.
>
> Coun[sellor] Whitney arose and corroborated the testimony of Sis Chase respecting the glorious manifestation in behalf of Sis[ter] Mills.
>
> Mrs. Chase then spoke in a very animated strain, by way of encouragement to the sisters, saying the angels are rejoicing over you etc.
>
> Sis[ter] Stanley proposed giving every tenth pound of flax, also one q[uar]t of milk per day.
>
> Miss Beman will make clothes.
>
> Sis[ter] Smith proposed getting muslin etc. from merchants not belonging to the church, who were friendly—proposed calling on Mr. Orr.
>
> Sis[ter] Green offered to donate thread of her own spinning.[71]

The contributions of the Relief Society sisters were significant, if not in monetary value, then in terms of the sacrifice required to realize them. Sarah Louisa Norris Decker reminisced, "Each one seemed to desire to help, and many sold

---

70. Nauvoo Relief Society Minutes, 16 June 1843, 91, microfilm of holograph, LDS Church Archives.

71. Ibid., 91-92.

things that they could scarcely spare to put the means towards the building. I can remember of my mother selling her China dishes and fine bed quilt to donate her part."[72] The recently widowed Elizabeth Kirby, age thirty-nine in 1843, recounted her experience: "It was taught in our meetings that we would have to sacrifice our idols in order to be saved. I could not think of anything that would grieve me to part with in my possession, except [my husband's] watch. So, I gave it up to help build the Nauvoo Temple and everything else that I could possibly spare and the last few dollars that I had in the world, which altogether amounted to nearly $50.00."[73]

The 1843 Building Season

The 1843 building season began at the end of April. At April conference, Joseph Smith's journal kept by Willard Richards recorded that the walls of the temple were "4 to 12 feet above the floor."[74] March and early April were spent "fixing runways for the cranes."[75] William Player, who had suffered from a protracted illness early in the spring, finally regained his health and commenced setting stones on 21 April.[76] About three weeks later, the *Nauvoo Neighbor* reported:

> The Temple is improving fast; the stones of that building begin to rise tier above tier; and it already begins to present a stately and noble appearance.
> The day being unusually fine, last Sabbath, we had a large concourse of people assembled at the Temple; the floor, as well as the walls, were literally covered with people. Mr. Joseph Smith delivered a discourse, in the morning; which was listened to with great interest by the congregation.[77]

David White of the *Pittsburgh Weekly Gazette* visited the temple site in late August and described the progress on the walls: "The windows of the upper stories

---

72. Sarah Louisa Norris Decker, "Reminiscences of Nauvoo," *Woman's Exponent* 37 (March 1909): 41. Sarah Louisa Norris Decker (ca. 1834-1914) was baptized in 1842 at age eight. Her family had joined the Church about two years earlier.

73. Elizabeth Terry Kirby Heward, "Reminiscence of Elizabeth Terry Kirby Heward" in *In Their Own Words*, 180. Elizabeth (1814-78) was born in Palmyra but raised in Canada. She and her parents' family joined the Church in 1838.

74. Faulring, *An American Prophet's Record*, 342.

75. George D. Smith, *An Intimate Chronicle*, 538.

76. Ibid. According to William Clayton, Player had been sick most of the winter and had "nearly lost the use of his hands and feet, and several times he fell, through weakness while on his way home. He considered that his sickness was caused by the change of climate and by his having drunk bad water while coming up the river." George D. Smith, *An Intimate Chronicle*, 533.

77. John Taylor, untitled announcement, *Nauvoo Neighbor* 1 (14 June 1843): 26.

are some fifteen or eighteen feet high, arched over the top in a perfect semi-circle.—
The first story above the basement is divided into two apartments, called the outer
and inner courts.... All the work is of good cut stone, almost white, and it will present a fine appearance when finished."[78]

Although most of the work this season focused on the stone walls, attention began to turn to some of the interior details. On 8 November, Joseph Smith
"examined a sample of fringe designed for the pulpits of the temple."[79]

According to William Clayton, "the work progressed steadily but slowly."
By the time winter set in, "the walls were up as high as the arches of the first tier
of windows all around. In this state the building was left through the winter and
until the spring of 1844."[80]

Support from the British Mission

Although many Saints in Britain never set foot in the Nauvoo Temple, they
felt a keen interest in its completion and donated liberally to its construction.
Presided over by various apostles, including Wilford Woodruff and Parley P. Pratt,
the fund-raising in Britain was carefully organized so that donations could be transferred safely from individual branch treasurers to the temple recorder in Nauvoo.
In late 1842, Pratt published the following notice in the *Millennial Star*:

> We here give notice that elder Hiram Clark has been specially commissioned by
> the authorities of the church at Nauvoo to come to this country as a general
> agent for the church; to aid in emigration and to act as an agent for the Temple;
> to receive and forward the tithings and consecrations for the same.... We sin-
> cerely hope that the tithings and collections for the Temple will continue to be
> made, and that all diligence will be exercised in this work, as the object is great
> and glorious, and can only be accomplished by continued exertion.
>
> All funds and communications on this subject should be addressed to Hiram
> Clark, 36, Chapel Street, Liverpool.[81]

After the deaths of Joseph and Hyrum Smith, Wilford Woodruff replaced
both Pratt and Clark in January 1845. He made extensive use of the *Millennial Star*
to keep the British Saints abreast of progress on the temple, encourage donations,

---

78. David N. White, "The Prairies, Nauvoo, Joe Smith, the Temple, the Mormons, etc.," *Pittsburgh Weekly Gazette*, 15 September 1843: 3; reprinted in Dean C. Jessee, ed., *The Papers of Joseph Smith*, 2 vols. (Salt Lake City: Deseret Book, 1989, 1992), 1:442. White visited Nauvoo on 28 August 1843.

79. *History of the Church*, 6:66.

80. George D. Smith, *An Intimate Chronicle*, 538.

81. Parley P. Pratt, "Tithings for the Temple," *Millennial Star* 3 (October 1842): 97.

and explain the procedures for forwarding donations to Nauvoo. This notice in
February 1845 is typical:

> I trust ... that all the presiding elders will use their exertions to have all the church-
> es continue their tithings, send the name of each individual with the money to us
> in Liverpool, that we may record the same in a book, and keep a copy with us,
> and also send a copy of the same with the money to Nauvoo, that it may be
> recorded in the book of the Law of the Lord.
>
> I wish the Female Society, in all the branches, to continue their subscriptions
> for the temple until it is finished; let their money and names be brought together
> the same as all other tithings and offerings, that, when the temple is finished, the
> whole amount they have paid may stand opposite their names in the Book of the
> Law of the Lord, that it may be known who are the owners of the house.
>
> I wish it to be distinctly understood, that collections of every description for
> the temple, in this land, whether from churches, individuals, or the Female
> Society, should be brought with their names to us here in Liverpool, that it may
> go through the proper channel, that our records may show that all things are
> done according to the order of God.[82]

Seven months later in another letter to the Saints, Woodruff explained:

> Any person has a right to forward their tithings to the President of the Churches
> in Britain, and receive a receipt for the same in their own name, if they wish to
> do so. Any person wishing to forward 10 s[hillings] or upwards, can do so by a
> post-office order: but as there is, or ought to be, an organization in all the con-
> ferences and branches to collect for the Temple, consisting of collector, secre-
> tary, and treasurer, all small sums can be paid into the hands of the treasurer of
> each branch or conference, and the name with the amount, in all cases, should
> be strictly taken; and then the treasurer of each branch or conference, (as the
> case may be) should forward those monies to Liverpool, not, by any means, omit-
> ting to send the name of each subscriber and the amount paid. Let the treasur-
> er's name be sent in full, that a receipt may be returned to him for the sum for-
> warded. I wish it to be distinctly understood, that each person's name will be
> recorded in our books, at Liverpool, and transferred into the Book of the Law of
> the Lord, at Nauvoo, with the amount of money paid, though it should not
> exceed one penny. All names forwarded to us by the treasurer are as strictly
> attended to as though each subscriber had a separate receipt. We would rec-
> ommend that all small subscriptions be paid into the hands of the collector or
> treasurer, and let the treasurer forward the same with the name to us, as by so
> doing we will be saved much trouble and expense, by giving one receipt for the

---

82. Wilford Woodruff, "To the Officers and Members of the Church of Jesus Christ of Latter-day
Saints in the British Islands," *Millennial Star* 5 (February 1845): 140.

total amount to the treasurer, instead of forty or fifty for the same number of shillings or sixpences, as we keep a printed duplicate, bound in a book, of each receipt we give. Some have forwarded us money for the Temple, without the subscribers' names, and others have forwarded us names, without informing us who the treasurer was, or in what name to make out the receipt. We wish all our friends, hereafter, to notice these items, and it will save us much trouble.[83]

Just before Woodruff left Great Britain on 27 October 1845, he recorded in his diary that he "spent the day at the office looking over the temple books." Since his term of office had begun, he had "received for the Temple during that time £157.16.8 1/4."[84]

Intention to Perform Endowments for the Dead

Ordinance work for the dead performed in Nauvoo consisted of baptisms, confirmations, and sealings. No vicarious washings, anointings, or endowments were performed. However, it is evident that the Twelve understood that these ordinances would be performed on behalf of the dead when the temple was completed. On 23 December 1843, Brigham Young preached at a meeting: "When the temple is done I expect we shall be baptized, washed, anointed, ordained and receive the keys and signs of the priesthood for our dead, that they may have a full salvation, and thus we shall be saviors on Mount Zion according to the scriptures."[85]

About a month later Joseph Smith, speaking to a congregation at the temple, taught that the Saints could become Saviors on Mount Zion "by building their temples, erecting their baptismal fonts and going forth and receiving all the ordinances, baptisms, confirmations, washings, anointings, ordinations, and sealing powers upon [their] heads in behalf of all [their] progenitors who are dead and redeem them that they may come forth in the first resurrection and be exalted to thrones of glory."[86]

83. Wilford Woodruff, "Temple Tithing—Bell Receipts," *Millennial Star* 6 (August 1845): 107.

84. Woodruff, Journal, 2:608. Currency notation for 157 pounds, 16 shillings, and 6 pence. In 1845, 1 pound was equivalent in buying power to $2.43. There were twenty shillings to the pound and twelve pence per shilling, hence 240 pence per pound. This system of currency originated during the ninth century when Charlemagne ordered that pounds of silver be minted into 240 individual coins.

85. Elden J. Watson, ed., *Manuscript History of Brigham Young, 1801-1844* (Salt Lake City: Elden J. Watson, 1968), 157.

86. Woodruff, 21 January 1844, Journal, 2:341-43. See also Faulring, *An American Prophet's Record*, 468. Three months later, on 8 April 1844, Joseph taught, "There must, however, be a place built expressly for that purpose, and for men to be baptized for their dead. It must be built in this central place; for every man who wishes to save his father, mother, brothers, sisters and friends, must go

Joseph Fielding noted in his diary during the Nauvoo period "It is necessary that [the dead] as well as we who are now alive should be made acquainted with the ordinances, signs and tokens of the priesthood and the terms of admission into the Kingdom in order that they may come forth with those who have received it here."[87]

From these statements, it is clear that the full range of ordinances would have been administered vicariously for the dead had the Saints not been forced to leave Nauvoo so quickly. The first endowments for the dead were performed in the St. George Temple in 1877.

---

through all the ordinances for each one of them separately, the same as for himself, from baptism to ordination. washing and anointings and receive all the keys and powers of the Priesthood, the same as for himself." *History of the Church*, 6:319.

87. Joseph Fielding, "'They Might Have Known That He Was Not a Fallen Prophet': The Nauvoo Journal of Joseph Fielding," *BYU Studies* 19 (Winter 1979): 133.

Chapter 6

THE DEATH OF JOSEPH: JANUARY 1844 TO JUNE 1844

Joseph's Plans for Circular Windows

One of the best-known incidents associated with the construction of the Nauvoo Temple occurred on 5 February 1844. Joseph Smith's history recounts this event:

> In the afternoon, Elder William Weeks (whom I had employed as architect of the Temple,) came in for instruction. I instructed him in relation to the circular windows designed to light the offices in the dead work of the arch between stories. He said that round windows in the broad side of a building were a violation of all the known rules of architecture, and contended that they should be semicircular—that the building was too low for round windows. I told him I would have the circles, if he had to make the Temple ten feet higher than it was originally calculated; that one light at the centre of each circular window would be sufficient to light the whole room; that when the whole building was thus illuminated, the effect would be remarkably grand. "I wish you to carry out my designs. I have seen in vision the splendid appearance of that building illuminated, and will have it built according to the pattern shown me."[1]

---

1. Joseph Smith, Jr., et al., *History of the Church of Jesus Christ of Latter-day Saints*, edited by B. H. Roberts (Salt Lake City: Deseret News Press, 6 vols. published 1902-12, Vol. 7 published 1932, 1st printing), 6:196-97.

One of Weeks's original drawings is a transverse section of the body of the building showing the arrangement of the structural timbers. The height of each of the two main stories was written in pen as twenty-five feet. Later pencil marks over the original dimensions prescribe a height of "30',"[2] accounting for a ten-foot increase in overall height. Whether the extra height was actually needed or not, the design change was implemented immediately because by May several of these rounds windows were complete.[3]

"Let the Nauvoo House Be"

On 4 March 1844, at a meeting of the temple committee and General Authorities, Joseph Smith proposed that it would be "best to let the Nauvoo House be till the Temple is completed." He continued, "We need the Temple more than anything else. We will let the Nauvoo House stand till the Temple is done and we will put all our forces on the Temple. Turn all our lumber towards the Temple. Stock the lumber we want for the Temple, cover it this fall and sell the remainder to get [blasting] powder, etc."[4]

Three days later on 7 March 1844, the Prophet made public his intention to put off construction of the Nauvoo House for the time being:

> Another man, [I] will not call his name, has been writing to New York Tribune some of the most disgraceful things possible to name. He has stated in that article that there are a great many appropriations to the Temple applied somewhere else etc. to stigmatize the Trustees and turn prejudice against us abroad. If any man who has appointed anything [to be applied to the construction of the temple—an] old harness horses wagon etc. let him come forward [and I will show that there is not] the first farthing and we cannot show where it has been appropriated, [or] I will give him my head for a football.
>
> He also states that the Temple cannot be built [because] it costs so much. Who don't know that we can put the roof on this building this season? By turning all the means of the N[auvoo] House and doubling our diligence we can do it.[5]

2. William Weeks, Transverse section of Nauvoo Temple, William Weeks Papers, Box 26, item 1, LDS Church Archives.

3. "The Temple of Nauvoo," St. Louis Gazette, ca. June 1844, Journal History, 12 June 1844.

4. Scott H. Faulring, ed., An American Prophet's Record: The Diaries and Journals of Joseph Smith (Salt Lake City: Signature Books, 1989). 451. The History of the Church, 6:230, reads: "We will let the Nauvoo house stand until the temple is done, and we will put all our forces on the Temple, turn our lumber towards the Temple, and cover it in this fall, and sell the remainder to get blasting powder, fuse, rope, steel, etc."

5. Faulring, An American Prophet's Record, 453. See also George D. Smith, ed., An Intimate Chronicle: The Journals of William Clayton (Salt Lake City: Deseret Book, 1995), 182; Mary Ann Weston Maughan, "Journal of Mary Ann Weston Maughan," in Our Pioneer Heritage, compiled by Kate B. Carter, 20 vols. (Salt Lake City: Daughters of Utah Pioneers, 1958-77), 2:364.

Willard Richard's, Joseph's scribe, recorded his belief that "God [had] whispered to the prophet, build the temple, and let the N[auvoo] House alone at present."[6] The silence of the historical record concerning work on the Nauvoo House during the summer of 1844 is a mute testimony to the Saints' compliance with this request.[7]

In March, the committee decided to construct a second crane to expedite raising the walls. Wandle Mace, who was again hired to design and build this crane, completed it before April conference.[8] Stone-setting began for the season a few days later on 11 April.[9] The second crane was used in part to "set the stone on the inside walls and also the inside courses of the main wall." Hence, Elisha Averett, who set most of the stone raised by that crane, bore the title "principal backer up." He was assisted by his brothers, Elijah and John, and by recent convert Truman Leonard.[10] The team that operated the crane included John Harvey, Thomas M. Pearson, George M. Potter and William L. Cutler.[11]

On 30 May 1844, Lorenzo Brown, one of the windlass men, "came near being killed by a large stone slipping out of the sling. I was standing, at the time, directly under it but stepped three feet [to] one side without knowing of danger and saved my life."[12]

---

6. Faulring, *An American Prophet's Record*, 455.

7. Work on the Nauvoo House resumed after Joseph Smith's death. Brigham Young placed renewed priority on its completion in early 1845. George D. Smith, *An Intimate Chronicle*, 159, 161, 175-77. Yet despite Young's new attention to the Nauvoo House, he still made the temple his first priority. In a letter to Wilford Woodruff dated 21 August 1845, he wrote: "The committee of the Nauvoo House are driving that building on briskly. They have got their brick now ready, also their lime, sand, and timber. The masons have commenced work, and in two months the walls will be complete and the roof will go on this fall, and be ready for *the inside work, which the joiners will commence as soon as they finish off[f] the Temple*." "Latest from Nauvoo," *Millennial Star* 6 (15 September 1845), 124; emphasis mine. Lyman O. Littlefield estimated in September 1845 that between 200 and 500 hands were at work on the Nauvoo House each day—"but the temple is not deserted; that goes on with as great a rapidity as ever." Lyman O. Littlefield, "From Nauvoo," dated 3 September 1845, *New York Messenger* 2 (20 September 1845): 67, photocopy, LDS Church Archives.

8. See chap. 4 for his first crane, built in 1842. Wandle Mace, "Journal of Wandle Mace," ca. 1890, typescript, 82, L. Tom Perry Special Collections, Harold B. Lee Library, Brigham Young University, Provo, Utah.

9. George D. Smith, *An Intimate Chronicle*, 540.

10. Elisha Averett (1810-90), a Tennessee native, was baptized 6 June 1835 and was a member of the Nauvoo Legion. His twin, Elijah (1810-86) was baptized the same day. John Averett (1821-52), their younger brother, was presumably baptized with his brothers in 1835. Truman Leonard (1820-97) was baptized 25 March 1843.

11. William Clayton, Journal, Journal History of the Church of Jesus Christ of Latter-day Saints (chronology of typed entries and newspaper clippings, 1830-present), 31 December 1844, 15, LDS Church Archives.

12. Lorenzo Brown, Journal, 1833-99, typescript, 15, Perry Special Collections, Lee Library. Brown (1823-1902) joined the Church in 1838.

By 4 May "four circular windows [were] finished on the upper story of the Temple."[13] One visitor in early June noted that "75 or 100" men were "zealously at work at the present time hewing stone or laying it for the Temple, all other public improvements being in perfect abeyance that the greatest and holiest of all may advance."[14]

Joseph's Last Charge to the Twelve

By 28 September 1843, Joseph Smith had entrusted to the apostles and to other close associates all the ordinances that would comprise Latter-day Saint temple worship. Benjamin F. Johnson summarized the Prophet's efforts:

> Apostate spirits within were now [June 1844] joining with our enemies outside for the destruction of the priesthood, for the Temple was progressing, and the devil, striving for empire began to stir up, in them as in Judas, desire for the Prophet's blood. The keys of endowments and plural marriage had been given, and some had received their Second Anointing. Baptism for the dead had been taught and the keys committed. All of these things I then comprehended, though in some I had not fully participated. These sacred principles were then committed to but a few, but not only were they committed to me from the first, but from the first I was authorized by the Prophet to teach them to others, when I was led to do so.[15]

In the early spring of 1844,[16] Joseph Smith held a series of councils in which he gave important instructions to the Twelve and others. During the councils, he instructed this circle of trusted friends more particularly concerning the ordinances they had received and gave them the authority to perform them for others. On one such occasion, probably at a meeting held on 26 March,[17] the Prophet gave what has been called his "last charge" to the Twelve. One interesting account of this momentous occasion was recorded, not by a participant, but by a passerby. In 1881, Dennison Lott Harris, age nineteen in 1844, recounted some little-known details about the fascinating events of that day:

---

13. Faulring, An American Prophet's Record, 476.

14. "The Temple of Nauvoo," Journal History, 12 June 1844.

15. Benjamin F. Johnson, My Life's Review (Independence, MO: Zion's Printing and Publishing Company, 1947), 98-99.

16. Orson Hyde stated that the councils took place before 4 April when he departed for the eastern states. "Trial of Elder Rigdon," Millennial Star 5 (December 1844): 104.

17. Andrew F. Ehat, "Joseph Smith's Introduction of Temple Ordinances and the 1844 Mormon Succession Question" (M.A. thesis, Brigham Young University, 1982), 162.

I was passing Joseph's brick building which was used for a store when Brother Willard Richards came out and beckoned me. As we approached each other he said, "Good morning, Brother Harris!" and shook hands with me.... I asked him if he was going my way and if he would ride. He said, "Yes, if you please." He got up and rode. As soon as he was seated in the wagon he said, "I have a message for you. Brother Joseph wanted me to come and see you. As soon as he saw you coming he remarked, 'There, brethren, we are all right now. The time has come. There is the man I want. There is the boy I can depend upon and trust. Brother Richards, will you go and see him and tell him what I want.'" Then Brother Richards told me that Brother Joseph had met in that building with most of the Twelve, and they had been waiting for someone that Joseph could depend upon to assist them. He then told me that Joseph desired me to drive around to the river where he would meet me with barrels and buckets to assist him to get some water up to the house in which the brethren had gathered, that Brother Joseph wanted to give them their endowments. I went to the river according to request, and found Brother Richards there with barrels and buckets. We loaded up the wagon and drove up to the house the back way. The Twelve were on the porch above with block and tackle with which they drew the barrels of water up. Brother Joseph was with them and assisted. Brother Joseph said to me: "This day I am going to roll this kingdom off my shoulders onto the shoulders of these my brethren, for them to preach the gospel and gather Israel and build up the king- dom upon the foundation which I have laid; for I shall not be known among the people for many years, or for 20 years; I am going to rest, and these, my brethren the Twelve have got to preach the gospel and gather Israel, etc." ... Joseph was addressing himself to me, while the Twelve stood around him on the porch. He then said to me, "You are the only witness on the earth to what I am about to do; I wanted you as a witness, and I have been waiting for you." Then turning to Brother Brigham he said, "Brother Brigham, when this temple is finished, will you see to the giving of this young man his endowments as I will give them to you today?" Brother Brigham answered, "I will, Brother Joseph." Brother Joseph remarked again "I request you to do it." Brother Brigham promised in his firm way that he would do it. Brother Joseph then told me that was all I could do for him, and I drove off.[18]

The following retrospective accounts by participants in the "last charge meeting" illuminate the substance of Joseph's teachings in these meetings and his motives for giving the ordinances outside the temple and conferring authority upon others:

---

18. "Verbal Statement of Bishop Dennison L. Harris of Monroe, Sevier County, Utah, made by him to President Joseph F. Smith in the presence of Elder Franklin Spencer, at the house of Bishop Dorius of Ephraim, Sanpete County, Utah, on Sunday Afternoon, May 15th, 1881. Reported by George F. Gibbs," typescript, 6-8, LDS Church Archives.

Apostle Orson Hyde, 10 March 1845: Before I went east on the 4th of April last, we were in council with brother Joseph almost every day for weeks, says brother Joseph, in one of those councils, there is something going to happen; I don't know what it is, but the Lord bids me to hasten and give you your endowment before the temple is finished. He conducted us through every ordinance of the holy priesthood, and when he had gone through with all the ordinances he rejoiced very much, and says, now if they kill me you have got all the keys, and all the ordinances, and you can confer them upon others, and the hosts of Satan will not be able to tear down the kingdom as fast as you will be able to build it up; and now, says he, on your shoulders will rest the responsibility of leading this people, for the Lord is going to let me rest a while.[19]

Apostle Parley P. Pratt, 10 March 1845: This great and good man [Joseph Smith] was led, before his death, to call the Twelve together, from time to time, and to instruct them in all things pertaining to the kingdom, ordinances, and government of God. He often observed that he was laying the foundation, but it would remain for the Twelve to complete the building. Said he, "I know not why; but for some reason I am constrained to hasten my preparations, and to confer upon the Twelve all the ordinances, keys, covenants, endowments, and sealing ordinances of the priesthood, and so set before them a pattern in all things pertaining to the sanctuary and the endowment therein."

Having done this, he rejoiced exceedingly; for, said he, the Lord is about to lay the burden on your shoulders and let me rest awhile; and if they kill me, continued he, the kingdom of God will roll on, as I have now finished the work which was laid upon me, by committing to you all things for the building up of the kingdom according to the heavenly vision, and the pattern shown me from heaven. With many conversations like this, he comforted the minds of the Twelve, and prepared them for what was soon to follow.

He proceeded to confer on Elder Young, the President of the Twelve, the keys of the sealing power, as conferred in the last days by the spirit and power of Elijah, in order to seal the hearts of the fathers to the children, and the hearts of the children to the fathers, lest the whole earth should be smitten with a curse. This last key of the priesthood is the most sacred of all, and pertains exclusively to the first presidency of the Church, without whose sanction and approval or authority, no sealing blessing shall be administered pertaining to things of the resurrection and the life to come.[20]

Benjamin F. Johnson, 1903: It was at Nauvoo early in 1844 in an assembly room, common to the meeting of the Council, or a select circle of the Prophet's most

19. Orson Hyde, "Trial of Elder Rigdon," 104.
20. Parley P. Pratt, "Proclamation," Millennial Star 5 (10 March 1845): 151.

trusted friends, including all the Twelve, but not all the constituted authorities of the Church, for Presidents Rigdon, Law or Marks, the High Council nor Presidents of Quorums were not members of that council.... Let us remember that by revelation he had reorganized the Holy Priesthood, and by command of the Lord had taken from the First Presidency his brother Hyrum to hold as Patriarch, the sealing power, the first and highest honor due to priesthood; that he had turned the keys of endowments, to the last anointing, and sealing together with keys of Salvation for the dead, with the eternity of the marriage covenant and the power of endless lives. All these keys he held, and under these then existing conditions he stood before that association of his select friends, including all the Twelve, and with great feeling and animation he graphically reviewed his life of persecution, labor and sacrifice for the church and kingdom of God, both of which he declared were now organized upon the earth. The burden of which had become too great for him longer to carry, that he was weary and tired with the weight he so long had borne, and he then said, with great vehemence: "And in the name of the Lord, I now shake from my shoulders the responsibilities of bearing off the Kingdom of God to all the world, and here and now I place that responsibility, with all the keys, powers and privileges pertaining thereto, upon the shoulders of you the Twelve Apostles, in connection with this council; and if you will accept this, to do it, God shall bless you mightily and shall open your way; and if you do it I now shake my garments clear and free from the blood of this generation and of all men"; and shaking his skirt with great vehemence he raised himself from the floor, while the spirit that accompanied his words thrilled every heart as with a feeling that boded bereavement and sorrow.[21]

Apostle Wilford Woodruff, 2 June 1889: I remember very well the last charge that Joseph gave to the Apostles.... When he delivered that charge to the Apostles he was filled with the power of God. His face was clear as amber, and the room was filled with the Spirit of God, like the holy fire. In his address he told us that he had received at the hands of the Almighty God all the keys, and powers, and priesthood, and ordinances and gifts belonging to the dispensation in which we lived. "Now," says he, "I have sealed all these blessings upon your heads, upon you Apostles of the Lamb of God, who have been chosen to bear off this Church and kingdom on the earth;" and after making this solemn proclamation to us, he said, "Now, you have got to round up your shoulders and bear off this kingdom, or you will be damned."[22]

21. Benjamin F. Johnson, Letter to George Gibbs, 1903, typescript, 6-7, Huntington Library, San Marino, California.

22. Wilford Woodruff, 2 June 1889, *Collected Discourses*, edited by Brian H. Stuy (Salt Lake City: B.H.S. Publishing, 1987-92), 1:292.

Land Consecrated to the Temple

While most donations to the temple took the form of cash, food, clothing, and other provisions, many Saints deeded land to the temple. Among the papers of the office of the trustee is a memorandum of deeds belonging to the temple. It lists nearly thirty parcels of land in and near Nauvoo that had been contributed between 1841 and 1844 with a total value of over $5,000.

Such notable elders as Hyrum Smith, Wilford Woodruff, Charles C. Rich, Levi Hancock, John Bernhisel, and Stephen Markham were among the contributors. Particularly generous were Knowlton Hanks and Edward Hunter, who each gave lots appraised at $800.[23] There were other land donations not recorded in this document. For example, Hunter donated more lots, bringing his real estate contributions to a total of $3,600.[24] Hiram Kimball also donated land to the temple, though his name does not appear on the list. (See chap. 3.)

Joseph, acting as trustee, sold this land to obtain useable commodities such as building materials and to pay the laborers. Newly arrived emigrants were encouraged to buy land from the trustee rather than other landowners so that these donations could be liquidated. As temple recorder, William Clayton announced in the *Nauvoo Neighbor*, late in 1843:

> I feel it my duty to say to the brethren generally, and especially those who are emigrating to this place, that there is in the hands of the Trustee in Trust, a large quantity of lands, both in the city and adjoining Townships in this county, which is for sale—some of which belongs to the church and is designed for the benefit of the poor, and also to liquidate debts owing by the church, for which the Trustee in Trust is responsible. Some also is land which has been consecrated for the building of the Temple, and some for the Nauvoo House.
>
> If the brethren who move in here and want an inheritance will buy their lands from the Trustee in Trust, they will thereby benefit the poor, the Temple and the

23. "List of Bonds and Deeds Belonging to the Temple," n.d., holograph, Newel K. Whitney Papers, L. Tom Perry Special Collections, Harold B. Lee Library, Brigham Young University, Provo, Utah. Other benefactors included Horace S. Eldredge, Frederick Kesler, Jacob Zundell, Alexander Mills, Albert G. Fellows, Dimick Jefferson, John McClure, William Spiers, Aaron Powers, Ethan Kimball, Alonzo LeBaron, James Dunn, David Fullmer, James S. Holman, Solon Powers, Abraham Washburn, Levi North, Lorenzo D. Driggs, Reuben W. Allred, George W. Nickerson, Lewis D. Wilson, Jacob Degrow, and James McClellan. Stephen Markham (1800-78) was born in New York, was baptized in July 1837 in Ohio, and was a member of the Nauvoo high priests' quorum. He stayed with Joseph, Hyrum, John Taylor, and Willard Richards in Carthage Jail until a few hours before the martyrdom. Frederick Kesler (1816-99), a builder by trade, was baptized in June 1840. Horace S. Eldredge (1816-88) joined the Church on 4 June 1836 and was ordained a Seventy early in 1844.

24. "Edward Hunter," *Our Pioneer Heritage*, 6:323. This biographical sketch (no author identified) contains lengthy excerpts from Hunter's autobiography.

Nauvoo House, and even then only be doing that which is their duty and which I know, by considerable experience, will be vastly for their benefit and satisfaction in days to come. Let all the brethren therefore, when they move into Nauvoo, consult President Joseph Smith the Trustee etc., and purchase their lands of him, and I am bold to say that God will bless them and will hereafter be glad they did so.

We hold ourselves ready at any time to wait upon the brethren and show them the lands belonging to the church and Temple etc., and can be found any day either at President Joseph Smith's Bar Room or the Temple Recorder's Office, at the Temple.[25]

Mary Ann Weston Maughan recalled that her husband, Peter, purchased their lot "from the temple" (meaning the trustee), and "being a stone mason, he went to work on the Temple walls to pay for it."[26]

The Sisters' Penny Subscription

During the latter half of 1843, the women of the Church launched a modest but remarkably effective fund-raising project for the temple. Mercy Fielding Thompson left this recollection of its genesis of the program:

At one time after seeking earnestly to know from the Lord if there was anything that I could do for the building up of the Kingdom of God, a most pleasant sensation came over me with the following words. Try to get the Sisters to subscribe one cent per week for the purpose of buying glass and nails for the Temple. I went immediately to Brother Joseph and told him what seemed to be the whispering of the still small voice in me. He told me to go ahead and the Lord would bless me. I then mentioned it to Brother Hyrum who was much pleased and did all in his power to encourage and help by speaking to the Sisters on the subject in private and public, promising them that they should receive their blessings in that Temple. All who subscribed the cent per week should have their names recorded in the Book of the Law of the Lord.[27]

Although this penny subscription began quietly in Nauvoo, it quickly gained impetus and spread to the surrounding settlements. In 1844 and 1845 it reached branches of the Church throughout the United States.[28] On Christmas Day 1843,

25. William Clayton, "Notice to Emigrants and Latter-day Saints Generally," 16 December 1843, *Nauvoo Neighbor* 1 (December 27, 1843): 68.

26. "Journal of Mary Ann Weston Maughan," 364.

27. Mercy Rachel Fielding Thompson, "Autobiography of Mercy Rachel Thompson," holograph, 7, LDS Church Archives.

28. "Boston Female Penny and Sewing Society," *Times and Seasons* 6 (1 March 1845): 820.

Mercy and her sister, Mary Fielding Smith, now the wife of Hyrum Smith, mailed a letter to the *Millennial Star* office in England where it was published the following June:

> To the Sisters of the Church of Jesus Christ in England:
>
> Greeting. Dear Sisters,—this is to inform you that we have here entered into a small weekly subscription for the benefit of the Temple Funds. One thousand have already joined it, while many more are expected, by which we trust to help forward the great work very much. The amount is only one cent or a halfpenny per week.
>
> As Brother Amos Fielding is waiting for this, I cannot enlarge more than to say, that myself and sister Thompson are engaged in collecting the same.
>
> We remain your affectionate sisters in Christ,
>
> MARY SMITH
M. R. THOMPSON

Appended to the notice was a statement by Hyrum Smith declaring that the subscription was "fully sanctioned by the First Presidency." Wilford Woodruff, editor of the *Star*, also endorsed the new fund-raising effort, expressing his "trust that the sisters in England will manifest that they will not be behind the sisters in Nauvoo in this laudable work" and exhorting the recorders in Britain to keep the names and subscription amounts "with the strictest accuracy."[29]

Hyrum Smith's endorsement of the penny subscription was critical. Not only was he was now a member of the building committee, but he also represented the First Presidency. He promised that "all the sisters who would comply with this call should have the first privilege of seats in the temple when it was finished."[30] At April 1844 conference, only a few weeks before his death, Hyrum made this fund a major theme of his address:

> I thought some time ago I would get up a small subscription, so that the sisters might do something. In consequence of some misunderstanding, it has not gone on as at first; it is a matter of my own, I do not ask it as a tithing. I give a privilege for any one to pay a cent a week, or fifty cents a year. I want it by next fall to buy nails and glass. It is difficult to get money, I know that a small subscription will bring in more than a large one; the poor can help in this way. I take the responsibility upon myself, and call again upon the sisters; I call again until I get about $1,000, it only requires 2,000 subscribers. I have sent this subscription to

---

29. Mary Fielding Smith and Mercy Rachel Fielding Thompson, "To the Sisters of the Church of Jesus Christ in England," *Millennial Star* 5 (June 1844): 15.

30. William Clayton's report of Smith's statement, George D. Smith, *An Intimate Chronicle*, 340.

England, and the branches; I am not to be dictated to by any one except the prophet and God; I want you to pay in your subscriptions to me, and it shall always be said boldly by me—the sisters bought the glass in that house—and their names shall be written in the Book of the Law of the Lord. It is not a tax but a free will offering to procure something which shall ever be a monument of your works. No member of the Female Relief Society got it up;[31] I am the man that did it; they ought not to infringe upon it; I am not a member of the Female Relief Society; I am one of the committee of the Lord's House. I wish to accomplish something; I wish all the saints to have an opportunity to do something; I want the poor to have a chance with the purse of five dollars.—The widow's two mites, were more in the eyes of the Lord, than the purse of the rich; and the poor woman shall have a seat in the house of God, she who pays her two mites as much as the rich; because it is all they have.[32]

Mercy Fielding Thompson recalled that she and her sister "took down and kept a record of all the names" and deposited the money in a bag. She remembered that during times of danger, they "hid up the bag containing that money in a pile of bricks which Hyrum had intended for building had his life been spared."[33] The Boston Female and Penny Sewing Society of Mormon women appointed Elvira Baldwin as treasurer of the subscription donations. Baldwin reported on the receipts at the society's quarterly meetings.[34] These local treasurers forwarded the donations to Mary and Mercy at Nauvoo with the names of the contributors. A list of the sisters in Pendlebury Branch in England dated 15 September 1844 with their contributions given in pence[35] has survived:

Isabella Ward 5½
Sarah Chapman 5½
Jane Chapman 5½
Ann Grundy 5½
Mary Grundy 5½
Mary Barker 5½
Mary Rothwell 5½
Mary Robinson ½

31. Hyrum Smith's claim of having started the society is enigmatic, since it is widely acknowledged that his sister-in-law Mercy and his wife Mary were responsible for creating the penny fund.

32. "Conference Minutes," *Times and Seasons* 5 (1 August 1844): 596.

33. Mercy Rachel Fielding Thompson, "Autobiography of Mercy Rachel Thompson," holograph, 9, LDS Archives.

34. "Boston Female Penny and Sewing Society," 820.

35. The total is in shillings and pence with twelve pence per shilling and twenty shillings per pound. A loaf of bread in England in 1845 weighing five pounds cost about 2 shillings (or twenty-four) pence.

Lucy Lythgo 4½
Esther Lythgo 2½
Betty Hamer 5½
Sarah Greenhalgh 5½
Hannah Greenhalgh 5½
Mary Grimshaw 5½
Martha Kay 3½
Jane Hilton 1½
Alice Patrick 5½
Total: 06   6½[36]

Patriarch Smith would continue to be an ardent supporter of the fund until his death in June 1844. After his demise, Alpheus Cutler, another member of the building committee, was appointed in Hyrum's stead to assist Mercy and Mary in recording the donations.[37] The Twelve under Brigham Young continued to endorse the fund as well. This notice appeared in the *Times and Seasons* two months after Joseph and Hyrum's death: "To the Saints in Nauvoo, and abroad: We would say that the penny subscription by the sisters, which has always been conducted and carried on by Mrs. Hyrum Smith, and Mrs. Thompson will still continue, and the payments be made and enclosed as usual with the persons names signed, and for which the Twelve will be responsible."[38]

The penny subscription represented a tremendous sacrifice for the sisters. One unidentified sister recalled, "[I] worked my fingers to the quick, to gain something from my scanty allowance, to assist in the completion of that building."[39] For Louisa Barnes Pratt, raising this sum represented her commitment to the Prophet, the temple, and the gospel:

We all struggled hard to bear our great bereavement and not suffer our lips to curse our enemies. Our hands and hearts were employed to hasten the completion of the temple. The sisters even resolved to pay fifty cents each towards buying nails and glass. By strict economy, I obtained the amount. I started in good faith to go to the temple office to bestow my offering. Suddenly a temptation came over me. I conned over in my mind how many things I needed for family

36. Lists of English Consecrations, Primarily from Female Members, n.d., Newel K. Whitney Papers, microfilm of holograph, Perry Special Collections, Lee Library.

37. George D. Smith, *An Intimate Chronicle*, 540.

38. Brigham Young and Willard Richards, "Notice," dated 20 September 1844, *Times and Seasons* 5 (20 September 1844): 670. Speaking at a Sabbath meeting, Young also "made a few remarks endorsing the sisters' penny subscription for the purpose of procuring glass and nails for the Temple and requested the saints to prepare themselves to entertain the elders who may be in attendance at conference." *History of the Church*, 7:279.

39. Emeline (pseud.), "Mormon Endowments," *Warsaw Signal*, 15 April 1846, 2.

use, and that money would relieve my present necessities. Then I resisted. Said I, "If I have no more than a crust of bread each day for a week, I will pay this money into the treasury." I went forward, paid over the money, and returned, feeling a secret satisfaction.[40]

Many of those who could, paid their full year's subscription for 1844 in advance, showing their anxiety to help.[41] In December 1844, Brigham Young and the Twelve faced the necessity of raising "the sum of $3,100, which [was] due from the Trustees to several individuals for church lands, which [was] to be paid within three months or the lands be forfeited, worth from ten to fifteen thousand dollars."[42] A payment of $1,000 was due in three days. Young met with the Twelve on 5 December to discuss possible means of quickly raising the required sum.

After conversing some time about possible ways of raising the needed funds, Brigham Young said that his "feelings were to draw the money lying in the possession of Sisters Mary Smith and Mercy R. Thompson and A. Cutler, which money has been donated by the sisters of the church, by paying one cent a week, for the purpose of purchasing the nails and glass for the temple and which amounted to five or six hundred dollars already collected. It is considered wisdom to do this to save the church property from the hands of our enemies; and the straitened circumstances under which the Trustees labor in consequence of persecution and oppression—we consider sufficient to justify the course. It is also considered certain that the money will be ready by the time the nails and glass are needed for the Temple, and that the money will be saving so much interest, whereas at the present it is lying useless. The suggestion by President Young seemed to meet the feelings of all the brethren, and it was concluded to draw an order for the money on Mrs. Mary Smith, and Mercy R. Thompson, which was immediately done.[43]

The order, addressed to Sisters Smith and Thompson, and signed by Brigham Young as President of the Quorum of Twelve. read:

Dear Sisters:
    We are under the necessity of raising a considerable sum of money for the use of the church within a few days. We have counseled together on the subject,

---
40. "Louisa Barnes Pratt," autobiography in *Heart Throbs of the West*, compiled by Kate B. Carter, 12 vols. (Salt Lake City: Daughters of the Utah Pioneers, 1947-51), 8:232. Louisa Barnes (1802-80), a Massachusetts native, married Addison Pratt in 1831. The two joined the Church in June 1837.

41. George D. Smith, *An Intimate Chronicle*, 540.

42. *History of the Church*, 7:322.

43. *History of the Church*, 7:322.

and have considered it wisdom to call upon you for the money in your hands, donated by the sisters as penny subscriptions. You will therefore, please deliver the same to Bishop Whitney when he presents this order.

Done by order of the Quorum of the Twelve, for and in behalf of the Church of Jesus Christ of Latter-day Saints.[44]

The money from the fund was sufficient to make the initial $1,000 payment. No known public announcement was made to the women about this diversion of the funds.

In 1845, the sisters' fund-raising efforts continued. On 15 March, Sisters Smith and Thompson published this announcement in the *Times and Seasons*:

> By the counsel of the Twelve, Mrs. Hyrum Smith and Mrs. Thompson request all those sisters who have received papers to collect the penny subscription, to forward them as soon as possible that they may be able to ascertain whether all those employed as collectors have been faithful: as it appears that there is suspicion resting upon a certain individual of having kept the money which she had collected. They would say for the satisfaction of the sisters that about one thousand dollars have been received, and most of the sisters with whom they have conversed, seem inclined to continue paying their cent a week until the temple is finished; and money being wanted to purchase other things besides glass and nails, they invite all those who are able and feel so disposed to pay up for the present year; and as there are some poor sisters who are extremely anxious to throw in their mite who cannot possibly raise money, they would say that any kind of useful articles will be received from such.[45]

On 31 May 1845, William Clayton wrote, "Many [of the sisters] have given the donation for the second year.... These contributions yet continue to come in each day."[46] All said, the fund raised nearly $2,000 for the liquidation of debts and the purchase of building materials.

The Martyrdom of Joseph and Hyrum Smith

Tension between Joseph Smith and his critics reached its acme in June 1844. On 7 June, several disaffected Church members published the first issue of

---

44. Ibid.

45. Mary Fielding Smith and Mercy R. Thompson, "Notice," *Times and Seasons* 6 (15 March 1845): 847.

46. George D. Smith, *An Intimate Chronicle*, 540.

the *Nauvoo Expositor*, a newspaper critical of the Prophet. The substance of the *Expositor's* complaints was, among other things, the then secret practice of plural marriage. As the name of the paper suggests, its purpose was to expose the practice to the public.

On 10 June, Joseph Smith and the Nauvoo City Council "passed a resolution ordering the [*Expositor*] press to be abated as a nuisance, which was done the same evening." This action created controversy throughout the state, and William Clayton remembered that "the [temple] works were suspended about the 20th of June." Rumors circulated that the owners of the press, who had fled from Nauvoo taking their families, had threatened vengeance. According to these rumors, William Clayton wrote, "in a few weeks there should not be left one stone of the temple standing upon another."[47]

Joseph agreed to stand trial for charges related to the *Expositor* incident. As he, Hyrum Smith, and several others departed from Nauvoo for Carthage on 24 June, they rode past the temple site. Here Joseph drew rein, looked with admiration on the temple, then over the city, and remarked, "This is the loveliest place and the best people under the heavens; little do they know the trials that await them."[48] When he arrived in Carthage, he was detained in the jail to await trial.

Governor Thomas Ford visited Nauvoo with two companies of the Carthage Greys while Joseph was held in Carthage Jail. While the party toured the temple, Alpheus Cutler asked William G. Sterrett to quietly watch them while they were on the building site. In the basement of the temple, the party inspected the baptismal font. According to Sterrett:

> One of the governor's company called his attention to one of the oxen that had part of one horn broken off. The governor stepped up to it and laying his hand upon it said: "This is 'the cow with the crumply horn' that we read of." One of the staff continued: "That tossed the maiden all forlorn!" At which they all laughed. Several of the horns were broken off by the governor's attendants and one at least was carried away as a souvenir.[49]

One of Ford's attendants reportedly remarked, "This temple is a curious piece of workmanship; and it was a damned shame that they did not let Joe Smith

47. Ibid., 541.

48. *History of the Church*, 6:554.

49. Quoted in B. H. Roberts, *A Comprehensive History of the Church of Jesus Christ of Latter-day Saints*, 6 vols. (Salt Lake City: Deseret News Press, 1930), 2:279. A few months later in September, a visitor observed, "[The oxen] are very handsomely carved of wood. I should not have known the nature of the material, if some lawless rascals had not defaced them by breaking off parts of the horns." "S.," Letter to the editor, *Springfield* [Massachusetts] *Republican*, in *Nauvoo Neighbor* 2 (13 November 1844): 71.

finish it." Another of the men remarked, "But he is dead by this time, and he will never see this temple again." Brother Sterrett interrupted indignantly, "They cannot kill him until he has finished his work." Ford smiled to his aides and said: "Whether he has finished his work or not, by God, he will not see this place again, for he is finished before this time."[50]

The Prophet and his brother Hyrum were murdered on 27 June, and John Taylor was injured. Willard Richards, also in the party, was unscathed. Orson Hyde depicted the scene that night in Nauvoo as word of the martyrdom spread:

> Before another day dawned, the messenger bore the tidings into the afflicted city; the picket guards of the city heard the whisper of murder in silent amazement, as the messenger passed into the city. There the pale muslin signal for gathering the troops hung its drooping folds from the Temple spire (as if partaking of nature's sadness), and made tremulous utterance to the humble soldiery to muster immediately. As the dawn made the signal visible, and the bass tone of the great drum confirmed the call, fathers, husbands, and minor sons ... fled to the muster ground.... The speaker announced the martyrdom of the Prophet and Patriarch, and paused under the heavy burden of the intelligence.[51]

The following day the bodies of the murdered brothers were brought from Carthage to Nauvoo, passing between rows of sorrowing Saints who lined the streets from the temple to the Mansion House.[52] The workmen's tools lay idle for several weeks while the Saints mourned the loss of their Prophet and Patriarch and wrestled with uncertainty about what course to pursue. William Adams later wrote: "Through the sad ordeal and persecution that the church had passed through, being about four weeks, nothing was done on the temple or the quarry until the middle of July."[53] William Clayton, writing in 1845, recalled that the emergency preempted work on the temple, for the temple workmen were forced to "stand on guard night and day."[54] William Huntington, recorded the mood of the city in his diary on 8 July 1844:

> Through this week past, the saints have remained quite as composed under our heavy trial as could be expected. Deep mourning pervades our city for the loss

50. Quoted in George Q. Cannon, *The Life of Joseph Smith the Prophet* (Salt Lake City: Deseret Book, 1888), 521. William Gibson Sterrett (1813-73) was a farmer and cabinetmaker.

51. Orson Hyde, Article in *Frontier Guardian* (Council Bluffs, Iowa), 27 June 1849, reprinted in *Scrapbook of Mormon Literature*, edited by Ben E. Rich, 2 vols. (Chicago: Henry C. Etten, 1913), 1:283.

52. "Edward Hunter." *Our Pioneer Heritage*, 6:324.

53. "Autobiography of William Adams," 1822-77, typescript, 15, Perry Special Collections, Lee Library. This document begins with an autobiographical reminiscence, then has daily entries.

54. George D. Smith, *An Intimate Chronicle*, 543.

of beloved Joseph and Hyrum. The people are waiting with anxiety for the return of the twelve. As soon as they return, a special conference will be called for the purpose of appointing a trustee-in-trust or one who shall preside over the church.[55]

The church never appointed anyone to take Hyrum Smith's place on the temple committee.

---

55. William Huntington Sr., "Journal of William Huntington," 1784-1846, 8 July 1844, typescript, 16, Perry Special Collections, Lee Library.

Chapter 7

THE ASCENDANCY OF THE TWELVE: JULY 1844 TO DECEMBER 1844

Work on the Temple Resumes

Parley P. Pratt, who was on a mission to the eastern states and therefore did not know when Joseph and Hyrum were murdered, felt prompted to cut his mission short and return to Nauvoo. During his homeward journey, news of the martyrdom reached him. In his autobiography he penned this description of the last leg of his journey:

> During the two or three days I spent in traveling between Chicago and Peoria I felt so weighed down with sorrow and the powers of darkness that it was painful for me to converse or speak to any one, or even to try to eat or sleep.... As I walked along over the plains of Illinois, lonely and solitary, I reflected as follows: I am now drawing near to the beloved city; How shall I meet an entire community bowed down with grief and sorrow unutterable? What shall I say?... Shall I tell them to fly to the wilderness and deserts? Or, shall I tell them to stay at home and take care of themselves, and continue to build the Temple? With these reflections and inquiries, I walked onward, weighed down as it were unto death. When I could endure it no longer, I cried out aloud, saying: "O Lord! in the name of Jesus Christ I pray Thee, show me what these things mean, and what I shall say

to Thy people?" On a sudden the Spirit of God came upon me, and filled my heart with joy and gladness indescribable; and while the spirit of revelation glowed in my bosom with as visible a warmth and gladness as if it were fire. The Spirit said unto me:"... Go and say unto my people in Nauvoo, that they shall continue to pursue their daily duties and take care of themselves, and make no movement in Church government to reorganize or alter anything until the return of the remainder of the Quorum of the Twelve. But exhort them that they continue to build the House of the Lord which I have commanded them to build in Nauvoo."

This information caused my bosom to burn with joy and gladness, and I was comforted above measure; all my sorrow seemed in a moment to be lifted as a burthen from my back.

The change was so sudden I hardly dared to believe my senses; I, therefore, prayed the Lord to repeat to me the same things the second time; if, indeed, I might be sure of their truth, and might really tell the Saints to stay in Nauvoo, and continue to build the Temple.

As I prayed thus, the same spirit burned in my bosom, and the Spirit of the Lord repeated to me the same message again.... In confirmation that the message was right, I found them already renewing their labors on the Temple, under the direction of John Taylor and Willard Richards.[1]

Pratt arrived at Nauvoo on Thursday, 11 July.[2] Just four days earlier at the Sabbath service, "the subject of the temple was brought into consideration, and the Church voted to commence work again and finish it as speedily as possible."[3] At this meeting, "Dr. Willard Richards advised some of the people to go out and harvest, and others who stay to go on with the Temple, and make work in the city."[4] Work on the temple resumed Monday, 8 July. William Clayton recalled: "The committee had not so much as a bushel of meal, nor a pound of flour, nor a pound of meat to feed the hands with; but all seemed determined to go to work and trust in God for the means."[5] This scarcity of means would continue for some time; and to make matters worse, the temple committee hesitated to disburse even the supplies they had available, fearing to exhaust their store completely. As a result, Brigham Young later recalled:

---

1. *Autobiography of Parley P. Pratt*, edited by his son Parley P. Pratt (1874, Salt Lake City: Deseret Book, 1985 printing), 293-94.

2. William Huntington Sr., "Journal of William Huntington," 1784-1846, 11 July 1845, typescript, 16, L. Tom Perry Special Collections, Harold B. Lee Library, Brigham Young University, Provo, Utah.

3. George D. Smith, ed., *An Intimate Chronicle: The Journals of William Clayton* (Salt Lake City: Signature Books, 1995), 543.

4. Joseph Smith, Jr., et al., *History of the Church of Jesus Christ of Latter-day Saints*, edited by B. H. Roberts (Salt Lake City: Deseret News Press, 6 vols. published 1902-12, Vol. 7 published 1932, 1st printing), 7:169.

5. George D. Smith, *An Intimate Chronicle*, 543.

Brigham Young, President of the Twelve

When the Twelve returned to Nauvoo, I found tithing-butter spoiled, potatoes rotted in the cellars, and pork spoiled in the barrels, while the brethren at work on the Temple would come to their labor without breakfast, and pork, butter, beef, etc., rotting under the feet of the Temple Committee. Said I, "Empty these barrels, or I will walk into your cellars and empty them for you: let these workmen have something to eat." "Oh," said the committee, "we are afraid there will not be enough to last a year." Then, if we starve, we starve together; and if we live, we live together. I ordered the wheat, the pork, the butter, etc., to be issued to the workmen.[6]

One by one, the Twelve reached Nauvoo until, by 15 August, all of them were present except William Smith, the Prophet's brother and Hyrum's successor as patriarch, who rightly feared for his life if he returned to Nauvoo. The Twelve met with the temple committee on 24 August and "voted that [Brigham Young] should take such measures as should seem best to gather men and means to Nauvoo to complete the Temple."[7] Under Young's direction, work was pushed forward "as fast as possible," the structure, goal, and stability proving, in Lyman O. Littlefield's words, to be "a very wise course for the promotion of peace and to restore confidence in the community generally."[8] Samuel W.

6. Brigham Young, 6 October 1860, *Journal of Discourses*, 26 vols. (London and Liverpool: LDS Booksellers Depot, 1855-86), 8:317.

7. *History of the Church*, 7:261.

8. Lyman Omer Littlefield, *Reminiscences of Latter-day Saints* (Logan: Utah Journal Company, 1888), 167.

Richards wrote to his brother, Franklin, who was then in New York en route to a mission in England: "We feel some better since the Twelve has come home and seem to have good faith that we shall build the Temple."[9]

The General Authorities took several additional measures to stimulate activity on the temple. Wilford Woodruff wrote in his journal that the Twelve visited the construction site in mid-August and "encouraged the workmen."[10] They promised the Saints: "If you will be united and go to with your mights in building the Temple you will have power to accomplish it and get an endowment."[11] Baptisms in the font resumed on 24 August with the Twelve leading the way; "several of the ... Apostles were baptized for their dead."[12] The apostles reassured the members of the Church in Great Britain by epistle, "The murder of Joseph will not stop the work; it will not stop the Temple."[13] Not only did the Twelve intend to finish the temple, but they also declared that it would "continue to be built up according to the pattern which has been commenced."[14]

The Saints responded with energy and good will. Elizabeth Ann Whitney recalled:

At this time [September 1844] the people were energetically at work upon the temple, and President Brigham Young and his brethren of the Quorum of the Twelve, with the bishops and all the leading men, were pushing everything forward towards completing the temple, in order to obtain certain blessings and confirmations that had been promised to the Saints when the temple should be so far finished as to enable them to work in it.[15]

The sisters of the branches in nearby La Harpe and Macedonia

sent word to the temple Committee and stated their anxiety to see the building progress still more rapidly. They proposed if the committee would build another crane, they would furnish the means to build it with. The committee and the Recorder counseled on the subject and it was decided to comply with the wishes

9. Samuel W. Richards, Letter to Franklin D. Richards, August 1844, Richards Family Correspondence, typescript, LDS Church Archives. News of the martyrdom prompted Franklin to return to Nauvoo.

10. Wilford Woodruff, 17 August 1844, *Wilford Woodruff's Journal, 1833-1898,* typescript, edited by Scott G. Kenny, 9 vols. (Midvale, Utah: Signature Books, 1983-85): 2:442.

11. *History of the Church,* 7:263.

12. Ibid., 7:261.

13. Ibid., 7:174.

14. Ibid., 7:250.

15. Elizabeth Ann Smith Whitney, "A Leaf from an Autobiography," *Woman's Exponent* 7 (15 November 1878): 191.

of those sisters. Sister Clark, wife of Raymond Clark was authorized to collect the contributions. She immediately started and returned on the 29th with money and other property amounting to the whole of $194, which was more than sufficient to build a new crane. The committee immediately set the carpenters to work and on August 3rd the crane was put in operation, under the management of Joshua Armstrong, the setter, and Horace Owens to back up, and William W. Dryer, William Austin and Archibald Hill to attend to the crane. They commenced work on the north side, and very soon satisfied the Saints of the utility of the movement.[16]

Another example of the Saints' eagerness to complete the temple is that of the stonecutters. On 14 August, the Twelve and the temple committee met with them to discuss their pay, which had been a matter of considerable confusion since the martyrdom. During the course of the meeting, the authorities decided to raise the wage of the windlass men to $1.50 per day and assured the stonecutters that their pay would be improved as well.[17] Wilford Woodruff recorded that "a good feeling was manifest."[18] Two days later the stonecutters voluntarily held a meeting to

> take into consideration our wages, having encouragement from the Twelve that our pay should be better than heretofore, and also from the interest that we have ourselves of hastening the building of the temple. We resolved to reduce our wages to the following specified prices, viz., that the cutting of capitals be reduced to two hundred dollars each, also that of the bush-hammer and droved [finishing] work be reduced to fifty cents per foot. That of the axed work [rough cutting] to twenty-five cents per foot. Resolved also that all other work for the future shall be estimated and priced according to these prices.[19]

The apostles ardently preached the importance of completing the temple. Scarcely a meeting passed without some word of encouragement or warning from the pulpit in this regard.[20] The following excerpts from sermons of Brigham Young are typical:

> 18 August 1844: Store your grain in Nauvoo for you will want it here, to eat while you are building the Temple. I want to say to the hands upon the Temple be united and I want to say to the committee don't turn away any person because he is

---

16. William Clayton, Journal, in Journal History of the Church of Jesus Christ of Latter-day Saints (chronology of typed entries and newspaper clippings, 1830-present), 31 December 1844, 15, LDS Church Archives.

17. *History of the Church*, 7:249.

18. Woodruff, 14 August 1844, Journal, 2:441.

19. Minutes of a meeting of the stonecutters, Journal History, 15 August 1844, 1.

20. See *History of the Church*, 7:254, 262, 268, 279, 284, 298, 299, 300 for examples of sermons by Brigham Young, Wilford Woodruff, Heber C. Kimball, and Parley P. Pratt on the construction of the temple between August and October.

an Englishman, Scotchman, Irishman, or any other nation, but employ every man you can and build the temple and your homes. I had rather pay out every cent I have to build up this place and get an endowment if I was driven the next minute, without any thing to take with me.[21]

6 October 1844: Why are we taking so much pains to build that Temple? That we may fulfill certain ordinances, and receive certain endowments and secure to ourselves an inheritance in the eternal world. Every man, woman and child within the sound of my voice, are interested in the building of that Temple. We know very little as a people yet, we don't know so much as the former day saints.... I know there are some here who know how to save themselves and their families, and it is this which occupies their attention all the day long and it was this which occupied the attention of our beloved prophet.... The first thing we have got to do is to build the Temple, where we can receive those blessings which we so much desire.[22]

Appointment of New Trustees

Joseph Smith's death removed him as trustee in trust from the Church and threw the disposition of Church's property into disarray. Most of his assets and property were in the name of the trustee in trust while his debts and obligations were considered personal.[23] Daniel H. Wells, in transferring the temple site, had deeded it to Joseph as trustee. As matter of legal course, his family was to have inherited the Church property and would have then been obligated to deed it to Joseph's successor. However, the question of who would be Joseph's successor had not been settled.

Appointing a new trustee became a matter of dispute because of the connection in many of the Saints' minds between the offices of President of the Church and trustee for the Church. There were, according to William Clayton's diary entry on 6 July, "4 or 5 men pointed out as successors to the Trustee and President."[24] During the final days of June and the first week of July, while the Saints were awaiting the return of the Twelve, speculation arose about who should be appointed trustee and whether the trustee could be someone other than the President of the Church. William Clayton's daily journal for the first week of July captures the uncertainty, rumors, and confusion:

21. Ibid., 7:259.

22. "October Conference Minutes," Times and Seasons 5 (15 October 1844): 685.

23. George D. Smith, An Intimate Chronicle, 137.

24. Ibid.

[2 July 1844, Tuesday.] [I] went to see Emma. She is in trouble because Mother Smith is making disturbance about the property in Joseph's hands.... There is considerable danger if the family begins to dispute about the property that Joseph's creditors will come forward and use up all the property there is. If they will keep still there is property enough to pay the debts and plenty left for other uses.

4 July 1844, Thursday.].... I went to Emma's and assisted Esquire Wood to examine Josephs affairs. The situation looks gloomy. The property is chiefly in the name of the Trustee in Trust while the obligations are considered personal.... [Evening] in Council with Brothers [William] Marks, [Alpheus] Cutler and [Reynolds] Cahoon at Mark[s's] house. It seemed manifest to us that Brother Marks place is to be appointed president, and Trustee in Trust and this accords with Emma's feelings.

[6 July 1844, Saturday.].... Yesterday a raft of Pine Lumber arrived for the Trustee in Trust. [Lucien] Woodworth laid claim to it, but the brethren say it is my duty as agent for the Trustee to take charge of it. I have accordingly done so and ordered [Albert P.] Rockwood to Guard it till we can get it to the Temple. The greatest danger that now threatens us is dissensions and strifes amongst the Church. There are already 4 or 5 men pointed out as successors to the Trustee and President, and there is danger of feelings being manifest. All the brethren who stand at the head seem to feel the delicacy of the business. [W. W.] Phelps and Dr. [Willard] Richards have taken a private course and are carrying out many measures on their own responsibility without council.

[7 July 1844, Sunday.].... 5 o'clock went to council with the Quorum on the subject of appointing a Trustee in Trust.... I was late at the Council. The brethren had agreed not to appoint a Trustee until the Twelve came home, and that I should act in the place of Trustee to receive property etc. until one was appointed.

[8 July 1844, Monday.] At the Temple all day. Emma came up.... She also objected to the conclusion of the Council last evening and says there must be a Trustee appointed this week on account of the situation of business.[25]

[12 July 1844, Friday.] A.M. at the Temple measuring Lumber. President [William] Marks came up to enquire which was best to do about appointing a Trustee. We concluded to call a meeting of the several presidents of Quorums and their Council this P.M. at 2 o'clock. As I returned to dinner, Brother [Newel K.] Whitney came down with me and stated his feelings about Marks being appointed Trustee. He referred me to the fact of Marks being with [William] Law and Emma in opposition to Joseph and the Quorum. And if Marks is appointed Trustee our spiritual blessings will be destroyed inasmuch as he is not favorable to the most important matters.[26] The Trustee must of necessity be the first presi-

---

25. Emma had understandable concerns over the disposition of Joseph's property. Five months pregnant with David Hyrum, she had an interest in maintaining whatever portion she could for the support of her adopted daughter, Julia, and three young sons, Joseph III, Frederick Granger Williams, and Alexander Hale.

26. By "spiritual blessings" and "most important matters," Clayton was probably referring to the law of celestial (plural) marriage, to which Clayton and Whitney were privy and to which Marks, William Law, and Emma Smith had reacted negatively.

dent of the Church and Joseph has said that if he and Hyrum were taken away Samuel H. Smith would be his successor.

After dinner I talked with Cutler and Cahoon on the subject, and they both agreed in the same mind with Brother Whitney and myself. At 3 we went to meeting. Emma was present and urged the necessity of appointing a Trustee immediately. But on investigation it was considered we could not lawfully do it. Another meeting was appointed for Sunday Eve. Dr. Richards and Phelps seem to take all the matters into their own hands and won't tell us anything what they intend or have thought to do.

[13 July 1844, Saturday.].... Emma.... talked much about Trustees being appointed and says if he is not a man she approves of she will do the church all the injury she can by keeping the Lots which are in her name.

[14 July 1844, Sunday.].... At 6 went to the Council. Phelps and Richards and P[arley] P. Pratt stated that they had concluded to appoint 4 Trustees when a majority of the Twelve returned. These three brethren seem to keep matters very close to themselves and I and several others feel grieved at it. After meeting I informed Emma of the proceedings. She thinks they don't use her right.

[15 July 1844, Monday.].... Emma sent for me. I went and conversed considerable with her. She feels dissatisfied with the conduct of Richard[s] and Phelps and says if they undertake to trample upon her she will look to herself. I conversed with Richards and Phelps and told them our feelings and they seem to feel more free. They told me the names of those they had thought of nominating for Trustees, Myself and A. Cutler are two of them. I told Emma of this and she seems better satisfied.[27]

Part of the business the Twelve undertook upon their return was settling the matter of the trustee's appointment. On 9 August, they resolved: "That Bishops N[ewel] K. Whitney and Geo[rge] Miller go forward to settle the property of the trustee in trust Joseph Smith and be prepared to enter into the duty of Trustees of the Church of Jesus Christ of Latter-day Saints in Hancock County."[28] Heber C. Kimball moved that William Clayton assist the newly appointed trustees in settling the Church's financial affairs.[29] Clayton wrote on 31 May 1845, "[A] few days afterwards, the trustees entered upon the duties of their office."[30]

27. George D. Smith, *An Intimate Chronicle*, 136-139. See also *Autobiography of Parley P. Pratt*, 294.

28. Willard Richards, Journal, 9 August 1844, holograph, LDS Church Archives. He recorded Brigham Young's declaration in this meeting: "[To] the oldest bishop of the Church belongs the general financial concerns of the Church." This decision was significant because it not only named trustees but it made a legally debatable distinction between the trustees and the church president.

29. Ibid. According to William Huntington, Journal, 6 December 1844, typescript, 21: "There has been a new organization. The business which has been conducted by Brothers Cutler and Cahoon is now in the hands of the Trustees in Trust, Bishops [Newel] Whitney and George Miller, who receive all proffered and pay off all the hands."

30. George D. Smith, *An Intimate Chronicle*, 546.

The newly appointed trustees carried out their responsibilities with the endorsement of the Twelve and with the support of the community at large. Even Thomas Sharp, an implacable enemy of Joseph Smith, did not mistrust Whitney and Miller: "Under their management, the funds [are] being honestly appropriated."[31]

The Devil and Charles Lambert

Charles Lambert, a stonecutter from England, arrived at Nauvoo in March 1844, three months before Joseph Smith's death. William Clayton later described him as a "liberal-hearted, faithful, good man from first to last" for the remarkable contributions he made to the building effort.[32] Because he had been a well-to-do contractor in England, Lambert came to Nauvoo with only fine clothing and therefore "had none suitable to wear while working as a tradesman."[33] Lambert recounted in his autobiography the awkward situation in which he found himself:

> The day after I arrived ... I went up to the Temple and saw there was work for me, but my dress and general appearance did not bespeak that of a working man. I inquired for those in charge. Reynolds Cahoon presented himself and some others. They tried me very much and sought to make game of me. They took me for a crank and enthusiast.[34] R. Cahoon at last said, "If you can work, we can do with

Charles Lambert cut several of the sunstones on the temple.

31. Thomas C. Sharp, "Items from Nauvoo," *Warsaw Signal*, 21 August 1844, 1.

32. William Clayton, Journal, Journal History, 31 December 1844, 15.

33. "Lambert Reminiscence," in *Gems of Reminiscence, Seventeenth Book of the Faith Promoting Series*, compiled by George C. Lambert (pseud. for George Q. Cannon) (Salt Lake City: Juvenile Instructor Office, 1915), 172.

34. A crank was an eccentric. An enthusiast was religious fanatic.

your work, but we have nothing to give you." I replied sharply, "I have not come here to work for pay, I have come to help to build that House," pointing to the temple. Then they laughed.[35]

In addition to being ridiculed by members of the temple committee, Lambert also had to endure mockery and unpleasant practical jokes from his coworkers. He appeared for work wearing a good suit of clothes and a high silk-finished hat. He hung his hat up in the workshop, donned an improvised cap and apron, and commenced work; but "many of those employed upon the temple were Americans who seemed to have a contempt for foreign mechanics, and especially for dandies in that line, and to show their contempt, or else in a spirit of fun or mischief, they threw spalls[36] at the 'stove pipe' hat as it hung in the shop until they cut it to pieces."

Lambert saw the folly of quarreling with his fellows over this act of vandalism, so he ignored it, and treated the perpetrators as if it had not occurred. His courteous and dignified conduct and lack of ostentation, combined with his superiority as a workman overcame the prejudice arrayed against him. He soon won the respect of his fellow workmen and got along agreeably with them.[37] He summarized: "I was now considered worthy to draw my rations with the other men."[38]

He was chosen to serve a mission to the Indians in 1844 but the call was withdrawn when he proved himself a valuable asset to the temple works.[39] In the turmoil that followed Joseph Smith's death, many of the temple workmen quit to find other jobs when they were no longer receiving tithing provisions. Lambert and William Player, however, "discussed this problem between themselves, and voluntarily pledged themselves to continue at work until the Temple was built whether they were paid for their services or not."[40] Part of the lore associated with building the temple is this story:

> Charles Lambert had married during the first year of his residence in Nauvoo and undertaken the support of two [young] brothers and a sister of his wife, who had recently been orphaned and were helpless. He felt keenly his responsibility, and wished for money as he never had done before. While feeling thus he was passing along the street in Nauvoo one day when he met a well-dressed, genteel stranger who inquired if his name was Charles Lambert. On being told that it was, he said his name was Higgins, and that his home was in Missouri. With an ingratiating smile he said "I have heard of your skill as a workman, and want you to go to Missouri and work for me. You are not appreciated or properly paid here. If you will quit the Temple and go and work for me you can name your own price

35. Lambert, "Autobiography of Charles Lambert," typescript, 9, LDS Church Archives.
36. Spalls are splinters of stone, the by-products of the chiseling process.
37. "Lambert Reminiscence," Gems of Reminiscence, 172-73.
38. Lambert, "Autobiography," 10.
39. Ibid.
40. "Lambert Reminiscence," Gems of Reminiscence, 173.

and you will be sure of your pay. You see I have plenty of money with which to pay you." Suiting the action to the word, he thrust his hand into his pocket, and drew it out full of $10.00 and $20.00 gold pieces, which he displayed in a tempting manner, and urged him to accept his offer and not to submit any longer to the unfair treatment accorded him at the Temple. With a gesture of impatience called forth by the intimation of unfairness, Father Lambert thanked the stranger for his offer, but said he couldn't think of accepting it. He said he had no complaint to make of his treatment at the Temple, and the price others would pay for work they wished done would not influence him in the matter, as he intended to continue on at the Temple from principle. Bidding the stranger "Good-day" he turned to continue his walk along the street, but almost immediately the query arose in his mind as to how the stranger knew his name, and where he got his information from about his skill as a mechanic, and turned to take a final look at the stranger, when lo! he was no-where to be seen. He had disappeared as completely as if the ground had opened and swallowed him, and yet he had not had time by any ordinary means of locomotion to get out of sight.[41]

Lambert maintained that his would-be employer was "no other than Satan, the prince of tempters."[42]

Faithful Saints such as Lambert saw themselves as engaged in an epic struggle against Satan to complete the temple. British convert William C. Staines recalled:

Just before leaving England [early 1843] I visited some friends in Sheffield, and met with Brother R. Rushton, who was on a mission from Nauvoo. He had been asked to visit a brother in the Church who was possessed of a devil. This was the first case of the kind I had heard of being in the Church, and I felt quite anxious to see the party so afflicted. While reflecting about it, Brother Rushton asked me to accompany him, which I cheerfully did, and what transpired I never shall forget. When we entered the room where he was sitting, he looked around and saw Brother Rushton whom he had met before, and with a coarse voice said: "So you have come again in the name of Jesus have you? Well you may come if you have a mind to. I know you came from Nauvoo where you are building a temple to get your endowments and more power. Well, get your power; and the more power you get the more power we'll get." Just as soon as he was through speaking Brother Rushton laid hands on him and rebuked the evil spirits that had possession of him, when the brother called out in a loud voice: "How did you know there was more than one?" Brother Rushton remarked calmly: "You said we." The brother then said, "We will go but we will come again."[43]

41. "Lambert Reminiscence," *Gems of Reminiscence*, 172-73.

42. Ibid., 175.

43. William C. Staines, "Reminiscences of William C. Staines," *Contributor* 12 (February 1891): 123. William Carter Staines (1818-81) was baptized in 1841 in England and reached Nauvoo on 12

Setting the Sunstone Capitals

By mid-September, several of the thirty pilasters were complete and pre-pared to receive their capitals. The others were nearing completion as well. The *Nauvoo Neighbor* reported that the temple was "nearly to the tops of the second story windows."[44] A Massachusetts paper noted, "Two of the walls are now up for the roof, and the work is going on with great vigor. There are on the Temple and at the quarry 140 men employed, besides numerous teams."[45]

The first design for the capitals proposed by William Weeks included a sun-burst with human features. The sun was rising so that the lower half was still obscured.[46] This design was later changed to reveal the full face. There is some evidence that Joseph Smith received revelation concerning the design of this particular symbolic detail. Josiah Quincy, who had visited Nauvoo in May 1844 and observed the carving of one of these capitals, recalled:

> Near the entrance to the temple we passed a workman who was laboring upon a huge sun, which he had chiseled from the solid rock. The countenance was of the Negro type, and it was surrounded by the conventional rays. "General Smith," said the man, looking up from his task, "is this like the face you saw in vision?" "Very near it," answered the prophet, "except" (this was added with an air of careful connoisseurship that was quite overpowering)—"except that the nose is just a thought too broad."[47]

Benjamin Mitchell, a stonecutter by trade, carved the first sunstone and three of the thirty capitals.[48] Charles Lambert did at least some work on eleven of the capitals.[49] Others who carved capitals included Harvey Stanley, James Sharp, Rufus Allen, and James Henry Rollins.[50] Rollins did the rough shaping of some capitals, which he then handed off to more experienced carvers. In 1898 he recalled:

---

44. "Public Buildings in Nauvoo," *Nauvoo Neighbor* 3 (25 September 1844): 19.

45. *Springfield Republican*, 14 September 1844, quoted in Joseph Earl Arrington, "The Story of the Nauvoo Temple," 144, unpublished manuscript, ca. 1970, microfilm of typescript, Perry Special Collections, Lee Library.

46. William Weeks, Detail drawings for Nauvoo Temple, MS 11500, Drawing 5, William Weeks Papers, LDS Church Archives.

47. Josiah Quincy, *Figures of the Past from the Leaves of Old Journals* (Boston: Roberts Brothers, 1883), 389.

48. William Clayton, Journal History, 31 December 1844, 14; Benjamin Mitchell, Autobiography, in "Autobiographies of Early Seventies," typescript, 53, LDS Church Archives. Mitchell (1816-80) was baptized on 15 June 1835. In another location, Clayton lists Charles Lambert as the carver of the first sunstone. Mitchell may have carved the trumpet stone and Lambert the sunstone.

49. Lambert, "Autobiography," 13.

50. Nauvoo Temple Committee, Daybook E, 1844, 58, entry made on 6 December 1844, micro-film of holograph, LDS Church Archives.

Sunstone capital

Benjamin Mitchell came to me to rough out a capstone [capital], he said he would give me $50.00, which I did for him, and one for Charles Lambert and another for a stone cutter from Quincy. One month after this, Brother Player and the architect came to me and told me to take one of the capital stones and dress it. I told them I didn't think I was capable of cutting one of those stones, but they persuaded me to try it and they would help me out.

I did so with reluctance but accomplished this task and it was raised on the northeast corner of the Temple wall, being the last capital stone raised on the wall.[51]

The temple committee daybook entry for 6 December 1844, indicates that the stonecutters worked together frequently in dressing the capitals:

Harvey Stanley [credited] by stonecutting
1 capital [$]300 pt. of 1 capital [$]150
pt. of Rufus Allen's capital [$]75"
"[James] Sharp's " [$]5
C[harles] Lambert [credited] by stonecutting pt. of 1 Capital [$]150
pt. of Rufus Allen's Capital [$]75
"" Sharp's "

---

51. James Henry Rollins, "A Sketch of the Life of James Henry Rollins," 1898, typescript, 12, LDS Church Archives.

[$]05 Rufus Allen [credited] to C[harles] Lambert and Stanley for assisting to cut capital [$]150

James Sharp [credited by] assisting in cutting capital by Lambert and Stanley [$]10[52]

Wilford Woodruff's journal indicates that some of the capitals were already complete by 16 August 1844. During a visit to the temple, he and Heber C. Kimball "saw two of the caps finished with a man's face with two trumpets over his head."[53] Brigham Young described the final design of the capitals:

> Each one composed of five stones, viz. one base stone, one large stone representing the sun rising just above the clouds, the lower part obscured; the third stone represents two hands each holding a trumpet, and the last two stones form a cap over the trumpet stone, and these all form the capital.... These stones are very beautifully cut, especially the face and trumpet stones, and are an evidence of great skill in the architect and ingenuity on the part of the stonecutters. They present a very pleasing and noble appearance, and seem very appropriate in their places.[54]

The sunstone portion of each capital cost $300 dollars to carve; the capital in its entirety cost an estimated $450.[55] The first sunstone was raised on 23 September with some difficulty. It weighed two tons and was most likely the largest stone that had been hoisted onto the walls at that point. According to William Clayton, "When the stone was at its height, and the men were attempting to draw it to the wall, the crane gave way at the foot of the wing or angle, which circumstance caused considerable danger. By great care the stone was safely landed and set without any further accident."[56] Two days later on Wednesday, 25 September, he recorded another incident. As the workmen were

> beginning to raise one of the capitals, having neglected to fasten the guys,[57] the crane fell over with a tremendous crash, breaking it considerably. As soon as it was perceived that the crane was falling, the hands fled to get out of the way. One of the brethren, Thomas Jaap, running directly in the course of the falling crane, barely escaped being killed. The crane struck the ground and was within a foot of striking his head. This circumstance hindered the workmen some; but in a few days the crane was mended, reared and the brethren again went to work on it.[58]

52. Nauvoo Temple Committee, Daybook E, 1844, 58, entry made on 6 December 1844.

53. Woodruff, 16 August 1844, Journal, 2:442.

54. *History of the Church*, 7:323.

55. Clayton, Journal, Journal History, 31 December 1844, 14.

56. George D. Smith, *An Intimate Chronicle*, 545.

57. A guy was a rope used to steady heavy objects while they were being lifted.

58. George D. Smith, *An Intimate Chronicle*, 545.

At October general conference, the Twelve reported that the "walls are ready to receive the capitals and the arches of the upper story windows; and in fact, seven of the capitals are already reared."[59] The workmen, headed again by William Player, continued to raise and set the capitals through the fall, though they were delayed as they waited for the stonecutters to complete the intricate stones.[60] According to William Clayton's record of May 1845, some feared that "Brother Player would not be able to finish them before winter set in but it seemed as though the Lord held up the weather until this important piece of work was accomplished."[61]

On 6 December, a cold and rainy day, the final and reportedly the heaviest sunstone was set in its place.[62] The *History of the Church* contains this description of its raising:

> The workmen commenced raising the stone at half after 10 o'clock, but when about half way up one of the block shives[63] broke in two. This placed the matter in a dangerous position, it was impossible to raise the stone higher without a new shive, and to attempt to let it down would have cut off the rope instantly. After much labor the workmen secured the tackle so that it could not move and having this done, they fixed a new shive in the block and after about an hour and a half's delay, at half after one p.m. the stone was safely fixed in its place in the wall.[64]

The crane that broke was most likely the third crane.[65] "Two hours after the capital was set," Clayton continued, "it commenced snowing very briskly, and at night the ground was covered about four inches, and it froze very keenly."[66] The

---

59. "An Epistle of the Twelve to the Church of Jesus Christ of Latter-day Saints," *Times and Seasons* 5 (1 October 1844): 668.

60. *History of the Church*, 7:323.

61. George D. Smith, *An Intimate Chronicle*, 546.

62. Ibid., 546.

63. A shive, properly a sheave, is the roller or wheel that fits inside a block. When a rope is passed between the sheave and block, a tackle or pulley system is formed.

64. *History of the Church*, 7:323. William Clayton's account reads: "When the hands were raising the last capital, and had got it about half-way up, one of the block shives in the tackle broke and rendered it impossible in the situation either to raise or lower the stone. This circumstance presented a great difficulty, but after some consultation the hands fastened the rope below the tackle, so that it could not slip, and left the stone suspended while they took down the blocks, put in a new shive and fixed the blocks again. The stone was then raised without further difficulty, and was set precisely at twenty minutes before one o'clock." George D. Smith, *An Intimate Chronicle*, 546.

65. Thomas Japp was one of the men who manned the third crane. William Clayton, Journal, in Journal History, 31 December 1844, 15.

66. George D. Smith, *An Intimate Chronicle*, 546.

67. *History of the Church*, 7:323.

work of raising the capitals had spanned ten weeks, three of which were lost "through bad weather, and having to wait for stone."[67]

Stone-setting ceased for the winter with this achievement on 6 December. While the sunstone portion of all thirty capitals had been set, "twelve of the capitals" still lacked their trumpet stones. Three of those trumpet stones were already cut and several others were nearly complete.[68]

The quarrying and preparation of stones continued throughout the winter. On 15 January 1845, Albert Rockwood, the quarry foreman, reported: "Sixty-two hands and six teams engaged today in the quarry."[69] The remaining trumpet stones would be among the first set the following season.

A New Location for the Donations Office

The recorder's office near the temple had been the designated place for the transfer of donations to the temple since October 1842. However, space must have been a problem, especially as the number of workmen and machines proliferated, requiring a larger amount of tithing supplies and more bookkeeping. On 1 December 1844, the trustees ran this notice in the *Times and Seasons*:

> We would say to all those who wish to bring tithes for the building of the temple in the city of Nauvoo, that we have deemed it wisdom to remove our office, for the better accommodation of business, and of all who visit us on business, to the new and commodious brick store of Elder P. P. Pratt, situated one block north from the west end of the temple; at which place we will attend every day in the week, (Sundays excepted) from morning till evening, to receive donations for the temple and also attend to all other matters of business pertaining to the trustees. We publish this notice that the brethren may not need to enquire where they shall deposit their donations. We have only one place of deposit in the city of Nauvoo and that is the above mentioned brick store.[70]

This location continued to double as the recorder's office and temple tithing store until late 1845. On 27 August 1845, William Clayton wrote in his journal:

> This morning Brother Parley came into the office to say that his women folks wanted the rooms over the store. This would deprive us of all but the one room

---

67. *History of the Church*, 7:323.

68. Ibid., 7:324.

69. Ibid., 7:360.

70. Newel K. Whitney, George Miller, William Clayton, "A Voice from the Temple," *Times and Seasons* 5 (1 December 1844): 728.

for office, store and council room. I suggested to the Bishops [Whitney and Miller] to move to the New York Store,[71] inasmuch as that property belongs to the church and is much larger and we are paying $200 a year rent for this. The Trustees immediately went over and examined the premises and decided to enlarge the cellar and make the "New York Store" our office. They mentioned the place to President Young and he agreed to it at once.[72]

The New York Store, which had been rented to William Allen, was located "a few rods south of the temple."[73] The trustees moved to this new location on Sunday, 9 November. Heber C. Kimball wrote in his journal the following Monday: "Went to the New York Store, as the Trustees moved there office on last Sabbath."[74] In addition to serving as the tithing store and office, the New York Store was also the site of prayer meetings and other councils during the final months of 1845.[75]

Carpenters Hired

Even though work on the framed-up interior of the temple began in 1842 with the preparation of the temporary floor, workers naturally concentrated on raising the exterior walls. However, in the fall of 1844, the Twelve and the temple committee began to allocate more resources to framing the floors and interior partitions. On 1 October the Twelve indicated that "the timbers are being framed, and reared on the inside" of the temple.[76]

On 16 December, the Twelve and the trustees met and decided to hire "a suitable number of carpenters this winter to prepare the timbers for the Temple, so as to have them all ready when the stone work was finished."[77] By timbers they meant such wood structural members as posts, trusses, and floor joists. According to William Clayton's record, the Twelve and the trustees decided

to employ fifteen persons, as steady carpenters, and that the architect be authorized to select such men as he may have confidence in, men who are well quali-

---

71. This was William Allen's store in Nauvoo where goods were sold at "New York Prices." Stanley B. Kimball, *On the Potter's Wheel: The Diaries of Heber C. Kimball* (Salt Lake City: Signature Books, 1987), 136.

72. George D. Smith, *An Intimate Chronicle*, 179.

73. "Samuel Miles, Tailor," *Nauvoo Neighbor* 3 (11 June 1845): 72. A rod is 16.5 feet, or 1/320th of a mile.

74. Stanley B. Kimball, *On the Potter's Wheel*, 140.

75. Ibid.

76. "An Epistle of the Twelve to the Church of Jesus Christ of Latter-day Saints," *Times and Seasons* 5 (1 October 1844): 668.

77. *History of the Church*, 7:326.

fied to do the work that is wanted. It was also concluded to fix up a shop in the Temple for the carpenters to work in. Accordingly, the south side of the lower story of the Temple was weather-boarded round. A very good shop was made by this means which was completed on the following Saturday, and on Monday the 18th the men selected went to work in this new shop. Their names are as follows: Truman O. Angell, William Felshaw, William F. Cahoon, Joseph S. Schofield, Samuel Rolfe, Zinni H. Baxter, Addison Everett, John Stiles, Hugh Riding, Miles Romney, Jabez Durfee, Stephen Longstroth, Benjamin Rolfe, Nicholas T. Silcock and William Carmichael. Hiram Mace, Wandel Mace and Gideon Gibbs were appointed to attend the sawmill, and Daniel Avery to turn grindstone for the carpenters, keep the shop clean and take care of strangers who visit the building.[78]

The carpenters began work almost immediately. A month later on 14 January, the Twelve issued another epistle which reported:

Great numbers of carpenters, masons, and other workmen are daily engaged in this arduous undertaking, so that not only is stone being prepared, but the sash, flooring, seats, and other things are progressing rapidly; and it is our design, if possible, so to rush the work forward that the building will be enclosed, and certain portions of it in that state of forwardness, so that we shall be prepared to commence giving the saints their endowments next fall.[79]

78. Journal History, 31 December 1844, 15.

79. "An Epistle of the Twelve to the Church of Jesus Christ of Latter-day Saints in All the World," *Times and Seasons* 6 (15 January 1845): 779.

Chapter 8

Setting the Capstone:
January 1845 to May 1845

Agents Again Designated

Despite a bewildering array of pressing tasks and decisions clamoring for the attention of the Twelve, they made completing the temple their first priority. Even during the deepest months of the winter when actual construction was limited, they did not turn to other tasks but kept up a relentless focus on its completion. In an epistle to the Church dated 11 January 1845, the Twelve outlined their plans for the coming season:

> We wish to inform you brethren that the work in which we are engaged is great and mighty, it is the work of God and we have to rush it forth against the combined powers of earth and hell, we feel it to be an arduous undertaking whilst you, many of you, have been enjoying ease, prosperity, and peace at home. We have had to combat mobs and to wade through blood to fulfill the work devolving upon us, and you; we have been exerting our energies, expended our money; and employing our time, our labor, our influence, and means for the accomplishment of this purpose; and feeling confident dear brethren, that you would like to share with us the labor, as well as the glory, we make the following requests:

We wish all the young, middle aged, and able bodied men who have it in their hearts to stretch forth this work with power, to come to Nauvoo, prepared to stay during the summer; and to bring with them means to sustain themselves with, and to enable us to forward this work; to bring with them teams, cattle, sheep, gold, silver, brass, iron, oil, paints and tools; and let those who are within market distance of Nauvoo bring with them provisions to sustain themselves and others during their stay. And let all the churches send all the money, cloth, and clothing, together with the raw material for manufacturing purposes; such as cotton, cotton yarn, wool, steel, iron, brass etc., etc., as we are preparing to go into extensive manufacturing operations, and all these things can be applied to the furtherance of the temple.[1]

Four days after writing this epistle, at a meeting of the Nauvoo high priests quorum on 15 January 1845, "a number of persons were selected to go forth in the United States to act as agents to collect funds for the temple."[2] To assure that only authorized agents would receive donations, a list of the appointees was published in a circular and mailed out on 28 January[3] along with this notice:

To Whom It May Concern: This certifies that the following named elders have been appointed by the proper authorities of the Church of Jesus Christ of Latter-day Saints, agents to collect donations and tithings for the temple in Nauvoo and for other purposes; and have complied with all necessary requirements by entering into bonds to our entire satisfaction. We hope they will be received as such by all people wherever they may travel. [Then follow the names of the forty-six elders so appointed].

We hope also that the brethren will have confidence in them, inasmuch as we hold ourselves responsible to credit on the Book of the Law of the Lord, for all donations put into their hands, to the names of the donors on their tithing.

Inasmuch as this is a very good opportunity, and inasmuch as we feel very anxious that all should double their exertions in order to finish the building of the temple the next season, that the saints may receive their endowments; we hope the saints universally will embrace the opportunity, and donate liberally, that they may the more speedily receive their reward, for great things depend on our finishing the building of the temple with speed.[4]

1. "An Epistle of the Twelve to the Church of Jesus Christ of Latter-day Saints in All the World," *Times and Seasons* 6 (15 January 1845): 779.

2. Dean C. Jessee, ed., "The John Taylor Nauvoo Journal," *BYU Studies* 23 (Summer 1983): 33; Joseph Smith Jr. et al., *History of the Church of Jesus Christ of Latter-day Saints,* edited by B. H. Roberts (Salt Lake City: Deseret News Press, 6 vols. published 1902-12, Vol. 7 published 1932, 1st printing), 7:369.

3. Stanley B. Kimball, *On the Potter's Wheel: The Diaries of Heber C. Kimball* (Salt Lake City: Signature Books, 1987), 94.

4. *History of the Church,* 7:369.

Between holding the meeting and publishing the notice, the Twelve issued yet another epistle on 14 January. Again, they reported to the Church on the matter that was their most urgent concern:

> The temple has progressed very rapidly since the death of our beloved Prophet and Patriarch. The diligence of those employed, and the willingness of the saints to contribute, have brought it to a state of forwardness, which has far exceeded our most sanguine expectations. You have already been informed that the capitals of the columns were all on; we have now to announce to you that by the time the spring opens we expect that every stone will be cut to complete the temple, and it will not take long to lay them, when they are all prepared.
>
> Great numbers of carpenters, masons, and other workmen are daily engaged in this arduous undertaking, so that not only is stone being prepared, but the sash, flooring, seats, and other things are progressing rapidly; and it is our design, if possible, so to rush the work forward that the building will be enclosed, and certain portions of it in that state of forwardness, so that we shall be prepared to commence giving the saints their endowments next fall; that the elders of Israel may be prepared by the power and spirit of the great Jehovah, to fulfill with dignity and honor, the great work devolving upon them to perform.[5]

Over the next few days and weeks, the appointed agent/missionaries started for their various destinations. In fact, twenty-four-year-old William Hyde had "started on a mission to the state of Mississippi as agent for the Church ... in company with Elam Luddington" on 25 January, three days before the circular was sent out.[6] He wrote in his autobiography: "The object of the mission was to collect tithing for the building of the [Nauvoo] temple, and also to get young men among the Saints, and such as could leave their homes to come and spend the summer in Nauvoo and labor on the temple."[7]

After two months and 2,400 miles of travel, the two agents returned to Nauvoo on 25 March 1845. Hyde recalled having been "blessed in my labors" and "having performed a successful mission."[8]

Another of these agent/missionaries, Erastus Snow, "started February 24th ... to Wisconsin Territory and the northern part of the state of Illinois to visit the

---

5. Ibid., 7:357.

6. William Hyde, Autobiography, in "Autobiographies of Early Seventies," typescript, 1, LDS Church Archives.

7. William Hyde, "Private Journal of William Hyde," 1873, typescript, 16, L. Tom Perry Special Collections, Harold B. Lee Library, Brigham Young University, Provo, Utah. Hyde (1818-74) was born in New York and baptized on 7 April 1834. He later served in the Mormon Battalion. William was not Orson Hyde's brother. I do not know their relationship, if any.

8. William Hyde, Autobiography, 1; William Hyde, "Private Journal," typescript, 16.

branches in that region." He returned just prior to April conference but was soon called to perform another mission, this time for the temple: "I started about the last of April for St. Louis by appointment of the Twelve Apostles to strengthen the Saints and collect tithing, etc. from them. I was gone about three weeks (going and returning by steamboat) and brought back to the temple at Nauvoo about $100.00."[9]

Noah Packard, one of the older agent/missionaries at age forty-nine, was "called upon to take a mission in the state of Michigan. I started on this mission the 27th day of January 1845, and after traveling 1,161 miles and holding 22 meetings, baptized one and collected about $225 in property, which was delivered to the tithing office in Nauvoo."[10] On 31 March, William Huntington, who was cutting stone for the temple, noted in his journal that "a number of agents have returned in the course of this week bring with them money and property in abundance as tithing from the churches in different States."[11]

A Covenant to Complete the Temple

This flurry of fund-raising on the part of the agents manifested both the resolution and the urgency of the Twelve to complete the temple. On 25 January, ten days after the high priests' meeting in which the agents were selected and sent out, Heber C. Kimball wrote in his diary: "I sat down in my house in the presence of my wife and inquired of the Lord ... as follows, If we should finish the Temple, it was verily yes."[12] Brigham Young recorded an almost identical experience that night: "I inquired of the Lord whether we should stay here and finish the temple. The answer was, we should."[13]

The next day, Brigham Young saw a way to advance this goal and promptly took advantage of it. He recorded:

> I attended the regular meeting of the high priests' quorum at the Masonic Hall. George Miller ... introduced the subject of building a hall for the use of the quorums of high priests one hundred and twenty feet long by eighty wide, and about thirty-three feet high. I asked all that were in favor of having such a hall built, and were willing to do something towards building it, and not merely look on and see

9. Erastus Snow. "A Journal or Sketch of the Life of Erastus Snow," 1875, typescript, 91-92, Perry Special Collections, Lee Library.

10. Noah Packard, "A Synopsis of the Life and Travels of Noah Packard," typescript, 8-9, Perry Special Collections, Lee Library.

11. William Huntington, Sr., "Journal of William Huntington" 1784-1846, 31 March 1845, typescript, 25-26, Perry Special Collections, Lee Library.

12. Stanley B. Kimball, *On the Potter's Wheel*, 93.

13. Brigham Young, Diary, 25 January 1845, quoted in Leonard J. Arrington, *Brigham Young: American Moses* (New York: Knopf, 1985), 119.

their brethren build it, to raise their hands; all hands were raised. I told them such a building as had been proposed would not cost less than fifteen thousand dollars. Two years ago or even one year ago we had not a public hall in this city. The room in Brother Joseph's store was the only one where a congregation could convene. A year ago last fall I said to the seventies that if I were as strong and numerous a body as they were, I would go to work and put up a building that I might have a place to worship in. They put up their building, but the plan being altered, at the suggestion of Brother Hyrum, they had to wait for timber and could not finish it that season. Should the high priests commence the erection of the building proposed, next fall will come and even winter and the quorum will still be without a place to meet in, and probably the next season would pass away before it could be finished. I proposed to the quorum to finish off the upper story of the Temple in which they could receive their washings and anointings and endowments instead of undertaking a building from the commencement: this proposition was received by unanimous vote.[14]

William Huntington described the outcome of the meeting in his journal: "The high priest quorum ... have covenanted to finish off the upper story of the temple this season coming for their own convenience for meeting and for the furthering of the work of receiving the endowment as there are ordinances which cannot be given only in an upper story which covenant was made on the 26th of January."[15]

On 15 March 1845, the Twelve met with the trustees, the temple committee, and architect Weeks. The outcome of this meeting was a united decision to "put all our help on the temple."[16] This meant sacrificing many other important concerns. For example, plans were underway to dam the Mississippi River near Nauvoo but these plans were put on hold for the time being.[17]

Another important Church activity that would be suspended for the time being was missionary work. Brigham Young, anxious for a quick start on the building that spring, addressed the congregation at the regular Sabbath service on 16 March 1845, about the need for renewed effort on the temple and advocated the temporary halt of many activities, including missionary work:

---

14. *History of the Church*, 7:364.

15. Huntington, *Journal*, 22. On 16 March, Brigham Young addressed Church members in Nauvoo from the stand in the grove and stated: "We covenanted to labor on the Temple until it was finished and do all we could towards its completion." *History of the Church*, 7:385-86. He may have been indicating that other quorums or the general Church membership had also made a similar covenant that winter.

16. *History of the Church*, 7:382.

17. Ibid.

I can call scores of men around me, who would sooner sacrifice every dollar they have, than the work on the temple should stop. We can set four hundred men to work on the temple. I do not want any man to go to preach till he is sent. If the world want to hear preaching let them come here, and if they really want the gospel, let them clean [up] Carthage jail.

I have proposed to the leading men of the Water Power Company [the Mississippi Dam project], to put their work on the temple. I will call the stockholders together, and give my reasons to them. We want to press forward the work on the temple. I now proclaim to all saints who control means, to go to the Trustees and see if they want means to procure provisions, etc., for the hands; and I ask you to use all your influence to strengthen the hands of the Trustees.[18]

In response, the next morning "one hundred and five extra laborers and about thirty teams commenced work at the temple this morning in obedience to the call of yesterday to hasten its completion."[19]

True to Young's declaration, missionary work all but ceased in 1845. Jesse Crosby recalled, "During the summer of 1845.... I remained at home and worked on the temple this season. There were but very few elders sent abroad this summer; the main object of the Church being to build the temple and Nauvoo House, which works were rushed on with great spirit."[20] Among those who had been called on missions but who were then requested to remain in Nauvoo and work on the temple were stonecutter Charles Lambert and joiner Wandle Mace.[21]

In his 15 March sermon, Young also addressed those Nauvoo citizens who needed to plow fields and plant crops during the spring and early summer for their livelihood:

We covenanted to labor on the temple until it was finished and do all we could towards its completion; but we have not done it; if the brethren [tithing laborers] had continued, they might have worked on those walls four days a week. The stonecutters and joiners have been at work; the joiners have far exceeded our expectations this winter. The timber holds out, we keep using and there is enough left; there will be no lack of timber. If the brethren will go to work now, there will be no lack of provisions. We want the brethren to pay up their tithing. If you will haul wood, timber, etc., and help on the temple you will find that it will be made up to you in your crops.

18. *History of the Church.*, 7:385-86.

19. Ibid., 7:387.

20. Jesse Wentworth Crosby, "The History and Journal of Jesse W. Crosby," typescript, 27, Perry Special Collections, Lee Library.

21. Charles Lambert, "Autobiography of Charles Lambert," typescript, 10, LDS Church Archives; Wandle Mace, "Autobiography of Wandle Mace," typescript, 82, Perry Special Collections, Lee Library.

Brigham Young later reminisced about having devoted his own teams to the construction that summer:

> When we were finishing the temple in Nauvoo, the last year of our stay there, I rented a portion of ground in what was called the church farm, which we afterwards deeded to Sister Emma. Brother George D. Grant worked for me then, and planted the corn, sowed the oats, and said this, that, and the other must be attended to. They called for teams to haul for the temple, and could not get them. Says I, put my teams on the temple, if there is not one kernel of grain raised. I said I would trust in God for the increase, and I had as good corn as there was on the farm, though it was not touched from the time we put it in to the time of gathering.
>
> The poor miserable apostates there prophesied, and the gentiles prophesied, and all creation of wickedness seemed to agree that the temple should not be finished; and I said that it should, and the house of Israel said that it should, and the angels of God said—"we will help you."[22]

The Twelve even encouraged the Saints "not to patronize, purchase, or support any publication pertaining to our cause, except .... the '*Times and Seasons*,' '*Neighbor*,' '*Millennial Star*,' and '*Prophet*' and that the means used to purchase them be applied to the temple."[23]

The call for renewed commitment was trumpeted not only to the Saints in Nauvoo but also to members of the Church throughout the United States and England. Wilford Woodruff wrote a letter to the Church in England, asking the Saints to

> bring forth your tithes and offerings into the storehouse of God, in such a manner that he will open the windows of heaven, and pour you out a blessing that there will not be room enough to contain it. I am not zealous of urging this matter upon our friends in this country, because I have any fears that the temple of God cannot be built; no, for I verily believe that if there should not a farthing be sent from this land or even from the United States, that the Saints in Nauvoo would never cease their work, diligence, and labours, until they saw the finishing stroke adorn that Temple; but, why, O ye Saints of God in Europe, should we stand still, withhold our tithings and offerings, and see our brethren in Nauvoo build that Temple, and then like Jacob of old secure alone unto themselves the promised blessing! may God forbid may God forbid, rather let all the Saints

---

22. Brigham Young, 17 February 1861, *Journal of Discourses*, 26 vols. (London and Liverpool: LDS Booksellers Depot, 1855-86), 8:337.

23. Parley P. Pratt, "Regulations for the Publishing Department of the Latter-day Saints in the East," *Times and Seasons* 6 (15 January 1845): 778.

throughout the world send up their tithings, with their names to be recorded in the Book of the Law of the Lord, by so doing they will not only keep the commandments of the Lord, but will own their share in the house, and have a right to all the promised blessings, ordinances, oracles, and endowments which will not only benefit them, but their posterity to the latest generation.[24]

The Saints responded vigorously to these pleas. On 31 May 1845, William Clayton looked back on the spring and noted, "This Spring has exceeded all past times for liberality and donations from the brethren."[25]

The result of this increased emphasis on the temple was noteworthy. The editor of the *Times and Seasons* exulted: "The spring has met us with an early emigration of saints, never before equalled: they come by land and water. Nor is this all: goods, wares, and articles of necessity, came also: and tithings for the Temple, in money and in meat, have recently cheered the hearts of the Trustees, and building committee, and nerved the arms of the labors with a celestial kind of feeling, that runs from heart to heart, and causes a whisper to mingle with the busy hum of business: (that God means to move on his work with rapidity.)"[26]

Completing the Exterior Walls

On 15 January 1845, Brigham Young reported that as many as sixty-two men and six teams of oxen were at work at a time quarrying and hauling stone.[27] Certainly there was no "off" season for the stonecutters and haulers. On New Year's Day, 1845, Joseph Grafton Hovey, one of the faithful stonemasons carefully recorded: "I cut stone with all my might on the temple of the Lord this winter. I, Joseph, cut one star and its base and also one window and caps and closures on the temple building."[28] William Huntington indicated that he "finished cutting stones for the body [exterior walls] of the temple"[29] toward the end of February.

On 12 March the laborers began setting the stones in the uppermost portion of the exterior walls, even though they were crowding the still-early season. William Clayton wrote about this first day's work: "On Wednesday, the 12th of

24. Wilford Woodruff, "To the Officers and Members of the Church of Jesus Christ of Latter-day Saints in the British Islands," *Millennial Star* 5 (February 1845): 140.

25. George D. Smith, ed., *An Intimate Chronicle: The Journals of William Clayton* (Salt Lake City: Signature Books, 1995), 551.

26. "The Saints Make Nauvoo," *Times and Seasons* 6 (1 April 1845): 856.

27. *History of the Church*, 7:360.

28. Joseph Grafton Hovey, "Autobiography of Joseph Grafton Hovey," 1 January 1845, typescript, 31, Perry Special Collections, Lee Library. Grandson M. R. Hovey copied and arranged this document from Hovey's journal in 1933. It begins with an autobiography, then moves to daily entries.

29. William Huntington, Journal, 23 February 1845, typescript, 23.

March, Brother William W. Player commenced work again on the walls. He got one stone up just as the bell rung for dinner."[30]

Two days later occurred what William Clayton called "the only accident of any moment that has ever happened on the temple or any of the works connected with it."[31] This accident resulted in the only death that would blemish the safety record of the Nauvoo Temple. Quarry foreman Albert P. Rockwood wrote:

> For the three and a half years that I have been in charge of the temple quarry, with from twenty to one hundred and fifty hands, Brother Moses Horn has been the first person that has met with an accident by blasting. During this time there has been burned, according to my judgment, about one hundred casks of powder. Brother Horn had retired to the usual distance while blasting; he was struck on the head by a stone weighing one and a half pounds which fractured his skull; we immediately conveyed him home, sent for Dr. Bernhisel and other physicians, who pronounced the wound mortal: he died in three hours.[32]

On 23 March, Huntington lamented, "Have not sat many stones on the Temple the weather has been too cool to work on the wall but little."[33] Nonetheless, work on the walls steadily continued. Joshua Armstrong and Charles Dana were engaged in setting "the upper part of the north wall" with the third crane. They were assisted by William W. Dryer, William Austin, Thomas Jaap, and William L. Cutler.[34]

William Clayton's record continues:

---

30. George D. Smith, *An Intimate Chronicle*, 547.

31. Ibid.

32. Quoted in *History of the Church*, 7:381. The tithing ledger contains this report: "Received of Moses Horn three days labor at eight and a half shillings per day = $3.00. As per A. P. Rockwood's timebook. In full on his tithing to the time of his death, which occurred on the 14th day of March 1845 whilst working on the stone quarry. His death was occasioned by the fall of a small piece of rock about the size of a hen's egg, which was forced into the air by the blast, and at the same time he was sixteen rods and one foot from the place of the blast. This happened at twenty minutes past three o'clock in the afternoon, and he expired the same evening at five minutes before six o'clock P.M. He had been a member of the Church about one year, and was greatly lamented [by] his widow and three children." Bishop's Ledger, Tithing Record Book, 1846-52, 15 March 1845, microfilm of holograph, LDS Church Archives.

33. Huntington, Journal, typescript, 25.

34. William Clayton, Journal, in Journal History of the Church of Jesus Christ of Latter-day Saints (chronology of typed entries and newspaper clippings, 1830-present), 31 December 1844, 14.

35. *History of the Church*, 7:401, contains this report under the same date about raising the star stone: "Elder William Player put up the first star on the southeast corner of the Temple. Elders Heber C. Kimball and William Clayton were watching the progress of the stone towards its destination: the 'stars' will add much to the beauty of the Temple."

On Thursday, the 27th of March, 1845, Brother Player put up the last trumpet stone, at about three o'clock, p.m. He also laid the first stringer for the large upper Venetian window in the east side.

On Monday, April 21st, Brother Player put up the first star in the architrave. At half past two o'clock, p.m., he notified me that they were about to begin to raise it. I immediately went to the east end of the temple. On my way I met Elder Heber C. Kimball, one of the Twelve, and we went and sat down together on Brother Cutler's fence, opposite where the stone stood.[35]

We entered into conversation together on various matters, chiefly pertaining to our spiritual interest. We watched the slow upward progress of the star with great pleasure. At precisely a quarter before three o'clock, it was properly set in its place; and the instant it was set, Brothers Edward Miller and Elisha Everett sprung for the top; but Brother Miller being a little the smartest he was on first and stood erect, viewing with pride the surrounding scenery. After he got down brother Everett also mounted the stone and stood on it for some time. The top of the star is fifty-five feet above the ground.

The first star was put up on Joseph's corner, being the first one north of the south-east corner.

On the morning of Tuesday, the 29th of April, the first upper circular window was finished setting by Brother Player.

On Friday, May 16th, a little after two o'clock, p.m., having been notified, I went on the temple and sat down on the top of the south-west corner stairway, on the highest part of the stone work. I then watched Brother Player set the last star, being on the west end and the second one from the south-west corner. It was set exactly at three o'clock, p.m. At this time the carpenters were very busy raising the timbers for the upper floor of the temple, having them all framed and quite a large amount was already upon the walls and body of the building.[36]

Three days later on 19 May 1845, Stephen H. Goddard, one of the hands, narrowly escaped death while working on the temple. William Clayton reported:

He was standing on the wall on the north side of the temple assisting some others to take down one of the scaffolding poles. By some accident the foot of the pole slipped and struck him on the left side of the head. He fell head foremost, being stunned by the blow. Fortunately they had just got two joists in the floor and he fell across them, which prevented him from going down into the cellar, a distance of about sixty-two feet. And in all probability, if he had fallen down he would have been killed. The brethren raised him up and on examination found that he had received a cut on the upper corner of his left eye. His face was also much bruised. He bled profusely. I laid hands on him with two other brethren and

36. George D. Smith, *An Intimate Chronicle*, 547-48.

he went home. He suffered considerable pain until evening, when it ceased, and in two days afterwards he was at work again, as usual.[37]

On Friday, 23 May 1845, the exterior walls were completed with the exception of the capstone. Clayton exulted, "This progress was a great rejoicing to the Saints. The Rigdonites have prophesied that the walls would never be built; but through the blessing of God we have lived to see the prediction come to naught."[38]

Sidney Rigdon's Prophecies Against the Temple

William Clayton's reference to Sidney Rigdon demonstrates yet another obstacle the Saints had to overcome in building the temple—the ill wishes of dissident Mormons. Sidney Rigdon, a former member of the First Presidency, had proposed himself as the Church's "guardian"; but when it became clear that the Twelve would lead the Church, he became disgruntled, moved to Pittsburgh where he gathered a small following, and declared that God had "rejected" the Church for not having finished the temple.[39] Shortly after Joseph Smith's death in 1844, Rigdon had "prophesied in a public meeting that there would not be another stone raised upon the walls of the temple." William Player "[was] determined that he (President Rigdon) should not prove a true prophet, in this instance at least. [He] took with him Archibald and John Hill, while returning from said meeting and raised and set a stone upon the wall making this prediction a failure."[40]

On 21 May, two letters appeared in the *Nauvoo Neighbor* in response to Rigdon's earlier claims. The first is by an unidentified correspondent who used the pseudonym "Americus."

I have enquired of the Temple Committee, and have also examined the records at the Temple, and learn that very few, if any of those persons who have apostatized from the church and gone after Rigdon, have ever paid any tithing for the purpose of erecting that edifice.

As they have withheld their substance from building this Temple at a time when they acknowledge God required it to be done, how came they to get a rev-

---

37. Ibid., 548-49. Stephen H. Goddard (1810-98), baptized 27 February 1836, was one of Brigham Young's vanguard pioneer company in 1847.

38. Ibid., 549.

39. Jesse Crosby, Letter, Journal History, 19 November 1844, 1-2. Crosby, who was on his way to England (he would be called home soon thereafter), visited Pittsburgh in November 1844.

40. Statement of William Player, 12 December 1868, microfilm of holograph, LDS Church Archives. This account was taken down in the third person by Joseph F. Smith and signed by William Player.

elation from Heaven that the temple was rejected of God because it was not sooner completed?—And how came they to find out that God has rejected those who have been faithful and done all in their power to complete the work? It must be that they have obtained this knowledge as a reward for their covetousness, or else they were drones in the hive and would not work, and the Mormons stung them and cast them out. Will you, Mr. Editor, give a few words of explanation upon these matters?

John Taylor, then editing the *Neighbor*, responded:

We would answer Americus by asking another question. A certain man had two sons, and he said to them both, "go and labor in the field, and if you complete your work at a certain time you shall receive a great reward." They both enter the field and one begins to labor and continues all the day long faithfully, but the other is idle and does nothing but tries to hinder the faithful one. The father knows precisely how both have conducted, and says to the idle one:—You shall be rewarded and continue to be my son, and even be exalted in my favor; but I will not speak to the faithful one at all; still I will tell you, that as he has not completed the work in the time specified, I will not accept it, neither shall he be any longer my son; but shall be disowned and sent away. Would Americus honor the justice of that father's decision? This is a true illustration of the character of Rigdon's God after whom his own character is, no doubt, formed.[41]

On 25 July, Amos Fielding, who was en route to Nauvoo from England and who had stopped in Pittsburgh, wrote Brigham Young after conversing with some of Rigdon's followers there about Rigdon's prophecy:

I will give you a statement of the cable which holds the ship of Rigdon, who as an anchor hold on to this cable at Rigdon's command. I trust and hope that ere this letter reaches you, the cable may be ready to part anchor. The cable is this, that if ever the roof of the temple is finished, all Rigdonism falls to the ground in this place.

I write this for the express purpose that you will write a few lines to my Brother Matthew Fielding, (he has not joined Rigdon) whenever the roof shall be finished, that is, all the shingles nailed on. It would be well to put a few lines in the Neighbor as there are many standing aloof on account of this prophecy.[42]

---

41. Americus (pseud.) and John Taylor, "Communications," *Nauvoo Neighbor* 3 (21 May 1845): 28.

42. Amos Fielding, Letter to Brigham Young, 25 July 1845, *Nauvoo Neighbor* 3 (13 August 1845): 59. Fielding (1792-1875) was one of the earliest converts in England, probably joined the Church in late 1839, and became a member of the Council of Fifty in Nauvoo.

On 20 May, a plough factory on the outskirts of Nauvoo was burned. The *Nauvoo Neighbor*, in reporting the blaze, claimed that a "set of Rigdonite renega-does [were] lurking about that place" and warned the Saints "to watch their property, lest the 'Keys of Conquest' in the form of a lucifer match be applied to their buildings."[43] Though unsubstantiated, this accusation demonstrates the mistrust of Rigdon that prevailed among Church members in Nauvoo. William Clayton indicated that there was some concern that Rigdon would attempt to burn the temple lumber in an attempt to fulfill his own prophesy.[44] Joseph Hovey recorded with some irony: "The Rigdonites are ... prophesying that we will be driven out before we will get the temple covered and that we would get burned up here and all that belongs to us, thus says the Rigdon prophets."[45]

Materials Purchased for the Temple

The majority of the raw materials for the temple came from the local quarries and from the "pineries" in Wisconsin. However, the temple committee commissioned their agents to obtain other materials and hardware such as glass, nails, tar, lead, and tin. On 18 June 1845, Newel K. Whitney "started for St. Louis with $1,549 to purchase materials for the temple."[46]

The Saints' need for haste, the quantity of materials they needed, and the pressing problem of poverty sometimes created difficulties for the agents charged with finding suppliers, negotiating prices, and getting satisfactory service from manufacturers, resellers, and shippers. One agent, George P. Dykes, wrote George Miller a hurried and frustrated letter from Ann Arbor, Michigan, documenting his plight:

> Dear Sir: In haste I [take] my pen to address you a line to inform you that I am still alive and thankful for it. I have been to Detroit and thence to the glass works. Business was all out of joint and they did not intend to send the glass on the pay they had got for it. Grovier and Hall were not the men to make the contract with (so Mr. Tinker tried to make it appear). On my arrival in the City I immediately went to Kircheval. He had heard nothing of it. I then [went] to the agency of Detroit for the Michigan glass works and there I found the glass marked 'L. Stodard.' I made inquiry why the glass was not sent according to agreement. The

43. Telemachus (pseud.), "Fire!," *Nauvoo Neighbor* 3 (28 May 1845): 30.

44. George D. Smith, *An Intimate Chronicle*, 545-46. See also John E. Page, Letter to A. J. Foster, *Nauvoo Neighbor* 3 (30 July 1845): 49.

45. Hovey, Journal, 31.

46. *History of the Church*, 7:427.

agent was very ignorant at first but at length said he would enquire into it. I told him the contract and produced the paper. He begin to think I was in good earnest about it but said Mr. Drigs was absent and would not return for two weeks and there could be nothing done till he come as he was the agent ... for the glass works. I told him I would go to the glass works [to] Mr. Grovier with whom the business was done and ask[ed] him if an order from Grovier would bring the glass. He said not; that Grovier was considered as a man not capable and they would fill none of his contracts or orders etc.—I then went to the livery stable and got a horse and buggy and ... paid this Tinker .... two dollars to go with me there. We found Mr. Grovier a gentleman. He made many apologies for not sending the glass, said ... that the bill was filled out but instead of its being sent to Kircheval it had to pass through this Mr. Tinker's hand and he was going to keep it until he could get other pay as the pay they got did not suit them etc. I was in a close place, as the contract was made with the wrong man. At length after some time disputing I got the glass and it is to be forwarded tomorrow on a propeller [boat] that's coming up the lakes. I am almost tempted to go back to Detroit and wait to see it all on board a boat as I fear that there is not honor enough in any forwarding merchant here to send it ... in haste I close yours with due respect

                                                                    G. P. Dykes

Since writing the above I have returned to Detroit and the Glass is now on the way up the Lake.

Thank the Lord but not the Devil of a Tinker.

                                                                    G.P.D.[47]

The glass arrived in Nauvoo on 31 August and 1 September.[48]

In marked contrast was service from the owners of the steamboat *Osprey*, which plied between St. Louis and Nauvoo. When Orson Hyde contracted for it to deliver a shipment of goods, the goods were not only delivered promptly, but the steamboat's clerk sent a cordial letter to Whitney, whom he addressed as "Rev. Bishop Whitney":

We have this day delivered to Mr. Chas. Allen at the stone house on the landing a lot of merchandise shipped by Elder Orson Hyde at St. Louis for your address. As we were informed that the articles just alluded to were to be used in the construction of the temple we have in consideration of this fact delivered the same free of any charge and should at any future time require any other articles for the above purpose from St. Louis we shall feel pleasure in bringing them up on the same terms as the present art.

47. George P. Dykes, Letter to George Miller as Trustee-in-Trust, 1845 (month and day obscured), holograph, Newel K. Whitney Papers, Perry Special Collections, Lee Library.

48. George D. Smith, *An Intimate Chronicle*, 180.

We feel that we are but performing a duty which we owe to the residents of your city for the very liberal share of patronage extended towards our boat during the past year 1844.

The clerk also added a postscript: "P.S. It is our intention to now (the present year) [continue] under the same arrangement as last season, arriving at Nauvoo every Sunday at 9 a.m. and leaving for St. Louis every Tuesday at 8 a.m. for St. [Louis]."[49]

Baptisms for the Dead

From the introduction of the ordinance of vicarious baptism for the dead, proxy baptisms had been performed without regard to gender, with men being baptized for women, and women being baptized for deceased male kin. One reason for this was probably that no one had given the matter much thought, but almost certainly another reason was that many Saints were the only members of their families who had joined the Church and keenly desired that their deceased kin could receive this ordinance. At April 1845 conference, Brigham Young mentioned that he had "stated" this policy "in the winter past" (1844-45), but that it had generated "discussion among the elders, and among the brethren and sisters in general." He wanted to clarify the appropriate practice of this doctrine. In the process, he also explained eloquently how understanding of new doctrine unfolds line upon line, precept upon precept—that condemnation does not come because of not having a complete grasp of a principle from the beginning but from not accepting the new understanding when it is taught:

> I do not say that you have not been taught and learned the principle; you have heard it taught from this stand from time to time, by many of the elders, and from the mouth of your beloved and martyred prophet Joseph; therefore my course will not be to prove the doctrine, but refer to those things against which your minds are revolting. Consequently I would say to this vast congregation of Saints, when we enter in to the temple of God to receive our washings, our anointings, our endowments and baptisms for the saving of ourselves, and for the saving of our dead: that you never will see a man go forth to be baptized for a woman, nor a woman for a man....
>
> Allow me to advance an idea, and it is this; except we attend to this ordinance according to the law of heaven in all things it will not be valid or be of any benefit either to the living or the dead; when it was first revealed all the order of it

---

49. J. H. Maittland, Clerk of the Steamboat *Osprey*, Letter to Newel K. Whitney, 2 March 1845, holograph, Newel K. Whitney Papers, Perry Special Collections, Lee Library.

was not made known, afterwards it was made known, that records, clerks, and one or two witnesses were necessary or else it will be of no value to the saints. Joseph in his lifetime did not receive every thing connected with the doctrine of redemption, but he has left the key with those who understand how to obtain and teach to this great people all that is necessary for their salvation and exaltation in the celestial kingdom of our God...

I have said that a man cannot be baptized for a woman, nor a woman for a man, and it be valid. I have not used any argument as yet; I want now to use an argument upon this subject, it is a very short one; and I will do it by asking this congregation, if God would call a person to commence a thing that would not have power and ability to carry it out? Would he do it? (No.) Well then, what has been our course on former occasions? Why, here goes our beloved sisters, and they are baptized in the river or in the fount for their uncles, for their fathers, for their grandfathers and great grandfathers.

Well, now I will take you and confirm you for your uncles, for your fathers, for your grandfathers, and let you go; after a while here comes our beloved sisters, saying. I want to be ordained for my uncle, and for my grandfather, and great grandfather; I want my father ordained to the high priesthood, and my grandfather, I want to be patriarch, and you may ordain me a prophet for my uncle! What would you think about all that, sisters, come now you have been baptized and confirmed for your father, won't you be ordained for him? You could cast on a stocking and finish it. You could take wool and card and spin it and make it into cloth, and then make it into garments. A person that commences a work and has not ability and power to finish it, only leaves the unfinished remains as a monument of folly. We will not commence a work we cannot finish: but let us hearken to the voice of the spirit and give heed to his teachings and we will make ourselves perfect in all things.[50]

The Vestibule and Stairways

The completed façade of the temple featured "a portico with three Roman archways"[51] which led into a large outer court or vestibule. David N. White described the interior of this court:

We enter ... at the west end, passing through either of three large open doors or arched pass-ways, each of which is nine feet seven inches wide and twenty one feet high. Passing through these we are standing in a large outer court, forty-three feet by seventeen feet wide.

---

50. Brigham Young. "Speech," *Times and Seasons* 6 (1 July 1845): 953-55.

51. Charles Lanman. *A Summer in the Wilderness* (Philadelphia, n.pub., 1847), 31. See also John Reynolds, *My Own Times: Embracing the History of My Life* (Belleville [Ill.] : Perryman and Davison, 1855), 587, microfilm, Perry Special Collections, Lee Library.

On either end of the vestibule on the wall facing the portals, were two large doors that opened into the main floor assembly hall. The walls between these courts are three feet thick, of solid mason work, with two immense doors for passage between them.[52]

The doors leading to the main assembly hall were made of elaborately carved wood. An unidentified visitor in 1853 commented ruefully in the *Illinois Journal* on the damage wreaked on the doors by vandals. It is the only known description of these doors, which were apparently very beautiful:

> We entered within its ample doors .... The wood-work of the doors and windows was composed of beautifully carved work. The top of the door jambs being ornamented with Corinthian capitals of the most exquisite workmanship. But these, alas! shewed the marks of sacrilegious hands of the visitors who wished to preserve some relic of the wonderful edifice. The beautiful vine-work had been deprived of many a delicately executed leaf and bud, and a smiling cherub of its nose—then, another the feathered tip of its wing.[53]

A visitor to the temple in May or June 1844, writing for the *St. Louis Gazette*, noted that on either end of the vestibule was "an apartment perfectly circular without window or loophole, or division of any kind, designed for some vestibular purpose, which none of our party could divine."[54] The circular rooms were actually the casings for the two stairways that provided access to the basement and upper stories of the temple. Charles Lanman, who visited the temple in 1847, saw the completed stairways: "At the two front corners of the edifice are two winding stairways, which meet at the base of the tower."[55]

The first window in each of the four rows illuminated these stairways. The visitor who published his or her account in the *Illinois Journal* included a rare description of these stairways:

> We ... began ... our ascent up the spiral staircase. We slowly progressed upward through the intermediary windings, passing by the circular windows, filled with glass of diverse colors, which threw an obscure light on our passage....

52. David N. White, "The Prairies, Nauvoo, Joe Smith, the Temple, the Mormons, etc.," in *Pittsburgh Weekly Gazette* 58 (15 September 1843): 3, as quoted in Dean C. Jessee, ed., *The Papers of Joseph Smith*, 2 vols. (Salt Lake City: Deseret Book, 1989, 1992), 1:442. White visited Nauvoo on 28 August 1843.

53. Author unknown, *Illinois Journal*, 9 December 1853, reprinted as "Recollections of the Nauvoo Temple," in *Journal of the Illinois State Historical Society* 38 (December 1945): 484; photocopy, LDS Church Historical Department Library.

54. "The Temple of Nauvoo," *St. Louis Gazette*, ca. 12 June 1844, Journal History, 12 June 1844, 5.

55. Lanman, *A Summer in the Wilderness*, 31.

Arrived at the top, we turned and cast a look downward. The distant floor was not distinguished from the extreme turnings of the spire. It seemed as if we were looking down into an immense corkscrew, the terminal windings of which were lost in obscurity.[56]

Only the stairway on the east was finished. Joseph Smith III recollected in his autobiography: "The stairway at the southwest corner of the building was finished to the extent that it provided a way for ingress and egress to and from the rooms above. It was this corner that remained standing longest after the fire. The stairway in the northwest corner was not finished. Rough inch boards were laid over the risers so that the workmen could pass up and down."[57] Thomas Bullock records that he took several guests "up one side, [and] down the other" when he was showing them through the completed temple in May 1846.[58]

Laying the Capstone

On Saturday, 24 May 1845, at sunrise on a day that William Clayton described as "very cold and chilly,"[59] the capstone of the temple was laid. Zina Diantha Huntington Jacobs Smith, the daughter of stonecutter William Huntington, wrote in her journal: "This memorable day the sun arose clear in the east. The morning was serene and silent. The sun and moon were at about equal height in the horizon, as if to rejoice with the Saints in praises to the most high. The Saints repaired (all that knew it) to the temple at six in the morning."[60] Among the few who learned about the exercises beforehand was Louisa Barnes Pratt who said she was "privately notified to be on the grounds at sunrise. With glad and anxious hearts we all hurried to the spot."[61] Thomas Bullock also "heard confidentially that the corner Stone was to be laid at 6 a.m."[62]

In contrast to the highly publicized cornerstone ceremony just four years earlier, the laying of the capstone was not publicly announced. Still, John Taylor indicated that, despite the deliberate lack of an advance announcement, the cere-

56. Author unknown, *Illinois Journal*, 9 December 1853.

57. Mary Audentia Smith Anderson, ed., *Joseph Smith III and the Restoration* (Independence, MO: Herald House, 1952), 101.

58. Gregory Knight, "Journal of Thomas Bullock, 31 August 1845-5 July 1846," *BYU Studies* 31 (Winter 1991): 63.

59. George D. Smith, *An Intimate Chronicle*, 551.

60. "'All Things Move in Order in the City': The Nauvoo Diary of Zina Diantha Huntington Jacobs," edited by Maureen Ursenbach Beecher, *BYU Studies* 18 (Spring 1979): 310.

61. Louisa Barnes Pratt, "Journal of Louisa Barnes Pratt," *Heart Throbs of the West*, compiled by Kate B. Carter, 12 vols. (Salt Lake City: Daughter of the Utah Pioneers, 1947-51), 8:234.

62. Thomas Bullock, Diary, 24 May 1845, quoted in Jesse, "The John Taylor Nauvoo Journal," 49-50.

mony, once begun, attracted immediate attention: "We repaired to the Temple with great secrecy for the purpose of laying the corner stone, there were but few that knew about it; the band playing on the walls and the people hearing it, hurried up."[63]

The Nauvoo Brass Band, under the direction of William Pitt provided music for the occasion. Band member Charles Hales, age twenty-eight, had "joined the [Brass] Band and continued to play with them at every public festival.... [He] played ... at the laying of the capstone of the Lord's house."[64] The band stood in a semi-circle on the platform at the southeast corner of the temple and played, first, a number called "The Nightingale," followed by "another tune ... while the people were collecting."[65]

By this time, according to Louisa Barnes Pratt, the "top of the building was covered with men while multitudes surrounded the walls below."[66] Among those present were members of the Quorum of the Twelve, Bishops George Miller and Newel K. Whitney as the trustees, Alpheus Cutler and Reynolds Cahoon as the building committee, architect William Weeks, the Nauvoo Stake Presidency, several of the Nauvoo High Council, and many other devoted Saints who had sacrificed much in hopes of living this moment.[67]

The capstone was raised with a crane and set in its place at the southeast corner of the temple walls. William Clayton's account of the actual laying of the capstone, penned one week later, gives a detailed description of the event:

> At eight minutes after six Brother William W. Player commenced spreading his mortar, perfect silence prevailing.
>
> President Young stood on the wall immediately north of the corner stone, with Elder Heber C. Kimball at his right hand.

---

63. Jesse, "The John Taylor Nauvoo Journal," 49.

64. Charles Hales, Autobiography, in "Autobiographies of Early Seventies," typescript, 208, LDS Church Archives. Other members of the band, according to William Clayton, were Stephen Hales, William F. Cahoon, Robert T. Burton, John Kay, James Smithies, Daniel F. Cahoon, Andrew Cahoon, Martin H. Peck, J. T. Hutchinson, James Standing, William D. Huntington, Charles Smith, and Charles C. Robbins. William H. Kimball was the color bearer. George D. Smith, *An Intimate Chronicle*, 549.

65. George D. Smith, *An Intimate Chronicle*, 549.

66. "Journal of Louisa Barnes Pratt," 8:234.

67. Clayton's list of dignitaries includes Brigham Young, Heber C. Kimball, John Taylor, Willard Richards, Amasa Lyman, George A. Smith, John E. Page, Orson Hyde, Orson Pratt, Newel K. Whitney, George Miller, Alpheus Cutler, Reynolds Cahoon, William Clayton, Patriarch John Smith, Charles C. Rich, William Huntington Sr., Aaron Johnson, George W. Harris, James Allred, David Fullmer, William Weeks, and William W. Phelps. George D. Smith, *An Intimate Chronicle*, 549.

When the mortar was spread, the stone was lifted to its place by President Brigham Young, William W. Player, Tarlton Lewis, Elisha Everett, John Hill, Edward Miller, Charles W. Patten, Samuel Hodge, Hans C. Hanson, and Thomas Jaap.

President Young then stepped on the stone, and taking a large pestle began beating it to its place. He finished laying the stone with the assistance and direction of Brother Player precisely at twenty-two minutes after six o'clock.[68]

The band then struck up the "Capstone March," composed and arranged by William Pitt, the leader, for the occasion.[69]

This capstone had great significance to the devoted Charles Lambert, who had prepared the stone. William Clayton praised his contribution: He "cut the stone and bought it, and when finished he gave the stone and the labor free of all charges. He has proved himself a liberal-hearted, faithful, good man from first to last."[70] Lambert not only did the finish work on the stone, but quarried it as well, hollowing it out so that it could contain some articles, which he records as "coins, books."[71]

John Taylor, who was then publisher of the *Times and Seasons*, was asked to provide printed materials for deposit in the capstone. He wrote:

I sent 5 volumes of the *Times and Seasons* (1st volume commencing November 1st, 1839) and seven numbers of the sixth volume, ending April 15th, 1845. A file of *Neighbors* from January 1st, 1845, to May 28th, 1845, inclusive; also a copy of my history of the Missouri persecutions; and three pamphlets I printed in the Isle of Man, one entitled *Methodism*, weighed in the balance and found wanting; the other two entitled *Calumny refuted* and *Truth defended.*[72]

Once the stone was set, Brigham Young instructed the congregation how to give the Hosanna Shout. His voice was "heard distinctly by the congregation below."[73] According to William Clayton, he then declared:

"The last stone is laid upon the temple, and I pray the Almighty in the name of Jesus to defend us in this place, and sustain us until the temple is finished and have all got our endowments."

The whole congregation then, following the motion of President Young, shouted as loud as possible; "Hosanna, hosanna, hosanna, to God and the Lamb! Amen, amen and amen!"

68. Thomas Bullock recorded the time as 6:27 a.m. Bullock, Diary, quoted in Jessee, "The John Taylor Nauvoo Journal," 49-50.

69. George D. Smith, *An Intimate Chronicle*, 550.

70. Journal History, 31 December 1844, 15.

71. Charles Lambert, Autobiography, ca. 1883, typescript, 13, LDS Church Archives.

72. Jessee, "The John Taylor Nauvoo Journal," 49.

73. Ibid.

This was repeated a second and third time.

The President concluded by saying; "So let it be, thou Lord Almighty!"

He continued and said: "This is the seventh day of the week, or the Jewish Sabbath. It is the day on which the Almighty finished His work and rested from His labors. We have now finished the walls of the temple, and we may rest to day from our labors."

He said he would take it upon him to dismiss the workmen for the day; and requested the people to hallow the day, and spend it giving thanks to God.[74]

Band member John Kay closed the ceremony by singing "The Capstone Song," written by W. W. Phelps for the occasion:[75]

Have you heard the revelation,
Of this latter dispensation,
Which is unto every nation,
O! prepare to meet thy God?

Go and publish how Missouri,
Like a whirlwind in its fury,
And without a judge or jury,
Drove the Saints and spilt their blood.

Illinois, where Satan flatters,
Shot the prophets too, as martyrs,
And repeal'd our city charters,
All because we worship'd God.

Bennett, Law and many others,
Have betray'd our honest brothers,
To destroy our wives and mothers,
As a Judas did the Lord.

And their chief is Sidney Rigdon,
Who's a traitor, base, intriguing,

---

74. George D. Smith, *An Intimate Chronicle*, 550-51. Thomas Bullock recorded Young's remarks as: "Prest. Young in his little speech remarked that as the Lord had completed his work in six days and on the seventh day he rested from his labors, so with us. We have finished the Temple, and now we complete it. This is the Sabbath day, and now brethren I do not require any man to work on the Temple, or any where else, but you may do as you please. You can now go home and pray that God may bless the labors on the Temple that you may get your endowment and exaltation." Bullock, Diary, quoted in Jesse, "The John Taylor Nauvoo Journal," 49-50.

75. George D. Smith, *An Intimate Chronicle*, 551. Kay (1817-unknown) later minted the first coins in Utah.

And will fight at Armageddon,
When the fire comes down from God.

While the devil such men jostles,
With his "keys of conquest" morsels,
We'll uphold the Twelve Apostles,
With authority from God.

And we'll feed the saints that's needing,
And improve our hearts by weeding,
Till we make Nauvoo as Eden,
Where the saints can meet the Lord.

CHORUS

We are a band of brethren,
And we've rear'd the Lord a temple,
And the cap stone now is finish'd,
And we'll sound the news abroad.[76]

The reason for the attempted secrecy of the ceremony that morning soon became apparent. A disgusted Bullock recorded: "The only thing that marred the whole ceremony, was some ill-bred, insulting backwoodsmen, laughing, talking, chattering like a rookery so that but little could be heard three yards from the speaker."[77] During the ceremony, according to Louisa Barnes Pratt, a group of officers gathered "a few rods from the crowd, watching to take Brigham Young when he came from the building. In this they did not succeed," she added, "for [as the crowd dispersed] he walked in the center of more than a hundred men; it was impossible for them to approach him."[78] John Taylor, who accompanied Young as he left, noted in his journal: "Although there were several officers watching for us to take us; yet we escaped without their knowledge; when the singing [by John Kay] commenced we left unnoticed, and they had not an opportunity of seeing us."[79]

Thomas Bullock remarked, "It [the ceremony] must have been a beautiful sight to the passengers on board the 'Osprey' which was coming up the River."[80]

---

76. W. W. Phelps, "The Capstone Song," *Nauvoo Neighbor* 3 (28 May 1845): 42. The reference to "key of conquest" morsels is an allusion to Sidney Rigdon.

77. Bullock, Diary, quoted in Jessee, "The John Taylor Nauvoo Journal," 49-50.

78. "Journal of Louisa Barnes Pratt," 8:234.

79. Jessee, "The John Taylor Nauvoo Journal," 49.

80. Bullock, Diary, quoted in ibid., 49-50. The *Osprey* must have been a few days off schedule to be coming up the Mississippi on a Saturday.

Chapter 9

THE ROOF AND TOWER:
JUNE 1845 TO SEPTEMBER 1845

Work of the Carpenters, Framers, and Joiners

The summer of 1845 was perhaps the most exciting building season on the temple. With the completion of the exterior walls early in the summer, the prospects of completing the edifice were good; and the temple site buzzed with activity. Wandle Mace recollected, "Men were as thick as blackbirds busily engaged upon the various portions, all intent upon its completion: although we were being in constant expectation of a mob."[1] Twenty-year-old Irene Hascall Pomeroy, who arrived in Nauvoo the day after the capstone was laid, captured the excitement in a letter to her mother: "I have been to view the Temple. It is a splendid building.... It never went on so fast before. Half has been built since Joseph was killed. It was not expected the stones would all be laid until fall. They are now encouraged and think they will be able to have meetings and commence endowment[s] before snow falls. More than three hundred are at work on it and the rest help by paying their tithing."[2]

1. Wandle Mace, Autobiography, 1890, typescript, 185, L. Tom Perry Special Collections, Harold B. Lee Library, Brigham Young University, Provo, Utah.

2. Irene Hascall Pomeroy, Letter to Ursulia Hascall, 2 June 1845, in (no editor), "Letters of a Proselyte—The Hascall—Pomeroy Correspondence," *Utah Historical Quarterly* 25 (January 1957): 61. Irene (1825-60) was baptized in 1842, and her husband Francis Martin Pomeroy (1822-82), was bap-

Brigham Young revealed his enthusiasm for the temple at the summer's out-set in a letter to Wilford Woodruff, who was then in England, presiding over the British Mission: "Many strangers are pouring in to view the Temple and the city. They express their astonishment and surprise to see the rapid progress of the Temple, and the beauty and grandeur of Mormon looks. Many brethren are coming from abroad, who seem highly delighted with the place and all its appendages."[3]

With the massive exterior walls completed, the complete focus of the tem-ple workmen next turned to installing the structural timbers. The attic story, gabled roof, tower, spiral stairways, interior partitions, mezzanines, ceilings, floor joists, and windows were all to be wood framed. The carpenters hired by the temple com-mittee during the winter of 1844-45 began work on the frame portions of the build-ing during the early spring. Samuel W. Richards, one of the carpenters/joiners,[4] summarized his spring labors on the temple: "After having attended the conference of the Church from the 6 to the 9th of April, and making due preparations, I com-menced work in the joiner's shop at the temple for the season, being about the middle of April, having previously worked ten days."[5]

William F. Cahoon, who had labored extensively on the Kirtland Temple, and carpenter Wandle Mace, who had been responsible for constructing the cranes, were assigned to oversee the construction.[6] William Weeks employed Mace to "draft and superintend the framing of all the timber work of the temple, commencing on the ground and throughout to the top of the tower." Mace remarked, "This was the most complicated piece of timber work or framing I ever done, and was the most easily accomplished."[7]

---

tized in 1844. They were married in late 1844 and arrived in Nauvoo on 25 May 1845.

3. Brigham Young, Letter to Wilford Woodruff, 27 May 1845, in Joseph Smith Jr. et al., *History of the Church of Jesus Christ of Latter-day Saints*, edited by B. H. Roberts (Salt Lake City: Deseret News Press, 6 vols. published 1902-12, Vol. 7 published 1932, 1st printing), 7:431.

4. In the 1840s, the terms carpenter, joiner, and framer were often used interchangeably but there are differences between them. "A distinction is often made between the man who frames, and the man who executes the interior wood-work of a house. The framer is the carpenter, and the fin-isher is called a joiner. This distinction ... seems to be a genuine English distinction. But in some parts of America ... the term carpenter includes both the framer and the joiner; and in truth both branches of business are often performed by the same person." "Carpenter," Noah Webster, *An American Dictionary of the English Language* (New York: n.pub., 1828). Although this distinction between join-er and carpenter was still in use while the Nauvoo Temple was under construction, "carpenter" was also used to refer to both the framing and the finishing.

5. Samuel W. Richards, Journal, Book 1, 5 April 1845, typescript, 40, Perry Special Collections, Lee Library.

6. William F. Cahoon, Autobiography, 1878, typescript, 88, Perry Special Collections, Lee Library; Mace, Autobiography, 82. Cahoon wrote: "In the spring of 1845, I was appointed to superintend the raising of all the timbers of the temple."

7. Mace, Autobiography, 82.

On 25 May, the day after the capstone was set, Young wrote to Parley P. Pratt in New York, apprising him of the temple's status and outlining the upcoming plans:

> The temple is progressing rapidly and bids fair for being finished far sooner than was anticipated.... The walls are finished and a large portion of the timber work is already on the walls. The carpenters are very busy raising the balance and any thing pertaining to it is far under way. We have purchased about $3000 worth of timbers which will be nearly enough. Brother Parker has arrived this morning with a raft of joists and square timbers and the balance of the lumber wanting is already contracted for and is expected within 8 or 10 days.[8]

William Clayton recorded that on "Wednesday the 28th day of May the first 'bent' [transverse frame] of the attic story of the temple was raised by the carpenters."[9] Heber C. Kimball recorded on the same day, "This day the timbers were raising in the at[t]ic story of the Temple. On the dome or steeple."[10]

William Huntington, writing in his journal during the early summer, described conditions at the site on 1 June:

> The work at and about the temple moves on with power. Perfect harmony prevails in all its various parts pertaining to the great work, which yet requires some two hundred men in all the work pertaining to the house....
>
> I am still cutting stone [and] shall soon finish my work on the temple the timbers are going up fast in to the tower and roof. The roof will soon be on. Brother Brigham said this day he believed before snow flies, the roof will be on and the Saints will hold meetings in the house in winter.[11]

On 27 June 1845, the anniversary of the martyrdom, Brigham Young reported to Wilford Woodruff: "Most of the woodwork for the temple is finished; all the window frames and sashes are made and the glaziers are ready to set the glass which we expect here in a few days."[12] The windows of the temple were

---

8. Brigham Young, Letter to Parley P. Pratt, 26 May 1845, microfilm of typescript, Newel K. Whitney Papers, Perry Special Collections, Lee Library.

9. George D. Smith, ed., *An Intimate Chronicle: The Journals of William Clayton* (Salt Lake City: Signature Books, 1995), 551. The attic in this case did not refer to the attic story but to the oblong box upon which the tower was constructed.

10. Stanley B. Kimball, *On the Potter's Wheel: The Diaries of Heber C. Kimball* (Salt Lake City: Signature Books, 1987), 117. This task continued through the day.

11. William Huntington Sr., "Journal of William Huntington," 1784-1846, typescript, 28-29, Perry Special Collections, Lee Library.

12. Brigham Young, Letter to Wilford Woodruff, 27 June 1845, *History of the Church*, 7:431.

made and installed during 1845. The frames and sashes for the windows began to be prepared early in the year. On 14 January, an epistle of the Twelve noted that under the care of the newly hired carpenters, the sashes were "progressing rapidly."[13] This work took several months as there were approximately 118 windows in the stone walls alone. These included the circular windows Joseph had requested, tall narrow windows with semicircular tops, the semicircular basement windows, two large "Venetian" windows on the east end of the building, and small round windows with panes arranged in the shape of a fivepoint star in the pediment. There were also about thirty-nine windows in the roof, tower, and attic, including the skylights and the large semicircular window at the east end of the attic.

The *Nauvoo Neighbor* indicated that by 13 August the frames and sashes were complete.[14] The glass for the windows, purchased by George P. Dykes in Michigan, was delayed and arrived in Nauvoo on 31 August and 1 September.[15] According to archeological evidence, the glass was one centimeter thick and "pale bluegreen" in color.[16] Joseph Young, who had some experience as a glazier, was among those who helped prepare and cut the panes.[17] During September the windows were installed in the stone walls so that by the 5 October meeting in the enclosed temple, Brigham Young could declare the "windows in" and the building entirely enclosed.[18]

Arza Adams, age forty-one in 1845, preserved in his journal the story of how he came to work as a carpenter:

> I continued sick with the three-day ague until sometime in June, 1845, and under a promise from Heber C. Kimball, one of the Twelve, that if we would work on the temple, that we should be well; and as soon as I thought I had strength sufficient, I took my carpenter tools on my back and commenced work on the temple, and although hard at first, I gained strength and worked on the public works until in the fall.[19]

The exact number of carpenters eventually hired to work on the temple is not known, but as late as August 1845, this imperious "want ad" appeared in the

13. "An Epistle of the Twelve to the Church of Jesus Christ in All the World," *Times and Seasons* 6 (15 January 1845): 779.

14. Ibid.

15. "The Last Shingle," *Nauvoo Neighbor* 3 (13 August 1845): not paginated.

16. George D. Smith, *An Intimate Chronicle*, 180.

17. Levi Edgar Young, "Joseph Young," *Utah Genealogical and Historical Magazine* 5 (July 1914): 106.

18. "First Meeting in the Temple," *Times and Seasons* 6 (1 November 1845): 1017.

19. Arza Adams, Journal, Vol. 4, 1843-56, typescript, 29, Perry Special Collections, Lee Library.

Nauvoo Neighbor: "A LARGE quantity of BRICKLAYERS and CARPENTERS wanted IMMEDIATELY, on the NAUVOO HOUSE and the TEMPLE. Do you see? Do you hear? if you do, pay ATTENTION!!! Recollect immediately!!"[20]

Wandle Mace "built a saw mill to saw plank and such small timbers as was needed."[21] This new sawmill was located on the temple grounds. Curtis E. Bolton, an 1840 convert from New Jersey, arrived in Nauvoo on 23 May and "went to work upon the Nauvoo temple as a carpenter."[22] Bolton

> tended the sawmill at the temple. For a while I had charge of receiving, keeping in order, and delivering the temple lumber under Bro[ther] Samuel Rolfe. [I] had my right foot very badly mashed by a pile of plank dropping on it. Had it administered to and it soon got well. I sawed into lengths and marked out for the buzz saw every piece of wood composing the staircase in each tower of the temple from cellar to steeple.[23]

Truman O. Angell recalled: "I had steady employment upon the Temple, having been appointed superintendent of joiner work under Architect William Weeks, and God gave me wisdom to carry out the architect's designs which gained me the goodwill and esteem of the brethren."[24]

On 6 August W. W. Phelps claimed that "three hundred and fifty men are zealously at work upon the building." He continued:

> The building of the Mormon Temple under all the troubles by which those people have been surrounded, seems to be carried on with a religious enthusiasm which reminds us of olden times, by the energy which controls all the movements towards its completion.... The whole community may be considered in their peculiar traits singular and remarkable and in after ages their Temple, like the ruins of Palenque may strike the beholder with wonder and history may be unable to explain what race worshiped there.[25]

20. George Miller, Peter Haws, Amasa M. Lyman, and George A. Smith, "Notice," *Nauvoo Neighbor* 3 (20 August 1845): 62. These men were all members of the Nauvoo House Association. Haws (1795-1862) had also worked in the "pineries" with Bishop George Miller from 1842 to 1843. Lyman and Smith (1813-77) were members of the Quorum of the Twelve.

21. Mace, Autobiography, 82.

22. Cleo H. Evans, comp. and ed., *Curtis Edwin Bolton: Pioneer, Missionary History, Descendants, and Ancestors* (Fairfax, VA: Author, 1968), 6.

23. Evans, *Curtis Edwin Bolton*, 6.

24. Truman O. Angell, "His Journal" (autobiography), in *Our Pioneer Heritage*, compiled by Kate B. Carter, 20 vols. (Salt Lake City: Daughters of the Utah Pioneers, 1958-77), 200. Angell (1810-87) later served as Church architect under Brigham Young, designing the St. George and Salt Lake temples.

25. William W. Phelps, "The Temple at Nauvoo," *New York Sun*, ca. 6 August 1845, in *History of the Church*, 7:434. Palenque is the site of some of the most impressive Aztec ruins in Mexico. Phelps's observation was prescient. During 1846-48, after the Saints had all but left Nauvoo and abandoned the temple, visitors marveled at the immense structure and conjectured what the various rooms and fixtures had been used for. See Appendix for the impressions of some of these visitors.

On 23 August, William Weeks gave Lyman O. Littlefield, correspondent for the *New York Messenger*, a tour of the structure. Littlefield described the first story: "The floor is not laid except with loose plank, for the convenience of carpenters, forty or fifty of whom were now to work on this floor."[26]

Heightened Security at the Temple

From the time of the martyrdom of Joseph and Hyrum Smith, security at the temple had been a concern. In August 1844, less than two months after the murders, Brigham Young declared: "We want to build the Temple in this place, if we have to build it, as the Jews built the walls of the Temple in Jerusalem, with a sword in one hand and the trowel in the other."[27] Young later reminisced that, when the Saints set to work again on the temple, they did so "with fire arms at hand, and a strong band of police."[28] Daniel M. Burbank, one of the carpenters, reminisced, "We had to labor days and guard nights. There was many attempts made to burn the temple."[29]

Beginning in the spring of 1845, Brigham Young assigned the Nauvoo police under the command of Captain Hosea Stout to guard the temple. Stout's daily journal details the day-to-day challenges of this responsibility:

> May 4, 1845.... Met the police and at dark went on guard at Brigham Young's until twelve o'clock m. then patrolled round by the temple.... Came home about eight o'clock a.m.
>
> May 19.... Came home at dark and then went to the temple as I had heard that there were suspicions that some evil was intended but nothing serious occurred.
>
> [July] 20.... I came home and in the evening met the police and after the duty was over spoke about one hour on certain principles were called forth by a circumstance taking place last night at the temple by some persons forcing themselves in the temple abruptly without authority from the police guard.
>
> [August] 25... Went to the temple and then went on patrol guard with Parker, [Shadrach] Roundy, Warthan, Pace, two of the Mechams and Langley; was out nearly all night. Came home and went to bed at three-thirty o'clock.

26. Lyman Omer Littlefield, "From Nauvoo—To the Editor of the *Messenger*," *New York Messenger* 2 (30 August 1845): 67-68, photocopy in LDS Church Archives.

27. Brigham Young, 18 August 1844, *History of the Church* 7:256.

28. Brigham Young, 6 April 1853, *Journal of Discourses*, 26 vols. (London and Liverpool: LDS Booksellers Depot, 1855-86), 2:32.

29. Daniel M. Burbank, "Autobiography of Daniel M. Burbank," 1863, holograph, 43, LDS Church Archives. Burbank (1814-94) was baptized in April 1841.

[August] 31 ... About nine o'clock then went ... to the temple and met some other of the police and we then removed a nuisance which took till about twelve o'clock.[30]

Wandle Mace recalled a precautionary measure that Brigham Young took during the summer of 1845:

Some old cannons had been brought to Nauvoo from New Orleans which had lain in the salt water until they had become very rusty. I was called upon by President Young to fit these cannons for action.

He told me to take them into the basement of the temple, and rebore them, and get them ready for action. I accordingly called upon two or three of the brethren to help me, and we took them by night into the basement, white washed the windows to prevent observation, and went to work. After much hard labor having to work upon the cannon at night, and superintend the work on the temple in the daytime, thus working day and night with very little time to rest, we had them ready to defend the city.[31]

In September, smoldering animosity erupted into violence, as Illinois citizens burned the homes and barns of dozens of Mormon families in surrounding towns. Five hundred temple workmen were temporarily reassigned that month to make preparations to defend the city.[32] Louisa Barnes Pratt stated: "The working men slept within the [temple] walls with their rifles at their heads at night."[33] From that point on, they could not give their undivided attention to building but felt they had to be constantly prepared for an attack. Curtis Bolton "worked many a day in the temple with my rifle and sword hid in the shavings."[34] Perrigrine Sessions, age thirty-one, wrote in his journal:

The months of September and October was a continual scene of work and turmoil and the labour on the Temple was almost oblige[d] to stop and the workmen many of them carried small arms with them all the time and all kept their muskets where they could put their hands on them at moments warning not knowing one moment but they would have to fight the next and seemed as though our enemies were determined that the work should stop but it continued

30. Hosea Stout, Diary, 1845, 2 vols., 1:50, 2:3-4, 2:17, 2:27, 2:28, typescript, Perry Special Collections, Lee Library.

31. Mace, Autobiography, 186.

32. Andrew Jenson, comp., *Historical Record: A Monthly Periodical Devoted Exclusively to Historical, Biographical, Chronological and Statistical Matters* 8 (January 1886): 10-11.

33. Louisa Barnes Pratt, "Louisa Barnes Pratt," in *Heart Throbs of the West*, compiled by Kate B. Carter, 8 vols. (Salt Lake City: Daughters of the Utah Pioneers, 1947-51), 8:234.

34. Evans, *Curtis Edwin Bolton*, 7.

through all the persecution and hardly stopped for a moment the Lord blessing
the labours of the faithful in all that was done both in building the temple and
defending ourselves and our wives and our children.[35]

On 16 September, "it was decided that there would be a guard kept night
and day around the temple, and that no stranger be allowed to come within the
square of the temple lot, and also that there be four large lanterns made for the purpose and placed about 25 feet from each corner of the temple, to keep a light by
night for the convenience of the guard."[36] In addition to the corner lanterns,
Brigham Young announced on 19 September his intention to place a light at the
top of the temple at night.[37]

The temple also became the rallying point for the defense of the city in the
case of an attack. Signals were established so the police, Nauvoo Legion, workmen,
and others would know to muster on the temple grounds. One of these signals was
the beating of a drum from the top of the temple. Priddy Meeks, a Nauvoo doctor
who lived "near a half mile from the temple," was also subject to the orders: "Every
man, when he heard the drum must be at the temple quick as possible night or day,
with their weapons of defense. Sometimes the alarm would be given in the darkest
hours of the night. We were broke of our rest a great deal, having to jump out of
our beds, half asleep, and run to the temple with our eyes hardly open."[38] Norton
Jacob recorded a scare on 22 September 1845 when a large muslin flag, which had
also been designated as "a signal for assembling the troops" was "hoisted about
sunset. When we were collected it was found to be a false alarm."[39] Fortunately,
the concerns over an attack on the temple were either foiled or unfounded.[40]

35. Perrigrine Sessions, "The Diaries of Perrigrine Sessions," 1814-86, ca. October 1845, photocopy of holograph, Perry Special Collections, Lee Library.

36. Hosea Stout, Diary, 2:36-37.

37. Ibid., 2:42-43.

38. Priddy Meeks, Journal, quoted in Dalton R. Meeks and Leonora Meeks, *The Life and Times
of Dr. Priddy Meeks* (Bountiful, UT: N.pub., 1996), 92, copy in Family History Center, Joseph Smith
Memorial Building, Salt Lake City. Meeks (1795-1886), a South Carolina native, had been baptized in
1840.

39. Norton Jacob, Journal, 1804-52, typescript, 18, Perry Special Collections, Lee Library. Jacob
(1804-79) was baptized on 15 March 1841.

40. In fact, it appears the citizens of Carthage and Warsaw were just as nervous about being
attacked by Mormons as the Mormons were about further attacks. On 25 September 1845, the
Burlington Hawkeye in Iowa carried this absurd report: "Carthage and Warsaw have been taken possession of by the Mormons, and the citizens driven from their homes. We have about two hundred
persons in our place from Hancock County, who have deserted their homes and taken shelter in Fort
Madison.... People are afraid to pass through the country on account of these troubles.... Report ...is
that ... other towns in Hancock County have been evacuated by the citizens and that the Mormons
have taken possession of these places." "Late from the Mormon War," *Burlington Hawkeye* 7 (25
September 1845).

Contribution of Joseph Toronto

Early in the summer of 1845, the goods in the tithing office began to dwindle. The increase in the number of temple workmen was apparently not matched by an increase in donated supplies. Brigham Young later recalled these worrisome circumstances: "We done a good deal of work at that time on the temple, and it was difficult to get bread for the hands to eat. I told the people or the Committee who had charge of the temple means to deal out all the flour they had and God would give them more and they done so."[41]

Brigham Young's faith was rewarded on 7 July. Heber C. Kimball recorded in his journal, "There was a brother [that] come and gave up all he had which was twenty six hundred dollars."[42] The brother was Giuseppe Taranto, whose name was anglicized to Joseph Toronto. He was a native of Sardinia, an island off the west coast of Italy. As a young man, he worked as a sailor in the Mediterranean Merchant Service and later on trans-Atlantic ships. He came to Boston in 1843 where he first heard of the Church and was soon baptized by George B. Wallace. Although he was counseled to gather with the Saints in Nauvoo, he decided to continue his trade of selling fruits and vegetables. However, when his boat collided with another, nearly drowning him, he felt motivated to follow the advice of the elders. Toronto had frugally saved his money during his years as a sailor and, upon reaching the city on 7 July, went immediately to Brigham Young, carrying several metal cans filled with money. "He rolled them across the table to President Young. When these were opened, there was [over] $2,500.00 in twenty-dollar gold pieces which he had saved during his seafaring life. He told President Young that he wanted to give himself and all that he had for the upbuilding of the Church and the Kingdom of God. Brigham Young blessed him and told him that he should stand at the head of his race, and that he and his family would never want for bread."[43]

---

41. Brigham Young, quoted in Wilford Woodruff, 8 February 1857, *Wilford Woodruff's Journal, 1833-1898*, typescript, edited by Scott G. Kenny, 9 vols. (Midvale, UT: Signature Books, 1983-85): 5:19-20.

42. Kimball, *On the Potter's Wheel*, 129.

43. "Joseph Toronto Chest," in *Our Pioneer Heritage*, 19:467-68. According to another version of Toronto's narrative, he was led to Nauvoo by a vision:

This philanthropist was Joseph Toronto, a native of Sicily, who had served for years as a sailor in the Italian navy. This frugal man had carefully hoarded his money for years, concealing his gold coins in his money belt.

As he approached New York harbor, he became fearful that some rogue in the large city might rob him of his golden spoil—the earnings of a lifetime. In the midst of his concern about the safety of his money, he dreamed one night that a man came to him, requesting that he leave his money with "Mormon Brigham" and he should be blessed.

The following day, Brigham Young and Willard Richards took the money to the recorder's office. William Clayton reported that they "brought a bag containing $2599.75 in Gold. Joseph Toronto, an Italian, came to President Young and said he wanted to give himself and all he had to President Young. He had this gold which was carefully wrapped up in old rags, tin bo[xes], etc. which he freely and voluntarily gave up."[44]

Brigham Young reported this event in dramatic fashion:

> The bishop and the committee met, and I met with them; and they said, that the law was to lay the gold at the apostles' feet. Yes, I said and I will lay it at the bishop's feet. So I opened the mouth of the bag and took hold of the bottom end and gave it a jerk towards the Bishop and strewed the gold across the room at his feet and I said now go and buy flour for the workmen on that temple and don't distrust the Lord any more for we will have what we need.[45]

Completion of the Roof

The framework for the roof was started early in the summer and must have been nearly finished by 16 June since, on that day, William Huntington's journal reads: "The frame of the roof is up, ready for shingles. The roof will soon be covered. The Temple will soon be enclosed."[46] Huntington's estimation was optimistic. Three days later, the better-informed Heber C. Kimball wrote in his journal, "The rafters are mostly on."[47] On 27 June, Zina Jacobs wrote: "The roof of the Temple is now about ready for the shingles."[48]

On 27 June Brigham Young informed Wilford Woodruff in England: "We have all the timbers for the temple on the ground, and above one hundred thou-

---

On reaching New York, he began to inquire about "Mormon Brigham," but no one knew him. Finally he met a person who told him that Brigham Young had recently become president of the Mormon Church, and was residing at Nauvoo, Illinois. Young Toronto left immediately for the city of the Saints. He arrived at the city of his desire during the April conference, at which President Young told how difficult it was to get enough bread for the workmen to eat, and made a strong appeal for assistance. At the close of the meeting, the twenty-seven year old Italian went to President Young's office where he removed his belt and placed it on the President's desk, informing him that it contained twenty-five hundred dollars in gold. The excited President met with the Bishop and the building committee, before whom he exhibited the leather scabbard which was gorged with gold coins. E. Cecil McGavin, *Nauvoo the Beautiful* (Salt Lake City: Deseret Book Company, 1946), 26-27.

44. George D. Smith, *An Intimate Chronicle*, 173.

45. Woodruff, 8 February 1857, Journal, 5:19-20.

46. Huntington, "Journal," 30.

47. Kimball, *On the Potter's Wheel*, 122, 126.

48. Maureen Ursenbach Beecher, ed. "'All Things Move in Order in the City': The Nauvoo Diary of Zina Diantha Huntington Jacobs," *BYU Studies* 18 (Spring 1979): 314.

sand shingles for the roof."[49] Contrary to reports that had circulated in the press alleging that the shingles would be made of oak, they were made of pine from Wisconsin.[50] They may have been purchased ready-made, prepared at the Church-owned saw mills in Wisconsin, or fabricated at Nauvoo from the raw lumber that continued to arrive from the "pineries." Allen Stout recorded that he "worked awhile at tending a shingle machine" in Nauvoo.[51] But as early as 1842, the Wisconsin sawmills were equipped to make shingles.[52]

Shingling began in mid-July and progressed rapidly.[53] The *Times and Seasons* reported on 1 August 1845: "The first roof of the Temple, has been made of white pine shingles and plank. The second, (for a building which will cost about two millions is worthy,) most probably, will be constructed of zinc, lead, copper, or porcelain. An experiment of sheet lead, covering a portion of the shingles, has already been made."[54] In October 1841, Parley P. Pratt had proposed "using lead for the roofs of the Temple and all other permanent buildings; I think it will be found more durable, more convenient, and cheaper than timber, and will perhaps save whole blocks from being consumed by fire."[55]

Materials for covering for the roof may have been purchased in St. Louis. On 2 August 1845, the trustees (Bishops Miller and Knight) instructed Howard Egan, then in St. Louis, to purchase materials which could have been used for roofing:

> We wish you to purchase the following articles for us in St. Louis, viz: 1 sheet of lead 20 feet long by 20 inches wide which you will find at Mr. W. W. Thompson's on front street.
> Also 2 barrels of tar which you will get [from] some grocery store.
> Also, 1 sheet of copper 14 inches wide and 8 feet long and ¼ inches thick.[56]

---

49. "Extracts from President Young's Letter," *Millennial Star* 6 (1 September 1845): 91.

50. The *Warsaw Signal* taunted: "The Saints say the Temple is NOT covered with oak shingles. We don't care; it is covered with pine, which will make it burn all the better." Reprinted without a title in *New York Messenger* 2 (27 September 1845), 100.

51. Allen Joseph Stout, Journal, 1815-89, typescript, 17, Perry Special Collections, Lee Library.

52. *History of the Church*, 5:57. On 3 July 1843, George Miller "arrived from the Pinery with ... seventy thousand shingles for the Temple." Ibid., 5:497.

53. According to Huntington, "Journal," 31-32, shingling began about 20 July.

54. "Roof of the Temple," *Times and Seasons* 6 (1 August 1845): 983.

55. Parley P. Pratt, Letter to Joseph Smith, dated 24 October 1841, Manchester, England, in *Times and Seasons* 3 (1 February 1842): 683.

56. Newel K. Whitney, Letter to Howard Egan, 2 August 1845, Newel K. Whitney Papers, Perry Special Collections, Lee Library.

When the shingling was completed on 13 August, the *Nauvoo Neighbor* happily reported:

The *Neighbor* has been delayed a few hours, in order to say that the last shingle has been laid upon the roof of the Temple. The roof is now completed, and, the sash and window frames having been made ready, the house of the Lord may be considered "enclosed." We thank the Lord who hath extended his arm to help us to accomplish so much in so short a time, and we pray for his continued aid for its final completion.[57]

The following day, Zina Diantha Huntington Jacobs wrote in her journal, "The last shingle was laid on the Temple. Praise the Lord."[58] Her father, William Huntington, recorded with similar thankfulness:

August 17th 1845 ... All business commences in the city with usual liveliness. The temple is in a rapid state of improvements. [It's] sturdy. The shingling of the roof ... put a veto on one of Sidney Rigdon's false prophecies that was that the last shingle never would be put onto the house in consequence of our enemies. But thanks be to God, no arm is as yet suffered to hinder the work of the Lord.[59]

At the summit of the roof, running from west to east, was a narrow surface known as the deck. Lyman O. Littlefield, writing for the Mormon *New York Messenger*, visited the temple on 6 August and described several features of the temple's roof:

Now climbing over a large beam, not daring in the mean time to look down through the many pieces of timber in to the great distance below, we stand upon the top of the building, or deck, in which is constructed six octagon sky-lights through which light will be reached into the large room below. The deck is finished in the same manner that some of our eastern rooms is ceiled; or in other words in ceiling form, perfectly water tight. At each side of the deck is a roof made of pine shingles perfectly matched and laid in the neatest manner. In each of these roofs, is six square sky-lights through which, light will be reached into the small rooms immediately below. Here are also, two elegant ornamental chimneys of hewn stone, running through each roof.[60]

---

57. "The Last Shingle," *Nauvoo Neighbor*, 3 (13 August 1845): not paginated.
58. Beecher, "'All Things Move in Order,'" 285.
59. Huntington, "Journal," 34.
60. Littlefield, "From Nauvoo—To the Editor of the *Messenger*," 67.

Visitors reached this deck through a door on the east side of the tower.[61] The deck at the pitched roof's summit spoken of by Littlefield was surrounded by a decorative balustrade and was used as a walkway. Thus, Charles Lanman, an essayist who visited Nauvoo in 1847, observed, "The roof of the main building is arranged for a place of promenade."[62]

The chimneys, completed on 1 July 1845, were the last stonework set in the temple. William Huntington, one of the stonecutters who had prepared these stones, "locked up his chest of tools at the Temple," wrote his daughter, Zina. "He has labored three years mostly. He has done 818 days work. Now in good health, aged 61 the 28 of last March."[63]

Along the eaves of the temple, running east-west along the top of the stone walls, were two troughs which functioned as rain gutters. Littlefield described them: "The eave troughs hold thirty barrels of water, and are sheeted with sixty-five hundred pounds of lead. The water will be let off from these troughs into a large reservoir at the east end of the building, from which the baptismal fount will be supplied with water."[64] In his 27 June letter to Wilford Woodruff, Brigham Young mentions the purchase of the lead used to line these troughs.[65]

The Temple Tower

The next project was framing the attic and tower. In the same letter, Brigham Young reported that "the frame and ornamental work of the tower [were] all ready to be put up." In fact, on that very day, he noted, "the frame work around the foundation of the tower is all up, and the first timbers for the tower itself were raised this day."[66]

On 6 August, Lyman Littlefield described the tower's dimensions:

Now let us go to the top of the attic story[67] which is sixteen and a half feet high from the eaves, and the eaves are sixty feet from the ground. This has not yet been shingled, and we have to stand upon some loose plank. This is a massive

---

61. *Nauvoo Patriot*, 9 October 1848, quoted in Journal History, 9 October 1848, 7.

62. Charles Lanman, *A Summer in the Wilderness* (New York: N.pub., 1847), 31.

63. Beecher, "'All Things Move in Order,'" 315.

64. Littlefield, "From Nauvoo—To the Editor of the *Messenger*," 68.

65. Brigham Young, Letter to Wilford Woodruff, 27 June 1845, *History of the Church*, 7:430.

66. Ibid.

67. By attic, Littlefield means the box-shaped structure at the west end on which the tower is constructed.

pine frame, from the centre of the roof of which rises the tower which is twelve and a half feet high. At that height it is lessened into the belfry which is twenty feet high. This is as far as the steeple is now completed. Above the belfry will come the clock section, ten feet high; next above that will be the observatory sixteen feet high; then the dome, thirteen and a half feet high, from which the balls and rod [lightning rod] will run ten feet higher, making the distance from the surface of the ground to the top of the steeple, one-hundred fifty-eight and a half feet.[68]

According to Hosea Stout, the tower was still at the level of the belfry four days later. After Sabbath services on 10 August, he "went with a number of other police and some of the band on the top of the belfry of the temple and the musicians played some beautiful airs to the congregation as they were dismissed."[69]

Over five hundred pieces of cut lumber were used in the frame for the tower, according to a surviving bill for the tower timbers. The bill specifies the dimensions of every sill, post, brace, trimmer, plait, joist, stud, and beam.[70] A non-Mormon visitor noted, "As the inside of this [tower] was not entirely finished, an excellent chance was afforded us to observe the massive strength of the framework, and perceive the solidity and view [the] durability, with which it was constructed. The bare timbers presented a never-ending system of braces, each supporting the other successively. The Mormons certainly knew how to build, if they were a deluded people in some other respects."[71]

Carpenter Norton Jacob acted as "foreman of all the framing of the roof and tower." He stated that "on the 16th of August I finished framing the tower."[72] Jacob Peart was among those who helped finish the tower. He recalled, "I did considerable work on the Temple, planing up boards and laying floors in the attic and tower."[73]

68. Littlefield, "From Nauvoo—To the Editor of the *Messenger*," 68. Littlefield's numbers may have come from "The Steeple of the Temple," *Nauvoo Neighbor* 3 (30 July 1845), not paginated: "The height may be calculated as follows: From the ground to the top of the eaves, 60 feet; From the eaves to the top of the attic story, 16½; Tower, 12½; Belfry 20; Clock section 10; Observatory 16; Dome 13½; Balls and rod 10; Total 158½ 130 feet of which is now raised."

69. Hosea Stout, Diary, 2:26.

70. Bill for lumber, submitted to the Temple Committee by M. B. Powell, 25 November 1845, Newel K. Whitney Papers, Perry Special Collections, Lee Library.

71. Unnamed visitor, Illinois Journal, 9 December 1853, reprinted as "Recollections of the Nauvoo Temple," in *Journal of the Illinois State Historical Society* 38 (December 1945): 482; photocopy in LDS Church Historical Department Library.

72. Jacob, Journal, 11.

73. Jacob Peart, "Life Sketch of Jacob Peart, Sr.," 8 October 1872, typescript, 1, Historic Nauvoo Lands and Records Office, Nauvoo, Illinois.

On 21 August, Brigham Young wrote another progress report to Wilford Woodruff: "The Temple is up, the shingles all on, the tower raised, and nearly ready to put the dome up. The joiners are now at work finishing off the inside, and within two months we shall have some rooms prepared to commence the endowment. The joiners will be enabled to finish the inside work during the winter."[74]

The exterior of the finished tower was elaborately decorated with Corinthian columns, carvings of stars, and windows. The framed tower was painted white and the shutters surrounding the belfry section were painted green.[75]

On 23 August, the dome of the temple was raised. The cupola was framed and covered with tin which had been purchased by late June.[76] The Nauvoo Tinners Association provided the labor to create the dome.[77] Massachusetts-born Philip Bessom Lewis, "being a tinner by trade" was among those who "covered the Nauvoo Temple tower with tin."[78] Thomas L. Kane reported that the dome had a gold appearance.[79] It is possible that an amalgam made with powdered bronze was used to coat the tin dome, giving it the look of a gilded surface.[80]

Raising the cupola, though not an event accompanied by the same pomp and ceremony as laying the capstone a few months earlier, caught the attention of the citizenry. It represented in a very visual way a culmination, not only of the three months of labor on the tower and roof, but also of the entire building project. In most respects, the temple looked complete.[81]

---

74. Brigham Young, Letter to Wilford Woodruff, "Latest from Nauvoo," *Millennial Star* 6 (15 September 1845): 124.

75. Lyman O. Littlefield, "From Nauvoo," *New York Messenger* 2 (8 November 1845): 152.

76. Brigham Young, Letter to Wilford Woodruff, 27 June 1845, *History of the Church*, 7:430.

77. "Amount of Labor Done on Temple by Tinners Association," ca. 1845, microfilm of holograph, Newel K. Whitney Papers, Perry Special Collections, Lee Library.

78. Philip E. Lewis, "The Life History of Philip Bessom Lewis," n.d., microfilm of typescript, Perry Special Collections, Lee Library.

79. Thomas L. Kane, "The Mormons: A Discourse Delivered Before the Historical Society of Pennsylvania, March 26, 1850," quoted in Daniel Tyler, *A Concise History of the Mormon Battalion in the Mexican War, 1846-1847* (Chicago: Rio Grande Press, 1964), 80.

80. Powdered bronze was obviously less expensive than gold and was often used to give metal surfaces a gilded appearance. The powder would have been mixed with quicksilver (mercury) and poured over the surface. The mercury would run off and be saved for additional applications while the powder would adhere to the surface of the tin.

81. Several others also recorded this event. See William Cahoon, Autobiography, 1813-1878, in Stella Shurtleff and Brent Farrington Cahoon, eds., *Reynolds Cahoon and His Stalwart Sons* (Salt Lake City: Paragon Press, 1960), 88; Norton Jacob, Journal, 11; William Holmes Walker, Journal, 1820-1897, typescript, 14; Huntington, "Journal," typescript, 34; and Samuel Holister Rogers, Journal, 1819-86, typescript, 44. The last three manuscripts are in Perry Special Collections, Lee Library.

Joseph Hovey wrote in his journal: "This day the dome of the temple is put on. About sixty or seventy hands partook of melons on the attic. Pretty high eating. They hoisted a flag and it stayed until Sunday night."[82] George A. Smith added: "In the afternoon attended meeting of the quorum of Seventies. The dome of the Temple was put in its place on the tower and our country's flag placed upon it."[83] Several other apostles were attending the same meeting of the Fourth Quorum of Seventy. Willard Richards interrupted Heber C. Kimball, who was addressing the meeting "while the facts were recorded that the dome of the temple was raised."[84] Elder John Taylor wrote: "While we were speaking we saw the cupola put on the Temple. After meeting, I went up to the Temple, and ascended to the top of the tower, while there I partook of some melons they had there, I returned thanks to God, who had enabled us to do so great a work, and have it so forward [nearly complete]".[85]

After the cupola was in place, several men took turns climbing to the top. William Holmes Walker "stood upon the top of the dome."[86] Willard Richards, from the ground, recorded that Stephen Goddard "stood on his head on the top of the spire post."[87]

By 12 September, the workmen had installed the "balls and rod" atop the tower. The weekly *Nauvoo Neighbor* ran a little announcement that day: "Nauvoo is great on improvement, and nothing bespeaks it more than the 'balls' on top of the steeple of the Temple."[88]

"A Grand Observatory"

Spiraling upward through the center of the tower was a staircase that provided access to the observatory.[89] A door on the east side of the dome allowed

82. Joseph Grafton Hovey, "Autobiography of Joseph Grafton Hovey," typescript, 32, Perry Special Collections, Lee Library. Grandson M. R. Hovey copied and arranged this document from Hovey's journal in 1933. It begins with an autobiography, then moves to daily entries.

83. George A. Smith, "My Journal," compiled and edited by Elden J. Watson, typescript, 88, print-out in my possession.

84. Willard Richard, Diary, as quoted in Dean C. Jessee, ed., "The John Taylor Nauvoo Journal," *BYU Studies* 23 (Summer 1983): 85.

85. Ibid.

86. Walker, "Incidents, Travels, and Life of Elder William Holmes Wilker," typescript, Perry Special Collections, Lee Library, 14. Walker (1820-1908) was born in Vermont and was baptized in 1835.

87. Quoted in Jessee, "The John Taylor Nauvoo Journal," 72.

88. "Improvement," *Nauvoo Neighbor* 3 (12 September 1845): 2.

89. Alexander H. Smith, quoted in Heman C. Smith, *History of the Reorganized Church of Jesus Christ of Latter Day Saints,* 7 vols. (Independence, MO: Herald House, 1903-14; second printing, 1967), 2:564.

workers or visitors to stand atop the tower. This door was presumably between the "v-shaped turrets" that skirted the bottom of the dome with "a small ladder" that could be "seen going up over the dome."[90] Alexander Hale Smith, one of Joseph and Emma's sons recalled:

> When a boy I was privileged to wander all over the building.... I well remember that on one ... occasion I ventured out of the small door on the east side of the rounded top which was covered with bright tin. I walked all around it, and as I approached the door the gentleman whom I was guide to caught me and drew me in, and lectured me for my imprudence, declaring that he would not dare do it.[91]

Given the temple's height and its already commanding site on top of the bluff, it offered a dramatic view of the surrounding countryside. Climbing to the steeple was a popular activity, not only during the few remaining months that the Latter-day Saints would be in Nauvoo but for visitors to the town for years afterward.

On 30 July 1845, John Taylor, editor of the *Nauvoo Neighbor*, recorded having taken a "tour up in the steeple" and added: "It may be well to say that the steeple of the Temple will be a grand observatory for those that wish to delight the eye."[92] A year later, the non-Mormon *Hancock Eagle* used virtually the same expression:

> The upper windows of the steeple serve as an observatory, from which a magnificent view of the surrounding country may be had. The Mississippi is seen winding its serpentine form along the wooded valley to the North and South—the hills of Iowa rise in bold relief to the westward, and lose themselves in the blue distance; while the prairies, fields, gardens and private buildings lie spread out like a map below.[93]

Hosea Stout frequently "went.... to the top of the steeple and had a fine and romantic view of the surrounding country."[94] Charles Lanman, who visited

90. Unknown author, untitled article containing quotations from J. M. Davidson, "Nauvoo: The Past and Present of That City: Visits of 1846 and 1864 Contrasted," *Carthage Republican*, 25 February 1864, 1, and quoted in E. Cecil McGavin, *The Nauvoo Temple* (Salt Lake City: Deseret Book, 1962), 93-95. McGavin mistakenly cites Davidson as the author of the article, rather than as "quoted by unknown author."

91. *History of the Reorganized Church*, 2:564.

92. John Taylor, "The Steeple of the Temple," Nauvoo Neighbor 3 (30 July 1845): not paginated.

93. William Matlack, "Public Buildings," *Hancock Eagle*, 24 April 1846, microfilm, LDS Church Archives. William E. Matlack, a Philadelphian, was a Princeton graduate and had previous editorial experience working for the *New Yorker*.

94. Hosea Stout, Diary, 2:94.

Nauvoo in 1846, described his view of the "city in the centre of an apparently boundless wilderness. To the east lay in perfect beauty the grand Prairie of Illinois, reaching to the waters of Michigan; to the North and South faded away the winding Mississippi; and on the west, far as the eye could reach, was spread out a perfect sea of forest land."[95] J. H. Buckingham, a businessman from Boston also praised the view he saw in the summer of 1847: "The whole valley of the Mississippi for miles and miles lay exposed to view on the north and south, where the prairie lands of Illinois, and Iowa, and Missouri, were to be seen to the east and west, overlooking the few hills lying near to the shore in the latter state, and showing the tortuous course of the Des Moines River for some distance."[96]

The view was spectacular enough that even young children remembered it many years later. Pamela Mason, who was four in 1846, wrote her memories for the *Deseret News* in 1897: "I remember my father taking my mother, brothers and sisters and myself up into the tower of our beautiful temple in Nauvoo. I also recall the grand scene presented to our view in all directions from the temple."[97]

Jonathan Layne recalled visiting the temple in the fall of 1845 when he was ten years old with his uncle Lee Bybee. Although the interior "was not then complete ... we were permitted to go in and see it and I went nearly to the top of the tower and was afraid to go up higher. Had a fine view of the country for many miles around. We could see farms, houses, grain stacks, etc."[98]

Visitors to the tower often obtained their view of the environs from the windows in the observatory but an adventuresome few actually ventured out onto the narrow walkway at the base of the dome. An unnamed visitor in 1853 wrote a record of his experience for the *Illinois Journal*:

> After ascending some distance, a series of steps which were very steep, a short stairway brought us to the end of our wearisome journey, and, emerging through a small opening on the side, we gained access to the open air.... A low balustrade [railing] encircled the huge dome, between which and the former wound a narrow path-way much worn by the feet of visitors. Many names were scratched on the dome and cut in the balustrade, by ambitious persons who wished to be remembered by posterity.[99]

95. Lanman, *A Summer in the Wilderness*, 33.

96. J. H. Buckingham, Letter to *Boston Courier*, 18 July 1847, reprinted in Harry E. Pratt, ed., "Illinois As Lincoln Knew It," *Papers in Illinois History and Transaction for the Year 1937* (Springfield, IL: N.pub., 1938), 172.

97. Pamela Mason, "Illinois to Utah," *Deseret News*, 30 March 1897, excerpts reprinted in *Our Pioneer Heritage*, 8:295.

98. Jonathan Ellis Layne, "Autobiography of Jonathan Ellis Layne," typescript, 2, Historic Nauvoo Lands and Records Office, Nauvoo, Illinois.

99. Anonymous author, *Illinois Journal*, 9 December 1853.

The visitor added that "the wind blew briskly" and "the massive super-structure began to tremble and seemed to rock to and fro. It made one's blood run cold to feel the mass quiver and shake beneath him at such a height. We felt a little dizzy, and quickly descended." James A. Scott, one of the temple workers said he "felt pretty ticklish when looking from the windows of the tower, being some hundred and twentyfive or thirty feet from the ground."[100]

After the Saints began to leave Nauvoo the following winter, Wandle Mace wrote, with some melancholy, "From the top of the tower of the temple I could overlook the spot where my family was camped."[101]

A Bell for the Temple Tower

Plans for the temple called for a bell to be placed in the tower. On 15 July 1845, Brigham Young wrote to the Saints in England:

> We have thought it might be very agreeable to the feelings of the English Saints to furnish a bell for the temple, if this is their pleasure, you can forward it [on] the first conveyance, and we will have it hung as the building is going up. We are but little acquainted with the weight of bells: we have thought of 2000 lbs. weight, but we leave this to your judgment. We want one that can be heard night or day.[102]

Wilford Woodruff, in printing this letter in the *Millennial Star,* added his own persuasion:

> I wish, now, to make an appeal to the hearts and minds of some ten thousand of my brethren and sisters that reside in this land, by asking you the question, "if you are willing to bring your tithes and offerings into the storehouse of the Lord, sufficient to purchase the mouthpiece or bell for the temple of the Lord?" My faith is that your answer will be "yes." It is justly due to the Liverpool branch of the church to say that, they not only say "yes" to a bell, but they also say, "ADD A CLOCK TO IT," and we will not be behind on our part. This is honourable indeed, and I have no doubt, but that, it will meet the feelings of the churches generally, and be pleasing unto them to prove that their tithings and offerings have been laid out to purchase a bell, that when they hear the sound thereof (which may it be the case) they may rejoice that it is the product of their own offerings to the temple of the Lord.[103]

100. James Allen Scott, Diary, 3, 31 March 1846, microfilm of holograph, LDS Church Archives.

101. Mace, Autobiography, 203-4.

102. Brigham Young, "Extract of a Letter from President Brigham Young," *Millennial Star* 6 (15 July 1845): 43.

103. Woodruff, untitled paragraph, ibid.

One month later in the 15 August issue of the *Millennial Star*, Woodruff specified: "Any contributions for a bell and clock for the temple, will be considered as contributions for the temple, inasmuch as they will be parts and parcels of the same, and that all future contributions for the temple will be applied for procuring the above, until a sufficiency be realized." He stated his hope that "the fact of providing a mouth-piece and time-piece for the temple of the Lord, will be an additional stimulus to the British Saints in this glorious cause."[104]

In September, Brigham Young arranged for a temporary bell to be used in the tower. On 17 September, Hosea Stout indicated that "the tolling of the temple bell" would be an alarm, signaling the Nauvoo police to "repair forthwith armed and equipped to the parade ground."[105] In December 1845 and January 1846, this temporary bell signaled the beginning of each endowment session in the temple.[106]

In the meantime, the Saints in England continued to raise funds for the permanent bell and the clock. At the Church conference at Manchester on 14 December 1845, Woodruff announced, "The British Saints have come forward nobly, when called upon to assist the brethren in the building of the Temple. Some £220 has been donated since we called for assistance for the bell and clock; this is well, and I feel convinced that you will continue your efforts. I should wish the Saints, during the winter, to continue their exertions."[107]

However, a few weeks later, Woodruff received a letter from Brigham Young outlining a new agenda: "I wrote you in my last letter that we intended to purchase the bell in this country and desired you to transmit the money collected for that purpose by the first safe opportunity. I feel as ever anxious this should be done."[108] Details about where, when, by whom, from whom, and the cost of the bell purchased are unknown.

Whether the clock for the tower was purchased is also a mystery. The clock section was to have four clocks facing each of the cardinal directions. Daguerreotypes of the temple show an elaborate clockface with roman numerals on the south side of the tower, but there appear to be no hands. Also partially vis-

104. Woodruff, "August 15, 1845," *Millennial Star* 6 (15 August 1845), 77.
105. Hosea Stout, Diary, 2:39.
106. George D. Smith, *An Intimate Chronicle*, 215.
107. "Special General Conference," *Millennial Star* 7 (1 January 1846): 5.
108. Brigham Young, Letter to Wilford Woodruff, 17 December 1845, holograph, Brigham Young Papers, LDS Church Archives. According to a Woodruff family tradition, the bell was "sent to the United States in the care of ... Wilford Woodruff." Edith Smith Eliot, quoted in Lois Leetham Tanner, "I Have a Question," *Ensign*, February 1981, 16. (Sister Eliot is a great-granddaughter of Wilford Woodruff). However, Woodruff's diary and correspondence make no mention of a bell purchase. He probably brought the donated money with him when he returned to Nauvoo in April 1846.

ible is a similar face on the west side. Whether the clockwork or hands were ever installed is unknown.

Work on the Stone Font

At some point during the winter of 1844-45, Brigham Young and the Twelve had decided to replace the wooden font in the temple's basement with a new one made of stone.[109] The *Times and Seasons* of 15 January 1845 contained this statement by the Twelve indicating that the old font had already been removed:

> There was a font erected in the basement story of the Temple, for the baptism of the dead, the healing of the sick and other purposes; this font was made of wood, and was only intended for the present use; but it is now removed, and as soon as the stone cutters get through with the cutting of the stone for the walls of the Temple, they will immediately proceed to cut the stone for and erect a font of hewn stone. This font will be of an oval form and twelve feet in length and eight wide, with stone steps and an iron railing; this font will stand upon twelve oxen, which will be cast of iron or brass, or perhaps hewn stone; if of brass, polished; if of iron, bronzed.[110]

At April 1845 conference, Brigham Young stated his reasons for the change:

> We have taken down the wooden fount that was built up by the instructions of Brother Joseph. This has been a great wonder to some, and says one of the stone cutters the other day, "I wonder why Joseph did not tell us the fount should be built of stone." The man that made that speech is walking in darkness. He is a stranger to the spirit of this work, and knows nothing. In fact he does not know enough to cut a stone for the house of God.... Brother Joseph said to me with regard to the fount, "I will not go into the river to be baptized for my friends, we will build a wooden fount to serve the present necessity"; brethren, does that satisfy you? This fount has caused the Gentile world to wonder but a sight of the next one will make a Gentile faint away.... We will have a fount that will not stink and keep us all the while cleansing it out: and we will have a pool wherein to baptize the sick, that they may recover. And when we get into the fount we will show you the priesthood and the power of it.[111]

109. William Clayton, Journal, in Journal History of the Church of Jesus Christ of Latter-day Saints (chronology of typed entries and newspaper clippings, 1830-present), 31 December 1844, 15, LDS Church Archives.

110. "An Epistle of the Twelve to the Church of Jesus Christ of Latter-day Saints in All the World," 14 January 1845, *Times and Seasons* 6 (15 January 1846): 779.

111. Brigham Young, "Speech," *Times and Seasons* 6 (1 July 1845): 953-56.

The records list only twenty-four baptisms for the dead in 1845.[112] It is probable that the removal and replacement of the wood font was one of the main reasons for this.

In addition to replacing the font, the Twelve, the trustees, the architect, and the temple committee met on 15 March 1845 and decided to "build a drain for the font."[113] When and by whom the drain was made are unknown. Archeological evidence suggests that the drain ran from the base of the font to the east end of the south wall and exited from the temple toward Mulholland Street on the south. As it approached the street, it broadened to nearly five feet.[114]

Once the stone for the exterior walls was cut, the cutters set to work on stones for the new font. Among those selected for this elaborate project were William W. Player, Benjamin T. Mitchell, Charles Lambert, William Cottier, Andrew Cahoon, Daniel S. Cahoon, Jerome Kimpton, Augustus Stafford, Bun Anderson, Alvin Winegar, William Jones, and Stephen Halles Jr.[115] Jonathan Sawyer Wells, who moved to Nauvoo in September 1845, also reportedly "helped to carve the oxen for the baptismal font."[116]

The stones for the font's foundation and basin were prepared first. In his letter to Wilford Woodruff on 27 June 1847, Brigham Young reported: "The new stone font is mostly cut, and the first stone was laid today at about four o'clock."[117] That same day Heber C. Kimball recorded in his journal visiting the temple "as they had just began to lay the first stones."[118]

John Carling, a Nauvoo cabinetmaker was the man chosen to create this model:

> While [he] was carving beautiful work on a mantle in Nauvoo, Brigham Young came to him and asked if he couldn't make a pattern of an ox as they wished life-sized oxen on which to rest the baptismal font. Brother Carling went home and drew a picture of one of his own oxen. He then pinned planks together with hardwood pins and glue and taking his carpenter's pencil, saw and drawing

112. Nauvoo Baptisms for the Dead, Book C, 1844-45, microfilm of holograph, Family History Library, Church of Jesus Christ of Latter-day Saints, Salt Lake City.

113. *History of the Church,* 7:382.

114. Harrington and C. Harrington, *Rediscovery of the Nauvoo Temple,* 41.

115. Clayton, Journal History, 31 December 1844, 15.

116. "Jonathan Sawyer Wells," in Susan Easton Black, *Membership of the Church of Jesus Christ of Latter-day Saints, 1830-1848,* 48 vols. (Provo, UT: Religious Studies Center, Brigham Young University, 1987), 44:217.

117. *History of the Church,* 7:431.

118. Kimball, *On the Potter's Wheel,* 126. John Taylor recorded a similar visit: "Saturday, June 28th, 1845 ... I went up with the Twelve to inspect their work, also to see the Arsenal and the font in the Temple, its foundation having just been laid." Jesse, "The John Taylor Nauvoo Journal," 65.

knife, he carved the first pattern of the first oxen used in Latter-day Saint Temples.[119]

The next task after laying the foundation stones was to make the oxen. Clarence Merrill, a four-year-old in 1845, later recollected that the masons used "an ox [carved] out of wood for a pattern to chisel the oxen out of for the Font to rest upon."[120] On 20 July, William Huntington indicated that "the oxen ... to be made of stone, will soon be commenced."[121] Mary Ann Weston Maughan remarked, "[The oxen] are good, and do credit to the brethren who are carving them."[122] Orson Pratt, in a letter to the *New York Messenger* published on 30 August, reported: "The stone[s] for the baptismal fount were all cut with the exception of the oxen, and the most of them placed in their proper position; stone oxen were in a state of forwardness, and will soon be completed."[123]

The unnamed *Illinois Journal* visitor left this detailed description of the completed font, including the relationship of the foundation, basin, and oxen:

> We first entered the basement, the floor of which we had no sooner gained than our eyes rested upon the great baptismal font, constructed of solid limestone, seemingly resting on the backs of six [sic] milk-white oxen, carved from solid blocks of stone.... I said the basin seemed to rest on them; but in reality it rested on a stone foundation of its own, composed of heavy blocks of stone, closely joined together, and fashioned in the form of a circle. The oxen were not fully developed but resting on their fore-feet, the middle of their bodies was firmly cemented to that circular foundation, and thus the basin seemed to rest directly on their backs.[124]

Another description, written by J. H. Buckingham in July 1847, provides some important details, including the information that the font stairways ran east and west, in contrast to those of the wooden font which had run north and south:

---

119. "John Carling," in *Heart Throbs of the West*, edited by Kate B. Carter, 12 vols. (Salt Lake City: Daughters of the Utah Pioneers, 1943), 4:260. Carling (1800-55) was baptized on 5 January 1840.

120. "Clarence Merrill, Pioneer," *Our Pioneer Heritage*, 9:319. The workmen probably used one of the oxen from the old font as a model. After the Saints had evacuated the city in 1846, the anonymous account in the *Illinois Journal* on 9 December 1853 noted: "Formerly there were placed wooden oxen, painted, which I saw in one of the upper rooms, but they were only temporary, and were replaced by these of stone."

121. Huntington, "Journal," 32.

122. "Journal of Mary Ann Weston Maughan," in *Our Pioneer Heritage*, 2:364.

123. Orson Pratt, "News to England" (Letter to Reuben Hedlock), *New York Messenger* 2 (30 August 1845): 67; photocopy in LDS Church Archives.

124. Unnamed visitor, *Illinois Journal*, 9 December 1853. He was mistaken; the number of oxen was twelve.

[The font] has two flights of steps, with iron banisters, by which you enter and go out of the font, one at the east end, and the other at the west end. The oxen have tin horns and tin ears, but are otherwise of stone, and a stone drapery hangs like a curtain down from the font, so as to prevent the exposure of all back of the forelegs of the beasts. In consequence of what I had heard of this font I was disappointed; for it was neither vast nor gorgeous; everything about it was quite simple and unostentatious.... and on each side and at the ends are small alcoves, intended for robing rooms for the faithful.[125]

According to William Gallup, who visited the temple in 1848, "The horns were made of tin fastened on by a screw."[126] Family tradition suggests that John Mills, British convert and tinsmith, "devoted much of his time" to fashioning the oxen's tin horns.[127] As a "skilled tin and copper craftsman" he "molded the horns and the ears of the oxen and worked on the font until its completion.[128]

In late August 1845 Lyman Littlefield gave this status report on the basement:

In the centre of [the basement], stands the base of the baptismal fount; it is of hewn stone, and the surface of it is in the shape of an egg divided in the middle from end to end. Its dimensions are fifteen by eleven feet and a half wide on the outside. Strewn over the floor is pieces of massive stone, ready hewn to complete it. When completed it will be supported by twelve oxen hewn from solid stone, which will be represented as being sunk to the knees in a floor of Roman cement [an extremely hard mortar]. The fount will be entered by a flight of steps in an arch form at each end. The whole will be surrounded by an iron railing to protect it from the soiling hand of the curious visitor. It will be an interesting and costly work when completed.[129]

Progress on the font was slow, in part because the task was complex and in part because the Saints were coming under increasing harassment from raiding parties that were attacking Saints in outlying settlements during the late summer. This was a constant distraction and source of tension to the workers. In early October, Brigham Young made an overly optimistic appraisal: "The font.... of the

125. Buckingham, Letter to Boston Courier, 18 July 1847.

126. William Gallup, Diary, 29 July 1848, photographic reprint of pages 12930 accompanied by introduction by William Powell, photocopy, Perry Special Collections, Lee Library.

127. "Elizabeth Hall," in Daughters of the Utah Pioneers and Their Mothers, edited by James T. Jakeman (Salt Lake City: Western Publishing, 1916), 235. Hall married John Mills in 1820.

128. "John and Elizabeth Hall Mills," Our Pioneer Heritage, 16:522. The reference to Joseph Smith is probably a mistake. The oxen for the wood font, which was conceived and created during Joseph's lifetime, did not have tin horns and ears. The stone font was not begun until early 1845, at Brigham Young's request.

129. Littlefield, "From Nauvoo—To the Editor of the Messenger," 67-68.

Temple will be in readiness in a few days."[130] However, work continued through the fall and early winter. On 1 December, Joseph Hovey, who was one of those selected to do the stone cutting for the font, recorded that he "finished my work on the baptismal fount."[131] In late December, Joseph Fielding wrote in his journal: "[The] font … is about finished and ready for use."[132] On 20 January 1846, an article in the *Times and Seasons* used virtually the same language: the font was "about ready."[133] The exact date of the font's completion is unknown, though it was probably before the end of January 1846. It seems apparent also that the stone font was not used much, given the departure of the main body of the Saints in February and March 1846.

    Of the completed font, the *Hancock Eagle* reported:

> The baptismal font is a most extraordinary work, and will stand a monument of Mormon extravagance and grotesqueness of taste. It is an immense stone reservoir, resting upon the backs of twelve oxen, also out of stone, and as "large as life." The effect of a first view of these rigid animals, standing in such a singular position, and wearing such mysterious countenances, is somewhat startling, but a feeling of superstition soon gives way to curiosity, and the beholder is lost in wonder at the magnitude of the design, and extraordinary amount of labor that must have been expended in the erection of the work.[134]

The completed font reportedly cost $30,000.[135]

Design Changes and Improvements

    After the death of Joseph Smith, it was clearly Brigham Young who assumed the executive decision-making role on the temple's design and progress. The design continued to develop throughout the construction process, and changes were implemented as various needs arose. Young met frequently with William Weeks to discuss the progress of the temple and to review the upcoming developments.[136]

---

130. Brigham Young, "Beloved Brethren," *Times and Seasons* 6 (1 November 1845): 1018-19.

131. Hovey, "Autobiography," 34.

132. Andrew F. Ehat, ed., "'They Might Have Known He Was Not a Fallen Prophet': The Nauvoo Journal of Joseph Fielding," *BYU Studies* 19 (Winter 1979): 160.

133. "January," *Times and Seasons* 6 (20 January 1846): 1096.

134. William E. Matlack, "The Temple," *Hancock Eagle*, 24 April 1846, microfilm, LDS Church Archives.

135. Gallup, Diary, 29 July 1848.

136. For example, Heber C. Kimball wrote in his journal on 26 May 1845: "Bishop Miller come down after B[righam] Young and myself with his carriage and took to his house where we met in council of the Twelve and Bishops, Temple committee, and Br[other] Weeks the Architect. Counseled on matters of the Temple." Kimball, *On the Potter's Wheel*, 116. See also *History of the Church*, 7:314, 321, 382.

On 15 March 1845, the Twelve, the trustees, and the temple committee discussed several improvements to the temple and grounds including the drain for the baptismal font, already described.[137] A second decision the same day was to erect "a wall on the south side of the Temple block."[138] The *Times and Seasons* reported, "A trench is being excavated about six feet wide and six feet deep, around a square of about six or eight acres, which will be filled with stone, and upon which will be placed an iron fence for the security of the Temple."[139] A month later on 14 April, "the public hands commenced the foundation of the wall."[140] Initial plans called for "pickets or [a] railing" atop a stone base;[141] but by 27 June 1845, Brigham Young described a different plan in his lengthy letter to Wilford Woodruff. The wall would be "eight feet high and about five feet thick at the base; the wall on the north side is nearly built."[142] Evidently this wall—never completed— was to encompass both the temple block and the block west of the temple where outdoor meetings were frequently held.[143]

On 16 May, Heber C. Kimball wrote in his journal, "We have one thing lacking in the House of the Lord, that is a stone in the west end for the superscription: Holiness to the Lord."[144] This idea was apparently discussed among the Twelve and the committee, for that same day, Brigham Young wrote "a letter to the Temple architect, directing him to place a stone in the west end of the Temple with the inscription 'Holiness to the Lord' thereon."[145] Obviously these instructions underwent further refinement, for the full inscription ultimately read:

THE HOUSE OF THE LORD
built by
THE CHURCH OF JESUS CHRIST
OF LATTER-DAY SAINTS
Commenced April 6th, 1841
Holiness to the Lord[146]

The exact date of the stone's completion and the name of the stonecutter(s) who worked on it are not known, but Lyman Littlefield, the Nauvoo corre-

---

137. *History of the Church*, 7:382.

138. Ibid., 7:382.

139. "The Saints Make Nauvoo," *Times and Seasons* 6 (1 April 1845): 856.

140. Ibid., 7:399.

141. Ibid., 7:407.

142. "Extracts from President Young's Letter," *Millennial Star* 6 (1 September 1845): 91.

143. *History of the Church*, 7:407. See "Plans for a Tabernacle" below.

144. Kimball, *On the Potter's Wheel*, 112.

145. *History of the Church*, 7:411.

146. Buckingham, Letter to *Boston Courier*, 18 July 1847; Lanman, *A Summer in the Wilderness*, 31.

spondent for the *New York Messenger*, commented on the progress that had been made on the inscription as of 23 August: "On the front of the attic story these words appear in gilt projecting letters: "THE HOUSE OF THE LORD, BUILT BY"— this is as far as the inscription is finished. Oh, the beauty and majestic elegance of that house!"[147]

J. H. Buckingham, the correspondent for the *Palmyra Courier-Journal*, described the temple in September 1847 as having two identical inscriptions, the second one being "on the front of the interior vestibule, over the doors of the entrance."[148] Thomas L. Kane, who visited Nauvoo in 1846, uses the felicitous term "a baptismal mark on the forehead"[149] to describe the plaque.

Adding the inscription stone was not the only design change. At a meeting on 6 June, Young and the Twelve instructed Weeks to substitute rectangular windows in the pediment instead of the semicircular windows called for in the plans.[150]

During the summer, workers spent time "clearing the ground round the Temple."[151] The Twelve also decided on 27 August "to pave the Temple floor with pressed brick instead of either stone or tile, to save expense and because [the Twelve] think it will be as good with brick."[152]

Also evolving as construction progressed were plans for the usage of the various rooms in the temple. On 15 January 1845, the Twelve announced: "In the recesses, on each side of the arch, on the first story, there will be a suite of rooms or ante-chambers, lighted with the first row of circular windows. As soon as a suitable number of those rooms are completed we shall commence the endowment."[153] However, before these rooms were used for that purpose, the Twelve decided to use the attic for the endowment, a change made, no doubt, to conform to Joseph's practice of using the "upper rooms" of the buildings in which he gave the endowment. Lyman O. Littlefield's letter in late August stated that the attic would be "done off into a number of rooms for the use of the higher order of priesthood."[154] Isaac C. Haight's journal entry for 11 September 1845 corroborates: "A

147. Littlefield, "Nauvoo Correspondence," dated 4 October 1845, *New York Messenger* 2 (25 October 1845): 133.

148. Buckingham, Letter to *Boston Courier*, 18 July 1847; see also Gallup, Diary, 29 July 1848.

149. Kane, "The Mormons," 80.

150. Journal History, 6 June 1845, 4.

151. *History of the Church*, 7:431.

152. George D. Smith, *An Intimate Chronicle*, 179. This decision may have been influenced by the recent exchange of bricks and wood by the temple and Nauvoo House Committees. George A. Smith's journal for 22 July 1845 reads: "The trustees of the Nauvoo House let the trustees of the Temple have 50,000 bricks and the trustees of the Temple let the trustees of the Nauvoo House have fifty cords of wood, in exchange." George A. Smith, "My Journal," 84.

153. "An Epistle of the Twelve," 779.

154. Littlefield, "From Nauvoo—To the Editor of the *Messenger*," 67-68.

room is being finished in the roof to begin to give those their endowments that are to go on their missions this fall."[155]

One reporter learned in November 1844 that the main assembly room was "to be one vast apartment, about 108 feet by 80, simply subdivided by three great veils, or rich crimson drapery, suspended from the ceiling overhead."[156] Thus, the Nauvoo Temple would have closely resembled the partitioning in the Kirtland Temple. However, the finished hall never had these partitioning draperies. It is unknown whether the plan was intentionally changed or if the hasty departure of the Saints in early 1846 prevented it from being carried out.

Plans for a Tabernacle

Although the temple was originally envisioned as a full-scale house of worship, capable of accommodating large congregational gatherings, Nauvoo's population had already outstripped the building's design. Speaking to a congregation of Utah Saints in 1855, George A. Smith said Joseph Smith had prophesied: "We may build as many houses as we would, and we should never get one big enough to hold the Saints."[157]

On 6 June, most of the Twelve met with the trustees and the architect at George Miller's house and decided to build a "tabernacle" to accommodate larger gatherings.[158] William Huntington wrote in his diary on 16 June 1845: "Calculation now is to build a tabernacle on the west end of the temple, twice as large as the temple, for the purpose of holding meetings, as the temple will no more than convene the priesthood."[159] Two days later on 18 June, the Twelve issued a letter to the Church which made public the plans for the tabernacle and attributed its inspiration to Joseph Smith: "Pursuant to the counsel of Joseph Smith given previous to his martyrdom, we now intend to erect a Tabernacle for the congregation made of canvas. It will take about four thousand yards, which, with other fixtures, will cost between one and two thousand dollars."[160] The letter also authorized Orson Hyde as agent on the tabernacle:

> We have appointed Elder Orson Hyde one of our own quorum, a faithful, trusty and competent man of God, to go forth and raise all the necessary funds for the above purpose, to procure the materials and return with them to this place as

155. Isaac Haight, Journal (1813-1862), 18, typescript, Perry Special Collections, Lee Library.
156. Unnamed visitor, *New York Spectator*, 9 November 1844, quoted in McGavin, *The Nauvoo Temple*, 51.
157. George A. Smith, 8 April 1855, *Journal of Discourses* 2:360.
158. Kimball, *On the Potter's Wheel*, 120; Jessee, "The John Taylor Nauvoo Journal," 51.
159. Huntington, "Journal," 30-31.
160. *History of the Church*, 7:427.

soon as possible. Elder Hyde is authorized to raise the necessary funds by loan, by contribution or tithing or donation if by loan, the church here will refund the same in lands at a low rate, or in cash as soon as we can command it; and any contract that he may make in relation to the above, the church will be responsible for.

It is hoped that no brother or sister who has funds that he or she can spare for a season will withhold them from Brother Hyde, for it is the aid that he seeks for us. Also we hope that the saints will be liberal in their donations, and every other person that wishes well to the Temple of God and to the Tabernacle of the congregation in Zion. May God bless all that feel interested in the matter.[161]

Hyde departed from Nauvoo in mid-July. On 16 August, he published a notice in the *New York Messenger*, appealing for members' support for the tabernacle:

I hope the elders residing in the different branches where I have made appointments, will take the earliest opportunity of laying this before the people that they may be in readiness to make me a witness of their liberality for the cause sake. Should any brother or sister, or branch of the church feel disposed to show their liberality on this occasion, and not have the opportunity of seeing me personally, they can address me through the post at the *Messenger* office, no. 7 Spruce-street, New-York, enclosing whatever they may be disposed to give on their tithing or otherwise, and it shall be faithfully entered to their credit on "the book of the law of the Lord."

Should a greater sum be raised then will be needful to purchase the canvas for the tabernacle, it will be applied toward completing the Temple.[162]

The Twelve also commissioned Howard Egan late in June to travel "to St. Louis to buy about 125 dollars worth of hemp to make cords for [the tabernacle]."[163]

On 30 August 1845, the *New York Messenger* published the most complete known description of the proposed tabernacle, written by Orson Pratt:

It is intended to erect a tabernacle of canvas in front of, and joining the Temple on the west. The form of this tabernacle will be that of an ellipse, its longer axis running north and south, parallel to the front of the Temple. Its height will be 75 feet in the centre; its sides sloping at an angle of 45 degrees. The area of its base will be sufficient to contain eight or ten thousand persons; its seats will gradually rise one above another in the form of an amphitheatre. This will be intended for preaching to the vast congregation; while the temple will be used for the meeting of councils and quorums, and the administrations of ordinances and blessings, and preaching to smaller congregations, etc.[164]

---

161. Ibid.

162. Orson Hyde, "The Tabernacle," *New York Messenger* 2 (16 August 1845): 52.

163. *History of the Church* 7:427.

164. Orson Pratt, "News to England," *New York Messenger* 2 (30 August 1845): 67.

Such publicity no doubt increased interest in and willingness to support the project. In about six weeks of strenuous travel and preaching, Hyde collected over $1,000 toward the purchase of the canvas. On 24 August, he wrote to Newel K. Whitney from Boston of the challenges of his mission: "I shall succeed in getting the canvas if God will. My constant exertion in this very hot weather has injured my health, and I think I shall ship the canvas in about 2 weeks or 3 to Whitney and Miller, and get it insured, and then stay long enough to catch the cool sea breezes and recruit a little."[165]

On 17 September, Elder Hyde shipped "between four and five thousand yards of canvas for the Tabernacle" from New York to Nauvoo.[166] The next day, he also started for Nauvoo. After making several stops along the way, he rejoined the Saints on 17 October.[167] Two days later, he addressed the Sabbath congregation, giving "an account of his success in procuring canvas for the tabernacle. He had got it not by loans from the rich who held onto their money, but by begging and some voluntary donations he had in his mission of some three months to the east."[168] The following day, he "made returns of money collected for the Tabernacle, $1415.38½."[169]

Because the Saints were forced out of Nauvoo four months later, they never started work on the tabernacle. However, they used the canvas to partition the attic of the temple for the endowment and to sew wagon covers for the trek west.[170] William Smith, who had been dropped from the Quorum of the Twelve and excommunicated in October 1845, published accusations that the "plans of getting the tabernacle canvas was all concocted in secret, and with the ultimate intention of appropriating the same for the construction of tents to be used in traveling."[171]

The concept of a large covered meeting place was realized in Salt Lake City with the construction of a bowery on the temple lot. One scholar has suggested

---

165. Orson Hyde, Letter to Newel K. Whitney, Boston, 24 August 1845, holograph, Perry Special Collections, Lee Library; printed by permission.

166. *History of the Church*, 7:482.

167. Ibid.

168. Norton Jacob, Journal, 1804-52, 18, Perry Special Collections, Lee Library.

169. *History of the Church*, 7:483.

170. Lisle G. Brown, "The Sacred Departments for Temple Work in Nauvoo: The Assembly Room and the Council Chamber," *BYU Studies* 19 (Spring 1979): 370; Watson, "The Nauvoo Tabernacle," 241. See also History of the Reorganized Church, 2:565.

171. William Smith, *A Proclamation: And Faithful Warning to All the Saints Scattered Around in Boston, Philadelphia, New York, Salem, New Bedford, Lowell, Peterborough, Gilson, Saint Louis, Nauvoo and Elsewhere in the United States; Also, to Those Residing in the Different Parts of Europe and in the Islands of the Seas* (1845; Bountiful, UT: Restoration Research, 1983), 12.

that the proposed Nauvoo tabernacle served as inspiration for the unique design and shape of the Salt Lake Tabernacle.[172]

Dreams about the Temple

Speaking to the elders' quorum in Nauvoo on 10 April 1843, Brigham Young declared, "A faithful man will have dreams about the work he is engaged in. If he is engaged in building the Temple, he will dream about it."[173] It would be normal for the temple to figure in the dreams of the Saints, especially those who were working on it or those whose hopes for the promised endowment were intense. Some of these dreams conveyed particular significance to their recipients and made their way into journals and family stories.

John Taylor recorded such a dream on Wednesday, 18 June 1845, about three weeks after laying the capstone:

I dreamt that I stood by the Temple and looked up, and saw that it was finished. I admired the elegance and symmetry of the building, and felt animated in my spirits and rejoiced to see the building finished. I remarked to a person standing by, what a beautiful structure this is, how elegant the design, and how well it is executed. I then said it is only a very short time since we laid the topstone; and now it is finished. I knew that a great deal of the wood work was prepared, but did not anticipate that the building would be so soon completed. I felt at the same time filled with the spirit of God, and my heart rejoiced before the Lord.

While I stood gazing with pleasure at the Temple, I saw another tower rising like unto the one that is on the west end of the Temple, and immediately exclaimed to the person that I had before conversed with, why there is another tower, and said I pointing my finger, still further there is another, and yet another; we have not yet began to see the whole; the scenery gradually changed, and a temple very much larger in dimensions, than the one which we are building, stood before me; there were a number of towers, placed apparently at equal distances on the outside, each of which were supported by buildings as large as this temple, and yet were united with, and were a part of the great temple; they were of as large dimensions as that which is on this Temple, from the midst of these towers and in the center of the building arose in majestic grandeur an immense large dome, that seemed to tower as high above the towers, as the towers were from the earth; it was not quite finished at the top, and there were some workmen employed near the top of the dome, who in consequence of the extreme height of the building appeared very small. I was much delighted with the scenery

172. Elden J. Watson, "The Nauvoo Tabernacle," *BYU Studies* 19, no. 3 (Spring 1979):421.
173. *History of the Church*, 5:350.

that presented itself to my view, and soon after awoke retaining for some time afterwards the same pleasing sensation that I had enjoyed during my dream.[174]

On 2 January 1846, Heber C. Kimball "asked God to enlighten his mind with regard to the work of endowment." He then had the following dream:

> He beheld a large field of corn that was fully ripe, he and a number of others were commanded to take baskets and pick off the corn with all possible speed, for there would soon be a storm that would hinder the gathering of the harvest. The hands engaged in gathering the harvest, were heedless and unconcerned and did not haste, as they were commanded; but he and the man he assisted had a much larger basket than the rest, and picked with all their might of the largest ears of the field, they once in a while would pick an ear that had a long tail on each end and but a few grains scattering over the center of the cob, which were very light.
>
> The interpretation of the dream is, that the field represented the church, the good corn represented good saints, the light corn represented the light and indifferent saints, the laborers are those appointed to officiate in the Temple, the storm is trouble that is near upon us, and requires an immediate united exertion of all engaged in giving the endowments to the saints, or else we will not get through before we will be obliged to flee for our lives.[175]

On 17 March 1846, Thomas Bullock "dreamed that some people were building a tower which they wanted to excel in height the Temple. I prophesied that when any want to have a building to excel in height or beauty the Temple of the Lord, it should surely fall and come to naught."[176] One night in the spring of 1846, Matthias Cowley dreamed that he was standing on the steeple of the temple when he "was caught away" and offered a glimpse of the "grandeur, brightness, and light" of the kingdom of heaven.[177]

---

174. Jessee, "The John Taylor Nauvoo Journal," 52-53.

175. *History of the Church,* 7:561.

176. Gregory R. Knight, ed., "Journal of Thomas Bullock: 31 August 1845 to 5 July 1846," *BYU Studies* 31 (Winter 1991): 62.

177. Matthias Cowley, Autobiography, 1853, typescript, 5, LDS Church Archives.

Chapter 10

CONFERENCE IN THE TEMPLE:
OCTOBER 1845 TO NOVEMBER 1845

First Meeting in the Temple

After the delays occasioned by security alarms in late September, "work on the temple redoubled in zeal."[1] On 24 September, Brigham Young and the Twelve decided that the Church would evacuate the city.[2] On 1 October, they negotiated a truce with anti-Mormons who agreed to stop the mob actions that had erupted in September if the Church would abandon Nauvoo within six months.[3] However, as Thomas C. Sharp noted correctly in the *Warsaw Signal* a few weeks later, "So far

---

1. "Reminiscence of Bathsheba Wilson Bigler Smith," in *In Their Own Words: Women and the Story of Nauvoo*, edited by Carol Cornwall Madsen (Salt Lake City: Deseret Book, 1994), 211.

2. Heber C. Kimball indicated that the Twelve "wrote a proposition to the mob." Stanley B. Kimball, ed., *On the Potter's Wheel: The Diaries of Heber C. Kimball* (Salt Lake City: Signature Books, 1987), 136. William Clayton, who was present when this proposal was authored, reflected: "It is very evident that the time is come for this people to separate themselves from all gentile governments and go to a place where they can erect the standard and live according to the law of God." George D. Smith, ed., *An Intimate Chronicle: The Journals of William Clayton* (Salt Lake City: Signature Books, 1995), 183.

3. Joseph Smith Jr. et al., *History of the Church of Jesus Christ of Latter-day Saints*, edited by B. H. Roberts (Salt Lake City: Deseret News Press, 6 vols. published 1902-12, Vol. 7 published 1932, 1st printing), 7:449. The settlement was reached with General John J. Hardin.

as the temple is concerned it appears to be part of their policy not to go and leave it unfinished."[4] Work on the temple was temporarily suspended for October general conference (5-7 October). According to Heber C. Kimball's diary on October 2, workmen "were laying the lower floor for the conference."[5]

On Sunday, 5 October, the day preceding general conference, a dedication meeting was held in the temple, attended by thousands of Saints. Their feelings on that great occasion are expressed in this passage from *History of the Church*:

> Through the indefatigable exertions, unceasing industry, and heaven-blessed labors, in the midst of trials, tribulations, poverty, and worldly obstacles, solemnized in some instances, by death, about five thousand saints had the inexpressible joy and great gratification to meet for the first time in the House of the Lord in the City of Joseph. From mites and tithing, millions had risen up to the glory of God, as a Temple, where the children of the last kingdom could come together and praise the Lord.
>
> It certainly afforded a holy satisfaction to think that since the sixth of April, 1841, when the first stone was laid, amidst the most straitened circumstances, the Church of Jesus Christ of Latter-day Saints had witnessed their bread cast upon waters, or more properly, their obedience to the commandments of the Lord, appear in the tangible form of a Temple, entirely enclosed, windows in; with temporary floors, pulpits and seats to accommodate so many persons preparatory to a General Conference.[6]

Lyman O. Littlefield, an eyewitness, described the dedication:

> At an early hour on the morning of the 5th, the Temple was opened for the ingress of the people, and soon the thronging multitude were passing through the massive doors, and finding seats wherever fancy led them through the spacious apartments; observing order however, and leaving the seats vacant, running through the centre of the two [a]isles, for the separate use of the ladies.... I found a seat in the north gallery and had a commanding view of the congregation which spread itself out below and around me, like the assembled delegations of a world. A more interesting spectacle never spread itself before the glance of mortal eye. A vast body of ladies clad in all the varying hues of dress, with eyes beaming with intelligence, and cheeks redolent with the rose of health and beauty, changing into diversified and graceful postures, like the swaying to and fro of a domain of flowers caressed by the fanning wind—spread itself far along the centre to the distant wall. On either side ranged a solid phalanx of seated males, and

---

4. Thomas C. Sharp, "Will They Go?" *Warsaw Signal*, 22 October 1845, 3.
5. Stanley B. Kimball, *On the Potter's Wheel*, 138.
6. *History of the Church*, 7:456.

all were oer-topt with down-gazing auditors that crowned the galleries.... [I]n the east end a stand was erected, containing three or four rows of seats for the seating of the Twelve, High Council, President of the stake, with his council, etc. etc, and for the elevation of the speakers. After the meeting was called to order, the lofty strains of modulated music rolled along upon the ear, filling the soul with a thrill of happiness inexpressible, and awaking in each heart a theme of praise and thanksgiving for the goodness and mercy of our heavenly bene-factor.... For five or six years have the saints toiled and labored through scenes of tribulation, poverty and death, casting in their mites for the erection of this noble edifice, and now to be permitted to assemble in it and hear the gospel of salvation from the apostles of the Lamb, was a source for rejoicing too great to be expressed.[7]

Littlefield's mention of galleries may have reference to the yet-unfinished mezzanine story that ran along and above the north and south sides of the assem-bly hall. The carpenters had installed the supports and perhaps some temporary flooring for the mezzanine during the summer, but the ceiling of the hall below was not yet lathed and plastered, which would have permitted some of the attendees to sit or stand on the floor of the mezzanine and have a view of the proceedings from above.

Helen Mar Whitney, who sang in the choir, recalled that "the choir and orchestra occupied a gallery at the west end opposite the stand."[8] Brigham Young opened the services with a dedicatory prayer. The prayer "presented the Temple, thus far completed, as a monument of the saints' liberality, fidelity, and faith" and con-cluded, "Lord, we dedicate this house and ourselves, to thee."[9] John Taylor spoke at considerable length on the "prospects before us that peace being now restored we had nothing to do but finish and dedicate the temple and prepare to move in a body next spring."[10] He also gave instructions for the members to provide "teams to work on the temple during the winter."[11] The official history summarizes: "The day was occupied most agreeably in hearing instructions and teachings, and offering up the gratitude of honest hearts, for so great a privilege, as worshipping God within, instead

7. Lyman O. Littlefield, "Highly Important and Interesting from Nauvoo," 19 October 1845, *New York Messenger* 2 (8 November 1845): 150.

8. Helen Mar Kimball Smith Whitney, "Scenes in Nauvoo, and Incidents from H. C. Kimball's Journal," Woman's Exponent 11 (May 1883): 185.

9. History of the Church, 7:456.

10. Norton Jacob, Journal, 1804-52, typescript, 15, L. Tom Perry Special Collections, Harold B. Lee Library, Brigham Young University, Provo, Utah. This journal begins with an autobiographical rem-iniscence, then begins daily entries.

11. Alexander Neibaur, Diary, 184161, holograph, 18, LDS Church Archives.

of without an edifice, whose beauty and workmanship will compare with any house of worship in America, and whose motto is: HOLINESS TO THE LORD.'"[12]

First General Conference in Temple

The following morning, 6 October 1845, general conference convened. The conference had been advertised in the *Times and Seasons*: "Notice is hereby given to the members of the Church of Jesus Christ of Latter day Saints, throughout the whole world, that there will be a General Conference of said church in the TEMPLE OF THE LORD, in the City of Joseph, commencing on the sixth day of October next, at ten o'clock in the forenoon."[13]

It would be a historic conference for three reasons. It was the first conference since Joseph Smith had declared three years earlier that the church would hold no general conference until such a meeting could convene in the temple. Second, this conference was also the only general conference held in the enclosed building while the leadership and majority of the Saints were still in Nauvoo.[14] Third and most importantly, it was at this conference that the Church made a united resolve to evacuate Nauvoo and discussed plans for the journey west. While the Church authorities were privy to the plan to depart, not all members were aware of the intended evacuation of the city. British convert George Whitaker, who was in attendance, later wrote, "At the October Conference a great many people gathered together. We did not know until then what the authorities of the Church had done. We knew that some important business would be transacted."[15]

Over four thousand Saints were present within the temple walls and thousands more gathered on the temple grounds.[16] The conference "assembled in the first main story in the temple,"[17] and the first order of business was to present the officers of the Church for a sustaining vote. An objection was raised to sustaining

---

12. *History of the Church*, 7:457.

13. "General Conference," *Times and Seasons* 6 (1 August 1845): 983.

14. A conference was held in April 1846, but most of the Twelve and many of the Saints had already left. The small congregation consisted mostly of the poor who had remained in Nauvoo and the workmen who were completing the temple.

15. George Whitaker, quoted in "Life of George Whitaker—A Utah Pioneer 1820-1907," typescript, 8, Special Collections, Marriott Library, University of Utah, Salt Lake City, edited with comments by an unidentified grandchild. Whitaker (1820-1907) was baptized in 1841 in England and immigrated to Nauvoo in 1845, arriving just prior to the conference.

16. Hosea Stout, Diary, 6 October 1845, typescript, 2:70, Perry Special Collections, Lee Library.

17. Erastus Snow, "A Journal or Sketch of the Life of Erastus Snow," 1875, typescript, 94, Perry Special Collections, Lee Library.

William Smith as Church Patriarch and apostle because he had conspired "to uproot and undermine the legal presidency of the Twelve."

He also criticized the temple project, exhorting Church members to "stop tithing" and to build "plain and comfortable meeting houses for the worship of the Lord."[18] Brigham Young made a colorful speech opposing William:

> [He] stepped forward to present his case before the people; he said that William Smith had made a great many threats about what he would do, but if he undertook to treat them as he had his brother Joseph, he would find out that he had got the wrong man to deal with for once. He further said that he carried a little toothpick around with him for his own protection, at the same time drawing a long, thin dagger out of a walking cane and presenting it before the congregation, and said it would not be healthy for any man to lay violent hands on him— if they did he would run that through them, so help him God, if he had power.[19]

Apostle Parley P. Pratt then addressed the natural concern and frustration felt by the Saints in leaving the temple they had sacrificed so much to erect:

> He referred to the great amount of expense and labor we have been at to purchase lands, build houses, the Temple etc.; we might ask, why as it that we have been at all this outlay and expense, and then are called to leave it? He would answer that the people of God always were required to make sacrifices, and if we have a sacrifice to make, he is in favor of its being something worthy of the people of God. We do not want to leave a desolate place, to be a reproach to us but something that will be a monument of our industry and virtue. Our houses, our farms, this Temple and all we leave will be a monument to those who may visit the place of our industry, diligence and virtue. There is no sacrifice required at the hands of the people of God but shall be rewarded to them an hundred fold, in time or eternity.[20]

18. "Conference Minutes," *Times and Seasons* 6 (1 November 1845): 1008. Alexander Neibaur, Diary, 18, indicated that "not a hand lifted in his favor." Before the end of the month, William Smith had printed 500 copies of his pamphlet *A Proclamation*, in which he claimed that Joseph III was the rightful heir to the presidency of the Church, that he (William) had been present with the Twelve when Joseph had initiated them "into the highest priesthood lodge," and that Joseph had conferred the priesthood keys "equally upon all the Twelve and not therefore bestowed on one." Consequently, William claimed "as much power and as many keys to bind and seal on earth, as can possibly belong to Brigham Young." William Smith, *A Proclamation: And Faithful Warning to All the Saints Scattered Around in Boston, Philadelphia, New York, Salem, New Bedford, Lowell, Peterborough, Gilson, Saint Louis, Nauvoo and Elsewhere in the United States; Also, to Those Residing in the Different Parts of Europe and in the Islands of the Seas* (1845; Bountiful, UT: Restoration Research, 1983), 15-16.

19. George Morris, "The History of George Morris," 1891, typescript, 31, Perry Special Collections, Lee Library.

20. "Conference Minutes," *Times and Seasons* 6 (1 November 1845): 1010. William Clayton took the minutes, for he recorded in his journal: "Went to the General conference in the Temple and kept minutes all day." George D. Smith, *An Intimate Chronicle*, 184.

The conference reconvened on Tuesday, 7 October at 10:00 a.m. "Patriarch John Smith appointed four bishops to stand at the door, to take a collection for the benefit of the poor."[21] Heber C. Kimball and Amasa Lyman addressed the attendees, and the choir sang.

As the crowd began to fill the assembly room on the first floor of the temple for the 2:00 p.m. session, an alarm—probably the temple bell—sounded.[22] Brigham Young announced that armed troops had entered the city, instructed "the brethren to go home," and ordered them to "let every man be prepared."[23] As a result of mob attacks in the outlying Mormon settlements, the Saints were still psychologically prepared for an attack on Nauvoo and their temple. Hosea Stout, who was present at the conference as chief of police, recorded that General Charles C. Rich of the Nauvoo Legion "gave orders for every man at the temple to go and get his arms and be prepared for the worst."[24] He further recorded that this order "created a great stir and conference was dispensed with till tomorrow. When I came to the square the people had assembled in considerable numbers but in a short time we had word to disperse and be ready at a moment's warning as the troops had passed out of town."[25]

This body of armed men were some of General John J. Hardin's troops under the command of Major W. B. Warren and were in Nauvoo to apprehend two men who had been accused of theft.[26] In his report of the incident, Warren wrote:

> By this time there were assembled at the Temple, under arms, not less than 1000
> or 1500 men.... I rode into the crowd assembled at the temple and ordered them

21. *History of the Church,* 7:469.

22. Gregory R. Knight, ed., "Journal of Thomas Bullock, 31 August 1845 to 5 July 1846," *BYU Studies* 31 (Winter 1991): 24.

23. Heber C. Kimball, as quoted in Whitney, "Scenes in Nauvoo, and Incidents from H. C. Kimball's Journal," 185. According to Jacob, Journal, 16, "In the afternoon the congregation was suddenly dismissed by Father John Smith before it was fully convened, telling them to go home immediately and prepare for the worst."

24. Hosea Stout, Diary, 2:70.

25. Ibid., 71.

26. Hardin was the commander of the Illinois State Militia (volunteers). Warren was a brigade-major under Hardin's command. They arrested Daniel Smith (1805-68), who had joined the Church in Nauvoo in 1841, and Benjamin Gardner (1800-75) who was baptized in Nauvoo in 1840. They had allegedly stolen property from citizens of Hancock County, thus supposedly helping to precipitate the burning of several Mormons' houses and barns in outlying areas in late September 1845. See Neibaur, Diary, 18; Jacob, Journal, 16. According to Hosea Stout, Diary, 2:71, however, Rich heard that Warren had writs of treason against the Twelve. *The History of the Church,* 7:492, confirms that Major Warren had writs against the Twelve for treason but did not intend to serve them because it would hinder the Twelve from leaving as they had announced.

to disperse, or I should be compelled to make them do so. They professed a perfect willingness to do so, and said their assembling was owing to the fact that they did not know me. They treated me with much respect and proffered me any assistance, at that or any other time that I should be pleased to call on them.[27]

After Brigham Young was apprised of the circumstances, he informed the congregation about the troops' identity and reason for their presence. He "requested them [the Saints] to retire to their homes in peace, concluding his remarks with these words, 'Be ye also ready.'"[28]

The remainder of the day passed in relative quiet. The conference resolved to discontinue the *Nauvoo Neighbor* immediately and the *Times and Seasons* as soon as the current volume (six) was complete, the coming February. The Saints also began to organize travel parties for the upcoming exodus.

Two items of business involved the temple. First, Brigham Young expressed concern that some believed that "the Twelve are supported out of the funds belonging to this house."[29] This he flatly denied. Young encouraged the Twelve, the temple committee, and all others who may have had incurred debts with the Church, to settle with the trustees in trust who would, in turn, report to the Presidency. A motion to this effect was seconded and carried with "not a dissenting voice in the congregation, and a perfect union exhibited by the Saints."[30]

Second, despite the agreement of the conference to depart from Nauvoo in the spring of 1846, the Saints' resolve to finish the temple was unswerving.[31] In an epistle to the Church on 8 October, Brigham Young wrote:

---

27. "Late from the Mormon War," *Burlington Hawkeye*, 23 October 1845, microfilm, Lee Library.

28. *History of the Church*, 7:470.

29. Ibid., 475. Such accusations were being circulated by William Smith, among others. According to Smith, *Proclamation*, 12, "That the Church funds have been misapplied, I have no hesitation in asserting, for of necessity I have been made acquainted with the fact, that several houses have been filled with women who have been secretly married to Brigham Young, H. C. Kimball, Willard Richards—women with little children in their arms, who had no means of support except from tithing funds." Rumors that the Twelve were embezzling continued through the winter of 1845-46. "Latter-day Saintism," *Burlington Hawkeye*, 20 November 1845, 2. Similar accusations had been made against Joseph Smith. Thomas C. Sharp and others found the estimated costs for the temple construction too high and believed Joseph was embezzling temple donations for his own support. An Exile (pseud.), "The Nauvoo Block and Tackle," *Warsaw Signal*, 25 April 1844, 3; Thomas C. Sharp, "Items from Nauvoo," *Warsaw Signal*, 21 August 1844, 2.

30. Whitney, "Scenes in Nauvoo, and Incidents from H. C. Kimball's Journal," 185.

31. According to Jesse Wentworth Crosby, "History and Journal of Jesse W. Crosby," 1820-59, typescript, 29, Perry Special Collections, Lee Library, "President Young asserted that we owed the United States nothing, not a farthing, not one sermon. They have rejected our testimony, killed our prophets; our skirts are clear from their blood. We will go out from them; let them see these matters."

> The utmost diligence of all the brethren at this place and abroad will be requisite for our removal, and to complete the unfinished part of the Lord's House, preparatory to dedication by the next General Conference.[32] The font and other parts of the temple will be in readiness in a few days to commence the administration of holy ordinances of endowments, for which the faithful have long diligently labored and fervently prayed, desiring above all things to see the beauty of the Lord and inquire in his holy Temple. We therefore invite the Saints abroad generally so to arrange their affairs as to come with their families in sufficient time to receive their endowments, and aid in giving the last finish to the House of the Lord previous to the great emigration of the church in the spring.... Wake up, wake up, dear brethren, we exhort you, from the Mississippi to the Atlantic, and from Canada to Florida, to the present glorious emergency in which the God of heaven has placed you to prove your faith by your works, preparatory to a rich endowment in the Temple of the Lord, and the obtaining of promises and deliverances, and glories for yourselves and your children and your dead.[33]

After the conference, the floor was replaced. On 18 October, Norton Jacobs "replaced the lower girders [floor joists under main story floor], they having lain four years in the weather and being exposed were so decayed as not to be safe."[34] Work on the floor continued through mid-November. On Sunday, 9 November the public meeting which was normally held on the temple's main floor was moved, "the floor of the first story in the Temple having been taken up to put in new timbers, the sleepers [floor timbers or joists] which were put in at the commencement of the Temple having become rotten."[35] The meeting was held "on the upper floor" instead.[36]

Norton Jacob wrote on 3 November that William Weeks assigned him "to go ahead and put in the truss timbers for the lower floor of the temple."[37] Two days later on 5 November, the Twelve, including Heber C. Kimball who recorded the event, "met at the Temple with the Bishops, and the Architect, to see how to seat the pews and concerning how many aisles. The conclusion was to have two aisles," and therefore three sections of pews.[38]

Planning continued on 14 November when Brigham Young, accompanied by Willard Richards and Heber Kimball, "went to the Temple ... to see how the pulpits should be built."[39]

---

32. By this, Brigham Young meant that the entire structure would be dedicated on 6 April 1846, but this conference was never held, due to the Saints' hasty departure from the city in February.

33. *History of the Church*, 7:478-80.

34. Jacob, Journal, 18.

35. *History of the Church*, 7:519.

36. Knight, "Journal of Thomas Bullock," 31.

37. Jacob, Journal, 20.

38. Kimball, *On the Potter's Wheel*, 139.

39. Ibid., 142.

Continued Meetings in the Temple

As noted, one of the important functions served by the Nauvoo Temple was that of a place of assembly. During the fall of 1845 and the winter and spring of 1846, it housed dozens of private councils and large meetings. Various church groups and quorums that had previously assembled in the upper room of Joseph Smith's store, the Masonic Hall, Seventies' Hall, and even private residences were allowed to use dedicated portions of the temple.

For example, the several emigrating parties met in the basement to organize themselves for the exodus. On 14 October 1845, Hosea Stout, who had been appointed leader of the twenty-fourth party "met with the company in the cellar of the temple to organize and make some preparations for our contemplated journey next spring."[40]

On Sunday, 19 October, a conference of the Seventies was held on the first floor assembly hall.[41] Immediately thereafter, the Saints gathered for a general preaching service in the same room. Orson Hyde, who had arrived at Nauvoo the previous day from his mission in the eastern states, addressed the Saints on a number of topics, including "his success in procuring canvas for the tabernacle."[42] John Taylor and Brigham Young spoke at length on the apostasy of William Smith. After failing to be sustained as Church patriarch and apostle at October conference, he had published a pamphlet in which he spoke out against the leadership of the Twelve. A motion to excommunicate Smith was sustained unanimously.[43] This general service lasted until four o'clock. Then that evening, Thomas Bullock recorded a meeting of "No. 1 Company" meeting, which included the Twelve.[44] At this meeting, Brigham Young "proceeded with the organization by appointing captains of fifties and tens."[45]

Appearance of the Finished Halls

The first and second floors of the temple, known as "the great stories,"[46] were supposed to be similar to each other in design, although the second story was never completed. The main floor room was about 100 feet long and 80 feet wide

---

40. Hosea Stout, Diary, 2:78.

41. Jacob, Journal, 18.

42. Ibid.; see also *History of the Church,* 7:483.

43. *History of the Church,* 7:483.

44. Knight, "Journal of Thomas Bullock," 27.

45. *History of the Church,* 7:483.

46. W. W. Phelps, "The Answer," *Times and Seasons* 5 (1 January 1844): 759.

while the second story hall was twenty feet longer and extended over the area occupied by the vestibule on the first floor. When completed, these halls were designed to seat about 4,000 occupants each.[47]

The main hall, in its finished state, resembled in many respects the assembly room in the Kirtland Temple. J. H. Buckingham described the first floor hall in 1846:

> On the lower floor was a grand hall for the assemblage and worship of the people.... Seats are provided in this hall for the accommodation of thirty-five hundred people, and they are arranged with backs, which are fitted like the seats in a modern railroad car, so as to allow the spectator to sit and look in either direction, east or west.[48] At the east and west ends are raised platforms, composed of series of pulpits, on steps one above another. The fronts of these pulpits are semicircular, and are inscribed in gilded letters on the west side, PAP, PPQ, PTQ, PDQ, meaning as we are informed, the uppermost one President of the Aaronic Priesthood; the second, President of the Priests Quorum; the third, President of the Teachers Quorum; and the fourth and lowest, President of the Deacons Quorum. On the east side the pulpits are marked PHP, PSZ, PHQ, and PEQ, and the knowledge of the guide was no better than ours as to what these symbolic letters were intended for.[49]

The inscriptions on the east pulpits signified President of the High Priesthood (or Presiding High Priest), President of the Stake of Zion (meaning Nauvoo), and President of the Elders' Quorum.

The hall, when finished in 1846, exhibited an extraordinary degree of craftsmanship and originality. J. M. Davidson, who visited the temple in the summer of 1846, recalled his visit for the *Carthage Republican* in 1864: "To one who had never seen anything larger than a country meeting house, this Mormon audience room presented a vastness and grandeur that was inspiring."[50] The *Hancock Eagle*,

47. Joseph Grafton Hovey, "Autobiography of Joseph Grafton Hovey," 1812-56, typescript, 34, Perry Special Collections, Lee Library. Grandson M. R. Hovey copied and arranged this document from Hovey's journal in 1933. It begins with an autobiography, then moves to daily entries in 1842. See also William Huntington Sr., "Journal of William Huntington," 1784-1846, 5 October 1845, typescript, 38. Both documents are in Perry Special Collections, Lee Library.

48. "The seats in the body of the chamber had movable backs that could be swung so that the hearers could face either stand, as the character of the service or standing of the preacher demanded." Unknown author, untitled article containing quotations from J. M. Davidson, "Nauvoo: The Past and Present of That City: Visits of 1846 and 1864 Contrasted," *Carthage Republican*, 25 February 1864, 1, and quoted in E. Cecil McGavin, *The Nauvoo Temple* (Salt Lake City: Deseret Book, 1962), 93-95. McGavin mistakenly cites Davidson as the author of the article, rather than as "quoted by unknown author."

49. J. H. Buckingham, Letter to *Boston Courier*, 18 July 1847, reprinted in Harry E. Pratt, ed., "Illinois as Lincoln Knew It," *Papers in Illinois History and Transactions for the Year 1937* (Springfield, IL: N.pub., 1938), 172.

50. Unknown author, untitled article, quoting Davidson.

a non-Mormon paper published in Nauvoo, noted in its April 1846 issue: "The grand hall designed for the congregation, is worthy the attention of all architects who delight in originality and taste. It has been thronged with visitors from abroad since its completion, and excites the surprise and admiration of every beholder."[51] An unnamed visitor writing in the Illinois Journal in 1853 commented that the finishing work in the hall was "of the most exquisite workmanship."[52]

Six posts supported the forty-one-foot arch that ran north-south above the middle of the assembly room.[53] According to William Weeks's drawings, these

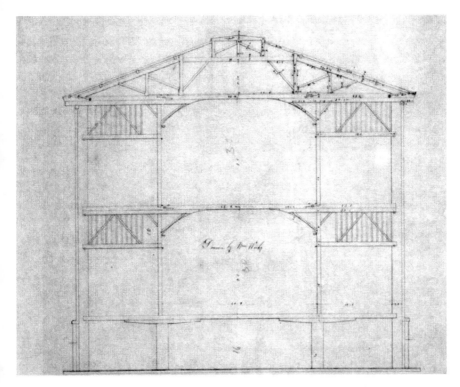

Transverse section drawing by William Weeks showing framing of the temple.

51. W. E. Matlack, "Public Buildings," *Hancock Eagle,* 24 April 1846, 2, microfilm, LDS Church Archives.

52. Unnamed visitor, *Illinois Journal,* 9 December 1853, reprinted as "Recollections of the Nauvoo Temple," in *Journal of the Illinois State Historical Society* 38 (Springfield: Illinois State Historical Society, December 1945): 482; photocopy in LDS Church Historical Department Library.

53. William Gallup, Diary, 29 July 1848, photographic reprint of pages 129-30 accompanied by introduction by William Powell, photocopy, Perry Special Collections, Lee Library.

posts were probably fluted columns, each topped with a capital similar in design to the sunstones on the temple's exterior.

Lyman Littlefield, who visited the temple in August 1845, described the east end as "abundantly lighted at the back by large windows nine feet seven inches wide and fifteen feet high." These windows, in addition to the eight tall windows with semicircular tops along the north and south walls, provided illumination. On the interior, the windows were designed to be surrounded by decorative wood casements which featured carved sunbursts similar to the tops of the columns supporting the room's ceiling.[54]

The unnamed 1853 visitor writing in the *Illinois Journal* commented on the acoustics: "The room was built very close and compact, and the ceiling very lofty, so that when we conversed in an ordinary tone of voice, the sound rebounded back and forth, until finally lost in echoes. When filled with people, a strong voice must have sounded remarkably clear and distinct."[55]

Alexander Hale Smith described another otherwise unknown room or set of rooms at the west end of the main floor auditorium. He recalled: "The offices in the corner to the left of [the] main entrance on the ground floor were finished but not furnished."[56] Thomas Bullock may have been referring to these rooms when he described a visit to the tower on 22 February 1846. He ascended the south staircase, and descended the partially finished north stairs, "then descended to the architect's room."[57] The room may have been used by William Weeks or his replacement Truman O. Angell.

Lyman Littlefield also described the second story as it appeared in August 1845:

> Now we ascend a ladder that carries us to the second story. Here is nothing particularly worthy of notice, except that the floor of the large room will be seventeen feet longer than the floor in the first story, in consequence of running out over the outer court. Here is formed a stone arch of forty-one foot span, which supports the tower. Looking down into the basement several children are seen at

54. Lyman O. Littlefield, "From Nauvoo—To the Editor of the *Messenger,*" 6 August 1845, *New York Messenger* 2 (30 August 1845): 67-68.

55. Unnamed visitor, *Illinois Journal,* 9 December 1853.

56. Alexander Hale Smith, quoted in Heman C. Smith, *History of the Reorganized Church,* 2:564. Although Alexander H. Smith does not indicate whether the offices were in the vestibule or the auditorium, it seems likely that their location was inside the hall, otherwise they would block the entrance to the north stairway.

57. Knight, "Journal of Thomas Bullock," 53.

play, who, from the extreme distance, look like mere specks or atoms crawling over the ground: I have watched them until my head swims, a queer feeling steals over me, convincing me that I never will do for a sailor; so I will cling tightly to the ladder and gain the third story.[58]

Alexander Hale Smith later stated that in "the upper auditorium (second story) the plastering was not done, the floor was only the rough boards, intended only for the lining, was laid."[59] Between the first and second stories there was the mezzanine level or half-story described above as overflow seating for conference. This level consisted of "two long rooms ... lighted with eight circular windows each,"[60] running east-west and contained "in the recesses over the arches"[61] that spanned the main assembly room below. Littlefield's guide told him that these long halls would be divided "off into fifteen rooms"[62]—actually fourteen, not including the main hall—of varying sizes. A similar half-story between the second floor and the attic was planned but never completed.

Based upon his examination of the William Weeks drawings, Church Architect Robert Dewey stated that a diagonal plank walkway leading from the spiral staircases at the west end of the temple would provide access to these half-stories.[63]

The Attic Story

The attic story was designed to accommodate the administration of the endowment. Lyman Littlefield, after his visit to the temple in August 1845, described this section of the temple:

This cannot properly be called more than a half story, the roof on each side not being sufficiently high near the eaves, for a person of six feet, to stand erect. But through the centre, from east to west, will be furnished a room the same size of that in the first story. At the east end of this room, is already construct-

58. Littlefield, "From Nauvoo—To the Editor of the *Messenger*," 68.

59. Quoted in Heman C. Smith, *History of the Reorganized Church of Jesus Christ of Latter Day Saints*, 7 vols. (Independence, MO: Herald House, 1903-14; second printing, 1967), 2:564.

60. Charles Lanman, *A Summer in the Wilderness* (Philadelphia, N.pub., 1847), 32.

61. Phelps, "The Answer," 759.

62. Littlefield, "From Nauvoo—To the Editor of the *Messenger*," 68.

63. Robert Dewey, Church architect, interviewed by Matthew McBride, 5 June 1999, notes in McBride's possession.

ed the frame of a window twenty and a half feet in the span, which forms four gothic windows, and three irregular triangles which partake of the elliptic and gothic. At each side of this room will also be constructed a row of smaller rooms.[64]

The unnamed 1853 visitor who published his observations in the *Illinois Journal* provides some insight into the appearance of the finished hall:

> We now entered the first room before us—the uppermost room in the whole building. It had never been finished; but the double row of composite[65] columns, of excellent workmanship, traversing its entire length, and the sky-lights of colored glass with which it was lighted, as well as the general appearance of the combined whole, shewed us that it was intended to surpass all the rest in the richness and taste of its decorations.[66]

The smaller rooms served as offices for various priesthood quorums and General Authorities, with one room reserved for the women's preparatory ordinances. Brigham Young explained the arrangement of the attic in his journal on 10 December:

> The main room of the attic story is eighty-eight feet two inches wide. It is arched over and the arch is divided into six spaces by cross beams to support the roof. There are six small rooms on each side about fourteen feet square. The last one on the east end on each side is a little smaller.
>
> The first room on the south side, beginning on the east, is occupied by myself, the second by Elder Heber C. Kimball, the third by Elders Orson Hyde, Parley P. Pratt and Orson Pratt, the fourth by John Taylor, George A. Smith, Amasa M. Lyman and John E. Page, the fifth by Joseph Young and presidents of Seventies, the sixth a preparation room.
>
> On the north side, the first east room is for Bishop Whitney and the Lesser Priesthood, the second is for the High Council, the third and fourth for President

---

64. Littlefield, "From Nauvoo—To the Editor of the *Messenger*," 68.

65. The composite order, also known as the Italic order, is the last of the five orders of columns (Doric, Ionian, Corinthian, and Tuscan being the first four). It is called composite because it borrows elements from each of the other orders: a quarter-round from the Tuscan and Doric, a row of leaves from the Corinthian, and volutes (spiral scrolls) from the Ionic.

66. Unnamed visitor, *Illinois Journal*, 9 December 1853.

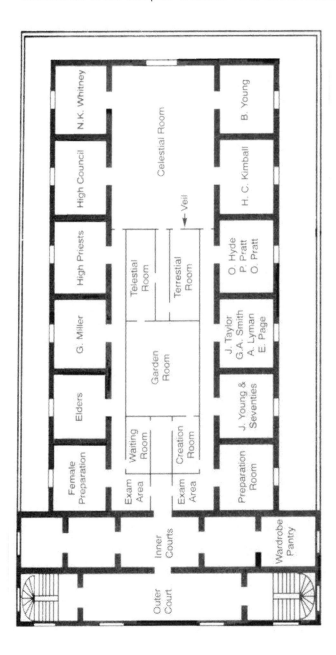

Attic floor plan showing the arrangement of the canvas-partitioned rooms used for endowments.

George Miller and the High Priest Quorum, the fifth the Elders room, and the sixth the female preparation room.[67]

The small round windows in the pediment lighted the twelve rooms. Charles Lanman, who visited Nauvoo in July 1846, observed that the offices had "circular windows and a massive lock on each door."[68] They also received light from square skylights in the ceiling.

Another visitor observed that the side rooms were "all finished in the plainest possible manner." The visitor then added, "As they were all besmeared with grease and oil, they might have been used in some baptismal ceremony, when the new convert was anointed with holy oil."[69] The residue on the walls was most likely from the burning of lamps and candles during the winter of 1845-46 when the rooms were used day and night.

On 19 November, Heber C. Kimball reported that the attic "rooms [were] most done."[70] The masonry finish on the walls and ceiling of the attic was completed on 22 November, and the painters set to work the same day.[71] Two days later they were finished, and workmen spent 24 November clearing the floor, removing construction materials, cleaning, and installing two stoves in the attic's largest room.[72] On 26 November, the painters applied the third and final coat.[73] Arrangements began for furnishing several of the small rooms.[74]

David Candland, a British convert, was assigned by Brigham Young to prepare Young's room in the southeast corner.[75] Abner Blackburn, age nineteen, was given "the job of sandpapering the floors of the endowment rooms and sacred

67. *History of the Church*, 7:542. Eleven days earlier, the History of the Church, 7:535, records the following arrangement, indicating that Brigham Young had made minor changes in room assignments in the intervening ten days: "The side rooms were occupied as follows: The first, in the southeast corner as a private office. The second by Heber C. Kimball, W. Richards and myself. The third and fourth by others of the Twelve; Fifth, by Joseph Young and Presidency of the Seventies; Sixth, for washing and anointing the elders. On the north side: first, bishops and lesser priesthood. Second, president of the stake and high council; third and fourth, high priests' quorum; fifth elders quorum; sixth, washing and anointing room occupied by the sisters."

68. Lanman, *A Summer in the Wilderness*, 33.

69. Unnamed visitor, *Illinois Journal*, 9 December 1853. The visitor confuses the location of these rooms stating that they were positioned to the sides of the second story hall. See the appendix.

70. Kimball, *On the Potter's Wheel*, 144-45.

71. Ibid., 149.

72. Ibid., 150-51.

73. Ibid.; see also *History of the Church*, 7:532.

74. *History of the Church*, 7:532.

75. David Candland, Journal, 1841-1902, 2, photocopy of typescript, Perry Special Collections, Lee Library. Candland (1841-1901) was baptized in 1841 and was called to be one of Brigham Young's clerks late in 1845.

apartments of the temple."[76] Another feature of the attic, installed a few weeks later, was a spiral staircase leading from the second story of the temple into Heber C. Kimball's office on the south side of the attic.[77]

Tithing Settlement

Joseph Smith and the Twelve had long stressed that paying tithing was a requirement for participating in the blessings that would soon be given in the temple. This emphasis continued during the final months of construction. Orson Pratt called upon the Saints in the eastern states to settle up their accounts: "If the Saints in the East desire a name and place in the temple, and wish to be legally entitled to the blessings to be administered therein, let them comply with all readiness and willingness with the whole law of tithing."[78]

At October general conference, Heber C. Kimball reminded the Saints: "We shall now expect a settlement from all those who have the wherewithal, or you need not expect an endowment in this house. President Joseph Smith said he would stand at the door with the books; you will not see him, but you will see his successors, who will carry out his designs."[79] Just as tithing payment had been required for baptism for the dead in the temple font, Elder Kimball made it clear that the blessings of the endowment were also contingent upon fulfilling this requirement.

On 6 November 1845, Thomas Bullock wrote in his journal: "I settled up my labor tithing to the 12 October 1845 and obtained a certificate entitling me to the use of the baptismal font. Thanks be to God that I am at last settled with my tithing and can go boldly forward for my blessings."[80]

As the temple drew closer to completion, there was general movement among the members of the Church to settle their tithing in anticipation of the endowment. George Whitaker recalled that during the fall of the 1845 he "turned all my labor in on tithing." He wrote:

> Those who had paid their tithing ... had the privilege of going through the temple. Everyone seemed to be trying to work and settle up their tithing that they might have the privilege of getting their endowments and blessings in the temple.... I paid my property tithing and my labor tithing and got my receipts for it,

---

76. Abner Blackburn, Autobiography, 1827-51, typescript, 5, LDS Church Archives. Blackburn (1827-1904) joined the Church in 1837 and later served as a member of the Mormon Battalion.

77. George D. Smith, *An Intimate Chronicle*, 222.

78. Orson Pratt, "Message," *Times and Seasons* 6 (15 August 1845): 998.

79. *History of the Church*, 7:475.

80. Knight, "Journal of Thomas Bullock," 30.

and had the privilege of going through the temple and getting my endowments a few days before they closed.[81]

Nor was tithing the only financial requirement. John D. Lee explained, "In many cases, also, where men require it, their just debts must be settled before they are allowed to be baptized, washed or anointed."[82]

Wilford Woodruff, still in Great Britian, expressed the anxiety of many of the Saints for the temple to be completed so that endowments be given. He reflected in his diary on 27 October: "I should judge from my feelings and [the] intimations of the spirit of God that the endowment had commenced and that the Lord had commenced pouring out some special blessings upon the Saints in Nauvoo but time will determine whether this is the case."[83] It was only a matter of weeks until the dedication of the attic story would allow the endowments to be administered to the Church membership at large.

---

81. Whitaker, "Life of George Whitaker," 8.

82. John D. Lee, *Mormonism Unveiled; or, The Life and Confessions of the Late Mormon Bishop, John D. Lee* (St. Louis: Bryan, Brand & Company, 1877), 169.

83. Wilford Woodruff, *Wilford Woodruff's Journal*, typescript, edited by Scott G. Kenney, 9 vols. (Midvale, UT: Signature Books, 1983-85), 2:609.

Chapter 11

ENDOWED WITH POWER:
DECEMBER 1845 TO FEBRUARY 1846

Final Preparations of the Attic Story

During November 1845, members of the Quorum of the Anointed or Holy Order worked feverishly to prepare the attic for the giving of endowments under Brigham Young's direction. Joseph Smith had charged him, as Brigham recalled in 1877, "to take this matter in hand and organize and systematize all these ceremonies." His experience in council with Joseph prepared him for the task "so that when we went through the Temple at Nauvoo I understood and knew how to place them there."[1] According to the *History of the Church*, he was "actively engaged in the Temple" from the last week of November through the second week of December "fitting up the apartments and preparing the rooms for administering endowments."[2]

---

1. Quoted in L. John Nuttal, Diary, 7 February 1877, typescript, L. Tom Perry Special Collections, Harold B. Lee Library, Brigham Young University, Provo, Utah.

2. Joseph Smith Jr. et al., *History of the Church of Jesus Christ of Latter-day Saints*, edited by B. H. Roberts (Salt Lake City: Deseret News Press, 6 vols. published 1902-12, Vol. 7 published 1932, 1st printing), 7:538.

To accommodate the endowment, the main hall of the attic was divided into several sections, or "departments," as they were called, by sheets of canvas hung from the ceiling. As mentioned, this canvas was probably some of that which Orson Hyde had obtained for the tabernacle.[3] William Clayton, writing in Heber C. Kimball's journal, described the arrangement of these "departments": "The big hall is converted into six separate rooms for the convenience of the Holy Priesthood [meaning the endowment]: two large ones and four small and a hall passing through between the small ones passing from the west down through the center, and doors into each room."[4] The portion of the room thus partitioned was probably enclosed entirely by canvas to create privacy in light of the frequent use of the side rooms.[5]

Recipients of the endowment would begin in the west end of the attic and move through the various departments until they were received into the large celestial room, which occupied the east end of the floor. In addition to hanging the canvas partitions, members of the Holy Order laid carpets, hung wall decorations, and otherwise furnished the various rooms. Kimball's journal records the following events related to the furnishing of the departments:

[29 November 1845:] At 10 in the morning I met the brethren at the Temple in the attic story to lay down the carpets in the sealing rooms, as it was set apart for that purpose.... We had carpet in plenty to lay down in all the rooms. The carpet [was] lent by different ones for the present.

[2 December 1845:] My William came with the wagon and then we went down to Hiram Kimball's and got about 25 or thirty flower pots with evergreens in them to adorn our garden [room].

[3 December 1845:] It is now 1 o'clock. We are now putting up the partitions in the big hall. Some part of partitions [is] finished.

[4 December 1845:] Engaged in putting up canvas and other things to prepare our room. W. W. Phelps brought in some cedar trees to adorn our garden [room]. About sunset Bishop Newel K. [Whitney] come in with the veil, the old one and new one. The holes were cut by B[righam] Young and others assisted.

[5 December 1845:] Commenced work putting up canvas adorning alters and so forth.... At half past 11 My wife, Sister Whitney, Helen my Daughter, Sarah Ann Kingsbury, come in for the purpose of hemming the veil. My son[s] W[illia]m and Heber P. come with them. W. W. Phelps come in with some cedar trees. . . .

3. Lisle G. Brown, "The Sacred Departments for Temple Work in Nauvoo: The Assembly Room and the Council Chamber," *BYU Studies* 19, no. 3 (Spring 1979): 372. See chap. 9.

4. William Clayton in George D. Smith, ed., *An Intimate Chronicle: The Journals of William Clayton* (Salt Lake City: Signature Books, 1995), 206. Clayton kept Heber C. Kimball's journal during December and January.

5. Brown, "The Sacred Departments," 372.

About 1, Samuel Ensign come in and put up some [moulding] to hang up looking glasses, portraits and maps, and a clock and other things.... It is sunset the canvas is all put up and the altars mostly done.

[6 December 1845:] Put up the looking glasses, and maps and portraits as
William W. Majors brought some up from his shop to adorn our room. The trees
[are] set in order in the garden. Sister Elizabeth Ann Whitney come in and sewed
on the fringe going over the top of the canvas running threw the room across
from north to south.... Sister Clarissa [Cutler] and Emily Cutler[6] made a cotton veil
going before the linen veil.... L[ucien] Woodworth put up the clock on west end
of the East room.... The coarse veil was put up this eve by B[righam] Young,
R[eynolds] Cahoon.

[8 December 1845:] Elder Phelps Brought in some grape vines, and hung clus-
ters of raisins to them as the choice fruit.[7] ... All things look well and heavenly. It
is now dusk. John D. Lee and others have been fitting up stoves in the two west
rooms, as they will be devoted to washing and anointing and to heat water.

[9 December 1845:] Elder Young is putting up a marble clock by the east window.[8]

Nathaniel Henry Felt, a twenty-nine-year-old tailor who had arrived at
Nauvoo during the summer, was among those who donated their belongings for
the adornment of these chambers: "Some of his furniture, such as carpets, tables,
chairs, sofa and mirrors, were used to furnish the sacred house preparatory to the
performance of ordinances therein."[9] Heber C. Kimball and Brigham Young donated two basins which they had made for their families which were used in part for
"baptizing the sick"[10] and presumably also in the washing rooms in the attic.

According to William Clayton, the walls of the celestial room or council
chamber, as it was known, were "adorned with a number of splendid mirrors, paintings and portraits."[11] Decoration also included several large maps of the United
States, Nauvoo, and the world. Clayton added, "In the centre and body of the
Celestial Room are two splendid tables and four splendid sofas. Also a small table

6. Sisters Clarissa Cutler Kimball (1824-74) and Emily Cutler Kimball both married Heber C.
Kimball in the Nauvoo Temple in 1845.

7. He is referring to the fruit of the tree of knowledge of good and evil.

8. Stanley B. Kimball, ed., *On the Potter's Wheel: The Diaries of Heber C. Kimball* (Salt Lake City:
Signature Books, 1987), 153-66.

9. "Nathaniel Henry Felt," in Andrew Jenson, *LDS Biographical Encyclopedia*, 4 vols. (Salt Lake
City: Greg Kofford Books, 2007), 2:380.

10. Kimball, *On the Potter's Wheel*, 165.

11. George D. Smith, ed., *An Intimate Chronicle: The Journals of William Clayton* (Salt Lake City:
Signature Books, 1992), 205. Mentioned are portraits of Brigham Young, Heber C. Kimball, Orson
Hyde, Willard Richards, John Taylor, George A. Smith, Lucius N. Scovil, John Smith, Bathsheba Wilson
Bigler Smith, Lucy Mack Smith, Caroline Grant Smith, William Collier, John L. Smith, Hyrum Smith,
Charles C. Rich, George Miller, Clarissa Lyman Smith, Sister Rich, Mary Catherine Miller, and Leonora
C. Taylor.

opposite the large window on the east end of the room on which stands the celestial and terrestrial globes. All the rooms are nicely carpeted and has a very splendid and comfortable appearance. There are a number of handsome chairs in it."[12]

Attic Story Dedicated

On the morning of 30 November, though final preparations continued into December as noted above, twenty-two men met to dedicate the attic of the Temple. John Taylor, who was among them, recorded: "I met with the brethren of the Quorum, not only of the Twelve but others who had received an endowment during the life-time of Joseph Smith, in the upper room of the Temple for the purpose of dedicating it preparatory to receiving or giving the endowments.[13] Several of them arrived at 10 o'clock with the others expected at noon. William Clayton spent the morning composing "some verses to the tune 'Here's a health to all good lasses' before the brethren assembled." At noon they sang, "Come all ye sons of Zion" and Brigham Young assigned Clayton to take minutes. Young then "offered up the dedication of the hall and small rooms."[14] He "dedicated the Attic story, the male room and ourselves to God, and prayed that God would sustain and deliver from the hands of our enemies, his servants until they have accomplished his will in this house.[15]

After the dedication, they "sat a short time," listened to John Taylor sing "A Poor Wayfaring Man of Grief," and then prayed again.[16] During the meeting, "Hans C. Hansen the door keeper reported that there were two officers waiting at the foot of the stairs for President Young. The President concluded that he could bear to tarry up in the warm as long as they could stay in the cold waiting for him."[17] The presence of state officers continued to be a threat to Young and others of the

---

12. Ibid., 205-6.

13. John Taylor, "Some Journalizing," 30 November 1845, holograph, 1, Nauvoo Temple Historical Documents, LDS Church Archives. He gives their names as Alpheus Cutler, Amasa Lyman, Brigham Young, Cornelius Lott, George A. Smith, George Miller, Heber C. Kimball, Isaac Morley, John Smith, John Taylor, Joseph Kingsbury, Joseph Young, Levi Richards, Lucian Woodworth, Newel K. Whitney, Orson Hyde, Orson Spencer, Parley P. Pratt, Reynolds Cahoon, Willard Richards, William Clayton, and William W. Phelps. Heber C. Kimball also noted that only "those that had received the Priesthood" were admitted. Kimball, On the Potter's Wheel, 154-55.

14. Kimball, On the Potter's Wheel, 155.

15. George D. Smith, An Intimate Chronicle, 192.

16. Ibid.; Kimball, On the Potter's Wheel, 155.

17. George D. Smith, An Intimate Chronicle, 192-93.

Twelve through December and January. (See "A Mormon Hoax on the Marshal," below.)

Initial Efforts to Sell the Temple

Once the decision had been made to leave Nauvoo, the Twelve considered arrangements to sell, rent, or lease the temple as early as 16 September.[18] In Brigham Young's letter of 24 September, delivered on 1 October to Illinois officials announcing the Saints' intention of leaving Nauvoo the next spring, he wrote, "We do not expect to find purchasers for our Temple and other public buildings, but we are willing to rent them to a respectable community who may inhabit the city."[19] By 31 October Young had changed his plan and was trying to find buyers for Church properties in Nauvoo, including the temple. At the suggestion of Judge James H. Ralston of Quincy, Illinois, Brigham Young wrote to John Purcell, bishop of the Catholic diocese in Cincinnati, Ohio:

> To Reverend Bishop Purcell, and all Other Authorities of the Catholic Church—Greeting:
>
> The Church of Jesus Christ of Latter-day Saints hereby take opportunity to inform you by letter and by our confidential messenger, Almon W. Babbit, Esq., that it is our fixed purpose to remove hence early next spring.
>
> The hand of oppression and the lacerations of the tongue of calumny have compelled us to the determination to dispose of numerous lots, tenements, etc., in this city together with our public buildings, for instance our Temple, the Nauvoo House, the Academy, Seventies' Hall, Concert Hall, and other buildings, also our farms and other possessions in Hancock county even all our effects and temporal interests. The individual members of our community have also determined en masse to do the same with their effects and have empowered agents to sell. The bearer, Mr. Babbitt, is empowered to represent as our authorized agent all our said property and interest in this city and county. Through the suggestion of Judge Ralston of Quincy and other friends to your faith we are disposed to invite the authorities of your church, either personally or by authorized agents, to visit our city that we may negotiate with them, at as early a period as possible, the sale of our property. We shall forbear any extensive sales to other communities until we learn your answer to this our epistle. The bearer may be

---

18. Minutes of a meeting of the Twelve, Journal History of the Church of Jesus Christ of Latter-day Saints (chronology of typed entries and newspaper clippings, 1830-present), 16 September 1845, 1, LDS Church Archives.

19. Brigham Young, Letter to John J. Hardin et al., 24 September 1845, *Nauvoo Neighbor* 3 (1 October 1845): 2.

relied upon as our confidential and highly esteemed brother who will furnish you any information preparatory to the proposed negotiation and sale.[20]

In addition to his mission to Cincinnati, Babbitt also visited St. Louis and Chicago in search of prospective buyers. On 20 November, the *Burlington Hawkeye* reported the Saints' decision to sell and speculated on the possible uses that a prospective owner might make of the temple:

A friend, who was at the holy city the first week, informs us that all is peaceable and quiet there—that the saints are making preparations to remove—but at the same time are finishing the Temple, putting in the carpets, etc., and intend to hang a bell and when all is completed will endeavor to rent it to some respectable society.... As long as it stands, the Temple will continue to be a great attraction of the upper Mississippi; and it is supposed that the purchaser might realize at least one half the annual interest on the money invested, by a small charge levied upon strangers for admission.

It is certainly an extraordinary specimen of human skill and industry; and so well appointed in its arrangements, that it can be made available for other purposes than those for which it was intended. As a college edifice it would stand unrivaled either in America or Europe.[21]

On 1 December, the Twelve, the temple committee, and the trustees met in the temple store. During the meeting, "letters were read from J. B. Purcell, Catholic bishop of Cincinnati, the Catholic bishop at Detroit, and other gentlemen, inquiring after the property and lands for sale in Nauvoo and vicinity." Almon Babbitt reported that "the Catholics were making considerable exertions to have the members of their church purchase our property. They were very anxious to lease the Temple, but were not able to buy it. Mr. Quarters, the bishop at Chicago, has sent an agent who may probably enter into some arrangements for our property, he is expected tomorrow."[22]

This agent did not arrive as expected; but on 8 December, two priests identified only as Father Tucker of Quincy and Father Hamilton of Springfield passed through Warsaw en route to Nauvoo to meet with the Twelve.[23] The two met with the Twelve on the afternoon of 9 December in Willard Richards's office in the temple.[24] They had come at the direction of the Bishop of Chicago to "inquire into the situation of the land

20. James R. Clark, comp., *Messages of the First Presidency of the Church of Jesus Christ of Latter-day Saints*, 6 vols. (Salt Lake City: Bookcraft, 1965-75), 1:288-89.

21. "The Mormon Temple," *Burlington* (Iowa) *Hawkeye* 7 (20 November 1845), 3, microfilm, Lee Library.

22. *History of the Church*, 7:536-37.

23. "Catholics and Mormons," *Warsaw Signal*, 10 December 1845, 2.

24. Kimball, *On the Potter's Wheel*, 166-67.

and property for sale in and around Nauvoo"; and that evening, the Twelve "wrote out propositions for the sale of our lands for the benefit of the Catholic deputation."[25] The next morning, Joseph L. Heywood, an 1842 convert, escorted the two visitors to the upper room of the temple where they met with Brigham Young, several of the Twelve, and others. "The propositions of the council in regard to the sale of our property were presented to Mr. Tucker in writing who read them over and then handed them to Mr. Hamilton who also read them."[26] The meeting then adjourned to Room 1 (Brigham Young's office) in the southeast corner. Young "gave [them] an explanation of the design of the rooms in the Temple,"[27] and Orson Hyde reviewed the content of the propositions. *The History of the Church* reports the ensuing conversation:

> Father Tucker said he thought it would be wisdom to publish our propositions in all the Catholic papers and lay the matter plainly before their people.
>
> He should also think it advisable for the Catholic bishop to send a competent committee to ascertain the value of our property, etc., etc. At the same time they will use all their influence to effect a sale as speedily as possible.
>
> Father Tucker thought they had men in St. Louis, New York and other cities, who could soon raise the amount we want, but the time is so very short he does not know whether it can be done so soon.
>
> He asked if we would be willing to have our propositions published in their papers.
>
> I [Brigham Young] answered that we would have no objections, providing it was understood that we reserved the right to sell when we had an opportunity. I said I was well aware that there were many men in the Catholic Church who could furnish all the money we wanted immediately, but I supposed it was with them as it was with a Mr. Butler, a wealthy banker, who, when asked, why he did not sign off more bills, replied it was a good deal of trouble to sign off bills!
>
> Perhaps it is too much trouble to dig their money out of their vaults, but I wished it distinctly understood that while we make liberal propositions to dispose of our property, we must have the means to help ourselves away.
>
> I said I would like to add a note to our proposals before they are presented for publication, to this effect, that if a party agree to them, we will lease them the Temple for a period of from five to thirty-five years, at a reasonable price, the rent to be paid in finishing the unfinished parts of the Temple, the wall around the Temple block and the block west of the Temple, and keeping the Temple in repair.

The council agreed to the amendment, which was accordingly added to the proposals, and handed to Father Tucker.[28]

25. *History of the Church*, 7:539.

26. George D. Smith, *An Intimate Chronicle*, 200.

27. *History of the Church*, 7:539.

28. Ibid., 7:539-41.

William Clayton observed, "Mr. Tucker seemed to give much encouragement that an arrangement would speedily be entered into, to accomplish what we want. Both the gentlemen seem highly pleased with the Temple and the City and appear to feel sanguine that the Catholics should get this Temple and vicinity. About half past 12 they departed evidently feeling well towards us."[29]

Despite this optimistic encounter, the sale fell through. One month later, Father Tucker wrote to inform the Twelve and the trustees that "the Catholic bishop could not raise money enough to purchase our property, but would either purchase or rent one of our public buildings, but would not insure it against fire or mobs."[30] With evident annoyance, Brigham Young responded that the Twelve "would not answer the letter, and that the Catholics might go to hell their own way."[31]

Endowments Administered in the Temple

On the evening of 9 December, with the attic story dedicated and arranged for the presentation of the endowment, Heber C. Kimball wrote in his journal: "Elder B[righam] Young and H[eber] C. Kimball washed ourselves in pure water . . . and also G[eorge] A. Smith, Am[asa] Lyman, and [were] the first washed in the Temple of the Lord. . . . We shall come tomorrow with our wives, that is, all the Holy Order, to go through with our washings and anointing again in the Temple of our God."[32]

The members of the Holy Order met in the attic on 10 December and administered the endowment for the first time in the temple. During the first two days, the endowment was given only to those who had already been endowed in other locales. Beginning on 12 December, the Twelve extended invitations to Saints who had not yet received it. Norton Jacob was among those selected to receive the ordinance on that first day for the general membership. He wrote:

> Brother William Weeks come to me and said he wanted me to go home and prepare myself and wife and come to the temple at 12 o'clock a.m. ready to receive our endowments. We most joyfully complied with the request and at about 5 o'clock p.m. we were washed and anointed in the House of the Lord. It was the most interesting scene of all my life and one that afforded the most peace and joy that we had ever experienced since we were married, which has been over fifteen years. Brethren William Weeks, Truman O. Angell, Charles C. Rich,

29. George D. Smith, *An Intimate Chronicle*, 200-202.

30. *History of the Church*, 7:565.

31. George D. Smith, *An Intimate Chronicle*, 256.

32. Stanley B. Kimball, *On the Potter's Wheel*, 167-68.

George W. Harris, James Allred and William Felshaw were the first that received their endowment in this House of the Lord, which took place on this day, the time before having been occupied in the washing and anointing those that had before received their endowments under the hands of Joseph Smith the prophet. ... After those six went in with their wives, Amos Fielding, Noah Packard, Samuel Rolf, Aaron Johnson, William Snow, Willard Snow, Erastus Snow, [William] Player and myself, with our wives, were called in and all passed through the endowment at the same time.[33]

As Norton Jacob's account makes clear, the endowments were given by appointment. John D. Lee recalled, "A list is made out the day previous of all those who wish to take their endowment."[34] Increase Van Dusen, who received his endowment on 29 January 1846, stated that he and his wife received "a notice to appear at the Temple at five in the morning."[35] Although Norton Jacob's boss on the temple, architect William Weeks, issued his invitation, these appointments usually came from the Twelve. Abraham O. Smoot was "called on by the Council of the Twelve Apostles ... to receive my endowments."[36]

According to John D. Lee, "Every person is required to wash himself clean, from head to foot. Also to prepare and bring a good supply of food, of the best quality, for themselves and those who labor in the house of the Lord."[37] On 7 January 1846, for instance, participants "brought all kinds of provisions for the use of those who are attending on the ordinances of the Lord's House."[38]

When candidates, often in "an immense crowd," arrived in the outer court (also called the "outside porch," the "reception room," the "vestry," or the vestibule) of the temple, guards welcomed them and instructed them "to pass up the main winding stairway, from the base to the attic story."[39] Here they were "received past the guard into a private room on the north side of the Temple," removed their wraps, and were seated.[40] At the proper time, they were ushered into the preparation rooms and then conducted through the various stages of the

33. Norton Jacob, Journal, 1804-52, typescript, 22, Perry Special Collections, Lee Library.

34. John D. Lee, *Mormonism Unveiled, or, The Life and Confessions of the Late Mormon Bishop* (St. Louis: Bryan, Brand & Company, 1877), 169.

35. Increase and Maria Van Dusen, *The Sublime and the Ridiculous Blended, Called, the Endowment* (New York: N.pub., 1848), 6.

36. Abraham O. Smoot, Journal, 1837-46, 17 December 1845, holograph, Special Collections, Marriott Library, University of Utah, Salt Lake City. Smoot (1815-95) was baptized 22 March 1835 and endowed 18 December 1845. His wife, Sarah Gibbons (also spelled Sariah Gibbon) Smoot (1800-unknown), was endowed four days later on 22 December.

37. Lee, *Mormonism Unveiled*, 169.

38. *History of the Church*, 7:565.

39. Van Dusen and Van Dusen, *The Sublime and the Ridiculous*, 7.

40. "Emeline" (pseud.), "Mormon Endowments," *Warsaw Signal*, 15 April 1846, 2.

ceremony. Joseph Fielding, upon receiving his endowment in the temple, remarked, "I and my wife received our endowment having formerly received it in the days of Joseph and Hyrum but it is now given in a more perfect manner because of better convenience."[41] Abraham O. Smoot recorded his journal:

> At the hour of 8 o'clock in the morning I was received into the preparation rooms with several others of my brethren, and I was there prepared to be conducted into the washing and anointing room, where I received my washings in clean and pure water, preparatory to my anointing, which I received under the hands of Samuel Bent, President of the High Council. I was then presented with a garment bearing the marks of the Priesthood, which I was instructed to wear as a prevention from evil. I was now prepared for the reception of further ordinances in the House of the Lord which were to me sublime, great and glorious, making on the mind endurable impressions, or as the prophet said "Engraving upon the heart and written on its inner parts."[42]

The ceremony, lengthier than the modern form, could last as many as nine hours depending on the size of the company, the number of available workers, and the recipients' familiarity with the ceremony. Samuel W. Richards indicated that the company with which he received the ordinance was engaged for six hours: "Went in about 10 in the morning with the second company, was the first of the company that was washed.... Received through the v[eil] by Amasa Lyman. Got through about 4 in the afternoon and left the house."[43]

The giving of endowments continued through the first week of February. During this span, over 5,000 Latter-day Saints received the endowment. Entire families received ordinances together.[44] Even the sick were carried to the temple to participate.[45]

Many of the endowment sessions were organized by quorum (high priests with their wives, and seventies with their wives).[46] For example, on 11 January at a meeting of the Sixth Quorum of Seventy held in the home of Samuel Rolf, "notice was given to some of the brethren to attend at the temple tomorrow." At the Sixth

---

41. Andrew F. Ehat, ed., "'They Might Have Known He Was Not a Fallen Prophet': The Nauvoo Journal of Joseph Fielding," BYU Studies 19 (Winter 1979): 158.

42. Smoot, Journal, 18 December 1845.

43. Samuel W. Richards, Journal, Book 2, 7 January 1846, typescript, 1, Perry Special Collections, Lee Library.

44. "Henry Jolley," in Our Pioneer Heritage, compiled by Kate B. Carter, 20 vols. (Salt Lake City: Daughters of Utah Pioneers, 1958-77), 8:541.

45. Warren Foote, Journal, 1816-1903, 23 December 1845, typescript, 73, Perry Special Collections, Lee Library.

46. George D. Smith, An Intimate Chronicle, 209, 215, 216.

Quorum meeting the following week, Quorum President Israel Barlow, already a recipient of the endowment, remarked that "he has a great anxiety for the brethren to go there [the temple], as much, he supposed, as they had themselves." He added that the the Sixth Quorum would "have the privilege to take in the coming week 8 more." Names were then taken of quorum members who had paid their tithing but had not yet received the endowment.[47] The various quorums also met frequently in the side rooms in the attic for instruction and prayer.[48]

On 26 December, Brigham Young reportedly said: "If the brethren do not get any thing more than they have already got, they have got all they have worked for in building this house, and if there is any more to be received it is because the Lord is merciful and gracious."[49] As the winter wore on and increasing tensions made it seem unlikely that the Saints would be allowed to remain in their city undisturbed until spring, the anxiety of the Saints to receive these ordinances heightened. As many as six hundred recipients were admitted in one day.[50] Louisa Barnes Pratt wrote:

> I was called to the temple to receive my blessings where I encountered grievous disappointment, not in the charter of the blessings, but in not being permitted to remain through the day as I had anticipated. The house being crowded, the overseer requested us to withdraw and make room for others. I remonstrated, but all in vain. I retired with a heavy heart. Afterwards I had frequent opportunities of attending the different exercises in the house, and felt that all was made right. It was a glorious sight to go through the stately edifice and examine the varied apartments, the architecture of which was dictated by the wisdom of God.[51]

Rules Drafted for Conduct in Temple

After the first few days of performing the endowment for the general membership under such crowded conditions, it became clear that maintaining reverence and order in the busy temple would be a challenge. On 13 December, Brigham Young dictated a set of rules to William W. Phelps:

47. Minutes of the Sixth Quorum of Seventy, 11, 18 January 1846, quoted in *Ora H. Barlow, The Israel Barlow Story and Mormon Mores* (Salt Lake City: Ora H. Barlow, 1968), 222, 223. Israel Barlow (1806-83) was baptized sometime prior to his ordination as a Seventy in 1835, and was one of the first Mormons to arrive in Commerce (Nauvoo).

48. John D. Lee, Diary, 1844-46, 27, 28, December 1845, typescript, 10-11, Perry Special Collections, Lee Library.

49. Quoted in George D. Smith, *An Intimate Chronicle*, 233-34.

50. *History of the Church*, 7:580. This was the total number admitted on 7 February, the last day endowments were offered. The day previous, 512 individuals were endowed.

51. Louisa Barnes Pratt, "Journal of Louisa Barnes Pratt," in *Heart Throbs of the West*, compiled by Kate B. Carter, 12 vols. (Salt Lake City: Daughters of the Utah Pioneers, 1947-51), 8:236.

RULES OF ORDER

Rule 1st. No person allowed to enter these apartments without changing or cleansing shoes in the Vestry.

Rule 2nd. No person allowed to wear his hat or cap, while in these rooms.

Rule 3rd. No person allowed to enter further than the reception or washing and anointing rooms till he or she has been washed and anointed.

Rule 4th. No person allowed to pass from one room to another while receiving the ordinances without being conducted by a superintendent.

Rules for those who have received the ordinances.

Rule 1st. No person allowed in the rooms without an invitation while in the hours of labor, excepting at the hour of prayer.

Rule 2nd. All persons who are invited are requested to remain in their rooms during the hours of labor.

Rule 3rd. At the ringing of the bell, all walking about, and loud talking, must cease. [The bell signaled the commencement of each endowment session.]

Rule 4th. No person allowed to remove things from one room to another without permission of the owner, and to be returned immediately when done with.[52]

The following morning, Young explained to recipients of the endowment that he had drafted some rules the previous evening that were being printed. He went over this list verbally, including "the order he wished carried out, and then took a vote whether this Quorum [of the Anointed] will sustain him in this regulation. The vote was unanimous in the affirmative."[53]

One endowment participant, commenting on the rules enforced in the temple, added, "The law is, that all those who have been ... initiated have the privilege of coming in [the celestial room] when they please ... for none are permitted to enter this holy place on any other condition than that he is one that can give the signs."[54]

As the weeks passed, Brigham continued to exhort the workers, and to introduce new measures and changes in procedure in order to increase reverence. Part of the difficulty was the crowd of people teeming through the congested little attic. John D. Lee noted on 19 December, "we have been thronged to the extent that it was almost impossible to move without running against some fifteen or twenty persons."

Noise was already a problem being in the drafty attic during the dead of winter. The "whistling of the weather" caused several companies to be dismissed because they couldn't hear. The crowds only added to this problem. Brigham

52. George D. Smith, An Intimate Chronicle, 211.

53. Ibid., 212.

54. Van Dusen and Van Dusen, The Sublime and the Ridiculous, 11.

Young even contemplated erecting "plank partitions" to replace the canvas ones between the various rooms to help reduce noise and increase privacy.[55]

Two weeks after Brigham drafted the first list of rules, he announced on 26 December new restrictions to increase order and reverence in the temple. William Clayton described the problem:

> Some men were doing things which ought not to be done in the Temple of the Lord. Some three or four men and perhaps more, had introduced women into the Temple, not their wives, and were living in the side rooms, cooking, sleeping, tending babies.... There was also a great many men introduced and passed through the ordinances who were not so deserving as some that were passed by. There were also many women and children passed through who were not well entitled to the ordinances, while none of the sons and daughters of the Twelve had been permitted to enter.
>
> There were also many persons lounging about, who had no particular duty to attend to, but who thought they had a right to be present, because they had once passed through the veil. There was also a number of men taking their stations at the veil without permission of the President; considering it their right to receive through the veil any female whom they might introduce into the washing and anointing room, while it is evidently the sole prerogative of the President to offi- ciate at that place or any one that he may authorize to do so.[56]

These regulations were put into effect two days later. In the early morning hours of 28 December, the workers were informed of the new regulations. John D. Lee wrote, "This morning produced new rules and regulations, prohibiting loafers from lounging and gawking around, meddling with other men's matters and indulging in levity, nonsense, and folly, and making light of things that are sacred and holy. Several persons that officiated in the beginning were dropped."[57]

"We Danced before the Lord"

On 17 December, John D. Lee recorded in his diary that, at the close of a long day of ordinance work, "an excellent fiddler came in by permission and ani- mated our feelings with melodious notes on his violin. We all rejoiced and praised

55. "General Record of the Seventies, Book B," in Anderson and Bergera, eds., *The Nauvoo Endowment Companies 1845-1846,* 81, 94.

56. George D. Smith, *An Intimate Chronicle,* 235.

57. John D. Lee, Diary, 1844-46, 28 December 1845, typescript, 10-11, Perry Special Collections, Lee Library. The situation had improved but Young continued to revisit the problem of disruption and irreverence while the temple was in use. See "General Record of the Seventies, Book B," in Devery S. Anderson and Gary James Bergera, eds., *The Nauvoo Endowment Companies 1845-1846* (Salt Lake City: Signature Books, 2005), 377.

the Lord in the dance."[58] This was the first instance on record of dancing in the temple. Dances would be held frequently during the remainder of December and January.[59] The 30 December entry in *History of the Church* reads:

> The labors of the day having been brought to a close at so early an hour, viz.:
> eight-thirty, it was thought proper to have a little season of recreation, accordingly Brother [Hans] Hansen was invited to produce his violin, which he did, and played several lively airs accompanied by Elisha Averett on his flute, among others some very good lively dancing tunes. This was too much for the gravity of Brother Joseph Young who indulged in dancing a hornpipe, and was soon joined by several others, and before the dance was over several French fours were indulged in. The first was opened by myself with Sister Whitney and Elder Heber C. Kimball and partner. The spirit of dancing increased until the whole floor was covered with dancers, and while we danced before the Lord, we shook the dust from off our feet as a testimony against this nation.[60]

On New Year's Day, 1846, the temple workers attended a feast of roast turkey in the temple attic. Brigham Young addressed the group of almost 150: "We [can] worship God in the dance as well as in other ways," he affirmed but reminded them that "this temple was a Holy place, and that when we danced, we danced unto the Lord.... He said the wicked had no right to dance, that dancing and music belonged to the Saints."[61] He warned the Saints of "the impropriety of mingling again with the wicked after having come in here, and taken upon them the covenants which they had."[62]

Evidently, Brigham Young heard criticism about the propriety of dancing in the temple. At another dance in the temple on 2 January 1846, Young defended the connection between worship and recreation:

> We will praise the Lord as we please. Now, as to dancing in this house—there are thousands of brethren and sisters that have labored to build these walls and put on this roof, and they are shut out from any opportunity of enjoying any amusement among the wicked—or in the world, and shall they have any recreation? Yes! and this is the very place where they can have liberty.... I will not have division and contention, and I mean that there shall not be a fiddle in this Church but what has Holiness to the Lord upon it, nor a flute, nor a trumpet, nor any other

---

58. Lee, Diary, 17 December 1845, typescript, 3.

59. Ibid., 19 December 1845, 4, records another dance this day.

60. *History of the Church*, 7:557-58.

61. George D. Smith, *An Intimate Chronicle*, 244.

62. Helen Mar Whitney, "Scenes in Nauvoo and Incidents from H. C. Kimball's Journal," *Woman's Exponent* 12 (1 September 1883): 50.

instrument of music.... The traditions of our forefathers, which we all inherited a portion of, were such that dancing was once thought among the unpardonable sins. In the early days of Kirtland, I remember that the ones guilty of indulging in so gross a sin as dancing were considered worthy of being disfellowshipped. They, like the sects of the day, had received their training from the old school where to sing a song or to laugh or run upon the Sabbath day was too much for the sanctity of those who believed in burning men, women and children as witches, etc.... We find nothing to condemn dancing; but we do read in Exodus, chapter 15, 20 and 21 verses: "And Miriam, the prophetess, the sister of Aaron, took a timbrel in her hand, and all the women went out after her with timbrels and with dances. And Miriam answered them, Sing ye to the Lord, for He hath triumphed gloriously."

He explained that "this same spirit was what filled the hearts of the Saints of Nauvoo, who had built a temple to the Most High.... [that] after being delivered even out of the seventh trouble, their joy and gratitude was poured out to their Deliverer in music and the dance."[63]

Hans C. Hansen, the violinist mentioned above who accompanied several dances in the temple, declared that "he had been in the habit of playing the fiddle for mixed companies among the wicked, and that in such companies he had seen very ungodly conduct." However, "when he saw the Saints enjoying themselves in the dance as they did here, he made a covenant with himself, that he would no more play the fiddle for the wicked, but that the Saints should have the use of his fiddle."[64]

Another violinist and member of the Church, Justus Morse had a different tale to tell. Though faithful to Joseph Smith, Morse was disenchanted with the new leadership. Nonetheless, he responded to an invitation to accompany a dance at the temple. On the evening of the event he found that his violin was unusable in some way. He had no time to repair it and borrowed one from a non-Mormon neighbor. According to Joseph Smith III,

> Brigham Young made quite a show of welcoming him, was glad to see him, glad he had brought his violin with him, etc., and then, taking the instrument from Mr. Morse's hand, he proceeded to pour some oil on it, anointing it thoroughly, and laid hands upon it after the manner of a sacred ordinance, and blessed it for the purpose of making music for the dancing of God's people!
> The whole thing happened so quickly Mr. Morse said he had not the opportunity to tell Mr. Young that it was a "Gentile" instrument he was blessing and dedicating, even if he had dared to, for he felt sure had he informed the domi-

63. Ibid. For Brigham Young's attitudes toward dancing, see Michael Hicks, *Mormonism and Music: A History* (Urbana: University of Illinois Press, 1989), 74-90.

64. Whitney, "Scenes in Nauvoo and Incidents from H. C. Kimball's Journal," 50.

nating leader of the fact, the borrowed violin would have been thrown down and smashed. The affair made him very indignant and disgusted, for he felt that it was bad enough for the Saints to dance in the Temple, but worse to make such sacrilege of it. He says he never played for them again.[65]

At the close of ordinance work on New Year's Eve, "the sound of Hansen's violin and Brother Averett's flute in the east room gave notice that business of a different nature would soon be attended to. The floor was cleared of chairs and tables, and filled up with two sets of dancers, one on each side of the stove."[66] Two days later on 2 January, the day Brigham Young defended dancing as belonging "to the Saints," members of the brass band were invited to perform "several very beautiful pieces of music, and at the request of President Joseph Young played a Fisher's Hornpipe, upon which he broke the gravity of the scene by dancing by himself. President Young then invited some others to join him in the dance."[67] Dances were also held on 5 and 6 January.[68]

George Laub noted in his diary on 19 January 1846 that, as he passed through the departments of the temple, he witnessed "the old and young men and maidens went forth in their dances. This was pleasing to the Lord."[69] The minutes of the Nauvoo Brass Band record another performance in the temple on 9 February:

By request of Brother Brigham Young, the band met in the upper room of the Temple; played a few tunes, after which Brother Young arose and said that, as we were about to leave Nauvoo, we had come together, to pass off the evening, and that he thought it no harm to have a little recreation in singing, etc., as long as it is done in righteousness. He then called on the Lord to take charge of the meeting; the brethren and sisters then joined in and danced; during the evening they handed round some of our Nauvoo grape wine, which was excellent. About 3 o'clock they dismissed and all went home.[70]

Dancing in the temple continued after even most of the Saints had evacuated Nauvoo. On 28 April 1846, Samuel W. Richards, who was still in Nauvoo working on the temple, wrote in his journal: "In the afternoon met in the attic story of the temple ... where we enjoyed ourselves with prayer, preaching, administration for healing,

65. Mary Audentia Smith Anderson, ed., *Joseph Smith III and the Restoration* (Independence, MO: Herald House, 1952), 104.

66. George D. Smith, *An Intimate Chronicle*, 244.

67. Whitney, "Scenes in Nauvoo and Incidents from H. C. Kimball's Journal," 58.

68. *History of the Church*, 7:564; George D. Smith, An Intimate Chronicle, 256.

69. George Laub, Diary, 1845-46, typescript, 35, Perry Special Collections, Lee Library. Laub (1814-80), a Pennsylvania native, was baptized in Nauvoo in 1843.

70. "An Interesting Record: Record of the Nauvoo Brass Band," *Contributor* 1 (June 1880): 196-97. This article contains excerpts from a handwritten record entitled, "A Book Containing the Minutes of Joseph's City Band." On 9 February, Samuel W. Richards, Journal, Book 2, typescript, 2, recorded: "In the evening met at the temple with a select party for a dance, several of the Twelve being present, and all the brass band."

blessing children, and music and dancing until near midnight."[71] On 1 May Richards and other workers and their wives "met in the upper room of the temple for a dance."[72]

Interestingly, Nauvoo resident J. K. Nichols taught "the rudiments of dancing" every other day during the first half of May, a class that was popular with the Saints still in Nauvoo.[73] Hiram Gano Ferris, an 1846 visitor, offered this humorous depiction of the Mormon dances: "I was told by a Mormon that the dignitaries of the church gave several grand balls in this room before they left, and that they actually did themselves 'Trip the light fantastic toe' with the young and the fair, and he further added that 'They liked right well to do it.'"[74] William Gallup, who visited the temple in 1848, noted that the attic story was still being "used as a dancing room by the young people of the place" and commented, "It is a fine place for the business."[75]

Bogus Brigham

On 23 December when endowments were proceeding every day, a Mr. Roberts, the deputy U.S. marshal from Illinois, accompanied by eight members of the Hancock Guard (the county militia) and a witness identified as "Mr. Benson of Augusta [Iowa]" came to Nauvoo from Carthage. Brigham Young, Parley P. Pratt, Heber C. Kimball, John Taylor, George A. Smith, Amasa Lyman, and Theodore Turley, had been "indicted at the late Term of the United States Circuit Court at Springfield, for Bogus making"[76] or "counterfeiting the coin of the United States,"[77] and the marshal had a warrant for their arrest. Benson's function was to identify Brigham Young for the marshal. This party reached Nauvoo at 1:00 p.m. and went straight to the temple where Young and others were in Young's room "in the southeast corner of the upper story."[78] Almon Babbitt, who was on guard at the temple entrance, informed Young of their arrival.[79] Young recalled, "I knelt down and asked my Father in Heaven, in the name of Jesus, to guide and protect me, that I might live to prove advantageous to the Saints."[80]

71. Richards, Journal, 28 April 1846, typescript 23.

72. Ibid., 25.

73. Ibid., 28.

74. Hiram Gano Ferris, "A Description of the Mormon Temple," *Carthage Republican*, 19 March 1890, 2.

75. William Gallup, Diary, 29 July 1848, photographic reprint of pages 129-30 accompanied by introduction by William Powell, photocopy, Perry Special Collections, Lee Library.

76. Thomas Sharp, "A Good Mormon Hoax," *Warsaw Signal*, 31 December 1845, 2.

77. *History of the Church*, 7:549.

78. Brigham Young, 23 July 1871, *Journal of Discourses*, 26 vols. (London and Liverpool: LDS Booksellers Depot, 1855-86), 14:218.

79. *History of the Church*, 7:549.

80. Young, *Journal of Discourses*, 14:218.

President Young did not interrupt his labors; and the guards at the temple door did not allow the marshal and his party to enter. Two hours later, "John Scott [another guard] informed George D. Grant [Young's assistant] that an officer and assistants were watching for President Young and others at the front door of the Temple. Brother Grant carried the information to President Young," adding that the officers were "intending to search [the Temple]."[81] In a story that certainly lost nothing in the retelling, Young later recounted to a congregation of the Saints in Salt Lake City:

> On entering the room, Brother Grant left the door open. Nothing came into my mind as what to do until, looking across the hall, I saw Brother William Miller leaning against the wall. As I stepped towards the door I beckoned to him: he came. "Brother William," I said, "the marshal is here for me: will you go and do just as I tell you? If you will, I will serve them a trick." I knew that Brother Miller was an excellent man, perfectly reliable, and capable of carrying out my project. "Here, take my cloak," said I; but it happened to be Brother Heber C. Kimball's; our cloaks were alike in color, fashion and size. I threw it around his shoulders, and told him to wear my hat and accompany Brother George D. Grant. He did so. "George, you step in the carriage," said I to Brother Grant, "and look towards Brother Miller, and say to him as though you were addressing me, 'are you ready to ride?' You can do this, and they will suppose Brother Miller to be me, and proceed accordingly"; which they did.[82]

Benson pointed out Miller to the guards, "accompanied by some ladies, in the act of getting into the carriage" and assumed it was Brigham Young.[83] Addressing Miller, George Grant "said in the presence of the officers who stood around the carriage ... 'Pres[ident] Young, the atmosphere is rather cold to be comfortable.'" Mr. Benson's assumption apparently confirmed, the officer "having the writ stepped [up] with the writ in his hand and said 'Mr. Young, you are my prisoner,'"[84] just as Miller "was about getting into [the] carriage."[85] "Miller told him there must be some mistake about it, as he was not guilty of anything of the kind, but the marshal insisted it was right."[86]

> The Saints learning what had been done assembled around the prisoner and swore that he should not be taken out of town. The Marshall and his posse were

81. History of the Church, 7:549.
82. *Journal of Discourses*, 14: 218-19.
83. Sharp, "A Good Mormon Hoax," 2.
84. Lee, Diary, 23 December 1845, typescript, 7.
85. *History of the Church*, 7:549.
86. Ibid.

however, determined and notwithstanding the threat of the crowd held on to their prisoner, and declared if any attempt was made to rescue him they would shoot Brigham the first man.[87]

The guards "made their boasts that they would get as many of the Twelve as they could, take them down to Warsaw, and have a new Years frolic killing them"[88] but the Saints, "by playing well their part, had prevented any suspicion from arising in the minds of the company that they had got the wrong pig by the ear."[89] "Miller [had] desired the marshal to go down to the Mansion where he could get counsel and ascertain if the proceedings were legal."[90] "After considerable bluster, the Saints began to cool off and the prisoner was taken to the tavern [Mansion House]. The Saints now began to show long faces and seemed very much affected. They spoke in a most affectionate manner to the prisoner—expressing their sympathy and sorrow for his mishap. As the officer and his posse left with their charge they broke out in such strains as these: 'Farewell Brother Brigham.' 'We hope you will soon return.' 'May the Lord bless you Brother Brigham and grant you a safe deliverance.' The sisters cried and Brothers swore no harm should befall him."[91]

Young's sons, Joseph and Brigham Jun., "and Brother Heber C. Kimball's boys and others, who were looking on, ... all seemed at once to understand and participate in the joke. They followed the carriage to the Mansion House, gathered around Brother Miller with tears in their eyes, saying, 'Father,' or, 'President Young, where are you going?' Brother Miller looked at them kindly, but made no reply."[92]

On reaching the Mansion they went into a private room where Esq. Edmonds examined the writ and pronounced it legal. Miller gave Edmonds the name of four witnesses for subpoena for him, and asked the marshall to remain until morning; he consented, but soon got uneasy and said he must go to Carthage. Miller then inquired if he would wait three quarters of an hour until he could get his witnesses, but in fifteen minutes he said he must go, and would wait no longer. Miller got into his carriage, Esq. Edmonds rode with the marshal's guard and they started for Carthage, Miller protesting there was some mistake about it, for he certainly was not guilty of any such things as were charged in the writ.[93]

87. Sharp, "A Good Mormon Hoax," 2.

88. George D. Smith, *An Intimate Chronicle*, 230.

89. Sharp, "A Good Mormon Hoax," 2.

90. *History of the Church*, 7:550.

91. Sharp, "A Good Mormon Hoax," 2.

92. *Journal of Discourses*, 14:219.

93. *History of the Church*, 7:550.

At 5 o'clock, Almon Babbitt, who had been present at the Mansion, returned to the Temple bringing word that "that the officer who arrested W[illia]m Miller ... [had] left the city, and gone to Carthage, with the prisoner, continuing ignorant of his mistake" and that "Mr. Edmonds, a partner of Mr. Babbitt, [had] gone with them to act as counsel for the prisoner."[94]

En route to Carthage "the marshal was very social, and remarked that the people had got quite a joke upon him for letting [Theodore] Turley give him the dodge. As they approached Carthage the troops began to whoop and holloa and went into town in high glee, performing the journey which was eighteen miles in two hours."[95]

On arriving at Carthage, "the marshal put up at Hamilton's Tavern and the rumor soon spread through the town that Brigham Young was in the custody of the marshal."[96] "The prisoner was put under a sufficient guard and was carefully watched."[97] "They kept him in a room to show him to the mobbers who would keep flocking in to look at him."[98] "Among others, George W. Thatcher, county commissioner's clerk, came into the tavern to see [Brigham Young]. The Marshall at his request took Miller into a private room."[99]

Thatcher, an apostate Mormon, who knew Young well, "came in, sat down and asked the landlord where Brigham Young was. The landlord, pointing across the table to brother Miller, said, 'That is Mr. Young.' Thatcher replied, 'Where? I can't see any one that looks like Brigham.' The landlord told him it was that fat, fleshy man eating. 'Oh, hell!' exclaimed Thatcher, 'that's not Brigham; that is William Miller, one of my old neighbors.' Upon hearing this the landlord went, and, tapping the Sheriff on the shoulder, took him a few steps to one side, and said, 'You have made a mistake, that is not Brigham Young; it is William Miller, of Nauvoo.' The Marshal, very much astonished, exclaimed, 'Good heavens! and he passed for Brigham.'"[100]

> The marshal soon returned and said to Mr. Miller, "I am informed you are not Mr. Young;" "Ah!" exclaimed Miller, "then if I should prove not to be Mr. Young, it would be a worse joke on you than the Turley affair," he replied, "I'll be damned if it won't."

94. George D. Smith, *An Intimate Chronicle*, 230.

95. *History of the Church*, 7:550.

96. Ibid., 7:550.

97. Sharp, "A Good Mormon Hoax," 2.

98. George Morris, "The History of George Morris," 1891, typescript, 34, Perry Special Collections, Lee Library.

99. *History of the Church*, 7:550.

100. *Journal of Discourses*, 14: 219.

The marshal asked Miller if his name was Young, he answered, "I never told you my name was Young, did I?" "No," replied the marshal, "but one of my men professed to be acquainted with Mr. Young, and pointed you out to me to be him." William Backenstos was called in and he told them William Miller was not Brigham Young. Another man came, and said he could swear Miller was not Brigham Young. The marshal said he was sorry, and asked Miller his name, he replied, "it is William Miller." He added, "You might have found that out sooner if you had been smart." The marshal left the room and soon returned accompanied by Edmonds who was laughing heartily at him. Edmonds inquired if he had anything more to do with "Mr. Young". The marshal replied that he did not know that he had anything further to do with Mr. Miller.[101]

Ruefully, the marshal added that "the Saints may 'have his hat'" and paid Miller this compliment: "I think you are a gentleman sir, for not making yourself known before."[102] William Miller was left to make his own way back to Nauvoo. But he (and presumably Edmonds) reached the city at midnight.

This was not the last brush that Brigham Young and the Twelve had with the law in Hancock County. Charges of counterfeiting and treason were made against them and, though based on false accusations, necessitated disguises and arms. Joseph Fielding wrote in his journal in late December:

Attempts are making to take the Twelve. It seems as though earth and hell are mad to see the work of the priesthood proceeding so rapidly. The United States Marshal has been here for some time searching and laying in wait for the Twelve and some others. He searched the Temple through[,] in vain. The Brethren have had to disguise themselves and conceal themselves to escape them. . . .

You may see the Twelve, etc., wherever they go with six shooter pistols in their pockets. But thus far, they have been preserved and are ministering in the temple and teaching the way of life and salvation.[103]

On one occasion, the marshal requested to search the temple for the individuals for whom he had warrants. John D. Lee wrote in his diary on 27 December: "The Deputy Marshall of the United States ... came into the temple by permission and searched the different departments for the apprehension of the Twelve and others.... [O]n entering the sacred departments they were required to take off their shoes and hats—for the ground on which they stood was holy—which they did. They searched about a half an hour—went away without making any discoveries."[104]

---

101. *History of the Church*, 7:551.
102. Sharp, "A Good Mormon Hoax," 2.
103. Ehat, "'They Might Have Known,'" 159.
104. Lee, Diary, 27 December 1845, typescript, 9.

The marshall returned later and was accompanied by guard Almon Babbitt to the temple tower and walked out on the deck. The majestic view "filled the Marshall with admiration and wonder. Seeing the splendour, magnificence and grandeur [sic] that saluted his eye as he caught sight of the Mormon population. . . and knowing the inconvenience under which we had to labor ... it was enough to astound [him] ... for in fact no other people, as they acknowledge, could have accomplished such a work under the same circumstances but the Saints."[105]

The First Temple Workers

Operating the temple during December, January, and February required a large team of workers. Due to the obligation of secrecy, these workers could be selected only from among those who had already received their endowment. Initially, the group included those who had been endowed by Joseph Smith or Brigham Young in various locations, including Joseph's store.

According to William Clayton, Brigham Young "presided and dictated the ordinances and also took an active part in nearly every instance except when entirely overcome by fatigue through his constant labors to forward the work."[106] In his absence, Heber C. Kimball presided. Young commented in his journal: "Such has been the anxiety manifested by the saints to receive the ordinances, and such the anxiety on our part to administer to them, that I have given myself up entirely to the work of the Lord in the Temple night and day, not taking more than four hours sleep, upon an average, per day, and going home but once a week."[107]

Among the first men who served as ordinance workers were Brigham Young, Heber C. Kimball, Orson Hyde, Parley P. Pratt, John Taylor, George A. Smith, Willard Richards, Newel K. Whitney, William Clayton, George Miller, Joseph Fielding, and William W. Phelps.

The first women who participated as ordinance workers included Mary Ann Angell Young, Vilate Murray Kimball, Elizabeth Ann Smith Whitney, Bathsheba Wilson Bigler Smith, Marinda Johnson Hyde, Leonora C. Taylor, Mary Fielding Smith, Mercy Fielding Thompson, and Mary Ann Frost Stearns Pratt. According to Bathsheba B. Smith, they were known as "priestesses."[108] Eliza R. Snow "administered in that Temple in the holy rites that pertain to the house of the Lord as priest-

---

105. "General Record of the Seventies, Book B," in Anderson and Bergera, eds., *The Nauvoo Endowment Companies 1845-1846*, 273.

106. George D. Smith, *An Intimate Chronicle*, 209.

107. *History of the Church*, 7:567.

108. Bathsheba Wilson Bigler Smith, Autobiography, 1822-1906, typescript, 11, Perry Special Collections, Lee Library. See also "Communications," Times and Seasons 6 (1 June 1845): 917.

ess and Mother in Israel to hundreds of her sex."[109] Elizabeth Ann Whitney stated, "I gave myself, my time and attention to that mission: I worked in the temple every day without cessation until it was closed."[110] Mercy Fielding Thompson "was called by President Young to take up my abode there to assist in the female department, which I did, laboring night and day, keeping my child with me, my beloved friend, Mother Granger, staying there also."[111]

Mary Ellen Abel Kimball, one of the plural wives of Heber C. Kimball, recalled how greatly she revered Kimball's first wife Vilate Kimball, from whom she received temple ordinances:

> I admired the building from the outside, but greater pleasure took possession of my mind when I entered and beheld the beautiful rooms within. I felt a reverential awe knowing this to be the temple of God, built by revelation. Sister Vilate Kimball gave me my washing and anointing in this house. I shall never forget how much admiration I felt for her. I knew her to be a saint.[112]

This privileged group of ordinance workers met a few days before the temple was completed and received instructions on their duties. According to Kimball, on Sunday, 7 December, Brigham Young "gave the brethren and sisters . . . a view of the separate rooms, and the object of them, then put up the veil and showed the order of it." They then partook of the sacrament. Kimball added, "Great solemnity rested on the brethren and sisters, great union in our meeting."[113]

Two days later, he recorded prayerfully: "We shall begin our operations to morrow morning if the Lord will. O Lord be with thy servants and inspire their hearts with light and knowledge, so that they may not go wrong in the ordinance of the Holy Priesthood and thy name shall have all the glory."[114]

This initial group was supplemented by those to whom they gave the endowment, both to conduct the ordinances and to maintain order in the temple. According to John D. Lee's recollection, "about twenty-five persons [were] required in the different departments to attend to the washing, anointing, blessing, ordaining, and sealing."[115] Erastus Snow recalled that on 12 December, he and his wife

---

109. Emmeline B. Wells, "Pen Sketch of an Illustrious Woman: Eliza R. Snow Smith," *Woman's Exponent* 9 (15 October 1880): 74.

110. Elizabeth Ann Smith Whitney, "A Leaf from the Autobiography of Elizabeth Ann Whitney," *Woman's Exponent* 7 (September 1878): 191.

111. Mercy Rachel Fielding Thompson, Autobiography, 1804-47, 10, holograph, LDS Church Archives.

112. Mary Ellen Abel Kimball, Journal, 1838-63, holograph, 21, LDS Church Archives.

113. Kimball, *On the Potter's Wheel*, 164-65.

114. Ibid., 167.

115. Lee, *Mormonism Unveiled*, 169.

Artimesia "received the first ordinance of endowments, and were called to labor and administer in the temple from that time forth." He "departed not from the temple, day or night, but continued in the labors and duties thereof—with the twelve and others selected for this purpose—about six weeks."[116] Mary Isabella Horne "spent two weeks [in the temple in January] in assisting in the work of administering in the ordinances for others, and was filled with joy to be able to act in this capacity for her sisters."[117]

The *History of the Church* records a meeting of the Twelve on 27 December at which they "selected the names of persons who would be called upon to labor in the Temple the ensuing week." These included Joseph Young, Lorenzo Snow, Abraham O. Smoot, Lewis Robbins, William Crosby, Benjamin L. Clapp, Henry Harriman, Charles C. Rich, Jedediah M. Grant, William Snow, Erastus Snow, Ezra T. Benson, Orson Spencer, Franklin D. Richards, Willard Snow, Elisha Averett, and John Lowe Butler.[118]

Most who received the call felt honored. John D. Lee recorded in his journal: "After passing through the sacred ordinances of the House of the Lord Pres[ident] B[righam] Young then informed me that my services was needed all the while here in the Temple during the time of giving Endowments. I accordingly returned home about 10 at night with feeling of gladness and joyful acclamations of praise to the Giver of All Good."[119]

Samuel W. Richards recorded on 7 January: "[Seventies] President Joseph [Young] informed me that, he should depend upon me to come and assist in giving the Endowment.... The next day commenced labour at the veil, and continued administrating and officiating in all the departments of the first endowment with the exception of the serpent, which I esteemed as a great blessing and privilege, affording to me a knowledge of those things which had been concealed before."[120]

Similarly, Abraham O. Smoot recorded:

> On Thursday the 18th of December 1845 ... I was called upon by the secretary of the Temple to return next morning to the Temple to assist them in the labor in that holy place, with which request I gladly complied.

116. Moroni Snow, ed., "From Nauvoo to Salt Lake in the Van of the Pioneers—The Original Diary of Erastus Snow," *Improvement Era* 14 (February 1911): 281.

117. "A Representative Woman: Mary Isabella Horne," *Woman's Exponent* 11 (October 1882): 25.

118. *History of the Church*, 7:555. Women were probably also selected but the official history does not list them.

119. Lee, Diary, 10 December 1845, typescript, 1-2. See also Joseph Grafton Hovey, "Autobiography of Joseph Grafton Hovey," 1812-56, typescript, 34, Perry Special Collections, Lee Library. Grandson M. R. Hovey copied and arranged this document from Hovey's journal in 1933. It begins with an autobiography, then moves to daily entries in 1842.

120. Samuel W. Richards, Journal, Book 2, typescript, 1.

On the morning of the 19th, at 7 o'clock, I was in the Temple ready to commence my labors, as soon as my position should be appointed to me, which I
received at 8 o'clock in the morning, in the anointing department, at which I
spent the day, conferring this sacred ordinance on the brethren of the Priesthood,
returned home at 9 P.M. and spent the night with my heart full of joy in the
Lord.[121]

Smoot worked for several days in the anointing room and acted in other
capacities as well.

Early each morning, Brigham Young or one of the senior members of the
Twelve would meet with the workers and assign them their various roles for the
day. Because the endowment consisted, in part, of a reenactment of the events of
the creation and the Garden of Eden,[122] some of the ordinance workers assumed
the roles of the various characters in the drama, explaining Samuel Richards's reference above to the "serpent." On 17 December, John D. Lee "acted as Tempter
while in the garden."[123] William Clayton recorded that, on 10 December 1845,
"H[eber] C. Kimball preside[d] as Elohim, Orson Hyde as Jehovah, and George A.
Smith as Michael and N[ewel] K. Whitney as the serpent" while, on 12 December,
"President Young act[ed] as Elohim, P[arley] P. Pratt as Jehovah, Orson Hyde as
Michael, William W. Phelps as the serpent."[124]

Other workers were assigned to prompt and assist the recipients as they
progressed in their symbolic journey. John D. Lee frequently acted as
"prompter."[125] At the final stage of the endowment, the recipients were received
through the veil and passed into the celestial room or council chamber. On 12
December, Clayton recorded: "President Young gave all the charges and received
Orson Pratt through the veil. The remainder of the men were received through by
Orson Hyde, the females by their husbands."[126] At least for a time, the roles were
also assigned numbers for convenience: John D. Lee's diary for January 10 notes:
"Thursday I acted the part of Elohim which is number 1 in the 1st and first [and] last
apartment.... Friday ... I acted the part of no. 2 in the last department also no. 4 in
the garden and middle department—Prompter and Tempter."[127]

121. Smoot, Journal, 18 December 1845.

122. James E. Talmage, *House of the Lord* (Salt Lake City: Deseret Book Company, 1968), 83.

123. Lee, Diary, 17 December 1845, typescript, 4.

124. George D. Smith, *An Intimate Chronicle*, 204.

125. Lee, Diary, 19, 20, and 21 December 1845, typescript, 5, 6, 7.

126. George D. Smith, *An Intimate Chronicle*, 209.

127. Lee, Diary, 20 December 1845, typescript, 16. Lee made similar references on 26
December and 10 January (pp. 6, 8), indicating that these code numbers were used for several days
at least.

In addition to conferring the endowment, these workers performed many other support tasks. For example George Washington Bean "worked in the outer court of the Temple running a windlass, drawing up the wood and water needed to carry on the endowments."[128] During the early morning hours, known as "the preparation time," workers cleaned the departments, washed temple clothing, kindled fires in the stoves, and did other maintenance chores. On 17 December, Hosea Stout helped prepare water for the washings.[129] Hans C. Hansen tended the fires and kept watch at the door.[130] The following entry from *History of the Church* illustrates some of the typical "off-hours" experiences of the workers:

> Lewis Robbins is cleaning and putting in order the washing rooms and furniture, Peter Hansen is translating the Book of Mormon into the Danish language, Elisha Averett is doorkeeper, John L. Butler, fireman, David Candland and L[ucien] R. Foster, clerks. Orson Pratt has been engaged in making astronomical calculations. From several observations he makes the latitude of Nauvoo 40° 35' 48" north.[131]

One of the "housekeeping" duties in the temple was to consecrate oil for use in the ceremonies. On 6 January, Heber C. Kimball requested that eight men assist him in preparing seventeen bottles of oil.[132]

John D. Lee, in addition to his responsibilities during the ordinances, also chronicled a variety of other duties:

> Friday [12 December] about 4 o'clock a.m., I entered the Temple and, in connection with several others, cleaned up the rooms in the various departments and prepared for the endowment. At half past 9 morning—the Twelve having come in they commenced operations. I will mention here that I had for several days to be the doorkeeper as well as chief cook and bottle washer. I do not mean in giving endowments but to see that all things were in readiness and kept straight in the preparation time.... I was set apart for clerk to keep the records of the Saints. I was truly thankful that I was thus favored as I had much writing in the rear [in arrears] to do through the day and a part of the night....
>
> Tuesday Dec[ember] 16, 1845 about 4 o'clock in the morning I entered the porch in [the] lower court where I met the Porter who admitted me in through the door which led to the foot or nearly so of the great flight of stairs which by

128. George Washington Bean, *Autobiography of George Washington Bean*, edited by Flora Diana Bean Horne (Salt Lake City: N.pub., 1945), 23. He probably hoisted the water and wood up the center of the spiral staircase on the north side.

129. Hosea Stout, Diary, 17 December 1845, typescript, 2:109, Perry Special Collections, Lee Library.

130. Stanley B. Kimball, *On the Potter's Wheel*, 158.

131. *History of the Church*, 7:554.

132. George D. Smith, *An Intimate Chronicle*, 255.

ascending led me to the door of (the) outer court which I found tyled[133] within
by an officer. I having the proper implements of that degree gained admittance
through the outer and inner courts which opened and led to the sacred departments. The Titles of these apartments are not lawful for me to give at present.
Having entered I found myself alone. I with the Tyler that kept the inner court set
about and soon got the fires up in the different rooms and setting things in
order—for the day—at about 9 o'clock in the morning the washing and anointing
commenced.

Wednesday Dec[ember] 17th 1845 about noon I got up with my writing
and had some considerable time to spend in officiating.... Pres[ident] B[righam]
Young said that he would retire into the East room and again celebrate the
praise of God by singing and Prayer which when he had done—we retired to
rest, all but the guard(s) who stood in turn 2 hours each till day when all was
up and at work in order to get things ready for the day—at 9 in the morning the
washing and anointing.[134]

Of his 12 December calling as head clerk, Lee later commented:

Brigham Young called and set me apart for the purpose of keeping the records
of sealings and anointings ... which were sacred and precious and will be of
course handed to future generations. Quite a number of cases have already
occurred without ever having been recorded and what was recorded was not in
a correct form, consequently had to be rectified, which of course produced much
labor which has been our occupation through the week. Finding the task more
arduous that [sic] what we expected, Brother Franklin Richards was appointed to
assist in getting the records properly arranged and up with the operations of the
day.[135]

Samuel Rogers, one who was appointed as guard, recalled "being on duty
at the temple ... six hours on guard, then twelve hours off."[136]

Because of the tremendous number of Saints who desired to be endowed
and the pressure to prepare for departure, the ordinance workers were engaged,
in Joseph Hovey's words, "forenoon, afternoon and at night."[137] They sometimes
did not even return home to sleep. William Clayton recorded that, on the night of
12 December, "after prayers the following took their blankets and lay down to rest
on the floor of the Temple where they tarried over night, viz. President B. Young,
Amasa Lyman, George A. Smith, Wm. W. Phelps, Charles C. Rich, John D. Lee,

133. Masonic term, meaning "guarded." A tyler is a guard or watchman.
134. Lee, Diary, 12, 16, 17 December 1846, typescript, 2-3.
135. Lee, Diary, 13 January 1846, 18.
136. Samuel Holister Rogers, Journal, 1819-86, typescript, 46, Perry Special Collections, Lee Library.
137. Hovey, "Autobiography," 34.

David Candland. Elder Joseph Young and his wife tarried in his own room over night."[138] On 20 December, according to the official history, "The brethren considered it prudent to devote [the] day to cleaning and washing, and suspend operation in the Temple, but on account of the anxiety of the Saints to receive their ordinances, the brethren and sisters volunteered to wash clothes every night."[139] Even Christmas Day, which fell on a Thursday in 1845, was devoted to giving endowments. Abraham Smoot wrote: "Still administering in the Temple, this day was spent by me in the most agreeable manner of all the Christmases that I ever spent. I had been engaged in pouring upon the heads of High Priests and Seventies the holy anointing oil."[140]

The spirit in the temple greatly rewarded the participants for their labor and fatigue. Abraham Smoot recorded on 22 December: "We labored during the day in the anointing room, where abounded much of the Spirit of the Lord, which made the hearts of the brethren rejoice."[141] William Clayton noted on 13 December 1845, "Peace, harmony and good feeling prevailed through the day."[142]

Young People Receive Ordinances

Although the majority of those who received ordinances in the temple were married adults, several unmarried youths were also selected to participate. Pleasant Green Taylor was "only 15 years old when he went to the Nauvoo Temple and received his endowments."[143] Eunice Waner Billings, was sixteen.[144] Zadoc Judd, who was nineteen in late 1845, recalled: "All my comrade tailors were all invited to the temple to receive endowments and I suppose through their influence, I also was invited, for it was seldom that boys of my age were given that privilege. It was generally the old and faithful that got their endowments there."[145]

Perhaps the most interesting account of a young person's Nauvoo Temple experience is that of Mosiah Hancock. Hancock, the son of Levi Ward Hancock and Clarissa Reed Hancock was only twelve when Brigham Young invited him not only to participate in the endowment, but also to be sealed to a young woman. In his autobiography, written when he was thirty-one, he recalled this event:

---

138. George D. Smith, *An Intimate Chronicle*, 209. See also entry for 13 December 1845, p. 210.

139. *History of the Church*, 7:548.

140. Smoot, Journal, 25 December 1845.

141. Ibid., 22 December 1845.

142. George D. Smith, *An Intimate Chronicle*, 210.

143. Pleasant Green Taylor, Autobiography, 1827-94, typescript, 1, LDS Church Archives.

144. Eunice Billings Snow, "Sketch of the Life of Eunice Billings Snow," *Woman's Exponent* 39 (January 1911): 22.

145. Zadoc Judd, Autobiography, ca. 1907, 19-20, Perry Special Collections, Lee Library.

On about January 10, 1846, I was privileged to go in the temple and receive my washings and anointings. I was sealed to a lovely young girl named Mary, who was about my age, but it was with the understanding that we were not to live together as man and wife until we were 16 years of age. The reason that some were sealed so young was because we knew that we would have to go west and wait many a long time for another temple.

Once while I was in the temple, Brigham Young came to me and said, I perceive that you are a sober boy and quick to observe, but do you think you can remember all you have seen and heard in this temple?" "I think I can," I said. "Be sober and remember all you can, for great things will be expected of you," he added.[146]

Matilda Loveless, who was sixteen in 1845, "was present ... the day my brother, William, and parents received their endowments (7th January, 1846). On their way home, how happy they were over receiving these blessings. They spoke to me about having my endowments, but I said 'No, I will wait until I am married,' which I did."[147]

The First "Temple Marriages"

On 1 January 1846, Ortentia White and Truman Leonard became the first couple sealed in the temple. "The ceremony was performed by Heber C. Kimball"; and according to a family tradition, "the reason for their being first was a privilege earned by Truman for a special service rendered in the erection of this beautiful edifice. Ortentia was given a lock of Mr. Kimball's hair, as well as a photograph, and she kept them in her scrap book as a memento of that outstanding event."[148]

That same night Brigham Young married his nephew William Young to Adelia Clark:

His nephew, Brigham H. Young, and Sidenia O. Clark officiated as groomsman and bridesmaid. After asking them repeatedly if it was the understanding that they were to be married for time and for eternity, and receiving an answer in the affirmative, he then asked Hazen Kimball and his wife (the latter being a sister of

---

146. Mosiah Lyman Hancock, Autobiography, 1834-65, 31, typescript, Perry Special Collections, Lee Library.

147. Matilda McLellan Loveless, Autobiography, ca. 1885, typescript, 1, Perry Special Collections, Lee Library.

148. Gertrude Earl Hansen West, "Ortentia," *Treasures of Pioneer History*, 6 vols., compiled by Kate B. Carter (Salt Lake City: Daughters of the Utah Pioneers, 1952-57), 4:223. Leonard (1820-97) was baptized 25 March 1843. Ortentia (1825-98) married Leonard on 1 January 1846 and the two had ten children together.

the bride) if the bride's parents understood their intentions and approved of
them; and received satisfactory answers. After the ceremony was over he pronounced various blessings upon them.[149]

Many already existing marriages were solemnized or sealed in the temple,
including several plural marriages. Abraham Smoot had his previous marriage to
Margaret Thompson McMeans sealed on 9 January 1846 and was, in the same ceremony, sealed to Sariah Gibbon.[150] Lorenzo Snow was sealed to four wives on the
same day. According to his sister, Eliza R. Snow:

> My brother and his wives, among the number, had their washings, anointings and
> endowments, and were sealed at a holy altar, a privilege and blessing which they esti-
> mated above all earthly honors. When Lorenzo walked across the inner court of the
> Temple proceeding to the altar, accompanied by his four wives, all stately appearing
> ladies, one of the Temple officiates exclaimed, "And his train filled the Temple!"[151]

George Laub recorded being sealed to his wife on 5 February:

> John D. Lee performed the ceremony.
> [M]y wife Mary Jane was sealed to me a wife for time and eternity to be my
> companion and comforter and to fill up the measure of our creation. And we were
> sealed up unto eternal life to come forth in the morning of the First Resurrection....
> Now when we were sealed to this order together with the promises given unto us
> by the power and spirit of the Lord, Father Lee being filled with the spirit embraced
> us in his arms and blessed us in the name of the Lord that we should become
> mighty upon the earth and our names to be honorable in all generations.[152]

Helen Mar Kimball Whitney, who had married Horace Whitney in 1843,
described her feelings the day they solemnized their marriage in the temple, 3
February 1846:

> At early twilight ... a messenger was sent by my father, informing H[orace] K.
> Whitney and myself that this day ... we were to present ourselves there that
> evening. The weather being fine we preferred to walk; and as we passed through

149. Helen Mar Kimball Whitney, "Scenes in Nauvoo and Incidents in Heber C. Kimball's
Journal," *Woman's Exponent* 12 (1 September 1883): 50. William Young (1827-94) was the son of
Lorenzo Dow Young, Brigham's brother.

150. Smoot, Journal, 9 January 1846. His wife's name is also spelled Sarah Gibbons

151. Eliza R. Snow, *Biography and Family Record of Lorenzo Snow* (Salt Lake City: Deseret News
Press, 1884), 85.

152. George Laub, Diary, 1814-77, 5 February 1846, typescript, 37, Perry Special Collections,
Lee Library.

the little graveyard at the foot of the hill a solemn covenant we entered into—to cling to each other through time and, if permitted, throughout all eternity, and this vow was solemnized at the holy altar. Though gay and highminded in many other things we reverenced the principles taught us by our parents and held them sacred, also the covenants which we had previously made in that house, so much so that we would as soon have thought of committing suicide as to betray them; for in doing either we would have forfeited every right or claim to our eternal salvation.[153]

In all, 2,420 living couples were sealed to each other in the Nauvoo Temple, and 369 deceased spouses were sealed to living companions.[154] One of these sealings that reached across the barrier of death was Perrigrine Sessions's sealing to his deceased wife on 3 February 1846: "Attended to some of the sealing ordinances for Juliann Sessions, deceased January 28, 1845 in the City of Joseph being thirty years six months and four days old when she died and left me with children one son and one daughter, Lucinda Sessions [his second wife] acting as proxy for her."[155]

Many children were sealed to their parents in the Nauvoo Temple. Brigham Young recounted to a congregation in Salt Lake City: "When we had a Temple prepared in Nauvoo, many of the brethren had their children who were out of the covenant sealed to them…. Children born unto parents before the latter enter into the fulness of the covenants, have to be sealed to them in a Temple to become legal heirs of the Priesthood."[156]

Other Ordinance Work in the Temple

In addition to endowments and marriages, the ordinance of adoption, which is akin to the sealing of spouses and children, was also performed in the temple.[157] According to the law of adoption, men and their families could be adopted by (sealed to) a prominent elder, most often one of the Twelve but also, posthumously, to Joseph Smith.

John M. Bernhisel, age forty-seven and a close friend of Joseph Smith, was adopted into the family of the Prophet on 3 February 1846:

153. Whitney, "Scenes in Nauvoo and Incidents from Heber C. Kimball's Journal," 81.

154. Richard O. Cowan, *Temple Building: Ancient and Modern* (Provo, UT: BYU Press, 1971), 29.

155. Perrigrine Sessions, Diary, 1814-86, entry ca. 3 February 1846, microfilm of holograph, LDS Church Archives.

156. Brigham Young, 4 September 1873, *Journal of Discourses* 16:186-87.

157. Gordon Irving, "The Law of Adoption: One Phase of the Development of the Mormon Concept of Salvation, 1830-1900," *BYU Studies* 14, no. 2 (Winter 1974): 473-88. See also Boyd K. Packer, *The Holy Temple* (Salt Lake City: Bookcraft, 1980), 194-95 for a recent authoritative explanation of adoption and the cessation of the practice.

John Milton Bernhisel this day came to the sacred altar in the upper room of the "House of the Lord" founded by President Joseph Smith (Martyred) the Prophet Seer and Revelator to the church and there upon gave himself to President Joseph Smith (martyred) to become his son by the law of adoption and to become a legal heir to all the blessings bestowed upon Joseph Smith pertaining to exaltations even to the eternal Godhead with a solemn covenant to observe all the rights and ordinances pertaining to the new and everlasting covenant as far as now is or shall hereafter be made known unto him done in the presence of Patriarch John Smith, President Brigham Young, Heber C. Kimball, Amasa Lyman, O[rson] Hyde and George A. Smith at 4 o'clock p.m.[158]

George Laub, who was adopted into the family of John D. Lee, added insights into the meaning and purpose of the ordinance:

Now in this time I attached myself to John D. Lee's family to become his adopted son in the order of God and obedience of the gospel.... I and my wife Mary Jane, with many others, were adopted into John D. Lee's family. Thus, I took upon myself the name of Lee in this manner; George Laub Lee and my wife's name Mary Jane Laub Lee. This order of adoption will link the chain of the priesthood in such a way that it cannot be separated. By covenanting before God, angels, the present witnesses we covenant together for him to be a father unto those who are sealed to him to do unto them as he would unto his own children and to council them in righteousness, and to teach them all the principles of salvation and to share unto them of all the blessings of comfort. These and all that are calculated to make them happy both in time and in eternity. Now we also did covenant on our side to do all the good for his upbuilding and happiness both in time and eternity. This was done in the House of the Lord across the altar as was prepared for this purpose of ordinances, sealing of marriages.[159]

As Laub notes, the adopted individuals were then considered children of the adoptive father and sometimes used the father's name.[160] Abraham O. Smoot wrote in his autobiography, "I also at that time had the son of my first wife adopted to me by the Priesthood, and he has ever since borne my name and been recognized and treated as one of my own sons."[161] John D. Lee "was the second one adopted to Brigham Young." Of the nature of that relationship he wrote, "I . . . . was

---

158. Journal History, 3 February 1846, 2.

159. Laub, Autobiography, 5 February 1846, typescript, 34, 36-37.

160. However, John D. Lee, Diary, 17, who was himself an adopted son of Brigham Young, notes: "I accepted James Woolsey and Lovina his wife into my family by the law of adoption, he choosing to retain his sir name for the present..... This however was a prerogative that I gave to him."

161. Abraham O. Smoot, "Early Experience of A. O. Smoot," in *Early Scenes in Church History*, compiled by George Q. Cannon (Salt Lake City: Juvenile Instructor Office, 1881), 24-25.

to seek his temporal interests here, and in return he was to seek my spiritual salvation, I being an heir of his family, and was to share his blessings in common with his other heirs."[162]

The practice of adoption continued intermittently, until 1890 when Wilford Woodruff received a revelation clarifying the order of family relations. Addressing a general conference of the Church on 8 April 1894, he announced:

> In the commencement of adopting men and women in the Temple at Nauvoo, a great many persons were adopted to different men who were not of the lineage of their fathers, and there was a spirit manifested by some in that work that was not of God. Men would go out and electioneer and labor with all their power to get men adopted to them.... Now, what are the feelings of Israel? They have felt that they wanted to be adopted to somebody. President Young was not satisfied in his mind with regard to the extent of this matter; President Taylor was not. When I went before the Lord to know who I should be adopted to (we were then being adopted to prophets and apostles), the Spirit of God said to me, "Have you not a father, who begot you?" "Yes, I have." "Then why not honor him? Why not be adopted to him?" "Yes," says I, "that is right." I was adopted to my father, and should have had my father sealed to his father, and so on back.... When a man receives the endowments, adopt him to his father; not to Wilford Woodruff, nor to any other man outside the lineage of his fathers. That is the will of God to this people.... What business have I to take away the rights of the lineage of any man? What right has any man to do this? No; I say let every man be adopted to his father.... "But," says one, "suppose we come along to a man who perhaps is a murderer." Well, if he is a murderer, drop him out and connect with the next man beyond him. But the Spirit of God will be with us in this matter. We want the Latter-say Saints from this time to trace their genealogies as far as they can, and to be sealed to their fathers and mothers. Have children sealed to their parents, and run this chain through as far as you can get it. When you get to the end, let the last man be adopted to Joseph Smith, who stands at the head of the dispensation.[163]

Another ordinance also performed in the Nauvoo Temple was the second anointing. Erastus Snow recalled that on 23 January 1846, he "received, with Artimesia and Minerva [his wives], the sealings and further endowments."[164] The Twelve notified those privileged to receive these "further endowments." For example, Heber C. Kimball instructed Joseph Grafton Hovey and Martha Ann Webster

---

162. Lee, *Mormonism Unveiled*, 197.

163. Wilford Woodruff, 8 April 1894, *Collected Discourses*, edited by Brian H. Stuy, 5 vols. (Burbank, CA: B.H.S. Publishing, 1987-92), 4:72-73.

164. Snow, "From Nauvoo to Salt Lake," 281.

Hovey to come to the temple. After being endowed, Joseph recorded: "We were conducted into another department and received our Second Anointing. This was a source of knowledge to us and it was a great consolation that we were counted worthy before our Father in Heaven to receive that which we did receive."[165]

Truman O. Angell, who, with his wife, Polly Ann Johnson Angell, received the second anointing in December, wrote that the receipt of the second anointing "far excelled any previous enjoyments of my life up to that time."[166] Abraham Smoot likewise recorded his experience:

> Spent the afternoon of the 13th [January 1846], in the Temple, and received a promise from Heber C. Kimball to receive my second ordinances during the week upon a condition of being prayerful and faithful which was complied with to the best of my ability. The 17th was a day of great enjoyment for me, it gave birth to the greatest blessings and an higher exaltation in the Priesthood than ever had been anticipated by me. I received my second ordinances in the Priesthood with my wife Margaret and Sister Sariah Gibbon, under the hands of George Miller, President of the High Priest Quorum in room no. 4 attic story of the Temple of the Lord. I was called on by the President to open meeting by prayer which I complied with with feelings of much gratitude to my Heavenly Father and my brethren that surrounded us. The services of this holy anointing commenced at the hour of 6 o'clock in the afternoon and closed at 7.[167]

Thomas Bullock, whom Brigham Young invited to receive his second anointing with his wife, Lucy Caroline Clayton Bullock, recorded his impressions: "His words were as the Lord whispering peace to my Soul. I feel very happy for the blessings and privileges that I am receiving at the hands of the Lord. May I ever have the same Spirit within me, and then I shall always feel well."[168]

Once the attentions of the Twelve turned to the giving of this ordinance, the "burden of the Endowment now [rested] on the First Presidency of the Seventies."[169]

165. Hovey, "Autobiography," 34.

166. Truman O. Angell, "His Journal," Our Pioneer Heritage, 10:200. The title is somewhat misleading. This piece is actually his autobiography.

167. Smoot, Journal, 17 January 1845.

168. Gregory R. Knight, ed., "Journal of Thomas Bullock, 31 August 1845 to 5 July 1846," BYU Studies 31 (Winter 1991): 44.

169. "General Record of the Seventies, Book B," in Devery S. Anderson and Gary James Bergera, eds., The Nauvoo Endowment Companies 1845-1846 (Salt Lake City: Signature Books, 2005), 273.

Dedication of the Altar

Brigham Young had an altar constructed in his room in the southeast corner of the attic. From its dedication on 7 January 1846, sealings and anointings were performed at this altar and the room came to be known as the "Holy of Holies." The *History of the Church* records:

> This afternoon [7 January], the new altar was used for the first time, and four individuals and their wives were sealed. The altar is about two and one-half feet high and two and one-half feet long and about one foot wide, rising from a platform about 8 or 9 inches high and extending out on all sides about a foot, forming a convenient place to kneel upon. The top of the altar and the platform for kneeling upon are covered with cushions of scarlet damask cloth; the sides of the upright part or body of the altar are covered with white linen.
>
> The Twelve and presiding bishops with their wives were present at the dedication of the altar this afternoon.[170]

Brigham Young offered the dedicatory prayer:

> Our Father in Heaven in the name of the Lord Jesus Christ we ask thee to forgive us of our sins and cleanse our hearts from every impure spirit that we may offer unto thee an acceptable offering. We present ourselves before thee and bow down upon this altar which we have been enabled to prepare for thy servants and handmaidens to receive their sealing blessings. We present it unto thee with ourselves and dedicate and consecrate it in the name of the Lord Jesus Christ unto thy most holy name; and we ask thee to receive this our dedication and sanctify this altar to thy servants and handmaidens and that all those who come unto it may feel the power of the Holy Ghost resting upon them and realize the covenants they enter into upon this altar; unto this end we ask thee to dedicate, consecrate, and sanctify this holy altar that our covenants and contracts that we enter into with each other may be dictated by thy Holy Spirit and sacredly kept by us and accepted of thee, and all these blessings be realized by all thy saints who come unto this altar in the morning of the resurrection of the just, and all the glory, honor, praise and power be unto God and the Lamb, forever and ever. Amen and Amen.[171]

Mary Ellen Kimball left a description of her sealing to Heber C. Kimball as one of his many plural wives:

---

170. *History of the Church,* 7:566.

171. "Record of Sealings, Wives to Husbands [proxy], Nauvoo Temple," holograph, 2-3, LDS Church Archives.

I was sealed to Brother H[eber] C. Kimball ... in the temple.... I ... remember those
who knelt at the altar at the same time, and Sister Vilate Kimball placed each of
our hands in that of her husband's. Three of these sisters were wives of the
Prophet Joseph Smith. Harriet Saunders and myself were the only ones who were
to belong to H. [Heber] C. Kimball. One of those was Sarah Lawrence, another,
Sister [Martha McBride] Knight, the last, Sylvia P. Lyon.[172]

Sunday Lectures in the Temple

While the temple was in operation, those who had received the ordinances
gathered each Sunday between 14 and 28 December 1845 for instruction from
those who had been tutored by the Prophet. The speakers were usually members
of the Quorum of the Twelve and others who had received the endowment from
Joseph Smith. The content of these addresses, according to Andrew Ehat, a scholar of Nauvoo Temple teachings, is "our best window on just what the Prophet
Joseph Smith taught a favored few in sacred meetings held in his 'Red Brick Store,'
when he tutored the first temple workers of our dispensation during the last two
years of his life."[173]

Abraham O. Smoot, who attended one of these meetings, wrote in his journal that he "derived much profitable instruction" from attending the meeting on 21
December 1845.[174] Seventy-five people met in the east, or celestial, room. Invitees
included "all those who could clothe themselves in the garments of Priesthood."[175]
Because everyone who had been endowed was invited, the next week's meeting
was apparently larger. Clayton observed: "Meeting at half past 10 o clock this day
in the attic Story of the Temple.... A very large congregation was present, the side
rooms were some of them filled, the curtain was withdrawn and the other rooms
besides the east room were filled. About 200 persons were present, clothed in
priestly garments."[176]

---

172. Mary Ellen Kimball, Journal, 1838-63, holograph, 21, LDS Church Archives. John D. Lee left
another detailed account of a sealing at the altar: "[I], Louisa Free, Abigail Sheffer Rachel Woolsey,
and Caroline Williams went into room no. 1 where being clothed in Priestly apparel, kneeled over the
altar, rather before the Holy Altar and over it the sacred, the solemn covenant and sealing was
entered into and ratified in presence of three witnesses, President Brigham officiating at the altar."
Lee, Diary, 18-19.

173. Andrew E. Ehat, "'Who Shall Ascend into the Hill of the Lord?,' Sesquicentennial Reflections
of a Sacred Day: 4 May 1842," in Temples of the Ancient World (Salt Lake City: Deseret Book
Company, 1994), 61 note 4.

174. Smoot, Journal, 21 December 1845.

175. History of the Church, 7:548.

176. George D. Smith, An Intimate Chronicle, 238.

No meeting was held the following Sunday. William Clayton explained: The brethren feared that the "floor is not stiff enough to support so large a company as would have come in without swaying too much." Brigham Young decided: "We shall not be able to have another public meeting here on account of the weight on the floor, it has already caused the walls to crack, prevents the doors from shutting, and will injure the roof."[177]

At these meetings, those assembled partook of the sacrament, sang hymns, and prayed. The apostles then discussed several aspects of temple worship, and the importance of keeping the covenants of the endowment. William Clayton wrote an account in Heber C. Kimball's journal of the meeting on 21 December 1845, as edited by his daughter, Helen Mar Kimball Whitney:

> Elder George A. Smith arose and addressed the congregation. He thanked God for the privileges this day enjoyed.... Already had more than five hundred persons passed through, and therefore, if half of them should be like the foolish virgins and turn away from the truth, the principles of the Holy Priesthood would be beyond the reach of mobs and assaults of the adversaries of the Church....
>
> We are different from what we were before we entered into this quorum.— Speedy vengeance will now overtake the transgressor. When a man and wife are united in feeling, and act in union, I believe that they can hold their children by prayer and faith, and will not be obliged to give them up to death until they are fourscore years old. Sometimes men trifle with and destroy the confidence which they ought to have in the other, this prevents a union of faith and feeling. . . . The woman ought to be in subjection to the man—be careful to guard against loud laughter—against levity and talebearing....
>
> Elder [Heber C.] Kimball next addressed the meeting. He concurred in all that had been said, the observation of these things is most essential....You have not got all you will have if you are faithful. He spoke of the necessity of women being in subjection to their husbands. "I am subject to my God, my wife is subject to me and will reverence me in my place, and I will try to make her happy. I do not want her to step forward and dictate to me any more than I dictate to President Young. In his absence I take his place according to his request. Shall we cease from loud laughter?... Will you never slander your brother and sister? I will refer your minds to the covenants you have made by observance of these things you will have dreams and visions.... We shall not be with you long. We cannot rest day nor night until we put you in possession of the Priesthood.... If we have made you clean every whit, go now to work and make others clean...."
>
> Amasa [Lyman] addressed the assembly, he said, "Doubtless with most of the present assembly it is the beginning of a new era in their lives—they have come to a time they never saw before—they come to a commencement of a knowledge

---

177. Ibid., 253.

of things, and it is necessary that they should be riveted on their minds. One important thing to be understood is this, that those portions of the priesthood which you have received are all essential matters.

["]It is not merely that you may see these things, but it is a matter of fact, a matter that has to do directly with your salvation, for which you have talked and labored many years. It is not for amusement you are brought to receive these things, but to put you in possession of the means of salvation, and be brought into a proper relationship with God—hence a man becomes responsible for his own conduct and that of his wife if he has one. It is not designed that the things that are presented today should be forgotten tomorrow but be remembered and practiced though all coming life—Hence it is a stepstone to approach to the favor of God. Having descended to the lowest state of degradation, it is the beginning of a homeward journey; it is like a man lost in the wilderness, and the means with which we are invested are here are to direct us in our homeward journey. You see then the reason why you are required to put away your vanities, cease to talk of all those things which are not conducive to eternal life. This is why you are required to be sober, to be honest, that you could ask and receive, knock and it should be opened, and that when you sought for things you should find them. It is putting you in possession of those keys by which you can ask for things you need and obtain them. This is the key by which to obtain all the glory and felicity of eternal life. It is the key by which you approach God.

["]No impression which you receive here should be lost. It was to rivet the recollection of these things in your memory, like a nail in a sure place never to be forgotten. The scenery through which you have passed is actually laying before you a picture or map, by which you are to travel through life, and obtain an entrance into the celestial Kingdom hereafter. If you are tempted in regard to these things here, you will be tempted when you approach the presence of God hereafter. You have, by being faithful, been brought to this point, by maintaining these things which have been entrusted to you.... It is not merely for the sake of talking over these things that they are given to you, but for your benefit and for your triumph over the powers of darkness hereafter.

We want the man to remember that he has covenanted to keep the law of God, and the woman to obey her husband, and if you keep your covenants you will not be guilty of transgression. The line that is drawn is for you to maintain your covenants, and you will always be found in the path of obedience, after that which is virtuous and holy and good, and will never be swallowed up by unhallowed feelings and passions. If you are found worthy and maintain your integrity, and do not run away and think you have got all your endowment, you will be found worthy after a while, which will make you honorable with God. You have not been ordained to anything but will be by and by.

["]You have received these things because of your compliance with all the requisitions of the law, and if faithful you will receive more. You have now

learned how to pray. You have been taught how to approach God and be recognized. This is the principle by which the church has been kept together, and
not the power of arms. A few individuals have asked for your preservation, and
their prayers have been heard, and it is this which has preserved you from being
scattered to the four winds. Those who have learned to approach God and
receive these blessings, are they better than you? The only difference is they have
[been] permitted to have these things revealed to them.

["]The principles which have been opened to you are the things which ought
to occupy your attention all your lives. They are not second to anything; you have
the key by which, if you are faithful, you will claim on your posterity all the blessings of the Priesthood."[178]

In addition to these special lectures for the already endowed, more public
congregations also gathered in the temple for Sabbath worship. On Sunday, 22
February 1846, during the meeting held in the assembly room on the main floor,
"the room was crowded and a great weight caused the new truss floor to settle
nearly to its proper position; while settling, an inch board or some light timber
underneath was caught and cracked, the sound of which created great alarm in the
congregation."[179] Thomas Bullock recalled, "Some jumped up to the windows and
began to smash them. One fellow, Uriel Chittenden Nickerson, smashed through
the east window, jumped through and hurt his arm. He is a Strangite. Several other
windows were smashed and persons jumped out."[180] One attendee, Philo T.
Farnsworth "smashed the northeast window, while others ran out of the doors, and
many of those who remained jumped up and down with all their might crying 'Oh,
Oh, Oh!' as though they could not settle the floor fast enough. But at the same time
so agitated that they knew not what they did."[181] "For a few minutes there was a
stampede among the people. In their endeavor to get out of the building, some got
trampled on," recorded Thomas Bingham, age twenty-two.[182]

Brigham Young "attempted to call the assembly to order and to explain the
cause of the settling of the floor; but failing to get their attention, he adjourned the
meeting to the grove." He then went to the basement to examine the floor supports "and found that it had hardly settled to its designed position. He then passed

---

178. Whitney, "Scenes in Nauvoo and Incidents from H. C. Kimball's Journal," 34.

179. *History of the Church*, 7:594.

180. Knight, "Journal of Thomas Bullock," 53. *History of the Church*, 7:594, corroborates: "One man who jumped out of the window broke his arm and smashed his face; another broke his leg; both were apostates."

181. *History of the Church*, 7:594. Philo Taylor Farnsworth (1826-87) was baptized in 1843 and later served as a member of the Territorial Legislature in Utah.

182. Thomas Bingham, Autobiography, 1824-ca. 1889, typescript, 1, Perry Special Collections, Lee Library. Bingham (1824-89) was baptized in 1833 and later served in the Mormon Battalion.

on to the assembly in the grove, where the snow was about a foot deep, and told the people that they might jump up and down as much as they pleased."[183]

In addition to large-scale services like the one mentioned above, the temple was also used for smaller quorum and prayer meetings. Brigham Young's history on 25 February records that "companies of brethren—high priests, seventies, and elders—met in groups, almost daily, in the Temple to engage in prayer in behalf of the saints everywhere in the church. Especial prayer service was also frequently celebrated in the camps by appointment. Indeed, if one notices the frequency of prayer both in the camps and in the Temple, he is led to exclaim—If prayer can really serve its high purpose, then there was never a time like this in the church where the service of prayer was so constantly used, or more fervent appeals made to God for the deliverance of the saints!"[184]

Work Continues on the Temple

Although the attic story of the temple was swarming with ordinance workers and members eager to receive the endowment and other ordinances, finishing work on the temple, particularly the main floor and basement, continued. On 1 January, Brigham Young reported: "The plasterers have commenced to plaster the arched ceiling of the lower hall, the floor is laid, the framework of the pulpits and seats for the choir and band are put up; and the work of finishing the room for dedication progresses rapidly."[185]

Workmen nailed laths (thin strips of wood) close together on the wood structure of the rooms. They then mixed plaster (a compound of lime, water, and sand, sometimes with hair as a binder), which they applied to the laths. The lime for the plaster came from the same kilns as the lime in the temple mortar. George Patten, age eighteen in 1846, recalled, "My father being a plasterer by trade, I helped lath and mixed mortar to plaster the temple."[186] Priddy Meeks, an 1843 convert to the Church, was one of the workmen who carried plaster in hods from the mixing troughs to the plasterers' location.[187] Joseph Fielding wrote in his journal on

183. *History of the Church*, 7:594. Although Young reported that the floor had "hardly settled to its designed position," the settling did cause some damage. Thomas C. Sharp, "A Crash in the Temple," *Warsaw Signal*, 25 February 1846, 2, passed on the report of a witness, adding, "The crowd .... succeeded in escaping before any serious injury was done to the building. Our informant estimates the damage at from $500 to $1,000." This estimate must include the cost of the new windows, repairs to the plastering, and repainting.

184. *History of the Church*, 7:610.

185. *History of the Church*, 7:560.

186. George Patten, "George Patten," *Our Pioneer Heritage*, 7:256. Patten (1828-1914) was baptized 15 June 1843 in Nauvoo.

187. Dalton R. Meeks and Lenora Meeks, *The Life and Times of Dr. Priddy Meeks and His Progenitors* (Bountiful, UT: N.pub., 1996), 82. Meeks (1795-1886) was baptized 17 December 1843 in Nauvoo.

4 January that there were still "many hands ... employed in the lower parts of the temple."[188] On 8 January 1846, Lorenzo Brown, one of the workers, met with an accident:

> Whilst working on the scaffold in the lower room of the temple, the scaffold gave way and myself and five others were precipitated from a height of from 12 to 15 feet onto the floor beneath, among tools, timber, plank, etc. I was the only one that escaped injury. Jesse Haven fell by my side with a very heavy plank lying across him. I sprang to his relief, thinking him dead. He revived shortly after being taken into the air, but was badly hurt. Brother Josiah Perry struck on his feet and has never recovered their use.[189]

Work on the temple met another obstacle on 18 February when the workers went on strike due to a lack of pay. Samuel W. Richards recorded:

> Wednesday.... made a strike with the temple hands, because of the want of Provisions and clothing, as many were suffering.... T[ruman] O. Angel, the architect of the temple immediately visited the Trustees to lay before them the wants of the temple hands, and upon the pledge of their word, that all should be done in their power, to relieve the wants of the hands they again resumed their labours on the following morning.
> The 19th in the afternoon received a visit at the temple from the Trustees in connection with Brigham and Heber who spoke to the hands upon what had taken place. The result of which was that John Stiles was placed in the office, that there might be an equal distribution of provision and continued work and prayers through the week.[190]

Despite these minor setbacks, the finishing work moved ahead rapidly. On 15 January, the *Times and Seasons* printed the following status report:

> January, thus far, has been mild, which, in the midst of our preparations for an exodus next spring, has given an excellent time to finish the Temple. Nothing has appeared so much like a "finish" of that holy edifice as the present. The attic story was finished in December, and if the Lord continues to favor us, the first story above the basement, will be completed ready for meeting, in the month of February. The Font, standing upon twelve stone oxen, is about ready, and the

---

188. Ehat, "'They Might Have Known,'" 159.

189. Lorenzo Brown, Journal, Vol. 1: 1823-46, typescript, 15, Perry Special Collections, Lee Library.

190. Richards, Journal, 18 February 1846, typescript, 3.

floor of the second story is laid, so that all speculation about the Temple of God at Nauvoo must cease.[191]

On 30 January "the weathercock was today placed upon the steeple of the temple."[192] It was the final external feature added to the temple. According to William Weeks's plans, the vane was in the form of an angel about five feet long.[193] While human or angelic figures (frequently Gabriel) commonly appeared as weather vanes on houses of worship, the angel on the Nauvoo temple bore distinctly Mormon characteristics. Perrigrine Sessions wrote the most detailed contemporary description: "The vane ... is the representation of an angel in his priestly robe with the Book of Mormon in one hand and a trumpet in the other which is overlaid with gold leaf."[194]

Joseph Smith III remembered vividly the "gilded angel that swung at the top of the spire,"[195] and Thomas L. Kane spoke of "the gilding of the angel and trumpet on the summit of its lofty spire."[196] The unnamed 1853 visitor who wrote for the *Illinois Journal* noted that the angel was "composed of tin gilded."[197] This gilded appearance may have been achieved using gold leaf or gold foil which Amos Davis had purchased on behalf of the trustees in November.[198]

The Departure of the Twelve

On 24 January, Brigham Young called a meeting of the endowed Church members with the purpose of "arranging the business affairs of the Church, prior

191. "January," *Times and Seasons* 6 (15 January 1846): 1096. The speculation he referred to was probably related to Sidney Rigdon's purported prophecy that the temple would never be completed. The last issue of the *Times and Seasons* appeared on 15 February 1846, pursuant to the resolution of the October 1845 conference to cease publication.

192. Rogers, Journal, typescript, 47. According to *History of the Church*, 7:577, it was positioned at 9:00 a.m.

193. William Weeks, Architectural Sketches of the Nauvoo Temple, Drawing 2, holograph, LDS Church Archives. An unidentified visitor several years later thought the actual angel was twelve feet long. Unnamed visitor, *Illinois Journal*, 9 December 1853, reprinted as "Recollections of the Nauvoo Temple," in *Journal of the Illinois State Historical Society* 38 (December 1945): 482; photocopy in LDS Church Historical Department Library.

194. Sessions, Journal, entry made ca. 3 February 1846.

195. Anderson, *Joseph Smith III and the Restoration*, 100.

196. Thomas L. Kane, "The Mormons: A Discourse Delivered Before the Historical Society of Pennsylvania, March 26, 1850," quoted in Daniel Tyler, *A Concise History of the Mormon Battalion in the Mexican War, 1846-1847* (Chicago: Rio Grande Press, 1964), 81.

197. Unnamed visitor, *Illinois Journal*, 9 December 1853.

198. Amos David "Invoice of Goods by Amos Davis, November 2, 17, 1845," microfilm of holograph, Newel K. Whitney Papers, Perry Collections, Lee Library. For more information on this gilding technique, see chap. 9.

A concept drawing of the weather vane for the temple by William Weeks.

to the exit of the Saints from this place."[199] The meeting was held in the unfinished second story of the temple.[200] Of primary importance was the announcement that the Twelve and other high-ranking Church officials would depart from Nauvoo within a few weeks. During this council, Young nominated Almon W. Babbitt, Joseph L. Heywood, and John S. Fullmer trustees for building the temple, and Henry W. Miller and John M. Bernhisel trustees for the Nauvoo House. These men would take the place of Bishops George Miller and Newel K. Whitney, although their role would be chiefly to dispose of Church property. These nominations were seconded and carried unanimously.[201]

> President Young explained to the brethren the object of appointing Trustees, informed them that the Trustees would act in concert with Bishops Whitney and Miller while they remained in Nauvoo; and that when the Twelve left, the Bishops would accompany them and that the Trustees now appointed would carry on the finishing of the temple and the Nauvoo House, also dispose of the property of the Saints, fit them out and send them west wards. "It is wisdom to take this course," said the President, "That we may have efficient men to act for and in behalf of the Church and people. I want Bishops Whitney and Miller here while we are here, and when we go, they will go with us.
>
> "We intend to finish the Temple and the Nauvoo House as far as putting on the roof and putting in the windows are concerned and we shall drop all political operations and Church government, and by so doing we may preserve our public buildings from the torch. I propose that all the Saints lay down their prop-

199. Brigham Young, "From Brigham Young's History," Journal History, 24 January 1846, 1, 3.
200. Hosea Stout, Diary, 2:131.
201. Ibid.

erty to be used in building the Temple and the Nauvoo House, and helping the
poor away, such as must go in the first company."[202]

At some point late in January or early in February, the Twelve decided that
the first companies should leave Nauvoo on 3 February.

Although they were delayed a few days, the Twelve were among the first
to leave. Before leaving their beloved temple, they gathered as a group one final
time around the altar and offered a parting prayer, Brigham Young acting as voice.
He asked "for the Holy Spirit to rest upon all those who had received their endowments ... and asked for the privilege of returning and dedicating the other rooms of
the Temple in the Lord's due time, that the records of the Temple might be preserved, [and] that the Temple might not be polluted."[203]

Ordinance Work Ceases in Temple

As the day of the Twelve's departure approached, concern increased that
all who desired to participate in the endowment would have the opportunity. On
20 January, Brigham Young noted, "Public prejudice being so strong against the
Saints, and the excitement becoming alarming, the brethren determined to continue the administrations of the ordinances of endowment night and day."[204] After
two arduous weeks of labor administering the ordinances, Young and the Twelve
resolved to cease work in the temple on 3 February to prepare for their departure
that same day. Young later related the reaction of the Saints:

> Notwithstanding that I had announced that we would not attend to the adminis-
> tration of the ordinances, the House of the Lord was thronged all day, the anxi-
> ety being so great to receive, as if the brethren would have us stay here and con-
> tinue the endowments until our way would be hedged up, and our enemies
> would intercept us. But I informed the brethren that this was not wise, and that
> we should build more Temples, and have further opportunities to receive the
> blessings of the Lord, as soon as the saints were prepared to receive them. In this
> Temple we have been abundantly rewarded, if we receive no more. I also
> informed the brethren that I was going to get my wagons started and be off. I

---

202. *History of the Church,* 7:575-76.

203. "Minutes of the Quorum of the Twelve Apostles" in Anderson and Bergera, eds., *The
Nauvoo Endowment Companies 1845-1846,* 619. An alternative account was left by George A.
Smith: "On Saturday, January 8, 1846, met in council with the Twelve in the southeast corner room,
no. 1, in the upper story of the Temple. Kneeling around the altar, we dedicated the building to the
Most High, and asked His blessing upon our intended move to the west, and asked Him to enable
us, at some day, to finish the lower part of the Temple, and dedicated it to Him, and prayed that He
would preserve it as a monument to Joseph Smith" (George A. Smith, "My Journal," compiled and
edited by Elden J. Watson, typescript, 93, photocopy in my possession).

walked some distance from the Temple supposing the crowd would disperse, but on returning I found the house filled to overflowing.

Looking upon the multitude and knowing their anxiety, as they were thirsting and hungering for the word, we continued at work diligently in the House of the Lord.

Two hundred and ninety-five persons received ordinances [that day].[205]

No endowments were given on 4 and 5 February because Brigham Young and "some of the Twelve and others [were] starting for the west."[206] Helen Mar Kimball Whitney later recalled: "On the morning of the 4th the sun shone brightly into the east windows of the temple, where a new scene was being enacted. A number of persons were busily engaged removing articles of furniture, stoves, carpets and pictures."[207]

Samuel Richards recorded that, on 6 February, "the [ordinance] work commenced again as usual at which I continued without rest or sleep, until Sunday morn [8 February], about 4 o'clock, when I retired for rest. About 4 hours after I left the endowment was closed."[208] The last endowments were administered on 7 February. George Q. Cannon later recalled that "some of the last company, who did go through never got further than the Terrestrial Room."[209] Norton Jacob observed that "after the endowment stopped in the House of the Lord ... the walls [canvas partitions] were taken down."[210] According to Alexander Hale Smith, this canvas was "subsequently used for wagon covers, by the saints on their journey across the plains."[211]

The altar was taken down soon thereafter. John Taylor sealed Charles Lambert and Mary Alice Cannon in the temple "but not at the altar; it been taken down."[212]

Although Young and several of the Twelve left Nauvoo with the first company on 4 February, they set up camp only a few miles from the western shore of the Mississippi at Sugar Creek, and each made one or more return trips to Nauvoo for various reasons.

---

205. *History of the Church*, 7:579.

206. Warren Foote, Journal, 1817-1903, typescript, 75, Perry Special Collections, Lee Library.

207. Helen Mar Kimball Whitney, "Last Chapter of Scenes in Nauvoo," *Woman's Exponent* 12 (1 November 1883): 81.

208. Richards, Journal, Book 2, typescript, 2.

209. Quoted in St. George Temple Minute Book, 21 February 1889, "Confidential Research Files."

210. Norton Jacob, Journal, typescript, 29.

211. Quoted in Heman C. Smith, *History of the Reorganized Church of Jesus Christ of Latter Day Saints*, 7 vols. (Independence, MO: Herald House, 1903-14; second printing, 1967), 2:565.

212. Charles Lambert, Autobiography, 1816-83, typescript, 11, LDS Church Archives.

Fire in the Temple

On 9 February, at about 3:30 p.m. the roof of the temple caught fire. According to Thomas Bullock's terse account, which was the primary source for the account in *History of the Church*, some temple clothing "was being washed and dried in the upper room. The stove got over heated. The wood work caught fire."[213] John Steele, one of those who helped extinguish the fire, explained in his journal: "There was a great sensation caused by the sisters who had been washing out the floors. Brother James Houston was keeping fires in the stoves for them. They thought the floors did not dry fast enough to suit them, and wood was applied freely to the fires. One of them became red hot, ignited the shingles and all was soon in a blaze."[214]

When the temple bell rang to sound the alarm, Willard Richards "called on the brethren to search every house for buckets and bring them filled with water."[215] Through incredible mischance, simultaneously a large "ferry boat.... with two wagons, two yokes of oxen and about twenty people on board" began to sink in the Mississippi River. The combined effect of the fire and the river accident "created an unusual excitement. The people ran to the river and temple in confusion."[216]

"A line was immediately formed and the buckets passed up in quick succession. The fire raged about half an hour. Axes were set to work and tore up the roof. The water [was] thrown on the burning parts."[217] Samuel Bateman was among the first workmen to clamber onto the roof to attack the fire directly.[218]

Brigham Young, who saw the flames from a distance but was unable to reach the temple, resolved stoically, "If it is the will of the Lord that the Temple be burned, instead of being defiled by the Gentiles, Amen to it."[219] During the conflagration "some of the Troops tried to force their passage into the Temple but were prevented by the Brethren who stood in the door way."[220] When the flames were extinguished "by great and uncommon exertions," the fire had "burned from the

213. Knight, "Journal of Thomas Bullock," 49.

214. (No editor), "Extracts from the Journal of John Steele," *Utah Historical Quarterly* 6 (January 1933): 5-6.

215. Quoted in Knight, "Journal of Thomas Bullock," 47.

216. Hosea Stout, Diary, 2:143, 146. The passengers and animals aboard the boat survived although their vessel sank. Many of the passengers held tenaciously to the flotsam and floated ashore.

217. Knight, "Journal of Thomas Bullock, 47-49; see also *History of the Church*, 7:581.

218. "Samuel Bateman," Andrew Jenson, *LDS Biographical Encyclopedia*, 4 vols. (Salt Lake City: Greg Kotford Books, 2007), 1:590.

219. *History of the Church*, 7:581.

220. The troops were still attempting to arrest Brigham Young and others of the Twelve on various charges, including counterfeiting.

railing to the ridge about 16 feet North and South and about 10 feet East and West. The shingles on the north side were broken through in many places. The damage to that part is about 100 dollars but other damage was also done in the anxiety to put out the fire." The workmen on the deck roof "gave glory to God and shouted Hallelujah which made the air rejoice."[221] According to Henry Bigler, "the band played several times on the top of the temple."[222]

About a week later on 17 February, Thomas Bullock visited the temple and noted, "The burnt part of the roof of the Temple was this day relaid and covered over with lead. The plastering is not yet put on. Many persons came to see the Temple and go to the top of the tower."[223] Four days later, he observed, "The roof [ceiling] is not yet plastered where burnt."[224]

Truman O. Angell Replaces William Weeks

Prior to his departure in February, Brigham Young stated his intention to build a temple at their new destination and declared: "Just as soon as I find the spot I want Bro[ther] W[illia]m Weeks to dig deep and lay the foundation of the Temple for I intend by the help of my brethren to build a Temple unto the Lord just as soon as the Saints by a united exertion can complete it."[225] He instructed William Weeks to prepare to depart from Nauvoo to join the Twelve at the Sugar Creek camp in Iowa. Weeks obediently crossed the river on the morning of 27 February, arriving at Sugar Creek later that day.[226]

His replacement was Truman O. Angell, who had been serving as Weeks's "superintendent of joiner work." Angell, the brother of Brigham Young's second wife, Mary Ann Angell Young, recorded: "At the time when the first encampment of the brethren—the Twelve and others—left Nauvoo, William Weeks, the architect, was taken away with them. This left me to bring out the design and finishing of the lower hall which was fully in my charge from then on to its completion."[227]

---

221. Hosea Stout, Diary, 2:145; Knight, "Journal of Thomas Bullock," 49.

222. Henry W. Bigler, Journal, Book A, typescript, 14, Perry Special Collections, Lee Library.

223. Knight, "Journal of Thomas Bullock," 52.

224. Ibid., 53.

225. Charles Kelly, ed., *Journals of John D. Lee, 1846-47 and 1859* (Salt Lake City: Western Printing, 1938), 101.

226. Willard Richards, Journal, Vol. 13, 27 February 1846, holograph, LDS Church Archives, notes Weeks's arrival at about 2:00 p.m.

227. Truman O. Angell, "Truman O. Angell—Master Builder," in *Our Pioneer Heritage*, 10:200.

It was fitting that the chief joiner should be appointed to take charge because most of the remaining work was finishing work on the temple's interior. Furthermore, Angell had impressed the authorities with his previous work on the temple. Of his prior experience he stated: "God gave me wisdom to carry out the architect's designs which gained me the good will and esteem of the Brethren." His patriarchal blessing encouraged him in his endeavors as a builder: "Thy calling is more particularly to labor in assisting the Saints to build cities and temples than traveling abroad to preach the gospel."[228]

Angell's appointment was formalized on 13 February 1845, with this document of authorization: "I, William Weeks, by the authority vested in me by Joseph Smith and his Councilors, the Twelve, do appoint Truman Angell to be my successor as superintendent over the finishing of the Nauvoo Temple and Nauvoo House in the City of Joseph according to the plans and designs given to me by him and no person or persons shall interfere with him in the carrying out of these plans and designs." After Weeks's signature, Brigham Young appended his own authorization, dated and signed the same day: "I wish Br[other] T[ruman] O. Angell to carry out the design of the Temple and Nauvoo House."[229]

Expressions of Disappointment

While the majority of those who received the ordinances in the Nauvoo Temple counted it a privilege and a blessing, some few were disenchanted by the experience. Ebenezer Robinson, former editor of the *Times and Seasons*, felt that the newly revealed ordinances represented a shift from the Christian foundations of the Mormon religion. "Let the history and downfall of Nauvoo be a solemn warning to the members of the church of Christ," he wrote, "and let us be content with the simple and plain teachings and gospel of the Lord Jesus Christ."[230] Catherine

228. Ibid.; "Truman O. Angell, Sr.," Patriarchal blessing given by John Smith, 13 May 1845, in *Heart Throbs of the West,* 3:67.

229. William Weeks, Letter to Truman O. Angell, 13 February 1846, Truman O. Angell Correspondence, holograph, LDS Church Archives.

230. Ebenezer Robinson, "Items of Personal History of the Editor—Including Some Items of Church History Not Generally Known," *The Return* 2 (July 1890): 301. Abner Blackburn, who was eighteen in December 1845, recalled that the authorities "hunted up all the young bloods to give them their endowments, myself being about the last one on the docket and told me to come along. I said I had to help finish the endowment room and that I knew all about it. The man I worked with had been through the sacred apartments the day before, and I thought the endowments did not improve him very much. Therefore, the Elders of Israel hunted some other worthies." Abner Blackburn, Autobiography, 1827-51, typescript, 5, LDS Church Archives. Though he was not endowed, his exposure to the ordinances from arranging the rooms and perhaps from listening to the conversations of coworkers apparently led to this attitude of indifference.

Truman O. Angell supervised the final stages of work on the temple.

Lewis, a convert from Boston, received her endowment on 22 December. She recalled, "It seemed so frivolous to me."[231]

The most scathing denunciation of the endowment was written under the pseudonym of "Emeline" for the *Warsaw Signal* in April. "Emeline" called the ceremony a "laughable farce" and characterized those who administered it as

> vile, corrupt, licentious libertines, taking upon themselves the livery of Heaven, and essaying to represent the characters of our God and Savior— knowing those characters as I did previously to be the most debased wretches upon earth, the whole farce appeared to me to be nothing less than fearful blasphemy.
>
> In the different apartments of this singular farce, we took upon ourselves oaths and obligations not to reveal the secrets of the priesthood. I do not consider them binding; as I have had ample and repeated opportunity to prove the administrators of these obligations are corrupt as the Devil in Hell.[232]

---

231. Catherine Lewis, *Narrative of Some of the Proceedings of the Mormons* (Lynn, MA: Author, 1848), 9. Lewis was forty-six in 1845 when she was endowed.

232. Emeline (pseud.), "Mormon Endowments," *Warsaw Signal*, 15 April 1846, 2.

"Emeline" proceeded to detail the ceremony which she had promised to keep secret, much to the delight of editor Thomas Sharp who exulted that he had found a Mormon who was willing to "let the cat out of the bag."[233]

Another exposé was published by Increase and Maria Van Dusen, in 1847. They followed it up with six more, each increasingly caustic and sensational.[234] In an 1848 edition of their book, Increase Van Dusen stated:

> This Temple farce ... is a cunningly devised fable of a few designing wicked men, and is in magnitude in keeping only with other enterprises of this advanced age.... There are many things concerning this Fraternity that I as fully believe in as I did when I first went with them, and always shall ... but at the same time I have seceded, and am free to say, that I am set against the proceedings of the Mormons at Nauvoo.... My apology for writing this Temple Secret, is, that it tends to evil in the highest degree; and as I know many consequences of enormous magnitude, I have, after much reflection, written it out and published it, to prevent others going after it.[235]

Expressions of Satisfaction

The disappointed participants in the endowment quoted above were a tiny minority compared to the larger part of the Saints. Despite tremendous exertion, great personal loss, and intense persecution, most of those who participated in the building of the temple expressed joy and fulfillment upon obtaining the blessings of the endowment. On 6 December, Heber C. Kimball, writing in his journal, remarked thankfully, "Peace dwells here in the House of the Lord. We all feel to rejoice before the Lord that he in his kind providence has permitted his servants to finish the attic."[236] Erastus Snow wrote in his journal, "All felt satisfied that during

---

233. Thomas C. Sharp, "The Ceremony of the Endowment," *Warsaw Signal*, 18 February 1846, 2.

234. Increase McGee Van Dusen and Maria Van Dusen, *The Mormon Endowment; A Secret Drama, or Conspiracy, in the Nauvoo Temple, in 1846* (Syracuse, NY: N.M.D. Lathrop, printer, 1847); *Positively True. A Dialogue Between Adam and Eve, the Lord and the Devil, called the Endowment* (Albany, NY: C. Killmer, 1847); *The Sublime and Ridiculous Blended; Called, the Endowment* (New York: Author, 1848); *Startling Disclosures of the Great Mormon Conspiracy Against the Liberties of This Country: Being the Celebrated "Endowment"* (New York: Authors, 1849); *Startling Disclosures of the Wonderful Ceremonies of the Mormon Spiritual Wife System. Being the Celebrated "Endowment"* (New York: n.pub., 1850); *Spiritual Delusions being a Key to the Mysteries of Mormonism, Exposing the Particulars of That Astounding Heresy, the Spiritual Wife System, as Practiced by Brigham Young of Utah* (New York: Moulton and Tuttle, 1854); *Startling Disclosures of the Mormon Spiritual Wife System, and Wonderful Ceremonies of the Celebrated "Endowment"* (New York: n.pub., 1864).

235. Van Dusen and Van Dusen, *The Sublime and Ridiculous Blended*, 17.

236. Stanley B. Kimball, *On the Potter's Wheel*, 162.

the two months we occupied it in the endowments of the Saints, we were amply paid for all our labors in building it."[237]

George Q. Cannon, later when he was an apostle, attributed the success of the Church's subsequent migration and colonization to the blessings received in the Nauvoo Temple. Upon receiving the temple ordinances, the Saints "had a power they never possessed previously." He continued:

> Up to that period or up to the time that the temple was partly finished and the blessings of God bestowed within its walls, our enemies to a very great extent had triumphed over us. We had been driven from place to place; compelled to flee from one town, county and State to another; but how great the change since then! We started out a poor, friendless people, with nothing but God's blessing upon us, his power overshadowing us and his guidance to lead us in the wilderness; and from the day that we crossed the Mississippi river until this day ... we have had continued success and triumphs.
>
> Whence, I ask, my brethren and sisters, has this power come? Whence has it been derived? I attribute it to the blessings and the power and the authority and the keys which God gave unto his Saints, and which he commenced to give in the Temple at Nauvoo.[238]

Here are some journal entries and reminiscences from participants in the Nauvoo Temple endowment:

Sarah Pippen Jolley: My husband and boys worked on the temple until it was done. Many days they worked and had nothing to eat but corn bread and water, but it was good. I don't complain. I had the privilege of going through the temple with my husband, so I am paid for all my trouble.[239]

Joseph Lee Robinson: We were thankful to get so great blessings in that holy, holy House. Surely it was a very beautiful, inspiring House. It cost us oh so much labor and so much means, but we never regretted what we had done for we considered ourselves well and amply paid for all we had done. We counted it the Lord's House and we considered ourselves the Lord's also.[240]

---

237. Andrew K. Larsen, *Erastus Snow: The Life of a Missionary and Pioneer for the Early Mormon Church* (Salt Lake City: University of Utah Press, 1971), 96.

238. George Q. Cannon, 8 April 1871, *Journal of Discourses*, 14:125-26.

239. "Sarah Pippin Jolley," 1871, *Treasures of Pioneer History*, compiled by Kate B. Carter, 6 vols. (Salt Lake City: Daughters of the Utah Pioneers, 1952-57), 3:184. Sarah Dudley Pippin (1812-unknown) married Reuben Manning Jolley in 1829 and the two joined the Church together in 1842.

240. Joseph Lee Robinson, "History of Joseph Lee Robinson," typescript, 18, Perry Special Collections, Lee Library.

Sarah DeArmon Pea Rich: Many were the blessings we had received in the House of the Lord which has caused us joy and comfort in the midst of all our sorrows and enabled us to have faith in God knowing he would guide us and sustain us in the unknown journey that lay before us, for if it had not been for the faith and knowledge that was bestowed upon us in [the Nauvoo] temple by the influence and help of the Spirit of the Lord our journey would have been like one taking a leap in the dark.[241]

Matthias Cowley: The spirit of persecution got into the anti-Mormons of Illinois, and they were determined to drive the Saints from that state; but it was in the hearts of the Saints not to leave Nauvoo until they had finished the temple which the Lord commanded his people to finish.... We finished the Temple of the Lord, and received our endowments in it which repaid me for all the persecutions and privations that I had ever experienced.[242]

Helen Mar Kimball Whitney: At all events we intend to prove true to our integrity and hold to the sacred covenants and institutions which we know have been established by the Almighty, and are calculated to put mankind in possession of the means of salvation, temporal as well as spiritual, and to bring us into our proper sphere and relationship to God our Heavenly Father, and which has given to women as well as men the true key that can unlock the mysteries of the eternal worlds—bringing back to our recollection these glorious things which we lost remembrance of in coming down to this dark world as wanderers in the paths of darkness, ignorance and degradation. It teaches us to be virtuous, honest and upright—to subdue and bring into subjection our fallen natures, and requires us to put away our vanities and not indulge in anything which is low or that would be offensive to God or the celestial beings. These things were taught to us in that holy sanctuary, and ought to be riveted upon our minds and upon those of our children, so as to be remembered and lived up to in all coming life.[243]

Martha Pane Jones Thomas: To my posterity I will say, we esteemed it a privilege to work on the House of God and the Nauvoo House, which your father and Morgan [her oldest son] did, until it was finished. We were then called to the house to receive the blessings the Lord has in store for the faithful, which amply paid them for all their labors. Those days were grand and glorious.... The Saints then were in the depths of poverty, but we rejoiced in building the House of the Lord.[244]

241. Sarah DeArmon Pea Rich, *Reminiscence reprinted in Journey to Zion: Voices from the Mormon Trail*, edited by Carol Cornwall Madsen (Salt Lake City, Deseret Book, 1997), 177.

242. Matthias Cowley, "Journal of Matthias Cowley," 1829-53, typescript, 5, LDS Church Archives.

243. Whitney, "Scenes in Nauvoo and Incidents from H. C. Kimball's Journal," 14.

244. Martha Pane Jones Thomas, Autobiography, in *Daniel Stilwell Thomas Family History* (N.p., 1927), 30, copy in LDS Church Archives. Martha Pane Jones (1808ca.-1890) joined the Church in Kentucky in 1835 with her family. She married Daniel S. Thomas in 1826.

Wilford Woodruff. The Saints had labored faithfully and finished the temple and were now received as a Church with our dead. This is glory enough for building the temple and thousands of the Saints have received their endowment in it. And the light will not go out.[245]

---

245. Wilford Woodruff, 8 May 1846, *Wilford Woodruff's Journal, 1833-1898*, typescript, edited by Scott G. Kenny, 9 vols. (Midvale, UT: Signature Books, 1983-85), 3:46-47.

Chapter 12

Monument to a People: March 1846 to August 1848

Spiritual Manifestations in the Temple

Those privileged to attend meetings in the Nauvoo Temple during the winter of 1845-46 experienced an outpouring of spiritual manifestations in the temple similar to those that occurred earlier in the Kirtland Temple, though perhaps not in the same concentration. On 5 December, William Clayton wrote:

After the dancing had continued about an hour, several excellent songs were sung, in which several of the brethren and sisters joined. The "Upper California" was sung by Erastus Snow, after which I called upon Sister Whitney who stood up and invoking the gift of tongues, sang a beautiful song of Zion in tongues. The interpretation was given by her husband, Bishop Whitney, and me, it related to our efforts to build this house to the privilege we now have of meeting in it, our departure shortly to the country of the Lamanites, their rejoicing when they hear the gospel and of the ingathering of Israel.

I spoke in a foreign tongue; likewise, Brother Kimball.[1]

1. Quoted in Joseph Smith, Jr., et al., *History of the Church of Jesus Christ of Latter-day Saints*, edited by B. H. Roberts (Salt Lake City: Deseret News Press, 6 vols. published 1902-12, Vol. 7 published 1932, 1st printing), 7:557-58.

317

Clayton, writing in Heber C. Kimball's journal, commented: "Altogether, it was one of the most touching and beautiful exhibitions of the power of the Spirit in the gift of tongues which was ever seen."[2]

Even with the departure of the majority of the Twelve and the first companies of pioneers, many poor Church members and temple hands remained in Nauvoo. These members continued to use the temple as a meeting place for regular Sabbath services, quorum meetings, and other purposes, and on a few occasions, experienced similar exhibitions of spiritual gifts.

Samuel W. Richards summarized two of these meetings in his diary. On 1 March "at sundown [I went] to the temple, where we spent the evening in holy conversation, administering the sacrament, and speaking in other tongues, enjoying the blessings of the gospel, etc." Two weeks later, the small group experienced an outpouring of spiritual gifts. Richards recorded that "great blessings were enjoyed, tongues, prophesying, and the angels attended us. Their glory filled the house insomuch that many witnessed it throughout the city and testified thereof that it was the brightness of fire."[3] Thomas Bullock recorded more details of the same meeting:

> At sundown went to the Temple. 14 partook of the Sacrament after which we had a most glorious time. Some of the brethren spoke in tongues. Bro[ther] Z[ebedee] Coltrin and Brown held a talk in tongues which was afterwards interpreted and confirmed. Some prophesied. Bro[ther] [Miles] Anderson related a vision. And all of us rejoiced with exceeding great gladness. A light was seen flickering over Bro[ther] Anderson's head while relating his vision, Phineas Richards' face shone with great brightness. Two men arrayed all in priestly garments were seen in the northeast corner of the room. The power of the Holy Ghost rested down upon us. I arose full of the Spirit and spoke with great animation, which was very cheerfully responded to by all, and prophesied of things to come. A brother testified that our meeting was accepted of God. And we continued our meeting until after midnight, which was the most profitable, happy, and glorious meeting I had ever attended in my life, and may the remembrance be deeply rooted in my soul for ever and ever. Beautiful day.[4]

During the following two days, 16 and 17 March, Bullock recorded three reported viewings of the temple wrapped in spiritual flame:

2. George D. Smith, ed., *An Intimate Chronicle: The Journals of William Clayton* (Salt Lake City: Signature Books, 1995), 244.

3. Samuel W. Richards, Journal, Book 2, typescript, 5, L. Tom Perry Special Collections, Harold B. Lee Library, Brigham Young University, Provo, Utah.

4. Gregory R. Knight, ed., "Journal of Thomas Bullock, 31 August 1845 to 5 July 1846," *BYU Studies* 31 (Winter 1991): 61.

Last night Chester Loveland was called out of bed by his mother in Law stating that the Temple was again on fire. He dressed as quick as lightning and ran out of doors and saw the Temple all in a blaze. He studied a few seconds, and as it did not appear to consume any, and as there was no others running, he was satisfied it was the glory of God, and again went to bed. Another brother saw the belfry all on a fire at a 1/4 to 10. He ran as hard as he could, but when he came to the Temple he found all dark and secure.... Thus was the Spirit, power and glory to God manifest, not only at the Temple while we were there but also in our families for which my soul rejoices exceedingly.

[I also] heard that Uriel C. Nickerson (a Strangite) said that on Sunday night last the Temple was illuminated from the top of the Belfry to the ground and swore that he saw men passing back and forwards having candles in their hands and wanted to make the people believe that there was a visitation by angels, but they were the Mormons themselves. Thus has a Strangite born strong testimony of the glory of last Sabbath.[5]

Evidently Bullock reported these incidents to a group gathered in the temple on Wednesday evening, 18 March. Samuel Richards, after hearing Bullock's report, wrote: "It was testified that there had not been so great faith manifested at any time before, and was testified of by many without that the temple was filled with an exceeding bright light."[6] Nancy Alexander Tracy, who was in Nauvoo until the beginning of June, recollected a similar experience which she claims occurred toward the end of May:

I was aroused from my slumbers one night, hearing such heavenly music as I had never heard before. Everything was so still and quiet when it burst upon my ear that I could not imagine where it came from. I got up and looked out of the window. The moon shone bright as I looked over at the Temple from whence the sound came. There on the roof of the building heavenly bands of music had congregated and were playing most beautifully. The music was exquisite![7]

"A Farewell View"

Beginning with the departure of the first pioneer company on 4 February, a steady stream of Saints poured out of Nauvoo for several months. As the exiles

---

5. Ibid., 62.

6. Richards, Journal, Book 2, typescript, 6.

7. Nancy Naomi Alexander Tracy, Autobiography, 1816-85, 32, typescript, L. Tom Perry Special Collections, Harold B. Lee Library, Brigham Young University, Provo, Utah. Tracy's recollection of the date may be wrong, since she wrote her autobiography in 1885, many years after these events.

prepared for departure from Nauvoo, they frequently cast a sorrowful glance at their beloved temple.

In writing of her final days in Nauvoo, Nancy Alexander Tracy remembered the bitter grief of leaving "the Temple, our homes, and the pleasant surroundings and bid farewell. It was to your tents, O Israel."[8] Louisa Barnes Pratt, who departed from Nauvoo in May, recalled poignantly, "As I was passing down the streets of Nauvoo, I cast a lingering look at the beautiful temple. I felt inclined to say as the poor Jews said of Jerusalem, 'When I forget thee, Oh Nauvoo, let my right hand forget her cunning, if I prefer not thee above my chief joy.'"[9]

"In going from Nauvoo to Sugar Creek [in Iowa]," comments James A. Little, "a short distance from the ferry across the river, the road passes over a hill." This hill came to be recognized as "the last point from which [one] could see the Nauvoo Temple."[10] Thomas L. Kane drew on this geographical feature to stress the Saints' anguish at leaving their beloved city and temple: "From morning to night they passed westward like an endless procession. They did not seem greatly out of heart ... but at the top of every hill, before they disappeared, were to be seen looking back, like banished Moors, on their abandoned homes, and the far-seen temple and its glittering spire."[11]

Here are some journal entries and reminiscences that capture the emotions of the departing Saints as they viewed the temple for the final time:

Luman Shurtliff: I turned my back to the west and took a last look at the Nauvoo Temple and its surroundings and bade them goodbye forever.[12]

Margaret Jane McIntire Burgess: The morning we started on our journey to the Rocky Mountains although a child I had to look back on the beautiful temple of Nauvoo, it being built on a hill, I could see it plainly as we journeyed westward.[13]

---

8. Ibid., 32.

9. Louisa Barnes Pratt, "Journal of Louisa Barnes Pratt," *Heart Throbs of the West,* compiled by Kate B. Carter, 12 vols. (Salt Lake City: Daughters of the Utah Pioneers, 1947-51), 8:237.

10. James A. Little, *From Kirtland to Salt Lake City* (Salt Lake City: Juvenile Instructor Office, 1890), 46.

11. Thomas L. Kane, "The Mormons: A Discourse Delivered Before the Historical Society of Pennsylvania, March 26, 1850," quoted in Daniel Tyler, *A Concise History of the Mormon Battalion in the Mexican War, 1846-1847* (Chicago: Rio Grande Press, 1964), 82.

12. Luman Shurtliff, "Biographical Sketch of the Life of Luman Andros Shurtliff," typescript, 66, Perry Special Collections, Lee Library.

13. Margaret Jane McIntire Burgess, quoted in Margaret V. Burgess McMurtie, "Sketch of Margaret Jane Mcintire (Burgess), Pioneer of 1849-1861," typescript, 2, Perry Special Collections, Lee Library.

The temple on the hill.

Wilford Woodruff: I left Nauvoo for the last time perhaps in this life. I looked upon the Temple and City of Nauvoo as I retired from it and felt to ask the Lord to preserve it as a monument of the sacrifice of his Saints.[14]

Samuel W. Richards: As I cast my eyes upon the City of Joseph from which the saints were exiled, and the temple of the Lord, upon which I had laboured so long, I felt that the saints had done a great work in a short time, and that it was accepted of the Lord.[15]

Priddy Meeks: While crossing over a ridge seven miles from Nauvoo we looked back and took a last sight of the Temple we ever expected to see. We were sad

14. Wilford Woodruff, 22 May 1846, *Wilford Woodruff's Journal, 1833-1898*, typescript, edited by Scott G. Kenny, 9 vols. (Midvale, UT: Signature Books, 1983-85): 3:49.

15. Richards, Journal, Book 2, 22.

and sorrowful. The emotions of our mind at the time I cannot describe. The thoughts of it almost disqualified me for writing although many years have passed away since that time.[16]

Jesse Crosby: [On] May 26, 1846, we ascended the bluffs, and some six miles from Nauvoo, we found ourselves on a high and sightly place where we had a most splendid view of the temple and almost every house in Nauvoo. This was a farewell view.[17]

John R. Young:
> The silvery note of the temple bell
> That we loved so deep and well:
> And a pang of grief would swell the heart
> And the scalding tears in anguish start
> As we silently gazed on our dear old homes.[18]

Lewis Barney: We camped on Sugar Creek, eight miles west of Nauvoo ... in sight of our own homes that were now in the hands of our persecutors. Our women and children trailing from one wagon to another knee deep in snow, many times nearly frozen to death.

At the end of three weeks we rolled out and set our faces westward trusting in the providences of Almighty God for our deliverance.

On reaching the summit between the Mississippi and Des Moines Rivers the company made a halt for the purpose of taking a last and peering look at the Nauvoo Temple, the spire of which was then glittering in the bright shining sun. The last view of the temple was witnessed in the midst of sighs and lamentations, all faces in gloom and sorrow bathed in tears, at being forced from our homes and Temple that had cost so much toil and suffering to complete its erection.[19]

Joseph Stratton, one of the temple hands who remained in Nauvoo until May to help complete as much of the temple as possible, recorded his last visit to the temple in his diary on 4 May:

Was passing by the temple at about 10 p.m. It was a most beautiful moonlight night and all was still. I walked around and contemplated that great building. My feelings were peculiar; I perceived a watchman at the door. I spoke, he knew me,

---

16. Priddy Meeks, Autobiography, 1812-86, microfilm of holograph, LDS Church Archives.

17. Jesse Wentworth Crosby, "The History and Journal of Jesse W. Crosby," 1820-69, typescript, 30, Perry Special Collections, Lee Library.

18. John R. Young, Memoirs of John R. Young, *Utah Pioneer 1847* (Salt Lake City: Deseret News Press, 1920), 14-15.

19. Lewis Barney, "History of Lewis Barney, typescript, 27-28, Perry Special Collections, Lee Library.

he very kindly lit a lantern and took me in to view the great room in the night. After looking over it I requested to be left alone a short time, which was granted. I bowed down before the Lord and poured out my soul in fervent prayer before him, and then came into my mind many who had desired me to pray for them, even in other lands. I felt well. Oh, Lord God of Israel, hasten the day when thy Saints shall have a house to worship thee in, upon the mountains.[20]

James Ferguson, who visited the deserted temple in late autumn 1846, penned these comments on the desolate structure:

I stood by the font ... but it was empty. It seemed but an urn that held the cold dead ashes of what had been.

I hurried from room to room in search of something, I knew not what, to cheer me up, but everywhere I met with disappointment. The altars where many a sacred vow had been pledged, were torn down or had vanished. The anointing oil had been removed. The veil of emblems had been folded away. The voice of praise was hushed. I withdrew, my spirit crushed and despondent.[21]

Work on the Temple through April

Almon W. Babbitt, Joseph L. Heywood, and John S. Fullmer, the trustees Brigham Young had appointed on 24 January 1846, were responsible for seeing that the workmen under Truman O. Angell had the resources necessary to complete the temple. Work on the Nauvoo House had been abandoned as resources and manpower diminished. On 9 March Brigham Young "wrote to the trustee[s] at Nauvoo ... that Brothers [Alpheus] Cutler and [Reynolds] Cahoon [of the Temple Committee] should roll out with their companies as quick as possible. The Twelve also wrote Orson Hyde to stay at Nauvoo and dedicate the Temple if the Twelve did not return."[22] Brigham Young had actually announced in late 1845 his intention to dedicate the temple on 6 April 1846, the Church's anniversary. Now he assigned that mission to Hyde.[23]

---

20. Joseph Albert Stratton, "Diary of Joseph A. Stratton," 1821-1850, microfilm of holograph, LDS Church Archives. Despite the title, this work is actually an autobiography. Stratton (1821-50) was baptized in 1840.

21. James Ferguson, *Liahona*, 20 January 1914, quoted in E. Cecil McGavin, *The Nauvoo Temple* (Salt Lake City: Deseret Book Company, 1962), 304-5. Ferguson was baptized in 1842.

22. Willard Richards, Journal, quoted in Journal History of the Church of Jesus Christ of Latter-day Saints (chronology of typed entries and newspaper clippings, 1830-present), 9 March 1846, 1, LDS Church Archives.

23. Brigham Young, "To the Brethren of the Church of Jesus Christ of Latterday Saints throughout the World," *Times and Seasons* 6 (1 November 1845): 1019.

During late February and March, the temple hands, working feverishly toward the 6 April deadline, concentrated on the first floor assembly hall and the basement. One important task that remained was to paint parts of the finished hall. A purchase order in the Temple Committee records dated 21 February 1846 shows the purchase of linseed oil, turpentine, and lead which were mixed to make paint for the hall.[24]

At some point during March, painters added the following inscription to the east wall of the main assembly hall:

THE LORD HAS BEHELD OUR SACRIFICE
COME AFTER US[25]

According to one visitor, this inscription was painted "in a circular line corresponding to the circle of the ceiling."[26]

This message would have meant different things to different people. While it may have beckoned Mormon immigrants, arriving in Nauvoo after the departure of the main body of the church, to follow their fellow saints into the wilderness, a more likely interpretation is suggested by the circumstances.

The inscription may also have been intended as a taunt, both to men such as James J. Strang and Sidney Rigdon who claimed the Church had been rejected for not finishing the temple ("The Lord has beheld [or accepted] our sacrifice") and to anti-Mormons who wished to see the Saints driven from Illinois ("Come after us").

Another important finishing touch was the laying of a brick floor in the basement. William Mendenhall, a bricklayer, began on 20 March to lay the "brick pavement of the temple" and completed the work on 4 April.[27] Archeological research revealed that the bricks were laid in a herringbone pattern.[28] The *Hancock Eagle* commented approvingly on the new floor: "The appearance of the basement hall, in the midst of which stands the baptismal font, has been entirely changed by a laborious use of the trowel, and the 'animals' now show to great advantage in contrast with the tiled floor."[29]

24. Nauvoo Temple Committee Records, Carpenter's Daybook K, 21 February 1846, holograph, LDS Church Archives.

25. Charles Lanman, *A Summer in the Wilderness* (Philadelphia, N.pub., 1847), 31-33.

26. J. H. Buckingham, Letter to Boston Courier, 18 July 1847, reprinted in Harry E. Pratt, ed., "Illinois As Lincoln Knew It," *Papers in Illinois History and Transactions for the Year 1937* (Springfield, II: N.pub., 1938), 171.

27. William Mendenhall, Diary, 1846, entries for 20, 21, 23, 24, and 25 March and 1, 2, 3, and 4 April, microfilm of holograph, LDS Church Archives.

28. Virginia S. Harrington and J. C. Harrington, *Rediscovery of the Nauvoo Temple* (Salt Lake City: Nauvoo Restoration, Inc., 1971), 23.

29. William E. Matlack, "The Temple in the Market," *Hancock Eagle* 1 (8 May 1846): 2.

Despite the valiant efforts of the workers to have the temple ready to be dedicated at April conference, there was still a tremendous amount of work left to do by the end of March. On 27 March, Orson Hyde wrote Brigham Young, then camped on the banks of the Chariton River in Iowa: "The temple will not be finished to dedicate on the sixth of April."[30] An alternate dedication date was chosen, and notices about the dedication—now scheduled to occur on 1 May—began to appear in the *Hancock Eagle* as early as April 10.[31]

On Wednesday, 1 April 1846 the Saints gathered again in the temple. According to Samuel Richards's account: "In the evening had an excellent time in the temple. Brother [Charles] Patten and Brother [William] Anderson with their women at the Quorum, all of them (there being six) were anointed for their infirmities and two children blessed. The sacrament was administered, and we had an interesting time."[32]

Five days later, general conference began. The brick flooring in the basement had just been finished, and the weather was so "stormy," that only a "few met at conference in the underground room of the temple."[33] Isaac Haight added: "The workmen were ... painting the lower rooms so the conference could not meet in the upper part of the temple and the day is so rainy we cannot meet in the grove."[34] Completing the temple was so urgent that the workmen did not attend general conference sessions but instead continued their work on these rooms. Jesse Harmon was among those who "had charge of finishing the work on the temple at Nauvoo."[35]

On the third day, 8 April, the weather cleared; and the congregation assembled out of doors. According to the *Hancock Eagle*, the object of the "grand Mormon conference ... now in session at the Temple ... is to wind up the affairs of the church in this region."[36] In fact, a major item of business was the conference's ratification of the Twelve's decision to dispose of Church property in Nauvoo:

> Brothers Almon R. Babbitt, Joseph L. Heywood and John S. Fullmer, were separately presented and received by vote, as trustees of the Church. A resolution was then adopted by the conference giving the trustees power to dispose of by deed

30. Orson Hyde, Letter to Brigham Young, quoted in Journal History, 27 March 1846, 5.

31. William E. Matlack, "Dedication of the Temple of God in the City of Nauvoo," *Hancock Eagle* 1 (10 April 1846): 3.

32. Samuel W. Richards, Journal, Book 2, 4, 9.

33. Ibid., 12.

34. Isaac Haight, Journal, 1813-62, 30, typescript, Perry Special Collections, Lee Library.

35. Jesse Harmon, Autobiography, in "Autobiographies of Early Seventies," typescript, 33, LDS Church Archives.

36. William E. Matlack, "Mormon Conference," *Hancock Eagle* 1 (8 April 1846): 3.

or otherwise, all the property belonging to the Church, both real and personal, excepting the two Temples, one in Ohio and the other in this city, (with power to rent the same for a term of years not exceeding twenty). Then voted that proceeds go to the payment of church debts, and the removal of this people.[37]

Samuel Richards recorded that, on 22 April, he "was at the temple to complete the joiner work which was done."[38] Jesse Crosby confirmed that "the works on the temple ceased April 23, 1846; that is, the joiner work. The painters and masons continued a few days longer."[39]

Probably one of the masonry projects still being worked on was completing the flight of stairs leading to the main entrance. On 24 April, the *Hancock Eagle* reported: "The immense doorways are gained by a flight of stone steps."[40] British convert George Morris later recorded in his autobiography that he and Peter Ofine "laid the flight of stone steps in the front of the temple," explaining that it was "the last work I done."[41] Samuel Richards's diary for the last week of April describes his final work in the temple:

Thursday, April 23rd. Met with the workmen at the temple, and swept out the house ... By request of Brother J. K. Nichols (the overseer of the painting), in the p.m. I commenced painting in the lower room of the temple to prepare it for the dedication.

Wednesday, 29th. Painting in the temple until 10 o'clock ... dancing until near midnight. The other hands completed the painting of the lower room.

Thursday, 30th. Spent most of the day at the temple sweeping out the rooms and making preparation for the dedication of the House.... This day finished my work on the temple and took a certificate of the same.[42]

After the workers had finished, the *Hancock Eagle* commented:

For two or three months past a strong force has been at work upon the interior night and day, and the greatest exertions have been made by the Mormons to complete it within a given time, that it might be dedicated before the period assigned for their removal....

37. Samuel W. Richards, Journal, Book 2, 12.

38. Ibid., 16.

39. Jesse W. Crosby, Journal, 1820-59, typescript, 30, Perry Special Collections, Lee Library.

40. William E. Matlack, "Public Buildings," *Hancock Eagle* 1 (24 April 1846): 2.

41. George Morris, Autobiography, 1816-91, typescript, 34. Perry Special Collections, Lee Library. Morris (1816-97) was baptized on 28 June 1841 in England and immigrated to Nauvoo in 1842.

42. Samuel W. Richards, Journal, Book 2, 16-18.

The Temple is now considered as finished. We were surprised, on inspecting it a few days ago, to perceive how much has been accomplished in a month.[43]

Apostle Wilford Woodruff returned to Nauvoo from England, arriving 13 April. While still downriver on the boat, he viewed the nearly completed temple and recorded his impressions in his journal: "At about 2 o'clock, we started to ascend the rapids. In about two hours we came in sight of the splendid temple built by the Latter Day Saints and also the city of Nauvoo. I immediately got my spy glass and examined the city. The temple truly looked splendid."[44]

Plight of the Workers

Some of the workers who remained in Nauvoo to help finish the temple, such as Truman O. Angell and Orson Hyde, were specifically assigned to that task. Others simply did not have sufficient funds to purchase provisions for the exodus because the cost of the anticipated overland journey was greater than the resale value of their property. Although money in the temple account was scarce, these workers hoped to earn some funds for the journey by their work.

Although financial records for that time are sketchy, it is clear that the tremendous cost of outfitting the companies of travelers all but emptied Church coffers. The Twelve and the trustees hoped that through the sale of Church property, they would be able to provide means for the poor to make the journey. Unfortunately, the trustees found it difficult to dispose of the property and were forced to devise other means to raise the money. As one example, the Nauvoo Brass Band organized "a grand concert of vocal and instrumental music" performed in the Nauvoo Concert Hall on 17 January 1846. It was such a decided success that it was repeated for large crowds three nights in a row. Proceeds from the last evening were earmarked "for the benefit of the Temple hands," but there is no record of how much was taken in.[45] In any case, these funds, acquired in mid-January, had probably been expended long before early April, when matters reached something of a crisis.

When it became clear that the trustees had not managed to sell much property, the "temple hands convened" on 4 April "and accepted a proposition from Brother Hyde" by which they "agreed to take half their wages if paid the cash and sacrifice the other half to the Church."[46]

---

43. Matlack, "The Temple in the Market," 2.

44. Woodruff, Journal, 3:38.

45. "An Interesting Record," *The Contributor* 1 (June 1880): 196-97.

46. Samuel W. Richards, Journal, Book 2, 10, 17.

Even under this new arrangement, the trustees feared that they would be unable to find enough cash. On 10 April, they announced that they would charge one dollar for admittance to the public dedication on 1 May with the avowed object "to raise funds to enable the workmen who have built the temple to remove with their families, and all who are disposed to see the Mormons remove in peace and quietness so soon as circumstances will allow, (which is the earnest desire of every Latter-day Saint) are respectfully invited to attend."[47]

Toward the end of April, the trustees further proposed that the workers take lumber as payment instead of cash. This caused, as Samuel W. Richards put it, "considerable dissatisfaction among the temple hands."[48] Their dissatisfaction was understandable, since their ability to move their families to safety depended on their ability to pay for goods and services. By working full-time on the temple, they were unable to find other work or even make preparations for the journey. On 28 April, Truman Angell wrote a letter "expressing the feelings of the hands in relation to that matter."[49] The trustees fell back on hoping for a good turnout at the dedicatory service and better prospects of selling Nauvoo property. The night before the dedication, they reminded the workers that the receipts from the ticket sales to "those who would pay $1 for admittance" would "go on payment of the T[emple] hands."[50]

Following the dedication, the receipts were gathered and tallied, probably exceeding $3,000.[51] The next day, Samuel W. Richards, "went to the Trustees office and settled for my work, and found them in debt to me ... thirty-four dollars and ninety six cents, of which I was to receive seventeen dollars and forty-eight cents, in cash according the previous arrangements made on the 4th of April with the temple hands."[52] But despite this small amount, Richards was one of the fortunate ones. The other workmen received less than half of their promised wages. George Morris recalled that Orson Hyde called the temple workmen together early in May

> to see if they would be willing to consecrate 2/3 of the wages that was owing them if he could succeed in raising enough money to pay them the balance, which we all readily consented to do. He with assistance of others succeeded in

47. "The Trustees in [T]rust" (Joseph Heywood, John Fulmer, and Almon Babbit), "Dedication of the Temple of God in Nauvoo," *Hancock Eagle* 1 (19 April 1846): 3.

48. Ibid.

49. Samuel W. Richards, Journal, Book 2, 17.

50. Samuel W. Richards, Journal, 30 April 1846, Book 2, 18.

51. The hall could seat over 4,000, and the hall was probably filled almost to capacity. Presumably, the workers who attended were not required to pay since the affair was for their benefit.

52. Ibid., 25.

raising the money and paid us accordingly. I received 3 gold sovereigns which made me feel like I was pretty rich as I had never before, all put together received to the amount of five dollars in cash for my labor in the 4 years and 4 months I had lived in Nauvoo.[53]

Despite the trustees' efforts, matters did not improve. On 26 June, John Fullmer wrote Brigham Young: "Our means are running so low that unless we can sell the Temple we shall not be able to meet all demands and help the poor away. I hope that God will favor the project, for I do assure you that Nauvoo is becoming anything but desirable."[54]

The Private Dedication of the Temple

Although portions of the temple such as the baptismal font and the attic had been previously dedicated, the temple as a whole had not. The final dedication took place in two stages: a private dedication on 30 April followed by a public dedication on 1 May. Endowed workers met for prayer in the temple's attic on the evening of 30 April. After prayer, they "repaired to the lower room for the purpose of dedicating [the Temple]." Vested in their white robes, they formed a prayer circle "immediately in front of the Melchizedek stand." There were between twenty and thirty of the "noble Elders of Israel present."[55] Joseph Young offered a dedicatory prayer, after which the men took their seats in the stands according to the offices they held in the priesthood. Samuel Richards, for instance, sat in the teachers' stand. Orson Hyde then offered another prayer of dedication.[56] Although no text for these prayers has survived, the substance of Joseph Young's prayer was captured in Brigham Young's history:

> [Joseph Young dedicated] the Temple, and all that pertained thereto to the Lord, as an offering to Him as an evidence of the willingness of His people, to fulfill His commandments, and build His holy house, even at the risk of their lives, and the sacrifice of all their labor and earthly goods. He prayed for the Twelve and all the

53. Morris, "Autobiography, 40-41.

54. John Fullmer, Letter to Brigham Young, 26 June 1846, Journal History, 6 July 1846, 1-2.

55. Woodruff, Journal, 3:41. Those known to have attended include Orson Hyde, Wilford Woodruff, W. W. Phelps, John W. Young, Joseph Young, Phineas H. Young, John M. Bernhisel, Joseph L. Heywood, and Samuel W. Richards. Elden J. Watson, ed., 30 April 1846, *Manuscript History of Brigham Young 1846-1847* (Salt Lake City: Elden Jay Watson, 1971), 147-48.

56. Whether Young's prayer or Hyde's prayer was the "official" dedicatory prayer is unknown. Samuel Richards's contemporary journal indicates that Hyde dedicated, while Brigham Young's account is secondhand.

authorities of the Church, and for the workmen that had wrought upon the Temple in the midst of persecution, want, and suffering, and for the deliverance of the poor; that the Lord would direct the brethren of the Camp of Israel, open the way before them and lead them to a place of His own appointment for the gathering of all the Saints. [He also prayed] that God would avenge the blood of His servants the Prophets and of the Saints who had been slain for the testimony of the truth and mete out to our enemies the same measure which they had meted out to us.[57]

After the prayers, those present responded "Amen," then shouted "Hosanna, Hosanna, Hosanna, to God and the Lamb, Amen, Amen, and Amen" three times, according to the pattern established at the dedication of the Kirtland Temple and repeated at the laying of the capstone.[58] Orson Hyde described these events a few days later at one of the public dedicatory services: "While the earth was wrapped in the mantle of darkness, the priesthood arrayed in prayer asking their Father to accept of the building. The glory of the Lord shone throughout the rooms in matchless splendor, of the order of Celestial things. He said that they were like unto rays of the sun emulating from every side."[59]

At the private dedication, Orson Hyde addressed the small gathering, prophesying "that inasmuch as we had built a temple and was now by Government compelled to sacrifice it by leaving it, at the end of five years the general Government should be as bad off as we then was as a people."[60] At the meeting's end, Hyde dismissed the participants to the attic where they "enjoyed a feast of raisins, cakes, and wine."[61] At midnight they dispersed, deciding to meet again in the attic at 2:00 p.m., following the public dedication. Wilford Woodruff "returned home thankful for the privilege of assisting in the dedication of the Temple of the Lord."[62]

The Public Dedication of the Temple

The public dedication was held the following morning. Nearly two weeks earlier, on 10 April, the trustees had announced the dedication in the *Hancock Eagle*:

---

57. Watson, 30 April 1846, *Manuscript History of Brigham Young*, 148.

58. Samuel W. Richards, Journal, Book 2, 23; *History of the Church* 2:427-28. See also chap. 8.

59. James Allen Scott, Diary, 3 May 1846, 8, microfilm of holograph, LDS Church Archives.

60. Samuel W. Richards, Journal, Book 2, 23.

61. Ibid., 19.

62. Woodruff, Journal, 3:41.

DEDICATION OF THE TEMPLE OF GOD IN NAUVOO

This splendid edifice is now completed, and will be dedicated to the MOST HIGH GOD on Friday, the 1st day of May, 1846. The services of the dedication will continue for three days in succession, commencing on each day at 11 o'clock A.M. Tickets may be had at the watch house near the door of the Temple, and also at the office of the Trustees in trust at $1 each.[63]

On Saturday, 1 May, the services commenced as scheduled, at 11:00 a.m. in the assembly hall on the first floor.[64] In a gesture of good will toward the impoverished temple hands, Wilford Woodruff purchased seven tickets for himself and several members of his family.[65] Many of the workmen attended with their families. Samuel W. Richards was "one of three who was appointed to seat the congregation, in the house and stood part of the time at the door to receive tickets."[66]

Thomas Kane reported the rumor that some of the "Elders of the sect traveled furtively from the camp of Israel in the wilderness, and, throwing off ingenious disguises, appeared in their own robes of holy office, to give it splendor."[67] Wandle Mace corroborated that "each one [of the endowed members] present was arrayed in priestly robes, and thus in proper order the temple was dedicated."[68]

The program began with a hymn by the choir, accompanied by an instrumental group, to which James Allen Scott listened "with peculiar feelings being seated in a house built by the express order of and being about to be dedicated to God. Differing from all others in the world."[69] Wilford Woodruff offered the opening prayer, the choir sang another hymn, and Orson Hyde, after making a few remarks, offered the following dedicatory prayer:

> Holy and Everlasting Father, before Thee this morning we present ourselves and acknowledge Thy mercy that has been extended to us since we have been on

63. The Trustees in Trust, "Dedication of the Temple of God in Nauvoo," 3.

64. Scott, Diary, 3 May 1846, 8.

65. Woodruff, Journal, 3:42.

66. Samuel W. Richards, Journal, Book 2, 24.

67. Kane, "The Mormons," 82. Kane described the dedication: "Then at high noon, under the bright sunshine of May, the next [day] only after its completion, they consecrated it to divine service. There was a carefully studied ceremonial for the occasion.... For that one day the temple stood resplendent in all its typical glories of sun, moon, and stars, and other abounding figured and lettered signs, hieroglyphs, and symbols."

68. Wandle Mace, Autobiography, 1809-90, typescript, 197, Perry Special Collections, Lee Library. Mace continued: "On this occasion a man had the garments but did not know how to clothe himself, [and] asked me to help him. I inquired, 'Have you had your endowments?' He answered, 'No.' He was in a manner speechless, he had to retire."

69. Scott, Diary, 1 May 1846, 7.

Thy footstool, and for this opportunity of dedicating this house. We thank Thee that Thou hast given us strength to accomplish the charges delivered by Thee. Forgive us our sins and the sins of thy people. Thou hast seen our labors and exertions to accomplish this purpose. By the authority of the Holy Priesthood now we offer this building as a sanctuary to Thy Worthy Name. We ask Thee to take the guardianship into Thy hands and grant that Thy Spirit shall dwell here and may all feel a sacred influence on their hearts that His Hand has helped this work. Accept of our offering this morning, and that soul that blesses this temple let blessings rest on his posterity to the latest generation, and that soul that shall practice evil against this temple and Thy House, set Thy face against him and let evil take the portion of his inheritance. Administer to Thy people and let Thy honor and glory fall on our heads, not in the eyes of men but in the day when the world shall become Thy dominion. May we have the honor to tune the lyre that Thou hast redeemed us from every nation and made us holy and pure and that we have washed our robes and made them white in the blood of the Lamb. It must needs be that offences come, we offer it as the fruit of our labors and may the oppression under which we groaned be to our good. We ask that the angel of mercy may be round about this temple and that light may descend upon us and let us pass to the courts of the heavenly. Let Thy Spirit rest upon those who have contributed to the building of this temple, the laborers on it that they may come forth to receive kingdoms and dominions and glory and immortal power. Accept of us we pray Thee, inspire every bosom to do Thy will, cause that truth may lead them for the glorious coming of the Son of God, when you come in the name of the King, the Lord of Hosts shall be the King. Gather us in Thy Kingdom through Jesus Christ our Lord, Amen.[70]

After the prayer, Almon Babbitt addressed the congregation for about an hour and a half. He reminded his listeners that the temple "was reared by the express order of God which if fulfilled would bring blessings upon their builders, but if not, they with their dead friends should be rejected." He "spoke of the necessity of a strict observation of every requirement of law, as the slightest deviation would forfeit the blessings thereof." He also looked forward to the "splendour and magnificence of the Lord's House that would be reared upon the mountain tops."[71] After Babbitt's address, Hyde adjourned the meeting until Sunday.[72]

The meeting ended between 1:00 and 2:00 p.m. The temple workmen then met in the attic, according to plan. Orson Hyde distributed cake and wine, a por-

---

70. Woodruff, Journal, 3:42.

71. Scott, Journal, 1 May 1846, 8.

72. Ibid. Scott is specific that the services were adjourned until Sunday, 3 May, even though services had been announced for 1, 2, and 3 May. Matlack, "Dedication of the Temple of God," 3. I have found no record of a meeting on Saturday, 2 May; and even assiduous diary-writers such as Wilford Woodruff mention no temple-related meetings on Saturday, although accounts of the Friday and Sunday sessions abound.

tion of which they carried home to their wives. Later in the evening, Hyde invited a few workmen to attend a dance in the temple.[73]

Dedicatory services resumed Sunday. James Scott recorded meticulously: "At 9 a.m. the doors of the temple (in accordance with a declaration made Friday) were thrown open to all."[74] Many had already gathered to gain entrance to the hall. The editor of the *Hancock Eagle* estimated that 5,000 were in attendance.[75] Orson Hyde delivered what would be his farewell address to the members in Nauvoo, speaking at length about the completion of the temple.[76] He asked, "Why have we laboured to complete it when we were not expecting to stay?" His answer: "If we moved forward and finished this House we should be received and accepted as a Church with our dead but if not we should be rejected with our dead. These things have inspired and stimulated us to action in the finishing of it which through the blessing of God we have been enabled to accomplish."[77]

He explained that the temple had been erected for the purpose of ordaining kings and priests unto God and declared, "This Temple was built for a certain purpose. That is gained. Will we now sell. All who are in favor of selling this House if it meets with the Council of the Twelve, manifest it by raising the right hand."[78] The vote was unanimous, reported William Matlack of the *Hancock Eagle,* except for one dissenter who "was not entitled to a vote."[79]

After the close of this service, Orson Hyde asked some of the workers to remain for a private meeting, in which they "administer[ed] the sacrament, being filled with praise and thanks giving to the most high for the privileges of the past week which we had enjoyed, especially in the dedication of the Lords House."[80]

Thomas Kane, who seems to have gathered his information about the temple dedication from eyewitnesses, indicated that workmen immediately set to work stripping the temple of its furnishings: "The sacred rites of consecration ended, the work of removing the sacro sancta proceeded with the rapidity of magic. It went on through the night; and when the morning of the next day dawned, all the ornaments and furniture, everything that could provoke a sneer had been carried off; and except some fixtures that would not bear removal, the building was dismantled to the bare walls."[81]

73. Samuel W. Richards, Diary, Book 2, 24.

74. Scott, Diary, 3 May 1846, 8. His statement casts further doubt on whether dedicatory services were held on Saturday.

75. Matlack, "The Temple in the Market," 2.

76. Samuel W. Richards, Journal, Book 2, 24.

77. Woodruff, Journal, 3:43.

78. Ibid.

79. Matlack, "The Temple in the Market," 2.

80. Samuel W. Richards, Journal, Book 2, 26.

81. Kane, "The Mormons," 83.

Was the Temple Completed?

Detractors were quick to point out that the temple was incomplete. They quoted the revelation in which the Saints were commanded "to build a house unto me" within the "sufficient time" appointed. If they failed, "at the end of the appointment ye shall be rejected as a church, with your dead, saith the Lord your God" (D&C 124:31-33). They attempted to discredit the validity of Young's leadership of the Church, insinuating that because the temple was not completed, the Twelve and the Mormons who follow them had been rejected. James J. Strang, who also claimed the right to succeed Joseph Smith, charged: "Nauvoo has ceased to be a stake of Zion, and is rejected as a church with its dead."[82]

The Reorganized Church of Jesus Christ of Latter Day Saints (now Community of Christ), organized in 1860 under the leadership of twenty-eight-year-old Joseph Smith III, also interpreted this revelation as meaning that the LDS Church, led by Brigham Young, had indeed been rejected by the Lord because the temple was never completely finished. Joseph Smith III, who remained a resident of Nauvoo after Brigham Young led out the portion of Saints who followed the Twelve, described the temple:

> In spite of assertions to the contrary I wish to emphatically state that the Temple was never finished.... I have gone over the entire building and was familiar with its every detail. From many visits to the place and contacts with its caretaker through the years I feel that I knew the Temple thoroughly, and can state that the claim made that it was finished as designed by Joseph Smith and those with him is a mistake. There were only two rooms in the building that could be said to have anywhere near approached completion.... Hence, whenever assertions are made that the Nauvoo Temple was finished, at any time, such statements are made by persons who are not acquainted with the facts.[83]

In reality, Brigham Young, did not claim that all of the finishing work on the temple was completed. On 1 January 1877, Young admitted to a congregation in St. George, Utah, that he "left brethren there with instructions to finish it, and they got it *nearly* completed before it was burned."[84] The point Young asserted was that the temple had been sufficiently completed that the ordinances could be per-

---

82. James J. Strang, "The Stake at Nauvoo," *Voree* (Wisconsin) *Herald*, 1 (April 1846): 3.

83. Mary Audentia Smith Anderson, ed., *Joseph Smith III and the Restoration* (Independence, MO: Herald House, 1952), 103, 105. See also Alexander Hale Smith quoted in Heman C. Smith, ed., *History of the Reorganized Church of Jesus Christ of Latter Day Saints*, 7 vols. (Independence, MO: Herald House, 1903-14, second printing 1967), 2:563-66.

84. Brigham Young, 1 January 1877, *Journal of Discourses*, 18:304; emphasis mine.

formed satisfactorily. Joseph Fielding Smith, writing in 1957, summarized the position taken by Brigham Young and his followers:

> "And if ye do not these things at the end of the appointment," obviously does not mean "if ye do not build a temple at the end of the appointment," as our critics infer it does, but it refers to the ordinances that were to be performed in the temple, and the failure on the part of the Saints to perform these ordinances for their dead was the thing that would cause their rejection with their dead, and not the failure to build the temple, which was merely the edifice in which the saving principles were to be performed.[85]

As Joseph Fielding Smith, then an apostle and future president of the Church, points out, the purposes of the temple, as stated in the revelation, were accomplished—that is, to provide a dedicated location in which to perform baptisms for the dead and administer other, higher ordinances. As far as the main body of the Saints was concerned, the temple was "so far completed," as Nauvoo member Wandle Mace put it, "that it was accepted of the Lord."[86] In other words, the finishing work that remained to be done in 1846 was not essential to the building's purpose or function.

Doctrine and Covenants 124, in addition to the warning to complete the temple or be rejected "with your dead," also contains a consoling promise which may, in light of later developments, be seen as a glimpse of the future:

> Verily, verily, I say unto you, that when I give a commandment to any of the sons of men to do a work unto my name, and those sons of men go with all their might and with all they have to perform that work, and cease not their diligence, and their enemies come upon them and hinder them from performing that work, behold, it behooveth me to require that work no more at the hands of those sons of men, but to accept of their offerings.
>
> And the iniquity and transgression of my holy laws and commandments I will visit upon the heads of those who hindered my work, unto the third and fourth generation, so long as they repent not, and hate me, saith the Lord God.
>
> Therefore, for this cause have I accepted the offerings of those whom I commanded to build up a city and a house unto my name, in Jackson county, Missouri, and were hindered by their enemies, saith the Lord your God. (vv. 49-50)

While this allowance refers to the curtailed attempt to build a temple in Missouri, it likewise foreshadows the fate of the Nauvoo Temple. This passage has

---

85. Joseph Fielding Smith, *Salvation Universal* (Salt Lake City: Deseret Book Company, 1957), 22. See also Joseph Fielding Smith, *Doctrines of Salvation: Sermons and Writings of Joseph Fielding Smith*, compiled by Bruce R. McConkie, 3 vols. (Salt Lake City: Bookcraft, 1954-56), 2:170-71.

86. Mace, Autobiography, 188.

also been interpreted as evidence that the Lord accepted the Saints' offering, even though they were "hindered by their enemies" from finalizing the temple. Interestingly, Brigham Young seemed to have applied this passage to the Nauvoo Temple while Joseph Smith was still alive. Speaking at a conference in Boston on 11 September 1843, he stated: "If the Temple at Nauvoo is not built, we will receive our endowments, if we have to go into the wilderness and build an altar of stone. If a man gives his all, it is all God requires."[87]

Continued Efforts to Sell the Temple

Although the Twelve's efforts to effect a sale to the Catholic Church had come to naught in January 1846, an important part of the charge to Almon W. Babbitt, Joseph L. Heywood, and John Fullmer as trustees in trust was for them to pursue a vigorous campaign to sell or lease Church properties in Nauvoo.

In early spring they attempted to lease the temple. On 10 April 1846, they published an advertisement "to lease on favorable terms, for the term of twenty years, 'The Temple' in this city for religious or literary purposes."[88] About two weeks later on 23 April, the *Sangamo Journal* of Springfield, Illinois, published a rumor that a "rich old bachelor from the South" was going to Nauvoo with the intention of buying the temple.[89] This wealthy bachelor was a Mr. Paulding from New Orleans. On 26 April, Brigham Young summarized a letter from Orson Hyde about this would-be buyer:

> A wealthy Catholic bachelor wished to purchase the temple and thereby immortalize his name. He would probably give two hundred thousand dollars for it.... Brother Hyde had offered to lease it to him, but he would not lease. Brother Hyde was afraid the temple would fall into the hands of enemies, as borrowed means were being called for, and numerous obligations were rolling in upon the trustees without means to liquidate them. Elder Hyde asked if it would not be better to sell the temple at Nauvoo and also the temple and church property at Kirtland, Ohio, and with the proceeds assist the saints to emigrate westward.[90]

The following morning, Young met with members of the Twelve and other leaders to consider Hyde's suggestion. According to Willard Richards:

---

87. *History of the Church,* 6:28.

88. Almon Babbitt, Joseph Heywood, and John S. Fullmer, "Temple to Lease," *Hancock Eagle* 1 (10 April 1846): 4.

89. S. Francis, "The Camp of Israel," *Sangamo Journal* 18 (23 April 1846), 2, microfilm, Lee Library.

90. Watson, *Manuscript History of Brigham Young,* 143.

The council decided that the trustees might sell the temples at Nauvoo and Kirtland [noting that] the temple would be of no benefit to the saints, if they could not possess their private dwellings, and when the time should come that they should return and redeem their inheritances, they would then redeem the temple also. A sale would secure it from unjust claims, mobs, fire, and so forth, more effectually than for the church to retain it in their hands.[91]

Some of the Twelve were now hesitant to sell the temple. For example, George A. Smith, who was in a different camp on the trail, wrote Brigham Young on 26 April, "We have felt much anxiety on that subject.... But if you in your wisdom should think it best to sell the same to help the poor in the present emergency we frankly concur notwithstanding we feel opposed to a Methodist congregation ever listening to a mob Priest in that holy Place; but are willing to sacrifice our feelings at times for the good of the Saints."[92]

Negotiations with Paulding continued for several months. In June, Heywood and Babbitt went to St. Louis to speak with Paulding's agent. They reported that the agent was generally positive about the possibility of a purchase but was waiting for instructions from Paulding. The trustees thought that it would probably take five or six weeks to close the sale.[93] As late as October, Paulding was still considering the purchase, but the sale was never completed for reasons that are not known.[94]

Meanwhile, from mid-May through the end of 1846, this advertisement appeared in the *Hancock Eagle*, signed by Babbitt, Heywood, and Fullmer:

TEMPLE FOR SALE
The undersigned Trustees of the Latter-day Saints propose to sell the Temple on very low terms, if an early application is made. The Temple is admirably designed for Literary or Religious purposes.[95]

On 8 May, the *Eagle* editorially encouraged the temple's purchase, paying a graceful tribute to the Saints' dedication in building it and alluding to the building's financial worth:

If any wealthy individual can be found who has a thirst for immortality, he can slake it by purchasing this great edifice for some literary, religious or charitable

---

91. Willard Richards, Journal, 27 April 1846, holograph, LDS Church Archives.

92. George A. Smith, Letter to Brigham Young and Council, 26 April 1846, holograph, Brigham Young Papers, LDS Church Archives.

93. John Fullmer, Letter to Brigham Young, 26 June 1846, in Journal History, 6 July 1846, 1-2.

94. Watson, Manuscript History of Brigham Young, 432.

95. Almon Babbitt, Joseph Heywood, and John S. Fullmer, "Temple for Sale," *Hancock Eagle* 1 (15 May 1846): 4.

institution. It can be had for less than one-fourth of the amount that would be required to erect a similar structure; and if bought on speculation, could probably be sold at a great advance in a few years.

Its cost to the Mormons (as appears by reference to their books,) exceeds one million of dollars; but a similar edifice might be built by contract for half the sum. The asking price for it now is $200,000.[96]

It is certainly an extraordinary specimen of human skill and industry; and so well appointed in its arrangements, that it can be made available for other purposes than those for which it was intended. As a college edifice it would stand unrivalled either in America or Europe. Will not the Catholics make a bid for it? They have ever manifested a laudable pride in magnificent architecture; and for an institution of learning the Temple would subserve their purposes quite as well as an edifice erected at treble the amount for which this can be purchased. It is for the interest of all parties that it should be sold—speedily sold—and we trust that some benevolent individual or charitable association will step forward and secure it for philanthropic purposes.[97]

Takers were few, however, for such a large building in a comparatively rural location. The fact that property values in Nauvoo were depreciating rapidly also made it difficult to effect the sale. Prudent buyers decided to watch and wait. Another problem was the temple's disputed title. In April 1846, James J. Strang, a former member of the Church who had proclaimed himself the successor of Joseph Smith, published the following report in his newspaper, the *Voree Herald* "expressing the opinion that the men who profess to be trustees in trust at Nauvoo are not legally in office and have no right to convey title to any property of the Church. We caution all against purchasing property of them."[98]

By September 1846, Strang had done some research on the title for the land upon which the temple stood. He published his findings in the *Herald*, reassuring his followers that they had the inside track to gaining possession of the building:

---

96. Estimates of the temple's total cost vary from $500,000 to over $1,000,000. *History of the Church*, 7:434; Parley P. Pratt. *Autobiography of Parley P. Pratt* (Salt Lake City: Deseret Book, 1985), 303; Andrew Jenson, "The Nauvoo Temple," Historical Record 8 (June 1889): 872. It is probable however, that nowhere near that sum in money or equivalent goods was actually spent. First, much of the labor was donated as tithing, and second, even if paid, the laborers often did not receive the agreed-upon wage. Henry Lewis, a visitor, estimates cautiously, "If the work had been paid for at the usual rate, the estimated cost of the Temple would have amounted to $800,000." Henry Lewis, quoted in *The Valley of the Mississippi Illustrated* (St. Paul: Minnesota Historical Society, 1967), 292.

97. Matlack, "The Temple in the Market." 2.

98. James Strang, "The Temples." *Voree Herald* 1 (April 1846): 4.

In regard to the titles of the Temples [Nauvoo and Kirtland], there need be no uneasiness. The lands on which they were erected, were conveyed to Joseph Smith, "sole Trustee in trust for the Church," and to his "Successors in the First Presidency," and as James J. Strang is the successor in the Presidency and no body else holds that office or pretends to hold it, there can be no difficulty as to the title, whatever there may be as to the possession....

The Church was organized in Illinois under a statute of that State for the purpose of holding real estate, etc., in a corporate capacity, by making Joseph Smith, Trustee in manner following:

From a Book of Mortgages and Bonds, page 95.

"City of Nauvoo, Hancock Co, Illinois,

Feb. 2, A.D. 1842.... At a meeting of the Church of Latter Day Saints at this place, on Saturday the 30th day of January, A 1841, I was elected sole Trustee for said Church, to hold my office during life, (my successor to be the First Presidency of said Church,) and vested with plenary powers as sole Trustee in Trust for the Church of Jesus Christ of Latter Day Saints, to receive, acquire, manage and convey property, real, personal, or mixed, for the sole use and benefit of said Church...

[signed Joseph Smith, Jr.]"

To Joseph Smith as such Trustee, and to his successor as above, the Temple of Nauvoo, was deeded. And this fact alone tells the whole reason why Babbit Haywood and Fullmer cannot sell that Temple. Capitalists are not much disposed to buy a mere naked possession without even a shadow of title. And until Babbit Haywood and Fullmer, can show that they are successors to Joseph Smith in the First Presidency of the Church they cannot set up any pretence to title to the Temple, or other Church property.[99]

Further compounding the problem was a report that Isaac Galland had a lien on the temple and other Church properties for $20,000.[100] The final expulsion of the Mormons during the Battle of Nauvoo in September 1846 (see below), the civic turmoil, and the resulting plunge in property values only made the possibility of finding a buyer more remote. A year later in October 1847 the *Warsaw Signal* passed along the word that the sale of the temple had failed several times because of problems with the title.[101]

---

99. Ibid., 2.

100. Watson, *Manuscript History of Brigham Young*, 482. Galland, who had sold land to the Church in Nauvoo but never received full payment, took legal action to obtain remuneration which, as Almon Babbitt explained to Brigham Young in the spring of 1847, had been an "impediment against a sale of the property." Almon Babbit, Letter to Brigham Young, 5 April 1847, Journal History, 5 April 1847, 3.

101. Thomas Gregg, "[title]," *Warsaw Signal*, 19 October 1847, 2.

Despite all of these problems, the trustees determinedly tried to fulfill Brigham Young's instructions. During the spring of 1847, Babbitt traveled through the eastern states looking for a buyer but without success. His best offer, reported to Brigham Young on 5 April, had been $100,000 for the temple and several other Church properties.[102] John Fullmer was upset that Babbitt had refused this offer and complained to Brigham Young that the prospective sale was "blighted by the inattention and darkness of mind of one in whom we had a right to confide."[103] However, Young's reply signaled a change in his attitude toward the sale:

> Has the Lord turned bankrupt? or are his children so needy that they are obliged to sell their Father's house for a morsel of bread? and if they should sell, how much would they get after they had paid some millions of unjust debts, mortgages, cancelled claims, demands, attachments, fines, forfeitures, imprisonments, massacres, lawsuits, judgments and the whole etceteras that united mobocracy could bring against you before you could get one dollar removed from the vault to a place of safety.... And if we get no other reward for past labors, we have left monuments which will memorialize the diligence of the Saints forever————————a greater glory than safes of gold.[104]

The situation remained a stalemate for the next six months. On 5 November 1847, Young wrote the trustees requesting them to "gather up all the books and papers pertaining to Church property as you can, and as many of the poor Saints, and gather to this place in season to start with the spring emigration, leaving the Temple of the Lord in the care of the Lord into whose hands we committed it before we left, and let the owls and the bats revel in the habitation of the Saints in Nauvoo ... until the Lord wills it otherwise."[105] He added, "Leave the keys of the temple in care of Judge Owens and the building itself in the hands of the Lord."[106]

However, in December 1847, Emma Smith shocked the Church by marrying Lewis Bidamon, a respected Nauvoo citizen, but not a member of the Church. After their marriage, the two almost immediately threatened to sue to stop the trustees from selling the temple on the grounds that a "Church could hold only ten acres of land, according to a limited construction of our state laws, and that consequently, the deed from Emma and Joseph Smith to Joseph as 'Trustee' was illegal." According to John Fullmer, this "destroys the confidence of everyone, and pre-

102. Watson, *Manuscript History of Brigham Young*, 546.

103. Joseph L. Heywood, Letter to Brigham Young, Journal History, 20 April 1847, 2.

104. Brigham Young, Letter to John Fullmer, quoted in McGavin, *The Nauvoo Temple*, 118.

105. Brigham Young, Letter to the Trustees, Journal History, 5 November 1847, 4.

106. History of the Church, 7:617. I have no additional information on this Judge Owens.

vents those who would have purchased from doing so."[107] Louis and Emma hoped to obtain some of the property to help pay off some of the personal debts that Emma had inherited from Joseph at his death. This new development prompted the trustees to remain for a few more months; but by early 1848, they realized that these new claims had all but destroyed the slim chance they had of selling the temple.[108]

On 25 January 1848, in response to these new developments, Brigham Young stated with resignation that he "did not wish the temple to be sold."[109] He gave the trustees permission to leave Nauvoo and come to Utah in the spring of 1848, though Babbitt chose to remain in the East for several more months.

The Bell and the Angel

The temple bell remained in the tower through the summer of 1846, but Brigham Young, who was then encamped in Iowa, had not forgotten it. On 28 September, he wrote the trustees in Nauvoo: "As you will have no further use for the Temple bell, we wish you to forward it to us by the first possible chance, for we much need it at this place."[110] Joshua Hawkes, one of the Mormons remaining in Nauvoo in September, reported that "he and James Hou[gh]ton took the Nauvoo Temple bell over the Mississippi river in 1846 and that it was in [the] charge of Joseph P. [sic] Heywood."[111] Heywood apparently forwarded the bell to Winter Quarters where it arrived in December 1846.

Brigham Young planned to take the bell with the vanguard party, which would depart as soon as there was enough grass for the animals. Brigham Young instructed in April 1847:

> The first company will carry the Temple bell, with fixtures for hanging at a
> moment's notice, which will be rung at daylight, or at a proper time, and call all

107. John Fullmer, Letter to Brigham Young, 27 January 1848, in Journal History, 27 January 1848, 4, LDS Church Archives.

108. Richard E. Bennett, "We'll Find the Place": *The Mormon, Exodus 1846-1848* (Salt Lake City: Deseret Book, 1997), 321-23.

109. Woodruff, Journal, 3:314.

110. Brigham Young, Letter to the Trustees, Journal History, 28 September 1846, 2.

111. Andrew Jenson, Nauvoo Bell Folder, Andrew Jenson Papers, LDS Church Archives. Houghton joined the Church in Kirtland and had been ordained an elder as early as September 1836. The tradition that the temple bell had been removed and placed in a local Protestant Church, from which it was spirited away by David and Andrew Lamoreaux, was reported as recently as 1981 in Lois Leetham Tanner, "I Have a Question," *Ensign*, February 1981, 16. This bell, however, was most likely the one known as Hummer's Bell. Ronald G. Watt, "A Tale of Two Bells: Nauvoo Bell and Hummer's Bell," *Nauvoo Journal* 11 (Fall 1999): 33.

who are able to arise to pray, after which the ringing of bell and breakfast, or the ringing of bell and departure in 15 minutes, to secure the cool of the day ... The bell may be needed, particularly in the night, if the Indians hover around, to let them know that [the sentries] are at [their] duty.[112]

Willard Richards explained the "fifteen-minute" provision more clearly: "The temple bell to be rung every morning to wake all up, then have prayers, breakfast, prepare teams. At the second ringing of the bell, in 15 minutes afterwards, start for their day's journey."[113]

Edward Stevenson, a company member, described how the bell accompanied the pioneer company:

[22 June 1847.] At 8 o'clock a.m. the signal for starting was given by ringing the Temple bell. The order of traveling was as follows: The first fifty of the first hundred took the lead; the second fifty formed a second line to the right. Next to these two lines came Charles C. Rich's guard with the cannon, the skiff and temple bell on the lead.

[23 June 1847.] ... The emigrating companies took up their line of march at 9 o'clock a. m., traveling two teams abreast, the cannon heading one line and the skiff and temple bell the other.[114]

The fate of the angel weather vane that once swung atop the tower has been something of a mystery. According to one witness, it had been removed in 1846. J. M. Davidson recalled a visit to the temple late in 1846 during which he crawled "out on a narrow parapet, which had only the slight protection [of] Vshaped turrets, and a small ladder was seen going up over the dome of a naked flagstaff (no angel on it—she was in the dome)."[115] It is possible that the angel was removed from the tower after 6 September 1846, when lightning struck the weather vane, scarring the cupola.[116]

---

112. Susa Young Gates, *The Life Story of Brigham Young* (New York: MacMillan, 1930), 83-84.
113. Willard Richards, Journal, Vol. 17: 13 December 1846-7 April 1847, 12 March 1847, holograph, 74, LDS Church Archives. These instructions clarify that the latest the bell could have arrived in Winter Quarters was early March.

According to Cincinnati resident and genealogist Marie Dickoré, the Salem Evangelical and Reformed Church in Cincinnati purchased it in 1867 and it was installed on the steeple of that church.[117] In 1966, a storm blew the Cincinnati angel from its perch. In November 1968, this angel was transported to Nauvoo by J. Byron Ravsten, then manager of Nauvoo Restoration. Upon examination, it was generally concluded that this was not the Nauvoo Temple weathervane—that its design, materials, and craftsmanship were not consistent with those supposed to have been used in 1840s Nauvoo. Unfortunately, the Cincinnati vane was discarded, preventing further examination.[118]

The Battle of Nauvoo

While most Mormons left Nauvoo during the late winter and early spring of 1846, many remained. According to Andrew Jenson, "They were generally of the poorest class—the persons who had not sufficient means to furnish themselves with teams and the necessary outfit to commence the journey, although they were all anxious to go and their labors were constantly directed to effect that end."[119]

As the summer passed, the anti-Mormon element in Hancock County grew impatient with the lingering Saints and resolved to force them out. Concern over a potential attack on the city and temple was widespread. George Morris wrote:

> Those were times to try men's souls.... I have lain in the temple night after night upon the hard wooden benches with my rifle by my side expecting an attack every minute, I have laid in my bed with my clothes on and my gun leaning against my pillow where I could lay my hand upon it at any hour of the night and jumped from my bed at all hours of the night at the sound of the big drum and

114. Edward Stevenson, Journal, quoted in Joseph Grant Stevenson, "The Life of Edward Stevenson" (M.A. thesis, Brigham Young University, 1955), 116-17.

115. Unknown author, untitled article containing quotations from J. M. Davidson, "Nauvoo: The Past and Present of That City: Visits of 1846 and 1864 Contrasted," *Carthage Republican*, 25 February 1864, 1, and quoted in E. Cecil McGavin, *The Nauvoo Temple* (Salt Lake City: Deseret Book, 1962), 93. McGavin mistakenly cites Davidson as the author of the article, rather than as "quoted by unknown author."

116. Arrington "Destruction of the Mormon Temple at Nauvoo,"417.

117. Marie Dickoré, Statement, 25 July 1961, in "Collected Material Concerning a Weather Vane in Cincinnati, Ohio," typescript, LDS Church Archives.

118. Milton V. Backman, Interview conducted by Matthew McBride, 15 April 2002, notes in my possession.

the ringing of the temple bell which was a signal for us to gather; and I have been armed and equipped and at the place of rendezvous inside of five minutes.[120]

On 15 June, the following report appeared in the *Daily* (St. Louis) *Missouri Republican*:

A gentleman from Fort Madison informs us that numbers had crossed the river to augment the force opposite that place, and they make no hesitation in saying the Temple must be destroyed. One of them boasted that he could put his hand upon the powder that was intended to be used for this purpose. If foiled in that, they threatened to burn the town. They say that they will not interfere with the new citizens who join them, and assist in removing the obnoxious persons.

A gentleman direct from one of the invading camps informs us that it does not contain a man who has any property interest in the county. He believes that the threatened invasion is not so much directed against the Mormons as against the prosperity of this city; which, under favorable auspices, might prove a formidable rival in other towns. It is supposed, therefore, that there are men of influence behind the curtain, who stimulate the prejudice against all who have purchased property of the Mormons. As to the correctness of this understanding of the case we are not prepared to speak, but we have heard it asserted that "when the new comers purchased property here, they purchased the incumbrance of a risk of the town being destroyed."

It certainly seems strange that it should be necessary to make demonstrations of this kind against some few hundred Mormons, who are hurrying off as fast as possible. The few that are now here, are incapable of making a stand, and the new citizens apprehend no danger from them.[121]

This threat never materialized, but concern over armed violence continued. On 10 September, sentries posted on the temple tower reported the approach of a mob.[122] This group camped near the city on the evening of 11 September. The few remaining Saints rallied to defend the city, erecting barricades and firing cannon shots in the direction of the strangers' camp. The following morning the mob, undaunted, sent word to Nauvoo demanding that they be allowed to occupy the city and that the Mormons surrender their arms. They moved into the city and easily overcame the little resistance that the poverty-stricken and ill-equipped Saints

119. Andrew Jenson, "Battle of Nauvoo," Historical Record 8 (June 1889): 845. Although the population of Nauvoo was changing rapidly during these months, prior to the dedication there were probably between two and three thousand; by June this number had probably dropped to fewer than a thousand.

120. George Morris, "The History of George Morris," 1891, typescript. 31, Perry Special Collections, Lee Library.

could offer. For four days, the victors ransacked houses, confiscated property, and drove families from their homes. On 16 September, Babbitt, Fullmer, and Heywood, representing the Church, signed a treaty surrendering the city and agreed to evacuate immediately.[123]

The next day, 17 September, "The keys of the temple were given up by Henry I. Young to the chairman of the Quincy committee."[124] This Quincy chairman apparently kept the keys only temporarily, for on 20 October, the trustees informed Brigham Young that "the keys of the Temple had been delivered up by the mob to Bro[ther] [Samuel L.] Paine."[125]

Joseph Fielding indicated that while the mob occupied Nauvoo, they "rendezvoused in the temple. We had guarded it by night and day, a long time feeling unwilling to leave it in their hands, but they now had it to themselves. They even preached in it and cursed the Saints, but did no great damage to it, thinking it would add to the value of their property."[126] Thomas Bullock also observed this violation of the Mormon sanctuary:

> The mob went through the temple and up to the dome of the tower, ringing the bell, shouting and hollowing; some enquired, who is the keeper of the Lord's house now?...
>
> A mobocratic preacher ascended to the temple tower and proclaimed with a loud voice: Peace, Peace, Peace to the inhabitants of the earth, now the Mormons are driven.[127]

Benjamin Ashby, who did not leave Nauvoo until October 1846, recalled, "At night we could hear the sound of the bell and the bass drum from the tower of the temple where the mob were carousing."[128]

In Winter Quarters, Helen Mar Kimball Whitney remembered receiving the news on 14 October 1846, that Nauvoo had fallen and that the temple had been desecrated: "The mob was pretty busy plundering houses, ripping open feather beds and scattering the contents in the street, knocking the horns from the oxen

121. *Daily Missouri Republican*, 15 June 1846, quoted in McGavin, *The Nauvoo Temple*, 138.

122. Ibid., 849-50.

123. Ibid., 855.

124. "Manuscript History of the Church," quoted in Journal History, 17 September 1846, 3.

125. Watson, *Manuscript History of Brigham Young*, 439. The trustees wrote on 20 October; Brigham Young refers to this letter in his response, dated 4 November 1846.

126. Andrew F. Ehat, ed., "'They Might Have Known He Was Not a Fallen Prophet': The Nauvoo Journal of Joseph Fielding," *BYU Studies* 19 (Winter 1979): 165-66.

127. "Manuscript History of the Church," Journal History, 18 September 1846, 2.

128. Benjamin Ashby, Autobiography, 15-16, photocopy of holograph, Perry Special Collections, Lee Library.

on which the font was built, and running about the streets imitating the blowing of horns with them and doing other acts of sacrilege. They had also torn down the altars and pulpits in the Temple, and converted the edifice into a meat market."[129]

On 5 October, William E. Matlack, editor of the *Hancock Eagle*, reported damage to the floors and font and graffiti scrawled on the walls. "Holes have been cut through the floors, the stone oxen in the basement have been considerably disfigured, horns and ears dislodged, and nearly all torn loose from their standing."[130]

Thomas L. Kane visited Nauvoo while the mob was still in possession of the temple:

> In and around the splendid temple which had been the chief object of my admiration, armed men were barricaded, surrounded by their stacks of musketry and pieces of heavy ordnance. These challenged me to give an account of myself and why I had had the temerity to cross the water without a written permit from the leader of their band.
>
> Though these men were generally more or less under the influence of ardent spirits, after I had explained myself as a passing stranger, they seemed anxious to gain my good opinion.... They also conducted me inside the massive sculptured walls of the curious temple, in which they said the banished inhabitants were accustomed to celebrate the mystic rites of an unhallowed worship. They particularly pointed out to me certain features of the building, which, having been the peculiar objects of a former superstitious regard, they had as a matter of duty sedulously defiled and defaced. The reputed sites of certain shrines they had thus particularly noticed, and various sheltered chambers, in one of which was a deep well, constructed, they believed, with a dreadful design.
>
> ... The victors had so diligently desecrated [the font] as to render the apartment in which it was contained too noisome to abide in.
>
> They permitted me also to ascend into the steeple to see where it had been lightning struck on the Sabbath before, and to look out, east and south, on wasted farms, like those I had seen near the city, extending till they were lost in the distance.
>
> Here, in the face of pure day, close to the scar of Divine wrath left by the thunder bolt, were fragments of food, cases of liquor and broken drinking vessels, with a bass drum and a steamboat signal bell.[131]

By the time the mob retreated from Nauvoo during the first week of November, they had done severe damage to the interior of the temple. Other visitors who came after the mob had come and gone also commented about the

---

129. Helen Mar Kimball Whitney, "Scenes and Incidents at Winter Quarters," *Woman's Exponent* 13 (July 1884): 131.

130. W. E. Matlack, "Home Matters," *Hancock Eagle Extra*, 5 October 1846, 2.

131. Kane, "The Mormons," 68-70.

temple's condition. An unnamed visitor noted, "Now and then, the surface [of the exterior stone walls] would present a bruise, showing the effects of the cannon of the sacrilegious Anti-Mormon host."[132]

Christiana Pyper, whose Mormon family was one of the few remaining in Nauvoo after 1846, was twelve that year. She described the results: "From basement to tower that sacred edifice was defaced with the most vile and wicked writing that could be imagined. We climbed the winding stairs and walked around the towers, where we had been more than once before, for the last time before it was burned. My mother and her two little girls wept like babes."[133]

Despite this wanton damage, Thomas C. Sharp defended the vandals:

The Jacks have reported that the Anties had done great injury to the Temple, by defacing its ornaments, and were exhibiting it for pay, as had formerly been the custom of the Mormons. This is utterly false. Some Jacks reported that $10,000 would not repair the injury done to the Temple by the Anties. Now the fact is, the only damage done to the building since the Anties have had possession, is a horn and an ear from one of the oxen has been removed and some ornamental letters taken from the inscription on the altar. The whole can be repaired for the sum of five dollars. When it is considered that since the Anties have had possession, hundreds of all sorts of people have gone through the building, it is surprising that no greater injury has been done.[134]

---

132. Unnamed visitor, *Illinois Journal*, 9 December 1853, reprinted as "Recollections of the Nauvoo Temple," in *Journal of the Illinois State Historical Society* 38 (December 1945): 482; photocopy in LDS Church Historical Department Library.

133. Christiana Dollinger Pyper, "Leaves from My Diary," *Juvenile Instructor* 57 (May 1922): 246. Christiana (1834-1925) was born in New York and moved to Nauvoo where she remained with her family until 1859 when they moved to Salt Lake City.

134. Thomas C. Sharp, "Jack Mormon Lies," *Warsaw Signal*, 20 October 1846, 2.

Chapter 13

THE TEMPLE'S FATE:
SEPTEMBER 1848 TO 1937

The Temple Burns

The few remaining Church members in Nauvoo and the city's other citizens used the temple intermittently until late 1848. Trustee Almon Babbitt leased the temple to his brother-in-law, David T. LeBaron, for $5,000 in March 1848.[1] LeBaron, who stayed in Nauvoo until 1852, acted as caretaker of the temple during the summer of 1848. Joseph Smith III remembers attending "meetings in it both for worship and for political purposes" while LeBaron was its landlord.[2] LeBaron, along with another of Babbitt's brother-in-laws, George W. Johnson, "exhibit[ed] the Nauvoo Temple to strangers."[3]

On 27 September 1848, the *Oquawka* (Illinois) *Spectator* published an announcement that the Home Missionary Society of New York would lease the

---

1. Janath R. Cannon, *Nauvoo Panorama: Views of Nauvoo before, during, and after Its Rise, Fall, and Restoration* (Salt Lake City: Nauvoo Restoration, Inc., 1991), 52. Cannon cites a photocopy of the original lease document in Nauvoo Restoration, Inc., files.

2. Quoted in Heman C. Smith, *History of the Reorganized Church of Jesus Christ of Latter Day Saints*, 7 vols. (Independence, MO: Herald House, 1903-14; second printing, 1967), 2:563.

3. George Washington Johnson, Autobiography, 1823-50, 5-6, typescript, L. Tom Perry Special Collections, Harold B. Lee Library, Brigham Young University, Provo, Utah.

temple for fifteen years for $3,000 and convert it into a school. The lease was final-ized on 2 October.[4] One week later on 9 October, the temple mysteriously burst into flames late at night. According to an eyewitness account published in the *Nauvoo Patriot*:

> Our citizens were awakened by the alarm of fire, which, when first discovered, was bursting out through the spire of the Temple, near the small door that opened from the east side to the roof, on the main building. The fire was seen first about three o'clock in the morning, and not until it had taken such hold of the timbers and roof as to make useless any effort to extinguish it. The materials of the inside were so dry, and the fire spread so rapidly, that a few minutes were sufficient to wrap this famed edifice in a sheet of flame.
>
> It was a sight too full of mournful sublimity. The mass of material which had been gathered there by the labor of many years afforded a rare opportunity for this element to play off some of its wildest sports. Although the morning was tol-erably dark, still, when the flames shot upwards, the spire, the streets, and the houses for nearly a mile distant were lighted up, so as to render even the small-est objects discernible. The glare of the vast torch, pointing skyward, indescrib-ably contrasted with the universal gloom and darkness around it: and men looked on with faces sad as if the crumbling ruins below were consuming all their hopes.[5]

The *Keokuk Register*, published just down the Mississippi River on the Iowa side, reported that the flames

---

4. Newspaper article described in George A. Smith, Ezra T. Benson, Joseph T. Young, Robert Campbell, Letter to Brigham Young, Willard Richards, and Heber C. Kimball, in Journal History of the Church of Jesus Christ of Latter-day Saints (chronology of typed entries and newspaper clippings, 1830-present), 2 October 1848, 14, LDS Church Archives. See also "The Mormon Temple," *Home Missionary* 3 (January 1849): 207, photocopy, Perry Special Collections, Lee Library; and Cannon, *Nauvoo Panorama*, 52. Cannon cites a photocopy of the original lease in Nauvoo Restoration, Inc., files.

5. Reprinted in *Warsaw Signal*, 19 October 1848, quoted in Joseph Earl Arrington, "Destruction of the Mormon Temple at Nauvoo," *Journal of the Illinois State Historical Society* 40 (December 1947): 418-19. Thomas Gregg, *History of Hancock County, Illinois* (Chicago: Charles C. Chapman & Co., 1880), 957, claims that the fire started in the cupola, but the *Patriot* account, which was closer to the event, is probably more reliable. Gregg states: "It was a beautiful night, and about 3 o'clock fire was discovered in the cupola. It had made but little head way when first seen, but spread rapid-ly, and in a very short period the lofty spire was a mass of flame, shooting high in the air, and illumi-nating a wide extent of country. It was seen for miles away. The citizens gathered around, but noth-ing could be done to save the structure. It was entirely of wood except the walls, and nothing could have stopped the progress of the flames. In two hours, and before the sun dawned upon the earth, the proud structure, reared at so much cost, an anomaly in architecture, and a monument of religious zeal—stood with four blackened and smoking walls only remaining."

threw a lurid glare into the surrounding darkness. Great volumes of smoke and flame burst from the windows and the crash of the falling timbers was distinctly heard on the opposite side of the river. The interior of the building was like a furnace, the walls of solid masonry were heated throughout by the intense heat. The melted zinc and lead was dropping from its huge blocks during the day. On Tuesday morning the walls were too hot to be touched.[6]

About two years later, John M. Bernhisel said that "a person who witnessed the conflagration of this sacred and magnificent edifice" told him "that when the flames first burst out through the steeple, a most profound silence reigned over this devoted city, then the dogs began to bark, and the cattle to low."[7]

The disappointed Home Missionary Society of New York described the fire in its report: "The Universalists held a meeting in it the night before. The walls, which are very thick, are not very much injured; but the wood work is all consumed. The twelve stone oxen and the Baptismal font standing on them are a heap of lime." However, it added optimistically: "The walls are now worth almost as much as the whole structure was. They may now be fitted up for, and adopted to, some proper purpose."[8]

Christiana Pyper, who was fourteen at the time of the fire and one of the few Mormons then living in Nauvoo, recorded her recollections of the disaster:

One morning, between two and three o'clock, we were suddenly awakened by a bright light in our rooms. We [she and her sisters and mother] slept upstairs—our house facing the east. Fearing the city was burning, and that we might be driven out again we could not move; afraid to look out, but, sitting up in our beds we saw the Temple burn until there was nothing standing but the walls. What a picture! What a sacrifice! No tongue can describe our fear, and trembling—expecting every minute to be dragged out of our beds and killed; no earthly protector, but the Lord, who was our help and our aid. Having implicit faith in Him we were safe.

As soon as we dared venture, we went with some of our schoolmates to view the ruins. The cellar and basement were a mass of melted debris, still smoking and burning like a hot pot of melted glass, lead, wood, etc.

The heat was so great we could not go very near, so we looked and went back home crying; mourning the sad fate of our beloved Temple.

6. *Keokuk Register*, 12 October 1848, quoted in Arrington, "Destruction of the Mormon Temple at Nauvoo," 418-19.

7. John Bernhisel, Letter to Brigham Young, from Nauvoo, Journal History, 10 September 1849, 2.

8. "The Mormon Temple," *Home Missionary* 3 (January 1849): 207, photocopy, Perry Special Collections, Lee Library.

People came from all parts to get souvenirs of the ruins and the neighbors boys melted some of the lead and run it into molten miniature flat irons and other things. I had many pieces, but parted with them before leaving there to come out west.[9]

Thomas Gregg, who had taken Thomas C. Sharp's place as editor of the *Warsaw Signal*, observed with typical acerbity, "The four blackened walls of stone will stand a monument to the rise, progress and downfall of one of the most nefarious systems of imposture of modern times."[10]

However, most in the surrounding region lamented the loss of the temple. Local papers published denunciations of the arson. The *Keokuk Register* declared:

However much the religion of the Mormons at Nauvoo may be condemned, every good citizen will condemn this act of incendiary as one of grossest barbarism.... Its destruction has inflicted material injury on the Mormons—to the surrounding country, it will be a serious loss. The citizens on both sides of the river reprobate the act as wanton and malicious in the extreme.... The naked walls still stand, a monument of the enthusiasm of its misguided worshippers—its destruction a striking comment on the spirit of the nineteenth century.[11]

The *Keokuk Dispatch* threatened, "The individual or individuals who planned this horrid outrage deserve to have the law in all its rigors enforced against them—aye, they deserve to have been confined within its walls while the conflagration was going on.... [We hope] that the incendiaries may be found out and punished.... [but] the prospect is a slender one."[12]

The editor of the *Nauvoo Patriot*, though describing the temple as "a monument of folly and of evil" relented to add: "Yet it was, to say the least of it, a splen-

---

9. Christiana Dollinger Pyper, "Leaves from My Diary," *Juvenile Instructor* 57 (May 1922): 246. Mary Field Gardner, another Mormon girl living in Nauvoo in 1848, recounted a similar experience: "We lived in a double house with a family named Lee. One night Mother went out to pump a pitcher of water. She heard a terrible crackling of timber. Looking up, she saw the beautiful Nauvoo Temple in flames. She ran back into the house, waking the children, the Lee family and several neighbors to watch it burn to the ground. It is impossible to describe the feeling of the Saints to see their sacred temple, of which they were so proud and which had cost the Saints so much hard work and money to build, being destroyed. Some of the anti-Mormons were also angry about it as they were proud to have this very beautiful structure in the community." "Mary Field Garner," *Our Pioneer Heritage*, 20 vols., compiled by Kate B. Carter (Salt Lake City: Daughters of the Utah Pioneers, 1958-77), 7:409. This article (no author identified) quotes from Garner's autobiography.

10. *Warsaw Signal*, 12 October 1848, quoted in Arrington, "Destruction of the Mormon Temple at Nauvoo," 420.

11. *Keokuk Register*, 12 October 1848, in ibid., 419.

12. *Keokuk Dispatch*, 12 October 1848, in ibid., 420.

did and harmless one."[13] Parley P. Pratt's classic rejoinder to this statement appeared a few months later in the *Millennial Star*: "Yes! This temple is destroyed; but this is not THE TEMPLE. We admire the good feelings of the *Nauvoo Patriot*; but even his conclusions are not correct. It was a monument of God's wisdom and not of man's folly."[14] Pratt asked rhetorically, "Is not the 'Priesthood' now established on the earth that shall never have an end?... Yes! And who can take it from the earth?" He knew that the invisible temple—the theological construction consisting of temple doctrines and temple ordinances— remained indestructibly in the hearts of the thousands who had worshiped in the Nauvoo Temple. It was only a matter of time before other houses of the Lord would be erected in its stead and the work of salvation for the living and dead would resume.

On 30 December 1848, the *Warsaw Signal*, despite Gregg's disapproval of all things Mormon, published an announcement by Nauvoo citizens, offering a reward for the arrest and conviction of the arsonist: "We, the citizens of Nauvoo, feeling it our indispensable duty to ferret out the nefarious incendiary who fired and burned the temple in this place, bind ourselves, our heirs and administrators to pay the sum set opposite our respective names to the person or persons causing the said incendiary to be arrested and legally convicted of the above charge." The total sum raised was $640.[15] No one was ever convicted of the crime.

The Arsonist

Tradition suggests that the arsonist was Joseph B. Agnew, described as "short of stature, rather stoutly built; dark blue eyes and brown hair."[16] He was thirty-six in 1848, had the reputation of persecuting the Mormons, and had participat-

---

13. "Destruction of the Mormon Temple," *Nauvoo Patriot*, 19 October 1848, reprinted under same title in *Millennial Star* 11 (1 February 1849): 46. Word of the temple's destruction reached England as early the beginning of 1849. Nathaniel Henry Felt's letter of 16 November 1848 informs Parley P. Pratt, the *Star's* editor, that members of "the mob ... have at last vented their fury upon that House.... Yes, the incendiary torch has been applied, and nought but the blackened walls of that once beautiful Temple stands [sic] forth upon its eminence, to show to every traveler the sacrifices of the people of God, and the ruthless violence and iniquity of their persecutors." *Millennial Star* 11 (15 January 1849): 15.

14. Parley P. Pratt, "Destruction of the Mormon Temple," *Millennial Star* 11 (1 February 1849): 46-47.

15. *Warsaw Signal*, 30 December 1848, in Arrington, "Destruction of the Mormon Temple at Nauvoo," 420.

16. Pyper, "Leaves from My Diary," 247.

ed in burning Mormon homes in September 1845.[17] In an interview with George A. Smith and Erastus Snow on 1 November 1856, Lewis C. Bidamon, Emma Hale Smith's second husband, implicated Agnew. He got his information from the deathbed confession of a woman named Walker who was boarding at Agnew's home when the temple was burned. She claimed that "the two Agnew boys [Joseph and his brother] drove off as if they were going to Queen Mills, which was several miles northeast of Dallas. She watched them. They drove to the southeast corner of the farm and there unhitched and left the wagon and rode off on horseback. About as long thereafter as it would take to ride from the farm to Nauvoo, a light of the burning temple was seen."[18]

Bidamon claimed that some of the inhabitants of the surrounding towns had made up a purse of $500 as payment for whoever would burn the temple. Although Bidamon was not a Mormon, he had strong reasons for resenting its destruction. "The burning of the Temple had the effect of diminishing the importance of Nauvoo," reported Smith and Snow, "for his [Bidamon's] 'Mansion' or 'Hotel' had not since the conflagration one-fourth the custom it previously had."[19]

In seeming confirmation of Bidamon's accusations, a report circulated in 1872 that, just before Agnew's death in the fall of 1870, he had made a detailed confession of the deed to George H. Rudsill, a resident of Fort Madison, Iowa. Rudsill's version of Agnew's confession was published in the *Peoria* (Illinois) *Transcript*.[20] The confession in full, as it later appeared in the *Fort Madison Democrat* read:

> Well, to the burning of the temple. I [Rudsill] will give it in Mr. J. B. Agnew's own words, as near as I can recollect, which was just before his death in the fall of 1870. After telling me his story he asked me as a friend not to let it be known until after his death of all parties concerned, as they had pledged themselves to secrecy in the matter. This I told him I would do, and now that these parties are

---

17. Joseph Smith Jr. et al., *History of the Church of Jesus Christ of Latter-day Saints*, edited by B. H. Roberts (Salt Lake City: Deseret News Press, 6 vols. published 1902-12, Vol. 7 published 1932, 1st printing), 7:530. See also "The Man Who Fired the Nauvoo Temple," Deseret Evening News, 26 April 1872, 3.

18. George A. Smith, Letter to Brigham Young, 1 November 1856, Journal History, 9 October 1848, 5.

19. *History of the Church*, 7:617.

20. "The Man Who Fired the Nauvoo Temple," *Deseret Evening News*, 26 April 1872, 3. This article is a reprint of an earlier article in the *Peoria Transcript*, which comments: "So successful was the party engaged in its firing, that probably he was never suspected. The recent death of the incendiary, however, has removed the necessity of further secrecy, and a day or two ago we were put in possession of his name, and the facts connected with the burning of the temple, by the only living person cognizant of them."

all dead, it will be no harm to let it be known, and it will satisfy many an old settler's curiosity.

Mr. Agnew was in failing health at the time he came to me. He told me that he was going to die soon, which I thought was true. I asked him if he had repented of his wrongdoings and he smiled and said: "Yes, all but one thing." I asked what that was and he said it was the burning of the Nauvoo Temple. Says I: "Did you do that?" And he said: "Yes, I did it with my own hands. Sit down and I will tell you about it,' which is as follows, as near as I can give it in his own words:

"The reason why I burned it was that there was a continual report in circulation that the Mormons were coming back to Nauvoo and we were afraid they might take it into their heads to do so, and as we had had all the trouble with them we wanted, Judge [Thomas C.] Sharp of Carthage, Squire McCauley[21] of Appanoose [Illinois, six miles north of Nauvoo], and myself of Pontoosuc [Illinois, eleven miles north of Nauvoo], determined the destruction of their Temple and by so doing they would not be able ever again to try and come back.

"So on the afternoon of the night that the Temple was burned, in order to make arrangements we three met on the prairie five miles south of Fort Madison, in Illinois, the judge coming from Carthage, the squire from Appanoose, and I from Pontoosuc, and we met about where the Mormon Church stood, five miles south of Appanoose, and there we pledged ourselves to destroy the Temple if it cost us our lives.

"So we journeyed toward it on horseback, and on the way tried to perfect some plan to work on. After a while we decided to get the steward [David LeBaron] to show us through the Temple, and then watch our chance to get in our work. So we hid our horses in the bushes in a secluded place a mile from town and walked in.

"We looked about town until 4 o'clock in the afternoon, and in the meantime had prepared a bundle of kindling by taking a corn sack and cutting arm holes in it so I could put it on like a coat under my coat. I then stuck in as many tarred rags on sticks as I could carry without being noticed. I then put it on and secured some matches from a store to light my pipe and we were ready. We had but little trouble to find the steward and after laboring with him some time he at last consented to show us through the Temple. We claimed to be strangers in the country and were going away that night and it would be our last chance perhaps of ever having an opportunity to visit the Temple. So on these conditions he would oblige us, provided we would hurry, which we agreed to do, as it was getting late and it would be dark before we could get through. So after a good deal of delay the key was at last inserted, it not seeming to fit, but at last the door

21. Probably John McCauley, who had been part of a mob that had kidnapped Richard Ballantyne, James Standing, Phineas H. Young, Brigham H. Young, and James Herring from Nauvoo in February 1846. Andrew Jenson, "Infancy of the Church," Supplement to Historical Record (Salt Lake City: Andrew Jenson, 1889), 55.

swung open. We went in with a rush and kept a going, the man being left behind working with the door. He called out for us to stop but we kept on going and I noticed that he left the door with the key in it.

I stepped back in a side room, and the other two kept on. The man ran on after them, and after he had passed me, I went back to the door and unlocked it and put the key in my pocket and then ran after them. By this time the man had discovered that I was missing, but when I came up to them and explained that I had stopped to look at the crucifixion, he seemed to be satisfied but looked suspicious at me, and from that time on he kept close to my side and would not allow us to stop but walked us right on around and out. It was getting dusk and we had no chance for me to light my fire and I saw that it was telling on my companions—that they were bitterly disappointed when we were compelled to walk out. I told them to come on in haste, that we were late and would miss our boat that we were going on. So they came along and we stopped behind a house, where I told them what I had done, which made them two of the happiest fellows I ever saw. We had to watch but a few minutes until we saw the steward start away on a run, and we knew he was going for a key or some one, and that this was our chance, so leaving the judge and squire on guard, I ran back to the Temple.

I started for the top which I soon gained and found a good place to start my fire where it would get a good start before it would shed any light and be seen from the outside. After seeing it start to success I began to retrace my steps with joy and a light heart, for I was sure that the Temple was as good as burned, with a chance for me to burn with it, for I had lost my way and did not know which way to turn to get out, although I had been through the Temple a number of times before. I had thought if I would succeed at last in getting out, that I would be sure to get caught by the steward, for he would soon be back and in all probability would have help with him, for I was certain that he would lay the missing key to us. You can imagine my feeling, being left in the burning Temple, and in case I did escape the fire I was sure of an arrest. I ran first one way, then the other, in hopes of gaining some passage that I would know so as to find my way out, but all to no purpose. I was getting worse lost all the time, and I could not tell one direction from another, for it was as dark as an Egyptian night. At last I came to the stairway going up and I took it with the hope that it would lead me back to where I had started the fire and I could then take a new start. After going up two pairs of stairs and through many halls I came to a square turn and a light shone way down the passage in the opposite direction from what I wanted to go, but I thought it best to go and see what it was or who it was, and I soon discovered that it was my fire which was burning at a fearful rate, sending its fiery tongue clear across the hall.

I drew as near as I could and I happened to see Squire McCauley's bandana handkerchief lying on the floor a short distance from the fire on the opposite side of me. So I knew that my way led through the fire as that room was the end of our trip. Now what was I to do? I knew no other way out but through the fire. I became horror stricken. Was I to be burned up by my own hands? O God, what shall I do? Not knowing as it were what I did, I threw my coat over my head and made a dive through that hell of fire, striking my full length on the floor and I rolled over and over until I got out of the reach of the fire. When I got to my feet I took off my coat and extinguished the fire that caught in the lining, after which I put it on again. With difficulty I tried to run, for I seriously hurt my arm and one of my legs from my fall on the floor, but was so excited at the time that I did not realize the pain until afterwards. With the assistance of a few matches I had, that I now thought of, I kept striking them along the way, and at last reached the door that I had been going through and found it standing open. The squire had come and thrown it open in hopes I might be able to see a star from without.

They were satisfied that something had happened on account of my delay. You can imagine our feelings when I stepped through the door. I pulled the door to and locked it and ran away in an easterly direction, the judge and squire following. I was sore, lame and burned and almost choked, not being able to speak and when I came to a well about one hundred yards away, I drank and threw the key in the well. I then told the boys to scatter and go to the horses, which they did. They got there long before I did for I was almost beyond going at all. After reaching the horses I told them the job was done and for them to go in different directions and get home as soon as possible and avoid meeting anyone. They objected to leaving me as they were afraid I was hurt internally, which I was fearful was the case, I had inhaled the fire and thought my time had come. I told them to go, that I would pull through all right. So the squire took the river road up the river to Appanoose ten miles distant; the judge took the road to Carthage, about sixteen miles distant to the south; while I took the prairie road in the direction of Pontoosuc, twelve miles distant.

After going about one-half mile, I looked toward Nauvoo and I saw a flickering light and the next minute the flames burst through the roof and lit up the country for miles as light as day. I put my horse into a dead run in the direction of the Missouri timber, which I gained in time without being seen, as the people on the road were all in bed, but I had no sooner jumped my horse over a fence into a field and secreted myself behind some bushes, when along came seven horsemen on their way to the fire, which had by this time been discovered twenty miles around. After they had passed I again tried to mount my horse, but found it impossible and found my leg had swollen so that I could not walk. I was in a fix, sure enough. What to do I did not know, but I had to do something, so I got down on my hands and knees and crawled on toward a cluster of trees, leading my horse. When I arrived at the timber I fortunately found a large tree which had been cut down, leaving a high stump; crawling upon this stump I managed to get on the back of my horse, and went back, jumping my horse over the fence back into the road.

I was suffering so terribly that I could but just cling to my saddle. I turned my horse in the direction of Squire McCauley's cabin, where I arrived just before daybreak, and found that the squire had got home nearly two hours before. He was surprised to be called out by me, but after giving him to understand my condition, he cried like a child. He took me in and hid me away for a week, where he and his wife cared for me, as they would for one of their own, until I was able to go about without suspicion. The judge got home the night following the night the Temple was burned, having to ride in the woods on Rock Creek all day, which was on the south side of Rock Creek township.[22]

This confession, part of the Nauvoo Temple lore since the 1870s, has been repeatedly cited by historians and Church members.[23] However, circumstantial evidence fails to support this colorful admission in some respects. George W. Johnson, David LeBaron's brother-in-law and co-caretaker of the temple at the time of the fire, repudiated Agnew's confession in his autobiography:

During the year of 1848, David T. LeBaron and myself, were engaged in exhibiting the Nauvoo Temple to strangers until it was burned which happened on the night of November 19th, 1848, and as a very incorrect account of its burning has been published I will here insert my account of it.

... On the 18th day of November, I was taking a party through. We had been to the top and returned as far as the second story when I heard voices below. Leaving my company, I ran down to the main room below where I found the door partly open and two men sitting in the pulpit talking. One of them was telling the other what a host of money and lives the building had cost. How much suffering and sorrow. [T]hen I entered and invited them to leave which they did.

He [one of the two men mentioned] was then boarding at a public house north of the temple across the street kept by a man by the name of Slocum. After the temple was burned he was heard to boast that he saw the fire when it did not look larger than a man's hand. His room was facing the temple. The fire started late at night when all were supposed to be in bed and asleep. Now add to this the fact that the west basement window on the south side which led to the stairway had been taken out and was

22. George H. Rudsill, "Brought to Light: How the Famous Mormon Temple at Nauvoo Was Destroyed," Fort Madison (Iowa) Democrat, ca. 1905, photocopy in LDS Church Archives.

23. See, for example, Pyper, "Leaves from My Diary," 246-47; and B. H. Roberts, A Comprehensive History of the Church of Jesus Christ of Latter-day Saints, 6 vols. (Salt Lake City: Deseret News Press, 1930), 3:22-23. Pyper accuses Agnew in no uncertain terms: "I knew the man who burned the Temple. With others I went to dancing school on Main street, where he kept a boarding house. A hall was in the north side of the house for dancing school and other amusements. He burned the Temple while living in that house—but it could not be proven—suspicion was all, and we had it from good authority that he was paid one hundred dollars to do the cowardly deed. Joseph Agnew was his name! He was short of stature, rather stoutly built; dark blue eyes and brown hair. I can see him now in my mind. I have his confession. He wrote it some years ago, and told how he did it!"

sitting against the wall of the building showing that no key was used to enter the building and the fire was started in the upper story now it is supposable at least that if a man saw the fire when it did not look larger than a man's hand at that time of night he must have been looking for it. And all these facts do away with the Agnew theory that he went to Apanoose on horseback and with a false key went through the door and set the fire. There are some now living who can corroborate these statements.[24]

Johnson was not the only one to reject Agnew as a suspect. Thomas Gregg, in his *History of Hancock County* states:

Who the vandal was that applied the torch has never been known.... There was a report, some years since, that Mr. Joseph Agnew, late of Pontoosuc, was the guilty person and had so confessed on his death-bed. After diligent inquiry we find that there is no foundation whatsoever for the story. Mr. A[gnew]'s friends, while admitting he was a daring Anti-Mormon, scout [scoff] at the idea that he was capable of such an act.

Gregg proposes another theory:

Public opinion abroad has fixed the stigma upon the Anti-Mormons. This has been unreasonable and unjust.... We do know and affirm that the great body of them everywhere condemned the act.... There is another theory in regard to its destruction that is quite as likely to be the true one. The truth is, that, now that the Mormons were leaving the city and State, the temple had become quite a large elephant in their hands.... There was dissension among the brotherhood [members of the Church]; two or three parties existed among them, all claiming to be the true Church, and the others as heretics, and they hated each other. It has been guessed, and we think not without reason, that some fanatical and over-zealous member of one of these parties may have destroyed it in order that the other should not reap the benefit of it.[25]

---

24. Johnson, Autobiography, 5-6. Though his autobiography was not published, it is clear that some of the details he mentions were widely known. For example, the *Peoria Transcript* article reprinted in the *Deseret Evening News*, notes: "It was always supposed that the party who burned the building had entered through the basement, but the facts are, Mr. Agnew surreptitiously obtained a key to one of the doors to the temple some time before the act..... Our informant, who is a responsible and prominent citizen of the western part of the state, says he thinks he can produce the key of the temple which Agnew secured in order to accomplish his work. "The Man Who Fired the Nauvoo Temple," *Deseret Evening News*, 26 April 1872, 3.

25. Gregg, *History of Hancock County*, 956-57. John Hajicek, "The Burning of the Nauvoo Temple," unpublished article, photocopy in my possession, has suggested that Brigham Young may have contributed the money to have the temple burned. He cites Young's repeated failures to sell the temple due to the faulty title and his practice of threatening to burn Mormon settlements in Utah before allowing them to be invaded, as well as statements like the one mentioned below.

In Salt Lake City in 1860, Brigham Young, expressed his feelings in characteristically strong terms:

> I never again want to see [a temple] built to go into the hands of the wicked.... I would rather see it burnt than to see it go into the hands of devils. I was thankful to see the Temple in Nauvoo on fire. Previous to crossing the Mississippi river, we had met in that Temple and handed it over to the Lord God of Israel; and when I saw the flames, I said "Good, Father, if you want it to be burned up." I hoped to see it burned before I left, but I did not. I was glad when I heard of its being destroyed by fire, and of the walls having fallen in, and said, "Hell, you cannot now occupy it." ... I would rather do this than to build a Temple for the wicked to trample under their feet.[26]

Many details of the Agnew confession are inconsistent with what is known about the layout of the temple and the statements of other witnesses, although these discrepancies may be accounted for by the passage of time and transmission of the account from one person to another. Agnew may have been involved somehow in the arson, although the particulars of his motive, payment, and method remain in doubt. Regrettably, his confession came to light after the deaths of all three supposed participants so there are no corroborative accounts by McCauley or Sharp nor do any contemporary records document a role for either in the temple's burning.

Tornado Destroys Temple

Although charred, the great stone walls of the temple survived the fire. In March 1849, David T. LeBaron, who was still acting as caretaker of the temple, sold it to the Icarians, as they were called, for $2,000.[27] This community of 280 French emigrants settled at Nauvoo during the spring of 1849 under the leadership of Etienne Cabet. Cabet, a French political activist, had authored *A Voyage into Icaria*, in which he proposed a society based on communal living. Attracted by the largely deserted city of Nauvoo, his followers decided to settle there and pursue their communal experiment. The Icarians undertook the task of refurbishing the temple for their use. They intended to "refit it for schools, its studying and meeting halls, for a refectory [dining hall] capable of containing about one thousand persons."[28]

26. Brigham Young, 8 October 1860, *Journal of Discourses*, 8:203. Young was of course referring to the earlier, short-lived fire on the temple roof.

27. *Oquawka* (Illinois) *Spectator*, 2 May 1849, quoted in Arrington, "Destruction of the Mormon Temple at Nauvoo," 423.

28. P. Dourg (Secretary of the Icarian Community), "Destruction of the Temple of Nauvoo, on the 27th of May, 1850, by a Storm," *Deseret News*, 24 August 1850, 5; this article is reprinted from the *Missouri Republican* of St. Louis on 29 May 1850.

Despite these ambitious plans, John M. Bernhisel, who was still in Nauvoo, observed in September 1849, "Though the walls of the temple are standing, yet they are much cracked, especially the east one; and not a vestige of the once beautiful font remains. There has been nothing done to rebuild it, except clearing away some rubbish, and it is highly probable there will never be anything more done. The temple is enclosed with a rude fence, and is used as a sheepfold and cow-pen."[29]

In early 1850, the Icarians began to work on the temple. By May, "masons began to lay the foundation to rest the columns or pilasters to support the floors.... The basement ... was divided into small rooms on either side. Two of these rooms had been covered with boards on the north side to store green hides. The others on the south side to store tools."[30] The Icarians had also sent an agent "to the pine forests in the North to buy timbers of dimensions necessary for re-establishing the roof and floors. Some other pieces of wood were ready; a steam mill was purchased to fit up a saw-mill; the saw-mill was nearly finished; a vast shed was raising near the Temple, to shelter the carpenters."[31]

Then on 27 May, a disastrous tornado swept through Nauvoo, knocking down one of the temple walls and damaging the others. The Icarian paper lamented:

> The dreadful tornado of May 27th which invaded the city of Nauvoo and neighboring places has been for us Icarians (little accustomed to such revolutions in the atmosphere) a spectacle of frightful sublimity, and also a source of mortal anguish, on account of the disasters and catastrophes which have resulted from it, to the inhabitants of this county and to us.
>
> The temple which we were preparing so actively and resolutely to rebuild ... has become the first victim of the tornado.
>
> How many projects are buried under these heaps of rubbish! How much outlay and days of hard labor have been lost to us! It was for that magnificent edifice to again give a soul to that great body, that one of our agents in the north pineries has just bought all the great beams necessary for its rebuilding.
>
> There now remains nothing of the gigantic work of the Mormons, except the west face, strongly united by its sides to another wall in the interior part and surmounted by an arch; between the two walls at the north and south are the two towers or seat of the staircases.[32]

---

29. John Bernhisel, Letter to Brigham Young, 10 September 1849, St. Louis, Missouri, quoted in *Journal History*, 10 September 1849, 2.

30. Emile Vallet, *Communism: History of the Experiment at Nauvoo of the Icarian Settlement* (Nauvoo, IL: Nauvoo Rustler, n.d.) 8-9.

31. Dourg, "Destruction of the Temple," 5.

32. "Destruction of the Mormon Temple," *Nauvoo Patriot,* 19 October 1848, reprinted under same title in *Millennial Star* 11 (1 February 1849): 46.

Several workmen were in the temple when the storm hit:

> The storm burst forth so quickly and with such violence that the masons didn't have time to flee before the northern wall sixty feet high bent down over their heads threatening to crush them.... Their loss appeared to be certain for the southern and eastern walls, which had always been looked upon as the weakest, now shaken by the fall of the former, seemed on the point of tumbling on them. But the running rubbish of the northern wall stopped at their feet.[33]

Icarian Emile Vallet, who was one of seven men in the temple when the storm hit, left a personal account of this terrifying experience:

> Suddenly a furious wind began to blow; four of the masons fearing non-solidity of the walls, left to seek shelter elsewhere. Seven of us remained, taking refuge in the tool room on the south side. If there is a Providence it was on our side, for hardly had we taken our position than the tornado began to tear small rocks from the top of the walls which flew in every direction. We became frightened. Some proposed to run away, others opposed it on the ground that it was dangerous as those loose rocks could fall on our heads and kill us. We had [not] decided whether we should stay or run, one of us who was watching, exclaimed, "Friends, we are lost, the north wall is caving in!" And so it was. A wall sixty feet high was coming on us, having only forty to expand. We fled to the south corner, deafened with terror. I for one, heard nothing. The fall of that wall was heard three miles away in the country. We looked at one another. All alive, but as white as sheets. The wind was terrific, the rain was blinding us. The clouds were touching the ground. The severest storm I ever witnessed in Nauvoo. We were mostly paralyzed. We expected every minute the other walls to come down. Some of the top rocks had fallen within three feet of us. The east wall was three feet out of plumb.
>
> "Forward march!" shouted one and on we ran over the heaped-up rocks more dead than alive. When out, it was so dark that we could not find any gates and jumped over fences.... The storm lasted three hours. Several houses had been blown down....
>
> The fall of that wall ended the rebuilding of the Temple.[34]

The Icarian Community secretary reported:

> The same evening, the masons, reunited and consulted by the Gerency [the Icarian leadership], acknowledged and declared that the southern and eastern walls would soon fall down, and that, to avoid any serious accident, it was better to destroy them.
>
> The next morning the General Assembly, having been convoked by the Gerency, met on the Temple Square, and unanimously resolved: first, that the demolition was urgent, for the safety both of the members of the Colony themselves,

---

33. Dourg, "Destruction of the Temple," 5.
34. Vallet, *Communism*, 8-9.

On the left is a tintype showing the west face of the temple ruins. On the right is Frederick Piercy's drawing of the ruins, showing the east side of the west wall.

and of the inhabitants and foreigners whom curiosity might bring to the spot. Second, that by unfixing the walls, stone by stone, they might preserve some good ones. But as this operation would take up much time, occasion much work, and expose them to many fatigues and dangers, and considering the lives of men as much more valuable than money, they decided to use some other method.

Those means having been discussed and agreed upon, they set at work immediately and the walls were pulled down.[35]

The Icarians also resolved to "begin again, on the place of the Temple, provisional and urgent construction" which was intended to serve "until they build another large and fine edifice."[36] However, before they could pursue this project much further, factionalism disrupted their unity. In 1857, a large group of them left Nauvoo, and by 1859 the community dissolved and deserted the city.[37]

At this point, the north wall had collapsed in the tornado, the south and east walls had been dismantled, but the west wall (façade) of the temple remained standing. Frederick Piercy, a twenty-three-year-old Mormon en route to Salt Lake City from Liverpool, described the ruins in 1853:

A tornado blew down the north wall, and so shook the building that the Icarians, who had been engaged in re-building the edifice for their use, deemed it advisable to pull down the east and south walls, leaving only the west wall. This beautiful ruin is all that is left of what was once a work the most elegant in its construction, and the most renowned in its celebrity, of any in the whole west, and which had been built by the Latter-day Saints in the midst of poverty and persecution.[38]

35. Dourg, "Destruction of the Temple," 5.
36. Ibid.
37. Gregg, *History of Hancock County*, 958.
38. Frederick Piercy, *Route from Liverpool to Great Salt Lake Valley* (London, Latter-day Saints' Book Depot, 1855), 62.

During the 1850s and early 1860s, the west wall was further weakened and started to crumble. After the departure of the Icarians, German immigrants began to move in, becoming the city's primary inhabitants. By 1864, only the southwest corner remained standing. Considered a safety hazard, it was razed and leveled in 1865. J. M. Davidson later reported in the *Carthage Republican*:

> It may be remarked that the southwestern corner of the temple stood as a magnificent ruin until 1865 ... a sightly landmark for many miles around. The ruin, when we saw it ... was said to be eighty feet high. It was torn down a year or two later for the stone in it, and the ground where the temple stood was converted into a vineyard.
>
> The last remaining vestige of what the famous Mormon temple was in its former glory has disappeared, and nothing now remains to mark its site but heaps of broken stone and rubbish. The southwest corner, which has braved the blasts of ten or fifteen winters,—towering in sad grandeur above the sad buildings,—a marked object for many miles, the shrine of the pilgrimage of thousands who have annually flocked to gaze in wonder and awe upon the beautiful ruin,—is no more. The eye of the stranger and traveler who approach the classic city of Nauvoo will no more rest upon the towering ruin that first gives notice of their proximity to the sacred soil, where once tread [sic] the hurrying feet of thousands of the "Lord's anointed."
>
> The old ruin has been in process of demolition at times during the past winter. One day last week a mine was placed beneath the remaining portion yet standing; and with the blast that followed the last of the famous Mormon temple lay prone and broken in the dust. We understand that the stone, much of which is uninjured, has been sold to parties who contemplate building residences and wine cellars. The facial and other decorations surmounting the columns are reserved by the proprietor, Mr. Dornseiff,[39] who has kindly promised us as perfect a specimen as can be saved from the ruin. Of the large number of decorations, stone carvings, etc., with which the temple was beautified, hundreds have been secured by curiosity seekers in all parts of the country; and numbers have even gone to Europe. Some fine specimens are in the possession of the citizens of Nauvoo; and numbers of the best wine cellars are ornamented over their entrances with suns in bas relief, trumpets, etc.
>
> Mr. Dornseiff will plant a vineyard upon the temple square as soon as the rock is removed and the season permits.[40]

---

39. Dornseiff (first name not known), a German immigrant and Nauvoo landowner, built an opera house from some of the temple stones. "Nauvoo 'Opera House' Acquired by Wilford C. Wood," *Improvement Era* 40 (June 1937): 356.

40. Unknown author, untitled article containing quotations from J. M. Davidson, "Nauvoo: The Past and Present of That City: Visits of 1846 and 1864 Contrasted," *Carthage Republican*, 25 February 1864, 1, and quoted in E. Cecil McGavin, *The Nauvoo Temple* (Salt Lake City: Deseret Book, 1962), 93-94. McGavin mistakenly cites Davidson as the author of the article, rather than as "quoted by unknown author."

Fate of the Stones and the Lot

Although Nauvoo had virtually no Mormon population after the Battle of Nauvoo in September 1846, the city was still a point of pilgrimage for the Saints for many years. Saints who traveled east from Winter Quarters and Utah as well as immigrants from the East and Europe en route to Utah frequently stopped at Nauvoo, usually lodging at the Mansion House, which was operated as a hotel by Emma and Louis Bidamon for many years. The visitors nearly always inspected the temple site, and their descriptions document the state of the building and grounds through the years, including the sale and subsequent use of the temple stones.

Jonathan C. Wright, a Latter-day Saint who paid a return visit to Nauvoo in early 1848, recalled that he and a "Brother Stewart ... visited the temple, went into the Northeast upper room and we there called in solemn prayer unto the Lord to remember his Church and to remember his scattered Saints."[41] Later that year Apostle Wilford Woodruff also visited Nauvoo and "went over [the temple] from the bottom to the top." He commented, "The temple was in a much better state of preservation than I expected to find it.[42]

Eliza R. Snow, en route to England in 1850, stopped in Nauvoo and penned a poignant description of the ruined city and its temple:

> My heart sickened as I contemplated that once beautiful city, filled with the songs of rejoicing, and all that was good and virtuous; where the voice of the Prophet had sounded forth upon the ears of thousands the deep and heavenly mysteries that had been concealed for ages.... But now, O how sad the change! The moss was growing upon the buildings, which were fast crumbling down; the windows were broken in, the doors were shaking to and fro by the wind, as they played upon their rusty, creaking hinges. The lovely Temple of our God, once the admiration and astonishment of the world and the hope of the Saints, was burned, and its blackened walls were falling upon each other![43]

In 1853 Frederick Piercy, in addition to providing an important sketch of the one remaining wall of the building, stated that the Icarians had "used the stones of the Temple to build workshops and a schoolhouse."[44] In 1859, Joseph Riter, a

41. Jonathan C. Wright, 11 February 1848, quoted in McGavin, *The Nauvoo Temple*, 130-31. Wright (1808-80) was baptized on 29 May 1843 and lived in Nauvoo until 1846.

42. Wilford Woodruff, 9 July 1848, *Wilford Woodruff's Journal, 1833-1898*, typescript, edited by Scott G. Kenny, 9 vols. (Midvale, UT: Signature Books, 1983-85), 3:356.

43. Eliza R. Snow, *Biography and Family Record of Lorenzo Snow* (Salt Lake City: Deseret News, 1884), 112-13.

44. Piercy, *Route from Liverpool to Great Salt Lake Valley*, 62. This schoolhouse stood for many years and later served as a visitors' center for Nauvoo Restoration, Inc.

Nauvoo resident during the 1850s and 1860s, recalled that the temple was "still standing a ruin" when he first moved to the city. He continued:

> The north wall and a part of the front were standing. When I returned at that time, several buildings were standing on the block. In the course of time, a great many stones of the temple have been carried away and used in other buildings, but there are quite a large number of them still to be seen on the ... lot southeast of the temple site. Quite a number of the stones that had the faces carved upon them were defaced, but there may be some of them still perfect.[45]

In 1876, eleven years after the last wall was razed, one observer noted, "No remains of the temple, except pieces of wall on the north side of the block could [be] discovered."[46]

During the 1880s, several important descriptions of the lot were written. At this point, the primary citizens of Nauvoo were German immigrants. Brigham Young's grandson, Richard W. Young, wrote of his 1882 visit to Nauvoo:

> The Temple we at once concluded must have been erected on one of the highest points of the ridge, and so we walked up to what we considered a likely location; our first conjecture was further strengthened as to the site by the presence in that neighborhood of a drug store and several other buildings constructed of finely wrought white stone, which we assumed to have come from the walls of the Temple. And so it proved, for after a short walk down a street in that neighborhood we met a man who turned out to be the owner of the Temple lot, which we had passed a block or two....
>
> And so we found it. Our guide, Mr. Bahmann, present proprietor of the lot and a store opposite, led us up the street to the middle of a certain block and turned into a gate, which opened through an ordinary fence. We saw nothing within to betray the former site of a costly edifice....
>
> The precise limits of the structure were pointed out; it was in the middle of the lot as regards north and south, with its front wall about half way from front to rear, and the rear wall coincident with the back fence. Upon this ground stood a wagon with freight for some neighboring town; a large sized peach tree was growing a little to the rear of the center of the building site, and a well, which was described as the only remnant of the Temple on the lot, except a few scattering pieces of rock from the walls which had been thrown near the fences in clearing the ground for cultivation..... The water of the well was quite sweet; Mr. Bahmann

45. Joseph D. Riter, Autobiography, 1910, typescript, 4, LDS Church Archives. Riter (1830-unknown), a nonmember, was born in Pennsylvania, moved to Nauvoo in May 1846, and was still living during the battle in September 1846. After traveling for several years, he settled permanently in Nauvoo in 1859.

46. William Adams, Autobiography, 1894, typescript, 36, Perry Special Collections, Lee Library.

described it as having been located near the font supported by the carved oxen. In his store he showed us a part of one of the (sunstone) rays, formerly on the second story front.[47]

During the summer of 1883, Louie Wells, the twenty-one-year-old daughter of Emmeline B. Wells and Daniel H. Wells, penned this account of visiting the site with a friend:

> We ... went up to see what was left of the Temple, but where it once stood is a nice new, frame house, and the store on the south west corner of the block is built entirely of the Temple rock; it is as smooth and white as ever, and they say it does not wear away, one particle. The store is used for a drug store and post office, and is very large, 103 ft. by 30. Ever so many foundations and houses around here seemed to be made of it, how we envied them; from there we went one block east, and saw a very small square house, built of the same rock....
>
> [A] Mrs. Clark ... went out with us and showed us where the rest of the Temple rock was that had been bought by Mr. Ritter, a very rich old man; one of the daughters went over with us and we saw all there was to see, hunted round for a piece with carving on, but found only one of those immense heads, and it was perfect; the stone was scattered over the whole block, and he has sold a great deal; it hardly seemed possible there could have been so much in the building. One large piece with carving on he sold to a man from Chicago for $300, and said he would not sell that head for less; he gave us some small specimens.[48]

In 1886, Apostle Franklin D. Richards, made a similar pilgrimage to the former temple grounds and provided this glimpse of its state:

> Near the southeast corner of the Temple Block we saw a tavern bearing the sign "Temple House, kept by Valentine Laubersheimer." We put up at this place of entertainment; but before we could bring our minds to think of food or rest, we visited the site where once stood the beautiful temple. Of the stately structure not one stone was left standing upon another. The pollution of man has done its work, and melancholy and decay now abide amidst the scattered fragments....
>
> The place is occupied by stores and houses. We met a Mr. Reimbold, who is the present possessor of a portion of the block, and the proprietor of a mercantile house located there. He consented to act as our guide and informant, and to take us with a vehicle about the place. His store is standing very near the spot where the entrance to the Temple premises was in former times; and his stable yard, in the rear of his warehouse, extends so far upon the sacred site as to

47. Richard W. Young, "In the Wake of the Church," *Contributor* 4 (January 1883): 151.
48. Louie Wells, Letter to Emmeline B. Wells, 25 July 1883, in "Nauvoo the Beautiful," *Woman's Exponent* 12 (15 August 1883): 37. Mr. Ritter was probably the Joseph Riter mentioned above.

include the well which supplied the water for the baptismal font. The basement has all been filled in with debris up to the level of the surrounding ground, and the well has been walled up to this surface with stones from the Temple. Cattle and horses are watered there daily. We drank from it and found the water clear and delicious to the taste. We filled a bottle with the crystal liquid, and brought it home, that others might partake of it. That which we have remaining of it, still retains its purity and sweetness.

Mr. Reinbold carried us to the house of a gentleman to view a collection of carved stones taken from the Temple. These are kept in view and are exhibited to hundreds of people who annually visit the locality. The great fire considerably softened and split the rocks, but the devices upon them are quite legible and are easily traced.[49]

Assistant Church Historian Andrew Jenson visited the site in 1888 and published his examination of the temple site in the *Deseret News*:

There are ten houses on the Temple Block; the exact spot where the Temple stood is owned by C. W. Reimbold, who keeps a little store and also a book in which he requests his visitors to the Temple site to register their names. Mr. Reimbold has taken considerable pains in posting himself concerning the old places, and we found him very correct and reliable. We learned a great many historical facts in regard to the Temple, the rocks of which have been shipped to nearly every State in the Union, and some have even been sent to Europe. Thus there is a Catholic Church in Rock Island, built of the Temple rock, a private residence in Davenport, Iowa, not to speak of a large two-story building standing in the southwest corner of the Temple Block itself, erected by the Icarians, and the many rocks used for ornamental purposes in many private residences in Nauvoo. A pile of picked rock, containing moons and other designs, lies in the south part of Nauvoo, being hauled there by a man who expected to erect a private residence with them.[50]

A decade later in 1909, John Zimmerman Brown, a professor at the University of Utah, added:

The block is now fairly well covered with dwellings and out buildings, the largest one, standing on the southwest corner, is built of stones taken from the walls of the temple. All that is now left of the sacred edifice is the old well that supplied water for the baptismal font. Not a single stone of the building is left in place. This well, which was in the east end of the basement, is now equipped with a pump and is used for culinary purposes.[51]

---

49. Franklin D. Richards, "A Tour of Historic Scenes," *Contributor* 7 (May 1886): 300.
50. Jenson, "Infancy of the Church," 54.
51. John Zimmerman Brown, "Nauvoo Today," *Improvement Era* 12 (July 1909): 714.

John D. Giles, a member of the Church's Young Men's Mutual Improvement Association general board, visited the site in 1929. He commented, "Nothing remains to mark the spot save the old well which supplied water for the baptismal font. Every stone, every bit of evidence that a Temple once occupied the spot has been carried away. No marker, no monument—nothing but grass and weeds."[52] Mormon historian T. Edgar Lyon, writing in 1965, summarized the uses to which the site had been put: "The Temple Block, during the 112 years following the exodus of the Saints, was occupied by a succession of saloons, slaughter houses, hotels, grocery and drug stores, pool halls, the telephone exchange, and private dwellings."[53]

Archeological investigations conducted in 1962 confirmed that "local stone salvagers had not only removed the surviving visible stones, but had even dug into the ground to reclaim the lowest footings and the font drain."[54]

The LDS Temple-Building Tradition Continues

After the arrival of the Saints in Utah, erecting a temple was one of the first orders of business. Within thirty years, four temples were under construction, an activity that revived many memories of the Nauvoo Temple. William Weeks, architect of the Nauvoo Temple, became disaffected from the Church in 1847, and Truman O. Angell, who later took his place as Church architect, became the primary architect of the Salt Lake, St. George, and Logan temples. He worked with Brigham Young in much the same way that Weeks and Joseph Smith had collaborated in Nauvoo.

Another Nauvoo Temple worker, carpenter, and joiner William H. Folsom, brought his experience to Utah where he assisted Angell in the architect's office and designed the Manti Temple and the Salt Lake Tabernacle. William Holmes Walker, one of the men who helped frame and raise the Nauvoo Temple tower, "labored in the Logan and Salt Lake temples, using the same tools he had used when working on the Nauvoo Temple."[55]

---

52. John D. Giles, "From the Green Mountains to the Rockies," *Improvement Era* 33 (April 1930): 385.

53. T. Edgar Lyon, "The Nauvoo Temple: 1841-1964," *Instructor* 100 (March 1965): 98.

54. Virginia S. Harrington and J. C. Harrington, *Rediscovery of the Nauvoo Temple* (Salt Lake City: Nauvoo Restoration, Inc., 1971), 2.

55. William Holmes Walker, in Andrew Jenson, *LDS Biographical Encyclopedia*, 4 vols. (Salt Lake City: Kofford Books, 2007), 1:565.

The Nauvoo Temple bell, which had been brought to Salt Lake with the vanguard pioneer company, was rung at the bowery constructed as a meeting place to signal the beginning of meetings.[56]

Joseph Smith's design for the Nauvoo Temple and his tutelage of Brigham Young exerted a tremendous influence on the appearance and functions of the temples in Utah. Several important decorative and architectural elements from the Nauvoo Temple were incorporated into later designs: the Angel Moroni on the spire, the sunstones, moonstones, and star stones, the assembly rooms with pulpits at each end, and the baptistery in the basement with the font supported by oxen.

The institution of the "temple store" or "tithing store" also continued during the settlement of Utah. Mosiah Hancock remembered that while his father worked on the Manti Temple, the family "drew provisions from the 'Temple Store.'"[57]

The sisters' penny fund in Nauvoo set the stage for the Relief Society's later temple fund-raising efforts. In 1917, the Relief Society raised over $13,000 for the construction of the temples in Alberta and Hawaii by means of a penny subscription.[58]

56. Ronald W. Walker, "'A Banner is Unfurled': Mormonism's Ensign Peak," *Dialogue: A Journal of Mormon Thought* 26 (Winter 1993): 84.

57. Mosiah Lyman Hancock, Autobiography, 1834-65, typescript, 87-88, Perry Special Collections, Lee Library.

58. Conference Report, October 1917, quoted in Jill Mulvay Derr, Janath Russell Cannon, and Maureen Ursenbach Beecher, *Women of Covenant: The Story of Relief Society* (Salt Lake City: Deseret Book Company, 1992), 202.

Epilogue:

THE TEMPLE RESURRECTED

Temple Lot Purchased

In early 1937, more than ninety years after the Saints had abandoned their Nauvoo home, the Church again purchased a portion of the lot on which the building once stood. Interest in selling the land to the "Utah Church" had began as early as 1930 when John Giles, a Mormon visiting Nauvoo from Salt Lake City in 1929, wrote that "a representative of the owner offered an option ... based upon a price of $1,640, the purpose being to resell it to the 'Utah Church.' Needless to say no option was taken and no sale was made, at least on that basis."[1] However, in February 1937, Wilford C. Wood, a wealthy LDS businessman from Bountiful, Utah, purchased part of the site on behalf of the Church. The *Improvement Era* carried this report of the sale:

> To a temple-loving people, the repurchase of the Nauvoo Temple site by the Church, announced by the First Presidency on February 20, 1937, comes as happy news. The purchase was effected by Wilford C. Wood, negotiating for the Church at a public sale of the property.
>
> The temple site, which of recent years has been the property of an embarrassed estate represented by the Bank of Nauvoo, has been offered at public sale on more than one previous occasion but each time the bank has protected its

---

1. John D. Giles, "From the Green Mountains to the Rockies," *Improvement Era* 33 (April 1930): 385.

own interest by bidding in this property over the low offers of competitive bidders. Elder Wood, a member of the High Council of South Davis Stake, has made several pilgrimages to this and other sites significant in Church history, and has for some time interested himself in the acquisition of the temple lot, and has kept the Church Authorities informed concerning the matter.

Telegraphic advice that the site was again to be offered at public sale sent Brother Wood to the First Presidency and the Twelve to learn their wishes concerning the matter. After discussion, Wilford Wood was authorized to represent the Church, and to pay not more than $1,000.00 for the property. Since definite word had already come to Brother Wood that the Bank of Nauvoo would open the bidding in its own interests at $1000.00 and that other interested parties might bid higher, this left a difficult problem.

Not ready to quit, however, Brother Wood, quickly drove the twelve hundred miles from Salt Lake City to Nauvoo, arriving on the evening of February 18, 1937, ready to begin negotiations for the Temple lot. At eight o'clock on the following morning he went to the State Bank of Nauvoo and there met Mr. Reinhardt, the cashier, and Mr. Anton, representing the bank's property interests, and Mr. Leslie Reimbold, administrator of the estate. These four met in a rear room of the bank from which the Temple lot was visible.

Wilford Wood advised these men that he could not afford to pay "the price of sentiment" for the lot, could not pay the price quoted in their telegram, and would not risk the ill-feelings that might be caused by competitive bidding. They advised him that the property was worth all they were asking and that they would buy it back at the sale for what they had in it, if necessary, to protect their interests. A recess occurred, and then Wilford Wood relates the following:

"Came back to the bank and in the back room sat in the most important Council Meeting held in Nauvoo since the Saints were driven from here nearly one hundred years ago. I pleaded for the price to be within reason so I could buy the property. I told them the Church would put up a Bureau of Information which would be a credit to Nauvoo and that what they might lose in the price of the lot would come back to them many times with the people who would come back and pay homage to a desolate city that once had 20,000 people, and only has 1,000 today. I told them of the true principles of the Gospel, of the agency of man, and of the worship of God according to the dictates of conscience.

"They all took cigarettes and offered them to me. I told them I had never tasted tea, coffee, or tobacco in my life. I asked them to name the price for which they would sell to me; they had previously said they could not see how they could sell for less than $1000 to $1500 and it seemed as though no agreement could be made as I was limited to the price I could pay. An impression came to me, and I said: 'Are you going to try to make us pay an exorbitant price for the blood of a martyred Prophet, when you know this property rightfully belongs to the Mormon people?' I felt the spirit of the Prophet Joseph in that room. Mr.

Anton said, 'We will sell the lot for $900.00.' I grasped his hand, then the hand of the cashier of the bank and the agreement was made and signed."

On February 20, 1937, Mr. Wood and Mr. Smith were on hand for the actual sale which was conducted at Carthage. From Nauvoo, they rode to Carthage in a rainstorm. The sale started at 11 o'clock, with several pieces of property being bidden in by the bank. When the Temple lot was put up, both Mr. Anton and Mr. Reimbold nodded to Mr. Wood. He was the sole bidder, offering $900.00, the bank officials having previously agreed not to bid nor to influence any other bidder to raise his bid. Mr. Anton, Vice President of the Nauvoo Bank, endorsed Mr. Woods' check, and the Certificate of Purchase was made out in the name of the Church of Jesus Christ of Latter-day Saints. The property became the Church's once more after nearly one hundred years.[2]

In the following months, Wood pursued the purchase of other portions of the lot.

An agreement entered into April 17, 1937, later followed by a deed dated April 19th, 1937, transferred title of four building lots on the temple block in Nauvoo, adjoining the temple lot, to Wilford C. Wood. In aggregate area the lots comprise one-fourth of the temple block, except for a twenty-five foot strip that was excluded from the sale. On the property, and included in the sale, stands the Nauvoo Opera House, also known as the Nauvoo City Hall, a commodious structure which is now used as a motion picture house, and which is estimated to have cost through its various stages of improvement, approximately $20,000.

Mr. Wood made the purchase in Nauvoo for eleven hundred dollars more than two weeks prior to the date of a public sale that had been advertised for April 26, 1937. The purchase was made on Mr. Wood's own responsibility and in his own name without active interest or authorization on the part of the Church.

The property was jointly owned by six interested parties and estates, represented by Mr. Jacob M. Fisher. The deed bears eight signatures as follows: Bernadine Ursaline Hierstein, Executrix; Jacob M. Fisher, Minnie C. Fisher, Rev. L. C. Tholen, Mrs. Ida Hart, Doris Hart, Dorothy Hart, [and] Adelaide Schneider.... Perhaps the most noteworthy feature of the entire transaction is the existence and conveyance of an abstract indicating a clear title and giving a complete history of the ownership and transfer of the property since it appeared in the name of "Joseph Smith, sole Trustee in Trust for the Church of Jesus Christ of Latter-day Saints," to whom it was transferred by "Daniel H. Wells and Eliza R., his wife." So far as is known this is the first and only quitclaim deed accompanied by abstract of title dating back to the Prophet's day that has in this generation come

2. Marba Cannon Josephson, "Church Acquires Nauvoo Temple Site," *Improvement Era* 40 (April 1937): 226-27.

out of Nauvoo to the Church of Jesus Christ of Latter-day Saints or any of its members.

Arrangements are now being made to transfer title of the property thus personally acquired by Wilford C. Wood to Heber J. Grant, Trustee-in-Trust for the Church of Jesus Christ of Latter-day Saints in which case there will be in existence a clear title of a piece of the Nauvoo temple block property beginning with the first President of the Church and resuming with the seventh President of the Church.[3]

Beginning on 29 October 1940, Wood made an attempt to purchase the old Icarian office building that stood on the southeast corner of the lot. He finally obtained a clear title to that property in 1942 and, in 1951, also acquired part of the northwest quarter of the site.[4] He gave both of these properties to the Church. In 1962, the Church bought the final section of the site, a small lot in the northwest corner, which had been owned by the Reorganized Church of Jesus Christ of Latter Day Saints (now Community of Christ).[5]

The Excavation of the Temple Site

In 1962, the Church sponsored the creation of Nauvoo Restoration, Inc., a nonprofit organization for the preservation of historic Nauvoo. Its first chairman was J. LeRoy Kimball, a Salt Lake physician and descendent of Heber C. Kimball. In the fall of 1961, Kimball had convinced Church authorities to undertake an archeological study of the temple site in preparation for making the Nauvoo Temple site a "great centerpiece" of the restoration of the city.[6] Church officials contacted Dr. Melvin Fowler, an archeologist at Southern Illinois University, and requested that he conduct an exploratory investigation:

In December of 1961 Dr. Fowler spent several days in Nauvoo running test trenches with the aid of a backhoe since the ground was frozen and too difficult to dig by hand. This preliminary testing resulted in the uncovering of four masonry piers thought at first to have supported the pilasters of the south wall. The ghost impression of the east wall was also discovered.... Dr. Fowler also located an area highly disturbed by the bulldozing of a few years back. This bulldozing

---

3. "Nauvoo 'Opera House' Acquired by Wilford C. Wood," *Improvement Era* 40 (June 1937): 356.

4. "The Church Moves On: Church Obtains Nauvoo Property," *Improvement Era* 45 (February 1942): 93.

5. Don Colvin, "A Historical Study of the Mormon Temple at Nauvoo, Illinois" (M.A. thesis, Brigham Young University, 1962), 190.

6. James L. Kimball, "Nauvoo Restoration Pioneer: A Tribute," *BYU Studies* 32 (Winter 1992): 11.

was done in an effort to locate the old walls but succeeded in destroying a good portion of the northeast end of the building instead.[7]

LeRoy Kimball later recalled the events of that first day of excavation:

The coldness of the day and whiteness of the snow provided a bleak setting for the stirring events which were to come....

The backhoe brought for the purpose was carefully swung into position to scoop up the earth where we dared to hope foundations could be located. To our amazement and relief, the blade of the machine immediately struck solid rock which turned out to be one of the south piers which supported the interior pillars of the temple. Our greatest expectations were realized as we gazed upon a sight that no one had beheld for a century.[8]

Fowler and Kimball presented the results of this preliminary dig to the Nauvoo Restoration executives and Church General Authorities and recommended that they conduct a more in-depth study the following summer. The purpose of the proposed second dig was to recover "artifacts which will give us clues ... to the method and detail of the temple's exterior and interior construction, ... to locate the original spot on which the baptismal font stood," and to expose "to public view many of the interesting details about the temple itself as well as artifacts."[9] The newly formed Nauvoo Restoration, Inc., named Fowler as the director of the project with "Dr. [Dee F.] Green supervising the digging and Mr. [Larry] Bowles in charge of mapping, grid, and transit readings for profiles."[10] The excavation commenced on 15 June 1962, under Fowler's direction, with Green and Bowles supervising a team of researchers.[11]

By the end of the summer, the team had located and uncovered the foundation of the north, south, and east exterior walls. "Several large foundation stones were recovered and left in place to mark the outlines of the walls," and an attempt was made to locate impressions of the missing stones.[12] The researchers also made other important discoveries, such as the remains of the partitions separating the

7. Dee F. Green and Larry Bowles, "Excavation of the Mormon Temple Remains at Nauvoo, Illinois: First Season," Florida Anthropologist 18 (June 1964): 78; photocopy in LDS Church Archives.

8. LeRoy Kimball, Foreword to Virginia S. Harrington and J. C. Harrington, Rediscovery of the Nauvoo Temple (Salt Lake City: Nauvoo Restoration, Inc., 1971), i.

9. Dee F. Green, "The Beginnings of Excavation at the Nauvoo Temple Site," Improvement Era 65 (June 1962): 401.

10. Green and Bowles, "Excavation of the Mormon Temple Remains, "78.

11. Green, "The Beginnings of Excavation," 401. For a summary of the first season of activities, see Dee F. Green, "Successful Archeological Excavation of the Nauvoo Temple Site Project," Improvement Era 65 (October 1962): 705, 744.

12. "Excavation at Nauvoo," 705.

suites of rooms along the north and south side of the basement, and a stone tunnel which they conjectured was the drain for the baptismal font.[13]

The excavation continued intermittently during the next four years until 1966, when NRI authorities appointed a husband-and-wife team, James Chipman Harrington and Virginia S. Harrington, to oversee the investigation. James was "recognized as one of the foremost historic archaeologists in the nation,"[14] while Virginia was an accomplished archeologist in her own right. Under their supervision, several new discoveries were made including remnants of the herringbone patterned brick floor and portions of the baptismal font and oxen.[15] The two continued work on the site until 1969; and in 1971, they coauthored a book, *Rediscovery of the Nauvoo Temple*, documenting their archeological study of the temple site. Fittingly, it was the first book published by Nauvoo Restoration, Inc.

T. Edgar Lyon, a former research historian for Nauvoo Restoration, summarized some of the important findings of this archeological dig:

> The interior weight of the floors and roof had been carried by columns or pillars which rested on two rows of stone piers, five in each row, running from east to west in the basement. The stone baptismal font, which had rested on the backs of twelve stone oxen, was located in the depression in the center of the basement. Nearby was a tunnel of stone masonry, more than a foot square, which apparently served as a drainage tunnel to carry the water from the font southeastward toward a ravine. Pieces of broken, polished stone—possibly portions of the oxen or the font, and others which may have been parts of the arched or circular windows of the building—were found. Many old-fashioned square nails, some of them hand-forged, and pieces of lath and plaster, were uncovered. Pieces of melted glass and ashes, and chunks of splattered lead from the 1,500 pounds used in the gutters, are mute evidence of the devastating fire.[16]

Plans to Partially Reconstruct

In 1968, Nauvoo Restoration, Inc., announced plans to rebuild a portion of the temple as a visitors' center. The *Improvement Era* reported:

> The purpose of the restoration is to create a center where the story of the Church can be told to the millions of tourists and nearby residents who travel through the Midwest....

13. Green and Bowles, "Excavation of the Mormon Temple Remains," 78.

14. T. Edgar Lyon, "Books," *Ensign*, February 1972, 77.

15. Harrington and Harrington, *Rediscovery of the Nauvoo Temple* (Salt Lake City: Nauvoo Restoration, Inc., 1971).

16. T. Edgar Lyon, "The Nauvoo Temple: 1841-1964," *Instructor* 100 (March 1965): 98.

Construction on the partial restoration of the Nauvoo Temple is expected to begin in 1970. A two-year construction period is anticipated. Preceding the restoration there will be an exhaustive program of archeological and historical research, which will near completion the latter part of 1969. The archeological work has already unearthed numerous artifacts....

The artifacts will be displayed in a museum and visitors' center to be located on the temple block. The information center will feature numerous displays, artwork, and rooms for the presentation of films designed to tell the temple story. Near the information center and inside the walled temple grounds will be appropriate statuary of the two martyrs, the Prophet Joseph Smith and his brother Hyrum, and of Brigham Young, president of the Council of the Twelve and successor to the Prophet Joseph Smith as head of the Church. Other statuary will represent scenes of the Nauvoo period. The temple block itself will be beautifully landscaped.

The main exhibit however, will be the restored portion of the Nauvoo Temple. The temple's footings and floor will be built over the exact spot where once stood the original temple, and will follow the exact measurements of the original building. Indeed, some of the original stonework, including some of the original footings, will be used in the reconstruction. The brick basement floor will also contain some of the original basement bricks. Portions of the legs of the original 12 oxen that surrounded the font will be used in the font restoration. Nearby will be the temple well, which provided water for the font.

The front façade of the temple is to be rebuilt to the original height of the upper pediment, so that tourists may ascend the stairway and obtain a glimpse of the view that so enchanted early-day Nauvoo visitors.[17]

This plan to partially reconstruct the temple was never carried out.

Improvements to the Site and Other Developments

In addition to the excavation of the temple site, several other important developments occurred during the course of the last sixty-nine years since the lot was repurchased. For many years, the old temple bell hung in the Bureau of Information on Temple Square and could be heard on KSL radio every hour.[18] In November 1941, Amy Brown Lyman, the general president of the Relief Society, announced "plans to mount the old Nauvoo Temple bell in a granite and bronze tower on the Salt Lake Temple Square, as part of [the Relief Society's] centennial celebration."[19]

---

17. Jay M. Todd, "Nauvoo Temple Restoration," *Improvement Era* 71 (October 1968): 11.

18. Lois Leetham Tanner, "I Have a Question," *Ensign*, February 1981, 16.

19. "The Church Moves On," *Improvement Era* 44 (November 1941): 670.

The contract for the tower was let in April 1942 with an announced completion date of about eight weeks.[20] However, the General Authorities decided that "the completion of the campanile will be postponed until the war emergency is passed."[21] Still, sculptor Avard Fairbanks "completed the plaques to be used in the Nauvoo Temple Bell Campanile" in September.[22]

In August 1948, two LDS missionaries tracting in eastern California knocked on the door of Leslie Griffin, William Weeks's grandson, who offered them a valuable series of drawings Weeks had done for the Nauvoo Temple. These plans augmented the small collection of original drawings that the Church already held.[23]

On Saturday, 14 August 1982, Gordon B. Hinckley, then a counselor in the First Presidency, dedicated seventeen restored historical sites in Nauvoo, including the temple site. He referred to the Nauvoo experience as "the crucible of Mormonism—a crucible of vision, a crucible of loyalty, a crucible of integrity, a crucible of leadership, a crucible of faith." The dedication was held on the temple grounds where the excavation had been filled in and the temple outline marked with stones. A hedge and chain link fence surrounded the landscaped lot, and a scale model of the temple gave visitors to the site an idea of the temple's appearance.

In 1988, the Historical Society of Quincy County announced its intention to sell one of the original temple sunstones, which had been on display at the governor's mansion for decades. The following December, the Smithsonian Institute purchased the stone for $100,000, one of its most expensive purchases to date. This sunstone, one of three known to be extant, is now displayed prominently in the Smithsonian Museum of American History in Washington, D.C., with other important American artifacts.[24]

In 1990, the Church began filming a new motion picture, *Legacy*, which was shown until 2000 in the newly refurbished Joseph Smith Memorial Building (formerly the Hotel Utah) in Salt Lake City. The film recounted the Church's odyssey from New York and Kirtland, to Missouri, then to Nauvoo, and finally across the plains to Utah. Most of the filming was done in Nauvoo, resulting the several interesting projects. According to an *Ensign* editor:

> The original stone quarries for the Nauvoo Temple were not hard to find, but they were overgrown with trees and vines and bushes. Crews stripped out all of the overgrowth, rebuilt scaffolding, and brought in oxen and huge-wheeled carts so

20. "The Church Moves On," *Improvement Era* 45 (April 1942): 221.

21. "The Church Moves On," *Improvement Era* 45 (September 1942): 574.

22. Ibid.

23. Carrie Moore, "Edifice Holds Dear Spot in Hearts of LDS Faithful," *Deseret News*, 2 July 2000, 7.

24. Lee Davidson, "Smithsonian Pays $100,000 for Sunstone from Nauvoo Temple," *Church News*, 2 December 1989, 5. This report does not say whether the Church sought to obtain the stone.

The temple lot as it appeared in 1988.

that the quarry scenes could be shot where the actual stones for the temple had been cut.... Great effort was made to be historically authentic and accurate in all reconstructions.[25]

Also in 1990, the Museum of Church History and Art in Salt Lake City unveiled a permanent exhibit featuring, among other things, a display on the Nauvoo Temple. It includes a reconstruction of the lower part of one of the exterior stone walls. LaRene Gaunt reported, "An unfinished sunstone rests in front of the Nauvoo Temple wall, along with actual tools used in the building of the temple, with chips from the sunstone scattered nearby on the ground. It is as if the stonemason has left his work temporarily and you have simply wandered over to the temple site to see his work."[26]

In 1994, a temple sunstone which had been on display in the Nauvoo State Park was moved to the temple grounds and installed in a protective Plexiglas display case. President Hinckley made the following remarks at the unveiling on 26 June:

> One purpose of our gathering today, of course, is to unveil a sunstone which was once a part of the Nauvoo Temple. As state senator Laura Kent Donahue has indicated, it is now the property of the state of Illinois and the state of Illinois has

---

25. LaRene Gaunt, "Legacy," *Ensign*, July 1993, 36.
26. LaRene Gaunt, "A Covenant Restored," *Ensign*, July 1990, 51.

graciously loaned it to us, placed it in our custody. I hope we have built the kind of enclosure around it which will preserve it for many generations yet to come.[27]

In November 1996, an ornamental iron fence four feet tall was installed around the block, replacing the chain-link fence. Manufactured in Ogden, Utah, by Petersen Engineering and Fabrication and installed by missionaries in Nauvoo, the fence was hailed by local missionaries as "a very attractive and dignified enclosure inviting visitors to enjoy this peaceful and sacred spot."[28]

Among the most significant recent discoveries concerning the temple was a daguerreotype of the temple. Though several other photographs from the same vantage point existed, the newly discovered image was the most detailed. The daguerreotype was taken ca. 1847 by Louis Rice Chaffin, a recent convert living near Nauvoo. Chaffin copied the plate in 1852 in Kanesville prior to his journey across the plains. Upon his arrival in Utah, he settled in Cedar City where, years later, his descendants donated the image to the local chapter of the Daughters of the Utah Pioneers. Housed for years in the Iron Mission Museum, it was discovered in 1999 by Scott Christensen of the LDS Church Historical Department. The daguerreotype was cleaned and restored by experts in Kansas City and is now the most detailed available view of the original temple.[29]

The Nauvoo Temple Resurrected

On 4 April 1999, at general conference, President Gordon B. Hinckley made a startling announcement:

> In closing now, I feel impressed to announce that among all of the temples we are constructing, we plan to rebuild the Nauvoo Temple. A member of the Church and his family have provided a very substantial contribution to make this possible. We are grateful to them.
>
> It will be a while before it happens, but the architects have begun their work. This temple will not be busy much of the time; it will be somewhat isolated. But during the summer months we anticipate it will be very busy, and the new building will stand as a memorial to those who built the first such structure there on the banks of the Mississippi.

---

27. Gordon B. Hinckley, "Nauvoo's Holy Temple," *Ensign*, September 1994, 59–60.

28. Don and Betty Ulmer (Public Affairs missionaries), "New Enclosure Surrounds Site of Nauvoo Temple," *Church News*, 9 November 1996, 6.

29. Scott Christensen, interviewed by Matthew McBride, 27 June 2000. See also "About the Cover," *Church News*, 17 April 1999, 2.

The new temple was to be built on the original footprint and with the same exterior appearance as the original.

The announcement was accompanied by delight and surprise throughout the Church. The response in Nauvoo itself was particularly poignant. Sobs, gasps, and clapping attended the announcement. The Nauvoo Stake president, Durell Noland Nelson, recalled, "We were not able to completely contain ourselves. There was a moment of shock, and then there was actually some applause, even though it was during the concluding session of conference. Then everyone caught themselves quickly, and for most of the rest of the meeting there was crying."[30]

Even the architect who had been assigned to the project was taken by surprise. Early in 1999, President Hinckley had asked Robert Dewey, an architect in the Church's Temple Construction Department, to prepare preliminary designs showing how a building of the dimensions of the original temple could be used as a modern temple. However, he did not know President Hinckley intended to make the announcement so soon.[31]

A full reconstruction of the Nauvoo Temple had been contemplated as early as 1938. Remarkably, President Hinckley's father, Bryant S. Hinckley, played a part in that earlier effort to spark interest in reconstruction. On 25 June 1938, in commemoration of the centennial of the founding of Nauvoo, Bryant Hinckley, then president of the Northern States Mission, held services for Latter-day Saints in that region on the recently repurchased temple lot. At this meeting, Lane K. Newberry, a Mormon artist and Nauvoo enthusiast, spoke of his dream of "the temple rebuilt in full size on this spot where it once stood."[32] He and Bryant Hinckley suggested the reconstruction to the First Presidency, but the Church's financial condition after the Depression did not allow serious consideration of the concept.[33] President Gordon B. Hinckley believes it "a strange and wonderful coincidence that I've had a part in the determination of rebuilding this temple."[34]

The history of the new Nauvoo Illinois Temple is a story for another place and time. It was completed in the spring of 2002 and dedicated on 27 June of that year, completing a miraculous series of events that have restored the temple to its majestic place on the bluff overlooking Nauvoo. There it stands, a monument to the faith and sacrifice of the early Nauvoo Saints.

30. R. Scott Lloyd, "Historic Nauvoo Temple to Be Rebuilt," *Church News*, 10 April 1999, 3.

31. Robert Dewey, Church Architect, interviewed by Matthew McBride, 5 June 1999, notes in my possession.

32. Quoted in Janath R. Cannon, *Nauvoo Panorama: Views of Nauvoo before, during, and after Its Rise, Fall, and Restoration* (Salt Lake City: Nauvoo Restoration, Inc., 1991), 75.

33. Ibid., 72; and Greg Hill, "Rebuilding of Magnificent Temple," *Church News*, 30 October 1999, 7.

34. Hill, "Rebuilding of Magnificent Temple," 7.

Appendix

Eyewitness Descriptions of the Nauvoo Temple

This appendix contains selected contemporary descriptions of the Nauvoo Temple. It is selective, rather than comprehensive, as I have focused on the most important, interesting, unique, and representative accounts.[1] While the narrative quotes excerpts from these descriptions, the full accounts offer a glimpse of how temple tours were often conducted and demonstrate which aspects of the temple captured the imagination of the visitors. For greater ease in reading, I have added paragraphing.

Charlotte Haven, "A Girl's Letters from Nauvoo," *Overland Monthly* 16 (December 1890): 620; photocopy in LDS Church Archives. Haven, a young non-Mormon from New Hampshire, lived in Nauvoo for a year with her sister (a member of the Church) while the temple was under construction. She wrote several letters to her

1. For other descriptions of the temple, see Henry Lewis, *The Valley of the Mississippi Illustrated* (St. Paul: Minnesota Historical Society, 1967), 292; *New York Spectator*, 9 November 1844, reprinted in E. Cecil McGavin, *The Nauvoo Temple* (Salt Lake City: Deseret Book Company, 1962), 50-51; John Reynolds, *My Own Times: Embracing the History of My Life* (Belleville [Ill.] : Perrylman and Davison, 1855), 586-87; W. W. Phelps, "The Answer," *Times and Seasons* 5 (1 January 1844): 759; Albert C. Koch, *Journey through a Part of the United States of North America in the Years 1844-1846*, translated and edited by Ernest A. Stadler (Carbondale: Southern Illinois University Press, 1972), 67; C. W. Dana, *The Garden of the World* (Boston: Wentworth & Co., 1856), 104; *The United Stated Illustrated*, ed. Charles A. Dana (New York: Herrmann J. Meyer, 1855), 39-40.

family that were later collected and published, one of which contains this account. She wrote this description after what appears to have been an informal tour of the work site and unfinished building in 1843.

> A few days ago I visited the celebrated Mormon temple, which is situated on the summit of the bluffs facing the west, and commands a view of the whole city, the river for several miles, and an extensive view of the State of Iowa. This temple is a large edifice of white limestone, a hundred and thirty feet in length by eighty-nine in breadth, with walls two feet thick. The style of architecture is unlike any other upon earth, having its origin with Joseph Smith, professed by him to have been revealed by divine revelation. The building is surrounded by thirty-two [actually thirty] pilasters, each resting upon an inverted crescent, and in bas relief is another crescent, on the inner curve of which is carved the profile of a human face made to represent the new moon. Upon the cap of each pilaster there is to be a round face and two hands, holding and blowing a trumpet, to represent the sun. The temple is to be lighted with four rows of windows, two of which will be arched and two round, alternately; but we can hardly form an idea of what its appearance will be when finished, for they have now only reached the first tier of windows.
>
> The Mormons look upon this undertaking as equal to the building of Solomon's Temple, and the day of its completion is far distant. The basement is divided into three halls, and two smaller rooms; the central hall contains the celebrated baptismal font, which is a large stone reservoir, surrounded by a carved wooden railing and supported on the backs of twelve oxen, beautifully carved in wood and standing knee deep in water; these oxen are to be overlaid with pure gold. Pumps are attached to the font to supply it with water when necessary. The temple, together with several other buildings in the city, is built by tithes, every Mormon being obliged to give either labor or produce (the latter being sold near the temple) and Joseph Smith holds in trust everything that is given.

David Nye White, "The Prairies, Nauvoo, Joe Smith, the Temple, the Mormons, &c.," *Pittsburgh Weekly Gazette* 58 (15 September 1843): 3, reprinted in Dean C. Jessee, ed., *The Papers of Joseph Smith*, 2 vols. (Salt Lake City: Deseret Book, 1989, 1992), 1:442-43. White (1803-88), a native of Massachusetts, was a printer by profession and owned the *Gazette*. He visited Nauvoo on 28 August 1844 and published this account the following month. His description of the basement is particularly detailed, since the rest of the building was incomplete.

> This modern structure, which is to revive the departed glories of the temple of Jerusalem, and which is an apparently dear to every Mormon heart, as was that famous and venerated house to the devout Jew, is building, as we stated before

on the bluff and is indeed "beautiful for situation." It is about 120 feet long by 90 broad. When finished it is to consist of a basement, and two twenty-five feet stories. The basement and one twenty-five feet story is up, and the remainder in process of completion. The basement story is about 12 feet in the clear, the half of which is under ground. It is divided off into various sized rooms running along each side, with a large hall or room in the center. In this large room stands the consecrated laver, supported by twelve oxen, carved with great fidelity to the living original. Four of the oxen face the north, four the south, and two each, east and west. They, as well as the laver, are composed of wood, and are to be overlaid with gold.

The laver is of oblong shape, some four or five feet deep, and large enough for two priests to officiate in the rite of baptism, for which it is intended, at once. A pump stands by it to supply it with water. Stairs approach it from either side. I walked up and looked in. It contained nothing but a few inches of water. The laver, oxen, and etc., are at present protected from the weather by a temporary roof. What the numerous rooms in this basement are intended for I did not learn. The walls are all exceedingly strong and massy, even the partition walls, generally from two to three feet thick. The basement is lighted by numerous windows, about five feet high, and as many wide, arched over the top between these windows are very heavy pilasters, on the top of which rest the basement stones of the less heavy pilasters between the windows of the upper stories. On each of these basement stones is carved a crescent or figure of the new moon, with the profile of a man's face, as seen in old almanacs.

The windows of the upper stories are some fifteen or eighteen feet high, arched over the top in a perfect semicircle. The first story above the basement is divided into two apartments, called the outer and inner courts. The walls between these courts are three feet thick, of solid mason work, with two immense doors for passage between them. The outer court is some twenty-five feet wide by ninety-feet long—the inner court is about ninety-feet square.

These facts about the dimensions of the building I obtained from Joe himself. All the work is of good cut stone, almost white, and it will present a fine appearance when finished. How the second story is to be finished I did not learn. I have been thus particular in my description of this building, as many exaggerated stories are circulated in regard to it.

Hiram Gano Ferris, "A Description of the Mormon Temple," *Carthage Republican*, 19 March 1890, 2. Ferris, a student at Knox College in 1846, visited the temple that spring or summer and wrote his description, even though it was not published until much later.

This building, situated at Nauvoo, Hancock County, Ill., is perhaps one of the most singularly constructed edifices in the United States. Its style of architecture is neither Gothic nor Greecian, but from the general analogy it bears to Mormon notions and character, it may properly be considered Mormonic. It very well corresponds to the marvelous and mystical notions held by the larger portion of the Mormons. The general appearance is neat and imposing. It is built of a fine quality of white limestone and the walls are solid. They are about five feet thick at the foundation, composed of large blocks, which are jointed and generally extend through. They are all polished on the surface, or outside, and laid with great care and exactness. On each side are nine columns, and six at each end. Projecting from the surface of the footstone of each of these is a fine representation of the new moon, and at the top of each is a large and well wrought profile of a man's face, in which each feature is prominent and distinct. On the same block, a little above and on each side is the representation of a trumpet lying principally above the surface with a hand grasped around it. Still above is a row of circular windows and a projecting cornice which evinces a high degree of workmanship.

The temple is one hundred and twentysix feet in length and eighty six wide. The basement story rises five feet above the ground. From this to the eaves it is fifty five feet. The tower is twenty, the cupola seventy five, and the dome and spire fifteen, making the whole height from the ground to the top of the spire one hundred and seventy feet. This does not include the slope of the roof, which is probably ten feet. The basement is full size of the edifice. On both sides and one end of this large room are smaller rooms made by thick partition walls. These small rooms on the sides are lighted by windows in the shape of an oblong semicircle; each has one door opening into the large, or central room. But the end room has neither any visible door or window. It is directly under the entrance. In the center of this large room is the baptismal font, constructed in imitation of the famous brazen Sea of Solomon. It is upborne by twelve oxen handsomely carved out of solid limestone. This font is made of large blocks of the same material, jointed and laid in water cement. The floor of this room is made of brick and has a gradual descent from the sides and ends to the font.

About twelve feet of the west end on the next floor above is occupied by the entrance, or "outer court," as the Mormons call it, and two circular stairways rising from the basement to the upper room. The rest of this floor is in one large and capacious room, finished in Mormon style. It is well seated, and at each end is a full set of pulpits, each having five seats, rising gradually one above another, and each calculated to accommodate the different orders and grades of their priesthood: one for the Aaronic, the other for Melchizedek order of priests. In front of each pulpit in large gilt letters are placed the initials of the office held by the occupants. This room presents many other peculiarities which render the whole style and appearance completely Mormonic, and impress one who has had a little insight into the character of Joe Smith and his followers with the fact that he got it up more to fill marvelous eyes than to serve any useful purpose in the convenience it might afford for religious exercises.

On the next floor above, the building is calculated for a hall of the same size as the one last described, but it is at present in an unfinished state. Still above, is a room one hundred feet long and twenty feet wide, which they call the "dancing hall." This hall is in the center, running lengthwise, and on each side are smaller rooms, say 14 to 16 feet in size, designed, as I suppose, for dressing rooms and other kinds of business connected with Mormon dancing entertainments. . . . This room is well finished and lighted by a large half round window in the south end and windows through the roof.

The tower, cupola and dome are all finished outside in a manner indicating neatness and good taste. On the top of the spire is a representation of the flying angel with a trumpet in his hand. Steps are arranged so that a person can go up into the belfry, from which there is a splendid view of the town and surrounding country. The broad Mississippi in all its native grandeur majestically winds its way on to the far distant south amid hills and valleys covered with forest trees, which seem to stand as silent spectators of their noble river, and bordering prairies, whose rich pastures by the refreshing breezes of July, present a variety of scenery both pleasing and sublime.

Unidentified visitor, *St. Louis Gazette*, ca. June 1844, copied in Journal History of the Church of Jesus Christ of Latter-day Saints (chronology of typed entries and newspaper clippings, 1830-present), 12 June 1844, 5, LDS Church Archives. This description, penned by an unknown author, was published while the exterior walls of the temple were not yet complete. It is notable for its reference to a diagram model of the temple which was shown to the author by Joseph Smith and for its description of the workshop where the stonecutters shaped the temple stones.

Ascending an acclivity somewhat abrupt, and turning to the right you are at the site of the Temple. The foundation is entirely of stone, constructed in the most massive manner, and the superstructure is to be of the same material and construction. The dimensions are perhaps 130 feet by 90 feet and the edifice is to have three stories of some 20 feet each in altitude. The spire is to be about one hundred feet higher than the walls, or 160 feet from the ground. The appearance presented by this edifice in the diagram model, which was shown me by the Prophet, is grand and imposing.

The tower, the casements, the doors, and all the prominent parts of the edifice, are to be richly ornamented, both within and without, but in a style of architecture, which no Greek, nor Goth, nor Frank, ever dreamed. I will be bound to affirm, indeed, as I learned from the lips of the Prophet himself, the style of architecture is exclusively his own, and must be known henceforth and for ever I suppose as the "Mormon order!"

The external layer of stone is dressed with considerable neatness, and each of the range of pilasters by which it is ornamented, bears upon it a sculptural representation of the crescent, with the profile of a man's face in strong relief, much in the style of that edifying picture of the moon you may have been wont to admire, as well as myself, in the primer when a boy! The effect of this image is semi-solemn, semi-laughable, and certainly more than semi-singular.

In the workshop beside the structure, in which a large number of stone cutters are employed, may be seen divers other carvings on stone, designed for the holy edifice, still more novel than that I have named. Among them are suns, full moons, and half the constellations of the firmament, to say nothing of the human faces of expression weird enough for an English obelisk. There are 75 or 100 of the fraternity zealously at work at the present time hewing stone or laying it for the Temple, all other public improvements being in perfect abeyance that the greatest and holiest of all may advance.

The walls of the structure are about two feet in depth, and the solidity of the buttresses and the port-hole aspect of the basement apertures for windows, lend the pile more the appearance of a fortalice [fortress] than a sanctuary. It has three entrances all on the west front. On each side of the main entrance is an apartment perfectly circular without window or loophole, or division of any kind, designed for some vestibular purpose, which none of our party could divine.[2] At the eastern extremity is a large arched window, and here no doubt is to stand the altar.

The basement story, as you look down into it, reminds you more of a wine cellar, with its dozen apartments or crypts, each divided from the other by ponderous masonry. In the centre of the basement, resting upon the backs of eight [actually twelve] white oxen carved from wood with passable skill, stands the baptismal font, a rectangular box of some twelve feet square, and half as many in depth.

From each side of this box appear the heads and shoulders of two oxen up to their knees in brick work, with most inexpressive eyes, most extensive ears, a remarkable longitude of face, and a protrusion of horns perfectly prodigious with a single exception, one horn of one unhappy ox having been torn off by some more than usually rude grasp at the "altar!" The effect of all this is of a character somewhat mixed.

It is certainly a little startling in the dim religious duskiness of the spot, to stumble upon these eight [sic] white oxen, standing so still, and stiff, and stark, and solemn, with their great stony eyes staring sternly at you for the intrusion; and yet, the first inclination, after recovering from your surprise is to laugh, and that most heartily. The idea of this font seems to have been revealed to the prophet directly by the plan of the molten sea of Solomon's Temple, which we are told in the old scriptures, stood upon twelve oxen, three looking to the north, three to the south, three to the east, and three to the west; all their hinder parts inward.

---

2. In these cylinder-shaped spaces, spiral staircases would later be constructed.

This Mormon Temple, should it ever be complete—and it has been three years reaching its second floor, will certainly present one of the most extraordinary architectural structures since the era of the erection of the massive sanctuaries of the Nile—of descriptions of the ruins of which the spectator is by this reminded! Its interior structure and arrangement, we were informed by the prophet, had not been decided on—(he did not tell me "had not yet been revealed to him," as he did to many others) and indeed he was by no means certain he should erect the edifice externally in accordance with the plan proposed and published.

The view of the roofs and streets of the city beneath, the farms and fields away to the north and east, the river winding its dark and serpentine course in front, the long and low wooded island lying midway of the stream, the little village of Montrose, on the opposite shore, and far away in the distance, blue along the western horizon, the retreating, undulating hills of lawn—all these objects are spread out like a map before the eye, at a coup d'oeil,[3] from the walls of the Temple; and the scene is as grand as it is beautiful.

Lyman Omer Littlefield, "From Nauvoo—To the Editor of the *Messenger*" *New York Messenger* 2 (30 August 1845): 67-68; photocopy in LDS Church Archives. Littlefield (1819-93) included this description in a letter on 6 August 1845 letter to Parley P. Pratt, editor of the *New York Messenger*, a Church-owned newspaper published in New York City. Littlefield was the paper's Nauvoo correspondent, writing letters regularly with the latest news from Nauvoo. Littlefield's account contains many details that are not in other descriptions. Particularly valuable are his observations about the details of the roof.

In my present letter, I design giving you a description of the Temple, together with a few general remarks upon our beautiful city. Last evening I took a survey of the Temple, and from the notes I took, assisted by the architect of the building himself, I have written the following description which I send for publication, that through the medium of your valuable paper the people of the eastern land may form some conception of the most curious and interesting building in the world.

Let us commence with the basement story. This is divided off into thirteen rooms, the one in the centre is one-hundred feet in length from east to west, and fifty feet wide. In the centre of this room, stands the base of the baptismal fount; it is of hewn stone, and the surface of it is in the shape of an egg divided in the middle from end to end. Its dimensions are fifteen by eleven feet and a half wide on the outside. Strewn over the floor is pieces of massive stone, ready hewn to complete it. When completed it will be supported by twelve oxen hewn from solid stone, which will be represented as being sunk to the knees in a floor of

---

3. Coup d'oeil: at a glance; as much as the eye can take in at one glance.

Roman cement. The fount will be entered by a flight of steps in an arch form at each end. The whole will be surrounded by an iron railing to protect it from the soiling hand of the curious visitor. It will be an interesting and costly work when completed. Large piles of ornamental carpenter work is heaped in different parts of the room designed for the finishing of different parts of the Temple. Curious devices or emblems are wrought or carved upon many of the different pieces.

Now let us examine what is properly called the first story, or the story that commences with the surface of the ground. We enter this at the west end, passing through either of three large open doors or arched pass-ways, each of which is nine feet seven inches wide and twenty one feet high. Passing through these we are standing in a large outer court, forty-three feet by seventeen feet wide. At each end of this is two large doors, passing through which, we are in the first story. The floor is not laid except with loose plank, for the convenience of carpenters, forty or fifty of whom were now to work on this floor. This story as well as the second, will be divided off into fifteen rooms. The large rooms running through the centre of each floor, will be one-hundred feet long, from east to west, and fifty feet wide, at each side of which will be a room, or smaller rooms, of different sizes constructed. At the east end of these large rooms pulpits will be erected, being abundantly lighted at the back by large windows nine feet seven inches wide and fifteen feet high.

Now we ascend a ladder that carries us to the second story. Here is nothing particularly worthy of notice, except that the floor of the large room will be seventeen feet longer than the floor in the first story, in consequence of running out over the outer court. Here is formed a stone arch of forty-one foot span, which supports the tower. Looking down into the basement several children are seen at play, who, from the extreme distance, look like mere specks or atoms crawling over the ground: I have watched them until my head swims, a queer feeling steals over me, convincing me that I never will do for a sailor; so I will cling tightly to the ladder and gain the third story. Here are several workmen. This cannot properly be called more than a half story, the roof on each side not being sufficiently high near the eaves, for a person of six feet, to stand erect. But through the centre, from east to west, will be furnished a room the same size of that in the first story. At the east end of this room, is already constructed the frame of a window twenty and a half feet in the span, which forms four gothic windows, and three irregular triangles which partake of the elliptic and gothic. At each side of this room will also be constructed a row of smaller rooms.

Now we enter the attic story. This story is eighty by forty feet, and is placed upon the west end of the main building. This will be done off into a number of rooms for the use of the higher order of priesthood.

Now climbing over a large beam, not daring in the mean time to look down through the many pieces of timber in to the great distance below, we stand upon the top of the building, or deck, in which is constructed six octagon sky-lights through which light will be reached into the large room below. The deck is finished in the same manner that some of our eastern rooms is ceiled; or in other words in ceiling form, perfectly water tight. At each side of the deck is a roof made of pine shingles perfectly matched and laid in the neatest manner. In each of these roofs, is six square sky-lights through which, light will be reached into the small rooms immediately below. Here are also, two elegant ornamental chimnies of hewn stone, running through each roof.

Now let us go to the top of the attic story which is sixteen and a half feet high from the eaves, and the eaves are sixty feet from the ground. This has not yet been shingled, and we have to stand upon some loose plank. This is a massive pine frame, from the centre of the roof of which rises the tower which is twelve and a half feet high. At that height it is lessened into the belfry which is twenty feet high. This is as far as the steeple is now completed. Above the belfry will come the clock section, ten feet high; next above that will be the observatory sixteen feet high; then the dome, thirteen and a half feet high, from which the balls and rod will run ten feet higher, making the distance from the surface of the ground to the top of the steeple, one-hundred fifty-eight and a half feet.

The wall is ornamented with thirty pilasters having upon the base of each, the representation of a half moon with the crescent downwards. Along the edge of the crescent is carved the representation of the chin, mouth, nose, and forehead of the human face. Upon the capitals of the pilasters, is carved a perfect view of the human face, which seems to represent some kind of a personage emerging out of a cloud, having a trumpet in each hand. A short distance above these are large stars, with five spangles or rays, below which is cut some beautiful drops or Masonic emblems.[4]

In all, there is forty-seven main windows, the tops of which is in a half circle, or oval form. Between the two rows of main windows, is a row of circular or round windows, twenty-two in number. Above the pilaster capitals, is a row of smaller circular or round windows. The basement story is lighted by twenty-two windows in the form of a half circle.

Round the eaves runs a large beautiful cornice, ornamented on the lower side with large stars. The eave troughs hold thirty barrels of water, and are sheeted with sixty-five hundred pounds of lead. The water will be let off from these troughs into a large reservoir at the east end of the building, from which the baptismal fount will be supplied with water.

William E. Matlack, "The Temple," *Hancock Eagle,* 24 April 1846, microfilm in LDS Church Archives. Matlack (-1846), the non-Mormon editor of the *Hancock Eagle,* was sympathetic to the plight of the Saints. The *Eagle* was the voice of the "new citizens" of Nauvoo—those who were taking the place of departing Mormon population, but who also deplored the violence and uncivil relationships that had exist-

4. The "drops or Masonic emblems" to which he refers must be the trumpets.

ed previously. Matlack wrote several descriptions of the temple during 1846. This is the most complete.

> We have made two different visits to this great monument of human industry; and although our attention has been drawn to every apartment in it, yet much is the vast extent of the immense edifice, and the complexity of its architectural designs, that our observations have been necessarily very superficial.
>
> It stands in a most prominent position on the bluff [and] overlooks the lower town and river; and such is the elevation of its spire, that it is distinctly visible from a distance of twenty or thirty miles in various directions.
>
> Viewed from the bank of the river its appearance is grand and imposing.—The material of which it is chiefly built, is white limestone, which has been worked and faced down to a perfect surface.
>
> Its dimensions, as far as we can recollect, are as follows:
>
> Length 128 feet;
>
> Width 88 feet;
>
> Height to comb of roof 77 feet;
>
> From the ground to top of spire 170 feet.
>
> The upper windows of the steeple serve as an observatory, from which a magnificent view of the surrounding country may be had. The Mississippi is seen winding its serpentine form along the wooded valley to the North and South—the hills of Iowa rise in bold relief to the westward, and lose themselves in the blue distance; while the prairies, fields, gardens and private buildings lie spread out like a map below.
>
> The walls of the temple are of massive stone, and at least two feet thick. On either side, and at the end, are rows of graceful pilasters, crowned with elaborately carved caps, upon the external surface of which is exhibited in bas relief, the face of "the man in the moon," and two hands grasping trumpets. Each pilaster rests upon inverted crescents, and are at least fifty feet long. They are thirty in number, and the united cost of them is estimated at about $100,000.
>
> The structure is lighted by four rows of windows, two of which are quadrilateral, and two circular. These, with the other ... architectural embellishments, give the whole pile an original and not unpleasing aspect.
>
> ... The immense doorways are gained by a flight of stone steps. The interior contains a basement (in the center of which, stands the celebrated baptismal font.) Two great halls ... extend nearly the entire length and breadth of the building, and a third hall underneath the roof, with small apartments on either side.
>
> The baptismal font is a most extraordinary work, and will stand a monument to Mormon extravagance and grotesqueness of taste. It is an immense stone reservoir, resting upon the backs of twelve oxen, also cut out of stone, and as "large as life." The effect of a first view of these rigid animals standing in such a singular position, and wearing such mysterious countenances, is somewhat star-

tling, but a feeling of superstition gives way to curiosity, and the beholders lost in wonder at the magnitude of the design, and extraordinary amount of labor that must have been expended in the execution of the work.

The hall on the first floor was intended as the regular meeting place of the congregation, and when freed from the rubbish and surplus timber that now encumbers it, will have a beautiful and imposing effect. The architectural decorations are chaste and rich, and the two grand pulpits at the East and West ends, gives to the whole an appearance of Oriental magnificence.

The attic (as it may be called) is lighted from the roof, and was designed for a large school room.

Leaving the body of the building, you ascend to the bell room of the steeple, thence to the clock room, and last to the observatory.

The immense structure is a chef d'oeuvre [master work] of architecture, and will rank in grandeur with the largest and most costly edifices of modern times.

Unnamed visitor, Letter to the *Springfield* (Mass.) *Republican*, reprinted as "City of Nauvoo, Ill." in *Nauvoo Neighbor* 2 (13 November 1844). The visitor who wrote this description was apparently a non-Mormon from Massachusetts, a "stranger from Yankee-land," who visited Nauvoo on 14 September 1844 with the purpose "of learning everything about the place and the people that circumstances would allow."

This morning, Mr. [William] Marks took his horse and wagon quite early, and carried me again to the Temple, and quite to the rear of the city. I saw and talked with the Architect, who showed me all the drawings and plans of the Temple, and explained them as much as I had time to spare. I also saw and conversed with several of the workmen, and particularly with the stone-cutters and sculptors, and mounted the ladder and went on to the topmost part where they were laying the walls, and after all, I do not feel competent to give you an intelligible description but will do the best I can....

The Temple is situated relatively much as the City Hall is in Washington, and is a magnificent structure so far as it is advanced. It is 128 feet long, 28 feet wide, and the walls 37 feet high. The materials are white long stone which are quarried on their own ground within a convenient distance. There are 30 pilasters projecting about 15 inches from the walls, the bases of which are wrought represent the rising moon in it, the first quarter, and the capitals which measured 5 feet high and 6 feet wide at the top, represent the meridian sun the whole executed in the most elaborate style, and indeed, the workmanship throughout is as well done as any thing in the United States. I speak with confidence, for I have seen and examined all the best specimens of stone cutting and masonry in this country.

There are to be circular windows between the upper and lower story windows, so finished as to represent stars. The whole is to be surmounted by a splendid dome. In the basement is the baptismal font, 18 feet long by 10 feet wide, standing on the backs of 12 oxen—4 looking south, 4 north, 2 east, and 2 west.— These are very handsomely carved of wood. I should not have known the nature of the material, if some lawless rascals had not defaced them by breaking off parts of the horns, &c. Two of the walls are now up for the roof, and the work is going on with great vigor. There are on the Temple and at the quarry 140 men employed, besides numerous teams.

Mr. William Weeks, a native of Martha's Vineyard, is the architect from whose kindness I had most of the statements I have made.

Charles Lanman, *A Summer in the Wilderness* (Philadelphia, N.pub., 1847), 31-33. Essayist, editor, and traveler Charles Lanman (1819-95) was born in Michigan and later achieved prominence as personal secretary to Daniel Webster. He visited Nauvoo and the temple in July of 1846, shortly after the main body of the Saints had departed. Lanman makes note of several interesting details like the locks on the doors in the attic and the mezzanine couched between the first and second stories.

Rock Island, Illinois, July, 1846.

On my way up the Mississippi, I tarried a few hours at the far-famed city of Nauvoo.... In the center of this scene of ruins, stands the Temple of Nauvoo, which is unquestionably one of the finest buildings in this country. It is built of limestone, quarried within the limits of the city, in the bed of a dry stream; and the architect, named Weeks, and every individual who labored upon the building, were "Mormons." It is one hundred and twenty-eight feet in length, eighty feet wide, and from the ground to the extreme summit it measures two hundred and ninety-two feet. It is principally after the Roman style of architecture, somewhat intermixed with Grecian and Egyptian. It has a portico with three Roman archways. It is surrounded with pilasters; at the base of each is carved a new moon, inverted, while the capital of each is formed of an uncouth head, supported by two hands holding a trumpet. Directly under the tower is this inscription, in golden letters:

The House of the Lord.
Built by
The Church of Jesus Christ of Latter-day Saints.
Commenced April 6th, 1841.
Holiness to the Lord.

In the basement room, which is paved with brick, and converges to the center, is a baptismal font, supported by twelve oxen, large as life, the whole executed in solid stone. Two stairways lead into it, from opposite directions, while on either side are two rooms for the recording clerks, and, all around, no less than twelve preparation rooms besides. On the first floor are three pulpits, and a place for the choir; and on either side eight Roman windows. Over the prophet's pulpit, or throne, is the inscription:

The Lord has beheld our sacrifice: come after us.

Between the first and second floors are two long rooms, appropriated to the patriarchs, which are lighted with eight circular windows each. The room of the second floor, in every particular, is precisely like that of the first. Around the hall of a spacious attic are twelve small rooms, with circular windows and a massive lock on each door. At the two front corners of the edifice are two winding stairways, which meet at the base of the tower and lead to the summit,—while the roof of the main building is arranged for a place of promenade; and the walls of the noble edifice vary from four to six feet in thickness.

Estimating the manual labor at the usual prices of the day it is said that the cost of this Temple was about $800,000. The owners now offer it for sale at $200,000, but it will be a long time, I fancy, before a purchaser is found.

Then it was that I had an opportunity to muse upon the superb panorama which met my gaze upon every side. I was in a truly splendid temple,—that temple in the centre of a desolate city,—and that city in the centre of an apparently boundless wilderness. To the east lay in perfect beauty the grand Prairie of Illinois, reaching to the waters of Michigan; to the north and south faded away the winding Mississippi; and on the west, far as the eye could reach, was spread out a perfect sea of forest land, entering which, I could just distinguish a caravan of exiled Mormons, on their line of march to Oregon and California. As before remarked, when I went forth from out the massy porches of the Mormon Temple, to journey deeper into the wilderness, I felt like one awakened from a dream.

Unknown author, untitled article containing quotations from J. M. Davidson, "Nauvoo: The Past and Present of That City: Visits of 1846 and 1864 Contrasted," *Carthage Republican*, 25 February 1864, 1, and quoted in E. Cecil McGavin, *The Nauvoo Temple* (Salt Lake City: Deseret Book, 1962), 93-95. (McGavin mistakenly cites Davidson as the author of the article, rather than as "quoted by unknown author.") Davidson seems intent on dispelling several current myths or rumors about the temple's appearance. He was the editor of the *Republican*, the only newspaper being published near Nauvoo in the 1860s.

The roof was so nearly flat that ourself and companion walked over it without difficulty or danger, approaching the sides where, grasping one of the chimneys, the sentries nearly ninety feet below looked like pygmies. It may be remarked that the southwestern corner of the temple stood as a magnificent ruin until 1865 or 6—a sightly landmark for many miles around. The ruin, when we saw it in February, 1864, was said to be eighty feet high. It was torn down a year or two later for the stone in it, and the ground where the temple stood was converted into a vineyard.

The main entrance to the temple was on the west, fronting the river. There were three archways opening into a vestibule; from thence two large doors opened into the main audience room. We took no note of the size of that room. It seemed very large. At either end were preaching stands with rows of elevated seats leading up to them. These were for the dignitaries of the church according to their rank. It is probable that the prophet and twelve apostles occupied the eastern stand, while some lesser preachers and dignitaries occupied the stand on the west.

The seats in the body of the chamber had movable backs that could be swung so that the hearers could face either stand, as the character of the service or standing of the preacher demanded. There had been inscriptions above these stands, as indicated by tracings on the wall, but, as with other ornamentation, had been torn down by the Mormons themselves, no doubt. The vast room was substantially though plainly finished, and appeared to be in good repair and free from acts of vandalism. To one who had never seen anything larger than a country meeting house, this Mormon audience room presented a vastness and grandeur that was inspiring. Ourself and companion stood in the midst thereof like animate atoms in a desolate expanse where there were no other inhabitants.

"Gentlemen should precede ladies in going up the stairway," was the quiet remark of our fair companion.... The temple spire was an airy structure; the stairways were lighted and unenclosed, and the wind was blowing up there at a merry rate. Three or four flights of stairs brought us to the dome, from whence, through square openings on the east and west, from an elevation of something over 150 feet, a vast and beautiful expanse of country could be seen. . . . Venturing to crawl out on a narrow parapet, which had only the slight protection V-shaped turrets, and a small ladder was seen going up over the dome of a naked flag-staff (no angel on it—she was in the dome) and comfortably seated on the dome with his legs around the flag-staff was Charley McDowell!

... W. C. Williams, who has lived in Hancock County all his life, says that when a boy he visited the Mormon temple often, and that the oxen supporting the baptismal font had their fore legs presented entire and fully half their bodies. It is probably an error that the oxen were of marble. The piece of head now in possession of Attorney J. D. Miller, of this city, looks more like the limestone of which the temple was built....

Nauvoo in 1846. At the period of our visit in that year, the great Mormon temple was as near its completion as it ever attained; finished however, in all its grand proportions of size and height. The basement hall, in which was situated the baptismal font—itself a miracle of art and beauty, with its appointments of life-sized oxen in purest marble, the marble basin and elaborate railings—the preparation and reception rooms; the immense audience chamber above with its pews and changing backs, its immense altars and oratories, its gorgeous tapestry and motes in gold and silver, its ponderous chandeliers and the innumerable columns and frescoes that elsewhere bewildered the eye with their gorgeous beauty.

Of all these appointments we have such a vivid recollection that it seems but the rehearsal of a last night's pleasant dream. We were but a boy then, and venturesome. We could not do it now,—but then we climbed to the top of that vast dome and planting our feet around the lofty rod which supported the bronze angel, we viewed a scene of magnificence vast and varied in its scope.... Such is our recollection of the great city and its proud temple in 1846.

J. H. Buckingham, Letter to *Boston Courier*, 18 July 1847, reprinted in Harry E. Pratt, ed., "Illinois As Lincoln Knew It," *Papers in Illinois History and Transactions for the Year 1937* (Springfield, IL: N.pub., 1938), 170-72. In 1847, Bostonian J. H. Buckingham traveled to Chicago in 1847 on business, after which he visited Nauvoo. His letter to the *Courier* contains what has long been considered the most comprehensive description of the completed temple.[5]

It is built of white lime-stone. The front is ornamented with sunken square columns of no particular style of architecture, having capitals representing half a man's head—the upper half—showing the forehead, and the top of the nose, and crowned with thorns, or perhaps what was intended for the points of stars.

Over the head are two bugles or horns, with their largest ends outwards, and the handles, or the upper side, forming a sort of festoon protection. On all sides of the Temple are similar columns and similar capitals. The base of each column is heavy, but in good proportion and of a fanciful design, which it would be difficult to describe.

There is a basement with small windows. Ten steps lead to the front and only one entrance to the main building. Three arches enable you to enter into a sort of vestibule, from which, by doors, you enter the grand hall, and at the side are the entries to the staircases, to ascend to the upper apartments.

The front of the Temple is apparently three stories high, and is surmounted by an octagonal tower or steeple, which itself is three stories, with a dome and having on four sides a clock next below the dome. There is a line of circular windows over the arched entrance, ornamented with carved work between each, and over that again a line of square entablature, on which is cut the following inscription:

---

5. J. H. Buckingham, "Letter from Nauvoo, July 1847," to *Boston Courier*, quoted in "Illinois As Lincoln Knew It," edited by Harry E. Pratt, *Papers in Illinois History and Transactions for the Year 1937* (Springfield: Illinois State Historical Society, 1937), 171.

THE HOUSE OF THE LORD
built by
THE CHURCH OF JESUS CHRIST
OF LATTER-DAY SAINTS
Commenced April 6th, 1841
Holiness to the Lord

A similar entablature is on the front of the interior vestibule, over the doors of the entrance with the same inscription. The letters are gilt.

The man in attendance demanded twenty-five cents as a fee for showing us the Temple, and asked everyone to subscribe to a visitor's book. I looked over the book, and saw but two names of persons hailing from Boston for the last six months, neither of which was familiar to me.

We were then taken to the very top of the building....

Coming down, we were ushered into the Council Chamber, which is a large, low room, lighted by one large half circle window at the end and several small sky-lights in the roof. On each side are six antechambers, said to have been intended for twelve priests, councillors, or elders, or whatever they had been called. The chamber itself is devoid of ornament, and I was unable to ascertain whether it was intended to have any, if it should have been completed.

In the entry on each side of the door to the Council Chamber, is a room called the wardrobe, where the priests were to keep their dresses. On one side was a room intended for a pantry, showing that the priests did not mean to go supperless to bed. Under the Council Chamber another large hall, with seven windows on each side, and four at the farther end.

On the lower floor was a grand hall for the assemblage and worship of the people. Over the window at the end, was inscribed in gilded capital letters:

THE LORD HAS BEHELD OUR SACRIFICE: COME AFTER US.

This was in a circular line corresponding to the circle of the ceiling. Seats are provided in this hall for the accommodation of thirty-five hundred people, and they are arranged with backs, which are fitted like the seats in a modern railroad car, so as to allow the spectator to sit and look in either direction, east or west.

At the east and west ends are raised platforms, composed of series of pulpits, on steps one above another. The fronts of these pulpits are semi-circular, and are inscribed in gilded letters on the west side, PAP, PPQ, PSR, meaning as we are informed, the uppermost one President of the Aaronic Priesthood; the second, President of the Priests Quorum; the third, President of the Teachers Quorum; and the fourth and lowest, President of the Deacons Quorum. On the east side the pulpits are marked PHP, PHQ, PSQ, and the knowledge of the guide was no better than ours as to what these symbolic letters were intended for.

We next descended to the basement, where there is the far-celebrated font. It is in fact the cellar of the building. The font is of white limestone, of an oval shape, twelve by sixteen feet in size on the inside, and about four and a half to five feet deep. It is very plain and rests on the back of twelve stone oxen or cows, which stand immersed to their knees in the earth.

It has two flights of steps, with iron banisters, by which you enter and go out of the font, one at the east end and the other at the west end. The oxen have tin horns and tin ears, but are otherwise of stone, and a stone drapery hangs like a curtain down from the font, so as to prevent the exposure of all back of the forelegs of the beasts. In consequence of what I had heard of this font I was disappointed; for it was neither vast nor gorgeous; everything about it was quite simple and unostentatious. The basement is unpaved, and on each side at the ends are small alcoves, intended for robing rooms for the faithful.

The whole is quite unfinished, and one can imagine what it might have been in course of time, if Joe Smith had been allowed to pursue his career in prosperity.

Unnamed visitor, *Illinois Journal*, 9 December 1853, reprinted as "Recollections of the Nauvoo Temple," in *Journal of the Illinois State Historical Society* 38 (December 1945): 482; photocopy in LDS Church Historical Department Library. This description, first published in 1853, is based on reminiscences of an earlier tour of the temple. While the author confuses some of the specifics, he or she provides a glimpse of several usually unmentioned details.

[Several] ordinary looking buildings stood on the hill; but these by their unprepossessing appearance only tended to make the Temple look more grand.

It was a beautiful sight! The gray massive pile, standing then in silent grandeur, looking over the whole scene with a quiet solemnity of aspect, affording a striking contrast to the use for which it was originally intended....

A short walk brought us to the base of the elevation on which it rested, and we had the majestic proportions of the entire structure before us. We paused in front to take a general survey of the whole, before we entered. What a grand and magnificent spectacle it presented! As we looked upon it we could hardly realize that the people who had built it and worshipped there had left it to go into a far off country, never to return, and we could sympathize with them as we imagined how they took one last, fond, lingering look at the object they had long loved, ere they departed forever.... The limestone of which it was constructed and in which the state of Illinois abounds, was well worked. Smith must have employed in its erection some of the most skillful architects and stone masons in the country.

Plain but massive columns of the Doric order, were fixed in the sides throughout the entire building,—on the broad basis of which was carved a very large crescent,—which on the capitals high up in the air, a cherub grasping in one hand a trumpet, in the other a book, seemed peeping out from under the eaves. Now and then, the surface would present a bruise, showing the effects of the cannon of the sacrilegious Anti-Mormon host,—reminding me of "the times that tried men's souls."

Casting our eye upward over the doorway, we beheld conspicuously emblazoned in large gilt capitals on the white stone this inscription: "Holiness to the Lord. The Temple of the Latter-day Saints," when founded and when completed. The dates I have forgotten. The front extended into the immense tower, rising huge and majestic before us, the summit of which was almost lost in the clouds.

We ascended the steps and had no sooner entered within the vestibule, than a very polite cicerone was ready to conduct us through its labyrinth of rooms. We first entered the basement, the floor of which we had no sooner gained than our eyes rested upon the great baptismal font, constructed of solid limestone, seemingly resting on the backs of six [actually twelve] milk-white oxen, carved from solid blocks of stone. They were well executed and with their bright eyes of glass and well-formed ears, looked exceedingly life-like, and altogether presented a handsome appearance. I said the basin seemed to rest on them; but in reality it rested on a stone foundation of its own, composed of heavy blocks of stone, closely joined together, and fashioned in the form of a circle. The oxen were not fully developed but resting on their fore-feet, the middle of their bodies was firmly cemented to that circular foundation, and thus the basin seemed to rest directly on their backs. Formerly there were placed wooden oxen, painted, which I saw in one of the upper rooms, but they were only temporary, and were replaced by these of stone. A flight of stone steps, with iron railing on each side, led up to the front, and similar flight on the other side descended therefrom. It was a damp, gloomy looking place and very chilly.

After having contemplated for a sufficient length of time this curious piece of sculpture, and having walked through the opening where many trusting saints received the ordinance of baptism ... we returned by the way we entered, and as our cicerone told us it was better to commence our examination at the top and come down, we assented, and began forthwith our ascent up the spiral staircase. We slowly progressed upward through the intermediary windings, passing by the circular windows, filled with glass of diverse colors, which threw an obscure light on our passage. It was said that the round windows were used a portholes, in any case of emergency. This might have been the intention of the Mormons; for they were certainly large enough to admit of the discharge of heavy ordnance with facility.

Arrived at the top, we turned and cast a look downward. The distant floor was not distinguished from the extreme turnings of the spire. It seemed as if we were looking down into an immense corkscrew, the terminal windings of which were lost in obscurity. Halting a few moments to take breath, we began to ascend the tower; and as the inside of this was not entirely finished, an excellent chance was afforded us to observe the massive strength of the framework, and perceive the solidity and view [the] durability, with which it was constructed. The bare timbers presented a never-ending system of braces, each supporting the other successively. The Mormons certainly knew how to build, if they were a deluded people in some other respects.

After ascending some distance, a series of steps which were very steep, a short stairway brought us to the end of our wearisome journey, and, emerging through a small opening on the side, we gained access to the open air. We now stood on the extreme summit of the tower, some 200 feet from the ground. . . .

A low balustrade encircled the huge dome, between which and the former wound a narrow path-way much worn by the feet of visitors. Many names were scratched on the dome and cut in the balustrade, by ambitious persons who wished to be remembered by posterity....

On the top of the dome was affixed a large representation of the angel Gabriel, with wings expanded, holding in one hand a trumpet, and in the other [a] book, twelve feet in length, composed of tin gilded. But the wind blew briskly, and the massive superstructure began to tremble and seemed to rock to and fro. It made one's blood run cold to feel the mass quiver and shake beneath him at such a height. We felt a little dizzy, and quickly descended.

We now entered the first room before us—the uppermost room in the whole building. It had never been finished; but the double row of Composite columns, of excellent workmanship, traversing its entire length, and the sky-lights of colored glass with which it was lighted, as well as the general appearance of the combined whole, shewed us that it was intended to surpass all the rest in the richness and taste of its decorations.... The next room directly below this was a very large one, with small rooms, eight or ten feet square, on each side—all finished in the plainest possible manner.—What they intended to do with this hall or these rooms, has ever remained a mystery. As they were all besmeared with grease and oil, they might have been used in some baptismal ceremony, when the new convert was anointed with holy oil....

But we descended the stairway, and the last room remained to be explored. This was the grand audience chamber—the inner Temple—the "Sanctum Sanctorum." We entered within its ample doors. It was a magnificent room, capable of seating a great concourse of people. The woodwork of the doors and windows was composed of beautifully carved work. The top of the door jambs being ornamented with Corinthian capitals of the most exquisite workmanship. But these, alas! shewed the marks of sacrilegious hands of the visitors who wished to preserve some relic of the wonderful edifice. The beautiful vine-work had been deprived of many a delicately executed leaf and bud, and a smiling cherub of its nose—then, another the feathered tip of its wing....

A series of seats, elevated one above another, was situated in the middle of each of the two sides, on the heads of which, were inscribed the initial letters of the office which the priest held. The highest seat was for the highest dignitary—

generally filled by the prophet himself. Various inscriptions in large gilt letters were placed upon the walls, in conspicuous places. There were numerous other seats for private members. The room was built very close and compact, and the ceiling very lofty, so that when we conversed in an ordinary tone of voice, the sound rebounded back and forth, until finally lost in echoes. When filled with people, a strong voice must have sounded remarkably clear and distinct.

William A. Gallup, Diary, 29 July 1848, photographic reprint of pages 129-30 accompanied by introduction by William Powell, photocopy, Perry Special Collections, Lee Library. While traveling across America during the summer of 1848, Gallup, a book salesman, made a stop in Nauvoo. This is probably one of the last descriptions of the temple penned before it was gutted by fire in October that year. Gallup makes note of the acoustic properties of the main hall on the first floor and the fact that the attic was being used as a dance hall in 1848.

Visit at Nauvoo. July 29th 1848

On the 29th of July I entered the Great City of Nauvoo.... I viewed the Great Temple myself. It is a most splendid building. 180 feet, height to the top of the steeple; 129 feet long and 90 feet wide. Four main stories the 1st 2nd and 4th were finished. In the lower or basement story is the baptismal fount, supported by twelve oxen cut out of pure marble. All in the natural state, looked as natural as life. The horns were made of tin fastened on by a screw. The stairs led up into the fount on the east and west side; stone steps with an iron railing. The cost of this fount was $30,000 dollars. On either side of this room, which the fount was in, were rooms for the person who had been baptized to change their clothes etc. The second story [main floor] was the room for public worship. On the east side of the house this inscription was written:

The Lord has beheld our sacrifice: Come after us

On the east side of the house.... the[re] is four rows of slips through and at each end of the body slips is four slips for the officers.... [6]

P. H. P. is the highest Officer
P. H. Q. 2d   "   "
P. S. Z. [sic] 3d   "   "
P. E. Q. 4th   "   "
P. A. P. 5th   "   "
P. P. Q. 6th   "   "

---

6. Slip is another word for a pew. Gallup is describing the arrangement of the seats in the hall: four sections (separated by three aisles) running from the back to the front and four rows of seating on the podiums at either end.

P. T. Q. 7th   "   "
P. D. Q. 8th   "   "

The[re] is 6 pillars on each side in the second story. The 4th story is finished off pretty much. That room is now used as a dancing room by the young people of the place. It is a fine place for the business. The second story is used for a preaching room at present enough preaching to prevent the buildings being taxed. Over the doors on the west of the building this inscription is written and also on the west end of the whole building:

The House of the Lord
Built by the
Church of Jesus Christ
Of Latter-day Saints
Commenced April 6th 1841
Holiness to the Lord
Admittance 25 cents.

BIBLIOGRAPHY

"About the Cover," *Church News*, 17 April 1999, 2.

Adams, Arza. Journal. Vol. 4, 1843-56. Typescript, 29. Perry Special Collections, Lee Library.

Adams, James M. Letter to Joseph Smith, 16 November 1842. *Whitney Papers*, Perry Special Collections, Lee Library, Brigham Young University, Provo, Utah..

Adams, William. "History of William Adams, Written by Himself" (1894). Typescript. Salt Lake City: LDS Church Archives.

_____."Autobiography of William Adams," 1822-77. Typescript, 15. Perry Special Collections, Lee Library.

_____. Autobiography, 1894. Typescript. Perry Special Collections, Lee Library.

Allred, William Moore. Autobiography. Typescript. Salt Lake City: LDS Church Archives, 1885.

Americus (pseud.) and John Taylor, "Communications," *Nauvoo Neighbor* 3 (21 May 1845): 28.

An Exile (pseud.). 1844. "The Nauvoo Block and Tackle," *Warsaw Signal*, 25 April.

Anderson and Bergera, eds. *The Nauvoo Endowment Companies 1845-1846.*

Anderson, Mary Audentia Smith, ed. *Joseph Smith III and the Restoration.* Independence, MO: Herald House, 1952.

Angell, Truman O. Letter to John Taylor, 11 March 1885. Holograph, *John Taylor Papers*, LDS Church Archives.

Arrington, Joseph Earl. "Destruction of the Mormon Temple at Nauvoo," 419, 420. Quoting *Warsaw Signal*, 12 October 1848.

_____. "Destruction of the Mormon Temple at Nauvoo," 420. Quoting *Keokuk Dispatch*, 12 October 1848.

_____. "Destruction of the Mormon Temple at Nauvoo," 423 Quoting *Oquawka (Illinois) Spectator*, 2 May 1849.

_____. "Destruction of the Mormon Temple at Nauvoo," *Journal of the Illinois State Historical Society* 40 (December 1947): 418-19.

_____. "The Story of the Nauvoo Temple," unpublished manuscript, ca. 1970. Microfilm of typescript, Perry Special Collections, Lee Library.

_____. "William Weeks, Architect of the Nauvoo Temple," *BYU Studies* 19 (Spring 1979): 340.

Ashby, Benjamin. Autobiography, 15-16. Photocopy of holograph. Perry Special Collections, Lee Library.

Babbit, Almon. Letter to Brigham Young, 5 April 1847. In *Journal History*, 5 April 1847, 3.

_____, Joseph Heywood, and John S. Fullmer. "Temple for Sale," *Hancock Eagle* 1 (15 May 1846): 4.

_____, Joseph Heywood, and John S. Fullmer. "Temple to Lease," *Hancock Eagle* 1 (10 April 1846): 4.

Backman, Milton V. Interview conducted by author, 15 April 2002.

Ballard, M. Russell "The Legacy of Hyrum." *Ensign* (September 1994): 55.

Barlow, Ora H. *The Israel Barlow Story and Mormon Mores.* Salt Lake City: Ora H. Barlow, 1968.

Barney, Lewis. "History of Lewis Barney," typescript, 27-28, Perry Special Collections, Lee Library.

"Baptisms for the Dead: An Epistle of the Twelve to the Saints of the Last Days," *Times and Seasons* 3 (15 December 1841): 626.

_____, *Times and Seasons* 3 (15 April 1842): 760-61.

Bean, George Washington. *Autobiography of George Washington Bean.* Edited by Flora Diana Bean Horne. Salt Lake City: N.pub., 1945.

Beecher, Maureen Ursenbach ed., *Personal Writings of Eliza Roxcy Snow* (Salt Lake City: University of Utah Press, 1995), 75-76.

_____. "'All Things Move in Order in the City': The Nauvoo Diary of Zina Diantha Huntington Jacobs." *BYU Studies* 18 (Spring 1979): 310.

Belnap, Gilbert. "Autobiography of Gilbert Belnap." Typescript, 30. Perry Special Collections, Lee Library.

Benjamin Winchester, Letter to Erastus Snow, 12 November 1841. *Times and Seasons* 3 (15 November 1841): 605.

Bennett, Richard E. *"We'll Find the Place": The Mormon, Exodus 1846-1848.* Salt Lake City: Deseret Book, 1997.

Benson, Ezra T. "Ezra Taft Benson I: An Autobiography," *Juvenile Instructor* 80 (July 1945): 103.

Bernhisel, John. Letter to Brigham Young, 10 September 1849. St. Louis, Missouri. In *Journal History,* 10 September 1849, 2.

Bigler, Henry W. Journal, Book A. Typescript, 14, Perry Special Collections, Lee Library.

Bingham, Thomas. Autobiography, 1824-ca. 1889. Typescript, 1. Perry Special Collections, Lee Library.

Bishop, M. Guy. "'What has Become of Our Fathers?': Baptism for the Dead at Mormon Nauvoo," *Dialogue: A Journal of Mormon Thought* 23 (Summer 1990): 85, 90.

Black, Susan Easton. *Early Membership of the Church of Jesus Christ of Latter-day Saints,* 50 vols. Provo, UT: BYU Religious Studies Center, 1984-88.

Blackburn, Abner. Autobiography, 1827-51. Typescript, 5. LDS Church Archives.

Blum, Ida. *Nauvoo: Gateway to the West.* n.p.: Ida Blum, 1974.

"Bond of William Smith," 13 April 1841, *Whitney Papers,* Perry Special Collections, Lee Library.

"Boston Female Penny and Sewing Society," *Times and Seasons* 6 (1 March 1845): 820.

Brown, John Zimmerman. "Nauvoo Today," *Improvement Era* 12 (July 1909): 714.

Brown, Lisle G. "The Sacred Departments for Temple Work in Nauvoo: The Assembly Room and the Council Chamber," *BYU Studies* 19 (Spring 1979): 363, 370, 372.

Brown, Lorenzo. *Journal, 1833-99.* Typescript, 15. Perry Special Collections, Lee Library. Brigham Young University, Provo, Utah.

Buckingham, J. H. Letter to Boston Courier, 18 July 1847. Reprinted in Harry E. Pratt, ed., "Illinois As Lincoln Knew It," *Papers in Illinois History and Transaction for the Year 1937.* Springfield, IL: N.pub., 1938.

Buerger, David John. "The Development of the Mormon Temple Endowment Ceremony," *Dialogue: A Journal of Mormon Thought* 20 (Winter 1987): 33.

_____. "The Fulness of the Priesthood': The Second Anointing in Latter-day Saint Theology and Practice," *Dialogue: A Journal of Mormon Thought* 16 (Spring 1983): 10-44.

Bullock, Thomas. "Journal of Thomas Bullock, 31 August 1845 to 5 July 1846." Edited by Gregory R. Knight. *BYU Studies* 31 (Winter 1991): 32.

_____. Diary, 1845-46. Typescript, LDS Church Archives. 70. *Woodruff Journal,* 3:39.

Burbank, Daniel M. "Autobiography of Daniel M. Burbank," 1863. Holograph, 43, LDS Church Archives.

Burgess, Margaret Jane McIntire. Quoted in Margaret V. Burgess McMurtie, "Sketch of Margaret Jane Mcintire (Burgess), Pioneer of 1849-1861." Typescript. Perry Special Collections, Lee Library.

Bushman, Jacob. Autobiography, 1902. Typescript. Perry Special Collections, Lee Library.

Cahoon, William. Autobiography, 1813-1878. In *Stella Shurtleff and Brent Farrington Cahoon,* eds., Reynolds Cahoon and His Stalwart Sons. Salt Lake City: Paragon Press, 1960.

_____. Minutes of a meeting of the stonecutters for the temple, *Journal History,* 15 August 1844, 8.

Candland, David. Journal, 1841-1902. Perry Special Collections, Lee Library.

Cannon, George Q. 14 January 1894, *Collected Discourses,* 6 vols. Edited by Brian H. Stuy. Salt Lake City: B.H.S. Publishing, 1987-92.

_____. Smoot, comp. *Early Scenes in Church History.* Salt Lake City: Juvenile Instructor Office, 1881.

_____. *The Life of Joseph Smith the Prophet.* Salt Lake City: Deseret Book, 1888, 1986.

Cannon, Janath R. *Nauvoo Panorama: Views of Nauvoo before, during, and after Its Rise, Fall, and Restoration.* Salt Lake City: Nauvoo Restoration, Inc., 1991.

Carter, Kate B., comp. *Heart Throbs of the West.* Compiled by 12 vols. (Salt Lake City: Daughters of the Utah Pioneers, 1947-51), 8:236.

_____. *Our Pioneer Heritage.* 20 vols. Salt Lake City: Daughters of the Utah Pioneers, 1958-77.

"Catholics and Mormons," *Warsaw Signal,* 10 December 1845, 2.

"Celebration of the Anniversary of the Church-Military Parade-Prest. Rigdon's Address-Laying the Corner Stones of the Temple," *Times and Seasons* 2 (15 April 1841): 375-77.

Certificate of Nathaniel Richmond for work on the temple, August 1845. Holograph, L. Tom Perry Special Collections, Harold B. Lee Library, Brigham Young University, Provo, Utah.

Cheney, Nathan. *Letter to Beloved Friends* (Charles Beebe et al.), 17 October 1841. In Eliza Jane Cheney Rawson, "Letters and Sketches," 2, LDS Church Archives.

Christensen, Scott. interviewed by author, 27 June 2000.

"The Church and Its Prospects," *Times and Seasons* 2 (15 September 1841): 543.

"The Church Moves On," *Improvement Era* 44 (November 1941): 579, 670.

_____, *Improvement Era* 45 (April 1942): 221.

_____, *Improvement Era* 45 (September 1942): 574.

"The Church Moves On: Church Obtains Nauvoo Property," *Improvement Era* 45 (February 1942): 93.

Clark, James R. comp., *Messages of the First Presidency of the Church of Jesus Christ of Latter-day Saints*, 6 vols. Salt Lake City: Bookcraft, 1965-75.

Clayton, William. Journal. *Journal History*, 31 December 1844, 5.

_____. "An Interesting Journal." Quoted in George D. Smith, *An Intimate Chronicle*, 526.

_____. "Notice to Emigrants and Latter-day Saints Generally," 16 December 1843, *Nauvoo Neighbor* 1 (December 27, 1843): 68.

_____. "The Temple of God in Nauvoo," *Times and Seasons* 4 (15 November 1841): 10.

_____. "To the Farmers around Nauvoo and Vicinity," *Nauvoo Neighbor* 2 (7 August 1844): 3.

_____. "To the Friends of the Temple," *Times and Seasons* 5 (15 October 1844): 675-76.

_____. "To the Saints in Nauvoo and Scattered Abroad," *Times and Seasons* 3 (15 October 1842): 957.

_____. Journal. In *Journal History of the Church of Jesus Christ of Latter-day Saints* (chronology of typed entries and newspaper clippings, 1830-present). 31 December 1844, 13, LDS Church Archives.

Clayton, William. Journal, 1840-45. 21, LDS Church Archives.

"Collected Material Concerning a Weather Vane in Cincinnati, Ohio." Typescript, LDS Church Archives.

Colvin, Don F. "A Historical Study of the Mormon Temple at Nauvoo, Illinois." Master's thesis, Brigham Young University, 1962.

"Communications," *Times and Seasons* 6 (1 June 1845): 917.

"Conference," *Times and Seasons* 4 (1 April 1843): 154.

"Conference Minutes," *Times and Seasons* 3 (15 April 1845): 763.

_____, *Times and Seasons* 5 (1 August 1844): 596-97.

_____, *Times and Seasons* 6 (1 November 1845): 1008-10.

Conover, Peter. "Autobiography of Peter Wilson Conover," 1884. Typescript. *Nauvoo Restoration Lands and Records Office*, Nauvoo Illinois.

"A Copy of a Letter of Authority Given to Benjamin D. Clapp," 18 October 1844. Microfilm of holograph, *Whitney Papers*, Perry Special Collections, Lee Library, Brigham Young University, Provo, Utah.

"Cost of a Charge for the 'Big Gun,'" *Nauvoo Neighbor*, 24 April 1844.

Cowan, Richard O. *Temple Building: Ancient and Modern*. Provo, UT: BYU Press, 1971.

Cowdery, Warren. "Love of God," *Messenger and Advocate* 3 (March 1837): 471.

Cowley, Matthias. "Journal of Matthias Cowley," 1829-53. Typescript. LDS Church Archives.

Crosby, Jesse Wentworth. "History and Journal of Jesse W. Crosby," 1820-59, Typescript. Perry Special Collections, Lee Library.

———. Letter. Journal History (19 November 1844) 1-2.

Daily Missouri Republican, 15 June 1846. Quoted in McGavin, *The Nauvoo Temple*, 138.

Dana, C. W. *The Garden of the World*. Boston: Wentworth & Co., 1856.

David, Amos. "Invoice of Goods by Amos Davis, November 2, 17, 1845." Microfilm of holograph. *Newel K. Whitney Papers*, Perry Collections, Lee Library. For more information on this gilding technique, see chap. 9.

Davidson, J. M. 1864 "Nauvoo: The Past and Present of That City: Visits of 1846 and 1864 Contrasted." *Carthage Republican*, 25 February.

Davidson, Lee. "Smithsonian Pays $100,000 for Sunstone from Nauvoo Temple," *Church News*, 2 December 1989.

Dean, Jessee. "Joseph Smith's 19 July 1840 Discourse," *BYU Studies* 19 (Spring 1979): 390-94. From a discourse of Joseph Smith reported by Martha Jane Knowlton, 19 July 1840.

"Death of Elias Higbee," *Nauvoo Neighbor* 1 (14 June 1843): 27.

Decker, Sarah Louisa Norris. "Reminiscences of Nauvoo," *Woman's Exponent* 37 (March 1909): 41.

"Dedication of the Temple of God in Nauvoo," *Hancock Eagle* 1 (19 April 1846): 3.

"Destruction of the Mormon Temple," *Nauvoo Patriot*, 19 October 1848. Reprinted under same title in *Millennial Star* 11 (1 February 1849): 46.

Dewey, Robert. interviewed by author, 5 June 1999.

Dickens, Charles. *American Notes for General Circulation*. Avon, CT: Limited Editions Club, 1975.

Dourg, P. 1850. "Destruction of the Temple of Nauvoo, on the 27th of May, 1850, by a Storm," *Deseret News*, 24 August.

Draper, F. W. "Timber for the Nauvoo Temple: From an Unwritten Page of Early Clark and Jackson County History," *Improvement Era* 46 (February 1943): 88.

Dusen, Increase and Maria Van. *The Sublime and the Ridiculous Blended, Called, the Endowment*. New York: N.pub., 1848.

Ehat, Andrew F. "'Who Shall Ascend into the Hill of the Lord?' Sesquicentennial Reflections of a Sacred Day: 4 May 1842." In Temples of the Ancient World: Ritual and Symbolism. Edited by Donald W. Parry. Salt Lake City: Deseret Book, 1994.

———. "Joseph Smith's Introduction of Temple Ordinances and the 1844 Mormon Succession Crisis." Master's thesis, Brigham Young University, 1982.

Ehat, Andrew F. ed., "'They Might Have Known He Was Not a Fallen Prophet': The Nauvoo Journal of Joseph Fielding," *BYU Studies* 19 (Winter 1979): 141, 145, 147,158-59, 160, 165-66

———. "The Nauvoo Journal of Joseph Fielding," *BYU Studies*, 19 (Winter 1979).

"Elders' Conference," *Times and Seasons* 4 (1 April 1843): 158.

Emeline (pseud.). Mormon Endowments. 1846. *Warsaw Signal*, 15 April.

Enders, Donald L. "The Steamboat Maid of Iowa: Mormon Mistress of the Mississippi." *BYU Studies* 19, no. 3 (Spring 1979): 329.

Erastus Snow, "A Journal or Sketch of the Life of Erastus Snow." Typescript. Perry Special Collections, Lee Library.

"Epistle of the Twelve," *Times and Seasons* 3 (2 May 1842): 767-69.

"An Epistle of the Twelve to the Church of Jesus Christ of Latter-day Saints," *Times and Seasons* 5 (1 October 1844): 668.

"An Epistle of the Twelve to the Church of Jesus Christ of Latter-day Saints," *Times and Seasons* 6 (15 January 1845): 779-80.

"An Epistle of the Twelve," *Millennial Star* 2 (February 1842): 146.

_____. *Times and Seasons* 2 (15 October 1841): 567.

_____. *Times and Seasons* 3 (2 May 1842): 767.

_____, *Times and Seasons* 6 (15 January 1845): 780.

Evans, Cleo H. comp. and ed. *Curtis Edwin Bolton: Pioneer, Missionary History, Descendants, and Ancestors*. Fairfax, VA: Author, 1968.

"Extracts from an Epistle to the Elders in England," *Millennial Star* 1 (March 1841): 270-71.

"Extracts from President Young's Letter," *Millennial Star* 6 (1 September 1845): 91.

"Extracts from the Journal of John Steele," *Utah Historical Quarterly* 6 (January 1933): 5-6.

Faulring, Scott H. ed. *An American Prophet's Record: The Diaries and Journals of Joseph Smith*. Salt Lake City: Signature Books, 1989.

Ferguson, James. *Liahona*, 20 January 1914. Quoted in E. Cecil McGavin, *The Nauvoo Temple*. Salt Lake City: Deseret Book Company, 1962.

Ferris, Hiram Gano. "A Description of the Mormon Temple," *Carthage Republican* (19 March 1890), 2.

Fielding, Amos. Letter to Brigham Young, 25 July 1845. *Nauvoo Neighbor* 3 (13 August 1845): 59.

Fielding, Joseph. Letter to the editor, 28 December 1841, *Times and Seasons* 3 (1 January 1842): 648-50.

_____. "'They Might Have Known That He Was Not a Fallen Prophet': The Nauvoo Journal of Joseph Fielding," *BYU Studies* 19 (Winter 1979): 133.

_____. "Joseph Fielding's Letter." *Millennial Star* 3 (August 1842): 77-78.

_____. Letter to the Editor, datelined January 1842, Nauvoo. *Millennial Star* 3 (August 1842): 78.

"First Meeting in the Temple," *Times and Seasons* 6 (1 November 1845): 1017.

Foote, Warren. Journal, 1816-1903, 23 December 1845. Typescript. Perry Special Collections, Lee Library.

Ford, Thomas. *History of Illinois, from Its Commencement as a State in 1818 to 1847*. Chicago: S. Griggs & Co., 1854.

Francis, S. "The Camp of Israel," *Sangamo Journal* 18 (23 April 1846), 2. Microfilm, Lee Library.

Frederick H. Piercy, "Route from Liverpool to Great Salt Lake Valley," *Improvement Era* 57 (August 1954): 557.

Fullmer, John Solomon. Letter to Almon Fullmer, ca. June 1843. Holograph, LDS Church Archives.

———. Letter to Brigham Young, 26 June 1846. In *Journal History*, 6 July 1846, 1-2.

———. Letter to Brigham Young, 27 January 1848. In *Journal History*, 27 January 1848, 4, LDS Church Archives.

Gallup, William. Diary, 29 July 1848. Perry Special Collections, Lee Library.

Gates, Susa Young. *The Life Story of Brigham Young*. New York: MacMillan, 1930.

Gaunt, LaRene. "A Covenant Restored," *Ensign*, July 1990, 51.

———. "Legacy," *Ensign*, July 1993, 36.

"General Conference," *Times and Seasons* 6 (1 August 1845): 983.

George D. Smith, *An Intimate Chronicle: The Journals of William Clayton*. Salt Lake City: Signature Books, 1995.

George Morris, Autobiography, 1823-91. Typescript, 40-41, Perry Special Collections, Lee Library.

Giles, John D. "From the Green Mountains to the Rockies," *Improvement Era* 33 (April 1930): 385.

———. "Successful Archeological Excavation of the Nauvoo Temple Site Project," *Improvement Era* 65 (October 1962): 705, 744.

"A Glance at the Mormons," Alton (Illinois) *Telegraph* 5 (14 November 1840): 2.

Green, Dee F. "The Beginnings of Excavation at the Nauvoo Temple Site," *Improvement Era* 65 (June 1962): 401.

Green, Dee F. and Larry Bowles, "Excavation of the Mormon Temple Remains at Nauvoo, Illinois: First Season," *Florida Anthropologist* 18 (June 1964): 78.

Gregg, Thomas. *History of Hancock County, Illinois*. Chicago: Charles C. Chapman & Co., 1880.

Haight, Isaac. Journal (1813-1862). Typescript, Perry Special Collections, Lee Library.

Hale, Aroet. "Diary of Aroet Lucius Hale." Typescript. Perry Special Collections, Lee Library.

Hales, Charles. Autobiography. In "Autobiographies of Early Seventies." Typescript, 208, LDS Church Archives.

Hamilton, Charles Mark. 1972. Quoting T. Edgar Lyon, Authorship and architectural influences on the Salt Lake temple. Master's thesis, University of Utah.

Hamilton, Marshall. "Thomas Sharp's Turning Point: The Birth of an Anti-Mormon," *Sunstone* 13 (October 1989): 5, 21.

Hancock County. *Deeds, Book M*, 397. Microfilm, LDS Church Archives. The deed was recorded on 8 July 1844.

Hancock, Mosiah Lyman. Autobiography, 1834-65. Typescript, Perry Special Collections, Lee Library.

Harmon, Jesse. Autobiography. In "Autobiographies of Early Seventies." Typescript, 33, LDS Church Archives.

Harrington, Virginia S. and J. C. Harrington. *Rediscovery of the Nauvoo Temple*. Quoting *St. Louis (MO) Morning Republican*, 24 September 1846. Reprinted Salt Lake City: Nauvoo Restoration, Inc., 1971.

Haven, Charlotte. "A Girl's Letters from Nauvoo," *Overland Monthly* 16 (December 1890): 624.

Hedlock, Reuben. "Address to the Saints," *Millennial Star* 5 (January 1845): 128.

Hendricks, Drusilla Dorris "Historical Sketch of James Hendricks and Drusilla Dorris Hendricks." Typescript, 16. LDS Church Archives.

Heward, Elizabeth Terry Kirby. "Reminiscence of Elizabeth Terry Kirby Heward" in *In Their Own Words*, 180.

Heywood, Joseph L. Letter to Brigham Young. In *Journal History*, 20 April 1847, 2.

Hicks, Michael. *Mormonism and Music: A History*. Urbana: University of Illinois Press, 1989.

Higbee, Elias. "Ecclesiastical," *Times and Seasons* 2 (1 February 1841): 296.

Hill, Greg. "Rebuilding of Magnificent Temple," *Church News*, 30 October 1999, 7.

Hinckley, Gordon B. "Nauvoo's Holy Temple," *Ensign*, September 1994, 59-60.

Holbrook, Joseph. Autobiography, 1871. Typescript, 58, Perry Special Collections, Lee Library.

Horne, Robert. *Millennial Star* 55 (September 1893): 584. Reprinted in N. B. Lundwall, *Temples of the Most High*. Salt Lake City: Bookcraft, 1993.

Hovey ,Joseph Grafton. "Autobiography of Joseph Grafton Hovey," 1812-56. Typescript, 31, Perry Special Collections, Lee Library.

Hunter, Howard W. "The Great Symbol of Our Membership," *Ensign* (October 1994): 2.

Huntington, William Sr. "Journal of William Huntington," 1784-1846. Typescript. Perry Special Collections, Lee Library Provo, Utah.

Huntington, William. Journal. 23 February 1845, typescript, 23.

Hyde, Orson. "The Tabernacle," *New York Messenger* 2 (16 August 1845): 52.

———. "Trial of Elder Rigdon," *Millennial Star* 5 (December 1844): 104.

———. 1849. Article in *Frontier Guardian*. Council Bluffs, Iowa. 27 June. Reprinted in *Scrapbook of Mormon Literature*. Edited by Ben E. Rich. 2 vols. Chicago: Henry C. Etten, 1913.

———. Letter to Brigham Young. Quoted in *Journal History*, 27 March 1846, 5.

———. Letter to the editor. *New York Messenger* 1 (6 September 1845): 77.

Hyde, William. "Private Journal of William Hyde," 1873. Typescript, 16. L. Tom Perry Special Collections, Harold B. Lee Library, Brigham Young University, Provo, Utah.

———. Autobiography. In "Autobiographies of Early Seventies." Typescript, 1, LDS Church Archives.

Hyrum Smith, "Extract of a Letter to a Member of the Branch in Kirtland," *Times and Seasons* 3 (15 October 1841): 589.

"An Interesting Record: Record of the Nauvoo Brass Band," *Contributor* 1 (June 1880): 196-97.

"Illinois As Lincoln Knew It." Edited by Harry E. Pratt, *Papers in Illinois History and Transactions for the Year 1937*. Springfield: Illinois State Historical Society, 1937.

"Immigration," *Times and Seasons* 1 (8 June 1840): 124.

"Improvement," *Nauvoo Neighbor* 3 (12 September 1845): 2.

Irving, Gordon. "The Law of Adoption: One Phase of the Development of the Mormon Concept of Salvation, 1830-1900," *BYU Studies* 14, no. 2 (Winter 1974): 473-88.

Jacob, Norton. Journal, 1804-52. Typescript. L. Tom Perry Special Collections, Harold B. Lee Library, Brigham Young University, Provo, Utah.

Jakeman, James T. ed. Daughters of the Utah Pioneers and Their Mothers. Salt Lake City: Western Publishing, 1916.

"January," *Times and Seasons* 6 (15 January 1846): 1096.

Jenson, Andrew comp. *Historical Record: A Monthly Periodical Devoted Exclusively to Historical, Biographical, Chronological and Statistical Matters* 8 (January 1886): 10-11.

_____. *LDS Biographical Encyclopedia*, 4 vols. (Salt Lake City: Andrew Jenson History Co., 1901-37; Reprinted Salt Lake City: Greg Kofford Books, 2007): 1:590.

_____. "Infancy of the Church," *Supplement to Historical Record*. Salt Lake City: Andrew Jenson, 1889.

_____. *Nauvoo Bell Folder. Andrew Jenson Papers*, LDS Church Archives.

Jessee, Dean C. ed., "The John Taylor Nauvoo Journal," *BYU Studies* 23 (Summer 1983): 33.
_____. *The Personal Writings of Joseph Smith*. Salt Lake City: Deseret Book, 1984.

Johnson, Benjamin F. Letter to George Gibbs, 1903. Typescript. Huntington Library, San Marino, California.

_____. *My Life's Review*. Independence, MO: Zion's Printing and Publishing Company, 1947.

Johnson, George Washington. Autobiography, 1823-50. Typescript. L. Tom Perry Special Collections, Harold B. Lee Library, Brigham Young University, Provo, Utah.

"Jonathan Sawyer Wells," In Susan Easton Black, *Membership of the Church of Jesus Christ of Latter-day Saints, 1830-1848*. 48 vols. Provo, UT: Religious Studies Center, Brigham Young University, 1987.

"Joseph Fielding's Letter," *Millennial Star* 3 (August 1842): 78.

Joseph Smith-History 1:68-71, in Pearl of Great Price

Josephson, Marba Cannon "Church Acquires Nauvoo Temple Site," *Improvement Era* 40, 284.

Journal of Discourses, 26 vols. London and Liverpool: LDS Booksellers Depot, 1855-86.

Judd, Zadoc. Autobiography, ca. 1907. Perry Special Collections, Lee Library.

Kane, Thomas L. "The Mormons: A Discourse Delivered Before the Historical Society of Pennsylvania, March 26, 1850." Quoted in Daniel Tyler, *A Concise History of the Mormon Battalion in the Mexican War, 1846-1847*. Chicago: Rio Grande Press, 1964.

Kelly, Charles ed., *Journals of John D. Lee, 1846-47 and 1859*. Salt Lake City: Western Printing, 1938.

Kimball, Heber C. Letter to Parley Pratt, 17 June 1842. Quoted in Stanley B. Kimball, "Heber C. Kimball and Family: The Nauvoo Years," *BYU Studies* 15 (Summer 1975): 458.

Kimball, James L. "Nauvoo Restoration Pioneer: A Tribute," *BYU Studies* 32 (Winter 1992): 11.

Kimball, Mary Ellen. *Journal, 1838-63*. Holograph, 21, LDS Church Archives.

Kimball, Sarah Melissa Granger. "Autobiography of Sarah M. Kimball" *Woman's Exponent* 12 (1 September 1883): 51.

Kimball, Stanley B. "Nauvoo as Seen by Artists and Travelers," *Improvement Era* 69 (January 1966): 38-43.

_____. "The Mormons in Early Illinois: An Introduction," *Dialogue: A Journal of Mormon Thought* 5 (Spring 1970): 9.

_____, ed., *On the Potter's Wheel: The Diaries of Heber C. Kimball.* Salt Lake City: Signature Books, 1987.

Kimball, Vilate. Letter written 6 September 1840, Nauvoo. Extract published in *Millennial Star* 1 (November 1840):

King, Larraine Wissler. "Life of Hiram Oaks," n.d., in her *Book of Remembrance,* in possession of Bill Burnard, Newton, Utah, photocopy of typescript at Nauvoo Restoration, Inc., Nauvoo, Illinois.

Knight, Gregory R. ed., "Journal of Thomas Bullock, 31 August 1845 to 5 July 1846," *BYU Studies* 31 (Winter 1991): 24, 61, 62, 63.

_____. "Journal of Thomas Bullock, 31 August 1845-5 July 1846," *BYU Studies* 31 (Winter 1991): 63.

Koch, Albert C. *Journey through a Part of the United States of North America in the Years 1844-1846.* Translated and edited by Ernest A. Stadler. Carbondale: Southern Illinois University Press, 1972.

Lambert, Charles. Autobiography, 1816-83. Typescript. LDS Church Archives.

Lambert, Mary Alice Cannon. "Recollections of Joseph Smith," *Young Woman's Journal* 16 (December 1905): 554.

"Lambert Reminiscence," In *Gems of Reminiscence, Seventeenth Book of the Faith Promoting Series.* Compiled by George C. Lambert (pseud. for George Q. Cannon). Salt Lake City: Juvenile Instructor Office, 1915.

Lanman, Charles. *A Summer in the Wilderness* (New York; Philadelphia: N.pub., 1847), 31.

Larsen, Andrew K. *Erastus Snow: The Life of a Missionary and Pioneer for the Early Mormon Church.* Salt Lake City: University of Utah Press, 1971.

"The Last Shingle," *Nauvoo Neighbor* 3 (13 August 1845).

"Late from the Mormon War," 1845. *Burlington Hawkeye,* 23 October. Microfilm, Lee Library.

"Latest from Nauvoo," *Millennial Star* 6 (15 September 1845), 124.

"Latter-day Saintism," *Burlington Hawkeye,* 20 November 1845.

Laub, George. Diary, 1814-77. 5 February 1846. Typescript. Perry Special Collections, Lee Library.

Launius, Roger D. and F. Mark McKiernan. *Joseph Smith's Red Brick Store.* Western Illinois Monograph Series, number 5. Macomb, Illinois: Western Illinois University, 1993.

Laura, a visitor (pseud.). "Nauvoo," *Nauvoo Neighbor* 2 (16 October 1844): 6.

Layne, Jonathan Ellis. "Autobiography of Jonathan Ellis Layne." Typescript. Historic Nauvoo Lands and Records Office, Nauvoo, Illinois.

Lee, John D. Diary, 1844-46, 28 December 1845. Typescript. Perry Special Collections, Lee Library.

_____. *Mormonism Unveiled: or the Life and Confession of the Late Mormon Bishop John D. Lee.* St. Louis: Bryan, Brand, & Co., 1877.

Leithead, James. "Life and Labors of James Leithead." Typescript. LDS Church Archives.

"Letter from P. P. Pratt," 12 August 1841, *Times and Seasons* 3 (15 December 1841): 625.

Lewis, Catherine. *Narrative of Some of the Proceedings of the Mormons.* Lynn, MA: Author, 1848.

Lewis, Henry. Diary, 51-52. Quoted in Joseph Earl Arrington, "Panorama Paintings in the 1840s of the Mormon Temple in Nauvoo," *BYU Studies* 22, no. 2 (Spring 1982): 202.

_____. Quoted in *The Valley of the Mississippi Illustrated.* St. Paul: Minnesota Historical Society, 1967.

Lewis, Philip E. "The Life History of Philip Bessom Lewis," n.d., microfilm of typescript, Perry Special Collections, Lee Library.

"Lime," *Nauvoo Neighbor* 3 (24 April 1844): 4.

Little, James A. *From Kirtland to Salt Lake City.* Salt Lake City: Juvenile Instructor Office, 1890.

Littlefield, Lyman Omer. "Nauvoo Correspondence," dated 4 October 1845, *New York Messenger* 2 (25 October 1845): 133.

_____. "From Nauvoo," dated 3 September 1845, *New York Messenger* 2 (20 September 1845): 67, photocopy, LDS Church Archives.

_____. "From Nauvoo," *New York Messenger* 2 (8 November 1845): 152.

_____. "From Nauvoo-To the Editor of the Messenger," 6 August 1845, *New York Messenger* 2 (30 August 1845): 67-68.

_____. "Highly Important and Interesting from Nauvoo," 19 October 1845, *New York Messenger* 2 (8 November 1845): 150.

_____. "Sights from the Lone Tree," *Times and Seasons* 3 (15 November 1841): 587.

_____. *Reminiscences of Latter-day Saints.* Logan: Utah Journal Company, 1888.

Lloyd, R. Scott. "Historic Nauvoo Temple to Be Rebuilt," *Church News*, 10 April 1999, 3.

Loveless, Matilda McLellan. Autobiography, ca. 1885. Typescript, 1. Perry Special Collections, Lee Library.

"Lumber Business of the Upper Mississippi," *Nauvoo Neighbor* 3 (28 May 1845): 4.

"Lumber," Nauvoo Neighbor 1 (12 July 1843): 4.

"Lyman Curtis, Pioneer of 1847." *In An Enduring Legacy. Compiled by Daughters of Utah Pioneers Lesson Committee,* 12 vols. Salt Lake City: Daughters of the Utah Pioneers, 1978-88.

Lyon, T. Edgar. "Oral History: Recollections of Old Nauvooers," *BYU Studies* 18, no. 2 (Winter 1978): 146.

Lyon, T. Edgar. "The Nauvoo Temple: 1841-1964," *Instructor* 100 (March 1965): 98.

Mace, Wandle. "Autobiography of Wandle Mace." Typescript. Perry Special Collections, Lee Library.

_____. "Journal of Wandle Mace," ca. 1890. Typescript, 82. L. Tom Perry Special Collections, Harold B. Lee Library, Brigham Young University, Provo, Utah.

_____. Autobiography, 1809-90. Typescript, 197. Perry Special Collections, Lee Library.

Madsen, Carol Cornwall. "Mormon Women and the Temple: Toward a New Understanding" in *Sisters in Spirit: Mormon Women in Historical and Cultural Perspective*. Edited by Maureen Ursenbach Beecher and Lavina Fielding Anderson. Urbana: University of Illinois Press, 1987.

Malin, Elijah Jr., *Letter to Joseph Smith, 15 May 1843*. Whitney Papers, Perry Special Collections, Lee Library.

"The Man Who Fired the Nauvoo Temple." 1872. Deseret Evening News, 26 April.

"Manuscript History of the Church," Journal History, 17-18 September 1846, 2.

Mason, Pamela. 1897. "Illinois to Utah," *Deseret News*, 30 March.

Matlack, William E. 1846. "Home Matters," *Hancock Eagle Extra*, 5 October.

———. 1846. "Public Buildings," *Hancock Eagle*, 24 April.

———. "Dedication of the Temple of God in the City of Nauvoo," *Hancock Eagle* 1 (10 April 1846): 3.

———. "Mormon Conference," *Hancock Eagle* 1 (8 April 1846): 3.

———. "Public Buildings," *Hancock Eagle* 1 (24 April 1846): 2.

———. "The Temple in the Market," *Hancock Eagle* 1 (8 May 1846): 2.

———. 1846. "The Temple," *Hancock Eagle*, 24 April. Microfilm, LDS Church Archives.

———. 1846. "Public Buildings," *Hancock Eagle*, 24 April. Microfilm, LDS Church Archives.

May, Dean. "A Demographic Portrait of the Mormons, 1830-1980." In D. Michael Quinn, ed., *New Mormon History: Revisionist Essays on the Past*. Salt Lake City: Signature Books, 1992.

McBride, Reuben. *Letter to Martha Knight, 1 November 1886*. Photocopy of holograph at Nauvoo Restoration, Inc., Nauvoo, Illinois.

McGavin, E. Cecil. *Nauvoo the Beautiful*. Salt Lake City: Deseret Book Company, 1946.

McGavin, E. Cecil. *The Nauvoo Temple*. Salt Lake City: Deseret Book, 1962.

Meeks, Dalton R. and Lenora Meeks. *The Life and Times of Dr. Priddy Meeks and His Progenitors*. Bountiful, UT: N.pub., 1996.

Meeks, Priddy. Autobiography, 1812-86. Microfilm of holograph. LDS Church Archives.

———. Journal. Quoted in Dalton R. Meeks and Leonora Meeks, *The Life and Times of Dr. Priddy Meeks*. Bountiful, UT: N.pub., 1996.

Mendenhall, William. Diary, 1846. Microfilm of holograph. LDS Church Archives.

Merritt, Arthur H. "A Postscript to American Churches Pictured on Old Blue China," *New York Historical Society Quarterly* 34, no. 1 (January 1950): 19-23.

"Minutes of a Conference," *Times and Seasons* 2 (15 October 1841): 578.

Miller, David and Della Miller. Quoting David W. Rogers, *Nauvoo: The City of Joseph*. Salt Lake City: Peregrine Press, 1974.

Miller, George. *Correspondence of Bishop George Miller with the Northern Islander from His First Acquaintance with Mormonism Up to Near the Close of His Life, 1855*. Compiled by Wingfield Watson. Burlington, WI: Wingfield Watson, 1916.

_____. Letter to James J. Strang, 26 June 1855. In H. W. Mills, "De Tal Palo Tal Astilla," *Annual Publications-Historical Society of Southern California* 10 (Los Angeles: McBride Printing Company, 1917) 364.

_____, Peter Haws, Amasa M. Lyman, and George A. Smith. "Notice." *Nauvoo Neighbor* 3 (20 August 1845): 62.

Moesser, Joseph. "Sketch of the Life of Joseph Hyrum Moesser," 1922. Typescript. LDS Church Archives.

"The Mormon Temple," *Burlington (Iowa) Hawkeye* 7 (20 November 1845). Microfilm, Lee Library.

"The Mormon Temple," *Home Missionary* 3 (January 1849): 207. Photocopy. L. Tom Perry Special Collections, Lee Library, Brigham Young University, Provo, UT.

"Mormon Temple, Nauvoo," *Graham's American Monthly Magazine*, 26 (April 1849): 257.

"Mormons," *Niles National Register*, 10 December 1842, 4, microfilm, Lee Library.

Monroe, James M. "Notice," *Nauvoo Neighbor* 2 (21 April 1845): 4.

Moore, Carrie. "Edifice Holds Dear Spot in Hearts of LDS Faithful," *Deseret News*, 2 July 2000, 7.

"The More We Reflect," *Warsaw Signal* 2 (9 June 1841): 2.

Moroni [pseud], "Spiritual Wife System," *Warsaw Signal*, 8 May 1844, 5.

Morris, George. "The History of George Morris," 1891. Typescript. Perry Special Collections, Lee Library.

_____. Autobiography, 1816-91. Typescript. Perry Special Collections, Lee Library.

Mulvay-Derr, Jill, Janath Russell Cannon, and Maureen Ursenbach Beecher. *Women of Covenant: The Story of Relief Society*. Salt Lake City: Deseret Book Company, 1992.

Munson, Eliza M. A. "Early Pioneer History," n.d. Typescript. LDS Church Archives.

"Nauvoo 'Opera House' Acquired by Wilford C. Wood," *Improvement Era* 40 (June 1937): 356, 638.

Nauvoo Relief Society Minutes, 16 June 1843. Microfilm of holograph, LDS Church Archives.

Nauvoo Temple Committee Records. *Carpenter's Daybook K*, 21 February 1846. Holograph, LDS Church Archives.

Nauvoo Temple Committee Records. *Day Book A, 1841-42*. Salt Lake City: LDS Church Archives.

"The Nauvoo Temple," *Journal History*, 12 June 1844, 3.

"Nauvoo," *Times and Seasons* 3 (1 October 1842): 936.

Neibaur, Alexander. Diary. Holograph, 18, LDS Church Archives.

Nelson, Mansel H. "Life of Edmond Nelson," 4. Typescript.

New York Spectator, 9 November 1844. Reprinted in Cecil B. McGavin, *Nauvoo Temple*. Salt Lake City: Deseret Book, 1962.

Newel K. Whitney Papers. L. Tom Perry Special Collections, Lee Library, Brigham Young University, Provo, UT.

"News from America," *Millennial Star* 1 (December 1840): 216.

Nibley, Hugh. *The Message of the Joseph Smith Papyri: An Egyptian Endowment.* Salt Lake City: Deseret Book, 1975.

Niswanger, "Lime," *Nauvoo Neighbor* 3 (24 April 1844): 4.

Nuttal, L. John. Diary, 7 February 1877. Typescript. L. Tom Perry Special Collections, Harold B. Lee Library, Brigham Young University, Provo, Utah.

"October Conference Minutes," 1844. *Times and Seasons* 5, 15 October.

"On Future Punishments," *Millennial Star* 3 (February 1843): 181.

Packard, Noah. "A Synopsis of the Life and Travels of Noah Packard." Typescript, 8-9, Perry Special Collections, Lee Library.

Packer, Boyd K. *The Holy Temple.* Salt Lake City: Bookcraft, 1980.

_____. *Things of the Soul.* Salt Lake City: Bookcraft, 1996.

Page, John E. *Letter to A. J. Foster, Nauvoo Neighbor* 3 (30 July 1845): 49.

Patterson, William McIntire. Journal. Holograph. *William Patterson McIntire Papers,* Perry Special Collections, Lee Library Brigham Young University, Provo, Utah.

Peart, Jacob. "Life Sketch of Jacob Peart, Sr.," 8 October 1872. Typescript. Historic Nauvoo Lands and Records Office, Nauvoo, Illinois.

Phelps, W. W. "The Answer," *Times and Seasons* 5 (1 January 1844): 759.

_____. "The Capstone Song," *Nauvoo Neighbor* 3 (28 May 1845): 42.

_____. "The Temple of God at Nauvoo," *Times and Seasons* 3 (15 June 1842): 830.

_____. Letter to William Smith, *Times and Seasons* 5 (December 1844): 759.

Piercy, Frederick. *Route from Liverpool to Great Salt Lake Valley.* London, Latter-day Saints' Book Depot, 1855.

Pomeroy, Irene Hascall. Letter to Ursulia Hascall, 2 June 1845. In "Letters of a Proselyte-The Hascall-Pomeroy Correspondence," *Utah Historical Quarterly* 25 (January 1957): 61.

Pratt, Orson. "Message," *Times and Seasons* 6 (15 August 1845): 998.

_____. "News to England," *New York Messenger* 2 (30 August 1845): 67.

Pratt, Parley P. "Destruction of the Mormon Temple," *Millennial Star* 11 (1 February 1849): 46-47.

_____. "Proclamation," *Millennial Star* 5 (10 March 1845): 151.

_____. "Regulations for the Publishing Department of the Latter-day Saints in the East," *Times and Seasons* 6 (15 January 1845): 778.

_____. "Tithings for the Temple," *Millennial Star* 3 (October 1842): 97.

_____. *Autobiography of Parley P. Pratt.* Edited by Parley P. Pratt, Jr. Salt Lake City: Deseret Book Company, 1985.

_____. Letter to Joseph Smith, 24 October 1841, Manchester, England. *Times and Seasons* 3 (1 February 1842): 683.

_____. untitled announcement, *Millennial Star* 2 (October 1841): 105-6.

"Public Buildings in Nauvoo," *Nauvoo Neighbor* 3 (25 September 1844): 19.

Pulsipher, John. Autobiography. Typescript, 6. Perry Special Collections, Lee Library.

Pyper, Christiana Dollinger. "Leaves from My Diary," *Juvenile Instructor* 57 (May 1922): 246.

Quincy, Josiah. *Figures of the Past from the Leaves of Old Journals.* Boston: Roberts Brothers, 1883.

Quinn, D. Michael. "Latter-day Saint Prayer Circles," *BYU Studies* 19 (Fall 1978): 79, 105.

———. "The Practice of Rebaptism at Nauvoo," *BYU Studies* 18, no. 2 (Winter 1978): 226.

Randall, Sally. *Letter to Dear Friends, 21 April 1844.* In Kenneth W. Godfrey, Audrey M. Godfrey, and Jill Mulvay Derr, *Women's Voices: An Untold History of the Latter-day Saints, 1830-1900.* Salt Lake City: Deseret Book, 1982.

"Recollections of the Nauvoo Temple," *Journal of the Illinois State Historical Society* 38 (December 1945): 482.

"Recollections of the Prophet Joseph Smith," *Juvenile Instructor* 27 (1 August 1892): 471-72.

"Record of Sealings, Wives to Husbands [proxy], Nauvoo Temple." Holograph, 2-3, LDS Church Archives.

"Relief Society Notes," *Woman's Exponent* 21 (15 March 1893): 149.

"Reminiscence of Bathsheba Wilson Bigler Smith." In *In Their Own Words: Women and the Story of Nauvoo.* Edited by Carol Cornwall Madsen. Salt Lake City: Deseret Book, 1994.

"A Representative Woman: Mary Isabella Horne," *Woman's Exponent* 11 (October 1882): 25.

Reynolds, John. *My Own Times: Embracing the History of My Life.* Belleville, IL.: B. H. Perryman and H. L. Davison, 1855.

Rich, Russell R. "Where Were the Moroni Visits?" *BYU Studies* 10, no. 3 (Spring 1970): 255.

Rich, Sarah DeArmon Pea. Reminiscence reprinted in *Journey to Zion: Voices from the Mormon Trail.* Edited by Carol Cornwall Madsen. Salt Lake City, Deseret Book, 1997.

Richard, Willard. Diary. Quoted in Dean C. Jessee, ed., "The John Taylor Nauvoo Journal," *BYU Studies* 23 (Summer 1983): 85.

Richards, Franklin D. "A Tour of Historic Scenes," *Contributor* 7 (May 1886): 300, 301.

Richards, Samuel W. Diary, 12 February 1846. Typescript, 3. Perry Special Collections, Lee Library.

———. Journal. Typescript. L. Tom Perry Special Collections, Harold B. Lee Library, Brigham Young University, Provo, Utah.

———. Letter to Franklin D. Richards, August 1844. Richards Family Correspondence. Typescript, LDS Church Archives.

Richards, Willard. "Temple Friends," dated 21 February 1842. *Times and Seasons* 3 (1 March 1842): 715.

———. "Tithings and Consecrations for the Temple of the Lord," *Times and Seasons* 3 (15 January 1842): 667.

———. Journal, 1838-46. Holograph. LDS Church Archives.

———. Journal, Vol. 17: 13 December 1846-7 April 1847. Holograph, 74. LDS Church Archives.

———. Letter to Levi Richards, 9 March 1842. *Richards Family Letters.* Typescript, ca. 1929. LDS Church Archives.

Riter, Joseph D. Autobiography, 1910. Typescript, 4, LDS Church Archives.

Roberts, B. H. *A Comprehensive History of the Church of Jesus Christ of Latter-day Saints,* 6 vols. Salt Lake City: Deseret News Press, 1930.

Robinson, Ebenezer. "Items of Personal History of the Editor-Including Some Items of Church History Not Generally Known," *The Return* 3 (January 1891): 12-13.

———. "Items of Personal History of the Editor-Including Some Items of Church History Not Generally Known," *The Return* 2 (April 1890): 252.

———. "Items of Personal History of the Editor-Including Some Items of Church History Not Generally Known," *The Return* 2 (July 1890): 301.

———. "History of Joseph Lee Robinson." Typescript. Perry Special Collections, Lee Library.

Rogers, Samuel Holister. Journal, 1819-86. Typescript, 46, Perry Special Collections, Lee Library.

Rollins, James Henry. "A Sketch of the Life of James Henry Rollins," 1898. Typescript. LDS Church Archives.

Rollins, James Henry. Autobiography, 1898. Typescript. LDS Church Archives.

"Roof of the Temple," *Times and Seasons* 6 (1 August 1845): 983.

Rowley, Dennis. "The Mormon Experience in the Wisconsin Pineries," *BYU Studies* 32 (Winter and Spring 1992): 127.

Rudsill, George H. "Brought to Light: How the Famous Mormon Temple at Nauvoo Was Destroyed," *Fort Madison (Iowa) Democrat*, ca. 1905. Photocopy in LDS Church Archives.

Rupp, I. Daniel. Quoting Joseph Smith *An Original History of the Religious Denominations at Present Existing in the United States*. Philadelphia: J. Y. Humphreys, 1844.

"S." *Letter to the editor*. 1844. Springfield [Massachusetts] Republican, in Nauvoo Neighbor 2, 13 November.

"The Saints Make Nauvoo," *Times and Seasons* 6 (1 April 1845): 856.

Samuel Miles, "Recollections of the Prophet Joseph Smith," *Juvenile Instructor* 27 (June 1892): 174.

"Samuel Miles, Tailor," *Nauvoo Neighbor* 3 (11 June 1845): 72.

"Sarah Pippin Jolley," 1871. *Treasures of Pioneer History*. Compiled by Kate B. Carter. 6 vols. Salt Lake City: Daughters of the Utah Pioneers, 1952-57.

Scott, James Allen. Diary, 31 March 1846. Microfilm of holograph. LDS Church Archives.

Scovil, Lucius N. Letter to the Editor, 2 January 1884. Quoted in "The Higher Ordinances," *Deseret Evening News*, 11 February 1884, 2.

Sessions, Perrigrine. Journal, 1814-86. Microfilm of holograph, LDS Church Archives.

Sharp, Thomas C. "The More We Reflect," *Warsaw Signal*, 9 June 1841, 2.

———. "The Mormons," 1841. *Western World*. Warsaw, IL, 7 April.

———. "Ceremony of the Endowment," *Warsaw Signal*, 18 February 1846, 4.

———. "Great Commotion in Nauvoo," *Warsaw Signal*, 24 December 1845, 2.

———. "Jack Mormon Lies," *Warsaw Signal*, 20 October 1846, 2.

———. "The Ceremony of the Endowment," *Warsaw Signal*, 18 February 1846, 2.

———. "Items from Nauvoo," *Warsaw Signal*, 21 August 1844..

———. "Will They Go?" *Warsaw Signal*, 22 October 1845.

———. "A Good Mormon Hoax," *Warsaw Signal*, 31 December 1845.

Shurtliff, Luman Andros. "Biographical Sketch of the Life of Luman Andros Shurtliff." Typescript. Perry Special Collections, Lee Library.

———. Autobiography. Typescript. Perry Special Collections, Lee Library.

Sissimus (pseud). "To the Editor of the Neighbor," *Nauvoo Neighbor* 2 (1 May 1844): 1.

Smith Joseph. Journal, *Journal History*, 12 July 1841.

———. "The Temple," *Times and Seasons* 3 (1 October 1842): 938.

———. "To the Brethren in Nauvoo City," *Times and Seasons* 3 (28 February 1842): 517.

———. "To Whom It May Concern," *Times and Seasons* 3 (15 December 1841): 638.

Smith, Alexander H. Quoted in Heman C. Smith, *History of the Reorganized Church of Jesus Christ of Latter Day Saints*, 7 vols. Independence, MO: Herald House, 1903-14; second printing, 1967.

Smith, Bathsheba Wilson Bigler. Quoted in Joseph Fielding Smith, *Blood Atonement and the Origin of Plural Marriage: Discussion between R. C. Evans and Elder Joseph Fielding Smith*. Salt Lake City: Deseret News, 1905.

———. "Recollections of the Prophet Joseph Smith," *Juvenile Instructor* 27 (1 June 1892): 345.

———. Autobiography, ca. 1906. Holograph, LDS Church Archives.

———. Autobiography, 1822-1906. Typescript, 11, Perry Special Collections, Lee Library.

———. Quoted in *Deseret Evening News*, 23 June 1903.

———. Letters to George A. Smith, 12 September 1843. LDS Church Archives.

Smith, Emma. *Collection of Sacred Hymns for the Church*. Nauvoo: Ebenezer Robinson, 1841.

Smith, George A. "My Journal." Compiled and edited by Elden J. Watson. Typescript.

———. Letter to Brigham Young and Council, 26 April 1846. Holograph, Brigham Young Papers, LDS Church Archives.

———. Letter to Brigham Young, 1 November 1856. In *Journal History*, 9 October 1848, 5.

Smith, George D. ed. *An Intimate Chronicle: The Journals of William Clayton*. Salt Lake City: Signature Books, 1995.

Smith, Heman C. *History of the Reorganized Church of Jesus Christ of Latter Day Saints*, 7 vols. Independence, MO: Herald House, 1903-14; second printing, 1967.

Smith, Job. Autobiography, 1854. Typescript, 5. LDS Church Archives.

Smith, John Rowson. *A Descriptive Pamphlet of Smith's Leviathan Panorama of the Mississippi River Now Exhibiting at Mason Hall Philadelphia*. (Philadelphia: n.pub., 1848), 3-4.

Smith, John. Journal, 11 October 1840. Typescript. *George Albert Smith Papers*, Special Collections, J. Willard Marriott Library, University of Utah, Salt Lake City.

Smith, Joseph F. "Redemption of Zion," *Improvement Era* 7 (May 1904): 512.

Smith, Joseph Fielding. *Doctrines of Salvation: Sermons and Writings of Joseph Fielding Smith*. Compiled by Bruce R. McConkie, 3 vols. Salt Lake City: Bookcraft, 1954-56.

———. *Salvation Universal*. Salt Lake City: Deseret Book Company, 1957.

Smith, Joseph. *Elders Journal* 1, no. 3 (July 1838): 43.

———. "A Proclamation to the Saints Scattered Abroad," *Times and Seasons* 2 (15 January 1841): 274.

_____. "Special Conference," *Times and Seasons* 4 (1 May 1843): 181-83.

_____. "The Temple," *Times and Seasons* 3 (2 May 1842): 775-76.

_____. "To the Brethren in Nauvoo City," *Times and Seasons* 3 (28 February 1842): 517.

_____. *Certificate of Authority for Heber C. Kimball*, 1 June 1843. Quoted in Helen Mar Kimball Smith Whitney, "Scenes and Incidents in Nauvoo," *Woman's Exponent* 11 (August 1882): 74.

Smith, Lucy Mack. *Biographical Sketches of Joseph Smith the Prophet and His Progenitors for Many Generations (1853)*. Photomechanical reprint. Orem, Utah: Grandin Books, 1995.

Smith, Mary Fielding and Mercy R. Thompson. Notice. 1845. *Times and Seasons* 6, 15 March.

_____. "To the Sisters of the Church of Jesus Christ in England," *Millennial Star* 5 (June 1844): 15.

Smith, William. "Nauvoo," *The Wasp* 1 (23 April 1842): 4.

_____. *A Proclamation: And Faithful Warning to All the Saints Scattered Around in Boston, Philadelphia, New York, Salem, New Bedford, Lowell, Peterborough, Gilson, Saint Louis, Nauvoo and Elsewhere in the United States; Also, to Those Residing in the Different Parts of Europe and in the Islands of the Seas*. 1845; Bountiful, UT: Restoration Research, 1983.

Smoot, Abraham O. Journal, 1837-46. 17 December 1845. Holograph, Special Collections, Marriott Library, University of Utah, Salt Lake City.

Snow, Eliza R. "The Temple of God," *Times and Seasons*, 2 (2 August 1841): 493-94.

_____. *Biography and Family Record of Lorenzo Snow*. Salt Lake City: Deseret News, 1884.

Snow, Erastus. 15 May 1878, *Journal of Discourses*, 26 vols. London and Liverpool: LDS Booksellers Depot, 1855-86.

_____. "A Journal or Sketch of the Life of Erastus Snow," 1875. Typescript, 91-92, Perry Special Collections, Lee Library.

Snow, Eunice Billings. "Sketch of the Life of Eunice Billings Snow," *Woman's Exponent* 39 (January 1911): 22.

Snow, Moroni, ed., "From Nauvoo to Salt Lake in the Van of the Pioneers–The Original Diary of Erastus Snow," *Improvement Era* 14 (February 1911): 281.

"Special General Conference," *Millennial Star* 7 (1 January 1846): 5.

"Speech Delivered by Heber C. Kimball," *Times and Seasons* 6 (15 July 1845): 972.

St. George Temple Minute Book, 21 February 1889. "Confidential Research Files."

Staines, William C. "Reminiscences of William C. Staines," *Contributor* 12 (February 1891): 123.

Stevenson, Joseph Grant. "The Life of Edward Stevenson." Master's thesis, Brigham Young University, 1955.

Stout, Allen Joseph. Journal, 1815-89. Typescript, 17. L. Tom Perry Special Collections, Harold B. Lee Library, Brigham Young University, Provo, Utah.

_____. Letters to Hosea Stout, Wisconsin Territory, 25 July, 10 September, and 13 September 1843. Microfilm of holograph. LDS Church Archives.

Strang, James J. "The Stake at Nauvoo," *Voree (Wisconsin) Herald*, 1 (April 1846): 3.

_____. "The Temples," *Voree Herald* 1 (April 1846): 4.

Stratton, Joseph Albert. "Diary of Joseph A. Stratton," 1821-1850. Microfilm of holograph. LDS Church Archives.

"Strayed," *Nauvoo Wasp*, 1 (8 July 1842): 4.

Talmage, James E. *House of the Lord*. Salt Lake City: Deseret Book Company, 1968.

Tanner, Lois Leetham. "I Have a Question," *Ensign*, February 1981, 16.

Tate,Lucile C. *Boyd K. Packer: A Watchman on the Tower*. Salt Lake City: Bookcraft, 1995.

Taylor, John. "Some Journalizing," 30 November 1845. Holograph, 1, *Nauvoo Temple Historical Documents*, LDS Church Archives.

_____. "The Steeple of the Temple," *Nauvoo Neighbor* 3 (30 July 1845) n.p.

_____. untitled announcement. *Nauvoo Neighbor* 1 (14 June 1843): 26.

Taylor, Pleasant Green. Autobiography, 1827-94. Typescript, 1. LDS Church Archives.

Telemachus (pseud.). "Fire!," *Nauvoo Neighbor* 3 (28 May 1845): 30.

Temple Committee, "To the Churches Abroad and Nearby," *Times and Seasons* 3 (1 September 1842): 909.

"Temple Funds," *Times and Seasons* 3 (2 May 1842): 782.

"The Temple of God in Nauvoo," *Times and Seasons* 4 (15 November 1842): 10.

"The Temple of Nauvoo," *St. Louis Gazette*, ca. 12 June 1844.

"The Temple of the Lord," *Times and Seasons* 2 (1 July 1841): 455.

"The Temple," *Times and Seasons* 2 (1 April 1841): 369.

"The Temple," *Times and Seasons* 3 (1 October 1842): 938.

"The Testimony of William Smith," *Millennial Star* 61 (26 February 1894): 132-34.

The United Stated Illustrated, ed. Charles A. Dana. New York: Herrmann J. Meyer, 1855.

The Words of Joseph Smith. Compiled and edited by Andrew F. Ehat and Lyndon W. Cook. Provo, UT: BYU Religious Studies Center, 1980.

Thomas Gregg, "[tirle]," *Warsaw Signal*, 19 October 1847, 2.

Thomas, Martha Pane Jones. Autobiography. In *Daniel Stillwell Thomas Family History* (N.p., 1927), 30. Copy in LDS Church Archives.

Thompson, Mercy Rachel Fielding. "Autobiography of Mercy Rachel Thompson." Holograph. LDS Church Archives.

_____. "Reminiscence of Mercy Rachel Fielding Thompson," In *Their Own Words: Women and the Story of Nauvoo*. Edited by Carol Cornwall Madsen. Salt Lake City: Deseret Book, 1994.

Thompson, Robert B. "Communication," *Times and Seasons* 2 (15 April 1841): 375-77, 380.

Todd, Jay M. "Nauvoo Temple Restoration," *Improvement Era* 71 (October 1968): 11.

"To the Saints Abroad," *Times and Seasons* 3 (15 September 1842): 923.

"To the Saints Among All Nations," *Times and Seasons* 4 (15 May 1843): 210.

Tracy, Nancy Naomi Alexander. "Life History of Nancy Naomi Alexander Tracy," 1885. Typescript, 25, LDS Church Archives.

_____. Autobiography, 1816-85, 32. Typescript, L. Tom Perry Special Collections, Harold B. Lee Library, Brigham Young University, Provo, Utah.

Twelve Apostles. "Baptism for the Dead," 13 December 1841, *Times and Seasons* 3 (15 December 1841): 626.

Ulmer, Don and Betty Ulmer. "New Enclosure Surrounds Site of Nauvoo Temple," *Church News*, 9 November 1996, 6.

Unknown author, untitled article containing quotations from J. M. Davidson, "Nauvoo: The Past and Present of That City: Visits of 1846 and 1864 Contrasted," *Carthage Republican*, 25 February 1864. Quoted in E. Cecil McGavin, *The Nauvoo Temple*. Salt Lake City: Deseret Book, 1962.

Unnamed visitor, Illinois Journal, 9 December 1853, reprinted as "Recollections of the Nauvoo Temple," in *Journal of the Illinois State Historical Society* 38 (December 1945): 482.

Unnamed visitor, *Illinois Journal*, 9 December 1853.

Vallet, Emile. *Communism: History of the Experiment at Nauvoo of the Icarian Settlement*. Nauvoo, IL: Nauvoo Rustler, n.d.

Van Dusen, Increase McGee and Maria Van Dusen. *Positively True. A Dialogue Between Adam and Eve, the Lord and the Devil, called the Endowment*. Albany, NY: C. Killmer, 1847.

_____. *Spiritual Delusions being a Key to the Mysteries of Mormonism, Exposing the Particulars of That Astounding Heresy, the Spiritual Wife System, as Practiced by Brigham Young of Utah*. New York: Moulton and Tuttle, 1854.

_____. *Startling Disclosures of the Great Mormon Conspiracy Against the Liberties of This Country: Being the Celebrated "Endowment."* New York: Authors, 1849.

_____. *Startling Disclosures of the Wonderful Ceremonies of the Mormon Spiritual Wife System. Being the Celebrated "Endowment."* New York: n.pub., 1850.

_____. *Startling Disclosures of the Mormon Spiritual Wife System, and Wonderful Ceremonies of the Celebrated "Endowment."* New York: n.pub., 1864.

_____. *The Mormon Endowment; A Secret Drama, or Conspiracy, in the Nauvoo Temple, in 1846*. Syracuse, NY: N.M.D. Lathrop, printer, 1847.

_____. *The Sublime and Ridiculous Blended; Called, the Endowment*. New York: Author, 1848.

Walker, Ronald W. "'A Banner is Unfurled': Mormonism's Ensign Peak," *Dialogue: A Journal of Mormon Thought* 26 (Winter 1993): 84.

_____. "Incidents, Travels, and Life of Elder William Holmes Walker." Typescript, Perry Special Collections, Lee Library, 14.

"War! War! And Rumors of War!!!" *Times and Seasons* 2, no. 19 (2 August 1841): 496.

Warsaw Signal, 30 December 1848, in Arrington, "Destruction of the Mormon Temple at Nauvoo," 420.

Watson, Elden J. ed. 1846. *Manuscript History of Brigham Young 1846-1847*. Salt Lake City: Elden Jay Watson, 1971.

_____. "The Nauvoo Tabernacle," *BYU Studies* 19, no. 3 (Spring 1979): 421.

_____, ed. *Manuscript History of Brigham Young, 1801-1844*. Salt Lake City: Elden J. Watson, 1968.

Watt, Ronald G. "A Tale of Two Bells: Nauvoo Bell and Hummer's Bell," *Nauvoo Journal* 11 (Fall 1999): 33.

Weeks, William. Transverse section of Nauvoo Temple, *William Weeks Papers*, Box 26, item 1, LDS Church Archives.

———. Letter to Truman O. Angell, 13 February 1846. Truman O. Angell Correspondence. Holograph, LDS Church Archives.

Wells, Emmeline B. "Pen Sketch of an Illustrious Woman: Eliza R. Snow Smith," *Woman's Exponent* 9 (15 October 1880): 74.

Wells, Junius F. "Wells Family," *Utah Genealogical and Historical Society Magazine* 6 (January 1915): 4.

Wells, Louie. *Letter to Emmeline B. Wells, 25 July 1883*. In "Nauvoo the Beautiful," *Woman's Exponent* 12 (15 August 1883): 37.

West, Gertrude Earl Hansen. "Ortentia," *Treasures of Pioneer History*, 6 vols. Compiled by Kate B. Carter. Salt Lake City: Daughters of the Utah Pioneers, 1952-57.

"Wheat and Provisions!," *Nauvoo Neighbor* 2 (28 August 1844): 7Whitaker, George. Quoted in "Life of George Whitaker-A Utah Pioneer 1820-1907." Typescript. Special Collections, Marriott Library, University of Utah, Salt Lake City.

White, "The Prairies, Nauvoo, Joe Smith, the Temple, the Mormons, etc.,"1:442.

White, David N. "The Prairies, Nauvoo, Joe Smith, the Temple, the Mormons, etc.," *Pittsburgh Weekly Gazette*, 15 September 1843: 3. Reprinted in Dean C. Jessee, ed., *The Papers of Joseph Smith*, 2 vols. Salt Lake City: Deseret Book, 1989, 1992..

———. *Letter, Pittsburgh Gazette*, 14 September 1843. Reprinted in Dean C. Jessee, ed., *The Papers of Joseph Smith*. Salt Lake City: Deseret Book, 1989.

Whitney, Elizabeth Ann Smith. "A Leaf from the Autobiography of Elizabeth Ann Whitney," *Woman's Exponent* 7 (August, September, November 1878; February 1879).

Whitney, Helen Mar Kimball. "Scenes in Nauvoo and Incidents from H. C. Kimball's Journal," *Woman's Exponent* 12 (15 July 1883): 14.

———. "Scenes and Incidents in Nauvoo," *Woman's Exponent* 11 (15 September 1882, May 1883).

———. "Scenes in Nauvoo, and Incidents from H. C. Kimball's Journal," *Woman's Exponent* 11 (May 1883): 185.

———. "Last Chapter of Scenes in Nauvoo," *Woman's Exponent* 12 (November 1883): 81.

———. "Scenes and Incidents at Winter Quarters," *Woman's Exponent* 13 (July 1884): 131.

———. "Scenes in Nauvoo and Incidents from H. C. Kimball's Journal," *Woman's Exponent* 12 (15 June 1883): 18.

———. "Scenes in Nauvoo and Incidents in Heber C. Kimball's Journal," *Woman's Exponent* 12 (1 September 1883): 50.

Whitney, Helen Mar. "Scenes in Nauvoo and Incidents from H. C. Kimball's Journal," *Woman's Exponent* 12 (1 September 1883): 50.

Whitney, Newel K. and George Miller. "A Voice from the Temple," *Times and Seasons* 5 (1 December 1844): 729.

Whitney, Newel K., George Miller, and William Clayton. "A Voice from the Temple," *Times and Seasons* 5 (1 December 1844): 728.

Whitney, Orson F. *Life of Heber C. Kimball.* Salt Lake City: Kimball Family, 1888.

Whittier, John Greenleaf. "A Mormon Conventicle," *Littell's Living Age* (October-November 1847). Reprinted in William Mulder and A. Russell Mortensen, eds., *Among the Mormons: Historic Accounts by Contemporary Observers.* New York: Alfred Knopf, 1958.

Wight, Lyman. Journal. Quoted in Heman C. Smith, *History of the Reorganized Church of Jesus Christ of Latter Day Saints*, 7 vols. Independence, MO: Herald House, 1903-14; 2d printing, 1967.

William Clayton. "To the Saints in Nauvoo, and Scattered Abroad," *Times and Seasons* 3 (11 October 1842): 957.

_____. Journal. *Journal History*, 23 October 1842, 4.

Winchester, Benjamin. Letter to Erastus Snow, 12 November 1841. *Times and Seasons* 3 (15 November 1841): 604-605.

Winters, Mary Ann Stearns. "An Autobiographical Sketch of the Life of the Late Mary Ann Stearns Winters," 1855. Typescript, 12, LDS Church Archives.

Woodruff, Wilford "To the Officers and Members of the Church of Jesus Christ of Latter-day Saints in the British Islands," *Millennial Star* 5 (February 1845): 140.

_____. "Temple Tithing-Bell Receipts," *Millennial Star* 6 (August 1845): 107.

_____. "To the Officers and Members of the Church of Jesus Christ of Latter-day Saints in the British Islands," *Millennial Star* 5 (February 1845): 140.

_____. "August 15, 1845," *Millennial Star* 6 (15 August 1845), 77.

_____. *Wilford Woodruff's Journal*, 1833-1898. Typescript. Edited by Scott G. Kenny, 9 vols. Midvale, Utah: Signature Books, 1983-85.

_____. *Collected Discourses.* Edited by Brian H. Stuy. 5 Vols. Salt Lake City, UT and Burbank, CA: B.H.S. Publishing, 1987-92.

Wortham, John. Autobiography. In "Autobiographies of Early Seventies," typescript, 75, LDS Church Archives.

Young, Brigham and Willard Richards. 1844. Notice. *Times and Seasons* 5, 20 September.

Young, Brigham. "Beloved Brethren," *Times and Seasons* 6 (1 November 1845): 1018-19.

_____. "Extract of a Letter from President Brigham Young," *Millennial Star* 6 (15 July 1845): 43.

_____. "From Brigham Young's History," *Journal History*, 24 January 1846, 1, 3.

_____. "Speech," *Times and Seasons* 6 (1 July 1845): 953-55.

_____. "To the Brethren of the Church of Jesus Christ of Latterday Saints throughout the World," *Times and Seasons* 6 (1 November 1845): 1019.

_____. Diary, 25 January 1845. Quoted in Leonard J. Arrington, *Brigham Young: American Moses.* New York: Knopf, 1985.

_____. Letter to John J. Hardin et al., 24 September 1845. *Nauvoo Neighbor* 3 (1 October 1845): 2.

_____. Letter to the Trustees. In *Journal History*, 28 September 1846, 2.

_____. Letter to the Trustees. In *Journal History*, 5 November 1847, 4.

_____. Letter to Wilford Woodruff, "Latest from Nauvoo," *Millennial Star* 6 (15 September 1845): 124.

_____. Letter to Wilford Woodruff, 17 December 1845. Holograph, *Brigham Young Papers*, LDS Church Archives.

Young, John R. *Memoirs of John R. Young, Utah Pioneer 1847*. Salt Lake City: Deseret News Press, 1920.

Young, Levi Edgar. "Joseph Young," *Utah Genealogical and Historical Magazine* 5 (July 1914): 106.

Young, Richard W. "In the Wake of the Church," *Contributor* 4 (January 1883): 151.

Zucker, Louis C. "Joseph Smith As a Student of Hebrew," *Dialogue: A Journal of Mormon Thought* 3 (Summer 1968): 41.

INDEX

Also available from
GREG KOFFORD BOOKS

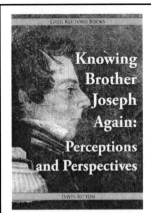

Knowing Brother Joseph Again: Perceptions and Perspectives

Davis Bitton

Paperback, ISBN: 978-1-58958-123-4

In 1996, Davis Bitton, one of Mormon history's preeminent and much-loved scholars, published a collection of essays on Joseph Smith under the title, *Images of the Prophet Joseph Smith*. A decade later, when the book went out of print, Davis began work on an updated version that would also include some of his other work on the Mormon prophet. The project was only partially finished when his health failed. He died on April 13, 2007, at age seventy-seven. With the aid of additional historians, *Knowing Brother Joseph Again: Perceptions and Perspectives* brings to completion Davis's final work—a testament to his own admiration of the Prophet Joseph Smith.

From Davis Bitton's introducton:

This is not a conventional biography of Joseph Smith, but its intended purpose should not be hard to grasp. That purpose is to trace how Joseph Smith has appeared from different points of view. It is the image of Joseph Smith rather than the man himself that I seek to delineate.

Even when we have cut through the rumor and misinformation that surround all public figures and agree on many details, differences of interpretation remain. We live in an age of relativism. What is beautiful for one is not for another, what is good and moral for one is not for another, and what is true for one is not for another. I shudder at the thought that my presentation here will lead to such soft relativism.

Yet the fact remains that different people saw Joseph Smith in different ways. Even his followers emphasized different facets at different times. From their own perspectives, different people saw him differently or focused on a different facet of his personality at different times. Inescapably, what they observed or found out about him was refracted through the lens of their own experience. Some of the different, flickering, not always compatible views are the subject of this book.

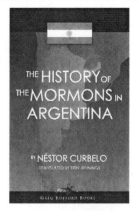

The History of Mormons in Argentina

Néstor Curbelo

English, ISBN: 978-1-58958-052-7

Originally published in Spanish, Curbelo's The History of the Mormons in Argentina is a groundbreaking book detailing the growth of the Church in this Latin American country.

Through numerous interviews and access to other primary resources, Curbelo has constructed a timeline, and then documents the story of the Church's growth. Starting with a brief discussion of Parley P. Pratt's assignment to preside over the Pacific and South American regions, continuing on with the translation of the scriptures into Spanish, the opening of the first missions in South America, and the building of temples, the book provides a survey history of the Church in Argentina. This book will be of interest not only to history buffs but also to thousands of past, present, and future missionaries.

Translated by Erin Jennings

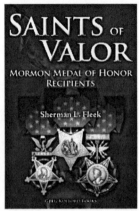

Saints of Valor:
Mormon Medal of Honor
Recipients

Sherman L. Fleek

Hardcover, ISBN: 978-1-58958-171-5

Since 1861 when the US Congress approved the concept of a Medal of Honor for combat valor, 3,457 individuals have received this highest military decoration that the nation can bestow. Nine of those have been Latter-day Saints. The military and personal stories of these LDS recipients are compelling, inspiring, and tragic. The men who appear in this book are tied by two common threads: the Medal of Honor and their Mormon heritage.

The purpose of this book is to highlight the valor of a special class of LDS servicemen who served and sacrificed "above and beyond the call of duty." Four of these nine Mormons gave their "last full measure" for their country, never seeing the high award they richly deserved. All four branches of the service are represented: five were Army (one was a pilot with the Army Air Forces during WWII), two Navy, and one each of the Marine Corps and Air Force. Four were military professionals who made the service their careers; five were not career-minded; three died at an early age and never married. This book captures these harrowing historical narratives from personal accounts.

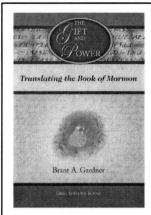

The Gift and Power: Translating the Book of Mormon

Brant A. Gardner

Hardcover, ISBN: 978-1-58958-131-9

From Brant A. Gardner, the author of the highly praised *Second Witness* commentaries on the Book of Mormon, comes *The Gift and Power: Translating the Book of Mormon*. In this first book-length treatment of the translation process, Gardner closely examines the accounts surrounding Joseph Smith's translation of the Book of Mormon to answer a wide spectrum of questions about the process, including: Did the Prophet use seerstones common to folk magicians of his time? How did he use them? And, what is the relationship to the golden plates and the printed text?

Approaching the topic in three sections, part 1 examines the stories told about Joseph, folk magic, and the translation. Part 2 examines the available evidence to determine how closely the English text replicates the original plate text. And part 3 seeks to explain how seer stones worked, why they no longer work, and how Joseph Smith could have produced a translation with them.

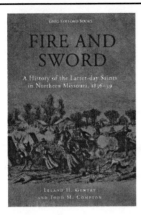

Fire and Sword: A History of the Latter-day Saints in Northern Missouri, 1836-39

Leland Homer Gentry and Todd M. Compton

Hardcover, ISBN: 978-1-58958-103-6

Many Mormon dreams flourished in Missouri. So did many Mormon nightmares.

The Missouri period—especially from the summer of 1838 when Joseph took over vigorous, personal direction of this new Zion until the spring of 1839 when he escaped after five months of imprisonment—represents a moment of intense crisis in Mormon history. Representing the greatest extremes of devotion and violence, commitment and intolerance, physical suffering and terror—mobbings, battles, massacres, and political "knockdowns"—it shadowed the Mormon psyche for a century.

Leland Gentry was the first to step beyond this disturbing period as a one-sided symbol of religious persecution and move toward understanding it with careful documentation and evenhanded analysis. In Fire and Sword, Todd Compton collaborates with Gentry to update this foundational work with four decades of new scholarship, more insightful critical theory, and the wealth of resources that have become electronically available in the last few years.

Compton gives full credit to Leland Gentry's extraordinary achievement, particularly in documenting the existence of Danites and in attempting to tell the Missourians' side of the story; but he also goes far beyond it, gracefully drawing into the dialogue signal interpretations written since Gentry and introducing the raw urgency of personal writings, eyewitness journalists, and bemused politicians seesawing between human compassion and partisan harshness. In the lush Missouri landscape of the Mormon imagination where Adam and Eve had walked out of the garden and where Adam would return to preside over his posterity, the towering religious creativity of Joseph Smith and clash of religious stereotypes created a swift and traumatic frontier drama that changed the Church.

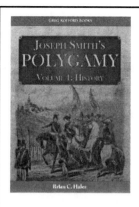

Joseph Smith's Polygamy, 3 Vols.

Brian Hales

Hardcover
Volume 1: History 978-1-58958-189-0
Volume 2: History 978-1-58958-548-5
Volume 3: Theology 978-1-58958-190-6

Perhaps the least understood part of Joseph Smith's life and teachings is his introduction of polygamy to the Saints in Nauvoo. Because of the persecution he knew it would bring, Joseph said little about it publicly and only taught it to his closest and most trusted friends and associates before his martyrdom.

In this three-volume work, Brian C. Hales provides the most comprehensive faithful examination of this much misunderstood period in LDS Church history. Drawing for the first time on every known account, Hales helps us understand the history and teachings surrounding this secretive practice and also addresses and corrects many of the numerous allegations and misrepresentations concerning it. Hales further discusses how polygamy was practiced during this time and why so many of the early Saints were willing to participate in it.

Joseph Smith's Polygamy is an essential resource in understanding this challenging and misunderstood practice of early Mormonism.

Praise for *Joseph Smith's Polygamy*:

"Brian Hales wants to face up to every question, every problem, every fear about plural marriage. His answers may not satisfy everyone, but he gives readers the relevant sources where answers, if they exist, are to be found. There has never been a more thorough examination of the polygamy idea."
—Richard L. Bushman, author of *Joseph Smith: Rough Stone Rolling*

"Hales's massive and well documented three volume examination of the history and theology of Mormon plural marriage, as introduced and practiced during the life of Joseph Smith, will now be the standard against which all other treatments of this important subject will be measured." —Danel W. Bachman, author of "A Study of the Mormon Practice of Plural Marriage before the Death of Joseph Smith"

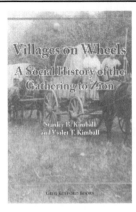

Villages on Wheels:
A Social History of the Gathering
to Zion

Stanley B. Kimball and Violet T. Kimball

ISBN: 978-1-58958-119-7

The enduring saga of Mormonism is its great trek across the plains, and understanding that trek was the life work of Stanley B. Kimball, master of Mormon trails. This final work, a collaboration he began and which was completed after his death in 2003 by his photographer-writer wife, Violet, explores that movement westward as a social history, with the Mormons moving as "villages on wheels."

Set in the broader context of transcontinental migration to Oregon and California, the Mormon trek spanned twenty-two years, moved approximately 54,700 individuals, many of them in family groups, and left about 7,000 graves at the trailside.

Like a true social history, this fascinating account in fourteen chapters explores both the routines of the trail—cooking, cleaning, laundry, dealing with bodily functions—and the dramatic moments: encountering Indians and stampeding buffalo, giving birth, losing loved ones to death, dealing with rage and injustice, but also offering succor, kindliness, and faith. Religious observances were simultaneously an important part of creating and maintaining group cohesiveness, but working them into the fabric of the grueling day-to-day routine resulted in adaptation, including a "sliding Sabbath." The role played by children and teens receives careful scrutiny; not only did children grow up quickly on the trail, but the gender boundaries guarding their "separate spheres" blurred under the erosion of concentrating on tasks that had to be done regardless of the age or sex of those available to do them. Unexpected attention is given to African Americans who were part of this westering experience, and Violet also gives due credit to the "four-legged heroes" who hauled the wagons westward.

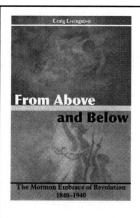

From Above and Below:
The Mormon Embrace of Revolution,
1840–1940

Craig Livingston

Paperback, ISBN: 978-1-58958-621-5

Praise for *From Above and Below*:

"In this engaging study, Craig Livingston examines Mormon responses to political revolutions across the globe from the 1840s to the 1930s. Latter-day Saints saw utopian possibilities in revolutions from the European tumults of 1848 to the Mexican Revolution. Highlighting the often radical anti-capitalist and anti-imperialist rhetoric of Mormon leaders, Livingston demonstrates how Latter-day Saints interpreted revolutions through their unique theology and millennialism."
--Matthew J. Grow, author of *Liberty to the Downtrodden: Thomas L. Kane, Romantic Reformer*

"Craig Livingston's landmark book demonstrates how 21st-century Mormonism's arch-conservatism was preceded by its pro-revolutionary worldview that was dominant from the 1830s to the 1930s. Shown by current opinion-polling to be the most politically conservative religious group in the United States, contemporary Mormons are unaware that leaders of the LDS Church once praised radical liberalism and violent revolutionaries. By this pre-1936 Mormon view, 'The people would reduce privilege and exploitation in the crucible of revolution, then reforge society in a spiritual union of peace' before the Coming of Christ and His Millennium. With profound research in Mormon sources and in academic studies about various social revolutions and political upheavals, Livingston provides a nuanced examination of this little-known dimension of LDS thought which tenuously balanced pro-revolutionary enthusiasms with anti-mob sentiments."
--D. Michael Quinn, author of *Elder Statesman: A Biography of J. Reuben Clark*

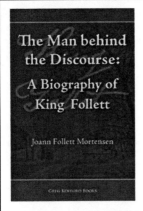

The Man behind the Discourse: A Biography of King Follett

Joann Follett Mortensen

ISBN: 978-1-58958-036-7

Who was King Follett? When he was fatally injured digging a well in Nauvoo in March 1844, why did Joseph Smith use his death to deliver the monumental doctrinal sermon now known as the King Follett Discourse? Much has been written about the sermon, but little about King.

Although King left no personal writings, Joann Follett Mortensen, King's third great-granddaughter, draws on more than thirty years of research in civic and Church records and in the journals and letters of King's peers to piece together King's story from his birth in New Hampshire and moves westward where, in Ohio, he and his wife, Louisa, made the life-shifting decision to accept the new Mormon religion.

From that point, this humble, hospitable, and hardworking family followed the Church into Missouri where their devotion to Joseph Smith was refined and burnished. King was the last Mormon prisoner in Missouri to be released from jail. According to family lore, King was one of the Prophet's bodyguards. He was also a Danite, a Mason, and an officer in the Nauvoo Legion. After his death, Louisa and their children settled in Iowa where some associated with the Cutlerities and the RLDS Church; others moved on to California. One son joined the Mormon Battalion and helped found Mormon communities in Utah, Idaho, and Arizona.

While King would have died virtually unknown had his name not been attached to the discourse, his life story reflects the reality of all those whose faith became the foundation for a new religion. His biography is more than one man's life story. It is the history of the early Restoration itself.

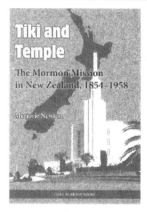

Tiki and Temple:
The Mormon Mission in New Zealand, 1854–1958

Marjorie Newton

Paperback, ISBN: 978-1-58958-121-0

From the arrival of the first Mormon missionaries in New Zealand in 1854 until stakehood and the dedication of the Hamilton New Zealand Temple in 1958, Tiki and Temple tells the enthralling story of Mormonism's encounter with the genuinely different but surprisingly harmonious Maori culture.

Mormon interest in the Maori can be documented to 1832, soon after Joseph Smith organized the Church of Jesus Christ of Latter-day Saints in America. Under his successor Brigham Young, Mormon missionaries arrived in New Zealand in 1854, but another three decades passed before they began sustained proselytising among the Maori people—living in Maori pa, eating eels and potatoes with their fingers from communal dishes, learning to speak the language, and establishing schools. They grew to love—and were loved by—their Maori converts, whose numbers mushroomed until by 1898, when the Australasian Mission was divided, the New Zealand Mission was ten times larger than the parent Australian Mission.

The New Zealand Mission of the Mormon Church was virtually two missions—one to the English-speaking immigrants and their descendants, and one to the tangata whenua—"people of the land." The difficulties this dichotomy caused, as both leaders and converts struggled with cultural differences and their isolation from Church headquarters, make a fascinating story. Drawing on hitherto untapped sources, including missionary journals and letters and government documents, this absorbing book is the fullest narrative available of Mormonism's flourishing in New Zealand.

Although written primarily for a Latter-day Saint audience, this book fills a gap for anyone interested in an accurate and coherent account of the growth of Mormonism in New Zealand.

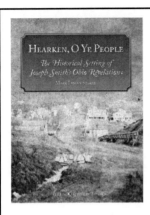

Hearken, O Ye People:
The Historical Setting of Joseph
Smith's Ohio Revelations

Mark Lyman Staker

Hardcover, ISBN: 978-1-58958-113-5

2010 Best Book Award - John Whitmer Historical Association

2011 Best Book Award - Mormon History Association

More of Mormonism's canonized revelations originated in or near Kirtland than any other place. Yet many of the events connected with those revelations and their 1830s historical context have faded over time. Mark Staker reconstructs the cultural experiences by which Kirtland's Latter-day Saints made sense of the revelations Joseph Smith pronounced. This volume rebuilds that exciting decade using clues from numerous archives, privately held records, museum collections, and even the soil where early members planted corn and homes. From this vast array of sources he shapes a detailed narrative of weather, religious backgrounds, dialect differences, race relations, theological discussions, food preparation, frontier violence, astronomical phenomena, and myriad daily customs of nineteenth-century life. The result is a "from the ground up" experience that today's Latter-day Saints can all but walk into and touch.

Praise for *Hearken O Ye People*:

"I am not aware of a more deeply researched and richly contextualized study of any period of Mormon church history than Mark Staker's study of Mormons in Ohio. We learn about everything from the details of Alexander Campbell's views on priesthood authority to the road conditions and weather on the four Lamanite missionaries' journey from New York to Ohio. All the Ohio revelations and even the First Vision are made to pulse with new meaning. This book sets a new standard of in-depth research in Latter-day Saint history."
          -Richard Bushman, author of *Joseph Smith: Rough Stone Rolling*

"To be well-informed, any student of Latter-day Saint history and doctrine must now be acquainted with the remarkable research of Mark Staker on the important history of the church in the Kirtland, Ohio, area."
          -Neal A. Maxwell Institute, Brigham Young University

CPSIA information can be obtained
at www.ICGtesting.com
Printed in the USA
FSOW01n2249221216
28773FS